IMPUNITY *and* HUMAN RIGHTS *in* INTERNATIONAL LAW *and* PRACTICE

IMPUNITY *and* HUMAN RIGHTS *in* INTERNATIONAL LAW *and* PRACTICE

EDITED BY

NAOMI ROHT-ARRIAZA

New York   Oxford

OXFORD UNIVERSITY PRESS

1995

Oxford University Press

Oxford   New York
Athens   Auckland   Bangkok   Bombay
Calcutta   Cape Town   Dar es Salaam   Delhi
Florence   Hong Kong   Istanbul   Karachi
Kuala Lumpur   Madras   Madrid   Melbourne
Mexico City   Nairobi   Paris   Singapore
Taipei   Tokyo   Toronto

and associated companies in
Berlin   Ibadan

Published by Oxford University Press, Inc.
200 Madison Avenue, New York, New York 10016

Oxford is a registered trademark of Oxford University Press

Library of Congress Cataloging-in-Publication Data
Roht-Arriaza, Naomi.
Impunity and human rights in international law and practice /
Naomi Roht-Arriaza.
p.   cm.
Includes bibliographical references and index.
ISBN 0-19-508136-6
1. Human rights. 2. Sanctions (International law) I. Title.
K3240.4.R63   1995
341.4'81—dc20   94-16401

2 4 6 8 9 7 5 3 1

Printed in the United States of America
on acid-free paper

*To Helen and George, for their love
and support,
to Gilberto, who started
me on this path, with love,
to Laura, for putting up with
Mom working too hard,
and to Rafa, who was born
with this project.*

Preface and Acknowledgments

The present volume looks at what should be done — and what is being done — to combat the problem of impunity, or lack of sanctions, for certain serious violations of human rights. Part I focuses on the legal issues. It moves from a general consideration of the theories of punishment and redress that shape and underlie the fight against impunity to a detailed look at the conventional and customary international law that defines state obligations to investigate, take action against, and provide redress for victims of at least the most serious violations of human rights. The part ends with a discussion of the legal status of amnesties and considers some gaps and problems in the existing law.

Parts II through IV consist of a series of country case studies on how the problem of impunity has been dealt with in practice in Europe, Latin America, and Africa and Asia. Each begins with an overview chapter summarizing a range of regional experiences. The focus is on situations of transition or change; the studies are neither exhaustive nor representative of the full range of experiences of transition. Rather, they illustrate some possible solutions and the difficulties associated with implementing these solutions. The studies were written by experts on the respective countries, some of whom were participants in the events that are discussed.

A concluding chapter sums up the lessons learned, reviews the role of international law and organizations, and recommends future actions.

The bulk of this book was written during 1992 and 1993. During that time, events internationally and in many of the countries under study changed dramatically. Although I have tried to update both the legal section and the country studies to December 1994, in some cases the flow of events was too rapid. In any case, the price of writing about recent — and still unfolding — history is that whatever one writes is outdated by the time it sees the light of day. It seems a small price to pay for tackling such an exciting and fast-changing area of law and practice.

Many people helped with the research and organization of this book. Nannette Ahmed, Sheila Shah, Anne Wagley, Margo Buckles, Jennifer White, Patrice Brymner, Meredith Richardson, Brian Hennessey, and Joseph Karnes provided able research assistance and support. Ellen Lutz, Frank Newman, Jaime Malamud-Goti, and Pat Merloe read portions of the manuscript and made useful suggestions. Diane Orentlicher was especially wonderful, reading large portions of the legal sections and providing detailed comments. Wiltrud Harms, the United Nations law librarian at the University of California, Berkeley, and Veronica

Maclay of the law library at Hastings College of the Law, University of California, were always on the lookout for relevant documents. Several people at Human Rights Watch were generous with documentation.

I began this project as the 1991–92 Riesenfeld Fellow in International Law and Organization at Boalt Hall, University of California, Berkeley. I profoundly thank Stephan Riesenfeld at Hastings and David Caron and Richard Buxbaum of Boalt for their support over the years. The writing was also partially supported by a grant from the summer writing program at Hastings College of the Law, for which I am also profoundly grateful.

San Francisco, California   N.R.A.
December 1994

Contents

Contributors

Belinda Aquino is an associate professor of political science and Asian studies at the University of Hawaii and director of the Center for Philippine Studies there. She received her Ph.D. at Cornell University. She was an expert witness in the U.S. civil suit against members of the Marcos family for human rights violations. She is the author of numerous articles on the Philippines.

Lynn Berat received her J.D. from the University of Texas and her Ph.D. from Yale University. She is the National Research Council Fellow at Yale Law School and an Associate Fellow of Yale's Southern Africa Research Program. The author of two books and more than fifty articles about international and comparative law with emphasis on Southern Africa, she has been a visiting fellow at the Centre for Applied Legal Studies of the University of the Witwatersrand and a visiting scholar at the Centre for Human Rights of the University of Pretoria.

Richard Carver is a researcher and writer on Africa and human rights. He has worked for Amnesty International and Human Rights Watch and currently directs the Africa program at Article 19, the International Centre Against Censorship. He is a consultant to various human rights and intergovernmental organizations and is a regular contributor to the British press and the BBC. He is the co-author of a book on health and underdevelopment and has written a number of academic articles on African themes. He is currently writing a book on the postindependence history of Malawi.

Jaime Malamud-Goti was a human rights adviser to President Raul Alfonsin with the rank of state secretary. He has also been Solicitor before the Supreme Court of Argentina. He is a professor of law at the University of Buenos Aires and has been a visiting professor at Columbia University and the University of Miami. He is currently a visiting professor at the University of Arkansas at Little Rock. He has pursued research and scholarship as a Fulbright and Guggenheim fellow and under the sponsorship of the United States Institute of Peace and the John D. and Catherine T. MacArthur Foundation. He is the author of *Smoke and Mirrors: The Paradox of the Drug Wars* (1992) and of numerous articles on criminal, moral, and legal theory.

Jorge Mera is a professor of criminal law at Diego Morales University in Santiago, Chile. He has worked closely with the Association of Families of the Disappeared in that country. He is the ex-director of the Human Rights Program of the

University Academy of Christian Humanism. He serves as an adviser to several international human rights groups.

Margaret Popkin, a U.S. lawyer, received her J.D. from Boalt Hall, the University of California, Berkeley. She completed seven years in El Salvador as assistant director of the Human Rights Institute at the José Simeon Cañas University in San Salvador. She monitored the case against the military officers and soldiers accused of killing seven Jesuit priests and their housekeepers. She was a consultant to the Truth Commission and prepared reports on the judicial system for the Lawyers' Committee for Human Rights and for Hemisphere Initiatives. She is the recipient of a 1994 MacArthur Writing Award. Some of the research for this chapter was carried out with funds from the John D. and Catherine T. MacArthur Foundation and while a fellow at the Orville H. Schell Jr. Center for International Human Rights at Yale Law School.

Edwin Rekosh, a U.S. lawyer, received his J.D. from Columbia University, where he was executive editor of the *Columbia Human Rights Law Review.* Currently he is a project director of the Washington-based International Human Rights Law Group. Since August 1992, he has been based in Bucharest, Romania, where he collaborates with Romanian and other Eastern European human rights organizations and lawyers groups. He has also worked as a consultant to Human Rights Watch and as an associate coordinator with the Lawyers' Committee for Human Rights.

Naomi Roht-Arriaza was trained as a lawyer (J.D., Boalt Hall, University of California at Berkeley, 1990) and as a public policy analyst (M.P.P., University of California, 1990). She teaches international human rights law, among other subjects, at the University of California, Hastings College of the Law, where she is Assistant Professor of Law. Her publications include "State Responsibility to Investigate and Prosecute Grave Human Rights Violations in International Law," 78 *California Law Review* 451 (1990), and "Truth as Justice: Investigatory Commissions in Latin America," 20 *Law and Social Inquiry* (1995). In 1991–92 she was the Riesenfeld Fellow in International Law and Organization at Boalt Hall. She has lived in Chile and Guatemala as well as elsewhere in Latin America.

Kathleen Smith received her Ph.D. in political science at the University of California, Berkeley, where her thesis was on coming to terms with Stalinist repression. She is one of the few English-speaking academics who has studied Memorial, a citizens' group seeking redress for past abuses. She received an Einstein Institute Fellowship for 1991–92. She is currently an assistant professor at Hamilton College, Clinton, New York.

Irwin Stotzky is currently a professor of law at the University of Miami School of Law. In 1986–87 he was a visiting scholar at Yale University Law School. In 1991–92 he was a Fulbright Scholar in Argentina. For the past sixteen years he has represented Haitian refugees on constitutional and human rights issues in many cases in the U.S. Supreme Court. He teaches in the areas of constitutional law and theory, criminal procedure, and philosophy. He has published numerous articles and is the author of *The Theory and Craft of American Law: Elements* (with Soia Mentschikoff) (1981). He is the editor of *Transition to Democracy in Latin America: The Role of the Judiciary* (1993).

Michael Vickery has been a senior lecturer in Southeast Asian History at the Universiti Sains Malaysia, Pulau Pinang, Malaysia, since 1988. He received his Ph.D. in history from Yale University and has lectured and taught in Australia and several European countries. He is the author of two books, *Cambodia 1975–1982* and *Kampuchea, Politics, Economics and Society,* as well as numerous contributions to books and articles on ancient and modern Cambodia.

Suzanne Walther received her Dr. jur. degree from the University of Freiburg and her LL.M. from Georgetown University. She is a research associate at the Max Planck Institute of Foreign and International Criminal Law in Heidelburg. Her research has focused on criminal law aspects of reunification.

IMPUNITY *and* HUMAN RIGHTS *in* INTERNATIONAL LAW *and* PRACTICE

1

Introduction

Naomi Roht-Arriaza

This book grew from an article I wrote in 1989. At that time, the difficult process of moving from military dictatorship to democracy was under way in a few countries of the Latin American Southern Cone. As a human rights lawyer with a long-standing interest in Latin America, I tried to do two things in the article: show how changes in the types of human rights violations committed in that region during the 1970s and 1980s required a new response from the international community, and establish how international law was beginning to provide that response. I posited that it did so by placing an affirmative obligation on states to investigate and prosecute those who, under state aegis, violated at least a subset of fundamental human rights.

It is now 1994, and the number of countries slowly and painfully coming to terms with their governments' past treatment of its citizens has grown. In Chile, the elected regime has moved to investigate violations and compensate victims but not in most cases to prosecute. In the former USSR and in several Eastern European countries the accountability of the prior regimes and methods of redress for their victims are urgent matters of public discussion. In South Africa, Cambodia, Haiti, El Salvador, and Guatemala, questions of investigation, accountability, and redress have been a major factor in negotiations toward domestic or internationally sponsored transitions, even as human rights abuses often continue. And in those countries that have confronted questions of impunity in the recent past — Argentina and Uruguay, for example — it is now possible to attempt an evaluation.

As the transitional regimes emerge, they inherit a legacy of widespread repression against the civilian population. In some cases, this repression has taken the form of massive killings of real or perceived political opponents; in others, opponents were forcibly kidnapped and disappeared; in still others, citizens were tortured and imprisoned; and elsewhere, selective killings combined with imprisonment were the norm. In each case, the official or quasi-official status of the perpetrators shielded them from sanction, creating a culture of impunity in which the most inhumane acts could be carried out without fear of repercussions.

This book is about efforts by people, governments, and international institutions to come to grips with these countries' recent history of repression and of impunity. In some of the cases studied, these actors have wrestled with whether, and to what extent, a government should engage in official investigations of prior wrongdoing by state officials. They have had to determine whether some, or most, of those responsible for the worst crimes should be brought to justice, even if this means annulling a previous amnesty law or risking a violent backlash by military or security forces. Finally, they have had to decide whether and how to compensate the victims of the prior regime. Where the shape of the future government or its commitment to human rights is still being negotiated, the parties to the negotiation must decide how much to insist on and how much to concede. And in still other countries, notably those of Eastern Europe, the question is not only one of risk to the new regime from a disgruntled party or military class but of the breadth of collaboration with the former regimes and the means for distinguishing the more from the less culpable.

Any transition from authoritarian rule to greater democracy necessarily involves efforts to establish and promote the rule of law. Societies in which massive human rights violations occur with impunity are by definition lawless societies. The lawlessness of the state itself serves to disempower ordinary citizens, making them fearful to think or speak out and breeding cynicism and passivity. As societies attempt to recover from these periods of lawlessness, one of the first opportunities to reestablish the primacy of law over individuals comes in the treatment of the former rulers, torturers, and jailers. If such people are treated summarily, extracting an eye for an eye, the transition to a society of laws is set back immeasurably. On the other hand, a blanket amnesty and silence from the new government perpetuate the existence of a separate class to whom the rule of law does not apply. Continued impunity equally undermines efforts to reestablish legality. Thus, the need to define legal procedures and criteria for dealing with past abuses takes on a special importance. Similarly, the mechanisms devised to settle accounts with those responsible for such abuses must meet certain criteria for fairness and predictability that are traditionally the province of law. Finally, much of the fight over impunity has been waged in terms of trials, domestic legislation, and international legal responsibilities. As a result, much of this book is written by and for lawyers.

At the same time, however, law is never made in a vacuum. It is always part of a larger political, moral, and social dynamic. Thus, the book is not exclusively about law or for lawyers. It includes the insights and efforts of political and social scientists, historians, and journalists, as well as human rights experts who combine the skills of several disciplines.

As governmental and nongovernmental actors frame the legal and policy debate, they look to the experiences of other countries. To design a strategy for dealing with their own past, actors learn from what has been successful or unsuccessful elsewhere.[1] The book aims in part to allow for that sharing of experiences, in the hope that lawyers, scholars, and activists in those countries in which dealing with the past is only now becoming an imperative may learn from those who have recently confronted similar challenges.

Discussion of how to deal with past human rights violations — in law as well as in politics and morality — takes place on two levels. First, national societies debate the effects of pursuing official investigations, prosecutions or civil penalties, or compensation mechanisms. The extent and severity of past violations, the prior history of democratic rule in the country, the number of victims, the extent of complicity by the citizenry, cultural and historical traditions, the stability of the new government, and the press of other — especially economic — matters provide a unique context in each case.[2] So too do the character of the liberalization (top down or bottom up), the strength of civil society, especially human rights or victims' groups, and the amount of time elapsed between the acts at issue and the transition or liberalization.

These debates raise the fundamental question of the appropriate decision makers in a given society. Are these decisions that should be made by government officials as part of their routine tasks, or are they so fundamental to a nation's self-definition that they should be subject to some specific mechanism for public choice? What if, as many argue was the case in Uruguay, for example, public approval mechanisms are subject to inordinate pressures from those who benefit from impunity? And even more basic, if the victims of repression constitute a discreet minority, isn't there a danger that majoritarian decision making will trample on whatever rights to redress victims may have in a morally unacceptable fashion? Or put differently, if we are talking about *rights* to redress, doesn't the right to demand justice or to forgive belong only to those directly harmed and not to the polity as a whole? Or is the harm against the whole society, both past and potential future victims alike? It is the resonance of these profound moral issues that makes the issue of impunity so complex and evocative of impassioned debate.

On a second level, the legal, political, and moral choices involved are to some degree shaped by the requirements of the international community. International law especially shapes limits to what national governments can openly do and establishes minimum requirements for compliance. As I hope to show, international law provides considerable guidance on issues of investigation, prosecution, and compensation, although admittedly its relevance has not always been recognized.

In formulating policies for dealing with past violations of fundamental rights, international law can be an important source of support for transitional regimes. If international law mandates investigation, prosecution, and redress, for example, the new government must somehow find ways to comply or else suffer real costs in terms of international isolation, opprobrium, or loss of trade or aid. These costs take the decision to comply with the law out of the realm of the merely possible, and therefore negotiable, and place it in the realm of the mandatory and nonnegotiable. For a weak transitional regime facing powerful constraints, a perceived lack of bargaining power on this point may be a boon. As a corollary, a decision to investigate or prosecute mandated by international law is less likely to be seen as political capitulation to a given faction or group or as mere vengeance.

Furthermore, reference to international law is mandated by the nature of the human rights violations at issue. In most of the cases studied in this book, past regimes engaged in a massive, systematic pattern of arbitrary killings, torture, and/or forced disappearances.[3] These acts are clearly prohibited under international law. Moreover, they constitute a small subset of violations of physical integrity, which historically have been subject to the highest possible degree of protection. Whereas other types of human rights have been the subject of controversy,[4] there is widespread agreement among both states and scholars that rights to physical integrity merit special protection. Such rights are nonderogable even in times of war or national emergency;[5] the norms protecting them are widely considered peremptory norms;[6] and the perpetrators are subject to universal jurisdiction.[7] There is a widely shared moral sense that such violations of physical integrity are affronts to human dignity on the most basic level. Thus, although it is possible that other types of human rights violations might merit similar treatment,[8] this book concentrates for the most part on investigation, punishment, and compensation for acts involving violations of an individual's physical integrity.

State-initiated and condoned killings, torture, and disappearances violate specific rights defined in widely subscribed instruments, including the Universal Declaration of Human Rights,[9] the International Covenant on Civil and Political Rights,[10] the American Convention on Human Rights,[11] and the European Convention for the Protection of Human Rights and Fundamental Freedoms.[12] Specific treaties concerning torture[13] and disappearances,[14] resolutions of U.N. bodies,[15] and court cases establishing torture[16] and disappearance[17] as violations of customary law all point to the clear international prohibition on states' killing, torturing, or forcibly causing the disappearance of their own citizens.

Treaty-based obligations give all other states parties to the treaty the right to scrutinize one another's performance and to demand compliance. To the extent the treaties involved contain individual complaint mechanisms, individuals and organizations as well as states may raise treaty violations. And to the extent the rights not to be subjected to torture, summary execution, or disappearance emanate from customary law, they give rise to obligations owed by each state to the international community as a whole.[18] These obligations also underlie the relevance of international law to the topic at hand.

In many countries, most notably in Latin America but also in South Africa, the Philippines, and others, the nature of these human rights violations has changed as governments have developed novel forms of repression. Most important are the related techniques of forced disappearance and use of paramilitary forces to carry out repressive activities. The emergence of these methods as preferred instruments of dictatorship provides yet another reason why the debate over impunity both concerns and can benefit from the perspectives of international law.

There are two main elements of a forced disappearance: first, "abduction or detention . . . by an agent of a State or by a person acting with the consent or acquiescence of a State" and, second, official refusal to acknowledge the abduction or to disclose information that would reveal the detainee's fate.[19] Those who are abducted are typically detained, tortured, and eventually killed. A death squad killing similarly involves state involvement or complicity and a denial of responsibility but differs in that the body, usually mutilated and tortured, is deliberately left where it can be found. In either case, the techniques serve to terrorize broad sectors of the population, leaving the families and friends of those who have disappeared in permanent anguish and chilling political and social activity. The overall effect of years of inexplicable disappearances and of the horror of mutilated corpses appearing at roadsides is to create a psychologically cowed population, where people retreat into themselves — and into denial of their own and others' rights — as a matter of self-preservation.[20]

The use of disappearances and death squads rather than outright arrest or official execution allows the regime to deny all accountability. The government can rid itself of actual, potential, or perceived opponents without the publicity of a public trial or the risk of creating martyrs; and through disguising and denying its responsibility it can make it difficult for citizens to press for either formal trial or release of detainees. These techniques leave little credible and specific evidence of official involvement. In the Argentine case, for instance,

> Orders were given orally in most cases, requiring the cooperative testimony of junior officers who are constitutionally entitled to the right against self-incrimination. Written orders were either unsigned or couched so vaguely as to communicate their true intent only by "subliminal intimation." . . . Official statements during military rule denied any illegality. . . . Kidnappers drove unmarked cars; torturers wore no uniforms and employed pseudonyms; victims were kept blindfolded; detention centers were often established on private rather than public property.[21]

Similarly, on an international level, the government may deny all responsibility and take refuge in the refrain that it is "investigating these lamentable occurrences." The strong international and domestic prohibitions on arbitrary execution, torture, and disappearances lose their effectiveness if governments may simply stonewall and delay, insisting that the burden of proof is on their victims to show official involvement. To make these prohibitions meaningful, law must respond by placing affirmative obligations on governments — obligations that include investigating, prosecuting, and compensating.

Whether or not these obligations are compelled by effective law, the question remains whether they are sound policy. The arguments for and against investigation, prosecution, and compensation are similar, although some questions are specific to each.

The debate over investigation turns on differing perceptions of the best way to prevent future abuses. Proponents of investigation argue that a society which moves forward without confronting its past is condemned to repeat it. Investigation draws a clear line between past and future, allowing the beginning of a healing process. During a period of repression, vast sectors of society will have closed themselves off from an inhospitable political world, choosing not to see the violence around them or justifying it on the grounds that the victims must have done something wrong to deserve their fate. Investigation reveals the extent of repression and the degree to which the victims were valuable members of the society (or merely random targets). Although such an investigation may be carried out by nongovernment groups,[22] an official imprimatur lends authority and a recognition that these were state-sanctioned abuses. The difference between unofficial and official recognition has been described as "the difference between knowledge and acknowledgement. It's what happens and can only happen to knowledge when it is made part of the public cognitive scene."[23] Investigation becomes a kind of unofficial apology, giving official voice and legitimacy to those who spoke up during the years of repression and were dissmissed as subversives, crazies, or dissidents.

As a form of redress, investigation also allows victims and especially their families to put the past to rest. In cases of forced disappearance, this is crucial because the victims' fate may be unknown, and families may pass anguished years believing their loved one is alive in some clandestine prison. In any case, investigation of the fate of the victims, publication of their names, and recognition of the fact that they were wronged rescues them from oblivion if not from death, at least in a symbolic sense. In a broader sense, too, investigation is part of a struggle for the control of history. It plays a central role in a society's redefinition of itself. By discrediting the official version of the former dictatorship's actions, it does not allow that version of history to be perpetuated in the military academies or in textbooks. "Dirty wars" may no longer be excused in the name of fighting communism, maintaining a way of life, or defending the proletarian state.

Opponents of official investigations have argued that such investigations may do more harm than good. By dwelling on the past, they argue, a deeply divided society will be unable to overcome its divisions and move forward. Old hatreds and vengeances will be dredged up and replayed ad infinitum, yet the overriding need is to let bygones be bygones and move forward in a spirit of conciliation. Furthermore, there are practical difficulties in investigations: How much proof of government involvement should investigations require? Should the names of the alleged perpetrators be made public as a form of social punishment when no other sanction seems forthcoming, or should no one be publicly accused without the chance to clear his or her name before a court of law? How broad should the inquiry sweep? Should it cover only government wrongs or also those of government opponents, especially armed opponents?

Prosecutions raise a related set of concerns. Proponents argue that prosecutions represent an efficient way of ascertaining the truth; the legal process ensures that fact finding will be thorough and reasonably impartial and will lead to a clear declaration of fault. In addition, prosecutions will punish or at least stigmatize the guilty, deter potential lawbreakers, and provide a warning that future transgressions will not be excused. More generally, prosecutions may be useful for reestablishing the rule of law, underlining the discontinuity between the new government and the old, and reinforcing the primacy of civilian institutions in the new order. Moreover, a failure to prosecute may well embolden the military or security forces or other remnants of the old regime, making it harder for civilian control to take root. The culture of impunity will continue unless the cycle is broken.

From the point of view of the victims, prosecutions channel the desire for private vengeance while "restoring citizens to full membership in society by suppressing the differences between those who had control over other persons' lives and those whose existence was at their mercy."[24] For the population in general, prosecutions help restore citizens' dignity after years of defenselessness based on state terror.

The main argument specifically against prosecutions is that they may destabilize a still-fragile transitional government past the breaking point. Thus, moving to punish violators may result in prolonged political instability or even a return of dictatorship. Furthermore, prosecutions hastily organized by a transitional state may be used as a cover for personal, political, tribal, or localized grievances, with the state unable to differentiate sufficiently between meritorious and spurious complaints. The promise of prosecutions may deter some dictators from abandoning power. Finally, opponents argue, overwhelming practical obstacles exist to prosecuting all those responsible for grave violations of physical integrity during periods of generalized repression. The courts will be clogged, and evidence will be difficult or impossible to collect if large groups or institutions are complicit. The authority of the civilian government will be undermined if it decides to press forward, only to find itself unable to subject the former rulers or torturers to legal process.

In the case of the military, difficult questions of how far up or down the ranks to prosecute must be answered. In part, these questions reflect the legal status in national and international law of the defense of superior orders; but in part they also reflect the practical problems of keeping a tightly knit institution from closing ranks and of devising incentive structures that facilitate cooperation. The fear is that deadlock will result, squandering society's material and political resources rather than building preventive rules and institutions for the future.

Several more thorny questions arise in the prosecution context. For instance, are the possibilities for state action limited to penal sanctions, or should we widen our views to include other state-imposed sanctions, including loss of pension, loss of military rank, inability to hold public office, or others?[25] If convicted, must ex-torturers or dictators serve their full sentences, or is a pardon permissible? If the latter, must they serve jail time at all? Is there some proportionality requirement in either domestic law or morality or in international law requiring the punishment to fit the crime? If so, is that requirement affected by the need to obtain eyewitnesses or other traditional prosecutorial concerns?

In addition to investigation and prosecution, transitional governments may attempt to confront a legacy of past violations by directly or indirectly compensating the victims. Compensation may be in the form of monetary payments (either from government or through civil suits) or it may be symbolic, ranging from public reburial to official apologies to monuments to a general fund in the victims' name dedicated to preventing future violations. In any case, proponents argue, compensation, although it clearly cannot bring back the victims' life or health, expresses in tangible form a societal recognition of wrongfulness. To the extent a compensation program honors the memory of the victims, its effects are similar to investigation. To the extent that monetary payments from either the perpetrator or state institutions serve a deterrent function, they parallel both investigation and prosecution.

Although compensation programs seem to be less controversial than either investigation or prosecution, more questions arise. For example, in countries in which most of the population has suffered under a past government, widespread compensation may be neither financially feasible nor morally justifiable. How can a society draw lines between those who suffered earlier or later or more or less? Second, should the compensation be paid from a general taxpayers' fund, or is it possible to target the budgets of those institutions (say, the military) most directly responsible? Third, should victims always be treated as individuals, or is there a role for collective compensation to discrete groups? Finally, there is a risk that requiring survivors and their families to come forward publicly and claim compensation may in itself be traumatic, rekindling old fears.

The rest of this book explores these dilemmas in law and politics. Part I establishes a general framework in the law. After a brief introductory look at why societies choose to provide redress to those harmed and to punish the harm-doer, it focuses on the international law limits and obligations of states with respect to investigation, prosecution, and compensation. It looks first at rules that may be found in international treaties, and then at those that arise from customary law or general principles of law. It then focuses on some of the knottier legal problems in the area, including the legality of amnesties, superior orders, and statute of limitations concerns.

Parts II, III, and IV consist of a series of country studies from Europe, Latin America, and Asia and Africa, respectively. The studies focus on national experiences with issues of investigation, prosecution, and compensation for grave human rights violations during the 1980s and 1990s. They look at the difficulties, dilemmas, and lessons learned in each national experience, and explore the role of international law and the international community in addressing these issues. They include societies in which a military dictatorship or pervasive party and security apparatus was replaced by a civilian regime that promised more openness and democracy, and those in which national and, increasingly, international negotiations to end a civil conflict include as a prominent component the question of the abuses of the prior regime. Each part begins with an introductory overview chapter which both situates the subsequent chapters in historical context and allows for brief discussion of other relevant experiences from the region.

Finally, the last chapter, Conclusion: Combatting Impunity, seeks to distill the experiences recounted and analyzed in the country chapters, in light of the legal obligations established in the legal chapters, into more general conclusions. This chapter examines what has worked, what has not, and what lessons the experiences to date hold for the future. I also consider the role of law, especially international law, in defining parameters and standards for action. Finally, I suggest ways to make the law on impunity more precise and responsive within a framework that includes both national and international approaches.

I

THE LEGAL SETTING

2

Punishment, Redress, and Pardon: Theoretical and Psychological Approaches

Naomi Roht-Arriaza

Most of this book is concerned with legal and political responses to the question of impunity, both as a matter of general international law and of national experiences. The present chapter looks at the normative bases for combating impunity. As a general proposition, societies may view the question from the point of view of the offender—which raises the general question of how and why a society punishes—and from the point of view of the victim, raising a series of issues around redress. The inquiries are distinct but not separate because punishment of offenders may itself be a form of redress for victims, whereas measures like truth telling, aimed at redress, may have punitive aspects.

The Relevance of Theories of Punishment

Criminal justice theorists generally divide punishment rationales into two broad categories—utilitarian and retributive. Utilitarians "believe that the right act is that which produces the greatest utility, or is most conducive to the welfare of all those affected by the act."[1] Punishment, in the utilitarian's mind, is future oriented and consequential, focusing specifically on end results. If punishment prevents an act that society has designated as a "wrong," it is justified.[2] Utilitarians are not concerned with the amount or character of the offender's culpability. After determining which rights and privileges to protect, a utilitarian society uses punishment to "persuade" people to respect those rights.

A theory based on end results alone lends itself to potential abuse. For example, society could use torture to deter crime.[3] Utilitarians counter accusations of moral abuse by integrating into their theory a balancing of the costs of curtailing certain citizens' civil rights against the benefits of punishment.[4] The harm to the individual offender cannot outweigh the benefit of the punishment to society. If it does, the punishment is not justifiable.[5]

Utilitarian punishment may be based on deterrence, rehabilitation, or incapacitation or on some combination of these.

Deterrence

Deterrence justifies punishment because it functions as a social control, using persuasion, propaganda, fear, and other forms of social coercion to prevent crime. Intuitively, deterrence works because "the risk of unpleasant consequences is a very strong motivational factor for most people in most situations."[6] Utilitarians assume that people assess their actions rationally in light of the possibility they will be caught and punished, and this assumption is the core of a deterrence model. The greater the likelihood of punishment, the more likely people are to refrain from committing crimes.

Deterrence may be special or general. Special deterrence targets the individual — "[n]ot the crime but the criminal to be punished."[7] The utilitarian assumes that an individual will not commit a crime because prior experiences provide incentives to avoid repetition. General deterrence targets society as a whole — it is the ability of criminal law and its enforcement to make citizens law abiding, either through the law's moral authority or through habit, social imitation, fear, and coercion.[8]

Deterrence theory provides several problems when applied to state-sponsored or initiated crimes in the human rights context. To deter, the content of the protected norm must be clear to both the enforcing entity and the potential offender. In cases of state violation of human rights, potential abusers may not always perceive that their act violates a norm. Often their confusion results from society's mixed messages: National security or the need to restore order, for example, may be invoked to justify what would otherwise be clearly punishable acts such as torture or murder.[9] Because government and society may justify or condone certain abuses, human rights abusers may not see their acts as ones that need to be deterred.

A second difficulty arises when individual members of organizations that abuse basic human rights ignore special deterrence factors because their organizational façade protects them. In the military, for example,

> [i]mmediate and certain approval from comrades overrides any reason for complying with legal standards or any fear of the consequences of engaging in criminal behavior. The certainty of approval and support from comrades and superior officers neutralizes the deterrent effect of a possible criminal sanction. Approval or disapproval from the military environment is much stronger than rejection from society at large.[10]

Similar results may occur within monolithic political party structures. These effects may be particularly pronounced at lower levels of the command structure, where autonomy is most reduced and the pull of institutional approval is greatest.[11] Because individual offenders do not believe the threat of punishment, deterrence in these situations becomes an empty shell. Moreover, past experience with de facto or de jure impunity may confirm to members of such organizations that they have little to fear from criminal sanctions. Therefore, for a deterrent threat to be credible, enforcement may have to come from outside the country in which the abuses occurred.

Rehabilitation and Incapacitation

Rehabilitation focuses on the offender's reeducation and his or her reintegration into society.[12] Besides reeducating the offender, rehabilitation has two other potential results: (1) the offender may attain some semblance of a "meaningful" life,[13] and (2) society can restrain the offender using social controls.[14]

Rehabilitation assumes that the offender is capable of absorbing and retaining social norms through education and rejects the possibility that an offender might resist reform. Originally, criminologists interested in punishment believed that scientific advances would facilitate rehabilitation. In recent years, however, theorists have begun to doubt the efficacy of a rehabilitation model because recidivism appears to occur at the same rate in programs that focus on rehabilitation as in those programs that do not.[15]

Rehabilitation poses several difficulties in the context of state-sponsored or condoned criminal violations. It assumes society has both the right and the obligation to rehabilitate an offender by changing his attitudes and perspectives. Yet here these attitudes are neither personal nor aberrational — rather, they are deliberately inculcated in an institutional setting, as part of a larger mission, say, of national security, that may still be seen as valid.[16] Rehabilitation in this context means institutional reformation. Although such rehabilitation is no doubt a worthy and necessary enterprise, it requires time, money, and political will and is a different enterprise than changing individual offenders. A similar objection applies to a theory based on incapacitation, which merely seeks to remove the offender from society's midst.

Retribution

In contrast to the utilitarians, adherents of retributive theories look backward to the nature of the offender's act and to his or her culpability.[17] The wrongdoer deserves a punishment proportionate to his or her culpability.[18]

Retribution is based on moral culpability. "If the criminal deserves punishment, it should be inflicted. If the criminal is not morally culpable, however, no punishment is justified, regardless of any potential good effect it may have on society."[19] Moreover, retribution is sometimes justified as a substitute for revenge — a socially acceptable way of avoiding blood feuds or vendettas while allowing society to express its deeply held moral revulsion at the criminal act. Other theorists explain the retributive urge as an expression of deeply held human sentiments of rage against behavior we see as oppressive or violative of our self-respect: Those sentiments are channeled through social institutions rather than allowed to fester.

The retributivist model links punishment to the offender's failure to accept and adopt generally accepted moral, social, or legal standards. Retribution is based upon an offender's understanding of his or her crime. The enforcer normally attempts to achieve justice by focusing either on the offender's moral reprehensiveness or on the offender's "unjust enrichment" through a voluntary rejection of the burdens of living within society's rules.

Theorists who focus on the reprehensiveness of offenders reject a strict separation between the moral and the legal, understanding the latter as a laudable and necessary attempt to give form to sentiments of resentment arising from the offender's denial of our self-worth.[20] Under an "unjust enrichment" model, society institutes rules and laws to govern social interaction. To guarantee peace among citizens, social rules burden each citizen by limiting his or her freedom to choose certain actions. Thus, the person who commits a crime is not sharing fully in the responsibilities and burdens of citizenship. The enforcer, usually government, punishes the offender to restore balance.[21] This approach assumes the offender receives some benefit from breaking the rules. In the context of state-sponsored crimes, individuals who participated in a repressive enterprise received job security, status, and a psychological sense of superiority — at times, as in Eastern Europe, material gain was indeed part of the bargain. On the other hand, in some cases the perpetrator may well not be pursuing any personal gain but merely doing his job; if so, an offender-based retributivist justification loses much of its force.[22]

Besides focusing on culpability, retributivists measure the proportionality of punishment. In its purest form, retribution took the form of *lex talionis,* or an "eye for an eye, a tooth for a tooth, a life for a life." Current retributive models differ slightly. In them, the central organizing principle of sentencing is that of "commensurate desserts." Sentences are to be proportionate in their severity to the gravity of the defendant's criminal conduct. Thus, retributivism aims to restore balance to society.

The Denunciation Model of Punishment

Both utilitarian and retributivist accounts of punishment have been widely criticized as limited by their own opposing premises: Retributivism requires the infliction of pain on offenders even if doing so cannot be shown to serve any future social good, whereas utilitarian accounts have difficulty coming to terms with the moral imperative of punishing only those who are guilty and doing so in proportion to the moral quality of the offense. Two alternative theories that attempt to combine and improve on the strengths of each approach hold more promise as the moral and theoretical underpinnings of a theory of punishment for state-sponsored or condoned human rights violations. A denunciation model of punishment focuses on the symbolic and norm-creating qualities of punishment for the larger society, whereas "goal-oriented retributivism" emphasizes the effects of punishment on the victim of crime. To the extent it is victim centered, this theory views punishment itself as a form of redress.

In the past, societies traditionally used punishment "as an opportunity for symbolic expression of moral outrage against non-conformity."[23] Modern accounts of denunciation theory see punishment as an expression of moral criticism. As such, it aims, first, at bringing wrongdoers to acknowledge their misdeeds and change their behavior and, second, at providing moral guidance more generally. The model is both backward looking, in that moral criticism is based on an offender's past acts, and forward looking, in that its goal is to change future behavior by establishing clear societal standards against which such behavior may be measured.[24] In addition, in its broadest expression denunciation theory focuses not only on the offender but on the "satisfaction" of the law-abiding members of a society. Whereas a utilitarian focuses on deterrence as a way of increasing safety, a denunciation theorist emphasizes the need to increase societal satisfaction with a just scheme of punishment, thus increasing social cohesion.[25] Law in this model serves as

> a forum for ordered, fair resolution of disputes that threaten the social fabric, but also, more subtly, by (a) announcing the norms of the community and thus reifying the values embedded in the culture and (b) establishing structures that create or sustain social behavior consistent with those values.[26]

A denunciation-type theory seems particularly appropriate in cases of state-sponsored or condoned human rights violations. The state, after all, plays a large role in articulating the moral values to be enshrined in laws: If those values become debased through state abuses and human rights violations, the state should play a major role in reformulating them for society. In addition, denunciation may sufficiently shame past perpetrators of abuse that they do not commit similar atrocities. Neither individuals nor regimes gladly accept the label torturer or murderer. For a denunciation theory to be effective, punishment must be public and must clearly enunciate standards of behavior. It must also be severe enough to make the intended point—a mere slap on the wrist might otherwise lead to the conclusion that the norms of the community do not, in fact, find the behavior at issue reprehensible at all.

Whereas denunciation theories of punishment focus on the norm-creating and enforcing effect of punishment, what Jaime Malamud-Goti has called "goal-oriented" retributivism focuses on the effect of punishment on the victim of the offense. Both utilitarianism and retribution classically acknowledge the victim of an offense only peripherally, to the extent needed to punish the offender or establish the greater good. Retribution, in its purest form, is offender centered, and all offenses that lie at parallel moral levels should receive equivalent amounts of punishment. When the victim is the center of the punishment equation, however, vindication becomes important, and similar offenses may be resolved in an entirely distinct manner.[27] One victim might be satisfied with a symbolic demonstration of the state's willingness to acknowledge the victim's trauma whereas another victim might require more.[28] Similarly, such a theory would not be able to override the victims' needs by subordinating them to a calculus of greatest overall societal good.

Punishment and Redress

The idea that wrongs should be redressed, that reparation should be made to the injured, is among the most venerable and most central of legal principles. It was a major proposition of the natural law dating from the time of Moses through Grotius and St. Thomas Aquinas; indeed, one interpretation of the *lex talionis* is that it refers to the need for restitution (an eye for an eye), not merely retribution. The Prophet Muhammad admonished that

> [i]f you see a wrong you must redress it, with your hand [action] if you can, otherwise with your tongue [vocal condemnation], otherwise with your eyes [reprobation], otherwise in your heart and that is the weakest manifestation of your faith [conviction].[29]

All modern societies allow for some form of civil redress for harm to individuals, and most contain administrative procedures for redress when the harm is occasioned by agents of the state as well as special forms of redress when the harm comes about as a result of a criminal act.

A victim-centered view of punishment blurs the line between criminal punishment and civil redress, seeing the criminal sanction as a form of redress and civil penalties as having punitive value. The distinction between civil and criminal penalties is based on the view that criminal acts transcend the harm to any one individual, harming the entire society and requiring punitive action by the state; in contrast, civil wrongs concern the victim alone. The distinction was almost unknown in ancient law: Under the Code of Hammurabi, the death-fine of ancient Greece, the Law of Moses, the restitution required by Indian Hinduism, and the early German "redemption of revenge," compensation to the victim was considered an integral part of the sanction for crime.[30]

The tort-crime distinction is usually traced back to twelfth-century England, when feudal barons decided to increase their revenues by obtaining fines and forfeitures from offenders at the expense of victims.[31] While well entrenched in nineteenth- and early twentieth-century Anglo-American legal practice, this distinction was never unanimously accepted by scholars.[32] In Continental practice (and in the countries of Latin America, Africa, and Asia that imported the precepts of the Napoleonic Code), the distinction was never as clear cut. In France, for example, an injured party may file an *action civile* for civil damages in criminal court concurrently with the criminal case or *action publique,* acting as a kind of private prosecutor; this practice avoids the delay and expense to the crime victim of using the civil courts. In a number of countries, the public prosecutor may represent the victim in the civil case as well as prosecute the criminal action.[33]

Even in common law countries, recent years have seen renewed interest in the plight and role of the crime victim. Most courts now provide for court-ordered restitution.[34] Redress for victims is justified to prevent the alienation of victims from society and to encourage voluntary citizen participation in crime reporting, as added deterrence for criminals, and to prevent individuals from refraining from revenge or self-help in the wake of victimization.[35] Victims are encouraged to participate in sentencing decisions, and their testimony is heard in deciding whether aggravating circumstances exist in capital cases. Conversely, civil sanctions like forfeiture of property are increasingly recognized as having a punitive result, thus requiring elaborate due process safeguards.

The Content of a Victim-Centered Approach

A victim-centered approach to punishment, as well as questions of redress for victims more generally, requires an analysis of victims' needs in the wake of state-initiated or sponsored crime against the victim or the victim's immediate family. To some extent, psychological studies of victimization are helpful in evaluating these needs.

Psychologists have long noted the traumatic effects of victimization.[36] Because violent crimes like those at issue here lay bare the fragility of life and the possibility of death, they deprive victims not only of "[their] belief in invulnerability, but also of [their] sense of control and autonomy in the world."[37] In response, victims may sink into helplessness and experience a loss of control over their destiny. Victimization also can lead to increased isolation because the world becomes a more frightening and less explicable place.[38] In a human rights context, this isolation may be particularly keen for victims and their family members, who may be shunned by the larger society as political outcasts who brought their problems on themselves, or from a generalized fear of being tainted — or even found guilty — by association with the victim. Survivors of traumatic experiences also feel isolated because others cannot bear to hear about and be linked with the massive pain of the experience and so tend to shun anyone they associate with it.[39]

In providing redress for victims, therefore, it is important to find ways to reassert their sense of control and autonomy, lessen their isolation, and increase their feeling of belonging to a community. Another important insight from the psychological literature is the need for victims to find some meaning in their victimization.[40] Whereas when the victim was a clearly defined and active political opponent of the regime the reason for victimization may be clear, in many cases victims of the most egregious human rights violations have no idea why they were victimized. The families may be similarly baffled.

Studies of torture victims in Chile, for instance, showed that production of a written document systematizing and summarizing their experiences was therapeutic because it helped the victims "integrate the traumatic experience into their lives by identifying its significance in the context of political and social events as well as the context of their personal history."[41] In addition, producing testimony about the traumatic events helped channel the victim's anger into a socially constructive action and provided a form of catharsis. Psychologists found that the power of the testimonies derived in part from the autoassertive quality of simple verbalization of the experience.

A conclusion to be drawn from the psychological literature on victimization, then, is that a victim-centered approach to redress must provide victims with a sense of control, an ability to lessen their isolation and be reintegrated into their community, and the possibility of finding reintegration and meaning through participation in the process. But what kind of process will lead to these results?

One aspect of the answer deals with the modalities of redress: These should focus on enhancing the dignity of the victims and on public recognition of the wrong done them as much as on monetary compensation or provision of public services. Redress may include public apologies and atonement by representatives of the state, monetary and nonmonetary compensation, preferential access to public services or resources, reinstatement or rehabilitation, disclosure of the truth, and commemoration, as well as punishment for those responsible for the victimization.[42] In all these areas, the touchstone of redress is its effect on the victim.

To the extent redress works through legal measures, some insights into what effective redress entails may come from work on procedural justice done in the context of civil and criminal litigation in the United States. Procedural justice theorists start from the premise that people are sensitive to the process and procedures they experience in encounters with the law. They posit that the fairness with which an individual is treated in encounters with the legal system, more than the outcome, is the most important factor in determining that person's perception of justice. People value the opportunity to state their views to a decision maker regardless of the influence of those views on the outcome of a dispute.[43] The dignity accorded the person within the procedure, the symbolic features of the procedure, and the degree of control the person has over the procedure (rather than the outcome) are all perceived components of fairness.[44] These value-expressive effects[45] reinforce citizens' positive self-image and standing in a social group. These findings are consonant with the need to reestablish autonomy and dignity, as discussed earlier.

Several studies address specifically the kinds of procedures most likely to promote a perception of procedural fairness. One early influential study compared the highly formalized procedures of adversarial litigation with less formal, less adversarial forms of mediation aimed at a prelitigation settlement. The study compared litigants' perceptions of fairness after trial and after negotiated settlement of a dispute. It found that, irrespective of whether they had won or lost, litigants viewed adversarial proceedings like trial and binding arbitration as fairer and more satisfactory than negotiated settlement. The most important explanations of this preference were that the trial-type proceedings were seen as more dignified and more careful. A formal court hearing was perceived as according importance to the persons and subject matter involved in a dispute, whereas an informal settlement conference might have seemed to trivialize the issue of right and wrong that litigants perceived was at the heart of their claim. In addition, formal trial procedures were seen as offering more participation in decision making than informal means and as being more understandable.[46]

Subsequent studies have attempted to control for cultural specificity in the preference for one type of procedure over another. While researchers found, for example, that Chinese subjects were more likely than U.S. subjects to prefer mediation over a full adversarial hearing, they found that both subject groups use the same criteria for decision making: control over presentation of evidence, the fairness of the procedure, the capacity of the procedure to reduce animosity between the disputants, and the extent to which the procedure favored the subject.[47] Other studies have reaffirmed the preference for adversary-type procedures and have isolated the ability to define the issues under dispute, to express arguments and present evidence, and to cross-examine or seek clarification as essential components of disputants' preference for such procedures. Finally, new studies show that adversary-type procedures are especially preferred when the relationship between the parties is such that negotiation and trade-offs are not possible[48] — as in the relationship between victims and victimizers in human rights cases.

Although it is important not to draw too much from these studies or to minimize the differences between U.S. legal culture and that of other countries,[49] the conclusions do suggest several things. First, any victim-centered procedure must put a heavy emphasis on people being able to tell their story fully before a decision maker who is perceived as neutral, honest, and attentive. Respectful treatment is more important than monetary or other gain. Public airing of victims' stories seems to serve important psychological and therapeutic ends. This finding again points up the usefulness of public recognition of the wrong done, public apologies, monuments, commemorations, reburials, and other forms of symbolic redress as important methods in a victim-centered approach. It further suggests that compensation alone is insufficient; indeed, compensation may be counterproductive if it infringes on victims' dignity through, for instance, excessive or too searching application procedures. The same is true of compensation that is seen as buying silence or "blood money." The finding also suggests that states may have some flexibility in meeting the needs of victims: Incarceration of offenders may not be the only option.

Second, more formalized procedures, including the ability to have an advocate and to confront and question their victimizers, may be more satisfying for victims than less formal, less adjudicative models. This finding might suggest the superiority of trial-type procedures, either civil or as an adjunct to criminal process, as preferable to more legislative or commission-type procedures from the point of view of victims.

Further confirmation of this last point comes from the experiences of Holocaust survivors. Although a number of techniques — history books, films, classes, and the like — are important to maintaining memory and teaching history, only trials, by bringing the past into the present and giving it present effects, satisfied the victims' need for justice. As Henry Rousso wrote of the 1983 trial of Klaus Barbie in France:

> Teaching history and raising consciousness are praiseworthy goals, but other institutions could achieve them as well as the courts. Nothing but a trial could satisfy the victims' need for justice, however. And their statements after the trial made it clear that this was what they felt too, far more than they cared about participating in any educational process.[50]

This kind of victim-centered model using modalities of redress combines easily with the utilitarian model as well as with a victim-centered retributive model of punishment. Public scorn for both the practices employed and those who employed them serves as a powerful deterrent. Publication of the names of those found to have committed murders, inflicted torture, and caused disappearances, although not a penal sanction, serves as a kind of punishment. For that very reason, some countries and commentators have hesitated to release names without a full judicial process.

Clemency and Punishment

Historically a "living fossil, a relic from the days when an all-powerful monarch possessed the power to punish and to remit punishment as an act of mercy,"[51] the power of clemency exists in almost all legal systems. Clemency may take a number of different forms, including pardon, amnesty, commutation of sentence, or remission of fines. For purposes of this book, there are two salient differences: First, pardon or commutation is granted to individuals on the basis of individualized considerations, whereas amnesty is granted to groups on the basis of public policy concerns. Second, pardon generally does not vitiate guilt for the underlying offense, whereas amnesty operates as an extinction of the offense itself.[52]

Both utilitarian and retributivist theories limit the use of clemency. General deterrence requires certainty of punishment: If potential lawbreakers are not convinced of this certainty, they will be encouraged to commit crimes. Although the rules themselves may be humane and may try to avoid unnecessary suffering, they must make no exceptions. Thus, Jeremy Bentham decried the extensive use of pardons in the late eighteenth century because they undermined the certainty of sanctions:

> From pardon power unrestricted, comes impunity to delinquency in all shapes: from impunity to delinquency in all shapes, impunity to maleficence in all shapes: from impunity to maleficence in all shapes, dissolution of government: from dissolution of government, dissolution of political society.[53]

For utilitarians, therefore, any exceptions to punishment must be carefully and narrowly drawn if used at all.

Early retributivists, like early utilitarians, believed that punishment was a "categorical imperative";[54] for Immanuel Kant, failure of a society to punish those who deserved punishment would make the members of that society themselves guilty of injustice. This was so because punishment was required to right a balance, to take away an injust benefit to the criminal. Pardons by a sovereign were in most cases unwarranted because they took away the citizen's right to have the balance of societal burdens and benefits restored. Even for Kant, however, pardon or remission of punishment was acceptable when the crime was encouraged by the state whose laws forbid it, as, for instance, those convicted of dueling.[55] Arguably, grave human rights violations committed by individuals in the employ of the state fall into a similar category.

Modern theorists have tried to develop a principled set of rules to distinguish appropriate uses of the power of clemency from those that erode justice. Kathleen Moore sums up the bounds of clemency compatible with justice as those where (1) the offender is legally or morally innocent, (2) the offender gained no unfair advantage by the crime, (3) the action was either morally justified or at least "conscientious," or (4) the offender would suffer excessively.[56] Reasons (1) and (4) seem the easiest to justify. Surely an appropriate use of the clemency power is to right individual cases of miscarriage of justice or of overly severe sentencing: to allow greater individuation in how we treat each offender given uniform sentencing laws and fallible truth finding. The closest analogue in the human rights context is probably mitigation of punishment in cases of obedience to superior orders.

So too with mercy based on the individual's frailties or personal tragedies: the dismissal of cases of those offenders too old or too infirm to be worth trying and punishing. On the other hand, the category of moral justification seems most slippery; who is to decide when a prohibited action is morally justified? No doubt the military establishments of Latin America believe their actions during the 1970s were morally justified in the name of saving the country from Communist expansion. Is that enough? I believe not.

Beyond these, several religious traditions encompass ideas of mercy and forgiveness that might form an independent moral basis for clemency. However, even within these traditions, forgiveness is possible only on the basis of an "offer of compensation"—that is, the recognition of wrongs committed and atonement through acts of reparation.[57] Although scholars disagree on whether mercy not tied to justice has a place in the law, even those who admit some independent role for mercy see it as a waiver of the right to punish that can be exercised only (either actually or by some process of agency) by those who have been victimized.[58]

Conclusion

The theories of punishment that best apply in the case of state-sponsored or condoned human rights violations are those which focus on the effects of punishment on the victim and on the wider society. Both denunciation theory and victim-centered retribution require punishment as one of an array of measures designed to provide redress for victims and to establish the force of societal norms. The following chapters illustrate how international law treats the concepts of punishment and redress as necessary parts of a legal regime based on respect for human rights.

3

Sources in International Treaties of an Obligation to Investigate, Prosecute, and Provide Redress

Naomi Roht-Arriaza

Until recently, a state's treatment of its own citizens was not considered a proper concern of international law. Only in the wake of widespread revulsion against the crimes committed immediately before and during World War II did nations finally begin to accept limits on their virtually absolute sovereignty regarding the human rights of those residing within their jurisdiction. Building on several strands in earlier law, the trial of the Nazi war criminals at Nuremberg established that certain grave human rights violations by a government against its citizens are a matter of international concern and action.

This chapter and the next examine the international law available on the subject of investigation, prosecution, and redress for victims of grave human rights violations. International law may be found in treaties among states and in non-treaty-based law, including custom and general principles of law.[1] This chapter looks at treaty-based sources of obligation, including judicial and quasi-judicial interpretation and commentary on treaty provisions, while Chapter 4 considers nontreaty-based sources.

A series of widely subscribed multilateral instruments now define many of the obligations of a government to its own citizens. Three different types of provisions in post-World War II multilateral treaties provide support for a state's obligation to investigate violations of personal integrity, take action against those reponsible, and provide redress to victims. First, a series of treaties specify the obligation of states to prosecute and punish perpetrators of acts defined as crimes under international law. Second, authoritative interpretations of broad human rights treaties hold that states parties fail to "ensure and respect" the substantive rights protecting individuals' physical integrity if they do not affirmatively investigate, prosecute, and provide redress. Third, the right to a remedy included in many human rights instruments provides a strong basis for inferring an obligation to investigate, prosecute, and provide redress.

International Criminal Law Provisions

Universal Jurisdiction and "Prosecute or Extradite"

International law has long allowed for the punishment of individuals who commit a certain limited subset of international crimes. Certain acts, notably piracy and slave trading, were considered so heinous and depredatory that any state which caught such offenders was authorized to try them and punish them. Universal jurisdiction of states over pirates and slavers dates back to the origins of international law. Such jurisdiction was based on both the nature and consequences of the proscribed acts: The acts in themselves involved morally reprehensive acts of violence against civilians, often including loss of life, and the consequences included interference with commerce and navigation on the high seas.[2] It mattered not which country pirates were nominally citizens of: Because they were *hostis humani generis* — an enemy of all humanity — any state, including their own, could punish them through its domestic courts.

Universal jurisdiction, however, is permissive, not mandatory. The trend in the last half century has been both to expand the offenses subject to universal jurisdiction and to make the assumption of jurisdiction (or extradition to a state that will assume jurisdiction) mandatory.

The principle *aut dedere aut judicare* — extradite or prosecute — dates back to Grotius, one of the earliest international legal scholars.[3] The purpose of the principle is to ensure that those who commit crimes under international law are not granted safe haven anywhere in the world. The principle goes beyond universal jurisdiction by making prosecution mandatory, not permissive.

The 1949 Geneva Conventions provide that the High Contracting Parties

> shall be under the obligation to search for persons alleged to have committed, or to have ordered to be committed, such grave breaches, and shall bring such persons, regardless of their nationality, before its own courts . . . [or] hand such persons over for trial to another High Contracting Party. . . .

"Grave breaches" under these Conventions include "wilful killing, torture or inhuman treatment, including biological experiments, wilfully causing great suffering or serious injury to body or health, unlawful deportation or transfer or unlawful confinement."[4] Protocol I to the Conventions specifies that "[in order to] avoid any doubt concerning the prosecution and trial of persons accused of war crimes or crimes against humanity," these persons should be submitted for the purpose of prosecution in accordance with international law, subject to guarantees of a fair trial.[5] The High Contracting Parties and the Parties to the conflict *shall* repress grave breaches, take measures necessary to suppress all other breaches, and pay compensation for violations of the Protocol.[6] However, the grave breaches provisions of the Geneva Conventions have been generally thought to apply only to international conflicts; although common article 3 of the Conventions establishes minimum humanitarian safeguards for noninternational conflicts, there is no explicit requirement to prosecute.[7]

The Convention on the Suppression and Punishment of the Crime of Apartheid[8] makes apartheid an international crime and establishes universal jurisdiction; more important, it requires states to adopt legislative, judicial, and administrative measures to prosecute, bring to trial, and punish those persons found within its jurisdiction accused of, or responsible for, the crime of apartheid. A series of treaties on slavery and slavelike practices, including forced labor, also require extradition or prosecution of those implicated.[9] In addition, international agreements to outlaw and punish hijacking,[10] aircraft sabotage,[11] the taking of hostages,[12] and terrorism[13] all include provisions calling for states parties to either submit the case of an alleged offender for prosecution under their own laws or extradite the person to a country that will prosecute him or her. These provisions are based on a rationale similar to that underlying universal jurisdiction for piracy; the crimes at issue both inherently threaten human life and create a threat to international peace, commerce, and stability. They represent the movement from permissive universal jurisdiction to mandatory action against the modern-day successors to the pirates of old.

Genocide, Torture, and Disappearance

After World War II, international lawyers sought mechanisms to ensure that the crimes of that period would not be repeated. The Convention on the Prevention and Punishment of the Crime of Genocide[14] drew from the immediately preceding period in two respects: Its definition of genocide was tailored to precisely the intentional targeting of a religious, racial, or national group that had characterized Nazi atrocities,[15] and it postulated an international criminal court, in the mold of that established at Nuremberg, as a forum for adjudicating accusations of genocide.

In article I of the Convention, the contracting parties confirm that genocide is a crime under international law, which they undertake to prevent and to punish. Article IV states: "Persons committing genocide or any of the acts enumerated in article III shall be punished, whether they are constitutionally responsible rulers, public officials or private individuals." Article V calls on states to "provide effective penalties" for persons guilty of genocide or related offenses. Article VI provides for trial by "a competent tribunal of the State in the territory of which the act was committed, or by such international penal tribunal as may have jurisdiction." In effect, because an international penal tribunal does not yet exist, the responsibility for prosecuting and punishing genocide devolves on national governments.[16] Interestingly, a proposal to require reparations for genocide was defeated because delegates feared it might detract from the Convention's emphasis on criminal punishment.

By the time the Convention Against Torture[17] was drafted in the 1980s, it was clear that at least for now the primary responsibility for dealing with offenders had to rest with the domestic courts of each state. The Convention requires investigating, prosecuting, and compensating the victims of torture as well as providing for universal jurisdiction over its perpetrators.

Article 1 of the Convention defines torture as acts[18] intentionally inflicted by or at the instigation of (or with the consent or acquiescence of) a public official or other person acting in an official capacity. Article 2 requires each state party to take effective measures to prevent acts of torture in territory under its jurisdiction.[19] Article 4 obligates states parties to ensure that torture, attempts to commit torture, and complicity or participation in torture are treated as criminal offenses, subject to penalties that "take into account their grave nature."

The Convention establishes state responsibility to extradite or prosecute suspected offenders. Article 7 reads:

1. The State Party in the territory under whose jurisdiction a person alleged to have committed any offense referred to in article 4 is found shall . . . , if it does not extradite him, submit the case to its competent authorities for the purpose of prosecution.
2. These authorities shall take their decision in the same manner as in the case of any ordinary offense of a serious nature under the law of that State.

The recently approved Inter-American Convention on the Forced Disappearance of Persons[20] similarly requires states to criminalize acts of forced disappearance, treat them as continuing offenses, and extradite or prosecute offenders.

In addition to an explicit directive to prosecute, the Convention Against Torture also explicitly calls for investigation of complaints and compensation for victims. Article 12 requires each party to "ensure that its competent authorities proceed to a prompt and impartial investigation, wherever there is reasonable ground to believe that an act of torture has been committed in any territory under its jurisdiction." Article 13 gives alleged victims of torture the right to complain to and have their cases examined by competent authorities. Article 16 makes the provisions of articles 12 and 13 applicable to other acts of cruel, inhuman, or degrading treatment.[21] Article 14(1) deals with compensation. It reads:

Each State Party shall ensure in its legal system that the victim of an act of torture obtains redress and has an enforceable right to fair and adequate compensation, including the means for as full rehabilitation as possible. In the event of the death of the victim as a result of an act of torture, his dependents shall be entitled to compensation.

By requiring states to provide redress as well as compensation to those subjected to torture, the drafters imply that redress consists of something other than simple compensation.[22] A commentary on the Convention indicates that

[w]hile redress seems to refer primarily to an official recognition of the wrong that has been done to the person concerned, the compensation is of a material (and primarily pecuniary) nature. Moreover, . . . [i]t is not sufficient that compensation can be granted as an *ex gratia* measure in appropriate cases.[23]

Under article 22 of the Convention, individuals may submit communications to the Committee Against Torture.[24] In one of the first cases submitted to the Committee, relatives of three Argentines killed under torture challenged the "due obedience" and "punto final" laws restricting prosecutions of the military.[25] The Committee declared the communications inadmissible because they were concerned with conduct that occurred before Argentina became a party to the Convention. Nonetheless, the Committee went on to observe that the laws in question were incompatible with the spirit and purpose of the Convention. The Committee urged Argentina not to leave the victims of torture and their dependants without a remedy, adding that if civil actions were no longer possible, it would welcome, in the spirit of article 14 (requiring an enforceable right to compensation), the adoption of measures to enable adequate compensation.[26]

Redress and compensation are also the focus of the International Convention on the Elimination of All Forms of Racial Discrimination.[27] That Convention requires criminalization of certain acts of racial hatred but does not explicitly require their prosecution. It does, however, specifically require a right to redress. Article 6 commits states parties to

> assure to everyone within their jurisdiction effective protection and remedies, through the competent national tribunals and other State institutions, against any acts of racial discrimination which violate his human rights and fundamental freedoms contrary to this Convention, as well as the right to seek from such tribunals just and adquate reparation or satisfaction for any damage suffered as a result of such discrimination.

Thus, states must not only provide redress for their own discriminatory acts, they must make available judicial or administrative remedies for private acts.

Overall, the trends with respect to international criminal law show a movement from permissive to mandatory jursdiction and from the idea of an international tribunal to reliance on national legal systems to prosecute offenders. The crimes covered by these conventions remain few: murder, torture, and inhumane acts such as rape or disappearance. Taken together, these provisions provide one basis for an emerging consensus that these human rights violations must be investigated and prosecuted.

Nonetheless, the applicability of penal law treaties is limited because not all states have signed the relevant treaties. But even where specific criminal treaty provisions have limited applicability, there are broader human rights treaties that provide additional treaty-based sources of an international obligation to investigate, prosecute, and compensate.

Comprehensive Human Rights Instruments

The comprehensive multilateral human rights instruments that have entered into force since the founding of the United Nations in 1945 define the substantive rights of individuals vis-à-vis their own states and, correspondingly, each state's commitment to the international community vis-à-vis the treatment of individuals living within its borders.[28] These commitments make human rights a proper subject for international concern and justify sanctions by other states, individually and collectively, for violations.[29] Because they generally do not specify the means by which rights are to be protected, these human rights instruments do not refer directly to a state's obligation to investigate or prosecute. However, the authoritative bodies created to monitor enforcement of these treaties have required states to investigate, prosecute, and compensate victims in cases of torture, summary execution, and disappearance. Moreover, they explicitly recognize an individual's right to a remedy and to judicial process when his or her rights have been violated.

Ensuring Substantive Rights

It is now widely accepted that references to "ensuring" the full enjoyment of the enumerated rights in comprehensive human rights treaties impose affirmative obligations on states. The International Covenant in article 2(1) requires parties to "respect and ensure to all individuals within its territory and subject to its jurisdiction the rights recognized" therein. The American Convention, in article 1(1), commits parties to "ensure to all persons subject to their jurisdiction the free and full exercise of those rights and freedoms [recognized in the Convention]. Article 1 of the European Convention frames the same duty as that of the parties to "secure to everyone within their jurisdiction the rights and freedoms" of the Convention. "The obligation 'to ensure' these rights encompasses the duty 'to respect' them, but it is substantially broader . . . [It] creates affirmative obligations on the state — for example, to discipline its officials."[30]

Thus, bodies charged with monitoring compliance with these human rights treaties have insisted that a series of steps are required to ensure the full enjoyment of the rights at issue, at least those — the right to life and to be free of torture — where violations are of the most basic rights and thus are of special concern.

The International Covenant includes provision for a Human Rights Committee to monitor state compliance with its provisions. By signing a separate optional protocol, states can also empower the Committee to hear individual complaints.[31] The findings and recommendations of the Committee in a number of cases involving summary execution, torture, and/or disappearance make clear that obligations to investigate, take action against perpetrators, and provide redress to victims are an integral part of ensuring the substantive rights at issue.

In an early "general comment" on article 7 (prohibiting torture), the Committee read that article together with article 2 to conclude that

> States must ensure an effective protection through some machinery of control. Complaints about ill-treatment must be investigated effectively by competent authorities. Those found guilty must be held responsible, and the alleged victims must themselves have effective remedies at their disposal, including the right to obtain compensation.[32]

In a later comment on the same article, the Committee added:

> The Committee has noted that some States have granted amnesty in respect of acts of torture. Amnesties are generally incompatible with the duty of States to investigate such acts; to guarantee freedom from such acts within their jurisdiction; and to ensure that they do not occur in the future.[33]

The Committee has reached similar conclusions in cases involving summary executions and disappearances. In the case of Eduardo Bleier,[34] for example, the Committee found that the state had a duty to investigate and if necessary prosecute as well as pay reparation. Mr. Bleier was arrested in Uruguay without a court order in October 1975, and his detention was unacknowledged by the authorities, although his name did appear for a time on a list of military prisoners. The Committee found that "[i]t is implicit in article 4(2) of the Optional Protocol that the State party has the duty to investigate in good faith all allegations of violation of the Covenant made against it and its authorities."[35] Moreover, it called on the Uruguayan government to

> take effective steps (i) to establish what has happened to Eduardo Bleier since October 1975; to bring to justice any persons found to be responsible for his death, disappearance or ill-treatment; and to pay compensation to him or his family for any injury which he has suffered; and (ii) to ensure that similar violations do not occur in the future.[36]

In another disappearance case, the Committee urged the government to take the same steps, adding that the families of those who disappeared were also themselves victimized by the practice.[37]

Thus, the body charged with interpreting the Covenant has interpreted it to require certain specific steps, including investigating, bringing to justice, providing compensation, and preventing future violations, as part of compliance with the substantive obligations to ensure as well as respect the right to life, to be free from torture and inhuman and degrading treatment, to be treated humanely, and to be free of arbitrary detention.

Velasquez and the American Convention

The American Convention on Human Rights, like the Covenant, obligates states parties to ensure the substantive rights enumerated. The Inter-American Court of Human Rights[38] elaborated on the content of this obligation in the 1988 *Velasquez-Rodriguez* decision.[39]

Velasquez concerned the arrest, torture, and execution of a Honduran student activist by the Honduran military. The Inter-American Commission's complaint, submitted to the court in April 1986, alleged violations of the rights to life, to humane treatment, and to personal liberty as protected by the Convention. The court found Honduras responsible for violating these substantive rights; more important, it found Honduras had also breached the general obligation of article 1(1) to ensure these rights.

The court asserted that the obligation of article 1 to "ensure" rights places an affirmative duty on the states parties to "organize the governmental apparatus and, in general, all the structures through which public power is exercised, so that they are capable of juridically ensuring the free and full enjoyment of human rights."[40]

> The State has a legal duty to take reasonable steps to prevent human rights violations and to use the means at its disposal to carry out a serious investigation of violations committed within its jurisdiction, to identify those responsible, impose the appropriate punishment and ensure the victim adequate compensation.[41]

This affirmative obligation is not fulfilled by the mere theoretical existence of a legal system to deal with complaints.[42] So long as the government exhibits a lack of diligence in preventing or responding to the violation, the government has violated its affirmative duty. While recognizing that "[t]he duty to investigate, like the duty to prevent, is an obligation of means or conduct which is not breached merely because the investigation does not produce a satisfactory result," the court demanded that the duty be undertaken seriously.[43]

The *Velasquez* judgment is significant in several ways. First, it employs a very broad definition of actions that engage state responsibility. The state breaches its obligation by failing to act even if the responsible organ or official has violated domestic law or overstepped the bounds of authority, and even if the identity of the individual perpetrator is unknown or the perpetrator is not a government agent.[44] Moreover, successor governments are responsible for the actions of their predecessors.[45]

Second, although the court relied on a pattern of violations as evidence of state involvement in Velasquez's disappearance, it did not limit its holding to cases in which a consistent pattern of violations was shown. Thus, even a single, isolated violation might trigger the state's obligation to act. Nonetheless, the evidentiary burden may be heavier for single violations than for those that form a pattern: Although the court allowed the use of the circumstantial evidence available in *Velasquez*[46] because the evidence fit the existence of a pattern or practice of similar violations, it did not reach the question of whether circumstantial evidence would suffice to establish state responsibility where no pattern or practice could be shown.[47]

The limits of *Velasquez*'s evidentiary holdings in cases not involving a pattern and practice are confirmed by a 1994 case brought against the Surinamese government for the death in detention of Asok Gangaram Panday. The Inter-American Court refused to infer government responsibility for the death from the fact that the victim had been illegally detained.[48] Although the court was willing to infer from circumstantial evidence that the detention itself was illegal, it refused to take the next step and hold the state responsible for the victim's hanging in his cell. It required the Commission, as petitioner, to meet its burden of showing that state actions or omissions — and not suicide, as some evidence indicated — were the cause of death.[49] Given that this information is likely to be exclusively in the hands of state authorities, the holding raises a significant evidentiary hurdle in cases where no pattern or practice evidence supports the Commission's case. Three dissenters argued that the state's affirmative obligation to protect and preserve life includes a due diligence obligation of reasonable prevention, and that, therefore, once the detention was declared illegal, state responsibility for the subsequent death followed.

The *Velasquez* court also hesitated to impose the sweeping remedy that would seem to be implied by the language of its judgment. At the remedy stage the court ordered only monetary compensation.[50] Lawyers for the victims' families, the Inter-American Commission, and a group of international law experts acting as *amici curiae* had asked the court for much broader injunctive measures, including an injunction requiring Honduras to prosecute criminally those responsible for disappearances, restructure the security apparatus, publicly condemn the practice of disappearances, and pay homage to the victims.[51] Although the narrow remedy seems inconsistent with the broad characterization of the offense, this was the first contentious case the court decided, and it may have found declarative relief less invasive of sovereignty than injunctive measures.[52]

In a subsequent judgment on compensation,[53] the court discussed the measures that constitute adequate reparation. Reparation "consists in full restitution (*restitutio in integrum*), which includes the restoration of the prior situation, the reparation of the consequences of the violation, and indemnification for patrimonial and non-patrimonial damages, including emotional harm."[54] The court also recognized that the harmful psychological effects of the disappearance on the victim's family must also be indemnified.[55] Punitive damages, however, were not appropriate.[56] Finally, the court reiterated that such measures as investigation, the punishment of those responsible, public statements by the Honduran government condemning the practice of disappearances, and the court's own judgment on the merits all constituted part of the reparation.[57]

Ensuring Rights in the European System

The European Convention for the Protection of Human Rights and Fundamental Freedoms, in article 1, commits the parties to "secure to everyone within their jurisdiction the rights and freedoms defined" in the Convention. The European Court[58] has interpreted article 1 to include an affirmative obligation to prevent or remedy breaches of the Convention. "The Convention does not merely oblige the higher authorities of the Contracting States to respect for their own part the rights and freedoms it embodies; . . . the Convention also has the consequence that, in order to secure the enjoyment of those rights and freedoms, those authorities must prevent or remedy any breach at subordinate levels."[59]

The European Commission has also addressed article 1. In a complaint brought by the sister of a man killed by the IRA, the Commission found that article 2, protecting the right to life, gives rises to positive obligations on the part of the state.[60] However, those obligations do not extend to providing protection *beyond* criminal prosecution of offenders, to include deployment of the armed forces to protect those exposed to terrorist threats.[61] Thus, by implication, criminal prosecution is part of the obligations the state assumes by signing the Convention.

It is also interesting to note that for the bodies charged with interpreting these conventions, the obligations to prevent future violations and to take action against past violators are entirely compatible; indeed, the latter, in that it provides a deterrent, is considered essential to ensuring the former. This contrasts with arguments, discussed later in this book, that the two can be contradictory and that to concentrate on prevention requires forgoing action against past violators.

The Right to a Remedy

Like the obligation to "ensure" rights, all the comprehensive human rights treaties include in some form the right to a remedy for violations. The Universal Declaration of Human Rights, the most accepted general articulation of recognized human rights, lists the right to a remedy in article 8: "Everyone has the right to an effective remedy by the competent national tribunals for acts violating the fundamental rights granted him by the constitution or by law."[62]

The International Covenant on Civil and Political Rights develops and specifies the civil and political rights enumerated in the Universal Declaration. It defines the right to a remedy in article 2(3). It reads:

Each State Party to the present Covenant undertakes:

(a) To ensure that any person whose rights or freedoms as herein recognized are violated shall have an effective remedy, notwithstanding that the violation has been committed by persons acting in an official capacity;

(b) To ensure that any person claiming such a remedy shall have his right thereto determined by competent judicial, administrative or legislative authorities, or by any other competent authority provided for by the legal system of the State, and to develop the possibilities of judicial remedy;

(c) To ensure that the competent authorities shall enforce such remedies when granted.

The drafting history of the International Covenant reveals that the Commission on Human Rights was concerned with ensuring accountability of government authorities for violations, especially by ruling out the defenses of sovereign immunity or superior orders.[63] The drafters therefore specified, in article 2(3)(a), that the right to a remedy extends to violations by government officials.

During the drafting of the Convention, some states wanted to strengthen the affirmative obligation on the part of government authorities to prosecute violations. The Philippine representative proposed adding the sentence "Violators shall be swiftly brought to the law, especially when they are public officials,"[64] making explicit a government obligation to prosecute those violating human rights. Although the proposal was defeated without discussion, the Philippine representative stressed that the defeat "should not be taken to mean that the Commission was indifferent to the fate of violators of human rights."[65]

Professor Oscar Schachter, writing about article 2(3) of the Covenant, suggests that "undoing, repairing and compensating for violations"[66] constitute appropriate remedies. This may include, at the least, injunctive relief, restoring the victim to his previous position if possible, and monetary compensation. Other remedial action under domestic law may also be appropriate. Thus, "cease and desist" orders, restructuring of the police or armed forces responsible for the violation, or mandamus ordering an investigation are all feasible remedies.[67]

In addition to the remedy provisions of article 2(3), the Covenant requires compensation for unlawful arrests or deprivations of liberty. Article 9(5) states that "[a]ny one who has been the victim of unlawful arrest or detention shall have an enforceable right to compensation." The drafting history of this provision reveals that a proposed list of exceptions, as well as a U.S. amendment to limit compensation to cases of malicious or grossly negligent conduct, were defeated. A majority of drafters understood that compensation was to be made by the state, not simply by the individual officials, especially since the latter interpretation would limit compensation to cases in which the offending official could be identified. A U.S. proposal to require only a right of action for compensation was also defeated.[68]

In addition, article 14(6) specifically requires compensation for those punished as a result of a miscarriage of justice. The European Convention, in article

5.5 (unlawful arrest or detention), and the American Convention, in article 10 (miscarriage of justice), similarly provide for compensation for these wrongs.

Article 25 of the American Convention also provides for the right to a remedy.[69] Although without referring explicitly to article 25, the *Velasquez* court discussed the types of remedies required under the Convention. Although the court acknowledged that remedies such as habeas corpus did exist in Honduran law, it found that in practice those remedies were ineffective "because the imprisonment was clandestine, formal requirements made them inapplicable in practice, the authorities against whom they were brought simply ignored them, or attorneys and judges were threatened and intimidated by those authorities."[70] Therefore, more was required: investigation, prosecution, compensation, and prevention, including through reorganization of the state apparatus. The court was authorized to order such relief by article 63 of the American Convention, which empowers the court to ensure the victim the enjoyment of the affected right or freedom, to repair the consequences of the violation of the victim's rights, and to assure payment of fair compensation to the victim or his or her family.[71]

The Inter-American Commission on Human Rights has long interpreted the "right to a remedy" language in the American Convention to include the obligation to investigate and prosecute, calling repeatedly for investigation of the facts and punishment of the responsible individuals in cases of torture or disappearance.[72]

Finally, the European Court of Human Rights has also interpreted the "right to remedy" language of the European Convention to include the obligation to investigate and prosecute. Article 13 of the Convention provides that "[e]veryone whose rights and freedoms as set forth in this Convention are violated shall have an effective remedy before a national authority notwithstanding that the violation has been committed by persons acting in an official capacity." The European Court has on at least one occasion adopted a liberal construction of the remedy provision.[73] In the *Klass* case,[74] the court held that article 13 requires the state to ensure a remedy before a national authority in order both to have his claim (of a violation of the Convention) decided and, if appropriate, to obtain redress.

While not decided under article 13, the case of *X and Y v. the Netherlands*[75] also sheds light on the types of remedies required. Dutch law provided that a criminal complaint must be filed within a given time by the victim; Miss Y was sexually assaulted, but because she was mentally handicapped her father filed the assault charges, which the prosecutor then dismissed. The government argued that the ability to institute a civil suit against the perpetrator was a sufficient remedy; the court disagreed. It cited article 8, requiring "respect for private life." The protection afforded by the civil law was insufficient in the case of wrongdoing of the kind in question, which affected fundamental values: Only criminal law provisions could achieve effective deterrence and, indeed, these provisions normally regulated such matters. Therefore, there was no adequate means of obtaining a remedy.[76] Thus, for serious criminal law violations, at least the possibility of prosecution may be a requirement under the European Convention; civil remedies may be insufficient.

A broad vision of redress is reinforced by the wording of those articles of both the European and American Conventions regarding the ability of regional human rights courts to provide redress. Under the American Convention, article 52 of the draft Convention originally referred only to the court's competence to determine compensation. An amendment, based on a Guatemalan proposal, strengthened and expanded the article to focus primarily on remedying the conduct at issue and only secondarily on compensation.[77] The current article 63 requires the court to rule

> that the injured party be ensured the enjoyment of his right or freedom that was violated. [The court] shall also rule, if appropriate, that the consequences of the measure or situation that constituted the breach of such right or freedom be remedied and that fair compensation be paid to the injured party.

Similarly, article 50 of the European Convention provides that, where the Convention has been violated and internal law allows only partial reparation, "the Court shall, if necessary, *afford just satisfaction* to the injured party" (emphasis added). This makes clear that international remedies are to be supplementary to those the states parties should provide in their national systems. Although monetary compensation is the usual measure of international satisfaction for isolated violations, if the violations are systematic or widespread, it will be insufficient. The European Commission has addressed the question of what constitutes satisfaction in cases of official torture or ill treatment. Where a state has taken reasonable steps to comply with its international human rights obligations but mistreatment of an individual nonetheless occurs, the Commission found that compensation generally will constitute an adequate remedy.[78] The state must put into place a system that prevents as far as possible the occurrence or repetition of the acts in question. Where the state has no such system, compensation will *not* be sufficient. Thus, by definition, if state authorities pursue a policy or administrative practice[79] authorizing or tolerating conduct in violation of the Convention, compensation alone will not be adequate.

The Right to Judicial Remedy

Another possible source of an obligation to investigate, prosecute, and provide redress is the provision common to the Civil and Political Covenant, the American Convention, and the European Convention requiring access to a court for determination of one's civil rights. The origin of this provision is article 10 of the Universal Declaration, which states: "Everyone is entitled in full equality to a fair and public hearing by an independent and impartial tribunal, in the determination of his rights and obligations and of any criminal charge against him."

Article 14 of the Covenant requires that "All persons shall be equal before the courts and tribunals. In the determination of any criminal charge against him, or of his rights and obligations in a suit at law, everyone shall be entitled to a fair and public hearing by a competent, independent and impartial tribunal established by law." The drafting history reveals little debate about the need for such a provision; the drafters emphasized its importance "since, in the last analysis, the implementation of all the rights in the covenant depended upon the proper administration of justice."[80] The first sentence was designed to ensure a right of equal access to courts and to limit the use of special courts.[81] However, there was debate over the scope of the provision: As discussed below, some delegates wished to restrict access to a court for individuals seeking administrative review of discretionary decisions by government officials.

Article 8.1 of the American Convention guarantees that

> Every person has the right to a hearing with due guarantees and within a reasonable time, by a competent, independent, and impartial tribunal, previously established by law, in the substantiation of any accusation of a criminal nature made against him or for the determination of his rights and obligations of a civil, labor, fiscal or any other nature.

The American Convention provision follows on an earlier one found in article XVIII of the 1948 American Declaration of the Rights and Duties of Man, which states:

> Every person may resort to the courts to ensure respect for his legal rights. There should likewise be available to him a simple, brief procedure whereby the courts will protect him from acts of authority that, to his prejudice, violate any fundamental constitutional rights.[82]

The language in article 6 of the European Convention is quite similar to that of article 14 of the Covenant.[83]

Despite the apparent broad reach and usefulness of the language of these provisions, the European and Inter-American systems diverge in their view of the provision's scope. The European Commission and the Court of Human Rights have addressed the meaning of article 6 in a number of cases. They distinguished rights arising under private law, which are covered by article 6, from those stemming from public or administrative law, which are not covered. Nonetheless, neither the mere fact that the state is a putative party, for example, in a tort suit, nor the fact that domestic law denies access to a court necessarily removes the rights to be adjudicated from the article 6 context: It depends on an examination of the exact nature of the suit at issue.

In the *Feldbrugge* case,[84] the European Court looked to the public law and private law aspects of Social Security insurance, deciding that article 6 applied only if the private law aspects, or analogies to private tort or contract law, predominated. The reasoning behind this distinction traces back to discussions around the parallel article of the International Covenant. According to a minority of judges in *Feldbrugge,* a number of representatives to the Covenant drafting process proposed that "everyone should have the right to have a tribunal determine his rights and obligations," but other delegates rejected the proposal because they were unwilling to require judicial review of discretionary administrative decisions, at least not without further discussion.[85] The drafting committee then added the words "in a suit at law" to what became article 14.

This distinction has been roundly criticized by commentators, especially given the increased importance of administrative law.[86] It has been disputed as a matter of the drafting history by Professor Newman, who points out that the appropriate distinction is not between administrative and other decisions but between *adjudications* (which are covered) and other forms of administrative action.[87] However, it has been consistently applied by both the European Commission and the court. For example, an applicant's complaint about court proceedings in which his claim for compensation under a specific German statute for victims of Nazi persecution had been rejected was found to belong to the domain of public law and thus was found inadmissible. The Commission distinguished the case from one in which damages could have been recovered under general principles of tort liability, which presumably would have come within the realm of private law, despite the fact that the claim was considered private under German law.[88] Thus, at least under the European Convention, to come under the protection of the respective articles on judicial protection a claim would have to be characterized as one of private law: Whereas tort claims in individual cases or against individual government officials could probably come within this stricture, more general claims for investigation, prosecution, and redress would not.

The Inter-American Court has not yet ruled directly on the scope of article 8.1. However, the Inter-American Commission has given quite a different interpretation to the right to judicial remedy, finding in a series of decisions that that right, together with others, precludes measures that limit certain prosecutions. Those cases are taken up in detail in Chapter 5.

The Right to Compensation

In addition to the provisions for redress and remedy, specific provisions in several multilateral treaties refer to compensation. The International Covenant on Civil and Political Rights, for example, requires in article 9(5) that "anyone who has been the victim of unlawful arrest or detention shall have an enforceable right to compensation." Discussions in the Commission on Human Rights indicated that the right "would seem likely to be invoked against individuals as well as against the State as a legal person."[89] Efforts by the United States to replace the words "enforceable right to compensation" with a mere "right of action for compensation" failed.[90]

Article 14(6) of the Covenant also calls for compensation for those convicted as the result of a miscarriage of justice. Although some delegates to the drafting commission felt that this was a matter for executive discretion in each country, a majority considered this compensation guarantee "essential" and necessary to complement the right to compensation in article 9(5).[91]

Thus, the comprehensive human rights treaties provide a broad definition of redress, especially in cases of government-sponsored or condoned violations. Redress, although it includes compensation, goes far beyond it to include prevention, investigation, and prosecution.

In sum, this chapter has established a number of complementary bases for finding a treaty-based state obligation to investigate grave human rights violations and to prosecute violators. Not all countries, however, are parties to one or more of the human rights instruments described here, and these treaty-based obligations do not apply to them. However, these countries are still bound to respect the obligation to investigate and prosecute human rights violators if the obligation has attained the status of a customary law norm or a general principle of law. Chapter 4 examines that possibility.

4

Nontreaty Sources of the Obligation to Investigate and Prosecute

Naomi Roht-Arriaza

The express undertaking of states, as found in multilateral treaties, provides the clearest form of legal obligation. However, treaty obligations as such bind parties to the treaty only: Governments that systematically violate human rights may be particularly disinclined to adhere to human rights treaty regimes. In addition, treaty obligations apply only to conduct that occurs after the treaty has entered into force for the state in question.[1] Treaty norms, therefore, must be supplemented by recourse to nontreaty sources of law. The two most important of these are customary international law and general principles of law.

Customary International Law

According to the classical definition, customary international law results from a general and consistent practice followed by states from a sense of legal obligation. Although state practice must be widespread, it need not be universal, and depending on the subject matter, it may be of relatively recent vintage.[2] Because practice alone is indeterminate, since states act from any number of motives, the second prong of the test — *opinio juris* — is necessary to assure that states are acting because they believe they are bound to act. Thus, custom has both an objective and a psychological/subjective dimension.

The use of state practice to determine unwritten rules of law makes the most sense in a setting in which what is at issue is one state's behavior toward another — the object of most nineteenth- and early twentieth-century international law. It is clear in these cases that the practice at issue is practice in the international arena, through diplomatic protests, economic or military coercion, or recourse to arbitration or international forums. The use of state practice becomes more problematic in the human rights area, where we are concerned with a state's international obligations to all other states vis-à-vis the treatment of its own citizens. Now it is unclear whether the state practice we are to consider is practice at the international level, through the state's statements and actions in international forums and through diplomatic channels and economic or military sanctions, or whether state practice should refer to a state's internal acts. This ambiguity has led to considerable confusion. For example, some writers have pointed to the discrepancy between many states' affirmations of support for a given norm on an international level and the contrary domestic practice of these same states to argue that customary law is inapplicable in the human rights context.[3] Other writers and courts have noted that because it is impossible to tell what effect human rights norms have had in restraining what would otherwise have been violations of those norms, state practice is necessarily inconclusive in this area. Thus, these commentators and courts have relied more heavily on indicators other than internal practice in the human rights area.[4]

Opinio juris is similarly hard to pin down in this area. The best source of what a state "believes" the law to be is no doubt statements to that effect made in diplomatic or international legal forums by state representatives. Yet because of a perception that talk is particularly cheap in international forums, many scholars discount such statements.[5] One is then left with few ways of knowing whether a state believes it is acting out of a need to comply with the law or from political, humanitarian, or even whimsical motives — except by reference to the consistency of its practice, which circles one back into the previous problem of indeterminacy.[6]

Although obligations to investigate, prosecute, and provide redress are relatively clear under treaty law, their customary law status is more ambiguous. A number of sources, if combined, suggest an emerging obligation under customary international law: (1) the treaty provisions just discussed, taken together; (2) diplomatic practice; (3) the customary law surrounding crimes against humanity; and (4) the practice of arbitral tribunals under the rules of state responsibility for the protection of aliens. All of these sources rely on states' practice in the external arena. Nonetheless, the failure of many states to act even against notorious human rights violators, or the passage of amnesties absolving violators from responsibility, makes it more difficult to define the line between the flouting of an established norm and the nonexistence of sufficient evidence, based on internal practice, of the existence of the norm itself. This conclusion leads to a search for other possible nontreaty sources of legal obligation. The extent to which states apply, and rely on, these norms in their internal practice is explored in later chapters.

Treaty Provisions as the Basis of a Customary Norm

Multilateral treaties, which allow any state to adhere and which are widely accepted, may in certain circumstances lead to the creation of customary international law because such agreements reflect the practice of states. Because of the wide acceptance and universal character of both the criminal and the comprehensive human rights treaties containing express or implied obligations to investigate, prosecute, and provide redress, the cumulative existence of these treaties provides one possible basis for a customary law obligation.

Both the International Court of Justice and the U.S. Supreme Court have held that treaties can create binding obligations for nonparties.[7] In the *North Sea Continental Shelf* cases, the International Court of Justice noted that treaty provisions of a "norm-creating character" might become general rules of international law, especially if there was a "very widespread and representative participation in the Convention."[8] The court considered the number of parties to the treaty, the structure of the treaty as a whole, and subsequent state practice, particularly that of states strongly affected by the treaty, to determine if a provision was "norm-creating." In the *Nottebohm* case,[9] the court also drew on treaties to elucidate an international rule of nationality despite the fact that the parties to the dispute were not parties to those treaties.[10]

Some scholars who do not accept the idea that treaties generally can bind nonparties through customary law are willing to accept that humanitarian treaties may do so. For example, R. R. Baxter thought that "[i]n so far as they are directed to the protection of human rights, rather than to the interests of States, . . . [humanitarian treaties] have a wider claim to application than treaties concerned, for example, with the purely political and economic interests of States."[11] This is true because such treaties clearly intend both the widest possible applicability and the generation or codification of custom. The International Court of Justice suggested this idea in its advisory opinion on the Genocide Convention, pointing out the need for more flexible rules in treaties aimed at universal acceptance and humanitarian purposes.[12]

In addition, these treaties build on one another and frequently have common provisions or embody parallel concepts. Similar provisions in numerous conventions provide even stronger evidence of a norm. Indeed, Meron writes that "the repetition of certain norms in many human rights instruments is itself an important articulation of state practice" and may serve as a "preferred indicator" of customary status.[13]

The clearest place where a treaty obligation may have transmuted into customary law is the "prosecute or extradite" provisions common to treaties that criminalize human rights violations like torture and disappearance. This is especially so since these provisions to a large extent codify principles long recognized by scholars, going back to Emmerich de Vattel in 1758.[14] The list of treaties requiring either prosecution or extradition is several pages long and includes treaties concerning humanitarian law, genocide, apartheid, slavery, prostitution, piracy, hijacking, drug trafficking, and terrorism.[15]

Compensation for official wrongdoing, codified in the torture convention as well as in all the comprehensive treaties, may also have attained customary status. It too has a long pedigree.

Diplomatic Practice

As just mentioned, there is no clear pattern of internal state practice of investigating, prosecuting, or redressing past human rights violations. Although several countries have done all or some of these things, others have not. This reticence, however, may be as easily explained by some states' lack of recognition of the international norm requiring such actions, thus weakening the case for customary status, as by extenuating political factors that make states unable to comply with a norm they clearly recognize. Thus, "state practice" as an indicator of custom is by itself inconclusive.

Proving the existence of customary norms in the human rights field through the traditional tests may be difficult. Yet most jurists, diplomats, and scholars agree that prohibitions on torture, summary execution, and arbitrary imprisonment are indeed part of customary law.[16] The difficulty in applying the state practice and *opinio juris* tests in the human rights area has led courts and commentators to turn to additional indicators of practice to determine which human rights norms have attained the status of custom. For example, although evidence of inconsistent state practice would normally militate against the existence of a customary norm, the International Court of Justice has found that it carries less weight in the field of human rights or humanitarian law. Instead, the court has focused on verbal statements of government representatives to international organizations, the content of resolutions and declarations adopted by these organizations, and the consent of states to such instruments.[17]

States are quite unwilling to say clearly that they have no obligation to investigate or prosecute human rights violators, just as they are unwilling to announce their rejection of other fundamental human rights. In their representations to international bodies, state representatives have stressed their compliance with the norm. So, for example, although the Uruguayan civilian government ultimately enacted a virtual amnesty, when it first took office it assured the U.N. Human Rights Commission that it would investigate the human rights violations committed under the previous dictatorship and bring the perpetrators of these abuses to justice.[18]

In 1984, the Chilean representative, responding to questions by members of the Human Rights Committee regarding Chile's compliance with its international obligations, assured the Committee that Chilean authorities were investigating disappearances, and that persons responsible who had been identified were brought to justice.[19] El Salvador's representative told the Committee in 1987 that then President José Napoleón Duarte's government had abolished a police section suspected of human rights violations and had brought nearly 1,000 members of the armed forces and security forces to trial for human rights violations.[20] Although these assertions may have been somewhat fanciful,[21] they demonstrate an apparent belief that such measures are a necessary part of human rights compliance.

In their diplomatic and political interchanges, some states also show recognition of an obligation to investigate and prosecute. For example, the U.S. government has conditioned foreign aid to El Salvador on satisfactory investigation and prosecution of those responsible for death squad killings of non-U.S. nationals.[22] The United States recalled its ambassador to Guatemala to protest the lack of prosecutions in human rights cases.[23] In response to U.S. pressure, the Chilean government agreed to compensate the Letelier family and assured the State Department that it was "making all efforts to bring to justice the murderers of [ex-Chilean foreign minister Orlando] Letelier."[24] The result was a payment by the Chilean government of over $2 million in compensation to the Letelier and Moffit families,[25] as well as the arrest and conviction of the army general suspected of masterminding the crime.[26] Polish leaders called on the Soviet Union to follow up on its admission that the Soviets were responsible for the Katyn forest massacre in 1940 with prosecution of those guilty of the crime.[27]

Practice at the United Nations

Another type of state practice may be found in resolutions and reports of U.N. organs, especially the General Assembly. The Assembly has repeatedly called for investigation and prosecution of human rights violators. For example, a 1981 resolution urged the Chilean government to "investigate and clarify the fate of persons who have disappeared for political reasons, to inform the relatives of those persons of the outcome of the investigation and to prosecute and punish those responsible."[28] Special *rapporteurs,* or experts assigned by the Commission on Human Rights to examine the situation in certain countries or with regard to the practices of torture, disappearance, or summary execution have repeatedly condemned a lack of investigation and prosecution as creating a climate of impunity conducive to further violations.[29] Like the courts and commissions that have considered the issue, the U.N. *rapporteurs* stress the deterrent function of investigation, prosecution, and punishment in preventing further abuses.

In 1989, the U.N. Economic and Social Council adopted, and the General Assembly endorsed, Principles on the Effective Prevention and Investigation of Extra-legal, Arbitary and Summary Executions.[30] Like the convention on torture, these principles provide that governments shall make extralegal, summary, or arbitrary executions punishable by appropriate penalties, investigate all suspected cases, extradite or prosecute those involved, and provide compensation to victims' families. The principles set out international standards for investigating and prosecuting these violations. The standards for investigation require, among other things, publication of the findings. Those governing prosecution specify that superior orders may not be invoked to justify participation in extralegal, arbitrary, or summary executions and prohibit any blanket immunity from prosecution for any person allegedly involved in such acts.

The United Nations has also dealt with the issue through its criminal justice-related activities. In 1985, the General Assembly unanimously adopted the Declaration of Basic Principles of Justice for Victims of Crime and Abuse of Power.[31] The declaration calls on member states to "enact and enforce legislation proscribing acts that violate internationally recognized norms relating to human rights." In cases in which "public officials or other agents acting in an official or quasi-official capacity have violated national criminal laws, the victims should receive restitution from the State."[32] Principles developed to implement the Declaration by a group of international criminal law experts call on states to conduct impartial investigations into all deaths and serious physical and mental injuries apparently caused by law-enforcement, military, administrative, medical, and other professional personnel; prosecute or extradite persons who commit serious crimes; and

> ensure that public and military officials and agents receive no immunity from prosecution or disciplinary proceedings for victimization that was caused will-

fully, and that in such prosecutions or proceedings there is no defence of obedience to superior orders in cases in which those orders are manifestly illegal.[33]

The implementation principles also call on states to provide access to justice
(through criminal, civil, or administrative proceedings), restitution and/or compensation for victims of violations of human rights conventions and of crimes
against humanity.[34]

The Declaration on the Protection of All Persons from Enforced Disappearance, adopted by the General Assembly in December 1992, specifically aims at
"setting forth standards designed to punish and prevent" forced disappearance.[35]
In addition to establishing individual criminal responsibility and civil liability for
the individual and the state, the Declaration contains detailed requirements
regarding prevention and investigation of disappearances, punishment of offenders, and compensation for victims and their families.

The Declaration contains several innovations when compared to similar earlier documents such as the Declaration on Torture,[36] which preceded the torture
convention. For example, article 4, which requires criminal penalties for perpetrators, also allows recognition of mitigating circumstances in national law for those
involved who "are instrumental in bringing the victims forward alive or in providing voluntarily information which would contribute to clarifying cases of enforced
disappearance." This article thus allows states some leeway for plea bargaining.
Articles 9 and 13 deal with investigation: Article 9 reaffirms the right to prompt
and effective judicial remedy *either* to determine the whereabouts of the person
who has disappeared *and/or* to identify the authority ordering or carrying out the
act, even in times of internal political instability or any other public emergency.
Thus, even if the disappeared person reappears (alive or dead), investigation is
still warranted. Article 13 sets out the right to a prompt investigation of an alleged
disappearance. It requires that the investigatory authorities be able to issue subpoenas and make on-site visits, protect the complainant and witnesses, and make
available the results of the investigation to "all persons concerned" unless doing
so would jeopardize an ongoing criminal probe.

Articles 14, 16, and 18, which require extradition or prosecution of offenders,
specify that violators should be tried by ordinary civilian courts, not be granted
immunity, and "not benefit from any amnesty or similar measures that might have
the effect of exempting them from criminal proceedings or sanction." Thus, for
the first time, some of the specific measures required to make prosecutions effective have been spelled out in no uncertain terms. These stringent commands are
slightly tempered by article 18(b), which allows states to exercise the right of pardon so long as the extreme seriousness of acts of enforced disappearance are
taken into account, thus recognizing the distinction between amnesty and pardon
(discussed in Chapter 21). The qualifying language, however, also ensures that the
pardon power will not be used to undermine the imperative of prior conviction
and punishment altogether — for example, through a pardon after a disproportion-
ately light sentence has been served. In addition, article 14 stipulates that "[a]ll
States should take any *lawful* and *appropriate* action available to them to bring to
justice all persons presumed responsible for an act of enforced disappearance,

who are found to be within their jurisdiction or under their control" (emphasis added). Although this language allows for the exercise of universal jurisdiction, it can also be read, emphasizing the italicized words, to allow the state some measure of discretion in prosecutions. Finally, article 17 characterizes disappearance as a continuing offense, requires "substantial and commensurate" statutes of limitation, and, most important, provides for tolling of the statute of limitations during periods when effective domestic remedies do not exist.

The U.N. Working Group on Enforced or Involuntary Disappearances tackled the question of impunity directly at its 1991 session, labeling it the most important factor contributing to the phenomenon of disappearance.[37] At its 1992 session, the working group recommended a number of measures to combat impunity, including guaranteeing the right of habeas corpus, protecting witnesses and complainants, and publishing the results of investigations, including the identity of both the victims and those responsible for designing, implementing, and abetting a policy of disappearances. Moreover, no laws or decrees should be enacted or maintained that, in effect, afford the perpetrators of disapparances immunity from accountability."[38] The U.N. Subcommission on Prevention of Discrimination and Protection of Minorities is currently considering the issue of impunity[39] and recently considered the issue of the right to restitution, compensation, and rehabilitation for victims of gross violations of human rights.[40] The latter study produced Draft Principles on the Right to Restitution, Compensation and Rehabilitation for Victims of Gross Violations of Human Rights and Fundamental Freedoms.

These draft principles define broadly the state's duty to make reparation to include restitution, compensation, rehabilitation, satisfaction, and guarantees of nonrepetition. The latter two aspects include verification of the facts and full disclosure of the truth; declaratory judgments and public apologies; bringing to justice the persons responsible for the violations; commemorations; and reorganization of the administrative, military, and judicial apparatus to prevent recurrences. The draft principles recognize the link between prosecutions of perpetrators and reparations to victims: Part of the state's duty includes ensuring

> that no person who may be responsible for gross violations of human rights shall have immunity from liability for their actions. . . . Reparation for certain gross violations of human rights that amount to crimes under international law includes a duty to prosecute and punish perpetrators. Impunity is in conflict with this principle.[41]

Finally, at the June 1993 World Conference on Human Rights, the first major global conference of governments on the human rights issue in twenty-five years, governments referred several times to the problem of impunity. The final Declaration and Programme of Action expresses the Conference's concern with the issue of impunity and reaffirms the duty of states to investigate allegations of forced disappearance and, if allegations are confirmed, to prosecute the perpetrators. In addition, it affirms that "[s]tates should abrogate legislation leading to impunity for those responsible for grave violations of human rights such as torture and prosecute such violations, thereby providing a firm basis for the rule of law." While many of the Declaration's provisions were the subject of intense controversy and negotiation, states expressed little or no public disagreement with these provisions.[42]

These indicators of diplomatic practice, although not conclusive in establishing a customary law norm, do demonstrate the repeated concern of states' diplomatic representatives and of international bodies with the need to investigate, prosecute, and provide redress for victims of past human rights violations. More important, the trend over time has been toward increasing specificity and stringency in the obligations states assume in this area. For example, this trend has been demonstrated in several recent pronouncements tying specific prohibitions on impunity, immunity, and amnesty to the general obligations to investigate and prosecute. Another interesting and welcome trend is the tying together of the previously separate concepts of compensation, prevention, and prosecution, in recognition of the close interrelationships among them.

General Principles of Law

Article 38(1)(c) of the Statute of the International Court of Justice lists "the general principles of law recognized by civilized nations" as a separate source of law. The most common function of general principles is as a "gap filler" where no conventional or customary rule of international law applies. Some scholars would limit the use of general principles to this supplementary function, employing general principles only where no other source of law (conventions, custom, unilateral acts, or even resolutions of international organizations or decisions of judicial or arbitral tribunals) applies.[43]

The International Court of Justice, in formulating article 38, apparently had no such hierarchy in mind. The drafting committee deleted the words "in the following order" from the listing of sources in article 38, thus eliminating any notion that treaties and/or custom are primary over general principles as a source of law.[44] Thus, general principles form a "primary" source of law coequal to treaties or custom. In practice, however, the International Court of Justice and its predecessor, the Permanent Court of International Justice, have used general principles cautiously.

The definition of a "general principle of law" has been the source of considerable difficulty. Most authors and the International Court of Justice agree that general principles consist of expressions common to the major legal systems.[45] General principles may also express rules of law developed within international law.[46] In addition, some scholars also use general principles to encompass "unperfected" other sources of law. Under both acceptations, general principles may provide a potent source of authority for obligations to investigate, prosecute, and provide redress.

To the extent general principles may be found beyond the comparison of national legal systems, the concept of general principles overlaps somewhat with that of customary law. Some scholars have looked to general principles to encompass a variety of international legal materials. Thus, Bassiouni includes among the possible sources of general principles U.N. General Assembly resolutions and "unperfected" custom, "such as when a custom is not evidenced by sufficient or consistent practice, or when States express *opinio juris* without any supportive practice."[47] Theoretically, this expansive view of general principles has the advantage of allowing law to be found where there is little or inconclusive state practice, yet a widespread sense that a legal rule is needed. Given the difficulties of defining and identifying state practice in the human rights area, it may make more sense to consider the statements of tribunals, diplomats, and the U.N.-related bodies discussed earlier under the rubric of general principles rather than of customary law. The disadvantage to this approach, of course, is that it blurs the line between the two categories without delimiting how much support is needed to transform such "unperfected" custom into a general principle of law.

The preferred mode of discerning general principles is through comparative study of the domestic law principles of the major legal systems. This approach offers several advantages. For one thing, principles actually applied within national legal systems are more easily ascertainable and less speculative than other sources of international law. Because such principles are derived from laws states have promulgated, there is a strong argument that states have implicitly consented to them and therefore that they should be binding sources of law. The problem comes in moving from the national to the international arena: A state may not have foreseen, and therefore may not be held to have consented to, the application of domestic legal principles on the international level. To this extent, general principles are not purely consensually based.

Objections to the use of general principles have focused on their universality and on the level of generality to be employed. Soviet scholars particularly objected to the notion that there was a common core of principles to be found in all legal systems, arguing that the relationship between state and individual in Soviet society was so fundamentally different from that found in Western societies that no common principles could exist. Scholars from Africa and Asia have similarly objected that general principles reflect Western biases imposed on other societies through colonialism. With the dissolution of the Eastern bloc and the increasing acceptance of some form of democracy as a universally shared standard,[48] these objections have become muted, although they persist.[49] In any case, the level of generality at which general principles are to be found reduces the risk of imposition of the precepts of a single legal system on others.

General principles operate on a fairly high level of abstraction: Rather than "import . . . private law institutions lock, stock, and barrel with a ready-made set of particular rules, it . . . looks to them for an indication of a legal policy or principle."[50] Thus, to define a general principle of law, one looks at how major legal systems resolve a problem and then seeks the unifying principles or precepts underlying the different constitutional, statutory, procedural, administrative, or private law applications. General principles, in this comparative law sense, are particularly useful in the human rights context. The content of human rights norms explicate, in the first instance, the relationship between state and individual[51] and commit each state to observe certain limits, provide certain benefits, and employ certain procedures in its treatment of individuals. Although these procedures vary greatly from one legal system to another, they share at least one purpose: protecting the individual from arbitrary domination by governing bodies.[52] By abstracting from the varied details of municipal procedural rules and looking to the purposes and structures of such rules, it is possible to derive general principles of law — those relating to general procedural maxims like estoppel or clean hands as well as those having to do with due process or similar procedural concerns[53] — applicable to states' human rights obligations. Although before 1945 many commentators considered only private law a proper source of general principles of law, it is now clear that a proper, and fruitful, subject for the application of general principles is "the legal protection of private parties against national and international governmental institutions and the 'objective' review of governmental action."[54]

Major legal systems all contain the idea that criminal conduct, even when (or especially when) perpetrated by state agents or officials, should be punished by the state. In both civil and common law systems, criminal acts carried out by officials or under color of law are subject to additional penalties.[55] The various qualifications, exceptions, and differences in application of such a principle admittedly make its transference to the international sphere only a starting point for analysis. Nonetheless, its very universality leads to the conclusion that international law is likely to follow similar rules, or at the least that deviations from the rule bear a heavier burden of justification.

A widely established general principle of law concerns reparations for illegal government misconduct. The Permanent Court of International Justice long ago established the principle of reparations for illegal acts of a state as a general principle of law. In the *Chorzow Factory* case, the court found the principle of reparation — as established by international practice and in particular by decisions of arbitral tribunals — to include "as far as possible, [to] wipe out all the consequences of the illegal act and reestablish the situation which would, in all probability, have existed if that act had not been committed."[56]

Over the last fifty years the major legal systems have begun to provide some form of civil redress against unlawful official acts. The French *conseil d'état* and *médiateur* and the Scandinavian ombudsman provide citizens with civil redress against abuse by officials.[57] The ombudsman model has been widely copied and now exists in Great Britain, Australia, Canada, New Zealand, Israel, Uganda, Namibia, and a number of other African countries.[58] Morocco is instituting administrative law courts in which people may seek redress for abuses of authority by public servants.[59] Under 42 U.S.C. § 1983 in U.S. law individuals can bring a civil suit against municipalities, officials acting under color of state law, and, in limited circumstances, the state and federal governments. Suits alleging ill treatment while in prison, for instance, are often brought under § 1983.[60] A number of countries have a specific office or official charged with investigating complaints about human rights violations.[61] The Soviet system once provided a procurator to investigate official wrongdoing as well.

Thus, the right of an individual to obtain some form of redress from the individual and/or the state for violations of his or her rights by the state exists in civil, common law, Islamic, and ex-Socialist countries. It is widespread enough among major legal systems to constitute a general principle of law. It is true that such rights of redress are often subject to official immunities, but such immunities, at least for individuals, do not normally extend to clearly wrongful or criminal conduct.[62] At the very least, the treaty provisions and customary law discussed earlier should be interpreted in light of this principle. Moreover, the general principle of redress for violations of individual rights by the state stands on its own as a source of law even beyond the limits of treaty. To this degree, general principles serve as a means for allowing international law to evolve new rules to meet new needs.

Arbitral Tribunals

International responsibility arising from a failure to investigate and prosecute was a major focus of the decisions of late-nineteenth- and early-twentieth-century mixed commissions formed to arbitrate claims based on injuries to aliens. An example is the United States–Mexican General Claims Commission.[63] The Commission was formed to mediate claims of damages to U.S. citizens arising from the Mexican Revolution. It was to base its decisions on the then established rules of international law.[64]

Several Commission decisions held that under international law the state is responsible for failure to attempt diligently to apprehend the assailant of an alien. In the *Neer* case,[65] the Commission held that the sufficiency of government action taken to investigate and apprehend an assailant should be put to the test of international standards. The Commission established that (1) international standards can obligate national authorities to take affirmative actions to investigate and apprehend; (2) failure to do so is a breach of a legal duty, giving rise to an international delinquency; and (3) even if the laws on the books are sound, the failure to provide effective execution constitutes a breach.[66]

The *Janes* case[67] provides the clearest example of liability based on a failure to prosecute an assailant. Janes, a U.S. citizen, was killed by a Mexican who was apparently allowed to escape by the Mexican authorities. The Commission held that the Mexican government was "liable for not having measured up to its duty of diligently prosecuting and properly punishing the offender."[68]

The Commission examined two possible theories on which to base state responsibility. The first, cited in earlier arbitral decisions, posited that the failure to punish wrongdoers should be deemed approval of the criminal conduct and should give rise to a presumption of government complicity in the murder itself. This presumption was especially applicable where the government had allowed the guilty parties to escape or had granted pardon or amnesty.[69]

The Commission refused to conflate the underlying offense and the subsequent escape, holding instead that the failure to prosecute and punish was a separate offense of the state. Damages should therefore include not only compensatory damages for Janes's death but separate damages to the family for the indignity of the lack of punishment.[70] In addition, "a reasonable and substantial redress should be made for the mistrust and lack of safety, resulting from the Government's attitude."[71]

Admittedly, there are differences between the law of state responsibility for injury to aliens and human rights law, which is concerned with the state's responsibility for the treatment of its own citizens.[72] Nonetheless, the parallel between the older concepts of state responsibility for injury to aliens and those of more recently developed human rights law is striking. Both are concerned with protecting individuals against improper state action. Both establish minimum standards for state conduct: The older concept of "international minimum standards" set out the permissible limits of a state's conduct, whereas the theory of "national treatment" postulated that aliens and nationals should be treated alike. Human rights law imported both ideas and merged them into one universal standard for state responsibility. The convergence of these two traditions extends the state's obligation to investigate and prosecute, already well developed with respect to aliens, to its own nationals.

Crimes against Humanity

Whether defined as customary law or as general principles, the law arising from the prosecutions of war criminals after World War II is relevant to a state's obligation to investigate and prosecute criminal human rights violations in several ways. First, the prosecutions acknowleged the importance of an official reckoning in the aftermath of heinous state-sponsored crimes. Truth telling was one of the major objectives of the trials. Justice Robert Jackson, chief U.S. counsel at Nuremberg, made clear that one of the major purposes of the trials was to establish a true and complete record of events, because

> [u]nless we write the record of this movement with clarity and precision, we cannot blame the future if in days of peace it finds incredible the accusatory generalities uttered during the war. We must establish incredible events by credible evidence.[73]

Second, the prosecutions affirmed that the crimes of state officials against their own citizens was a proper subject of international criminal law, giving rise to both state and individual responsibility and that official status provides no immunity. The prosecutions provided at least an initial definition of crimes against humanity and characterized these as international crimes.

The trials characterized crimes against humanity as offenses punishable under international law. The charter of the international tribunal at Nuremberg defined crimes against humanity as

> murder, extermination, enslavement, deportation, and other inhumane acts committed against any civilian population, before or during the war, or persecutions on political, racial or religious grounds in execution of or in connection with any crime within the jurisdiction of the Tribunal, whether or not in violation of the domestic law of the country where perpetrated.[74]

The Allied powers based the jurisdiction of the tribunal and lesser courts on two main rationales: Crimes against humanity could be punished because they violated elementary principles of humanity, and because they threatened world peace.[75]

The first justification explained why the law of the tribunal, and subsequent prosecutions in national courts, did not constitute ex post facto applications of criminal penalties to acts that were, after all, justified under Nazi laws. The Allies argued that because the Nazi crimes violated general principles common to the major legal systems of the world, they were already crimes under international law. In addition, the notorious nature of the crimes meant that the defendants must have been aware of their criminal status.[76] The precept that the prohibition on ex post facto laws does not encompass those that violate general principles of law was subsequently codified in several human rights treaties.[77]

Certain characteristics distinguish crimes against humanity from the underlying common crimes as well as from human rights violations, even gross human rights violations, per se. First, murder, mayhem, enslavement, and the like are crimes in the world's major legal systems. To become crimes against humanity, there must be an additional, international element, which Bassiouni characterizes as "state action or policy"—that is, that these acts are carried out by state officials or their agents in furtherance of an action or policy based on discrimination and/or persecution of an identifiable group.[78] Unlike war crimes, crimes against humanity need have no transnational element; and unlike genocide, they are not limited to cases in which an intent to destroy a racial, ethnic, or religious group can be proved. The international dimension is provided by the inability of normal state-based mechanisms of control to deal with the official criminality of high-ranking state leaders: Only international mechanisms can do so.[79] In requiring this element of "state action," crimes against humanity are similar to other gross violations of human rights. They differ, however, in their necessarily collective and massive nature; the reference to "populations" in article 6(c) of the charter recognizes this element of massiveness.

Although the Nazi crimes punished at Nuremberg required an international tribunal because of their international character and the nonexistence of a German state able and willing to try offenders, most subsequent efforts to combat crimes against humanity have focused on encouraging states to try violators in national tribunals, with international universal jurisdiction as a backup. Crimes against humanity have been the subject of numerous national prosecutions, including the trials of German criminals carried out under Allied Control Council Law 10 and later under German law, under British, French, and Russian jurisdiction, under German and other European national courts, and in other states in the *Eichmann, Barbie, Demjanjuk,* and other cases. Although the charter itself, and its subsequent codification by the International Law Commission and approval by the U.N. General Assembly,[80] characterize the enumerated acts as international crimes whose perpetrators are liable to punishment, they do not by their terms *require* states to punish such acts; they merely permit such prosecutions, and provide their legal basis.

In 1970, the U.N. General Assembly in a resolution on war criminals and crimes against humanity noted that such crimes were still being committed in various parts of the world and that thorough investigation, as well as the arrest, extradition, and punishment of persons guilty and the establishment of criteria for compensation of victims, were important elements in the prevention of such crimes and in the safeguarding of international peace and security. It called on states to take appropriate measures to arrest and extradite war criminals and persons who have committed crimes against humanity and to agree that such crimes should not be subject to statutes of limitation.[81] Three years later, the General Assembly adopted the Principles of International Cooperation in the Detection, Arrest, Extradition, and Punishment of Persons Guilty of War Crimes and Crimes Against Humanity.[82] The Principles do establish a duty to prosecute, preferably by the state in which the crimes were committed. They indicate that "crimes against humanity, wherever they are committed, shall be subject to investigation and the persons against whom there is evidence . . . shall be subject to tracing, arrest, trial and, if found guilty, to punishment."[83]

Shortly after the Nuremberg trials ended, the U.N. General Assembly asked the International Law Commission to prepare a Draft Code of Offenses Against the Peace and Security of Mankind, to include the international law principles laid down at Nuremberg.[84] The Code has been in the works ever since; at the end of the 1991 session, with the cold war no longer an obstacle, the International Law Commission provisionally adopted draft articles and sent them to governments for comments.[85]

The Code, unlike the charter, embodies an obligation to extradite or prosecute offenders, including those acting as state officials or heads of state.[86] Article 2 of the draft Code declares that the definition of crimes against peace and security is independent of internal law, and article 3 holds that individuals who commit crimes against the peace and security of mankind are liable to punishment.[87] Other articles deal with statutes of limitation and the role of superior orders.[88] Individual responsibility, however, does not preclude separate state responsibility. Although the state cannot be punished like an individual, it can, for instance, have a duty to pay reparations for injuries caused by its agents.

The Draft Code faces several hurdles before it is likely to be adopted by a sizable number of states. Several of the substantive definitions of crimes are controversial or vague: For example, crimes such as "intervention" and "willful and severe damage to the environment" will need to be defined in much greater detail if they are to meet minimum standards establishing fair notice of criminal behavior.[89] In addition, the relationship between the Draft Code and a possible international criminal court is still evolving, although the two projects are proceeding along separate tracks. The criminal court, the ad hoc tribunal on the former Yugoslavia which has given new impetus to it, and the possibility of other ad hoc international tribunals, are the latest indications that the international community is taking more seriously the need for accountability for crimes against humanity, as well as other grave violations of human rights.

Ad Hoc Tribunals and a Proposed International Criminal Court

In the years after Nuremberg, a number of well-known instances of mass killings, characterizable as crimes against humanity if not genocide, went unpunished. In Cambodia, Uganda, Guatemala, and other places, government-led or -affiliated troops killed thousands of civilians with little international response. However, after many years of cold war–induced paralysis, the early 1990s produced a resurgence of interest in the creation of effective international mechanisms for prosecuting and punishing individuals accused of certain grave violations of human rights and humanitarian law. The International Law Commission presented a preliminary draft of a statute for an international criminal court to the General Assembly for discussion. And the creation of an ad hoc tribunal on the former Yugoslavia will no doubt provide lessons for the practical operation of such a court.

Reports of "widespread and flagrant violations of humanitarian law," including reports of mass killing, mass detention and rape, and "ethnic cleansing," led the U.N. Security Council in 1992 to establish a Commission of Experts to investigate and collect evidence of grave breaches of the Geneva Conventions and other violations of international humanitarian law.[90] After the Commission submitted an interim report, the Council in early 1993 decided to establish an international tribunal and asked the secretary-general to draw up a proposed statute for such a tribunal.[91] In Resolution 827, the Council approved the secretary-general's report and mandated establishment of the International Tribunal for the Prosecution of Persons Responsible for Serious Violations of International Humanitarian Law Committed in the Territory of the Former Yugoslavia since 1991 ("tribunal"). The Council noted in that resolution its belief

> that the establishment of an international tribunal and the prosecution of persons responsible for the above-mentioned violations of international humanitarian law will contribute to ensuring that such violations are halted and effectively redressed.

It thus combined the deterrent and redressive rationales for prosecution. It also noted its determination to put an end to the crimes being committed "and to take effective measures to bring to justice the persons who are responsible for them" as a means of "contributing to the restoration and maintenance of peace."[92] Finally, the Council recognized that prosecution is related to other measures of redress, specifically noting that the right of victims to seek compensation for damages remains intact.

The Rules of Procedure and Evidence the tribunal adopted in February 1994,[93] among other innovations, are noteworthy for their heightened attention to the needs of victims. In part, provision for protection of victims and witnesses arises from the prevalence of rape and gender-related violence among the violations at issue. But beyond that, several provisions speak to the needs of victims in general for a public airing of grievances and for redress. For example, in cases in which a trial chamber finds the accused guilty of a crime and concludes that unlawful taking of property was associated with the crime, it may order restitution, either of the property itself or of the proceeds. Restitution may be ordered even if the property is in the hands of innocent third parties; it is to be effectuated through national authorities.[94] Similarly, victims may bring actions in a national court "or other competent body" to obtain compensation, and the tribunal's judgment shall be binding as to criminal responsibility.[95] This raises the possibility of a future claims tribunal, which could be set up based on the experience (positive and negative) of the Iraqi–Kuwait Claims Commission.[96]

In addition, the rules recognize the demonstrative and norm-creating aspects of prosecution through their treatment of public indictments. Especially in a situation in which many of the most important potential defendants are unlikely to be captured and brought before the tribunal, public exposure of their identities and crimes may be important both to stigmatize their conduct and to provide some satisfaction to their victims. The rules provide that if an arrest warrant cannot be executed, the prosecutor is to submit the indictment to the Trial Chamber in open court, together with the evidence underlying the indictment. If the Trial Chamber is satisfied that there are reasonable grounds for believing that the accused has committed all or any of the crimes charged in the indictment, it is to so determine. The relevant parts of the indictment are then to be read out publicly and an international arrest warrant issued and transmitted to all states.[97] Thus, even if such criminals are never convicted or imprisoned, at the very least they will become international pariahs, unable easily to leave their places of refuge. And the public nature of the indictment serves to express the community's condemnation and its recognition of the victims.

Consonant with its determination that events in the former Yugoslavia constitute a threat to international peace, the tribunal is established under the Security Council's power pursuant to Chapter VII of the U.N. Charter. Under that authority, the Council requires all states to cooperate with the tribunal, including by compliance with warrants for surrender or transfer of persons to the custody of the tribunal.[98] Noncompliance with requests for evidence or for surrender of defendants subjects the noncomplying state to the possibility of further enforcement actions under Chapter VII.

In defining the tribunal's jurisdiction *ratione materiae,* the secretary-general's report expresses concern that there be no doubt about the prior existence of the law to be applied. It therefore purports to apply only "rules of international humanitarian law which are beyond any doubt part of customary law." The statute bases its definitions of prosecutable offenses on four sources that the secretary-general considers entirely part of customary law. These are grave breaches under the Geneva Conventions of 1949, the 1907 Hague Convention (IV) Respecting the Law and Customs of War on Land, the Genocide Convention, and the definition of crimes against humanity contained in the charter of the Nuremberg tribunal. The definitions of the crimes in the statute itself, however, raise problems.[99]

The statute's (and the Council's) definition of the crimes at issue as violations of *humanitarian* law is perhaps the most troubling from the point of view of the law on impunity. Humanitarian law traditionally has been defined as the law of armed conflict, whereas laws applying whether in peace or in war have been considered part of human rights law and/or international criminal law. Thus, as the secretary-general recognizes, the Genocide Convention and the Nuremberg charter defining crimes against humanity both apply whether or not a conflict exists — technically, at least, they are broader than humanitarian law.

The failure to differentiate between the jurisdictional limits on this tribunal and the substantive nature of the offenses at issue extends to the definition of crimes against humanity in article 5 of the statute. That article lists the offenses considered crimes against humanity at Nuremberg, with the welcome addition of rape, but precedes the list with a limiting phrase: The tribunal "shall have the power to prosecute persons responsible for the following crimes *when committed in armed conflict,* whether international or internal in character, and directed against any civilian population" (emphasis added). If so interpreted, the definition would be a step back from prior definitions of crimes against humanity in both Control Council Law 10 and subsequent codifications, which had abandoned the original tie to acts done "before or during the war." It is understandable that the secretary-general sought to make clear the difference between systematic acts on political, national, ethnic, or religious grounds and isolated common crimes, but this limiting language was not necessary to do so. The secretary-general himself in the accompanying report made clear that crimes against humanity do not require a nexus to war. It is possible to read the articles merely as a jurisdictional limitation on the international tribunal and not as part of the definition of crimes against humanity.[100] The imprecise language, however, may have unfortunate consequences both for the prosecution of acts of "ethnic cleansing" that preceded the outbreak of military hostilities in a given local area and, more important, for the development of the law in this area.

Despite this shortcoming (and others), the series of Security Council resolutions on the conflict in the former Yugoslavia and the statute of the tribunal provide a reaffirmation that the investigation and prosecution of crimes against humanity, as well as other offenses, remains a vital aspect of international peace and security. That conclusion is buttressed by the announcement that the new government of Rwanda has agreed to support an international war-crimes tribunal to judge the persons accused of genocide during the recent civil war.[101] Following the Yugoslav precedent, an international commission, composed of three prominent Africans, has been asked to gather evidence and report to the Security Council. The government had earlier announced its determination to try the persons accused of atrocities in Rwandan national courts. Although an important indicator of national practice, this determination was problematic in a situation of continuing ethnic strife; it is to be hoped that an international tribunal will be able to avoid any accusations of partiality that might have undermined a purely national effort.

The success or failure of these ad hoc international tribunals will be important to revived efforts to create a permanent, treaty-based international criminal court. After languishing for decades, the International Law Commission's draft statute for a court was transmitted to the General Assembly for comment in 1993. Although the final statute at this writing awaits comments from governments and further revisions by the ILC, its current approach is conservative in both the substantive crimes subject to international criminal jurisdiction and in the states that must consent to the jurisdiction of the court.[102] The intent seems to be to make the statute as nonthreatening to governments as possible.

The draft statute distinguishes between treaties defining international crimes — genocide, grave breaches of the 1949 Geneva Conventions, apartheid, hijacking, and the like — and treaties that commit parties to suppress crimes under national law. Jurisdictional requirements are less onerous in the case of the first set. Despite the opinion of some ILC members,[103] the Torture Convention is relegated to the second list, which requires both special acceptance of the court's jurisdiction and that the crime be "exceptionally serious." In addition, article 26 allows for special acceptance of jurisdiction over "crimes under general international law." The commentary notes that this provision is intended to cover, inter alia, genocide in the case of states not parties to the Genocide Convention, or other crimes against humanity. Thus, some of the most important international crimes are relegated to a secondary status. Nonetheless, like the statute for the tribunal on the former Yugoslavia, the ILC draft embodies at least a minimal understanding that genocide, crimes against humanity, war crimes, and torture cannot remain unpunished.

5

Special Problems of a Duty to Prosecute: Derogation, Amnesties, Statutes of Limitation, and Superior Orders

Naomi Roht-Arriaza

The existence of an international law obligation to investigate, prosecute, and provide redress for at least certain human rights violations raises but does not solve a host of thorny legal issues. Can a state exempt itself from its obligations by passing domestic laws granting total or partial amnesty? Could such an amnesty be justified as a permissible derogation from existing international commitments? And could a state avoid most if not all its obligations if potential defendants successfully raise the defenses of superior orders or the statute of limitations?

Amnesties in Recent International Declarations and Decisions

Neither the language of criminal law treaties nor the general human rights treaties requiring prosecution, discussed in Chapter 3, prohibit by their terms an amnesty granted to those accused of gross human rights violations. Of course, a prohibition at least of a blanket amnesty may be implied as the converse of an obligation to prosecute. But in addition, it is possible to piece together the explicit and emerging outlines of international rules limiting the use of amnesties. At the same time, the case should not be overstated: Especially in the aftermath of an armed conflict, many states are still reluctant to give up the prerogative of a blanket amnesty.

A first distinction to be drawn is between amnesties granted by the state to its opponents, usually for political offenses, and those that exonerate conduct attributable to the state itself. Whereas the former are within a state's rights due to its role as both the victim and the enforcer of the state's penal laws, those rights do not extend to situations in which the state itself, through its officials, is the perpetrator of the violations.[1]

Moreover, amnesties for conduct carried out at the behest of (or with the condonation of) the state or by its agents allow the state to judge its own case, a result inconsistent with general principles of law forbidding self-judging. This general principle belongs to the group of general maxims long used as "gap fillers" by international courts. The Permanent Court of International Justice in the 1925 *Frontier between Iraq and Turkey* case[2] used the "well-known rule that no one can be judge in his own suit." Like similar principles of equity and fairness, the rule is found in one form or another in all major legal systems. It applies in both the civil and criminal law area, where legislators and judges often disqualify themselves, or are subject to disqualification, from hearing cases or voting on laws in which they might be perceived to have a personal interest and where the principle that no one may judge his or her own crimes is long settled. The principle should be applicable as well in cases of a self-amnesty granted by a government to its own forces: Such amnesties are simply a version of judging one's own case (at least by implication, since no judgment is in fact allowed) and therefore would seem to be prohibited under general principles of law.

The prosecutions of Nazis after World War II confronted the question of self-amnesty. Allied Control Council Law 10, which governed the prosecutions within Germany for Nazi crimes against Germans, foresaw the problem in domestic prosecutions of the perpetrators escaping justice through self-granted measures of exoneration. Article II(5) of the law reads:

> [i]n any trial or prosecution for a crime herein referred to, the accused shall not be entitled to the benefits of any statute of limitation in respect of the period from 30 July 1933 to 1 July 1945, nor shall any immunity, pardon or amnesty granted under the Nazi regime be admitted as a bar to trial or punishment.[3]

Moreover, where amnesties are granted through non-legitimate means — for example, through a decree of a de facto government or a law passed by a non-democratically elected legislature — they may legitimately be denied legal force due to their irregular means of promulgation and may be summarily overturned under the principle of "formal parallelism."[4]

Although self-amnesties are particularly objectionable as self-serving means of covering up crimes with no social gain in return, amnesties may also be instituted by successor regimes as the price of transition or of social peace. The wisdom of such amnesties is discussed in Chapter 21; here I wish to deal with their legal status.

Until recently, there were few direct references to the question of amnesty in international instruments. An exception is Protocol II to the Geneva Conventions, dealing with non-international armed conflicts. Article 6(5) of the protocol states:

> At the end of hostilities, the authorities in power shall endeavour to grant the broadest possible amnesty to persons who have participated in the armed conflict, or those deprived of their liberty for reasons related to the armed conflict, whether they are interned or detained.[5]

This recommendation appears at the end of an article dealing with penal prosecutions; the rest of the article deals with due process protections for those prosecuted for criminal offenses related to the armed conflict. Although these protections are framed in mandatory terms, the section on amnesty is merely advisory (as was pointed out by several delegations during the drafting conferences).[6]

Although not reflected in the final article, there were several attempts during the drafting process to limit the availability of amnesty for certain offenses. The Soviet representative contended that persons guilty of crimes against humanity and genocide should not receive protection, but rather "rules should be laid down for their punishment."[7] A group of Socialist bloc states introduced a proposal for a new paragraph to read: "None of the provisions of this Protocol may be used to prevent the prosecution and punishment of persons accused of war crimes or crimes against humanity."[8] The proposal, however, was eventually relegated to a section forbidding application of the death penalty until the end of the conflict, where it apparently became caught up in debate over the general propriety of the death penalty and died. On the other hand, a proposal to allow anyone sentenced to seek pardon or commutation of the sentence, including "amnesty, pardon or commutation" of a death sentence, met the same fate.

Subsequent debate over the amnesty provision centered on some delegates' contention that it was an unnecessary intrusion into domestic law, in that "provisions of that nature were included in the legislation of all States"(Pakistan) or were "within the competence of Heads of State" (Nigeria).[9] The final text of Article 6(5) was approved by 37 votes to 15, with 31 abstentions.

Thus, there was some concern that an amnesty not be overbroad, which is reflected in both the non-mandatory nature of the provision ("shall endeavor to . . .") and its flexible contours ("the broadest possible . . ."). There was also an understanding that an amnesty was desirable to integrate former insurgents back into national life[10]; no attention was paid to the special problems of amnesty for state agents accused of penal offenses. Nonetheless, the language of Article 6(5) is broad enough to cover both insurgents and state agents. The debate also reflects the first major defeat of the argument that amnesty, pardon, and the like are purely domestic matters subject entirely to government discretion and not fit for international regulation. That trend continues to this day.

There is an increasing trend in international human rights bodies explicitly to condemn amnesties for certain particularly grave offenses, even those granted by successor regimes.[11] A 1985 report on amnesty laws by a U.N. special *rapporteur* suggested that international crimes or crimes against humanity should not be subject to possible amnesty to avoid a situation in which "the infringement of the 'human condition' is such the right of oblivion may become a right to impunity."[12] The report cited a number of provisions of national laws excluding persons guilty of international crimes and crimes against humanity from amnesty laws. In addition to provisions affecting former Nazis in the German Democratic Republic and Romania and more recently in Hungary, a 1982 Colombian amnesty law excluded persons guilty of torture, forced disappearances, and executions. In Portugal, a constitutional provision excluded from any amnesty high-level security-force officials accused of ordering torture.[13] Indeed, the original 1984 Argentine law establishing military prosecutions of those accused of human rights violations excluded from its due obedience clause those accused of "atrocious and aberrant acts."[14]

As mentioned in chapter 4, U.N. declarations on the Protection of All Persons from Enforced Disappearance,[15] on the Effective Prevention and Investigation of Extra-legal, Arbitrary and Summary Executions,[16] and on Basic Principles of Justice for Victims of Crime and Abuse of Power[17] all specifically disallow blanket amnesties. On the other hand, while a 1992 draft of the Inter-American Convention on Forced Disappearance similarly prohibited amnesties in cases of forced disappearance, the final text adopted in 1994 does not.[18]

The U.N. Human Rights Committee has noted that "amnesties are generally incompatible" with states parties' duties under articles 2(3) (right to a remedy) read together with article 7 (prohibiting torture) of the International Covenant.[19] The Human Rights Committee has also addressed the question of amnesties applied to specific situations. In response to Uruguay's third periodic report under article 40 of the Covenant, the Human Rights Committee expressed its "deep concern" over Uruguay's Expiry law,[20] which precluded prosecution of military and police officers and required dismissal of existing criminal complaints against them. The Committee recommended that the law be corrected to ensure that victims of past human rights violations have an effective remedy. It

> note[d] with deep concern that the adoption of the Law effectively excludes in a number of cases the possibility of investigation into past human rights abuses and thereby prevents the State party from discharging its responsibility to provide effective remedies to the victims of those abuses. . . . Additionally, the Committee is particularly concerned that, in adopting the Law, the State party has contributed to an atmosphere of impunity which may undermine the democratic order and give rise to further grave human rights violations. This is especially distressing given the serious nature of the human rights abuses in question.[21]

The Inter-American Cases

The Inter-American Commission on Human Rights has found that amnesties violate the American Convention on Human Rights. In the wake of the 1989 *Velasquez* judgment,[22] the Inter-American Commission on Human Rights ruled in 1992 that laws restricting or prohibiting prosecutions of the military in El Salvador, Uruguay, and Argentina violate the American Convention.[23] In all three cases, the Commission found the Convention's provisions gave rise to a duty of international law to prosecute that could not be extinguished or overruled by a domestic amnesty. The Commission based its conclusions on article 25's right to a remedy provision, read together with protections of the right to life and physical integrity, the obligation to ensure rights of article 1, and the "right to due process" or judicial process of article 8. These provisions are analyzed in Chapter 3.

The Salvadoran petition concerned a massacre of some seventy-four peasants in 1983 near Las Hojas, Sonsonate province. After compelling evidence implicated the military, thirteen people, including several army officers, were arrested and held for trial. While trial was pending, the legislature passed an amnesty decree, whereupon the local courts dismissed the charges based on that decree. Noting that both the Salvadoran Constitution and the Vienna Convention on the Law of Treaties support the view that treaty obligations may not be overridden by contrary domestic law, the Commission found the government to be in breach of the above-mentioned obligations.

Uruguayan petitioners challenged the Expiry law. Petitioners argued that the law denied them the right to turn to the courts, impeding a thorough and impartial investigation of the human rights violations of the past government and thus violating their rights under articles 1.1, 8.1, and 25 of the Convention.

The Uruguayan government had argued that domestic remedies were not exhausted because civil damage suits were technically possible. The Commission disagreed, finding that "the ability to establish the crime in a civil court was considerably curtailed since vital testimony from the moral and material authors, military and police personnel of the State, cannot be adduced or used."[24] The Commission rejected arguments that article 8 applies only to the rights of criminal suspects and that article 25 was limited in this case to monetary compensation.

The Uruguayan government also cited articles 30 and 32 of the Convention, whereby rights can be restricted by laws enacted for reasons of general interest or when those rights are "limited by the rights of others, by the security of all and by the just demands of the general welfare in a democratic society." According to the government, the need for national reconciliation was sufficient to allow the restrictions on rights contained in the amnesty law. The Commission rejected this argument with little discussion, noting merely that article 29 of the Convention prohibits interpreting anything in the Convention as restricting the rights recognized therein or those recognized in other conventions or declarations.[25] Although this result is surely correct — an expansive interpretation of article 30 would make the Convention's guarantees next to meaningless — the Commission unfortunately did not elaborate.

Significantly, the Uruguayan government also argued that the amnesty question had to be viewed in the political context of reconciliation, as a necessary law approved by democratic processes and as conducive to the public good, since "investigating facts that occurred in the past could rekindle the animosity between persons and groups" and thus obstruct the strengthening of democratic institutions.[26] The Commission rejected these contentions, noting that the domestic legality of laws, however democratically enacted, do not affect a state's international obligations. It held that, after carefully weighing the political and ethical dimensions of the amnesty provision, it had reached a conclusion different from that of the government as to whether the obligation to defend and promote human rights, guaranteed by the American Convention, was being served.

The Argentine petitioners, for their part, alleged that local laws limiting the number of prosecutions, providing a "due obedience" defense, and subsequently pardoning most of those involved in the country's "dirty war"[27] similarly violated the Convention. As in the Uruguayan case, the Commission found that the decrees weakened the victim's right to bring civil actions in conjunction with the criminal case. Thus, by precluding prosecution, the Argentine government violated articles 8 and 25, read in conjunction with article 1.1.

The Argentine government's main objection was that the petitions were inadmissible *ratione temporis* because the torture and disappearances complained of took place before the Convention's entry into force for Argentina in 1984. Indeed, President Raúl Alfonsin in his letter of ratification took pains to note that "the obligations assumed by virtue of the Convention will only become effective in relation to events occurring after the ratification of the Convention." The Commission rejected this argument, reasoning that the denial of the petitioners' rights to a fair trial and to judicial protection concerned acts arising after 1984 — the underlying act being the amnesty decrees rather than the torture and disappearances.[28] Some commentators have criticized this aspect of the decisions but even so have noted that the same result could be reached by applying provisions of the OAS Charter read together with the right to a fair trial contained in the 1948 Declaration of the Rights and Duties of Man, which Argentina long ago signed.[29]

In both cases, however, the Commission left unclear the extent to which its findings rest on the existence of provisions of domestic law that allowed petitioners to participate in (in the Uruguayan case) and to initiate (in the Argentine case) the public criminal process. It so happened that in these cases the procedure for civil redress was intimately tied to criminal prosecution, but the decisions do not adequately address the state's obligations where the civil remedy is not habitually tied to the criminal case as a matter of domestic law — as, for instance, in common law systems. Even there, if the rationale is one of developing evidence and testimony that cannot be otherwise compelled, it would seem that a curtailment of criminal prosecution affects the rights to fair trial and remedy.

Derogability

Despite the growing international condemnation of blanket amnesties, such amnesties might nonetheless be legal under international law if obligations to investigate, take action against, or provide redress are derogable. The International Covenant on Civil and Political Rights and the European and American conventions on human rights all contain provisions permitting derogation from some but not all human rights obligations under conditions of "public emergency."[30] For example, fragile incoming governments facing a hostile military or continued ethnic or factional strife might plausibly argue for applicability of this "public emergency" escape clause.

The European Court of Human Rights has held that to qualify as a public emergency the danger must be actual or imminent, its effects must involve the whole nation, and it must threaten the continuance of the organized life of the community. In addition, "[t]he crisis or danger must be exceptional, in that the normal measures or restrictions permitted by the Convention for the maintenance of public safety, health and order, are plainly inadequate."[31]

The public emergency exception is limited. The comprehensive human rights treaties permit derogations only where such measures are not inconsistent with other obligations under international law, including nontreaty law.[32] This provision is less useful than it first appears. International criminal law treaties contain their own derogability provisions: For instance, the Convention Against Torture makes the prohibition on torture nonderogable under any circumstances but not so the obligation to investigate, prosecute, or compensate. However, derogation might be inconsistent with customary obligations or with redress or reparations under general principles of law.

More important, certain basic rights, including the right to life and the prohibition against torture, are always nonderogable.[33] A measure that eliminates a derogable right would be invalid if it also undermined a nonderogable right. Although neither the right to a remedy nor the state's obligation to ensure rights is included among the nonderogable rights, the American Convention at least makes clear that those judicial guarantees essential for the protection of nonderogable rights are also nonderogable.[34] For example, the Inter-American Court has found the right to habeas corpus to be nonderogable even though it is not explicitly mentioned as such in the list of derogable rights in article 27(1). The court reasoned that because habeas is "an effective means of preventing torture," its nonderogability is an essential corollary of the nonderogable nature of the prohibition against torture.[35] Thus, certain rights or procedures, even if not expressly made nonderogable, are so closely tied to other nonderogable rights that limits on the former necessarily impair the latter. This is arguably the case for the obligation at issue here.

This view is supported by the policy reasons for making some rights nonderogable. Certain actions — torture, for example — are prohibited by a nonderogable right because such actions are so repugnant to the international community that no circumstances, no matter how exigent, can justify them. Thus, when these underlying rights are at issue, the right to state-imposed sanction and remedy by the state must also be nonderogable. The nonderogable nature of the underlying right would be meaningless if the state were not required to take action against those who violate the right. If one accepts this view, exculpation or amnesty is not allowed for violations of nonderogable rights.

Similarly, a state may not generally invoke the customary doctrine of necessity to avoid its obligations. Necessity arises as a defense to the obligations of customary law when a state is threatened by a grave and imminent peril and its sole means of safeguarding an essential interest is to adopt conduct not in conformity with international requirements. A state may not invoke necessity as a defense to international responsibility if the state itself contributed to creating the condition of necessity.[36]

To invoke necessity as a way of avoiding its obligations under customary law, a state must show that there were no alternative means of confronting the danger, that it did not contribute to creating the danger, and that its actions are not prohibited by treaty. This is a heavy burden. There is no allowance for a common situation in which amnesty arises: one part of the state (military or security forces) threatens another part (a civilian government) with rebellion if its demands are not met.

Statutes of Limitation

A kind of de facto amnesty may come about through the application of statutes of limitation in civil and/or criminal cases. In some societies certain crimes, such as murder, are never time barred; in others all crimes and civil wrongs are subject to repose. Statutes of limitations are designed to provide closure for defendants and witnesses and ensure that evidence is not unreasonably stale. Such statutes may constitute a difficult bar to recovery for victims or punishment for perpetrators, especially when actions may not be brought for many years after the complained-of conduct.

There are at least two answers to the statute of limitations problem. One is treaty-based abrogation of the statute for certain enumerated offenses. The U.N. Convention on the Non-Applicability of Statutory Limitations to War Crimes and Crimes Against Humanity[37] commits state parties to ensure that statutory or other limitations do not apply to the prosecution and punishment of genocide or crimes against humanity.[38] The similar European Convention applies to genocide, grave breaches of the Geneva Conventions, or other comparable violations of a rule or custom of international law.[39] The International Law Commission's Draft Code of Offenses precludes statutory limitations for crimes against the peace and security of mankind.[40] The French Court of Cassation in the *Barbie* case found that the nonapplicability of statutes of limitations to crimes against humanity was a rule of customary international law.[41] The Hungarian Constitutional Court in 1992 held that statutes of limitation, as an essential element of the predictability and certainty of the law, applied to bar many prosecutions from the Communist era. In October 1993, it reversed this stance on the grounds of international law, permitting the prosecution of those responsible for killings after the 1956 uprising. The Court held prosecution for the killings was not time-barred to the extent they constituted war crimes.[42]

A second approach is to allow for tolling of the existing statute of limitations while the possibilities of judicial recourse are inoperative. This approach is well known in national laws: Several U.S. states, for instance, toll the statute of limitations for charges involving misconduct by a public official for the period the official remains in office. The Romanian government recently argued that the statute of limitations should be tolled for the duration of Communist rule, thus allowing prosecutions for the murder of dissidents during the 1950s and 1960s.

A U.S. court recently applied a tolling approach in a civil case involving human rights claims. In *Forti v. Suarez-Mason,* victims of torture and the family of a woman who disappeared in Argentina sued the Argentine general believed responsible, who was found hiding out in the United States. The court found that the appropriate limitations period was that for California personal injury and wrongful death suits. That statute of limitations had long since expired, yet the court found that because it was impossible for the victims to sue during the military dictatorship, equitable tolling of the statute was appropriate. "[G]iven the pervasiveness of the military's reign of terror, it may be possible for plaintiffs to demonstrate that members of the judiciary neglected to apply laws granting relief out of fear of becoming the next victim of the 'dirty war.'"[43]

The Declaration on Enforced Disappearance, as noted, takes a similar approach to disappearances, allowing for suspension of the statute of limitations while remedies are not effective. In addition, by characterizing disappearance as a continuing offense as long as the perpetrators continue to conceal the fate and whereabouts of persons who have disappeared, the statute does not begin to run until the facts are clarified. The Inter-American Convention on Disappearances abolishes the statute of limitations for penal action against the perpetrators of forced disappearance except in certain limited circumstances.[44]

Superior Orders

Finally, a state may attempt to avoid prosecutions by arguing that, with perhaps the exception of the country's leader or commander-in-chief, all possible criminal violations would be excused under the theory of due obedience to superior orders. The so-called superior orders defense applies to individual criminal responsibility and has no bearing on the state's responsibility per se. However, to the extent the state argues that its own responsibility is discharged because individual culpability has been cut off, and thus prosecution would be futile, the defense is worth considering here.

Nuremberg, of course, established that even during a time of war orders from a superior are not sufficient to exempt a subordinate from criminal responsibility.[45] The Charter of the International Military Tribunal established that the "fact that the Defendant acted pursuant to order of his Government or of a superior shall not free him from responsibility, but may be considered in mitigation of punishment if the tribunal determines that justice so requires."[46] In its judgment, the tribunal stated the test as "whether moral choice was in fact possible." It added: "Individuals have international duties which transcend the national obligations of obedience imposed by the individual State."[47] Tribunals of the United States that were set up under Allied Control Council Law No. 10 to try "lesser" German officials elaborated on the limits of the superior orders defense. In the *Einsatzgruppen* trial,[48] the tribunal held:

> If the nature of the ordered act is manifestly beyond the scope of the superior's authority, the subordinate may not plead ignorance of the criminality of the order. If one claims duress in the execution of an illegal order it must be shown that the harm caused by obeying the illegal order is not disproportionately greater than the harm which would result from not obeying the illegal order. . . . If the cognizance of the doer has been such, prior to the receipt of the illegal order, that the order is obviously but one further logical step in the development of a program which he knew to be illegal in its very inception, he may not excuse himself from responsibility for an illegal act which could have been foreseen by the application of the simple law of cause and effect.

The International Law Commission's Draft Code of Offenses Against the Peace and Security of Mankind reiterates the Nuremberg law on superior orders; acting pursuant to government or superior orders is no defense if, in the circumstances at the time, it was possible for the offender not to comply with the order. Conversely, a superior is responsible for the acts of his subordinates if he knew or had information allowing him to conclude that the subordinate was committing or would commit a crime and did not do everything feasible to prevent or repress it.[49]

Neither the Genocide Convention nor the 1949 Geneva Conventions explicitly mentions the superior orders defense, although in both cases drafting proposals raised the issue.[50] However, article 2 of the torture convention explicitly provides that "[a]n order from a superior officer or a public authority may not be invoked as a justification for torture." The Inter-American Torture Convention and the Inter-American Convention on Forced Disappearances also exclude the defense.

Further useful elaboration of the limits of the superior orders defense comes from an Israeli Military District Court in *Chief Military Prosecutor v. Melinki.*[51] Two Israeli soldiers were tried for opening fire pursuant to an order to shoot to kill anyone moving out of doors in an Arab village after curfew. They opened fire on Arab villagers returning from work in the fields unaware of the curfew. The court held that soldiers could be excused only if their orders were not "manifestly illegal." It elaborated:

> The distinguishing mark of a "manifestly unlawful order" should fly like a black flag above the order given, as a warning saying "Prohibited." Not formal unlawfulness, hidden or half-hidden, nor unlawfulness discernible only by the eyes of legal experts, is important here, but a flagrant and manifest breach of the law, definite and unnecessary unlawfulness appearing on the face of the order itself, the clearly criminal character of the acts ordered to be done, unlawfulness piercing the eye not blind nor the heart stony and corrupt.

The court added that in considering a subordinate's act, a court should consider the relative ranks of the commander and subordinate; whether the subordinate had good grounds to consider the order lawful; whether the subordinate might consider that the superior had such grounds of which he was unaware; whether the subordinate had time to clarify in his own mind, given the circumstances, whether the order was lawful; whether there was an emergency at the time the order was given; whether the subordinate was in fear of death or actual physical injury should he refuse to obey; and whether the subordinate had a reasonable and honest view of the facts.

Applying these criteria, orders to kill, force the disappearance of, or torture political opponents would most likely be considered manifestly unlawful. The most troubling issue is the lack of moral choice: At least in the case of enlisted men and junior officers, a refusal to follow orders might well have resulted in their own deaths or disappearances. In these cases, another way to conceive the problem is not as one of superior orders but of coercion or duress, an excuse recognized in international criminal law.[52] For coercion to be a valid excuse, the soldier's state of mind becomes determinative, as does the immediacy of the threat. Even so, under most national criminal law systems coercion is not a permissible defense in cases of murder.[53] For higher-ranking officers, however, the consequences might be less grave (transfer, lack of promotion). If so, coercion would not apply, and superior orders would be inadmissible as a defense.

The Limits of State Responsibility

Chapters 3 through 5 have established the bases in international law of an obligation to investigate, prosecute, and provide redress for a certain subset of particularly grave human rights violations. However, lacunae in this emerging law remain. First is the question of exactly which violations are covered. The clearest obligations are those provided by treaty: These establish an obligation to investigate and prosecute grave breaches of the Geneva Conventions, enslavement or slaverylike practices, torture, genocide, and racially based discrimination amounting to apartheid; a right to redress for racial discrimination is also explicit. Following the jurisprudence and recommendations of the relevant treaty interpretation bodies, summary execution and disappearance may be added to the list. The Nuremberg Charter itself did not require but only permitted prosecutions for crimes against humanity. Nonetheless, subsequent U.N. resolutions and treaties establishing the nonprescriptability of such crimes, together with their necessarily massive and grave nature and their substantial overlap with the other categories, probably suffice to support an obligation to prosecute in these cases also.

Beyond that the lines get murkier. The language used in some cases on ensuring rights, on the right to a fair trial, and on the right to a remedy seem to recognize no distinctions or gradations, either in intensity or scope, among human rights violations. Thus, if taken literally, any violation of human rights recognized in treaty or custom (or, in some formulations, in national law) would be subject to an obligation to investigate, prosecute, and provide redress. Of course, in practice courts and treaty-interpretation bodies have applied such obligations only to the most serious offenses — crimes against humanity, summary execution, disappearance, torture, or (occasionally) prolonged arbitrary detention. Yet because the language used allows for a much broader reading, it seems advisable to focus the *international* dimension of these obligations more narrowly, to avoid state objections that national systems of civil and criminal justice must be allowed a wide range of latitude and discretion and that international obligations have become too intrusive and too restrictive.

Commentators and lawmakers have tried to distinguish among types of violations on a number of grounds: "serious violations of physical integrity,"[54] nonderogable rights under article 4 of the International Covenant on Civil and Political Rights,[55] gross, massive, and systematic violations. Each of these formulations has limits. The first, although it reflects a widespread moral sentiment that human life and physical integrity are at the root of all human rights, does not correspond to an explicit dividing line in either treaties or custom (although it may reflect distinctions observed in case outcomes — all the violations to date that have been recognized as giving rise to accountability obligations involve physical integrity). Nonderogability of certain rights even in times of public emergency encompasses some of these basic rights, like the right to life and to be free of torture, but it also has limitations: The right not to be imprisoned for debt, for example, is nonderogable, whereas the right to be free of arbitrary arrest and detention is derogable.

Nor does the designation of certain acts as criminal in either international or domestic law resolve the problem: The raiding of state coffers or acts of drug trafficking, for instance, may be unlawful under domestic or international law, yet many courts and scholars would agree that these offenses should be treated differently than torture or murder as a matter of international state responsibility for investigation, prosecution, or redress. One way to frame an appropriate list of violations that trigger international obligations is through their place at the intersection of human rights law and criminal law: At a minimum, human rights

violations that are also criminal under either international law or general principles of law are subject to an obligation to investigate, prosecute, and provide
redress.

The relationship between human rights violations and international crimes
has never been made explicit. A recent study on the "Definition of Gross and
Large-Scale Violations of Human Rights as an International Crime"[56] attempts
to do precisely that. The study starts from the premise that certain serious types
of violations should be taken up by the international community as breaches of
the general principle of respect for human rights, in addition to infringements of
a more specific international obligation. To define which violations merit this
priority treatment, the *rapporteur* classifies violations along four dimensions:
individual versus large-scale, gross versus less serious, systematic versus sporadic, and the product of state versus private action (including state complicity
or condonation). The first three categories tend to produce similar results — that
is, large-scale violations also tend to be both gross and systematic, whereas
gross violations tend to be, or to become, large-scale violations. Such violations,
when carried out with an element of state action, should be characterized as
international crimes for purposes of establishing both state and individual
responsibility. This makes explicit the special gravity of these types of human
rights violations: The practical consequences of state commission of an international crime remain to be tied to the state obligations that form the basis of the
present study.

This narrow approach, admittedly, has its drawbacks. Violations of economic,
social, and cultural rights, which would be excluded from such obligations, may
be as serious and as harmful to a people over the long run as the violations of
basic civil rights focused on so far. For example, accountability for the raiding of
the public treasury for private gain may be equally necessary to the reestablish-
ment of the rule of law and equally difficult to obtain absent international pressure. The effect on victims, however, may be different: In cases of financial
malfeasance the victims are diffuse (and therefore less traumatized), making it
more difficult to apply the victim-centered rationales for investigation and prosecution. Penal sanctions may also be inappropriate for violations of economic,
social, and cultural rights, but their investigation, and the imposition of civil
penalties, may well be appropriate.[57]

Some violations of economic, social, and cultural rights overlap violations of
the right to life and so would come within the purview of existing law — for example, when an indigenous or tribal people is deprived of its life and livelihood by
the destruction of its ancestral lands. The question that would arise is not so much
whether the right to life is affected but whether there is an intent requirement: If
the loss of life occurs through criminal negligence rather than intent, does it come
within the strictures of accountability recognized to date?

Similar problems arise with respect to systematic violations that do not rise
to the level of "gross" or "serious" — that is, do not involve deliberate killing,
torture, disappearance, or similar acts but that nonetheless create a devastating
cumulative effect on a people. The example comes to mind of Ceaucescu's
forced natalism, in which Romanian women not only were prevented from ter-

minating unwanted pregnancies but were constantly monitored and harrassed about their reproductive status. These "second-tier" violations at some point should be considered widespread and systematic enough that accountability for them is required, even if they do not result in widespread loss of life or suffering akin to torture. Perhaps the test for triggering international responsibility for investigation, prosecution, and compensation should be framed as gross, massive, *and/or* systematic violations of human rights. An alternative would be a "sliding-scale" approach, in which only a narrow set of human rights violations (defined as international and/or domestic crimes, as nonderogable, or as violations of physical integrity) require the full panoply of accountability measures, whereas lesser violations require civil sanctions as well as compensation. Although precedent exists for compensation — a wide variety of international and domestic wrongs require compensation, either to the offended state or the individual offender — no international forum has so far employed such a sliding-scale approach. Nonetheless, this approach seems best to balance the need for a limited set of *international* obligations within the wider realm of national discretion with a recognition that whatever line is drawn will necessarily leave outside its purview situations in which some international accountability obligation should be imposed.

State responsibility may arise either through complicity, condonation, or sanction of the underlying violations or through the separate delict of failure to protect or to prosecute. The difference is important in cases in which the underlying conduct, for instance, occurs before the state's accession to a given treaty regime. The law of state responsibility is clear that a state may be responsible for acts committed by private parties so long as the state's failure to prevent or punish those acts is systematic enough to be considered complicity in or condonation of the private acts, converting them into de facto state action.[58] While the Restatement of Foreign Relations law requires that such condonation be a matter of state policy to be considered a violation of customary international law, other commentators have disagreed.[59] In certain circumstances, responsibility for the underlying acts may arise even without proof of condonation, on the basis of a failure to warn or to protect.

Nonetheless, responsibility for the underlying acts is separate from responsibility to investigate, prosecute, and provide redress, which does not in principle require even condonation by the state. Thus, in the report of the Commission of Inquiry established by the Israeli government to investigate the role of Israeli forces in the massacre of civilians by Phalangist militia at the Sabra and Shatila refugee camps, the Commission found the Israeli army "indirectly" responsible for not protecting the camps' residents. Even if active condonation by the Israeli military commanders of the Phalangists was unprovable, the failure to provide adequate protection for civilians, categorized as "indirect responsibility", could more properly have been termed a separate wrong of failure to prevent a grave human rights violation.[60] Therefore, even when conduct cannot be imputed to the state, a separate liability arises for after-the-fact failure to remedy the harm.[61] There is a distinct advantage to such a broad rule: It allows victims of "private" violence — violations against women by their family members comes to mind — to hold the state responsible for preventing and punishing the violations without a showing of the existence of a state policy. The distinction also is crucial when, for example, in the Argentine amnesty case, the initial acts of torture and disappearance occurred before Argentina became a party to either the torture convention or the American Convention on Human Rights.[62] If the failure to prosecute is merely evidence of condonation of the underlying offense, there is a stronger argument that the state is not bound than there is if the state's failure to prosecute constitutes a separate breach of international responsibility.

And yet we might wish to attach special condemnation to criminal conduct carried out using the resources and authority of the state, perverting the role of the state as guarantor of the security of the population. The moral and policy arguments for enforcing an obligation to investigate, prosecute, and provide redress rest heavily on the fact that the crimes at issue were committed by state officials, acting as part of a perhaps unwritten but nonetheless real state policy, who therefore found it easier to remain above the law. Although not necessarily true in cases in which certain arms of the state like the military or the secret police are practically autonomous, as a general rule the state should have a greater responsibility as well as an ability to ferret out wrongdoing among its own officials than within private groups. Both of these considerations point to the need to impose stricter legal obligations to investigate, prosecute, and provide redress when state officials are allegedly responsible.

Finally, there are cases in which private conduct is not adequately investigated or prosecuted because of ineptitude, inability, or inertia rather than a conscious effort at obfuscation. The *Velasquez* court recognized that the obligations to investigate and prosecute were those of conduct and not result and that a fruitless investigation, if carried out with due diligence and good faith, would not per se give rise to international responsibility.[63] The further development of the definition of due diligence, especially for transitional governments or governments with minimal investigatory or judicial infrastructures, is another urgent task for the law in this area. So too is developing a theory of state responsibility that can account for the violations of "state-like" actors — for example, the Bosnian Serbs — outside the context of humanitarian law.

Conclusion

Chapters 3 through 5 have examined the extent and depth of state obligations in international law to take action with respect to past human rights violations. It is possible to discern an emerging trend requiring investigation, prosecution, and redress for certain international crimes and grave human rights violations. Have states followed these precepts in practice, and with what results? What are the practical problems that arise when transitional governments attempt to deal with the past? Are these international guidelines workable, and what can be done to enhance their success? Answers to these questions are the subject of Parts II through IV, which explore different national responses to the issues of investigation, prosecution, and redress for victims of past human rights violations.

II

CASE STUDIES: EUROPE

6

Overview

Naomi Roht-Arriaza

Europe has faced issues of investigation, prosecution, purge, and redress periodically throughout the twentieth century. Responses to the Armenian genocide and World War I, to the vast crimes committed during World War II, and to the transition from military to civilian regimes in Southern Europe in the 1970s all provide lessons for the current wave of transitions in Eastern Europe. This chapter provides an overview of these early attempts to confront these issues.

Armenia and World War I

After World War I, a Commission on the Responsibility of the Authors of War and on Enforcement of Penalties was set up to report on the violations of international law during the conflict.[1] Although the Commission found that all of those who had violated the "laws of humanity" were liable to criminal prosecution, no action was ever taken, largely because of U.S. objections that the "laws of humanity" was too vague a concept on which to prosecute. The Versailles Treaty contained provisions for prosecuting German military personnel for war crimes (article 228). At one point the Allies informed the German government that 896 alleged war criminals had been identified for trial in accordance with the treaty.[2] Nonetheless, no international trials ever took place, because the Netherlands declined to hand over the Kaiser for trial and Germany refused to surrender its citizens, although some were tried in domestic courts.

The Commission also contemplated the trial of Turkish officials for the killing of over half a million Armenians. The Treaty of Sèvres,[3] in article 230, obligated the Turkish government to

> hand over to the Allied Powers the persons whose surrender may be required by the latter as being responsible for the massacres committed during the continuance of the state of war on territory which formed part of the Turkish Empire on the 1st August, 1914. The Allied Powers reserve to themselves the right to designate the Tribunal which shall try the persons so accused.

The Sèvres treaty was never ratified, however, and was replaced by the 1927 Treaty of Lausanne, which contained no such provisions; indeed, as part of the treaty, the Allies gave Turkey a "declaration of amnesty" for all offenses committed during the war period.[4]

Post-World War II: Germany

In July 1943, during the height of World War II, Australia, Canada, China, India, New Zealand, South Africa, the United Kingdom, and the United States joined the exiled governments of several European states in forming the United Nations War Crimes Commission. In their wartime declarations, the Allies emphasized their resolve to punish both war crimes and inhuman acts, including those carried out against civilian populations of the Axis countries themselves. The Charter of the International Military Tribunal was contained in the London Agreement issued by the four major Allied powers in August 1945.[5]

The International Military Tribunal tried twenty-four major war criminals, including Hermann Göring, Rudolf Hess, Wilhelm Keitel, and Albert Speer. In the subsequent trials conducted under Allied Control Council Law 10, the United States prosecuted 1,814 persons and executed 450; the United Kingdom prosecuted 1,085 and executed 240; the French tried 2,107 but executed only 109, and the USSR, although exact data were long kept secret, is thought to have tried over ten thousand persons in Germany.[6] Those tried included high-ranking officials in the SS and in the High Command, as well as government ministers and industrialists. The task of prosecuting German offenders was subsequently turned over to the German courts, which prosecuted some 60,000 cases between 1947 and 1990. However, despite widespread convictions, by 1951, half of all of those convicted had been released. In 1950, clemency boards were established, which almost uniformly recommended release. Although there have subsequently been Nazi war crimes trials in Israel — the Eichmann and Demjanjuk trials[7] — as well as the Barbie trial[8] in France and the Finta prosecution in Canada,[9] witnesses have become scarce and less reliable with age and convictions harder to obtain.

In addition to criminal prosecution, the Allies attempted to prevent any resurgence of Nazism through a broad purge of German life. A "liberation law" enacted in 1946 at the insistence of the Allies provided for the screening and categorization of the entire adult population in the area under Western control.[10] Public prosecutors grouped persons into five categories by degree of offense. Sanctions ranged from minor fines to imprisonment, internment in labor camps, confiscation of property, and restrictions on employment. Local lay boards rendered decisions on punishment, which could be appealed.

The results were predictable. The local boards were difficult to staff from local communities because most people, not recognizing any distinction between administrative and criminal sanctions, felt they were being unfairly punished by "victors' justice." The boards, overwhelmed with appeals and with information, testimony, and exculpatory evidence on those affected, became both ineffectual and easily corrupted. The vast majority of those sanctioned received minor fines only; once the fine had been paid, they received a certificate of rehabilitation that removed any future stigma.

In addition to the problems posed by such a broad-based target and by the imposition of the purges by the victorious Allies, the desire to effectuate a thoroughgoing purge ran up against two other insurmountable obstacles. First, there were few individuals who were untarnished available to restart the economy and rebuild the administration of the reborn state. Therefore, persons who had been accomplices or even minor participants in the Nazi regime were soon recruited back into the bureaucracy of state and industry. Second, the United States especially soon turned its energies to fighting the cold war and required German cooperation and skills to bolster the anti-Soviet alliance. Thus, by 1947 the United States was urging the termination of the screening boards, and there resulted a series of amnesties in late 1947 and 1948.

In East Germany even less was done to purge former Nazis from public life. The Soviet-backed government insisted that all Nazis had fled to the West and that East Germany had no responsibility for Nazi crimes. It is possible to speculate on the relationship between the incomplete processes of coming to terms with the past in both eastern and western Germany and the recent resurgence of neo-Nazi violence in that country, especially in East Germany.

Finally, the German state did pay reparations to the state of Israel, pursuant to a 1952 treaty,[11] for crimes committed against the Jews. Some industrialists also paid for the use of slave labor to fuel the war effort, although trying to obtain just compensation was drawn out and difficult.[12]

Post-World War II: France after Vichy

The French experience dealing with a collaborationist government, although complicated by particularities stemming from prewar French history and the 1940 armistice, is to some degree representative of the processes in other countries, including Belgium, the Netherlands, and Norway, which had quisling regimes. Unlike in Germany, the French experience of settling accounts after World War II was not imposed from outside by the victors. France had maintained the collaborationist Vichy government in part of its territory from 1940 until liberation in 1944. Marshal Philippe Pétain, the head of the Vichy government, at first commanded widespread support for keeping French territory intact and France out of the war, as well as from those sectors who saw Pétainism as the answer to the disastrous National Front government of the left in the 1930s. After the Allied victory, Resistance forces composed of Gaullists, Communists and others, assumed the government. They then had to come to terms with the members and supporters of Vichy, who comprised a significant portion of the population. The fact that prosecutions, investigations, and purges were carried out by the French against other French using domestic institutions makes the post-Vichy transition more like those studied in this book. Nonetheless, there are significant differences: With the German defeat, the armed might of the old state was totally abolished; at the same time, the existence of a government in exile waiting in the wings meant that the problems experienced in Germany and elsewhere of trying to reconstruct the economy and society while purging suspect members of the civil administration were much less acute.

The Committee of National Liberation, established by General Charles de Gaulle in May 1943, became the government of the anti-Vichy state. As areas became liberated, new institutions were established, the elected or appointed officials of Vichy ousted, and the mechanisms for both prosecutions and purges set up.

Although every effort was made to set guidelines and principles upon which the purge was to be carried out, including the establishment of a committee of eminent jurists to devise guidelines for removing and punishing individuals, in the last half of 1944 there were widespread summary executions of known collaborators.[13] Although initial estimates of those killed ranged as high as 40,000, more recent historians have concluded that some 10,000 collaborators were executed, most before the end of the war. To avoid further illegal bloodletting, one of the post-Vichy government's first acts was to try some 160,000 cases for collaboration-related offenses. A few cases were tried by military courts, which tended to be more lenient, but most were tried in regular or specially set-up courts. Some were tried under the provisions of the existing penal code dealing with murder, torture, or slander; others under article 75, a 1939 provision penalizing "intelligence with the enemy."[14] The meaning of the provision was expanded, however, to include "collaboration," defined as giving "to the enemy material and moral help, even if indirectly, by helping actively and spontaneously in domestic or foreign policy the government of Vichy."[15] This meant that the Vichy regime itself was illegitimate, so that persons who actively supported it were traitors, even if they had seen their motives as eminently patriotic.

A third crime, *indignité nationale,* or national dishonor, included participating in any capacity in the government or the commissariat for Jewish affairs; being a member, participant, or contributor to organizations or publications favoring collaboration; or writing or publishing books, articles, or pamphlets or giving public speeches favoring collaboration. The penalty was a fine, loss of civil rights, and public disgrace but not prison.

Of the cases before military and civilian courts, 45 percent were dismissed or acquitted, 25 percent were convicted of national dishonor, and 24 percent were sentenced to prison terms. Some 7,000 persons were sentenced to death, and 1,500 were actually executed. In addition, hundreds of educators and civil servants lost their job or became ineligible to hold public office. Nonetheless, despite the convictions and purges, there was never any systematic examination of why so many good Frenchmen had collaborated, nor any overall recounting of the period by the new regime.

As Henry Rousso and others have described, the widespread extent of French support for Vichy meant that after the war a number of myths were propounded by government figures to minimize the degree of collaboration and characterize France as a nation of resisters. The trials, by criminalizing beliefs and membership as well as criminal acts such as murder and torture, did nothing to create a unified view of the past; rather, they gave the former collaborators a perceived injustice of their own to complain about and thus shifted the postwar political debate in their favor.

Those subject to purges or prosecutions soon protested what seemed to them to be the arbitrary nature of the sentences meted out, which varied significantly by court, by region, by the social status of the defendant, and by their timing, with courts becoming less severe as time went on. The new National Assembly, dominated by parties of the right, first introduced an amnesty bill in October 1950. It cited five major arguments: clemency, reparation for the injustices of the purge, national reconciliation, the political nature of some of the offenses committed, and the example set by Germany and Italy, which were promulgating similar amnesties. Despite strong opposition from the left, a first amnesty law passed in January 1951, affecting minor offenders but not those who had committed grave crimes.

In July 1953, in the midst of cold war attacks on the left, a second amnesty billed was passed, which led to the release of all prisoners except those guilty of the most serious crimes. After a number of forced conscripts were convicted of massacring the village of Oradour, an amnesty was also passed for all of those who had been forcibly conscripted into the German army.

Well over half of those killed during the war were civilians, who were executed, massacred, bombarded, deported, or killed in battles with other French. Given the widespread French complicity in many of these acts, the government chose to maintain a "discreet silence"[16] about the war. Very few commemorations or monuments to the dead exist; the commemorations that did take place were fragmented and partial. The plight of the Jewish camp survivors was perhaps most embarrassing to those who were trying to get back to "normality" and so was quickly ignored and repressed. Documents regarding the 1940–44 period were inaccessible to researchers until 1979, when some limited access was granted.

The consequences of that early silence can be felt to this day. The issue of French collaboration and of participation in the deportations of the Jews continues to haunt France, flaring up periodically in books, movies, and belated indictments and trials of collaborators. The most well known of these are the indictments of four Vichy or *milice* (militia) officials. Former prefect Jean Leguay, who had supervised the deportation of large numbers of Jews, was indicted after considerable delays in 1979 when the French foreign ministry ruled that under international law Leguay had possibly committed not only war crimes (for which the statute of limitations had long since run) but crimes against humanity, which under a 1964 law were not subject to any limitation. With this ruling in hand, the courts also indicted, on similar charges, Paul Touvier, an officer in the Vichy *milice*, who had earlier been pardoned by President Georges Pompidou, and Maurice Papon, who had committed atrocities in the Bordeaux region.

Also indicted was René Bousquet, head of the police for Vichy during the height of the deportations and the highest-ranking French official ever charged with crimes against humanity. Neither Leguay nor Bousquet ever came to trial: Leguay died in July 1989, after the investigation in his case was complete (the investigation found him guilty of rounding up Jews for deportation) but before the case could be sent to a jury, and Bousquet was assassinated in June 1993. In April 1994, Paul Touvier was found guilty of crimes against humanity and sentenced to life imprisonment.[17]

The 1983 trial of the German Klaus Barbie, accused both of the murder of Resistance leader Jean Moulin and of deportations of Jews in Lyons, was a major event in French consciousness. Several problems arose in connection with this trial: First, because only charges of crimes against humanity would overcome the statute of limitations, the war crimes charges involving the murder of Moulin were excluded, although debates over who had betrayed Moulin dominated both the press coverage and the tactics of the defense counsel. Second, it was difficult to comply with strict evidentiary rules requiring authentication of documents and the like so long after the event. But despite these problems,

> the Barbie trial was above all an occasion for witnesses to come forward and tell their stories . . . [T]he prosecutor preferred to rely on documentary evidence, so the testimony of Barbie's victims had little to do with the conviction, although it gave the trial a dimension all its own. The victims spoke in a place that was not simply a memorial site but a seat of justice, with all the corresponding solemnity. Pent-up feelings were vented as those who had suffered took revenge on history. The witnesses . . . were the heroes of the trial because they gave, symbolically, faces to the dead, who were on everyone's mind.[18]

If there are lessons to be drawn for the present from the French experience, they are at least these: First, do not confuse either prosecutions or administrative sanctions for serious crimes like murder and torture with sanctions for membership in organizations or espousal of ideas. It may well be better not to risk a backlash by trying to sanction the latter, instead concentrating judicial and political resources on the former. Second, an enforced silence to avoid confronting uncomfortable truths, in the long run, keeps a society divided and does not let the issue be put to rest.

The Fall of the Military Regimes of Southern Europe in the 1970s

Another wave of transitions came during the 1970s with the downfall of long-standing military regimes in Portugal and Spain and of the seven-year reign of the colonels in Greece. The Portuguese experience is perhaps sui generis, in that it was bound up with the loss of Portugal's overseas colonies in Angola, Mozambique, and Guinea-Bissau and was led by a sector of the military itself. The contrasting Greek and Spanish examples, summarized here, provide important illustrations of the uses and nonuses of prosecutions in transitions from dictatorship.

Greece

The rule of the colonels lasted from April 1967 to July 1974. During that time, the military regime subjected real or perceived opponents to arbitrary arrest, torture, and denial of civil liberties. By 1974, the military, weakened by its adventure in

Cyprus, was forced to relinquish power. The incoming government of Constantine Karamanlis moved quickly to free political prisoners, provide amnesty for political offenses with the exception of the crimes of the dictatorship, reinstate persons who had been dismissed or discriminated against under the prior regime, and dismiss the most conspicuous pro-junta civil servants.[19]

The new government's freedom of action vis-à-vis the military, however, was limited by the continuing Turkish threat over Cyprus and the fact that the military command structure remained intact. Thus, Karamanlis, without provoking a new coup, had to reassert control over the military and take action against the torturers within it. To complicate matters more, the government's apparent foot dragging in bringing the military and projunta civilians to trial provoked popular discontent and led to a large number of actions brought by private citizens against the junta leaders for treason and/or torture of political prisoners. These suits forced the government to act.

Karamanlis, arguing that only a government with a popular mandate could deal properly with the question of "dejuntafication," announced parliamentary elections for November, four months after the fall of the colonels. At the same time, the government announced that the dictatorship's crimes would not be subject to amnesty and that all those charged with crimes would be tried by five-judge appellate courts under traditional criminal procedure. Finally, all high officials of the junta were to lose their pensions. Two days later, the junta leaders and thirty army and police officers were indicted for "moral responsibility" for premeditated murder in the deaths of students during the Athens Polytechnic University uprising of November 1973. The top junta leaders were subsequently also indicted for subversive activities and high treason.

The elections gave Karamanlis a parliamentary majority and made it easier for him to maneuver. In January the parliament declared the laws of the junta void and its crimes not subject to statutory limits. Four categories of crimes were to be prosecuted: those associated with the coup itself; killings during the Athens Polytechnic incident; torture; and the coup in Cyprus, although by March all Cyprus-related prosecutions were dropped. Prosecutions began in February against 104 ministers, undersecretaries, and secretaries-general who had served the junta; in April they were joined by fifty army and police officers. During the same period, some one hundred senior army officers, thirty senior naval officers, thirty air force officers, and a number of heads of the security force were forcibly retired.

The trials lasted from July through September 1975. Three of the leaders of the 1967 coup were sentenced to death, which the government promptly commuted to life imprisonment. Eight others received life sentences, and the rest were either acquitted or given lighter sentences. The most dramatic trial was that of thirty-two officials of the ESA (Military Police) detention center for torture. The trial brought to light shocking practices that outraged both the public and the professional military, who especially objected to the torture of anticoup senior military officers by their subordinates. The commanders of the detention center received long sentences, whereas lower-ranking officers and enlisted men either were given lighter sentences or were acquitted. Other trials for torture followed, with similar results.

Karamanlis took a number of steps to placate and divide the military and security forces and thus forestall coup attempts. The government set a three-month deadline for filing private lawsuits against torturers (six months for high junta officials), arguing that speedy trials were necessary to preserve evidence of torture. The effect was to invalidate two thirds of the privately initiated cases against accused torturers. In addition, offenders could escape prosecution by testifying for the prosecution, and a fair number did so. A number of those convicted were set free after paying modest fines or given suspended sentences. Finally, Karamanlis increased the defense budget and announced that the careers of army officers would henceforth be judged solely by their future behavior.

Despite its shortcomings, the government's policy of limited public prosecutions and purges was successful in removing and punishing the worst offenders, making a public record of the military's crimes and setting the stage for their return to a nonpolitical role. Several favorable factors helped ensure the relative success of the policy: a prior tradition of civilian rule; the weakness of the military after the Cyprus debacle; the existence of a real external threat from Turkey, which required some degree of national unity and gave the military a new professional mission to replace that of internal security; functioning civil courts; a parliamentary majority able to act quickly on legislation; and the ability to distinguish a small core of corrupt and repressive officers from the bulk of the armed forces. The Greek experience remains a model and a source of useful lessons for future transitions.

Spain

In sharp contrast, the Spanish transition from the dictatorship of Generalissimo Francisco Franco to parliamentary democracy was marked by the absence of any attempt to deal with the past. In part this was no doubt due to the peculiar nature of the crimes and human rights violations committed: The acute period of serious violations took place during and just after the 1936 civil war. Rather than a military coup, the civil war was just that, with both sides fielding armies, holding territory, and committing real (and alleged) atrocities. There followed more than thirty years of Francoism, in which the severity and frequency of human rights violations wound down over time. Most of the population rejected the notion of a *ruptura* because they were afraid of reviving old civil war divisions in a situation where memories of harsh repression had already faded.

Another key factor was the continuing role of the military and the king. The military, key in Franco's rise to power, continued to exercise a veto over the pace and direction of reform. Threats of a coup if any purge of the army was attempted were backed up by two attempted coups in the early 1980s; evidence of several more plots were uncovered in the trials of the instigators that followed.[20] The implicit threat of more coup attempts combined with continuing unrest and terrorism in the Basque region — where the military was called on to restore order — insulated the military from attempts to purge it or try those responsible for past wrongs. Finally, the king acted both as a symbol of reconciliation and moderation and as a buffer insulating the armed forces to some extent from criticism. For all these reasons there was never widespread support for prosecuting or purging members of the military, nor for delving into investigations that would no doubt have turned up crimes on all sides of the past conflict.

The next wave of countries confronting repressive pasts came in the 1980s with the fall of the regimes of Eastern Europe. Prior experiences, especially those arising out of World War II, would be extremely relevant to current attempts to deal with the past. We now turn to a number of those cases.

7

Decommunization after the "Velvet Revolutions" in East Central Europe

Kathleen E. Smith

Perhaps the most surprising feature of the dramatic demise of communism in Eastern Europe was its form — pacts between reform Communists and democratic movements in Poland and Hungary and swift, civic-led peaceful revolutions in Czechoslovakia and East Germany.[1] In the aftermath of communism's collapse, demands have been raised in every post-Communist state for identification and disenfranchisement, if not prosecution, of those who thwarted earlier reforms, violated human rights, collaborated with the secret police, or abused their official positions under the old regime. The pervasiveness of such demands can be traced in part to the fact that, unlike violent and protracted conflicts, the "velvet revolutions" left the "vanquished" Communists alive and well, with their privileges virtually intact. A thorough settling of accounts with the old regime, however, has proved not only complex but potentially dangerous. For example, calls for prosecution of the old guard have jeopardized coalition rule in Poland and Hungary. Meanwhile, velvet revolutionaries in Germany and Czechoslovakia have grappled with contradictions between rule of law and purge. Václav Havel, the first post-Communist President of Czechoslovakia, described his nation's law on screening state institutions for former secret police collaborators as "a somewhat revolutionary law, a law that is attempting to do something from above that our society failed to do and did not have the strength to do from below."[2] This problem of carrying out a second, democratic revolution against entrenched remnants of Communist rule in Central Europe is examined in this chapter.

I am investigating how new Central European democracies are coping with the legacies of Communist rule. I argue that the nature of the antecedent regime and the kind of transition to democracy exert considerable influence on the options and pressures facing new regimes. Thus, I begin by outlining the extent and forms of repression employed under Communist rule. Second, I address the types of transitions from communism and their consequences for new regimes in terms of breaking with the past. After examining the concrete issues and practical obstacles that have arisen in terms of "settling accounts" in post-Communist states, I assess the efficacy of government policies in accomplishing professed aims. To illustrate the process of de-communization, I analyze the most advanced case thus far, that of pre-1993 Czechoslovakia. After comparing Czechoslovakia's wide-ranging efforts to the strategies employed in Poland, Hungary, and the former German Democratic Republic, or GDR, I speculate on the lessons of East Central Europe for other nations that are struggling with the legacies of repressive rule.

From Repression to Revolt

In Eastern Europe the excesses and injustices under Communist rule began with the postwar takeovers themselves. The revolution mandated expropriation and *etatization* of private property. Moreover, in accordance with Soviet directives, "building communism" included liquidation of class enemies and constant vigilance against counterrevolutionaries, especially within the Communist parties themselves. The Soviet-style "replica regimes"[3] not only reproduced the command economic system but also adopted the brutal methods employed by Stalin and his secret police to suppress real and potential opposition. In East Germany former Nazi concentration camps soon housed new political prisoners,[4] and across the Soviet bloc show trials resulted in death or imprisonment for hundreds of thousands of people.[5]

Stalin's death in 1953 opened a new era in East European politics. A waning of brutality and repression, as well as a rise in public expression of discontent and unrest, characterized this phase of "destalinization." Khrushchev's 1956 denunciation of Stalin's crimes and miscalculations sent shock waves through Eastern Europe. It raised the issue of reforming the political and economic system and revealed the fallibility of Moscow. While each Eastern bloc nation followed a distinct course of experimentation with liberalization, all were characterized by what J. F. Brown calls a tension between "viability" and "cohesion"—that is, pressure for national domestic efficacy versus the demand for conformity with central Soviet domestic and foreign policy.[6] The two most striking manifestations of this unresolvable tension were the 1956 Hungarian revolution and the 1968 Prague Spring reforms, both of which made sharp rejections of Stalinist brutalities and purges part of their campaigns for legitimacy before being crushed by Soviet military intervention. Indeed, during its brief "thaw," Czechoslovakia adopted the "only law on rehabilitations in postwar Eastern Europe."[7] Restoration of conservative Communist rule cut short efforts to restore justice to the victims of Stalinist purges. Nevertheless, although the failed revolutions generated a second series of purges to punish the rebels and discourage potential radicals, the arbitrariness and mass executions associated with Stalinism had ended.

In the wake of failed radical reform, the East European Communist regimes engaged in a particular form of counterreformation—that is, they offered their citizens an improved standard of living and some economic freedom in exchange for an end to political pluralism and meaningful political participation. Repression did not end, but it took on less visible and more predictable forms.[8] As one Czechoslovak dissident described the effects of the new system:

> At some point in their life everyone had to make an agonizing choice: to prove their loyalty to the regime by humiliating themselves or to lose everything. Everybody knew what "everything" meant. . . . It meant to lose not only your own career, but to blight the future of your children, because they would not be allowed to attend university.[9]

Despite the milder nature of their sanctions against dissidents, the East European Communist regimes continued to strive for total control and therefore blocked the functioning of any civil society.[10] Not only intellectuals but vast numbers of citizens from all walks of life were recruited — often through blackmail — to become informers for the secret police. Sophisticated police networks kept tabs on all strata of society but persecuted only those individuals who overtly expressed their dissatisfaction or disagreement with the regime. Yet at the same time the regime made real neutrality impossible. In his sophisticated analysis of the dynamics of totalitarianism, Havel has explained how, by extracting constant professions of loyalty, the Communist regime created the image of unanimity and simultaneously made its citizens complicit in the propping up of the Communist system.[11] The majority of the population of the Eastern bloc surrendered to the demands of the regime and channeled their energy into their private, material lives. The few open dissenters responded to the counterreformation by abandoning the tactic of trying to reform the regime and instead advocating construction of a "second society" or "parallel polis" — that is, reform of one's own life space regardless of one's inability to affect high politics directly. The success of dissidents in creating an independent civil society varied widely — from the mass Solidarity movement that united workers and intellectuals in Poland to tiny networks of intellectual and religious dissidents in Hungary and East Germany.

The Path of Velvet Revolution

Economic crisis, which had been building in East Central Europe throughout the 1970s, blossomed into breakdown in the late 1980s under the stimulus of Soviet leader Mikhail Gorbachev's dual domestic and foreign reform programs. Gorbachev's domestic economic and political liberalization proposals fueled the efforts of liberal Communists in Eastern Europe to reform their own systems; thus the split in the Soviet Communist Party reproduced itself elsewhere. Moreover, Gorbachev's "new thinking" about global cooperation produced the "Sinatra doctrine," which — in contrast to the "Brezhnev doctrine" coined during the Prague Spring to formalize the Soviet prerogative to intervene in the case of breakdowns of Communist orthodoxy in Eastern Europe — allowed the Warsaw Pact countries to "do it their way."

Not surprisingly, Poland with its highly developed opposition Solidarity movement first exploited the breakdown of authority to displace its Communist leaders. After the Polish regime failed to win even a minimal level of popular support, in 1989 it entered into round-table talks with the opposition. The resulting compromise set free elections for a newly created upper house of the parliament — the senate — and for 35 percent of seats in the lower house — the Sjem. It also stipulated parliamentary election of a president, who would be granted broad powers. The June 1989 parliamentary elections left the Communist Party and its puppet coalition partners with their guaranteed 65 percent of the seats in the Sjem and a single seat out of the 100 places in the upper house. As had been agreed, the new cabinet allowed the Communists to fill the posts of minister of defense and minister of interior. On the whole, however, its devastating defeat cast the Communist Party into such a decline that even its hold on the Sjem disintegrated, allowing Solidarity an almost free hand in economic reform.

The Hungarian Communist Party similarly moved from confrontation to compromise to collapse. In this instance, the post-1956 conservative leadership had managed to coexist peacefully with Moscow and with its own cowed citizenry. Encouraged by Gorbachev's perestroika and frightened by signs of Hungary's own economic decline, however, beginning in 1988 frustrated reformers within the Communist Party began to shake up the hierarchy. The reformers then moved to shore up popular support by formulating plans to reform the economy and to "'constitutionalize' public life."[12] The regime, in effect, legitimized the opposition — which unlike Solidarity consisted of several relatively small organizations — by inviting them to participate in a series of talks about radical economic change. The Hungarian round-table talks ran from mid-June to mid-September 1989, and the opposition, though fragmented, refused to be limited to discussing economic measures alone. It too won considerable concessions, including free presidential and parliamentary elections. In the March 1990 elections various opposition parties won nearly 85 percent of the seats.[13]

In mid-1989, as their neighbors tested the limits of political reform, Czechoslovakia and East Germany still appeared to be solidly under the sway of unwavering Communist regimes. Czechoslovak and GDR hard-liners dominated their organizations and had neither compromised with dissidents nor flirted with glasnost and democratization. East German identity as a separate state has been grounded in its promise of *socialist* economic success and its practice of gradual political liberalization; in the 1980s it became clear to many citizens that neither of these trends was progressing as expected. As one analyst observed: "Honecker raised expectations, Gorbachev hijacked them."[14] East German leaders could not sacrifice their socialist orientation easily, but many GDR citizens showed less restraint. In the summer of 1989 many GDR residents took advantage of unrestricted travel to their more liberalized bloc allies to flee to West Germany. While shaken by this hemorrhage of refugees, the East German regime was ultimately toppled by massive street protests by those who stayed behind. The Communist Party, unable to produce a viable reformist leader to negotiate with the opposition, finally gave way to a weak coalition regime that would orchestrate the end of East Germany as a nation.

Czechoslovak leaders had their own specific reasons to fear Gorbachev's push for liberalization. Glasnost would undoubtedly raise the issue of the 1968 invasion and produce a postmortem that was bound to reflect badly on the conservative leadership, which still held the posts it had gained through the crushing of the reform movement. As in East Germany, the rising tide of change in the Socialist bloc raised the expectations of the populace. Here too, massive, unprecedented popular protests catalyzed the collapse of the Communist regime. In Czechoslovakia a strong dissident movement, relatively untouched by emigration, provided leadership for popular protest—through Civic Forum in the Czech lands and Public against Violence in Slovakia. Use of violence against student demonstrators on November 17, 1989 further discredited the regime and inspired public reaction. For the first time workers joined dissidents in a two-hour general strike. Deprived of this base of passive acquiescence, if not support, the government scrambled to devolve political control peacefully. On December 29, the Federal Assembly unanimously chose Havel as the nation's new president, with free parliamentary elections to follow.

The Dimensions of "Settling Accounts" with Communism

In the rapid, nonviolent demise of communism one can find both a source of popular elation and optimism as well as seeds of coming frustration. The two major forms of regime change, pact and protest, *nowhere overturned the majority of power structures of the old regime.* Although the democratic oppositions obviously took over parliamentary and high executive posts, this altered only the tip of the iceberg of Communist domination. Top Communist officials had resigned their political posts, but what of the Communist Party's immense financial assets and properties? What of all the managers, administrators, and civil servants that had executed the old regime's commands? The secret police obviously needed to be purged and restructured, but what about other institutions and their staffs? Moreover, no "revolutionary justice" had been meted out against the old regimes. New governments had to sort out and decide the fate of all levels of participants in the old regime. Essentially, three major questions regarding settling accounts with the old Communist regimes erupted during and after the democratic transitions: institutional reform, reparations to victims, and screening and/or prosecution of collaborators and criminals. Whereas these issues are common to transitions from repressive rule, the extent, duration, and intensity of Communist penetration of politics, society, and the economy as well as the "soft" nature of the transitions make settling accounts particularly complex.

First, as regards "institutional reform," a thorough overhaul could conceivably encompass a huge variety of organizations, from universities to the military to the completely state-run media. Beginning with political structures, democratization required stripping the Communist Party of its position as final arbiter over all policy making and making it subject to rule of law. Departyization entailed not just personnel changes but creation of new structures of accountability within the army, police, and judiciary to make them subordinate to elected officials rather than to the party hierarchy. Under communism the term *nomenklatura* was invented to refer to the enormous list of local and central cultural, political, and economic posts where hiring was subject to Communist Party confirmation. All of these jobs now had to be filled by other means, but changing selection procedures could have little effect unless these posts were first vacated.

Prosecution of those guilty of committing clear criminal offenses under the law is contentious, but legally purging bureaucrats requires great ingenuity and daring. "Fair" screening of personnel entails resolution of numerous complex problems. Agreement must be reached on standards for evaluation of culpability; procedures for this evaluation, including a decision on who is to be evaluated and by whom; and a set of graduated sanctions. The extent of Communist Party control exposed a huge number of people to accusations of responsibility for crimes ranging from economic mismanagement and environmental destruction to mistreatment of political prisoners and embezzlement of state funds. In this respect, the situation in Eastern Europe is more like that of postwar France than of former authoritarian regimes in Latin America. This is so because the most frequent charge is not violation of human rights but "collaboration" — which is not only hard to define but problematic because prosecution of such an offense frequently relies on assumptions of "collective guilt" and employs ex post facto laws.

Finally, just as it is problematic to identify who is responsible for the many "evils of communism," it is equally difficult to decide who should be considered a victim and subsequently what should be done about compensation. Again, some cases seem fairly clear cut — that is, those imprisoned without trial or fired for political reasons merit legal rehabilitation if not reinstatement. But what about those who were barred from higher education, denied work in their field of specialization, or blackmailed by the secret police? And given the general economic devastation left by Communist rule, how can the state now expect to take money from the general public to make amends for injustices that cannot be corrected by any sum of money?

Rather than speculate on possible resolutions to these questions in the abstract, I will use the case of Czechoslovakia to show how one post-Communist regime has struggled to address these issues simultaneously. I focus on Czechoslovakia because it has produced a wide range of debates and compromises on institutional reform, screening, and reparations. I will then briefly contrast Czech approaches to official attempts to come terms with the past in other East Central European nations. While events have continued unfolding, this account focuses on the period before the January 1993 division of Czechoslovakia into two separate states.

The Czechoslovak Approach to Settling Accounts with Communists

As noted earlier, Czechoslovakia did not quickly succumb to democratization or perestroika. Indeed, the regime continued to persecute dissidents up until the November revolution. Despite decades of pressure, Czechoslovak dissidents, primarily through the Charter 77 organization, had built a strong reputation for integrity and anticommunism. In the days of the revolution dissidents led the broad popular opposition movements, thus cementing their status as democrats and leaders. Playwright Václav Havel, the nation's most famous dissident, was overwhelmingly chosen to head the new government. Havel brought with him tremendous moral authority and a particular ethical view of culpability for totalitarian rule. His initial stance might be labeled forgiveness without forgetting. In an early address to the nation, Havel argued that whereas one should not forget either the martyrs or the murderers, accounts should be settled on the pages of history books; in practice, forgiveness was the best policy. Resorting to witch hunts meant accepting the mistaken principle employed by the Communists that the ends justify the means. In this same speech, Havel admitted that the federal government nevertheless faced difficulties in regard to the transition:

> We live in a peculiar and paradoxical time. We are building a legal state, so to speak, in a revolutionary way. Due to this an emphasis on the law is impeding and frustrating the revolution from time to time, while contrarily the revolutionary nature of things flouts the law from time to time.[15]

Havel proposed to remedy this dilemma with quick and energetic work by the parliament to set up a "normally functioning democracy." Such optimism about a rapid, relatively painless break with the past was justified in Havel's opinion because "the totalitarian system has fallen and its structures — if they still exist at all — are in the service of new times, or are paralyzed to such an extent that they cannot achieve anything more than mud stirring."[16] Havel's approach, while fitting his own moral philosophy,[17] proved somewhat naive and did not satisfy many citizens.

Examples of Institutional Reform: Police, Judiciary, Industry, and Party

Democratic reformers made the dismantling of the secret police one of their first objectives. While admitting that every state needs a counterintelligence agency, the democrats sought to disarm the mechanisms of internal repression, embodied primarily in the State Security apparat (StB). The first new minister of internal affairs was Richard Sacher, a compromise candidate from the Catholic People's Party. (This party was one of several puppet organizations allowed to exist after the Communist takeover as part of a façade of pluralism.) Under the old regime the ministry of internal affairs had 18,000 employees and relied on a network of over 140,000 informers to spy on a population of 15 million.[18] Sacher promised to cut the overall number of staff to 6,000 and to carefully screen all employees.[19] Many democrats, however, perceived Sacher as moving slowly and hesitantly. They criticized him for abolishing the StB altogether only after pressure from Civic Forum. Further, the public expressed dissatisfaction about the six months of compensation pay received by fired StB employees.[20] More damaging to Sacher, however, were revelations that he had gone to great trouble to find a new post for former deputy minister of internal affairs Alojz Lorenc — who was later indicted on three criminal charges, including destruction of StB archive materials — and that he had loosed a smear campaign against a Civic Forum member who had strongly criticized him.[21] Finally, Sacher's own deputies accused him of ordering investigations into the activities of current government and parliamentary leaders. The furor over the choice of a reluctant reformer to hold this sensitive position led Havel to replace Sacher with former Charter 77 spokesman Jiri Ruml in the summer of 1990. Even Ruml, however, became entangled in controversy over his position when he released information gained from secret police files that a leader of the People's Party, and candidate for parliament, had been a long-time secret police informer.[22]

Most institutional reform, however, could not be achieved by razing old organizations and starting from scratch. In the restructuring of the judiciary one finds a more typical situation: Some parts of the institution were compromised by their service under the old regime, but the majority of departments contained professional, hard-to-replace specialists. Thus, overhauling the judiciary required positive restructuring as well as some housecleaning. Parliament intervened slowly and incrementally to increase judges' independence and to expand judicial purview. In July 1991, for instance, it created commercial and administrative courts to supplement civil and criminal courts and to handle a whole range of legal activity that had not existed under communism.

Reorganization alone, however, could not address the main obstacle to restoring trust in the legal system — the judges themselves. Those judges who had presided over political trials inspired disdain, whereas those who had granted special treatment to the Communist elite were open to blackmail. Beyond providing incentives to recruit new judges, the government began a case-by-case screening of judges already on the bench. This individualized and time-consuming process was stipulated by law — judges were elected for ten-year terms subject to recall only on "serious grounds." A July 1991 law, in an effort to retain and attract capable judges, finally mandated that henceforth all judges — except those on the constitutional court — would be appointed for life, but that all those appointed before January 1, 1990 had to be reappointed within the next twelve months if they were to continue in the judiciary. This vetting, however, targeted only those guilty of blatant collaboration, not those who had been informers or secret police agents (the comprehensive screening law that further affects the judiciary is discussed below).[23] With regard to criminal prosecution of judges and prosecutors involved in trying and sentencing dissidents, including Havel, the prosecutor general rejected this as incompatible with the "ethical revolution which proclaims love and forgiveness."[24] The most visible result of all these reform efforts thus far has been a shortage of judges because of voluntary resignations and purges, accompanied by a surge of claims resulting from new rehabilitation and property-restitution laws.

The problem of whether and how to replace experienced personnel also arises in regard to reforming the economy. Popular expectations that Communist dominance in the management of state enterprises would decline dramatically after the first free elections in June 1990 were sorely disappointed. Conflict over the necessity and means for turnover in management rapidly peaked when in July 1990 a local branch of Civic Forum produced a list of 250 top managers in its district and identified over half as Communists. The government protested that the only conceivable use for such a list was a purge based on political beliefs, whereas the criterion for judging managers should be how well they performed their jobs. Civic Forum responded that the predominance of Communist appointees made for a "Communist mafia" that used its position not only to discriminate against non-Communists but to block economic reform and subvert privatization in order to enrich themselves. In an August speech, Havel recognized these concerns about replacing managers and spoke of the need for a "second revolution"; however, he argued that rapid market reform and privatization, not an administrative purge, would best replace bad managers. Thus, Havel reflected the government's twofold concerns: that the already troubled economy not fall into the hands of incompetent amateurs and that democratic principles and individual rights be respected.[25]

Popular resentment over decades of state surveillance and political misrule exended beyond the specific institutions that executed policy to the single institution responsible for policy making — the Communist Party. In many minds, the party bore the blame for past and present problems, from violating individual human rights to pollution and economic crisis. In the debates over the party's fate, propositions ranged from banning the party outright — as many West European nations banned fascist parties after World War II — to confiscating its assets and/or putting its leaders on trial. Havel held firm that the principle of political pluralism should not be sacrificed unless the reconstituted Communist Party violated the constitution. Others argued that the Communist Party had never been a political party in the normal sense of the word and hence should not be treated as such. As one former dissident put it:

> There's been a fatal confusion of two things: the right of demagogic parties to exist, and the right to proceed with the transmogrification of a particular mafia organization called the Communist Party . . . [T]he Communist Party should be abolished, and its assets should be confiscated as symbolic recompense for wrongs committed. Its elected members of parliament could then form some sort of new party to represent the preposterous left.[26]

In the spring of 1990, the Confederation of Political Prisoners mobilized some twenty thousand demonstrators to support a local prosecutor who had been reprimanded for initiating an investigation of the Communist Party for violating laws against spreading fascism, and seventy thousand people signed a petition of hunger strikers calling for banning the party.[27] Finally, in October 1990, the Federal Assembly passed a law nationalizing party property, though by this time the party's assets had shrunk by over half since the revolution as party functionaries siphoned off what they could. (Prosecutions for bribery, embezzlement, and misuse of state funds are proceeding on an individual basis.) Despite the precipitous decline in the size and strength of the Communist Party, the government continued to chip away at the party, outlawing the propagation of fascism and communism in cases where they violate human rights.[28]

Compensation and Reparations

The new democratic government moved quickly to rehabilitate and compensate former political prisoners. In April 1990, the Federal Assembly passed a law on judicial rehabilitation that provided for the outright annulment of verdicts in convictions for political crimes. Beginning in July 1990, former prisoners or their heirs could turn to the courts for rehabilitation. Upon receipt of a certificate of rehabilitation they could apply, again through the courts, for compensation for lost wages, costs of legal defense, and of any fines paid. The state agreed to pay limited compensation in cash over the next ten years.[29] By the end of 1991, 202,295 citizens had been rehabilitated, but of 37,805 claims for compensation only 7,374 had been settled because of the overburdening of the new commercial courts.[30] Moreover, individual institutions ranging from the military to the patent office made provisions for those expelled for their political stances in 1968 to resume their old careers.[31] The provisions of the law on judicial rehabilitation, however, have only partially satisfied the demands of the Confederation of Political Prisoners, which requests "decent pensions" and additional medical care, especially for persons who were exposed to uranium during forced hard labor.[32] Moreover, no compensation existed for opportunities lost because of blacklists that barred people from studying or working in their professions.

Although compensation to former prisoners aroused little controversy, a tremendous dispute broke out in parliament over restitution to former property owners. An early bill restoring property nationalized between 1955 and 1961 passed fairly easily because its time limit meant it affected mainly small business and apartment house owners. When the Federal Assembly had to consider restitution for large businesses, however, fierce debate erupted over the form, extent, and subjects of restitution. Added pressure arose from the need to resolve the restitution question before privatization of large enterprises could be undertaken.[33] The government was concerned that the costs of restitution would fall on taxpayers. A Slovak leader expressed his objections bluntly: "The past was cruel, but it was what it was. . . . We cannot reconstruct the relations that existed in the past, and atonement understood this way is not possible."[34] Yet most Czechs felt a moral obligation to make some compensation for lost property, and thus a compromise was reached that granted limited restitution. Although the Czechoslovaks are fortunate in having well-preserved records on property ownership, the danger of overwhelming litigation still looms, especially in cases involving property that has been improved over time. Moreover, more legislation is needed to address restoration of political parties' and Church property as well as restitution of land.[35]

Screenings and Prosecutions

Along with calling for disbandment of the secret police, democratic revolutionaries early on demanded screening of top officials to detect secret police agents and collaborators. Actual vetting, however, has been not only prolonged but partial and painful. Some political parties and candidates in the parliamentary elections asked to be screened, but this ad hoc lustration relied on incomplete records and did not mandate disclosure of results. Thus, although deputies to the new parliament were democratically elected, doubts remained about their pasts. Widespread fear of hidden agents and blackmail, punctuated by sporadic scandals, led to a second stage of screening. Parliament had begun its term by setting up a commission to investigate the violence against demonstrators during the November revolution; it charged this commission with the delicate job of screening Federal Assembly deputies, the ministers and their deputies, as well as the employees of the presidential and Assembly offices. (Ironically, two members of an earlier task force to address the November events turned out to be secret police agents.) Collaborators in the ministries and offices could be fired, but deputies had parliamentary immunity and could not be forced to resign. Of the seventeen deputies found to have collaborated with the secret police, five resigned immediately; the others were publicly exposed, and several are now suing for defamation.[36]

The second round of vetting satisfied neither those who wanted full disclosure nor those who believed the whole process was fatally flawed. Ultimately, however, public pressure pushed deputies toward more comprehensive legislation, and a federal screening law followed up efforts by Slovak and Czech National Councils.[37] The national law applied to

> people who, between February 1948 and November 1989, were: members of the State Security Corps [StB]; are registered as StB resident agents, agents, holders of a rented conspiratorial apartment, informers, ideological collaborators, or conscious StB collaborators; secretaries of the Communist Party of Czechoslovakia [CPCZ] and the Communist Party of Slovakia [CPSL] bodies from district committees upward; members of the CPCZ and CPSL presidia from district committees upward; members of the CPCZ Central Committee, and the Central Committees of other republic-wide party bodies; those in the bodies who were involved in the political guidance of the National Security Corps; People's Militia members; members of Action Committees and screening commissions; and students of some military colleges in the USSR.

It bars these individuals, with the exception of those who held positions only during the Prague Spring period of 1968–69,[38] from holding elected or appointed positions until 1996 in the following organizations:

> state administration bodies, the Czechoslovak Army, the Federal Police Corps, the presidential office, the offices of the Federal Assembly, the Czech National Council and the Slovak National Council, the offices of all three governments, [state] radio and television, CSTK, state-owned enterprises, shareholding companies in which the state is the sole shareholder, foreign trade enterprises, budget-funded and subsidized organizations, state funds, state-owned banks, the Czechoslovak State Bank, supreme judicial bodies, and the Czechoslovak Academy of Sciences and Slovak Academy of Sciences Presidiums.[39]

Anyone over the age of eighteen may apply under the law to receive a certificate verifying that he or she is not registered as an informant in the secret police files; and only with the consent of the individual concerned can material in these files be published.[40]

The adoption of a comprehensive national law, however, could not quiet the debate over complicity and its influence. Although Havel asked for amendments to the national law to ensure further the right of individuals to appeal the results of the vetting, he revealed his own growing bitterness about the difficulties involved in rooting out Communist influence. For instance, after the passage of the screening law, Havel lamented:

> [Our revolution] was carried out in the spirit of reconciliation, understanding, forgiveness, and repentance. All those involved in one way or another with the totalitarian system were given a magnanimous opportunity. They could leave their post quietly and inconspicuously. Nothing would have happened to them. . . . They have not made use of this opportunity. They have just perked up. They have settled down in various new posts and positions and have even started to laugh at us.[41]

One deputy felt compelled to remind his colleagues that the point of screening is to prevent scandals over the long run, not to create them.[42] Ideally, short-term discrediting would be compensated for by a government worthy of trust and respect over the long run.

An alternative view, however, holds that the undemocratic nature of the screening law itself will ultimately do more to damage the new democracy than the presence of former collaborators. As foreign minister Jiri Diestenbier argues:

> Failure to respect the presumption of innocence, the introduction of the principle of collective guilt, the denial of legal counsel and the humiliation of a great number of honest people who made mistakes in the past but who hurt no one, is no way to move towards a law-abiding state.[43]

The view that screening constitutes unfair discrimination was recently echoed by the International Labor Organization.[44] Due process concerns arise from the fact that only one small category of cases have the right to appeal the results of lustration and from the allegation that secret police records may be inaccurate or faked. Moreover, the law does not distinguish between motivations for informing or gradations of guilt—parliament rejected an earlier version that called for sanctions only against those who could be proved to have "suppressed human rights." Those who carry out lustration have no leeway to pardon even those who signed only one record of interrogation and who never revealed anything damaging to others.[45] Finally, lustration punishes "little informers" as much as, if not more than, their former bosses. One cartoon on this theme depicts a member of the Federal Assembly responding to the question of whether he is concerned about screening: "'Why worry? I was never recruited by the secret police; I was giving them orders.'"[46]

The head of the interior ministry's commission in charge of appeals freely admits that legislation should be revised to address due process complaints. The law could, for instance, easily be changed to allow more appeals and to permit them before charges are disclosed.[47] With regard to other complaints, examination of police procedure regarding informers reveals that, although the motivation and effects of informers are open to interpretation, a complicated filing and indexing system made creation of false records nearly impossible. Moreover, secret police periodically had to produce agents for inspection and often taped and filmed encounters; invention of agents would have been difficult and would have brought about severe punishment if discovered.[48] The vetting law was designed not to settle accounts but to cleanse public life; it seeks to avoid creation of a large unemployable pariah class by applying limited sanctions to a particular group of public servants. Lustration is confidential and carries no penalty besides ban from the offices named above.

There have been only three major attempts to subject former officials to criminal proceedings. The first concerned the use of force against demonstrators during the November revolution. The first secretary of the Prague branch of the Communist Party received a sentence of four years for ordering suppression of demonstrations, whereas a number of policemen received much shorter or suspended sentences for their roles in the November 17 incident.[49] The former minister of the interior and his deputies were tried for the arbitrary detention of dissidents to block their participation in the demonstration. Their defense was that they were following the orders of the Communist Party's Central Committee.[50] Other attempts to bring Communist leaders to justice have been less successful because of the twenty-year statute of limitations on most crimes. Thus, an indictment against the 1960s minister of the interior for crimes against detainees and prisoners was dismissed. Charges against twenty-two top party officials for treason for "inviting" Warsaw Pact troops into Czechoslovakia in 1968 also ran up against the statute of limitations barrier. Instead, charges were brought against the former prosecutor general, who failed to act on charges against these officials pressed by Charter 77 back in 1988, before the statute of limitations had expired.[51] Thus, it appears that actual convictions of human rights abusers will be limited to the most recent years, when repression rarely took on a violent form.

Elsewhere in Eastern Europe

The same general questions of settling accounts encountered in Czechoslovakia arose in East Germany, Poland, and Hungary, but in each case the treatment of the issues has varied. The German experience is treated at length in Chapter 8. Let me simply note briefly that the GDR most resembles Czechoslovakia, not merely in the form of its transition to democracy but in the substance of its debates over coming to terms with the past. Here too, lack of preelection screening damaged the credibility of the new parliament. In terms of prosecutions, the East Germans, like the Czechoslovaks, have concentrated on recent events — in this case, the fatal shootings of border crossers, aid to international terrorists, and corruption. Indeed, perhaps because of the myth of GDR economic superiority, East Germans have taken an enormous interest in economic "crimes" ranging from *nomenklatura* privileges to cases of outright embezzlement and fraud. The GDR's long-term resolution of issues of account settling are unique, however, because reunification has made possible the introduction of West German institutions and personnel to replace tainted East German counterparts. Despite charges of West German "colonization,"[52] the West German assumption of responsibility may defuse the potential instability caused by the process of settling accounts.

In Hungary and Poland, until 1992 the actual settling of accounts consisted largely of efforts to rehabilitate and compensate victims. Many Hungarians argue that the rarity of violence in recent years combined with the peacefulness of the transition make prosecutions unnecessary.[53] Arguably, institutional change in Hungary is proceeding steadily with the aid of former Communists turned reformers. The slow pace of reform, however, produced a scandal when it came to light that the ministry of internal affairs had continued to spy on opposition parties after the latter had been legalized. Lustration has been raised by the radical opposition but more as a veiled threat than as a real possibility.

The issue of criminal prosecution of those involved in violently suppressing the 1956 uprising turned out to be extremely volatile. In 1991, the Hungarian legislature passed the "Zetenyi-Takacs Act," which declared that "the statute of limitations shall start again for the criminal offenses committed between December 21, 1944 and May 2, 1990 . . . provided that the state's failure to prosecute said offenses was due to political reasons."[54] The statute covered treason, torture resulting in death, and murder, which under Hungarian law is subject to a 20-year limitations period. Proponents of the law argued that because Communist Party control over prosecutors meant that high-ranking party officials were never prosecuted, the normal presumption that known criminals would be prosecuted within the statutory time period did not apply. The law was referred to the Constitutional Court for pre-enactment review, and the court found it unconstitutional. The initial decision held that a state based on the rule of law must have predictable and foreseeable laws, and that the "certainty of the law based on formal and objective principles is more important than necessarily partial and subjective justice."[55]

Proponents of prosecutions then returned to the legislature. In March 1992, Parliament passed an authoritative resolution excluding the period between 1944 and 1989 from the operation of the statute of limitations, on grounds that the statute was tolled by the inability of the justice system to bring charges against Communist Party officials. This, too, the Constitutional Court struck down. Again in February 1993 the legislature sought to amend the law to force prosecutors to bring charges in the cases arising from the 1956 uprising, even if the trial itself would be barred by the statute of limitations. And again the Court rejected the bill.[56]

Finally the legislature adopted a new approach, based on international law. The Act on Procedures Concerning Certain Crimes Committed During the 1956 Revolution permitted prosecutions for acts that violated the Geneva Conventions of 1949, especially Common Article 3 and Article 147 of the Fourth Convention defining grave breaches, as well as crimes against humanity as defined in article 6(c) of the Charter of the Nuremberg Tribunal.[57] It then interpreted the killing of demonstrators and the torture and killing of political prisoners during the 1956 uprising to be war crimes and/or crimes against humanity under the Conventions or the Charter. These acts were not subject to statutes of limitations under the 1968 New York Convention on the Non-Applicability of Statutory Limitations to War Crimes and Crimes Against Humanity, which Hungary adopted in 1971.

The Constitutional Court upheld the law in October 1993. The Hungarian constitution provides that "the legal system of Hungary shall respect the universally accepted rules of international law, and shall ensure furthermore, the accord between the obligations assumed under international and domestic law."[58] While the non-applicability of statutes of limitation to war crimes and crimes against humanity could not be considered part of international common law or universally accepted rules of international law, states that had ratified either the 1968 New York Convention or the similar 1974 European Convention assumed an obligation to prosecute according to the standards of international law. Moreover, the court held, "in this respect we are dealing with the development of international law in a clear direction, the process of which has not yet reached its final stage."[59]

The court did not typify which acts qualified as war crimes and which as crimes against humanity. However, the judgment stressed that, unlike the more narrowly drawn "grave breaches" provisions, the obligations of Common Article 3 of the Geneva Conventions, applicable in non-international conflicts,[60] are minimal requirements that conflicting parties must apply "always and under all circumstances."[61] They are based on elementary considerations of humanity and cannot be violated in any armed conflict.

Since October 1993, at least a dozen people have been arrested, accused of taking part in mass shootings of unarmed civilians in 1956. Veterans groups as well as the Justice Ministry have been compiling documents from 1956.[62] It remains to be seen, however, whether prosecutions can weather both changes in the ruling coalition and the evidentiary difficulties involved.

Poland also moved slowly to confront former human rights abusers. This reluctance to settle accounts actively apparently also stems from the compromise transition process. Walesa defends Poland's negotiated "35 percent democracy" by arguing:

> We have done everything very prudently, and we have not even antagonized the Communist Party members too much. This will bring us advantages. Accounts will be settled with the old regime but this should not be our main goal. However, I fear that Europe expects us to settle accounts drastically.[63]

Hesitancy regarding radical political reform allowed the Polish secret police and military security forces to destroy hundreds of thousands of incriminating documents. Moreover, by 1991 Poland's parliamentary commission investigating over 100 mysterious deaths under the old regime had still received little help from the Communist-controlled ministry of internal affairs.[64] In June 1992, a divided parliament finally addressed the subject of lustration, with disastrous results. Having learned that the new minister of internal affairs was preparing an investigation of secret police files on the urging of a more radical prime minister, the Sjem demanded immediate disclosure, despite the fact that the investigation was incomplete and had been hastily and sloppily conducted. The list given to parliament included all of the deputies listed in secret police registers — regardless of whether they were agents or objects of surveillance. In the resulting furor, parliament voted the government out of power for having favored lustration. Given the inaccuracies of the first attempt at lustration, anger turned against its instigators and executors — and no one named as a collaborator resigned from parliament. The question now is whether to make a second effort at lustration to clear up the confusion sowed by the first.[65]

Lessons from East Central Europe

Although few Communist regimes remain to be overthrown, the experience of post-Communist governments in East Central Europe holds several potentially valuable lessons for transitions from repressive rule. Paradoxically, both Walesa and Havel thought they had successfully negotiated a path to democracy when they avoided a Communist backlash; instead, they encountered an unforeseen anti-Communist backlash. The spectacle of Communist officials and functionaries continuing to profit and dominate through their economic and political posts gradually aroused popular embarrassment and resentment. Even Hungary and Poland — where the very process of transition by compromise instilled some patience for gradual change and blurred the distinction between "bad" Communists and "good" alliance partners — faced pressure to implement greater "justice." Disillusionment with pacts grew over time, spurred by the realization that the "late developers" — East Germany and Czechoslovakia — had surpassed Poland and Hungary in the extent and speed of reform.

The speed and nonviolence of the civic revolutions in Czechoslovakia and the GDR, on the other hand, unrealistically heightened public expectations of radical change in personnel and institutions. As Havel has reluctantly concluded,

> the mistake was [not] made immediately in the first revolutionary days, when we allegedly were too tactful toward the adversary. Those who claim this have forgotten too soon the fact that the previous regime had at its disposal, to the last minute various . . . power instruments. . . . The mistake was perhaps made a bit later, in the first months of 1990, when we all underestimated the exceptional artfulness of our former adversaries.[66]

Ultimately, the debate over purging collaborators seems inescapable because the former Communist nomenklatura has neither transformed itself nor been unseated by modesty or market mechanisms. Even economic pragmatism has not provided a durable rationale for ignoring the abuses of the past in postcommunist states as elites incompatible with the new regime remain entrenched in the economy as well as in government, and indeed over time have managed to win elections in several countries.

In practical terms, because the democrats feel "we are not like them," the new rulers have been frustrated by their inability quickly and fairly to unseat the old apparat. As pointed out earlier, collaboration does not lend itself to legal prosecution. Indeed, unlike Latin American transitions where human rights abusers could be clearly targeted for prosecution, the vast majority of former East European officials rest secure in the knowledge of having technically committed no crimes. This sense of impunity contributes to their reluctance to withdraw from public life — after all, unlike military rulers, they have no "barracks" to which to return. Many feel that compensation to victims is not enough to restore justice and prevent a return to repression. In Czechoslovakia lustration served as a compromise between "forgiveness" and "prosecution."

Advocates of lustration argue that the presence of former secret police agents and collaborators in high posts could be a potential time bomb: Not only might such people be open to blackmail but they also arguably lack the appropriate character for public service. On the other hand, opponents note that all who lived under communism carry some guilt, some complicity, for the maintenance of an oppressive system. They contend that the government's authority and dignity might be undermined more by controversies and scandals over the past than by the presence of a few former collaborators. Some opponents even argue that lustration means a "belated victory" for the secret police because police records provided the grounds for "certificates of moral hygiene."[67]

If one concludes that allowing the immense secret police network of informers to exist untouched breeds a suspicion that undermines new democracies, the evidence from East Central Europe indicates that the method of lustration matters a great deal. Looking at the shortcomings of the Czechoslovak experience, one sees, for instance, that preelection screening of candidates, by giving parties a chance to submit lists to be checked against secret police records, can prevent unnecessary scandals. In terms of screening and punishment, evenhandedness toward collaborators is important, even if "justice" is elusive. This means formulating and enforcing a comprehensive screening law from the beginning rather than relying on ad hoc dismissals. Lustration on a case-by-case basis is open to political manipulation and offers no mechanism for victims of rumor to clear themselves. The Czechoslovak attempt to formalize lustration uncovered further potential pitfalls. It allowed lustration to far overreach legislators' original intentions because whereas it mandated lustration for certain posts, the law did not preclude screening of others — so that school cooks, among others, are now subject to vetting.[68] Moreover, lack of a strong appeals system in the administrative screening process created due process problems. A judicial mechanism might better protect individual rights and could allow the flexibility necessary for evaluation of mitigating circumstances.

8

Problems in Blaming and Punishing Individuals for Human Rights Violations: The Example of the Berlin Wall Shootings

Susanne Walther

Postunification Germany appears to differ from other countries whose repressive governments were toppled by a revolution of the people. But just as do the citizens of other such countries, East Germans and unified German society must find the strength to start anew while facing the economic, social, and political ruins of the former state. A nation seeking to rectify past governmental wrong by applying the rule of law encounters particular tensions. The rule of law may rival the sense of justice: Protective procedural guarantees present obstacles to punishing persons responsible for human rights violations who went unprosecuted under the former government or state. Another impediment to the mastering of the past (*Vergangenheitsbewältigung*) is that the law, particularly the criminal law, was designed with classical, not governmental, criminality in mind. Governmental criminality, with its links to the political and societal dogmas of an entire government and legal system and to the world political scene, may well be beyond the reach of the criminal law.

These links generate problems regarding not only the scope of the criminal law but also the function of the judiciary. Can it remain true to its judicial function and avoid the appearance of political trials? Can law and justice on the one hand and political morality and legitimacy on the other be neatly separated? Altogether, the *Vergangenheitsbewältigung* after German reunification is so complex that we are faced with a dilemma. Should we approach the German Democratic Republic (GDR) case as we would any other with our set of analytic tools derived from West German experience? By doing so, do we run the risk of a kind of local bias? Questions like these do not lend themselves to easy answers and perhaps ultimately cannot be solved at a national level.[1]

Nevertheless, the occurrence of grave human rights violations in the GDR is undisputed, and focusing on these violations is within the legitimate function of the criminal courts. The unique situation in Germany arises because the state whose past is at issue dissolved voluntarily and joined the Federal Republic by way of consensual treaty. This creates the awkward situation that one party to the treaty has assumed the position of judge over the past of the other. The absence of an explicit stipulation of jurisdiction in the reunification treaty itself, particularly with respect to the responsibility of leading state officials for acts of state, gives rise to the suspicion that the stronger party is subduing the defeated.

Criminal prosecution of grave human rights violations is now in progress. The term *"Regierungskriminalität"* ("government criminality") encompasses a number of vastly different, wrongful acts of state (or acts attributable to the state). State Security Service (Stasi) repression of critics and opponents of the regime, activities that are still under investigation, may turn out to be the most egregious forms. At first, however, the focus of criminal prosecution was on the trials of GDR border soldiers accused of killing East German citizens who attempted illegally to cross the border into the West, particularly at the Berlin Wall. The Berlin Wall shootings will likely not prove among the gravest violations of human rights. They are, however, not only among the most visible; more important, perhaps, these cases allow us to single out immediately individuals who are prima facie responsible for them — the low-level soldiers who pulled the trigger.

The *Vergangenheitsbewältigung* is not limited to criminal prosecution but encompasses other forms of legal redress as well.[2] Among the most important of these is the review of GDR convictions.[3] Judicial powers of redress include cassation (annulment) and the authority to award compensation for wrongful prosecution,[4] retrial, a declaration of incompatibility with rule of law standards or inappropriateness of legal consequence, and rehabilitation of persons convicted for making use of their basic political rights.[5] Other forms of redress include legislative efforts toward compensation for the victims of the SED regime, as well as the unprecedented opening of the Stasi documents. Each area raises its own set of questions. In this chapter, I shall cast some light on the problems of criminal prosecution as exemplified by the Berlin Wall cases. While in the meantime, more cases involving killings at the Wall have been tried and reviewed,[6] the focus of this chapter is on the Bundesgerichtshof's[7] first appellate opinion reviewing the criminal responsibility of the border soldiers *(Mauerschützen I)*;[8] I also address the high court's opinion reviewing the manslaughter convictions of high-level political leaders in the so-called Honecker case.[9]

First I briefly outline the relevant postunification criminal law issues and then discuss the international and constitutional law issues the courts had to face in establishing the border soldiers' criminal responsibility. A look at problems of individual attribution and personal culpability is followed by a consideration of the special problems in trying Honecker and other top-level officials. I then discuss the problems of sentencing in the *Mauerschützen* cases and raise the issue of appropriate sanctions in human rights cases in general. I conclude with some perspectives on the legitimacy of ex post facto criminal justice and on the problems of state prosecution of human rights cases in general.

Postunification Criminal Law Issues

Between the construction of the Berlin Wall in August 1961 and its destruction in November 1989, over 200 people were killed by GDR soldiers at the inter-German border. The last death occurred just a few months before the Wall fell. In reunified Germany prosecutors began the process of determining who, if anyone, can be held criminally responsible for these killings.

Homicide investigations against border soldiers initiated prior to October 3, 1990 by the General Prosecutor of the GDR were taken over by prosecutors at the Landgericht Berlin according to the regulations of the Unification Treaty.[10] The first case against border soldiers, *Mauerschützen I*,[11] which implicated four defendants, arose out of an attempt of two young GDR citizens to overcome the Wall not long before its fall. Defendant H., who was initially sentenced to three years, six months of imprisonment for manslaughter in a minor degree, had shot at a fugitive from a distance of less than 40 meters as he was about to overcome a metal fence, the last border security device on GDR ground. According to the judicial findings, after fruitlessly firing two warning shots, the defendant aimed at the fugitive's upper body and thereby took into account that his shot could be deadly. Defendant K., who was initially sentenced to two years on probation, had shot with automatic gunfire from his Kalaschnikow from a distance of at least 125 meters, which according to the Landgericht constituted attempted manslaughter. Two other defendants were acquitted.[12] In the second case, *Mauerschützen II*,[13] according to the judicial findings of fact as stipulated in the BGH's fifth senate appellate decision, defendant W. was a junior officer and H. a soldier in the GDR border troops. On December 1, 1984 at 3:15 A.M. they shot at twenty-year-old GDR citizen S., who was climbing a ladder and about to cross the Wall into West Berlin. Defendant W., after ordering S. to stop and after firing warning shots, fired at S. at a distance of approximately 150 meters, while defendant H. shot from a distance of 110 meters. Within five seconds each guard had fired more than twenty bullets. The bullet that caused the fugitive's death entered his back when he had already put his hand on the top of the wall. Although S. would have lived had he received immediate medical care, because of secrecy and regulations defining specific job duties, he was not taken to a hospital until more than two hours later and died there.

Both defendants testified that they did not want to kill S., whom they believed to be a spy, saboteur, or "criminal," but that they were aware of the possibility of a deadly hit. Before entering into service at the border they had been asked whether they were willing to shoot "border violators," which they answered in the affirmative. Before each turn standing guard they were subject to a "guard mount," which outlined the course of action to take in the event of a border violation; included was the possible use of deadly force if it was necessary to thwart flight.

The pivotal questions for the prosecution were what law to apply and whether the border soldiers accused of willful homicide could claim grounds of justification or excuse. Under East German law, justification was conceivable based on the GDR's border law firearms provisions. If West German law applied, however, justification would be ruled out, leaving only the possibility of excuse based on unavoidable lack of consciousness of wrongdoing (mistake of law).[14]

After 1973, West German courts generally applied West German law as far as provided by the rules of international jurisdiction when adjudicating crimes committed in the GDR.[15] On the basis of the Unification Treaty, however, it is widely agreed that crimes committed in the GDR before October 3, 1990 must be analyzed twice: first according to the applicable laws of the GDR and then according to those of the unified Germany.[16] The results are then compared and the more lenient law applied.[17]

Under East German law, the use of firearms by border soldiers at the inter-German border was authorized under certain circumstances. Whether such circumstances included the use of deadly force to stop those unlawfully trying to leave or whether such shootings instead constituted criminal homicide[18] became a crucial issue.

Neither the internal orders and regulations of the ministries for national defense and the interior regulating the use of firearms nor the border-security regulations in section 27 of the border law of 1982 authorized killing with intent or contingent intent.[19] However, the internal regulations authorized the use of firearms if and when necessary to arrest persons disregarding the orders of border patrols, and the 1982 border law authorized the use of firearms "to prevent the imminent commission or continuation of a crime which under the circumstances constitutes a felony."[20] The GDR Criminal Code had only to declare the "unlawful frontier-crossing" a felony, which it did for "grave cases": crossing the frontier with accomplices or crossing by way of "dangerous means and methods," for example, constituted grave cases[21] justifying the use of firearms. According to the prevailing view, overcoming the high-security frontier fortifications practically always constituted a felony. Nonetheless, according to the letter of the law, the use of firearms had to be reasonable. Specifically, the use of firearms was defined as "the utmost measure of force against persons," with a person's life to be "spared as far as possible."[22] Thus, the law of the GDR did not contain a literal statutory exemption for "contingently intentional" or reckless use of deadly force. And yet "to spare as far as possible" could justify killing the transgressor where the fleeing person could not otherwise be stopped. The LG Berlin, as well as the BSH, assumed this was the official GDR interpretation. It was repeatedly conveyed to the border soldiers during their routine guard mount; according to the judicial findings, the *"Befehlslage"* ("command status") for the thwarting of flight authorized even the conscious use of deadly force against fleeing persons if milder means were not sufficient.[23]

International and Constitutional Law Problems of Establishing Criminal Responsibility: Do We Have to Respect Possible Impunity Grounds Provided by GDR Law?

If GDR law in *practice* permitted the use of deadly force against those fleeing over the Wall, the question becomes whether that law must now be accepted by the German courts, leading to acquittal. Acceptance of the justification provided by GDR law could be mandated by the notion that persons accused of crimes are protected by the principles of *nullum crimen sine lege* and *nullum crimen sine lege scripta,* principles laid down in the Federal Republic's Basic Law or Grundgesetz[24] and in the European Convention for the Protection of Human Rights and Fundamental Freedoms (European Convention).[25] Some authors therefore have cited the prohibition of retroactive establishment of criminal liability (ex post facto prohibition), encompassed by the *nullum crimen* principle, to support the view that justifications grounded in the GDR border law must be respected by the German courts today.[26] According to this view, only "excessive perpetrators" — those whose conduct went beyond the limits of the border law itself — may be punished. For instance, if border soldiers shot at fleeing persons "with automatic machine-gun fire or with intent to kill," they can be punished.[27] This was the view adopted by the LG Berlin in *Mauerschützen II;* the court held that the GDR border law was binding, but that the shootings in question had violated it.[28] The BGH, on appeal, disagreed, finding that GDR state practice justified even the use of automatic machine gun fire and contingent (reckless) intent to kill to prevent border violations.[29] Thus it needed to find another way to avoid the ex post facto problem.

Several doctrinal approaches are possible to avoid the ex post facto prohibition. First, the accusations could be elevated to the level of international crimes, as "crimes against humanity." The existence of international crimes of this kind was recognized in the statutes of the International Military Court at Nuremberg and at Tokyo and in Control Council Law No. 10.[30] However, the use of firearms by individual border soldiers cannot be compared to the crimes adjudged crimes against humanity in Nuremberg and Tokyo.[31]

Second, inalienable principles derived from natural law may override state-granted impunity. As did our judiciary in trials of Nazi collaborators, the courts could rely on a "core of law, which according to universal conviction cannot be breached by any legislative act or any other authoritative measure."[32] According to a leading judgment of the BGH in 1952, the "core of law" encompasses

> certain principles of human conduct, viewed as inviolable, which were built over time in all civilized peoples on the basis of commonly shared moral beliefs, and which remain legally binding even if particular provisions of the national legal systems seem to authorize their defiance.[33]

The court conceded that it may be unclear where to draw the line; but in accordance with Radbruch's famous definition, it regarded it as transgressed where government orders do "not even aspire to justice, consciously deny the idea of equality, and clearly disregard the convictions, common to all cultured peoples, regarding the worth and dignity of the human person"; such orders "do not create law, and conduct in compliance with them remains Unrecht (un-law)."[34] In another opinion the BGH had stated that assaults on life must be subject to particularly strict scrutiny: Except for the execution of a court-ordered death sentence, killings may be permissible only "if ensuing from an absolutely necessary use of force."[35]

The LG Berlin in its first trial against border soldiers, citing this "core of law" jurisprudence, held that the ex post facto argument vitiates the principle that laws in violation of the core of law are null and void.[36] The court referred to a 1953 BVerGE[37] decision that drew this lesson from the Nazi experience in Germany:

> [T]he legislature also may create Unrecht so that, if the practice of law is not to be left unarmed in the face of such conceivable historic developments, it must remain possible in extreme cases to value the principle of *Gerechtigkeit* (material justice) higher than the principle of *Rechtssicherheit* (certainty of the law), as generally represented by the validity of the written law.[38]

In reviewing the LG's second conviction of border soldiers, the BGH, however, applied a third approach, which is doctrinally related but more concrete. The court did not base its decision on the "core of law" jurisprudence of the 1950s; in dicta, it called the application of "core of law" principles to cases of this kind "not easy, since the killing of human beings at the inter-German border cannot be put on an equal footing with the Nazi murder." Instead, the court relied on the GDR's own constitutional law in combination with international human rights law.[39] It pointed out that the constitution of the GDR protected human life and that according to recognized doctrine, statutory limitations on this right were subject to scrutiny by a principle of reasonableness.[40] Application of this standard had to include the consideration of human rights guarantees as laid down in international covenants binding on the GDR.[41] The GDR had in 1974 ratified the International Covenant on Civil and Political Rights of 1966,[42] and it entered into force in both German states in 1976. Since GDR state practice at the border violated the right to the protection of life (Covenant, art. 6, cl. 1) and the right to leave (Covenant, art. 12, cl. 2), the border law could at no time be interpreted as a justification for the use of deadly force against unarmed fugitives.[43]

By focusing on the "correct interpretation" of the border law as required by higher legal standards that had to be observed by the GDR, the court could overcome the hurdles posed by the ex post facto prohibition. The court recognized that the ex post facto prohibition protects not only against retroactive changes in the elements of a crime, but also of changes in the grounds of justification.[44] However, since the letter of the border law (as interpreted in accordance with human rights guarantees) did not provide justification here, the defendants could only be shielded from prosecution if their actual reliance on state *practice* were encompassed by ex post facto protection. This the court did not accept; the expectation that the law will be *applied* in the future as it was at the time of conduct is not worthy of protection, where this would in effect lead to acceptance of justification grounds contrary to human rights.[45]

The court's references to the right to the protection of life and the right to leave are, however, problematic. Although the GDR ratified the Covenant in 1974 and it entered into force in both German states in 1976, the GDR subsequently did not transform it into national law, as provided in article of the GDR Constitution. Arguably, without transformation the standards in the Covenant were not binding on the GDR.[46] The BGH never directly addressed when the actual commitment to observance of rights guaranteed by the Covenant arose, assuming that ratification or promulgation made the Covenant internally binding even without transformation.[47] Laudable as the court's elevation of international human rights over concerns of national sovereignty may be, the court largely ignored the international law problem of whether and when treaties are "self-executing."[48] Instead, it was satisfied that the prevailing view in the GDR itself, as pronounced in an international law treatise, was that a state cannot avoid an international commitment by using its national legal order as a pretense.[49] However, it is far from clear internationally if and when international human rights agreements take precedence over the lawmaking prerogative of sovereigns when it comes to the protection of the rights of the individual.[50]

Moreover, a closer look reveals that the international consensus on the rights to the protection of life and to leave is less than airtight and that there are noticeable gray areas where protection of these rights conflicts with national security interests. As to the protection of life, it seems widely agreed that the use of firearms with *direct* intent to kill is in violation of article 6 of the Covenant, which protects against "arbitrary" deprivation of life. There seems to be no general consensus, however, on the limits of *possibly* deadly use of firearms — that is, the lawful use of firearms where border officials are aware of the possibility of a deadly outcome.[51]

As to the right to leave, international law guarantees leave something to be desired as well. The right is embodied in the Universal Declaration of Human Rights of December 10, 1948,[52] as well as in numerous other human rights treaties, including article 12, clause 2 of the Covenant. Whether customary international law recognizes the right seems to be widely regarded as nonverifiable.[53] Again, neglecting the problems of transformation, the BGH held the GDR to its ratification and regarded its border system as a violation of the right to leave. The court considered the fact that "other states as well restrict their citizens' right to leave," that different opinions exist among members of the United Nations regarding the developing countries' desire to prevent the emigration of the intelligentsia, and that the authors of our own Basic Law did not want to embody the right to leave for fear of undesirable emigration of the working force. But the court believed the GDR practice distinguishable on at least two grounds: The denial of leave was the rule, not the exception, and the GDR border system was of "particular harshness." The court said:

> Germans from the GDR [had] a special motive for their desire to cross the borders to West Berlin and West Germany: They and the people on the other side of the border belonged to one nation and were connected with them through manifold kinship and other personal relations. [The situation created by] the restrictive passport and leave regulations cannot be assessed under the aspect of human rights without regarding the real circumstances, characterized by the Wall, barbed wire, death zone and shooting order.[54]

The court did not, however, examine the issue of travel restrictions enforced in the name of "national security," as upheld, for instance, in the *Elfes* judgment of the Federal Constitutional Court in 1957.[55]

In sum, the court largely passed over the tremendous complexities regarding the historical background of East-West politics as well as thorny definitional problems regarding both the right to the protection of life and the right to leave.

Problems of Individual Attribution and Personal Culpability

The criminal law is concerned with the individual's culpability. The primary question is whether a given "result" is attributable to the alleged perpetrator or whether the role of the perpetrator was only that of aiding another person's crime. If one believes that the border soldiers were instruments of their superiors, one could argue that the actual perpetrators should be sought among the rear-rank commanders and decision makers and that the soldiers were mere aiders and abettors. In fact, under the strictly "subjective" theory that the BGH adopted thirty years ago, persons who had fulfilled all the elements for commission of a crime as principals could still be held responsible as accessories only, where, without their own crime interest, they merely executed the will of another.[56] In the prosecutions of Nazi crimes at the time, application of this doctrine lead to the result that basically no one could be held as a principal for the most atrocious crimes. The highest-ups (who were dead) were deemed the "real" criminals, while those who had executed their will were regarded as accessories because they had acted without the requisite "interest" in bringing about the crime result.[57] As part of the major criminal law reforms of the early seventies, the legislature ruled out such extreme results, particularly with regard to the responsibility of direct actors.[58] Thus, today the BGH could address this point in routine fashion. The defendants had, acting in concert, fulfilled the elements of the crime; moreover, unlike persons who receive an order immediately before shooting, they also had a "certain room for action" because they were left on their own in case a fugitive suddenly appeared.[59] This said, it can be deplored that the court passed over the historic chance to address directly the full dimension of complicity doctrine in cases of grave human rights violations.

Perhaps the biggest problem lies in the border soldiers' individual consciousness of wrongdoing. The LG Berlin as well as the BGH have adopted a rather rigorous view and rejected both the defenses of "action under superior orders" and of "mistake of law" (lack of consciousness of wrongdoing).

As to the defense of "superior orders," the BGH applied West German (military) law, the more lenient law, which exempts the subordinate from punishment except in cases where he recognizes that following an order would constitute unlawful action or where this is "obvious under the circumstances known to him." Interestingly, West German law recognizes no duty to "think twice" where the legality of an order is in doubt, granting the superior orders defense unless there is *no* doubt about its unlawful nature. East German law, in contrast, assumes that there is a duty to examine "whether the order, recognizable for everyone, violates criminal and international law."[60]

The BGH found the superior orders defense did not apply to the defendants.[61] The court argued that, despite the high degree of political indoctrination to which the border soldiers had been exposed, even for them "the elementary prohibition to kill was obvious," and that besides "the great majority of the GDR population disapproved of the use of firearms at the border."[62] This result raises the question whether anything is really left to the more lenient nature of the West German law, at least in cases involving the protection of life.

Rejecting the "superior orders" defense did not, however, settle the question of culpability. The possible defense of unavoidable lack of consciousness of wrongdoing, according to which the defendants would have acted "without guilt," remained.[63] Here, too, the courts did not see much difficulty: the LG Berlin held that even the "intellectually simple-minded" defendants, whose personal development had been influenced by a rigid military training, could have realized that military duty does not justify all conduct. If they believed their conduct to be justified, their mistake was not unavoidable since life is the highest of all legal interests.[64] The BGH felt it could not take exception to this view, adding that the trial judge could also have pointed out that in the course of their training the border soldiers had been told they did not have to follow orders requiring them to act inhumanely.[65]

The court only briefly considered GDR criminal law doctrine as possibly more lenient. GDR doctrine apparently would have cast the issue as one of lack of intent, intent requiring that the perpetrator knew that he was violating basic social norms. The difference is important because for the defense of lack of intent it is irrelevant whether the underlying erroneous assumptions were avoidable, making lack of intent a much stronger defense than lack of consciousness of wrongdoing. But the court dismissed the issue because it was not convinced that under GDR law it would have constituted lack of intent to believe that an order must be followed even if it violates the criminal law.[66]

In sum, the BGH deserves criticism not only for failing to scrutinize more closely the nature of the actual orders and the defendant's ability to recognize them as wrong[67] but also for dismissing in such shortcut fashion the possibility that the application of GDR criminal law doctrine might have led to an exoneration of the defendants based on lack of intent.

Special Problems in Prosecuting Top-Level Decision Makers

In the meantime, a number of top-level decision makers have been prosecuted in a trial that became known as the Honecker case. Erich Honecker, the former state council and SED party chairman, and other top-level officials close to him were charged with manslaughter based on selected cases of killings at the inter-German border. Particularly the fact that Honecker himself was to stand trial in unified Germany was spectacular and caused fervent public debate.[68] On the one hand, there was a strong feeling that the "big fish" should not be able to act with impunity while the little fish are caught. On the other, some questioned whether the Unification Treaty provided sufficient basis for the unified German state to assume jurisdiction and punitive power over the representatives of the former East German state, and whether staging a criminal trial against Honecker could really further societal peace. Moreover, the prospect arose that adherence to rule of law and fair trial standards could hamper prosecution of these defendants, who were aged and ailing; allegedly, Honecker was terminally ill with cancer.

Issues of jurisdiction and sovereign immunity had been cleared by the high courts early on,[69] and Honecker's ability to stand trial became the main issue.[70]

After two months of a trial that became largely entangled in medical questions over the nature and severity of Honecker's illness, the proceedings against him had to be dismissed. Berlin's newly established state constitutional court, in one of its first cases, ruled that continued detention would constitute a violation of human dignity.[71] Honecker left for Chile on January 12, 1993; the German people were left divided over the question of whether respecting the rule of law's procedural guarantees in Honecker's case, too, has been a deplorable surrender or a healthy triumph of the Rechsstaat.[72]

The trial continued against former members of the National Defense Council Heinz Keßler, Fritz Streletz, and Heinz Albrecht.[73] Based on their roles in the decision-making process and execution of government policy regarding border violations, the LG Berlin held them responsible for the deaths of seven people who had been killed between 1971 and 1989 in an attempt to flee across the inter-German border. According to the criminal law in the former GDR, however, full criminal liability for the indirect commission of a crime was limited to circumstances in which the direct perpetrators were not responsible themselves.[74] Since this was not the case here, the LG convicted these higher-ups only as accessories (instigators) to the crimes of the lower ranks who had actually shot at the fugitives or operated the land mines. The defendants received sentences of imprisonment between seven and a half and four and a half years.[75]

The BGH, on appeal, tightened this judgment.[76] The court reiterated that the GDR state practice at the border constituted an "obvious, unbearable" violation of elementary norms of justice and internationally protected human rights and therefore could not provide grounds of justification for any of the individuals who were responsible for the killings of fugitives, directly or indirectly. The court then examined whether the rear ranks should have been held responsible as principals. Under the law of the Federal Republic[77] this turned on the issue of control: Could these defendants be deemed to have acted "through" others,[78] although those others had all acted themselves with full legal responsibility? Based on standards of factual control, the court answered in the affirmative, thereby settling a longstanding doctrinal controversy over the "principal behind the principal." Rear ranks are responsible as principals where they act within the framework of an organizational structure in which their acts lead to a regular course of events; where they take advantage of such structures, in particular of the unconditional readiness of others to fulfill the elements of crime; and where they "want" the end result "as a result of their own actions."[79] Applying these criteria to the defendants here, the court found that they were perpetrators of manslaughter, based on the fact that they had been members of the National Defense Council on whose decisions the implementation of the border practice rested. Those who actually killed fugitives in execution of this policy acted as subordinates in a military hierarchy and as such were "fixed" in their roles.[80]

The style and language of the court's opinion suggests that a new precedent with potentially far-reaching consequences beyond government criminality is being set.[81] In the context of the killings at the Berlin Wall, it is yet an open question to what extent intermediate officers can be held criminally responsible under this precedent. So far, homicide prosecutions have concentrated on the border soldiers and on the top-level leaders.[82]

Criminal Sanctions: To What Avail?

Considering the sentences in the first two *Mauerschützen* proceedings before the LG Berlin, it looks as though the courts have sought to soften the rather rigorously found manslaughter verdicts by means of lenient sentencing. In both proceedings the accusations were reduced from attempted manslaughter to attempted manslaughter in a minor degree.[83] In support, the courts primarily pointed to the fact that the defendants were brought up in a repressive system that through its schools, mass organizations, and "political education" in the military had contributed to the deformation of their *Rechtsbewußtsein*, or sense of right.[84] This reduction lowered the sentencing range for manslaughter from "not under five years"[85] to "six months to five years" for manslaughter in a minor degree, with an additional reduction for attempt.[86] With the exception of one defendant who was sentenced to a three-and-a-half-year term of imprisonment,[87] the other defendants received sentences between one and a half and two years and were granted probation.[88]

In determining the individual sentences, the courts had to consider the degree of the defendants' culpability. In its appellate opinion, the BGH in its first *Mauerschützen* case summarily accepted the LG Berlin's reasoning, which had considered in mitigation the fact that the defendants grew up after the Berlin Wall was built and that therefore their personal backgrounds made them unable to assess critically their indoctrination. Furthermore, the court recognized that the defendants were soldiers at the "very bottom" of the military hierarchy and that "in a certain way" were themselves victims of the "circumstances."[89] Finally, the court shared the LG Berlin's desire for leniency because the soldiers were being held criminally responsible at a time when functionaries "who had a greater overview and a more differentiated training" had not been tried or sentenced.[90]

Sentencing in these types of cases is fraught with difficulties. What *functions* does punishment serve in politically "tainted" human rights cases, and what *kinds* of sanctions are appropriate?[91] A probationary sentence, for example, is arguably a "system-bound" sanction in that it is primarily designed to resocialize the defendant.[92] From this point of view, the purpose of probation becomes futile to the extent that the society and its norms toward which resocialization was aimed has ceased to exist.[93] The benefit of a sentence of probation is then the avoidance of the negative effects of imprisonment. Probation in this context actually amounts to abstention from execution of punishment. Whereas abstaining from punishment is a sentencing option, albeit very limited, in our present law,[94] mere abstaining from *execution* of punishment is not.

Yet in many cases it is uncertain whether any of the traditional forms of punishment, especially imprisonment, can serve a legitimate penal purpose for human rights violations that are a product of norms sanctioned by a vanished political system.[95] The justification of punishment of human rights violators based on the theory[96] of deterrence is questionable when a need for deterrence is not discernible. This is especially so where the political system that engaged in human rights violations has been replaced by another system whose institutions are not likely to follow the same example, as in the case of unified Germany. Another, so-called positive general prevention theory[97] seeks to justify criminal sanctions on the basis of the need for symbolic norm affirmation. But on the one hand, the GDR norms need not and should no longer be affirmed, and on the other, the defendants cannot be required retroactively to accept the norms of the Federal Republic. Thus, the theory is plausible only if, on a higher suprapolitical level, punishment can be deemed to affirm the continuing validity of inalienable human rights. If the purpose of punishment is to enforce and reaffirm norms, not to make norms, the normative basis here would have to be an internationally recognized set of rules with regard to the protection of life and the right to leave one's country. As we have seen, however, a firm consensus on this remains elusive. But to the extent that the normative basis is lacking or incomplete, the symbolic powers of punishment are really employed for non-formation, not norm-affirmation purposes.

Another problem is that by overemphasizing the abstract norm level, theories of "positive" general prevention run the risk of justifying results disconnected from the concrete harm. In contrast, the harm level is taken into account by theories that seek to balance concerns for both prevention and justice. The need to safeguard societal peace and restore equity is taken into account. Penal sanctioning is based on the individual offender's guilt in violating essential norms and thereby causing harm or danger to both individuals and community and on the need to provide a fair remedy. Such an approach is significantly distinct from notions of "retribution" and "just deserts." Unlike these (purely punitive) theories, this approach allows and seeks an integration (not simply addition) of punitive and restorative remedies; it assumes that a fair remedy need not necessarily be either a "proportional" or a "stigmatizing" one in order to fulfill the purposes of the criminal law. Such a theory of punishment might also be better suited to addressing "politically tainted" human rights violations, provided that it combines concerns for the victim's rights with further humanization of sanctions for the offender.

In general, we should therefore seek alternatives to imprisonment where possible. One option is to extend the range of sentences eligible for suspension. While maintaining the symbolic power of imposing a sentence that is adequate to the guilt of the offender, the negative consequences of desocialization through execution of that sentence are avoided. Suspension can be combined with lesser stigmatizing and restorative sanctions for the benefit of the victims, their families, and the community. It seems that these avenues have been ignored in the *Mauerschützen* cases.

Some types of sanctions may be particularly suited to address human rights violations. For instance, as Roht-Arriaza has suggested,[98] the loss of pension rights and other sanctions related to the official function that was abused, directly or indirectly, seem worthy of further consideration. On pension rights, the Unification Treaty in its chapter on "Employment and Social Order," in fact, provides that as a matter of social security law (i.e., not depending on a conviction in criminal court) "unjustified" and "excessive" pension benefits from "special" and "supplemental" insurance systems shall be denied or reduced. The former insurance covers persons serving for the government in a special "service and trust" relationship—for instance in the Stasi or the military—whereas the latter covers various professional groups, in particular those deemed "intelligentsia."[99] In particular, pension benefits shall be reduced or denied for beneficiaries who violated the "principles of humanity or the rule of law" or gravely abused their positions to their own advantage or to the detriment of others.[100]

Whether such "welfare sanctions" globally imposed on "system-closed" segments of society will withstand judicial scrutiny, including review by the constitutional court, remains to be seen. Among the pivotal questions should be whether and to what extent such sanctions are tantamount to a public judgment of personal, blameworthy wrong-doing and may therefore represent punishment. This would make imposition of such sanctions subject to procedural and substantive constitutional guarantees, especially that of *nulla poena sine culpa,* and require a finding of individual criminal culpability in a fair proceeding respecting the presumption of innocence.

In general, however, suffice it to say that our general criminal sanctions presently focus on the deprivation of physical liberty and financial means and are relatively antipathetic to the deprivation of professional, political, and property rights as forms of punishment.[101] However, not only the recent deliberations at the 1992 meeting of the Deutscher Juristentag,[102] but also the newly introduced for-feiture of property as punishment[103] indicate growing dissatisfaction with the tra-ditional criminal sanctions.

Conclusion: Some Perspectives on Criminal Justice in Human Rights Cases

The *Mauerschützen* cases in unified Germany illustrate that blaming and punish-ing individuals for human rights violations within the framework of the criminal justice system is fraught with difficulties. First, the traditional principles of crimi-nal responsibility were designed to deal with conduct and the conduct-result rela-tion where individuals act alone or in concert with a few others; they were not intended for larger organizational structures that tend to dilute the individual's personal responsibility for a particular result. Second, Germany's particular his-toric situation of reunification forecloses direct scrutiny of GDR law and practice by the principles embodied in the constitution of the Federal Republic. Forced to rely on international law, we have to realize that there are considerable gray areas concerning the recognition of, commitment to, and national enforcement of important human rights that ought to be beyond the reach of national govern-ments. Third, not only unified Germany but successor governments in general, willing to prosecute criminal human rights violations that occurred under a former regime, will face problems regarding the prohibition of ex post facto punishment entrenched in the rule of law. Fourth, another major problem arising in the area of criminal human rights violations relates to the question of appropriate sanctions.

At present, academic discussion in Germany is largely concerned with the problem of ex post facto punishment. The BGH in the *Mauerschützen* case found a way out without fully addressing the problem, by framing the decisive issue as one of "right interpretation" of the GDR border law at the time of conduct. Yet it would be more straightforward to assume that criminal prosecution conflicted directly with the ex post facto prohibition, and to ask whether its protection is subject to inherent limitations.[104] Such a limiting approach could build on the idea that the individual's reliance deserves strongest protection where ex ante defini-tion of criminal conduct is at issue but potentially less protection regarding the reliance on exemptions from punishment. Arguments in support could rely on both natural law and international law, in that there appears to be an emerging obligation under customary international law to investigate grave human rights violations and take action against those responsible.[105] Arguably, such an obligation, including the obligation to provide redress to victims, is incorporated into German constitutional law; the German Grundgesetz in article 1, clause 2 professes the German people's respect for "inviolable and inalienable human rights as the basis of all human community, peace and justice in the world." Under this approach, not all crimes committed by an oppressive government can justify overriding the ex post facto prohibition, but only cases of sufficient gravity.[106] Undoubtedly, this would be the case where the violation amounts to an international crime – namely, a crime against humanity. Below this level, sufficient gravity exists where human rights are being violated in reliance on laws, regulations, orders, or state practice that were recognizably meant to exempt such violations from being subject to punishment, or where the interpretation and application of the law amounts to an obvious, grave human rights violation.[107]

And yet, considering the numerous problems in blaming and punishing individuals for human rights violations, are there really viable alternatives to criminal prosecution? The idea of amnesty has not found support in Germany; in particular, it is argued that there is no basis for amnesty before the allocation of criminal responsibility.[108] To be sure, only many years down the line will the extent of de facto amnesties (amnesties resulting from nonprosecution) be verifiable. In addition, the idea of a "national tribunal" and other forms of community catharsis that have been advanced by voices from the former GDR seem to have lost their initial appeal.[109]

Considering the hundreds of norms that criminal laws do protect by the threat of punishment, it seems paradoxical that some of the gravest violations leave modern societies more or less perplexed. The prosecution of "little fish" raises serious quandaries because the definition of what is right or wrong as a matter of law has traditionally been within the domain of national sovereignty and national policies. The protection of universal human rights, therefore, will always be subject to compromise so long as the sovereigns cannot be forced to observe these rights in making national law. The considerable doubts and gray areas concerning the international status of the right to the protection of life, as evidenced, for instance, in the use of deadly force against border violators, must be clarified.

Adjudicating the criminal responsibility of "big fish," particularly leading state representatives, for grave human rights violations requires considering an international solution. The legitimacy of holding individuals responsible in a criminal court would then be based on international legal consensus that no nation could disregard without justifying itself on the basis of specific, internationally recognized grounds. Nations would not, as is the case in Germany today, be suspected of engaging in political self-righteousness or even *Siegerjustiz* (victor's justice) and "political trials"; instead, the state could assume the role of complaining party – which seems a more fitting role than that of judge with respect to the offensive state practices in question. Thus, the example of the Honecker case provides additional impetus to proceed with the long-deliberated establishment of an international criminal court.[110] In the course of working out further details, the question of sanctions should merit special attention, a topic that opens new and challenging fields for academics as well as practitioners.[111]

9

Destalinization in the Former Soviet Union

Kathleen E. Smith

Where should one begin in describing mass repression in the former Soviet Union — with the Red Terror inflicted on civil war opponents? With forced collectivization of the peasantry? With famine exacerbated by state policies? With executions and imprisonment of millions of "enemies of the people" in the 1930s? With wartime deportations of entire ethnic groups? With postwar incarceration of returned prisoners of war? Or with the exile of inhabitants of newly annexed territories? It is easier to pinpoint the end of widespread terror, which came with Stalin's death in 1953. Grave human rights violations, however, continued on a lesser scale throughout the Soviet period.[1] Until recently examination of past repressions in the USSR took place during periods of liberalization, but not transformation, of the old repressive regime. Under these circumstances vast state-sponsored repressions were not matched by equally extensive efforts at investigation, prosecution, and compensation.

Under Nikita Khrushchev, from 1956 to 1964, and Mikhail Gorbachev, from 1986 to 1991, liberal elements within the Soviet leadership attempted to distance themselves from the worst aspects of the Stalinist system and to increase support for Communist Party rule through economic, political, and legal reform. Yet because the Communist Party drew legitimacy from its status as a direct successor of the party of Lenin (and Stalin), it could not tolerate a radical break with the past. Disclosure of previous Soviet atrocities also threatened the personal authority of reformers, who owed their own positions to the old system. In both periods of liberalization, cautious, partial rejection of previous state repression by liberals within the leadership became a source of conflict with conservative officials and civic radicals. Official restraint in revealing the whole horror of previous repressions demonstrates the limits of in-system reform. Only the demise of the Soviet empire and the ban of the Communist Party in late 1991 finally severed the continuity of party rule and transformed the dynamics of coming to terms with the past in the former USSR.[2]

By comparing distinct periods of reform in light of official policies toward recognizing and rejecting previous state repression, one should be able to see how the passage of time since repression affects coming to terms with the past during in-system reform and how a revolutionary break changes the dynamics of settling accounts with the old regime. In this chapter, I examine four key battlefields in the Soviet Union's struggle to cope with its repressive past. In roughly chronological order, the following issues emerged as sources of tremendous controversy during periods of liberalization: rehabilitation of victims, rewriting of Soviet history, commemoration of victims, and judicial measures against human rights offenders. Policies toward interpretation of and reparations for previous state repressions reflect the level of the government's commitment to reform at the time in question, as well as the status of ongoing confrontations over basic rights, including freedom of speech and association.

Background to Liberalization

At the moment of Stalin's death in March 1953, Soviet labor camps and jails held an estimated eight million political prisoners from all walks of life. And in the months beforehand, Stalin had clearly signaled the start of a new campaign of terror, his first target being a group of prominent Jewish physicians. After Stalin's demise, however, the members of the Politburo quickly moved to arrest the head of the secret police, Lavrentii Beria, and to denounce the so-called Doctors' Plot as a fabrication. The trial and execution of Beria disposed of the man most feared by other top Communist Party officials; it did not serve as a pretext for delving into the rampant criminal acts committed by the secret police under Stalin's orders. By removing Beria, Khrushchev guaranteed the physical security of other members of the party-state apparatus and showed his commitment to collective rule at the level of the Politburo, or Presidium as it was briefly called under Khrushchev.

Only in March 1956 at its twentieth Congress did the Communist Party admit the existence of and condemn Stalin's purges. In his so-called secret speech to a closed session of the Congress, Khrushchev blasted Stalin's cultivation of a harmful "cult of personality." Criticism of Stalin's self-glorification had been voiced earlier, but Khrushchev elaborated on the damage that resulted from Stalin's arrogance and his elevation of himself above others. According to Khrushchev, Stalin's grasping for power, intolerance of his colleagues, and "sickly suspiciousness" led him to use violence not just against his real opponents but against "many thousands of innocent people." While Khrushchev hid the extent of Stalin's purges and painted the party as the main victim, his sharp attack on Stalin's leadership — ranging from his role in falsifying history to his mishandling of military strategy in World War II — remains the harshest portrait of Stalin ever drawn by a Soviet leader.

Khrushchev's detailed revelations of Stalin's sanction of torture, brutality toward honest old Bolsheviks, and mass repression of party and state workers shocked the audience and marked the beginning in the USSR of the slow, somewhat erratic process of confronting the past. In his report, Khrushchev obviously felt compelled to address the troubling question of why other party leaders had not acted to curb Stalin's "perversion of socialist legality" during the ruler's lifetime. At times pleading ignorance and at times admitting fear, Khrushchev blamed only Stalin, Beria, and a few corrupt secret police investigators for the atrocities. He stressed that the party itself suffered most under Stalin. These tenuous justifications of the party's failure to prevent human rights abuses both set the stage for and marked the boundaries of officially approved truth seeking.

Throughout the Khrushchev thaw, conservatives and liberals battled on several fronts over the legacies of the purges and the boundaries of reform. When the Politburo ousted Khrushchev for his "hare-brained schemes" in 1964, it also moved to quash what it viewed as disruptive debates over interpretation of Soviet history stirred up by destalinization. Although Leonid Brezhnev did not revert to a Stalinist form of administration, he retreated from many of Khrushchev's liberal reforms, including allowing criticism of Stalin. Under Brezhnev, silence and inaction replaced discussion of the purges and rehabilitations. Human rights abuses became a topic raised only by daring dissidents until Gorbachev and a new team of reformers came to power in 1985. Gorbachev's policy of glasnost, or openness, gave citizens the opportunity to express their concerns, and they challenged authorities to face up to the consequences of mass terror.

Rehabilitation and Reparation

The top priorities of purge victims and their families in 1953 were release and rehabilitation. The government granted amnesties to a large number of ordinary criminals immediately after Stalin's death, but only a few thousand "politicals" — mainly loyal Communists and prominent public figures — had been freed by 1955. This so-called silent destalinization neither reduced the pressures in the camps nor raised public awareness of what had taken place under Stalin. In several abortive camp rebellions, prisoners attempted to draw the attention of high authorities to their plight. But only after Khrushchev's "secret speech" were some seven to eight million political prisoners liberated, and perhaps another five to six million posthumously rehabilitated.[3]

To process the huge number of prisoners, Khrushchev formed special three-person commissions made up of an official from the prosecutor's office, a representative from the party Central Committee, and a party member who had already been rehabilitated. These commissions fanned out to camp sites and places of exile across the country, where they used their extraordinary powers to rehabilitate or pardon ordinary prisoners on the spot following a brief review of the prisoner's file and a short interview. The time and form involved in the reversal of a sentence often paralleled the manner of its imposition — ten minutes in front of a commission with extralegal powers. Posthumous rehabilitations, on the other hand, were granted only on receipt of a request and after a potentially lengthy review of the case.[4] Moreover, far from all who applied for rehabilitation received it. Most notably, the government refused to rehabilitate the victims of the famous show trials of the 1930s, including old Bolsheviks Nikolai Bukharin, Lev Kamenev, and Grigorii Zinoviev.

In assessing the status of victims, one must bear in mind that there exist several kinds of rehabilitations: formal juridical rehabilitation — not a pardon or amnesty but a revised sentence; social rehabilitation — that is, compensation for lost wages and suffering; restoration of property, position, pension, and, in the Soviet case, party membership; and, finally, public rehabilitation — in which the victim's good name and standing within the community are restored.[5] Under Khrushchev, legal rehabilitation was common, whereas public and full social rehabilitation were extremely rare. The government did provide assistance with housing and limited financial compensation for survivors of the purges. Survivors received two months' wages from their old jobs and could count their years of work in labor camps toward pensions and job seniority. Few former prisoners, however, returned to their old positions, especially if they had held high office earlier. Lingering suspicion of "enemies of the people" remained, as can be seen in the statistics on restoration of membership in the Communist Party. The Party Control Commission reviewed over 70,000 petitions between 1956 and 1961 but reinstated only 30,954 members.[6] Rehabilitation was not an open process — it proceeded behind closed doors, without the victim's participation or right to appeal. And while biographical notes about public figures might mention that a person had been a victim of illegal repression, no articles on rehabilitation per se or lists of victims appeared in the Soviet press. The government did not even inform citizens how to proceed in seeking rehabilitation.

Under Brezhnev, rehabilitations slowed to a trickle. Preferential treatment for survivors regarding housing ceased, and the press no longer mentioned illegal repression in biographical sketches. Beginning in 1986, however, Gorbachev's policy glasnost spurred frank discussion in the press of Stalin's purges. Decline of fear, along with the public rehabilitation of famous figures such as Nikolay Bukharin, prompted more citizens to appeal for rehabilitation on behalf of themselves or their relatives. At first rehabilitation proceeded as before — that is, slowly, only after a specific request had been filed, and without much publicity. Glasnost, however, allowed the press to champion cases of victims and their families who still awaited rehabilitation. In response to public pressure, the authorities turned to official decrees in 1988 and early 1989 to reform the process of rehabilitation. First, the local KGB and procurators' offices were ordered to review all cases from the 1930s to the mid-1950s regardless of whether a complaint had been registered. The Politburo also requested that local party organizations accelerate their review of petitions for readmittance to membership. Most significant, the Politburo decreed that all sentences which had been decided by a *troika* — a three-man committee set up to alleviate the burden on the courts during the height of the repressions — or other nonjudicial organs be annulled and the persons sentenced be considered rehabilitated.[7] This order allowed the KGB and procuracy to resolve a great many cases in a short period of time. By spring 1991, the Moscow city procuracy had reviewed and resolved 90 percent of its cases that involved sentences from nonjudicial bodies — a large share of its approximately 100,000 cases subject to review.[8] Finally, in August 1990, President Gorbachev ordered that full rights be restored to those who had suffered exile or arrest as a result of forced collectivization in the 1920s.[9] Public pressure had long been building for rehabilitation of any and all victims of Soviet rule from 1917 to 1986 (when Gorbachev released most of the current Soviet political prisoners), but this was the first official move to broaden the definition of victim of repression.

The statutes on reparations to victims of illegal imprisonment, however, remained as before: They stipulated revision of pension status and awarded two months' pay at the rate prior to arrest — only now currency reform had reduced such wage compensation to a pittance. Many angry letters appeared in the Soviet press from newly rehabilitated survivors who rejected such compensation as an insult. On a local and republican level, however, new legislatures took their own steps to assist former purge victims. Many cities awarded survivors (and sometimes their spouses as well) the same privileges that veterans of World War II received, including the right to shop in special stores, free passage on local transport, and priority access to better housing and medical care. At the time of the August coup, the national parliament, despite over a year of discussion, had been unable to adopt a law on rehabilitation and reparations.[10] Although Gorbachev found that he could turn legal rehabilitation of individuals to his advantage — building his reputation as reformer — he was unwilling to shoulder real financial responsibility for previous state repressions.

Finally, the media under glasnost devoted considerable space to accounts of victims' sufferings and to rehabilitation of public figures. Coverage of the purges, however, drew on unofficial sources, not on official statements or documents. Both Khrushchev and Gorbachev formed party commissions to investigate violations of legality under Stalin, but except for occasional reports about rehabilitations the results of this research remained secret. Significantly, investigation of repressions remained the province of the party, not the government or an independent committee. Party-state archives remained closed to most other researchers.

In Russia, the end of Communist Party rule had tremendous repercussions on policies involving coming to terms with previous state repressions. Less than three months after the coup attempt, the Russian parliament passed a comprehensive law on rehabilitation and reparations for victims of repression.[11] The law covers political repressions from November 7, 1917 onward and includes as victims children who shared exile with their parents or suffered due to their parents' convictions. Moreover, the government formally adopted a broad definition of repression as

different means of compulsion used by the state for political reasons to wit: deprivation of life or freedom, placement in forced care in psychiatric medical institutions, deportation from the country and deprivation of citizenship, eviction of groups of the population from their places of residence, exile, deportation to special settlements, forced labor in conditions of restricted freedom, and any other deprivation or limitation of rights and freedoms of people who were declared to be socially dangerous to the government or political structure for class, social, national, religious or other reasons, as carried out by the decisions of courts or other organs sharing judicial functions, or by administrative command issued by organs of the executive power and responsible officials.[12]

The law stipulates numerous measures designed to restore justice and to compensate victims of repression, including return of confiscated property; the right to return to one's place of residence prior to repression;[13] financial compensation of two-thirds of current minimum monthly wage multiplied by the number of months spent in incarceration or exile, but not exceeding 100 times the minimum wage; priority access to housing and, for invalids and pensioners, to health care; free legal services for problems regarding rehabilitation; limited access to secret police files; return of photographs, manuscripts, and other personal artifacts; and information about cause of death and place of burial where relevant. In terms of official acknowledgment of state repression, the law also guarantees periodic publication of lists of rehabilitated people and biographical data in the official press. In practice, access to archives requires the cooperation of the KGB, which has not committed substantial resources to this endeavor and hence is very slow in processing requests. Nevertheless, victims and their families have begun to take advantage of the opportunity to see their files.[14] Also gradually, the bureaucracy involved in administering reparations has begun to function. In a gesture of sincerity, the parliament has reinforced its commitment to helping victims by amending its law to index compensation to inflation.

Rewriting Soviet History

Lack of access to archives by scholars is only one problem facing Soviet historians. "History is politics projected into the past," wrote the renowned Russian historian Mikhail Pokrovsky, and his view of history aptly describes both Stalin's and later reformers' approaches to historiography. Under Communist rule, history, like the arts, was expected to serve the interests of the people as defined by the Communist Party of the Soviet Union (CPSU) leadership. For instance, all Soviet schools used the *Short Course on the History of the CPSU(b)* from the time of its publication in 1938 until 1956. This text exalted Stalin's role in Soviet history from the time of the revolution onward at the expense of other old Bolsheviks. In Stalin's version of the past, Leon Trotsky, Bukharin, and many prominent revolutionaries disappeared from Lenin's side and surfaced only as "enemies of the people" unmasked by Stalin's vigilance. Not surprisingly, when castigating writers and social scientists for deifying Stalin, Khrushchev singled out the *Short Course* as one of the main vehicles of propaganda behind Stalin's "cult of personality."[15]

Whereas a generation of Soviet citizens had been raised on a textbook that glorified Stalin, a generation of historians had been devastated by purges and by pressures to conform to the vagaries of the party's ideological line. As one Western observer noted shortly before Stalin's death:

> For over two decades, Soviet historiography has been in steadily deepening crisis. Histories succeed each other as if they were being consumed by a giant chain smoker who lights the first volume of the new work with the last of the old. Historians appear, disappear, and reappear; others vanish without a trace.[16]

The historical profession continued to suffer a crisis of credibility and courage in the years after Stalin's death. Despite the party's condemnation of the role of historians in creating Stalin's cult of personality, few historians readily engaged in serious self-criticism. Older historians were compromised by their previous writings, and even younger scholars were accustomed to respond to commands from above rather than seize the initiative in choice of topic and in political tone for their works. Thus, although they were willing to parrot the party stance on the consequences of the cult of personality, most historians avoided making new analyses of the 1930s.

When one historical journal attempted to promote candid discussion, better research methods, and freedom from official commands regarding research topics, conservatives fought back. They attacked the journal's political orientation, accusing it of catering to enemies of socialism and of fostering "nihilism" among the young. In early 1957, an alliance of conservative historians and party ideologists removed the journal's liberal editors; the orthodox party press exulted: "While criticizing Stalin's mistakes, the Party at the same time defends him against the attacks of revisionists and declares that it will not give up Stalin's name to [its] enemies."[17]

Conservative historians successfully defended the idea that history should be written to serve the party's goals, however they might be defined, against the notion that history should present facts and trust to readers to make their own judgments. In 1957, calls for writing the whole truth lost, and literary writers, who required less institutional support and training than did historians, took the lead in publishing the most revealing and thoughtful accounts of the purges.[18]

By the beginning of perestroika, popular awareness of previous state repressions had waned due to the reimposition of strict censorship regarding negative aspects of Soviet history. The history textbook in use in 1986 barely reflected Khrushchev's destalinization campaign. Although it mentioned that Stalin had made "serious errors" and cited the Central Committee resolution of 1956 condemning the cult of personality, it failed to criticize Stalin's role in collectivization or in the famine of the 1930s.[19] Gorbachev himself did not originally make rewriting history a priority. On the contrary, he apparently took a very utilitarian stance against reopening painful questions; in 1986 he allegedly told a meeting of Soviet writers:

> If we start trying to deal with the past, we'll lose all our energy. It would be like hitting people over the head. And we have to go forward. We'll sort out the past.
> ... But right now we have to direct our energy forward.[20]

Gorbachev did not want animosities from the past to hinder his current program for perestroika, but — to the public's great interest — writers, poets, journalists, social scientists, and film makers all exploited glasnost to reexamine the past, and in particular Stalinism.

Finally in 1987, Gorbachev publicly declared the need for filling in "blank spots" in history. Again he approached the question pragmatically, arguing that one needed to draw lessons from the past to avoid mistakes in the present. Gorbachev consistently endorsed a balanced view of Soviet history: He both bemoaned the errors and recalled the achievements of the 1930s. Under pressure from liberal scholars, Gorbachev came to support "truth" in history as an important precondition of democratization. Official and unofficial criticism of the purges, collectivization, and Stalin in general, however, did not pass without protest from conservatives. In the summer and fall 1987, Politburo member Yegor Ligachev and KGB head Viktor Chebrikov both spoke out harshly against "one-sided" views of history. Chebrikov even claimed that Western secret services were encouraging "certain representatives of the artistic intelligentsia into positions of carping criticism, demagoguery and nihilism, of denigrating certain states of the historical development of our society."[21] Conservatives did not deny that the purges had taken place, but they challenged any depiction of the past that gave repressions central stage. Conservative protests, however, eventually paled in light of aggressive responses by liberals within the Gorbachev administration and within the liberal media.[22]

As for official historiography, revelations in the popular press along with public debates over interpretation of Soviet history led to the canceling of exams for Soviet history in the spring of 1988 and to plans for a new textbook.[23] Teachers faced a tremendous credibility problem due to what liberal historian Iurii Afanas'ev labeled a gap between popular, oral history and history as taught in the schools. He argued that this contradiction, not negative truths, led young people to mistrust authority. Historians and educators could not fill the demand for new textbooks and teaching materials quickly. Unlike popular writers, who had long written novels and memoirs "for the drawer"—that is, without expectation of publication—anti-Stalinist historians had not possessed the materials to prepare quality studies during the years of stagnation. Under glasnost, a new wave of memoir literature appeared and was complemented by new projects to collect oral histories.

Given the pressure to produce a revised educational program immediately, as one observer noted, "[the educational system] faced the unenviable task of making definitive statements about topics under intense debate in society at large."[24] Thus, the first new history textbook came under fire for being out of date as soon as it came off the presses.[25] The book also failed to incorporate pluralist teaching methods, which would encourage students to draw their own conclusions from primary source material. While not yet reflected in the 1989 textbook, however, for the first time professional historians admitted the need to incorporate first-person accounts and literary treatments of the past in their own debates.

Under Khrushchev, historians tried to break away from the command system by which they essentially performed research on demand and within strict political guidelines. Under Gorbachev, historians reassessed the impact of repressions on Soviet society and government. Most important, the popular conception of history during the 1990s gradually expanded to include reminiscences, documents, and oral interviews of ordinary people. Shaping collective memory has become a task for nonprofessionals as well as professionals. Even if archival access remains limited, future historiography seems destined to give greater weight to the significance of repression.

At present, although the Yeltsin government has not passed a comprehensive law on archives or launched an official investigation of previous state-sponsored repressions, a team of pro-Yeltsin politicians, lawyers, and academics have amassed some seventy volumes of documentary evidence, including information about political repression, for use in the trial of the CPSU (see later in this chapter). A team of historians from the civic group "Memorial" (the All-Union Historical-Enlightenment Society), appointed to new postcoup state commissions for the study of KGB archives, were granted extraordinary access to a range of official archives to help prepare for the trial. The volumes of incriminating documents they collected provide documentary proof of, among other things, Stalin's direct role in setting quotas for arrests and in signing execution lists, as well as evidence of party involvement in all stages of the purges. Trial preparations led to the release and publication of numerous documents from party and state archives revealing the workings of the secret police in the purges and in the persecution of dissidents—which will undoubtedly improve the treatment of repression in new versions of Soviet history.

Commemorating Victims: Symbolic Politics and Civic Activism

Besides condemning Stalin in words, Khrushchev took numerous steps to dismantle the trappings of the cult of personality. After his secret speech, authorities at all levels—from ministers to school principals—removed from display portraits of Stalin and banners bearing his statements. In some schools students cut Stalin's picture out of their textbooks, just as they had removed pictures of "enemies of the people" in the past. At the twenty-second Party Conference in 1961, Khrushchev even orchestrated a campaign to demand eviction of Stalin's corpse from its resting place alongside Lenin. Without ceremony, Stalin's body was removed from Lenin's mausoleum and buried nearby within the Kremlin walls. Khrushchev also called for consideration of "erecting a monument in Moscow to commemorate the memory of the comrades who became victims of arbitrariness."[26] Unlike the negative measures aimed at denigrating Stalin, nothing came of the proposal to officially honor victims. Moreover, restrictions against unofficial organizations left victims and their families isolated, with no forum in which to voice their common interests and no public space in which to gather to mourn their dead.

During perestroika the issue of commemorating victims reemerged, and once again attention focused on monuments and graves. But under Gorbachev, ordinary citizens had the opportunity to mobilize and speak out. Thus in 1987, the idea of commemorating victims of repression arose not at a party congress but among young people in an informal political discussion club. A small group of Muscovites began a petition drive to publicize and gain support for their proposal to build a monument to all victims of repression under Soviet rule that would combine a statue with a research center devoted to study of the purges. At first the group was stymied by local authorities, who detained signature gatherers and refused to cooperate. Through relentless efforts, however, the volunteers spread the word about their plan and won the support of prominent cultural figures as well as of ordinary citizens. The plans for a monument sparked a civic movement, and Memorial became one of the biggest social movements in the USSR both in terms of members and number of branches. Indeed, 103 cities sent delegations to Memorial's founding conference in January 1989.

Memorial campaigned not only for a broad conception of victims of repression — one that included those who suffered during collectivization of agriculture in the 1920s as well as modern-day political prisoners — but for civic control over the design and creation of a monument. Given its members' concern that repression never happen again, Memorial formulated an agenda that included historical research, education, aid to survivors of repression and their families, defense of human rights, and active participation in the country's democratic transformation. At every stage of its development, however, Memorial encountered fierce resistance from local and central authorities. In some cases officials harassed and threatened activists; in others they used bureaucratic means to hamper the society's operation. Despite the fact that official disapproval and material shortcomings limited Memorial's impact on state policies regarding destalinization, Memorial profoundly changed public awareness of the past and became a symbol of civic courage.

Citizen initiative also paved the way for discoveries in a second battlefield of symbolic politics — detection of mass graves. Starting in 1989, revelations of common burials of purge victims seemed to emerge from all corners of the Soviet Union as Memorial and individual citizens drew on the testimony of witnesses to uncover grave sites. These shocking revelations proved a powerful stimulus for antistalinism. Moscow writer Aleksandr Mil'chakov began a one-man crusade to identify the anonymous corpses. He was researching a novel when he learned from cemetery employees that in the 1930s hundreds of bodies with bullet holes in their foreheads had been thrown into unmarked common graves in central Moscow cemeteries. Under glasnost, Mil'chakov made his knowledge public and, in cooperation with *Vecherniaia Moskva* — Moscow's main evening newspaper — Mil'chakov published a series of articles recounting his efforts to get information on burials from the KGB. After months of silence and subterfuge, the KGB finally produced lists of persons buried in central cemeteries. In December 1990, *Vecherniaia Moskva* began to publish weekly a column of photographs and short biographical sketches of those buried in Moscow cemeteries. Mil'chakov's lists — with their haunting black and white photos and terse obituaries — shattered once and for all the myth fostered by Khrushchev that the party was Stalin's main victim. Chauffeurs and professors, blue-collar workers and executives, party members and the unaffiliated, young and old, all appear in the execution lists. Again the truth had come to light due to the efforts of a citizen gathering public support and taking on seemingly invulnerable state institutions.

Since the coup, the public face of the Russian government has changed. In one of the most striking moments following the coup attempt, a crowd gathered in front of KGB headquarters and pulled down the statue of Felix Dzerzhinsky — the founder of the Soviet secret police. The parliament has since resolved to remove symbols of Soviet rule from its buildings except when to do so would damage the architecture. It also made October 30 an official holiday. First dissidents and then Memorial had long marked this day as a day of memory of Soviet political prisoners. The memorial complex to victims of repression, however, remains in the planning stage as the money collected melts away due to massive inflation.

Trials

In Latin America pursuit of justice for victims of human rights abuses has focused on prosecution of secret police/military perpetrators. In the USSR neither authorities nor the public concentrated on the judicial system as a means of redress or of prevention. Khrushchev engaged in both legal reform and selective prosecutions of human rights abusers to reassert control over the secret police. As noted earlier, Politburo members arrested secret police chief Beria in 1953. They acted against Beria out of fear that he would manipulate the police to install himself as a new Stalin, not out of disgust with his role in masterminding the purges. Nevertheless, Khrushchev prosecuted Beria and his top six associates partially on the basis of their roles in illegal repressions.[27] The Supreme Court sentenced Beria and his codefendants to execution. And four more closed trials followed in which the Soviet press reported that a total of twenty-three high police officials, all Beria's protégés, were sentenced to execution or long prison terms.

The fates of other former NKVD officers tried in the 1950s remain hidden. One amateur historian has discovered that at least fifty other high-ranking NKVD investigators — whose names surfaced during the review of cases of major party and cultural figures — were also arrested for falsifying cases and/or torturing prisoners.[28] According to procuracy official Terekhov,

> If facts became known that one or another officer of state security was mixed up with baseless accusations against Soviet people . . . then such workers, depending on their degree of guilt, were excluded from the party, removed from their posts, or judged by law. But only in the event that there was irrefutable proof. There were no special purges, the staff was not reduced.[29]

The party did admit to expelling 347 of its members (including 10 ministers of internal affairs and state security at union and republic levels and 72 senior NKVD officials) for violations of socialist legality between 1956 and 1961.[30] But even today, no data have come to light on the quantity of secret police subject to this range of sanctions.

Prosecutions clearly had to be initiated from above. Memoir literature includes numerous instances of prisoners who wrote endless complaints to officials at all levels about torture and abuse by NKVD investigators. After Stalin's death, rehabilitation of victims did not include the opportunity to file legal complaints against those resposible for illegal arrest or sentencing. Although the state preserved these petitions, it did not use them as a basis for prosecutions. Moreover, by 1956, many people involved in carrying out the purges had themselves become victims of Stalin or had retired. Finally, the introduction of a statute of limitations for criminal cases as part of a new criminal code at the end of the 1950s halted all official prosecutions.

During perestroika, however, the idea of a trial of Stalin and Stalinism became a subject of public debate. While the statute of limitations still blocked efforts to open or reopen cases against individual executioners and torturers, international law mandates that there can be no deadlines in cases of crimes against humanity. When the Tomsk branch of Memorial attempted to prosecute party officials, including Yegor Ligachev, for crimes against humanity for the cover-up of mass graves in the 1970s, however, the courts refused to hear the case.[31] Moreover, it came to light in Moscow that the imposition of a statute of limitations had interrupted a number of prosecutions. Revelations in the press that several former investigators who had been indicted for torture and falsifying cases and then released under the statute of limitations currently held high civilian posts in Moscow created a public furor. Publicity led to the men involved losing their positions, degrees, and honors, but they remained immune to prosecution.[32]

Oddly enough, one of the only cases to gain even a preliminary court hearing was based on a citizen's initiative to *defend* Stalin. A former procurator charged a liberal writer and newspaper with slandering Stalin and those who defended Stalin. The plaintiff argued that Stalin could not be called a criminal because he had never been tried or convicted of any crimes. The proceedings really were nothing more than a media event in which both sides struggled to present their opinions before the judge ultimately dismissed the suit. The popular press celebrated the suit's dismissal as a defeat of modern-day incarnations of Stalinism, but it admitted that the plaintiff's spirited defense of Stalin's honor had great resonance for some members of the older generation.[33] Moreover, while the idea of slandering the dead received short shrift, support remained for exposing the names of NKVD men. Although publication of the names of executioners is often proposed as an alternative to a Nuremberg trial, such a proposal falsely assumes that the identity of the guilty could be determined without benefit of legal procedure. Controversy over lustration in Czechoslovakia and elsewhere demonstrates that "outing" informers and secret police without due process only increases mistrust of the judiciary.[34]

Distrust of the Soviet legal system is one of the reasons behind support for an extraordinary forum. The idea of a popular, "social trial" of Stalin and Stalinism gained popularity among those committed to preventing a return to repression. In school classrooms and public auditoriums across the Soviet Union, history teachers and various clubs have experimented with using a trial format to reach moral and historical judgments of Stalin. In early 1991, the most elaborate and pointed social trial was held in Moscow by a group of city council deputies, who charged not Stalin but the Communist Party with grave crimes, ranging from systematic human rights violations beginning in 1917 to the invasion of Afghanistan. According to the accusers, the party not only had put itself above the law but had committed crimes against humanity.[35] Ultimately the trial was a one-sided affair with little public impact (though it turned out to be a harbinger of postcoup charges against the Communist Party.) The idea of a social or a moral trial is appealing because of the feeling among many people that Russians share some sort of basic moral standards—not embodied in written law. Moreover, a social trial provides the means to empower ordinary people by encouraging them to reevaluate and judge their national past.

Besides the technical legal obstacles, many liberal intellectuals cited a possible return of inflammatory rhetoric and political purges as cause not to pursue a Nuremberg-style trial. If prosecutions took on the same scope as persecutions, the Soviet Union would be awash in a sea of lawsuits. The scale of potential hostility that could be unleashed by mass prosecutions deters even those who would in principle like to see the perpetrators of repression held to account. Still, many people consider a legal trial or investigation vital to breaking with the repressive past. Concerned with the results of condoning impunity, one letter writer bemoaned, "When will there be an all-peoples' trial of the executioners? . . . How can we talk about perestroika if no judicial evaluation is given to all these crimes? . . . Who will impose control over the KGB?"[36]

Since the August coup, the Russian parliament has not amended the criminal code to alter the statute of limitations regarding prosecution of human rights abusers. The law on rehabilitation does require that data be published periodically in the media about workers of the secret police or judicial system who are acknowledged as "bearing criminal responsibility on the basis of criminal law" for falsifying cases or using illegal forms of investigation. Nonetheless, no such measures have occurred to date. The only real legal attempt to assess the Soviet past emerged, paradoxically, from an attempt to overturn the ban on the Communist Party declared by Yeltsin at the time of the August coup.

Beginning in the summer of 1992, the new Russian constitutional court heard a case stemming from charges by a group of Communist Party members that President Yeltsin's decrees banning the CPSU and its Russian branch, and confiscating their property, were unconstitutional. The conservative members of the former Communist Party based their challenge on the separation of powers enshrined in the Constitution and the USSR law on parties and voluntary organizations — neither of which gave the president power to dissolve parties or expropriate their assets.

Fearing that the ban on the CPSU would be overturned for procedural reasons, liberal deputies brought a countersuit asking that the Communist Party as an organization be declared unconstitutional. The president's advocates asserted that the Communist Party was never a real political party but rather part of state structures, as shown by the party's role in making foreign and domestic policy, in selecting personnel for state posts, and in controlling mechanisms of repression. As part of the state, the party was subject to the president's administrative orders. Moreover, they argued, "the organization calling itself the Communist Party" should be considered unconstitutional because both its ideology and activity contradict article 7 of the Russian Constitution, which forbids parties that have as their goals violent overthrow of the Soviet constitutional system and socialist government or which incite social, national, or religious tension. As evidence they pointed to the party's alleged participation in the coup attempt and its ideology, which elevated one class above another. The party responded by defending its glorious past and arguing that the party that initiated perestroika and democratization should not be confused with the party of the 1930s; it had abolished article 6 of the Constitution, which had enshrined the party's leading role and had become a parliamentary party.[37]

The constitutional court combined these appeals and in December 1993 issued a compromise ruling that overturned nationalization of party property and partially upheld the ban on the Communist Party. The court ruled that leadership structures could be dissolved but not local party cells. Although return of Communist Party assets may prove problematic, Yeltsin probably has little to fear from a rebirth of the CPSU. Many top party leaders had already resigned their membership and, like Gorbachev, refused to take part in the suit. Moreover, Yeltsin's *ukases* did not ban communist ideology, and some seven successor parties exist already – none with mass membership. As one commentator noted, the court was delivering not a death blow to the party but giving a postmortem on the party; the party had already decisively lost members and legitimacy by the fall of 1991.[38] In fact, the collapse of the party in 1991 meant that public interest in the trial was small. After all, Yeltsin did not aim to prosecute or settle accounts with the party or its former leaders but rather to break party control over state structures, a problem that had all but resolved itself by the time of the court's ruling.

Why have trials – either prosecutions of individual cases or grand affairs – not been a major part of coming to terms with past repressions in the USSR? Obviously, the scale of the crimes involved, as well as the passage of time, present obstacles. An equally important factor stems from society's deep lack of respect for the legal system. On the whole, courts have never been the first choice for Soviets seeking justice. Under the Soviet regime, citizens expected change to come from central authorities – petitioners addressed their grievances to the real source of power in the USSR, the party and its representatives. Many former prisoners see Soviet law as a party-state tool, capable of manipulations, not so different from laws under which original abuses were committed. A new government has the chance to validate itself and discredit the old regime by holding an extraordinary trial by fiat. But, given the continuity of Communist Party rule under Khrushchev and Gorbachev, the party-state regime could not use trial as a form of restoring legitimation. And Yeltsin is clearly more concerned about ongoing political and economic crises than settling accounts.

Conclusion

In any transition, unearthing past atrocities may so alarm members of the old regime that they threaten to disrupt the process of reform. In the Soviet case, both impulses for reform and pressure to bury the past came from within the top leadership. Particularly under Khrushchev, high party officials who had participated in organizing mass repressions wished to avoid awkward questions about their own complicity. Khrushchev carefully shifted blame from the party and its current leaders and sharply restricted prosecutions for human rights violations. Conservatives also constantly warned that official acknowledgment of the massive extent and arbitrariness of repressions would fatally undermine the legitimacy of Soviet rule. Even liberalizing leaders who sought to use condemnation of repression to justify their reform programs and distinguish themselves from the old regime recognized this danger. A conservative backlash is not the only potentially disruptive consequence of calls for acknowledgment of grave human rights abuses: Particularly during top-down reform, disclosure of past abuses may act as a catalyst for citizens to challenge officials to make a dramatic and revolutionary break with the past. During the Khrushchev period challenges from below came from writers, historians, and a small number of dissidents who tried to break the boundaries of permitted discourse, but the authorities easily squashed these initiatives when they contradicted official policy.

Twenty-five years later, deeper reform and weaker fears of repression encouraged the Gorbachev regime to allow greater openness about previous state-sponsored repressions. The passage of time meant that few perpetrators survived, and those that did had long been retired. Whereas stimulus for prosecution thus lessened, the wounds left by repression had still not healed. Thus, commemoration of victims and exploration of past repressions proved to be a tremendous catalyst for a true civic movement. New freedom of association allowed survivors and their sympathizers to assert their rights and their interpretation of Soviet history. Memorial began by supporting reformers, acting in the belief that they had shared goals, but it also demanded reparations, prosecutions, and a full accounting of past crimes by the state. Memorial's goals interfered with the desires of reformers to use history as a tool to guide reform from above. Communist Party officials attempted to discourage the formation of a social initiative for the commemoration of victims of Stalinist repressions by arguing that such an effort would distract citizens from the priorities of perestroika. Beyond a reflexive reaction against unofficial political participation, the position of these party workers reflected fears that, by lifting the taboo on discussions of Soviet history, perestroika and glasnost had opened a pandora's box. Indeed, the call for commemoration of the regime's past victims did threaten the party's reform program, but not by diverting attention from critical economic matters. Instead, just as under Khrushchev, this issue revealed the limits of top-down reform. Acknowledgment of past repressions and attempts to remedy these abuses reflected well on reformers only insofar as they were willing to meet the concerns for openness, democratization, and accountability that arose from consideration of past abuses. The passage of time reduced the threat of individual criminal prosecutions, but even fifty years after the apex of mass repression revelation of previous Soviet atrocities threatened the authority of reformers who owed their positions to the old system and who remained committed to one-party rule.

Although the practical results of efforts to achieve acknowledgment and reparations for past human rights abuses in the USSR pale in comparison to prosecutions and official acknowledgment elsewhere, public awareness has grown remarkably over the past five years. Moreover, the end of Communist Party domination of government and social life has only just opened up the political arena. The new non-Communist government in Russia has already tackled the issues of reparations and archival access. Continuing political flux means that relations with the old regime are still subject to negotiation in Russia and the former republics of the Soviet Union. Should the Soviet successor states decide to turn their attention to prosecution or revelation of human rights abusers and secret police informers, they will face the same difficulty in balancing a commitment to rule of law with a desire to break down old structures that has already emerged in the trial over banning the CPSU. The issue of lustration has so far arisen only in the Baltic states; Russia is preoccupied with other issues. Interest in the past in Russia has waned tremendously since 1990. Russian society appears tired of glasnost and self-criticism. Arguably, the gains of the past years have made rejection of repression a less pressing issue than before, but more significantly the constantly deepening economic crisis overshadows all other issues for both politicians and ordinary citizens.

10

Romania: A Persistent Culture of Impunity

Edwin Rekosh

Romania's recent history differs significantly from that of its Central and Eastern European neighbors, most of which experienced "velvet" revolutions in 1989. In Romania, the revolution was not velvet. When the change came, it was as bloody as it was swift and unexpected. After an apparently spontaneous uprising in December 1989, a new elite quickly emerged to guide the country through its transition. At first the new elite had the broad support of Romanian society. Before long, however, the leadership split, and an opposition developed in response to a growing perception that the Romanian revolution was being managed by a clique that, at best, represented an anti-Ceausescu faction of the establishment.

As a result, the main source of pressure to settle accounts has come from a fragmented opposition, most fervently when a grass-roots movement emerged in the spring of 1990 with the expectation that it could influence the shape of the future regime through politics of protest. That chapter came to a close, however, when a newly elected government welcomed the assistance of miners from the Jiu Valley, who converged on Bucharest for the third and bloodiest time that year to restore order.

The emergence and consolidation of the new ruling clique proved to affect significantly Romania's ability to come to terms with the past. A true coming to terms would have required a difficult confrontation with a large, immovable bureaucracy and the *nomenklatura* from the prior regime. In Romania, that confrontation has been sharply tempered by Romanian leaders who themselves owe allegiance to the same bureaucracy and *nomenklatura*. Instead of fulfilling the expectations of many Romanians who were filled with revolutionary zeal and who expected a clean break with the past, the transitional regime manipulated public opinion with the false appearance of justice. The end result did nothing to end Romania's culture of impunity, inherited from the Ceausescu regime. The effects persist into the present.

The events of December 1989 are still clouded in mystery, and no one has been held accountable to the public for the bloody clashes that took place between miners and protestors in June 1990. The execution of the Ceausescus and the trials that followed the revolution may have satisfied an immediate thirst for revenge spawned by the violent turmoil or may have fulfilled the political needs of those in power. These actions did not, however, represent a coming to terms with the past or even the present.

Moreover, issues of decommunization or punishment of past human rights abuses are especially complex because Romania is in the midst of confronting a primary problem: establishing the truth about what happened (and what is happening). Indeed, "the truth" is a loaded term in Romania.[1] Too often, generalized conclusions stand in for specific information. This attitude toward truth is deeply ingrained in the consciousness of the Romanian people: so much so that in late 1992, a group of young Romanian democrats proposed in all earnestness to tackle Romania's "image problem" by creating a centralized coordinating center for all independent non-governmental organizations, to be called "The Truth About Romania." The proposal demonstrated a failure to distinguish between discovering truth and creating it.

Ceausescu Falls and Justice Fails

The Events of December 1989

The events surrounding the Romanian revolution of 1989 are so murky and controversial that many question even calling it a revolution. Many Romanians, when referring to the upheaval that accompanied the change in regime, speak of the "events of December" or *tulburarile* ("the disturbance.") The conspiracy theorists, who abound in Romania, postulate that December 1989 represented everything from a palace coup to a foreign intervention by security forces from Hungary, the Soviet Union, Israel, or the United States. Most observers agree, however, that what happened in Romania in December 1989 began as a genuine popular uprising, even if it was later seized by a political elite who could be most charitably described as an internal opposition within the ranks of the Communist Party, the Army, and the security apparatus.[2]

The events of December began on December 16, 1989 in Timisoara, a town in southwest Romania close to the Hungarian and Serbian borders. On December 15, 1989 protests arose over the forced transfer from Timosoara of Bishop Laszlo Tokes of the Hungarian Reformed Church of Romania. Although the police were initially restrained, the protests soon escalated and troops opened fire on the demonstrators under orders that came directly from Nicolae Ceausescu and that were approved by the Political Executive Committee of the Communist Party (the Romanian equivalent of a Politburo).[3] At least dozens of demonstrators were killed.[4]

The Timisoara phone lines had been blocked, and the roads leading to Timisoara had been closed. Nevertheless, word was out by the time Ceausescu returned from a diplomatic visit to Iran on December 20. When he ill-advisedly called for a televised public demonstration the next day as a show of support, a small protest broke out in the back of the crowd. Caught off guard by the disruption, Ceausescu appeared to falter. The national television station interrupted its live coverage of the event for several minutes while order was restored, but not before some boos and catcalls could be heard and Ceausescu's vulnerability became obvious to the viewing public.

The people of Bucharest took the irregularities as their cue to go to the streets. Protest demonstrations formed at University Square and Romana Circle. Savage repression by the Army and security forces resulted in many deaths and injuries and continued into the early morning hours of December 22, 1989.[5] By daylight, however, the clashes had ended, and the Army together with some units of the Securitate appeared to have switched sides. People left their jobs en masse, and soon hundreds of thousands of people were in the streets, with the Army fraternizing with the crowds. Elena and Nicolae Ceausescu were forced to flee but were caught in Tirgoviste, a town northwest of Bucharest, later that day.[6]

Videotapes later made public recorded the first meeting of the elite clique that constituted itself as the National Salvation Front that same afternoon. Ion Iliescu, elected five months later as Romania's first post-Communist president, had already emerged as the public face of the National Salvation Front, having signed the new entity's first public statement. He had been a prominent member of the *nomenklatura* and a high-ranking Communist Party official before being dismissed from the Central Committee in 1984. Others present at the first meeting included top-ranking generals and some of Ceausescu's closest advisers.[7]

The arrest of the Ceausescus was announced by a spokesman for the newly formed National Salvation Front who promised a public trial. The next day, Iliescu confirmed the arrest in a televised speech. "The time will come for their just and harsh judgment by the people," he said.[8]

The New Regime Faces Its First Trial

The trial of the Ceausescus presented the new regime with its first opportunity to make a firm break with the abuses of the past and to provide a public accounting. That opportunity was lost. Instead, the Ceausescus were tried by a secret, specially constituted military tribunal, and the first official acknowledgment of their status came when the media broadcast a National Salvation Front statement three days after their arrest. Much later that night,[9] Romanian television showed selected excerpts of the Ceausescus' trial and dramatic footage of the former ruling couple lying dead, with multiple bullet wounds, in pools of blood.

According to the videotape of the proceedings, most of the two-hour long trial consisted of bare accusations of crimes committed by the Ceausescus against the Romanian people and the Ceausescus' protests that they did not recognize the authority of the tribunal, that they had been victims of a foreign-sponsored coup, and that they should be heard by the Grand National Assembly.[10] Ultimately they were accused of genocide, with over 60,000 victims,[11] and of attempting to flee the country with foreign-held assets. They were formally convicted under articles 162, 163, 165, and 167 of the Romanian Penal Code for undermining state power through organization of armed actions, destroying public assets, undermining the national economy, and conspiracy.[12]

The Ceausescu trial was a travesty of justice: The defense lawyers acted like a second prosecution,[13] and there was no appeal and no request for clemency.[14] The entire period from arrest to execution lasted three days. A small number of top National Salvation Front leaders apparently decided on the death sentences on December 24, 1989, before the trial had even started.[15]

Moreover, the Ceausescu trial could not have constituted a true settling of accounts where there is a public disclosure of the facts coupled with a reasoned, normative judgment. The trial was not public,[16] as had been originally promised, and there was no opportunity for a full airing of the wrongs committed by the Ceausescu regime. Equally important, the trial failed to elucidate what had caused the switch from street violence on the evening of December 21, 1989 to a jubilant celebration with Army backing the next morning. Finally, as the first major public act of the provisional government, the trial did nothing to fulfill the new regime's stated goals of moving toward a rule-of-law state with a democratic order. On the contrary, the trial tarnished the image of the new regime in international public opinion, with the executions uniformly criticized by foreign governments and international human rights groups.[17]

More Trials

The Ceausescu trial was just the first of many trials. Although none of the later trials demonstrated as egregious a disregard of fair judicial procedures, they were nonetheless responsible for undermining public confidence in the judiciary. Trumped-up charges and then later releases on contrived grounds neither elucidated the historical record nor provided any indication that decisions were grounded in principle.

The machinery of justice began with an emphasis on the prosecution of so-called terrorists that ultimately came to nothing. Extraordinary military tribunals were set up in each of the forty-one Romanian counties and Bucharest according to a decree-law published on January 8, 1990.[18] They were empowered to use the summary procedures employed for offenses *in flagrante delicto* and to try criminal offenses

> which were committed with a view to suppressing the people's revolution and destabilizing the state, threatening its very existence and the life, physical integrity and health of persons, the public and personal patrimony and the assets of the national cultural patrimony.[19]

The very existence of terrorists was later doubted, however, especially after some time had passed and none of the supposed scores of terrorists were brought to justice.

A number of highly publicized trials, however, did take place in the aftermath of Ceausescu's fall from power. The first of them, commencing on January 27, 1990, concerned Ceausescu's four closest aides: former minister of the interior Tudor Postelnicu, former deputy premier Ion Dinca, former Communist Party organization chief Emil Bobu, and former first deputy premier Manea Manescu. In a well-publicized show trial with rehearsed, self-critical testimony, which the defendants later renounced, the four pleaded guilty to complicity in genocide for their role in issuing orders to fire on demonstrators in December 1989. All four were sentenced to life imprisonment, and all of their property was confiscated. Soon after, in March 1990, proceedings that came to be known as the Timisoara trial charged more than two dozen Securitate and police officers with complicity in genocide for the killings in Timisoara and the secret removal of corpses to Bucharest for burning. Subject to numerous delays, the trial lasted nearly two years, with over 500 witnesses having been heard. Charges were eventually modified to aggravated murder and complicity in murder. When the verdict was read on December 9, 1991 eight defendants were jailed, with sentences ranging from fifteen to twenty-five years. Six of the remaining defendants were acquitted, one died, and ten others were convicted but were pardoned or released when the time served during the investigation and trial was taken into account.[20]

In April 1993, however, the Supreme Court reconsidered the case of Ceausescu's four closest advisers and commuted the charges from complicity in genocide to aggravated manslaughter and complicity in aggravated manslaughter, reducing the sentences to between ten and seventeen years. By 1994, all four had been released, benefiting from medical releases or a parole procedure that commutes three quarters to two thirds of a jail term for anyone over the age of sixty. All of those convicted in the Timisoara trial had also been released on health grounds. Each of the releases, gradually announced over the course of many months, was marked by little more than a small press notice.

Another group trial centering around the events of December 1989 involved the entire Political Executive Committee of the Romanian Communist Party (other than the four persons charged in January) and started in July 1990. The procedural history of this case provides perhaps the most telling example of the arbitrary justice meted out in these trials. The members of the committee were originally charged with genocide for approving Ceausescu's orders to fire on demonstrators in Timisoara on December 17, 1989 and in Bucharest on December 21, 1989. The military prosecutor later reduced the charge to instigation to aggravated murder. In March 1991, the military court of first instance convicted nine of the members on charges it further reduced to complicity in murder and negligence of duty. The rest were acquitted or received suspended sentences. The convictions were overturned on appeal in December 1991, but the general prosecutor launched an extraordinary appeal to the civilian section of the Supreme Court. The result was that all twenty-one defendants were convicted in a final judgment on new charges of complicity in aggravated murder and attempted complicity in aggravated murder. Yet in the end, three of the defendants are officially on parole, and the others have been released for health reasons.

Ceausescu family members, many of whom held public positions, were also brought up on charges. Most notable, the notorious younger son of the ruling couple, Nicu Ceausescu, was prosecuted for ordering the shooting of demonstrators in December 1989 in the Transylvanian city of Sibiu, where he was the local first secretary of the Communist Party. N. Andruta Ceausescu, a brother of Nicolae Ceausescu and a former Securitate lieutenant-general, was sentenced to fifteen years for aggravated murder, complicity in murder, and firearms violations for his role in the violence on December 21–22, 1989, including having personally shot seven people.[21] Other family members, including the two other Ceausescu children, were investigated or charged with the undermining of the state economy, embezzlement, or fraud.

But even son Nicu Ceausescu rode the ups and downs of a seemingly ambivalent judiciary. He was originally sentenced to twenty years for genocide. Appeals filed in his case first reduced the charges against him to instigation to aggravated murder and illegal possession of firearms and later reinstated the genocide charge. In the end, the only charge that stuck was the illegal possession of firearms, carrying a five-year jail term. Nicu served only half of that sentence, however; he was paroled, partly for health reasons, in November 1992. His release received little public attention. One newspaper account quoted a shopkeeper's reaction: "People are so worried about where they can get food and if they will lose their jobs. . . . They do not have time to bother about the fact that it is unjust for him to be released. There are too many other problems. Winter is here and we are cold."[22] Brother Andruta Ceausescu, currently out of jail, has also quietly benefited from at least two temporary releases from prison on medical grounds.

These trials differed significantly from the Ceausescus' trial in that they were held before the regular military courts, and many of the sessions were broadcast live on television, with journalists welcome to attend the sessions. In addition, the death penalty had been abolished on the day after Christmas, giving Elena and Nicolae Ceausescu the distinction of being the executioner's last two victims. Nevertheless, the later trials, too, contributed to the impression that a highly politicized judiciary was implementing a purge of the top leadership at least as much as it was accounting for human rights abuses. That impression was aggravated by the lack of a clear underlying theory of prosecution and the conflation of human rights prosecutions with investigations into the financial dealings of the Ceausescu children. In addition, trying most of the defendants in large groups contributed to confusing guilt by job title with individualized responsibility. In the end, the subtlety of the accusations against the Political Executive Committee, whether its members were criminally culpable for acquiescing in Ceausescu's decision to fire on demonstrators, was undoubtedly lost on the general Romanian public.

At the same time, the gradual reduction of charges and suspiciously consistent parole and medical release practices have resulted in an apparent failure to hold anyone responsible other than Nicolae and Elena Ceausescu. The post-Ceausescu trials present the worst aspects of two contradictory political impulses. They started as highly politicized show trials caught up in the hysteria of the moment, but in the end the concrete results were effectively subverted through indirect means, presumably due to political influence. The main result has been a further erosion of public confidence in the rule of law; with it, any deterrence value of the trials has been undermined.

Ambiguous "Amnesties"

On the heels of the revolution, on January 4, 1990, Ion Iliescu, acting as the president of the National Salvation Front Council, announced a general amnesty for political offenses committed from December 30, 1947 until December 22, 1989. Political offenses were defined in article one of the decree as deeds that had as their purpose:

(a) protest against dictatorship, the cult of personality, terror or the abuse of power by the authorities;
(b) the respect of fundamental human rights and freedoms, exercising civil, political, economic, social and cultural rights, or abolishing of discriminatory practices;
(c) the satisfaction of democratic claims.[23]

In addition, article two provided a general amnesty for any crime subject to a sentence of up to three years. Likewise, article three commuted any sentences of up to three years currently being served. The amnesty's cutoff date of December 22, 1989 was apparently intended to ensure that the so-called terrorists would not benefit from its provisions, but more significantly, the amnesty did include the key period leading up to Ceausescu's fall.

Ten days later, on January 15, 1990, Bucharest Radio reported that the National Salvation Front Council had issued a second decree-law, this time characterized as a pardon, but not limited to political offenses. Like the previously announced amnesty, the decree clearly provided that it would not benefit those convicted of murder, severe bodily injury, rape, theft, and prison escape as well as abuse of power contrary to the public interest, bribery, intercession, illegal arrest and abusive investigation, ill treatment and unfair repression.[24] Unlike the previously announced amnesty, however, the decree also provided that it would not benefit:

The individuals who, having participated in the leadership or service of the old dictatorial regime, actively suppressing human rights and freedoms or carrying out other of the objectives of that regime, or simply acting within it in the service of their own interest or in order to avoid responsibility, perpetrated crimes against peace and humanity, or against the state, as well as crimes of illegal arrest, abuse on duty, violation of arms regulations, terrorist acts or complicity in terrorist acts.[25]

Although the January 15 pardon appears to be carefully limited so as not to cover any human rights abuses, the prior general amnesty — which did not contain the same qualifications — still holds for crimes subject to sentences of three years or less. The ambiguous relationship of the two decrees was never explained to the general public; indeed, few people are aware that two different decrees existed. Moreover, all political prisoners were released immediately after Ceausescu's departure, before either decree was announced.

The full benefits of the January 4 amnesty decree became clearer when Securitate officers and other former officials began to benefit from its provisions. For example, in March 1991, five Securitate high officers were convicted for "unlawful deprivation of liberty" under article 189 of the criminal code for detaining Dumitru Mazilu and his family from December 21 to December 22, 1989. Mazilu, a one-time Securitate officer himself, was a former U.N. diplomat turned dissident who later participated in the formation of the National Salvation Front.

Although seemingly appropriate, the officers were not charged under article 266 of the criminal code, which prohibits "illegal arrest and abusive investigation" and is excluded by the general amnesty.[26] As a result, Emil Radulescu and Gheorghe Manea, sentenced to two and a half years each, were amnestied according to the January 4 decree-law.[27] Defendants in the Timisoara trial and other trials concerning the events of December 1989 also benefited from the decree.[28]

In the end, then, the popular move of providing an amnesty for offenses of political protest provided a vehicle for simultaneously forgiving human rights abuses with little attention. Indeed, the restrictions contained in the later pardon misleadingly gave the impression that no human rights abuses would go unpunished.

Nonetheless, the decrees do leave room for the prosecutions of many persons who would have committed human rights abuses under the authority of the Communist regime, at least if they committed crimes subject to a sentence of more than three years. Indeed, the pardon refers, in part, to the exclusion of "crimes against peace" and "crimes against humanity" that were established by the Nuremberg courts after World War II.[29] The opportunity they provide, however, has not been seized.

Confronting the Communist Regime

The Aborted Trial of Communism

Like the summary trial of the Ceausescus, the morally evocative charge of genocide initially leveled at most of the post-Ceausescu defendants served to deflect much of the newly awakened public outrage at decades of victimization. Genocide does not, however, refer merely to large-scale killings, as the Romanian authorities and media implied at the time. Genocide has a specific meaning under international law, which is mirrored in the Romanian Penal Code. It requires an intent to destroy, in whole or in part, a national, ethnic, racial, or religious group (as such).[30] The only group distinction shared by the victims of state violence in December 1989 was a political one, making a genocide claim incompatible with international law. Indeed, the genocide charges were, for the most part, ultimately dropped, especially when it became clear that the numbers of dead and wounded during December 1989 had been exaggerated.

But the misuse of the genocide charge superficially masked a more important omission. The charges in the 1990 trials were exclusively limited to the "events of December." There was no investigation or prosecution relating to the political persecutions of the Ceausescu years, for which many of the same defendants arguably were responsible. Moreover, the abuses of the harsh, Stalinist regime of Ceausescu's predecessor, Gheorghiu-Dej, which included mass deportations, extrajudicial executions, disappearances, political arrests, torture, and forced labor, were not mentioned.

Even before the 1990 trials were under way, well-known dissident Doina Cornea spoke of her concerns: "It is impossible to judge people only on what they did on the day the revolution started. Everybody must be judged by the people. I am not in favor of vengeance, I have always advocated human rights. But you cannot pass the death sentence on a couple and say that everything else is fine."[31] Once the trials began, critics like Octavian Paler, an intellectual writing for the newly formed independent newspaper *Romania Libera,* advocated strongly for a more comprehensive approach to the trials: "Does justice want that these trials be limited, that they should not accuse the Communist system? Why? Does it believe that the massacre in Timisoara can be understood by avoiding the roots of the evil which lie in the totalitarian order?"[32]

By the time the one-year anniversary of December 1989 came around, the government was at least superficially acknowledging the problem. In what may have been an early sign of an impending split between the president and the more reform-minded prime minister Petre Roman, the justice minister, speaking on Roman's behalf, issued a stern public criticism of the prosecutor's office:

> The penal bodies, more particularly the prosecutor's office, are in duty bound to take each case separately and establish one's contribution to the country's disaster and to the attempt to repress the revolution, and bring the culprits to court because they are to be held responsible for what they have done against the country and the Romanian people for more than forty years, including the hot revolution days when they shot at an unarmed population. To conceal the truth and to procrastinate the moment of doing justice means to work against the Romanian people's interests of today and tomorrow, and that is why the passive attitude of the penal bodies, of the prosecutor's office, can no longer be tolerated.[33]

The statement concluded that "the country's rebirth, national reconciliation and the restitution of Romania's true image to the rest of the world" could not be achieved without prosecutions. The prosecutor's office reacted defensively, citing the thousands of depositions, expert appraisals, searches, and other inquiries that had been necessary merely to indict those responsible for the repression in December 1989. "The prosecutors are doing all they can to find out the truth and punish those guilty of crimes against the Romanian people," their official response insisted.[34] But the exchange of public statements ultimately proved to be mere window dressing, because no new criminal investigations were initiated.

By the end of 1991, pressure began to mount on the prosecutor's office to initiate a "trial of communism" that would address the human rights abuses of the Communist regime. The Association of Former Political Prisoners filed a formal complaint regarding crimes committed under communism, and there were a series of meetings between the justice ministry, the prosecutor's office, and leaders of several civic organizations, such as the Association of Former Political Prisoners, the League for the Defense of Human Rights, the Romanian Helsinki Committee, and the December 21 Association. Negotiations continued for about eight months. The nongovernmental organizations wanted to start by making examples of the most notorious figures from the Stalinist period of 1946 to 1964, such as Teoharie Georgescu, Alexandru Nicolski, and Alexandru Draghici. Georgescu was responsible for operating a prison in Pitesti and devising the "Pitesti phenomenon," a particularly brutal psychological and physical torture process that resulted in the conversion of the torture victims themselves into torturers. Nicolski was the chief of the Securitate under Gheorghiu-Dej, and Draghici was the minister of the interior, responsible for signing the orders for the internal displacement of tens of thousands and sending untold thousands, including political prisoners who had served their sentences, to forced labor camps near the Black Sea where they helped dig the Danube canal.[35] Many died in the camps from the ill treatment and hard conditions. In total, Nicolski and Draghici were responsible for the arrest and detention of at least hundreds of thousands of political prisoners, according to estimates by the Association of Former Political Prisoners and others.[36]

The discussions with the prosecutor's office proved futile and broke off. Georgescu had been long dead, and Nicolski died of a heart attack around the same time an arrest warrant was issued. No action was taken against Draghici until after he fled to Hungary. Finally, in August 1992, the prosecutor's office issued an arrest warrant and sought Draghici's extradition for ordering the 1954 murder of a Turkish citizen following a dispute in a café.

Hungarian authorities balked at the request for extradition in early 1993 because the Hungarian proscriptive period for murder, thirty years, had expired. The Romanian-Hungarian Treaty of Mutual Juridical Assistance stipulates, in relevant part: "Extradition shall not take place if, according to the laws of the side to whom the application was submitted, the penal action cannot be carried out owing to the prescription terms having been reached or other legal grounds." Romanian authorities argued, nevertheless, that bringing any high officials before justice was unthinkable under the Communist regime, thus constituting a *force majeure* and suspending the running of the prescriptive period.

Unable to convince the Hungarian authorities, the prosecutor's office went forward in May 1993 and prosecuted Draghici in absentia along with three Securitate aides who had been involved in the killing. The prosecution relied in large part on documentation provided by the Romanian Intelligence Service, the successor to the Securitate, based on a 1968 investigation.[37] By March 1994, however, Draghici had died. On March 19, 1994 the Military Section of the Supreme Court in Bucharest issued an order of no indictment for all four defendants based on the passing of the prescriptive period.

In April 1993, another prosecution for abuses committed under the Communist regime commenced. Tudor Postelnicu, who was in prison at the time for his role in the events of December 1989, and George Homosteanu, another former minister of the interior, were charged along with seven Securitate officers. They were accused of carrying out Ceausescu's orders for the summary execution of three people who attempted to highjack a bus to the West in 1981.[38] Two of the three Securitate officers accused of carrying out the killing admitted their guilt. In July 1993, the Bucharest Military Tribunal convicted all nine, handing down sentences of up to eighteen years. Yet along with the others involved in the trial of Ceausescu's four closest advisers described earlier, Postelnicu remains free nonetheless.

These token prosecutions, which have had only a very limited success, represent a tiny fraction of the potential cases. Indeed, out of frustration over less than vigorous official efforts, nongovernmental groups have attempted to launch prosecutions by doing their own fact finding. To date the prosecutor's office has accepted for consideration four cases based on information provided by the

League for the Defense of Human Rights. One case documented the extrajudicial execution of three men near Targu Mures who were arrested in 1948. In July 1993, the Targu Mures prosecutor exhumed the three skeletons and found that each had been shot in the skull. Nevertheless, bringing the case to trial is difficult because the identities of the officials responsible are not known. Generally, the ability of human rights groups or other nongovernmental organizations to establish enough of a factual basis for further prosecutions is hampered by a 1991 decision by the Romanian parliament to seal Securitate records for forty years.[39]

In addition to prosecuting the systematic gross violations of human rights that were especially prevalent before Ceausescu took power, some Romanians urge that the scope of a trial of communism include some of the subtler abuses of the Ceausescu regime. Indeed, as former dissidents and others contend, many Ceausescu policies caused widespread suffering and abused the rights of millions of Romanians. For instance, Ceausescu's "systemization" policy resulted in the bulldozing of entire villages. Urban planning policies resulted in the razing of entire sections of Bucharest, including many historic churches and other buildings of historical or architectural significance.[40] Demographic policies under the Ceausescu regime criminalized abortions and financially penalized childless women and men over twenty-five years of age. Doctors faced criminal sentences if they failed to inform the prosecutor's office of emergency medical procedures — meaning that many women died from unattended complications rather than confess to an illegal abortion.[41] Economic policies that subsidized the development of a large but substandard industry and ignored Romania's rich agricultural resources arguably caused unnecessary misery for most Romanian citizens, who suffered through food shortages and winters without heat.[42] Uncommonly widespread and intrusive surveillance created a climate heavy with fear and intimidation.

Some Romanians argue that decision makers for such policies should be held accountable along with those responsible for authorizing or carrying out extrajudicial executions, torture, and other gross violations of human rights. As atrocious as the policies were, however, determining individual criminal responsibility for devising the policies would not be an easy task. Prosecutors would face an enormous line-drawing problem since the scope of complicity could be potentially enormous. Romanian laws currently on the books that punish crimes such as "hostile actions toward the state" or "undermining the state economy" could probably be invoked. But using excessively vague criminal provisions of the prior regime would not contribute to the creation of a rule-of-law state. Trying crimes that easily lend themselves to political interpretation could, in fact, be a dangerous precedent and would not help to depoliticize the judiciary.

Regardless of the scope of a trial of communism, proponents of such a trial argue that its value is fundamental to the political tranformation currently underway in Romania. Constantin Ticu Dumitrescu, the president of the Association of Former Political Prisoners and an opposition senator in the Romanian parliament has written:

> The trial of communism, in its correct and complete sense, pursues restoration of the historic truth, the recuperation of the memory of our past, of the sense of

social justice, with a view to the moral curing and civil and political emancipation of our people. The trial of communism is, in fact, a condition of democratization, the Romanian revolution's last chance.[43]

Gabriel Andreescu, founder of the Civic Alliance and president of the Romanian Helsinki Committee, adds that from a juridical point of view, a trial of communism must concern itself with individual responsibility for particular crimes. But the *force majeure* justification for the suspension of the prescriptive period, that the very existence of the Communist regime prevented such prosecutions, refers to a collective event. It is in this sense, says Andreescu, that a trial of communism can be thought about collectively without sacrificing the principle of individual responsibility.[44]

Although no trial of communism has taken place — and there have been only a very few efforts to prosecute any human rights abuses of the Communist regime — compensation for human rights victims has been addressed relatively swiftly. The Association for Former Political Prisoners was formed at the beginning of January 1990 with the express purpose of seeking reparations for the suffering of its members.[45] Its efforts were successful, and law 118/90, passed in early 1990, provided a supplementary pension of 200 lei a month for every year persons persecuted by the Communist regime served in a prison or forced labor camp. Applicants must provide a ministry of the interior certificate proving they were detained for political reasons.

The government also announced that it would offer moral compensation by inscribing former political prisoners' names in a list to be known as the White Book. As of 1994, however, publication was withheld because the Association of Former Political Prisoners complained that the list was misleading. Containing 37,000 names, the list covered only three detention sites, a small fraction of the total number. Indeed, when the Association formed in 1990, more than double that number of former political prisoners registered with the organization.[46]. The Romanian Intelligence Service, in a 1993 report to parliament, claimed to have processed more than 70,000 applications for "moral compensation and due rights" by victims of political repression.[47] Also in 1993, the parliament passed a law rehabilitating judges who had been fired for political reasons after the Communists took power. For more recent victims, "revolutionary certificates" were awarded to those who fought in the revolution, were wounded in it, or had a relative who was killed in it. The certificates entitle their holders to tax breaks.[48]

Decommunization

A trial of communism represents perhaps the most extreme measure available to punish human rights abuses committed under the Communist regime, and other Central and Eastern European countries have generally avoided criminal proceedings in favor of vetting government officials and reforming institutions. Yet Romania is unique in some respects. On the one hand, the Communist regime in Romania was one of the most repressive regimes in the region. On the other hand, with four million members in a country of twenty-three million people, the Romanian Communist Party had the highest per capita membership. As a result, there are strong political forces in Romania that both demand and resist decommunization.

When the National Salvation Front first announced its intention to provide provisional leadership as the country made a transition to a pluralistic, democratic system, its legitimacy was supported by a wide range of political actors, including several well-known dissidents, who became members. By the end of January 1990, however, the dissidents had abandoned the National Salvation Front and were accusing it of perpetuating the firm grip on power by elements from the old regime. Historical opposition parties from the interwar period had reformed and began to gain in strength. Despite the lack of a tradition of organized dissident groups like Charter 77 in Czechoslovakia or Solidarity in Poland, civic organizations began to form outside of the party process. One of them, the Timisoara Society,[49] elaborated a statement enumerating demands that were believed necessary for the creation of a new democratic society. On March 11, 1990, workers' and students' associations gathered in Timisoara and adopted the thirteen-point "Timisoara Proclamation," which became the most coherent reflection of the popular sentiment that had moved the population to take to the streets in December. Point 7 of the Timisoara Proclamation questioned the role of the National Salvation Front: "Timisoara started the revolution against the entire Communist regime and its entire *nomenklatura,* and certainly not in order to give an opportunity to a group of anti-Ceausescu dissidents with the PCR [Romanian Communist Party] to take over the reins of political power." Point 8 provided that all former Communist activists and Securitate officers should be barred from running for public office, nationally and locally, for three consecutive legislatures. It also singled out the office of the president, opposing the right of those who had served the Communist regime — as party activists, not as simple members — to lead the country.[50] The proclamation was immediately adopted by hundreds of independent associations, and nearly four million individuals registered their support over the next two months for incorporating point 8 into the election law.[51] Nonetheless, the organizers of the 1990 elections pointedly ignored point 8, which would have excluded most of the leadership of the National Salvation Front, including its candidate for president, from running for office.[52]

Point 8 of the Timisoara Proclamation also became a rallying cry during a massive demonstration at University Square on April 22, 1990 that turned into a marathon sit-in that blocked traffic in the center of Bucharest for months.[53] The peaceful demonstration, which drew participants from a wide range of Romanian society, carried on through the first post-Ceausescu elections and ended in the violence of the "Mineriad" (see below) in June 1990. Iliescu's public reaction was to call the demonstrators tramps (*golani*) and charge them with attacking the majority of citizens, who had been linked to communism through party membership of themselves or family members: "People try to identify all of the evils of the old regime with the members of the Communist Party. But this can turn into a dangerous witch hunt."[54] The leaders of the demonstration insisted that they were not interested in punishment, only in having party activists "stop claiming that they represent us."[55]

After Iliescu won the May elections,[56] the demonstration dwindled in size. At

dawn on June 13, 1990, the police moved in, beating and arresting many of the protestors. Protestors retaliated throughout the day. After President Iliescu made a public appeal that evening, the miners from the Jiu Valley east of Bucharest arrived the
next day to restore order.[57] The events that ensued, known as the Mineriad in Romania, have become the blackest spot in the history of the new regime. Hundreds of
demonstrators and others in the street were beaten, and at least a dozen or so were
killed. Violence spread as miners went after targeted personalities, and opposition
party headquarters were ransacked. The events ended in a pogrom against Gypsies
(Roma) in a neighborhood of Bucharest with a large Roma population. By June 15,
when the miners left, the public that had been demonstrating for months in University Square lost any hope that their message would be heard by those in power.

But the Mineriad stands for more than just the end of dialogue with the ruling
government. There has never been a public acknowledgment of responsibility by
the government for the miners' violence. A parliamentary commission designated
to investigate the events issued two contradictory reports, one authored by the
National Salvation Front (the majority) and the other authored by opposition parties (the minority). Despite complaints filed with the prosecutor's office by human
rights groups and others, no one has been prosecuted.[58] Thus, June 1990 confirmed the pattern that had been developing in the trials that followed the fall of
Ceausescu. It was a pattern that would be mirrored again and again when vigilante mobs torched Roma homes in dozens of villages in Romania, police beat or
tortured prisoners, and miners descended on Bucharest in another bloody confrontation in September 1991.[59] One argument in favor of prosecuting past human
rights abuses is that leaving the abuses unpunished invites repetition, and the post-
Ceausescu record in Romania provides ample support for it. When asked whether
there was any guarantee against a future repetition of June 1990 and other violent
episodes, one human rights activist responded, "We have hopes, but the only
guarantee would be to punish those responsible."[60]

Establishing the Truth

One prime motivation of the advocates of a trial of communism was simply to
establish the truth of what happened under the Communist regime. Moreover, the
most egregious of the human rights abuses committed under the Communist
regime took place decades ago, and many of the persons responsible for it are
dead. As Constantin Ticu Dumitrescu, president of the Association of Former
Political Prisoners, acknowledges, "Our purpose is not revenge or punishment
because we have no one to punish. All we want is the truth."[61] Opposition senator
Alexandru Paleologu, who served time as a political prisoner during the Gheorghiu-Dej regime and was the first post-Ceausescu ambassador to France, emphasizes the wide implications: "The past cannot be forgotten because a society with
amnesia is a primitive society. In a true society, there is a collective memory and a
law and an agenda for those elected."[62]

There have been efforts to establish the truth without resorting to criminal proceedings. A draft law that would allow individuals to see their own secret police

files was introduced in December 1993 and then modified in July 1994, but does not appear to be very high on the legislative agenda.[63] Nevertheless, even without access to the secret police files, a powerful and moving series of television documentaries initiated in late 1990, *Memorial of Pain,* has been able to clarify many of the human rights issues of the past through oral history. The twenty-fourth episode, broadcast in July 1993, for example, interviewed former political prisoners who had been arrested in a crackdown on dissidents and protest organizers who had been inspired by the 1956 Hungarian uprising. The series is extremely popular, and as one of the only sources of credible information, each episode becomes a point of reference for anyone interested in the human rights abuses committed under communism. Books have also been published, for instance, one on the Pitesti phenomenon[64] and another presenting the notebooks of a *Memorial of Pain* subject.[65] Periodical sources containing primary documents and analytical articles also became popular after the revolution[66] but are less widely read than they once were. A new history textbook with a revised discussion of the Communist regime was announced in the spring of 1993.

New museums have been established, too. In the early fall of 1992, as an election campaign was under way, one of the destroyed buildings on "Revolution Square," where Ceausescu gave his last speech, was transformed into a Museum of the Resistance at the initiative of the Civic Alliance. For its first exhibit, the burnt-out shell of the red brick building formerly housing the Fifth Division of the Securitate was draped with three-story–long sheets containing the names of political prisoners who died in Romanian prisons under the Communist regime. In addition, a Museum of Totalitarianism was announced in the spring of 1993, to be established in Sighet, one of the most notorious penitentiaries for political prisoners in northwest Romania.[67]

Nevertheless, rediscovering history has been difficult, even for relatively recent events. The Romanian senate finally established a commission to investigate the events of December 1989 in early 1991, but the commission did not hear its first witnesses until the summer of 1993. Although a December 1993 deadline was set for the commission's report, the senate postponed the due date by an additional year in November 1993. In the meantime, Senator Dumitrescu had resigned as chairman of the commission in protest over the lack of cooperation from state authorities. In addition, a senate commission to investigate the miners' attacks in September 1991 has not yet presented its long overdue findings. The majority and minority reports issued by the commission investigating the events of June 1990 merely emphasized how politicized the official truth-seeking process was.

Romania had an especially intense experience with the manipulation of information for political purposes under communism. As Senator Alexandru Paleologu, Romania's ambassador to France in 1990, put it: "What was true was what you *said,* not what 'is.' There was an official version of the truth. Even after 1989, there was a reflex — people were not accustomed to discussing the truth."[68] The manipulative techniques of official elites are imitated throughout society, according to Paleologu, sometimes causing popular reactions that are equally uninformative.

In the context of impunity for past human rights abuses, the "truth" about the past must consist of information concerning who were the victims of abuses, what happened to them, and who was responsible for the abuses. In addition, such information should be accompanied by some sort of official acknowledgment. In Romania, however, the "truth" often consists of a series of politicized conclusions, without much discussion of the underlying facts. Sometimes the "truth" is merely obfuscation or mystification. Even for those operating in good faith, the end result is preaching to the choir without the satisfaction of universal acknowledgment.[69]

Conclusion

Generally, countries in transition are faced with choices about how to address past human rights abuses. Options generally include criminal prosecution, vetting of officials and institutional reform, compensation of victims, and investigation and creation of an historical record. But the issues that most of those choices raise have barely been addressed in Romania, mainly because of a general perception that there is no choice. Proponents of criminal proceedings have been stymied, and there appears to be little hope of a satisfactory official investigation and accounting for past abuses, or for more recent ones.

The thesis laid out in Chapter 1 is that international law can be useful to encourage a "weak transitional regime facing powerful constraints" to address firmly the prior regime's human rights record. Yet Romania may be a paradigm case of a country struggling with reactionary forces but eager for international approval. In the early 1990s, two of the most important foreign policy issues, for instance, have been the restoration of most-favored-nation trade status by the United States and admission to the Council of Europe,[70] both of which have subjected Romania to a thorough scrutiny of its human rights record. In addition, it is posited that a solid basis in international law is necessary to avoid the appearance of mere "political vengeance." Yet the prosecutions that have taken place to date in Romania do seem to have more in common with political vengeance than with accountability.

If international legal obligations to investigate and prosecute serious human rights violations had clearer political consequences, perhaps Romanian authorities would have taken greater measures to end the cycle of impunity. But regardless of any international political consequences, the most important factor preventing Romania from confronting its past has been its strange hybrid transition. Despite diplomatic pressure to investigate or prosecute abuses, the political will necessary to ensure that such obligations are carried out in good faith has been lacking.

The impunity enjoyed by the Communist regime appears to pertain with equal force to the recent past, with profound implications for the Romanian present and future. Although the passage of time and a history of frustrated hopes have decreased demands for a public accounting, the largely unresolved trauma of the Communist regime and the murkiness of the "revolution" and its aftereffects continue to spawn mistrust. One important consequence is that the Romanian public has failed to regain confidence in the rule of law. Indeed, Romanians often regard seeking a remedy for a human rights violation through the courts as a futile gesture. Thus, the persistent culture of impunity has significantly impeded the project of establishing a stable democratic order.

III

CASE STUDIES: LATIN AMERICA

11

Overview

Naomi Roht-Arriaza

The urgently felt need to come to terms with the recent past in Latin America stems in part from the extreme nature and particular characteristics of the prior human rights violations. Military and security forces, aided and encouraged by civilian elites who were afraid of growing oppositional movements, jailed, tortured, forcibly disappeared, and summarily killed persons who were considered politically dangerous. Often these crimes were justified in the eyes of the perpetrators as necessary to stave off a Communist insurgency, although the victims extended far beyond those waging armed antigovernment actions. There was little attempt to legalize such crimes; rather, in the case of disappearances, massacres, and summary executions, the regimes denied any involvement, blaming private death squads, "unknown men," or guerrilla groups. The worst violations generally took place under a state of emergency, with the executive ruling by decree. Although nominally civilian governments may have existed, the real power was the military and/or security forces. Even after a transition to an elected civilian government, in most countries the military continues to play a leading role in national life. In contrast, both the legislative and judicial branches of government, although nominally independent, have been weak and played—if any—a negative role in protecting human rights during the dark years.

This part looks at the cases of Chile, Argentina, Haiti, and El Salvador as perhaps the best-known and most complete experiences to date of coming to terms with the past. Whereas Argentina's transition took place in the wake of the armed forces' defeat in the Malvinas/Falklands war, the Chilean armed forces handed back power to civilians following a plebiscite that confirmed popular dissatisfaction with military rule. In both cases, the incoming governments have had to deal with a still powerful and restless military. In El Salvador, in contrast, the coming to terms took place in the context of an internationally brokered settlement of a protracted war, where the past figured prominently in the negotiating agenda. The Haitian case is still unfolding, but dealing with the past is one of several necessary strands in any transition to a more democratic society.

These are not the only countries in which coming to terms with past human rights violations has been a major subject of national debate. In Uruguay, Honduras, Guatemala, Nicaragua, Paraguay, Brazil, and Bolivia, the issue has figured prominently in the last few years. A brief synopsis of events in these countries helps give a broader context to the case studies.[1]

Uruguay

Uruguay had long been a liberal democracy with a relatively stable political system. The military that ruled Uruguay from 1973 to 1985 believed it was saving the country from subversion, especially from the armed leftist "Tupamaro" movement, which waged urban guerrilla warfare in the early 1970s. The military was responsible for the widespread prolonged imprisonment of perceived political opponents under extremely harsh conditions and for the torturing of thousands of Uruguayans. Although disappearances were not a principal feature of government policy, some 164 Uruguayans disappeared after being arrested. Many more lost their jobs because of suspect political ideas.

The transition from military to civilian rule in 1985 came about by means of a negotiated settlement between the military and a broad range of political parties, known as the Naval Club pact.[2] The pact called for congressional and presidential elections and the withdrawal of the military from public life. In exchange, the political parties implicitly agreed to leave the military high command intact and that the executive branch of a future government would not prosecute members of the military, although it would not stand in the way of adjudications by civil courts. Perhaps because of this unofficial pact, the military did not grant itself a self-amnesty, as did the Argentine and Chilean militaries.

Before and during the 1984 elections the political parties, unions, and other social groups had agreed that human rights abuses should be investigated, prosecuted, and punished. All the presidential candidates, including the winning candidate of the Colorado Party, Julio Maria Sanguinetti, declared that they would seek justice for those who had violated human rights. Shortly after Sanguinetti's inauguration, government representatives told the U.N. Human Rights Commission the same thing.

Sanguinetti quickly reinstated with back pay the thousands of civil servants who had lost their jobs for political reasons, signed the U.N. Convention Against Torture, and pardoned those awaiting trial in military courts. A Law of National Pacification, which granted amnesties to almost all the remaining political prisoners, exempted from its provisions military and police personnel responsible for human rights abuses during the military's rule. A parliamentary Commission on the Situation of "Disappeared" People and Its Causes was established, but without the power to subpoena records or compel testimony from the armed forces. In 1986 it reported on 164 cases but did not make specific evidentiary findings as to the fate of any of the persons who had disappeared. A private Church-related group, the Peace and Justice Service (SERPAJ), also published a detailed account of the extent and nature of torture and other violations, entitled *Uruguay Nunca Mas,* in March 1989.[3]

Within the first few months of Sanguinetti's government, attorneys representing those detained and tortured, and families of the disappeared, filed some forty cases against military defendants for criminal activities. Although the military refused to appear personally before civilian judges, responding to requests only in writing, proceedings continued until a civilian court issued arrest warrants for two officers in a disappearance case. At that point military courts challenged the civilian courts' jurisdiction over military personnel, but in November 1986 the Supreme Court upheld the civilian courts' claim to jurisdiction. The military let it be known that it would not cooperate or appear before civilian courts, setting the stage for a possible institutional crisis.

The government began seeking ways to avoid a confrontation with the Army high command. A first-draft amnesty bill failed when opposition political parties rejected it. At that point, polls showed that an overwhelming majority of voters in Montevideo, the capital, favored punishing the guilty members of the security forces. A second amnesty measure, introduced in August 1986, also narrowly failed, as did a substitute bill that would have allowed trials for murder, rape, disappearances, and serious woundings but not for torture. Finally, as the civil cases made their way through the courts and approached trial dates, and with the threat of open military defiance of a court order imminent, Congress finally passed law 15,848, the Law Nullifying the State's Claim to Punish Certain Crimes (Ley de Caducidad de la Pretensión Punitiva del Estado). The law, which did not use the word "amnesty" to avoid prohibitions on reconsidering a law on the same subject more than once in a legislative session, was in effect an amnesty for crimes committed during the de facto period by military and police officials "either for political reasons or in fulfillment of their functions and in obeying orders from superiors."[4] It required dismissal of all pending cases, with a few exceptions that proved meaningless either because they applied to no pending cases or because the cases subsequently have not progressed even though they are nominally excluded from the terms of the amnesty. In addition, there remains the possibility of a suit directly against the state, although statute of limitations and evidentiary problems make such suits problematic.

Disappearance cases, although covered by the law, were to be investigated by the executive branch and the results of the investigations communicated within 120 days. In May 1987, President Sanguinetti, in a further concession to the military, delegated the investigatory responsibility to the defense ministry, which appointed an active duty officer, Colonel José Sambucetti, as prosecutor. Predictably, Sambucetti's investigations were perfunctory, and in the six cases he investigated, he concluded that there was insufficient evidence to hold the armed forces responsible. Theoretically, this outcome should have allowed the cases to go back to the civilian courts unencumbered by the amnesty law; in practice this has not happened.

Outraged by the government's actions, a group of family members of victims, with the support of other prominent Uruguayans, decided to challenge the amnesty law. The Uruguayan constitution permits a popular referendum on any law within a year of its promulgation if 25 percent of the electorate so request. The National Pro-Referendum Commission set out to obtain the required petition signatures — some

550,000. Although initially the Commission obtained almost 100,000 more signatures than necessary, the electoral court, whose members were affiliated with antireferendum political parties, repeatedly disqualified large numbers of signers for minimal or spurious irregularities. President Sanguinetti repeatedly spoke against the referendum, and the defense ministry, in a show of force, scheduled highly visible war games for shortly before the referendum date. Despite the opposition of most of the political elite and the military, and little help from the mass media, the required number of signatures was reached just before the deadline.

The referendum was held on April 16, 1989. Although voters in Montevideo overwhelmingly voted to repeal the amnesty law, the provincial vote was against repeal, and the referendum failed, 58 percent to 42 percent.

The Uruguayan case raises squarely the question of the role of popular consent to amnesty measures. The amnesty law was not only promulgated by a popularly elected government recognized as legitimate by the population. It was also reaffirmed four years later in a popular referendum. Although it is possible to point to irregularities and intimidations that might have put pressure on the electorate to vote against repeal, the referendum was generally recognized as valid. But whereas popular approbation is surely a necessary condition for a successful policy on past abuses, is it enough?

As discussed in Chapter 3, international human rights law grants to individuals the right to a remedy and the right to a fair trial. To the extent a state's obligations to investigate, prosecute, and provide redress rest upon these individual rights, the obligations are not subject to limitation through majoritarian political processes but only through the specific relinquishment of such rights by the individuals involved. This position makes sense from the perspective of classical political theory: The direct victims of imprisonment, torture, and execution, and their families, are a minority of the population in any country. Moreover, these people have usually been stigmatized by their actual political, religious, or other attributes or — as Jaime Malamud-Goti points out in the Argentine case — because most people needed to believe others were targeted because they had "done something." Constraints on popular and legislative action exist in legal systems precisely to avoid majoritarian overriding of the needs and interests of such discrete, and powerless, minorities. The fact that an amnesty law is approved by a majority of the population, therefore, cannot imbue it with legitimacy; approval merely reaffirms the minority status of those most directly affected by the acts for which amnesties are granted. Rather, it is the role of law — both domestic and international — to assure that majoritarian impulses adequately protect the rights of minorities.

This does not mean that a society may never, under any circumstances, choose not to investigate or prosecute. But such choices are constrained, both by international obligations of the state itself and by the rights of individual victims.

Paraguay

In February 1989, the thirty-year dictatorship of General Alfredo Stroessner was overthrown by his right-hand man, General Andrés Rodriguez. General Rodriguez legalized opposition parties and vowed elections, prosecutions for human rights violators, and freedom of expression. He won in the initial elections held three months after the coup; a new Senate and House of Deputies were also elected.

The newly elected deputies called on the executive branch to "initiate trials in all the cases involving torture, illegal punishments, disappearances and similar crimes, in order that the facts be investigated and those directly responsible, their accomplices or those that engaged in cover-ups be duly punished." Although the government was slow in complying, the commissions heard from human rights victims, and in September 1992 the Congress created a bicameral Commission on the Investigation of Illicit Acts to investigate the police.

One particularity of the Paraguayan case is that many abuses were carried out by the police rather than the military; this has made it easier for some prosecutions to proceed even under a military-led government. As of May 1993, there were twenty-seven active cases and a half dozen officials in jail, either having been convicted or awaiting trial. On May 21, 1992, four high-ranking police officers were convicted of the 1976 torture and murder of Mario Raul Schaerer and sentenced to twenty-five years in prison.[5] The former head of the secret police, a retired Army general, was sentenced to five years for covering up the case. Legal proceedings against other Army officials for corruption and smuggling have also been initiated.

Although there has been no overall official truth-telling process, the Paraguayan press has been vociferous in detailing both the past abuses of the Stroessner regime and the identity of those responsible. Truth-telling efforts were given a huge boost in December 1992 with the discovery of the so-called horror files. Acting on a tip, a former political prisoner found boxes of documents in a local police station giving details of the detention, torture, and disappearance of suspected "Communists" and opponents of the prior regime. A series of raids by the attorney general's office produced still more files, including several relevant to the pending lawsuits. Other files included detailed information about U.S. aid to the secret police and collaboration with the security forces of other Southern Cone countries in the arrest and torture of political detainees. The Paraguayan press has published the names of informers taken from the secret files, and the government has pledged to open the archives to investigators, although not to conduct its own investigation.

President Juan Carlos Wasmosy, elected in May 1993, has stated that he will not oppose prosecutions but will leave them to the judiciary. Nonetheless, he added that it was time to "turn the page" and "look forward, not backward."[6] It remains to be seen how the courts, staffed mostly with judges from the Stroessner era, and the new legislature will deal with the current prosecutions and the new information being gleaned daily from the "horror files." For now, the government seems to have chosen a middle course, avoiding amnesties but also providing little support for official truth-telling or investigations.

Bolivia

From 1980 to 1981 Bolivia was ruled by a de facto government headed by General Luis Garcia Meza. The assassination and forced disappearance of political opponents, lack of civil liberties, and economic mismanagement characterized his rule. After a return to civilian rule, victims of those killed or imprisoned during the dictatorship together with trade unions and nongovernment organizations began pushing for the trial of those responsible. In 1986 the Bolivian Congress instituted criminal proceedings against General Garcia Meza, his interior minister Luis Arce Gomez, other ministers and chief commanders of the junta, and numerous members of the armed forces, the police, and paramilitary groups. After initially appearing before the trial court and giving testimony, Garcia Meza and a number of other defendants went into hiding. They were declared in contempt of court and tried in absentia, represented by government-appointed defense lawyers.

After years of delay, in April 1993 the Supreme Court convicted those accused, sentencing Garcia Meza and his interior minister to thirty years' imprisonment. In doing so, the court rejected pleas of obedience to superior orders, citing constitutional provisions limiting the use of this defense. The convictions spanned three different types of offenses: those arising out of the illegal coup d'état itself; those connected to grave human rights violations; and those arising from acts of corruption. The human rights violations included murder, torture, arbitrary detention, criminal association, and creation of armed paramilitary groups.[7]

Two incidents gave rise to the human rights portion of the indictment. The first occurred during the coup, when paramilitary forces attacked the Bolivian Trade Union Federation headquarters. Three well-known political and trade union leaders were killed, and others were detained by the Army and tortured. The second took place in January 1981, when the Army planned and executed the premeditated murder of eight leaders of a left-wing group, the Movimiento de la Izquierda Revolucionaria (MIR). The court characterized the latter killings as genocide.

The Supreme Court referred to international law at several places in its opinion. As a preliminary matter, defendants raised the statute of limitations as a bar to several of the charges. The court rejected the defense, noting that Bolivia is a party to the U.N. Convention on the Non-applicability of Statutory Limitations to War Crimes and Crimes Against Humanity, which are defined in the Statute of the Nuremberg Tribunal. The court did not specify which of the charged offenses constituted crimes against humanity. It indicated that it considered at least forced disappearances in this category, noting that the U.N. Economic and Social Council had recently declared that disappearances, as crimes against humanity, were prohibited by international law.[8]

The court's treatment of the crime of genocide is especially interesting. The opinion refers to the Genocide Convention twice, once within the context of defining it as crime against humanity (and therefore not subject to a statute of limitations) and again in discussing the killing of the MIR leaders. The court characterized as genocide "the destruction of a group of politicians and intellectuals"; however, the drafters of the Genocide Convention explicitly refused to include political opponents within the groups protected by the Convention.[9] Nor does the killing of eight individuals, taken alone, easily fit into the traditional definition of a crime against humanity, which requires large numbers of victims.[10] Despite its reliance on international law, the legality of the conviction is based on article 138 of the Bolivian Penal Code, which includes "bloody massacre" within the domestic definition of genocide. Thus, international law serves here to justify and legitimize suppressing the conduct at issue, but not directly to undergird the criminal charges.

The conviction is interesting for a final reason: The thirty-year sentences for the most serious crimes include a provision denying pardons for those convicted. In handing down the verdict, Supreme Court president Edgar Oblitas described the trial as an attempt to "end the history of impunity which has protected putsch makers and autocrats."[11] Although the military officially accepted the verdict, there are some indications that Garcia Meza's whereabouts are being protected by high-ranking officers within the security forces. To counter accusations that it was not searching diligently enough for Garcia Meza, the current government has offered a reward for the general's capture.[12] Meanwhile, eleven of those convicted are serving prison terms.

Nicaragua

When the Sandinista National Liberation Front overthrew the Somoza dictatorship in 1979, it promised to be "generous in victory," to avoid trials and punishment for most members of the defeated National Guard. However, some 2,000 of the worst offenders — including many known torturers — were jailed, although most of the highest-ranked Guardia commanders and their civilian allies fled the country. The Sandinistas considered the old court system an adjunct of Somocista rule and set about revamping it; soon, however, they found that a shortage of trained personnel and of resources would make court reform a long process. To try the remaining Somicistas expeditiously, the Sandinista government set up People's Anti-Somocista tribunals. These special courts were composed of one lawyer and two laypersons. They were soon roundly criticized by human rights groups because their members were Sandinista party activists, because they used rather loose evidentiary standards for conviction, and because — despite a conviction rate of close to 90 percent — there was no appeal to regular tribunals from their verdicts.[13] In addition, as the *contra* war intensified, the tribunals were increasingly used to jail suspected *contra* supporters rather than those accused of violating human rights in the past regime. Finally, in 1988, the tribunals were suspended, remaining cases were transferred to the regular court system, and many of the ex-national guardsmen were released.

The Nicaraguan case points up some of the quandaries involved in using the judiciary to settle accounts. The incoming Sandinistas faced a nonfunctioning judicial system that had to be rebuilt practically from nothing, with acute shortages of judges, lawyers, and resources. Meanwhile, there was an urgent need to proceed with the trials of national guardsmen who had been arrested in Nicaragua shortly after the Sandinista victory. The Sandinistas had control over the state's armed forces and so were not subject to the kinds of pressures felt by Southern Cone transitional regimes; however, they did face enormous pressure from the United States and, after 1983, from an armed *contra* insurgency. Their solution —

special courts to try political cases, using nonlawyers and special evidentiary rules — contained features contrary to international requirements of due process and helped undermine the regime's long-term domestic and international legitimacy. Even freed from the political constraints of an armed threat from a recalcitrant military, transitional governments, if their policies are to be successful, must still walk a fine line between effectiveness and respect for the due process rights of their opponents.

Honduras

Unlike other Latin American examples, the Honduran investigation into human rights violations committed by the military was carried out by an individual rather than a Commission. In 1992 then-President Callejas created an ombudsmen's office, known as the commissioner for the protection of human rights. To guarantee its independence, the commissioner was to be selected by the president from a list provided by a National Reconciliation Commission and could only be removed by a two-thirds vote of that Commission. All civil and military authorities are to cooperate with and cannot suspend the Commissioner's investigations.[14]

Shortly after his election, Commissioner Leo Valladares, as part of the regular duties of his office, began investigating a pattern of disappearances that had taken place in Honduras from 1980 to 1993, most during the early 1980s. Valladares, a member of the Inter-American Commission on Human Rights, was profoundly influenced by the jurisprudence of the Inter-American Commission and Court requiring investigation and sanction of those responsible for disappearances.[15] He justified his efforts on two grounds: First, investigation was necessary to "know the Truth and do Justice to achieve the needed reconciliation of all Hondurans," because it is impossible to forgive without knowing what happened or who was responsible. Second, investigation was necessary to restore public confidence in state institutions, especially the judiciary.

Valladares found 179 cases of disappearances, carried out by the armed forces. Because of a lack of resources, he did little firsthand investigation but relied heavily on newspaper accounts, existing court documents, and the work of national and international human rights groups and the U.N. Working Group on Forced Disappearances. His report, entitled "The Events Speak for Themselves," named several members of the Army high command and specific units like the Intelligence Battalion 3–16 as responsible for the practice of disappearances. The court system also came in for criticism for its inaction in the face of the disappearances.

The Commissioner examined in detail the role of the Nicaraguan "contras," their U.S. advisers, and that of Argentine military trainers in both engaging in and abetting disappearances. The report published the names of a number of Argentine "trainers," as well as detailed documents regarding U.S. participation in the anti-Sandinista war waged from southern Honduras. However, Valladares was careful to note that the *contras* and their backers enjoyed the protection of Honduran state officials, thus implicating the state's responsibility. Nonetheless, the report's recommendations extend to asking for more information from both the United States and Argentina on their role in the events described and identifying and extraditing those ex-members of the Nicaraguan *contra* alleged to have been involved in disappearances on Honduran soil.

The report's recommendations are far-reaching, and the Commission set a year as the term within which they should be carried out. The commissioner recommended that those apparently involved in the disappearances be tried by the appropriate courts; it provided a list of persons who occupied certain military posts during the years involved. Although Honduras, like other Central American countries, passed an amnesty benefiting the individuals involved in the region's 1980s conflicts, the Commission pointed out that any such amnesty had to be interpreted consistently with international law, which precludes amnesty for those involved in disappearances.

In addition, the report recommended investigations of all those judges and magistrates who denied habeas corpus petitions filed by family members of the disappeared; changes in the laws of administrative and penal detention; periodic visits of human rights groups to detention centers; creation of a special commission to find clandestine cemeteries; requesting the extradition for trial in Honduras of foreign military advisers or *contras* involved in disappearances; the separation of military and police functions; and civilian control over military intelligence. Finally, it recommended an official apology, compensation, and an official monument to the disappeared; the institution of human rights education; and adherence of Honduras to several human rights treaties.

The report was well received by official political sectors and even by some members of the armed forces, who were anxious to put a closed period of the past behind them; other armed forces representatives were predictably hostile. The report received wide circulation in the press. However, it remains to be seen how many of the report's recommendations will actually be implemented within the one-year period set for their completion. To date, the courts have yet to convict anyone for the violations detailed in Valladares's report. Valladares is now preparing a follow-up report.

Guatemala

Guatemala fits uneasily into a book examining transitions to democracy. Despite the advent of civilian rule in 1986, the military still plays a preponderant role in the country's political and economic life. Human rights violations continue, although not on the massive scale of the early 1980s, when over 200 Mayan Indian villages were obliterated, tens of thousands of people were killed, and thousands were victims of forced disappearance. Nonetheless, even in Guatemala the issue of investigation and prosecution of those responsible for these crimes has become central to the political debate. Three aspects merit particular attention: A few court cases have led to convictions of low-ranking military officers while confirming the judicial system's inability to confront high-ranking officers accused of human rights violations; national and international forensic anthropologists have begun systematically uncovering evidence of the massacres of the

1980s; and a sputtering and uneven process of negotiations between the government and insurgents has resulted in agreement to set up a "truth commission" and led to proposals for amnesty.

Perhaps the best-known example of both the possibilities and limits of Guatemala's judiciary is the Myrna Mack case. Anthropologist Myrna Mack, who had spent years studying displaced populations in Guatemala's highlands, was knifed to death by two men in 1990. The Human Rights Ombudsman's office classified the crime as a political offense. After considerable pressure from the Mack family and international academic and human rights groups, Noel de Jesus Beteta Alvarez, a former sergeant major specialist in the security section of the Presidential High Command (EMP), was indicted. In 1993, despite innumerable delays, Beteta was convicted and sentenced to twenty-five years in prison. The conviction gave some hope to Guatemalans that the justice system might eventually respond, if complainants were tenacious and determined enough.

As important as Beteta's conviction was the attempt to indict those who had given him orders. Beteta had maintained a two-week surveillance of the victim before killing her, yet was never sanctioned for neglect of duties during this period nor for abandoning his job after the murder.[16] Extensive threats and surveillance of witnesses and of Mack's co-workers, the unsolved murder of a principal investigator in the case, the fact that Beteta was an active-duty member of the EMP, and the politically sensitive nature of Mack's work all pointed to more extensive military involvement. However, the trial court refused to look into whether the former chief and subchief of the EMP were involved in either ordering or covering up the crime. After the Mack family, as private prosecutor,[17] brought numerous appeals, in February 1994 the Penal Chamber of the Supreme Court reopened the case against Beteta's higher-ups and accomplices. That decision is, as of this writing, on appeal to the Constitutional Court.

While the legal results in the Mack case are incomplete, the political effect has been contradictory. The case both demonstrated the weakness of the judicial system and inspired hope that it could eventually be used to prosecute at least a few cases. Together with other notorious cases involving the military,[18] it has kept the issue of impunity before the press and public.

The difficulty in prosecuting human rights cases was also part of the impetus for recent reforms to the criminal procedure code. The reforms allow greater use of oral testimony and make access to the courts easier for victims. It remains to be seen if the reforms can be effectively implemented and if they will make it easier to obtain convictions in cases involving military defendants.

Another aspect of Guatemala's as yet incipient efforts to deal with the past has been extensive exhumations of massacre victims. Combined national-international teams of forensic anthropologists, acting on tips from families of victims, have unearthed thousands of bodies from clandestine cemeteries throughout the highland region. The victims are identified where possible and given to the families for reburial. This nongovernment effort, despite threats from paramilitary groups, is providing catharsis for villagers. It is to be hoped that the results will be used to substantiate the extent and forms of military and paramilitary actions against the civilian population.

The problem of impunity has also been central to negotiations between the government and a twenty-year-old guerrilla movement, now known as the Guatemalan National Revolutionary Union (URNG). Peace talks have been going on for several years, with delays attributable mainly to the military's reluctance to grant concessions to an opponent now posing little military or political threat. Nonetheless, under intense international pressure to end Central America's only remaining war, in January 1994 the two sides signed a framework agreement designed to lead to the signing of a definitive peace accord by the end of 1994.

In March 1994 the government and URNG signed a Global Accord on Human Rights.[19] Point three of the accord, entitled "commitment against impunity," states:

3.1 The two sides coincide in that firm action is needed against impunity. The Government will not instigate the adoption of legislative or any other kind of measures aimed at impeding the trial and punishment of those responsible for human rights violations.

3.2 The Government of the Republic of Guatemala will promote before the Legislature the legal modifications in the Penal Code necessary to define and punish, as especially serious crimes, forced or involuntary disappearances as well as summary or extrajudicial executions; the Government will also promote within the international community the recognition of forced or involuntary disappearances and summary or extrajudicial executions as crimes against humanity.

3.3 No special courts or exclusive jurisdiction can provide a shield of impunity for human rights violations.[20]

In addition, the government agrees to strengthen the office of the human rights ombudsman; combat the existence of clandestine security forces and death squads; not create new civil defense forces "so long as there is no reason to do so"; and provide special protection for human rights activists and organizations and special help to the victims of human rights violations. While the government agrees to "continue the cleansing and professionalization of the security forces," no independent mechanism for weeding out notorious human rights violators from the military is apparently envisioned.

The accord is to be subject to international verification through a U.N. Observer Mission, which will have a one-year renewable mandate. The mission's functions are to include receiving complaints about violations, evaluating both the existence of violations and the effectiveness of national institutions in dealing with them, helping to transform national institutions to make them more effective, and verifying observance of the peace accords. It will be limited, however, to considering events subsequent to its installation and will not therefore be able to deal with past violations.

Past violations will be the province of the Commission for the Historical Clarification of the Human Rights Violations and Violent Acts That Have Caused Suffering to the Guatemalan People (Truth Commission). The outlines of the Truth Commission were agreed upon by government and URNG negotiators in Oslo in June 1994. Although hailed by many Guatemalans as an initial step toward accountability, the Truth Commission's outlines are in many respects quite problematic.

The agreement calls for the Commission to "clarify . . . the human rights violations and violent acts that have caused suffering to Guatemalans, related to the armed conflict." The phrase "related to the armed conflict" could be used either to limit consideration of violations to those committed during formal military operations or to create the impression that all the victims of human rights violations — including union, peasant, and student leaders; priests; and politicians — were killed or disappeared in relation to the armed conflict rather than because of their peaceful organizing efforts or opposition to government policies.

The Commission's mandate dates from the "beginning of the armed conflict," a formulation with the potential to overwhelm investigators because by at least some accounts the conflict is forty years old. It is to present a report on its findings, recommend measures "to preserve the memory of the victims, promote a culture of mutual respect and observance of human rights and strengthen the democratic process." The Commission will have up to one year to complete its work.

The Commission's mandate specifically excludes the possibility of using its results for subsequent prosecutions.[21] No individuals are to be named. Although presumably prosecutions could still be brought based on independent evidence, the obvious intent of the military at least is to preclude this possibility. Previous Latin American Truth Commissions, notably the Salvadoran and the Chilean, specifically allowed for the possibility of subsequent court action rather than attempting to foreclose it.

The Commission is to have three members: the U.N.'s moderator of the peace talks, Jean Arnault; a "citizen of irreproachable conduct" named by the moderator; and an academic proposed by the university presidents. Inclusion of the U.N. monitor, although no doubt important to inspire trust in both parties to the agreement, may make it more difficult for him to play a forceful role in enforcing the agreement. Both national figures must be approved by the two sides. Apparently, Guatemalans will also be able to staff the Commission: While this may provide needed expertise, it may also give rise to worries about security and infiltration, especially given a widespread perception that members of the Army's intelligence service have joined the ranks of national investigative bodies.

Despite the existence of a mechanism for "civil society" to propose reforms as part of the peace process, this mechanism was given no role within the context of the Truth Commission. And although both sides to the agreement commit themselves to collaborate with the Commission, neither makes any commitment to implementing its recommendations.

Although as of this writing the details remain to be worked out and a definitive cease-fire will take place in December 1994 at the earliest, the Guatemalan provisions on past violations appear significantly weaker than those negotiated in neighboring El Salvador or in other Latin American countries. In addition to the specific prohibition on naming individuals or turning over information to the courts, the truth-telling mechanism is not (at least to date) accompanied by any measure to force the government to restructure or cleanse the military. Moreover, efforts to demilitarize the police were abandoned early in 1994, and military officers now lead the police. In part, the shortcomings reflect the relative weakness of the Guatemalan insurgents compared to the Salvadoran FMLN, the insurgents' overriding need to reach a settlement to prove themselves a still-potent force in the country's political life, and intense international pressure to come to an agreement. The Guatemalan government has also no doubt learned from the political difficulties caused its counterpart by the report of the Salvadoran Truth Commission, which did "name names" as well as making far-reaching recommendations.

To further reassure the military and its backers, President de Leon Carpio and members of Congress have begun floating the idea that "something like amnesty"[22] will be required. Although the peace accords prohibit the "government" from introducing such measures, it is unclear whether the prohibition extends to the legislature. In July 1994, several amnesty bills were introduced in the Guatemalan Congress, covering "political crimes and related common crimes;" one bill exempts the killers of Myrna Mack and political leader Jorge Carpio.[23] Considerable opposition to amnesty exists,[24] and it will be up to a new Congress, elected in August 1994, to tackle the issue. In any case, those involved in the massacres and massive disappearances of the early 1980s are already protected by a self-amnesty granted during the military regime of Oscar Mejia Victores in 1986 and another issued by the civilian government of Vinicio Cerezo in 1988. Barring an effort to overturn the existing laws or to interpret them consistent with Guatemala's international obligations,[25] the actual impact of a new amnesty may be above all symbolic and political.

12

Punishing Human Rights Abuses in Fledgling Democracies: The Case of Argentina

Jaime Malamud-Goti

In the 1990s, Argentine society exhibits two odd and striking characteristics. The first is the extremely fragmented views of the citizenry concerning what happened during the 1974–83 period, in which state-sponsored human rights violations took place. As a consequence, the significance of the human rights trials set up during the subsequent Alfonsin administration is also controversial. The second peculiarity is a clear inconsistency between the fervent popular support of those trials (of human rights abuses) and present indicators that the populace is ready to elect authoritarian rulers and acquiesce again to police brutality. A new campaign of police abuse has met with little public reaction, and in the 1991 elections, candidates representing extremely authoritarian views had an astonishing appeal. Military officers running for provincial governorships and seats in the lower house captured a substantial portion of the electorate. This appeal was not diminished by the fact that these candidates had either represented the delinquent military dictatorship in the same jurisdictions where they were running in 1991 or had stood up against the elected government of President Raul Alfonsín to have the trials terminated.[1]

The most surprising event was the success of ex-Lieutenant-Colonel Aldo Rico, who ran for governor of the Buenos Aires province (Argentina's largest province) in the September 10, 1991 elections. Rico had been cashiered during the Alfonsín administration for leading military rebellions against his commanders in April 1987 and January 1988. Pardoned by President Saúl Menem in 1989, hardly anybody considered him or his newly founded party, MODIM, as having a chance of obtaining over 2 percent of the electorate in Buenos Aires. Identified with a staunchly undemocratic faction of the Army, Rico's party obtained three seats at the National Congress when almost 11 percent of the province's population voted for his ticket.[2] This is particularly astonishing considering that Rico headed revolts in an attempt to remove the Army's commanders for failing to stop the trials of officers accused of violating human rights. According to Rico, such failure jeopardized the dignity of the Army.[3] After the elections, most political observers conjectured that the success of Rico's party was a desperate move by the urban poor of Buenos Aires province. Recent polls have demonstrated, however, that the ex-officer's voters were mostly middle class.[4]

Another striking example involves General Domingo Bussi. In the northern province of Tucumán, where he earned a grim reputation for the assassination of prisoners as the delegate of the 1976–83 dictatorship, Bussi obtained 43 percent of the vote, but still lost to the Peronist Party candidate, pop singer Ramon ("Palito") Ortega, whom Menem backed personally. Bussi challenged the elections, claiming they had been rigged.[5] This opinion is shared by many observers who suspect the rigging occurred because of the federal government appointee who supervised the elections in Tucumán.

My own conclusion is that if genuine (institutional) authority is not asserted in Argentina, democracy cannot be expected to be more than formal, and strong leaders will maintain their appeal to large sectors of this fragmented society. The lack of initial clarity concerning the purposes and limits of the human rights trials, rapidly followed by immunity,[6] and the pardon decrees of 1989 and 1990 in particular, undermined the reliability of Congress and the judiciary. To understand the ultimate outcome of the policies of the transitional governments, a short review of the Alfonsin government's policy regarding the human rights violations of the prior military juntas is required.

Justifications for the Trials

Raúl Alfonsín was elected president of Argentina in 1983, replacing a series of military juntas that were responsible for grave human rights abuses during the 1970s, including assassinations, arbitrary detention, and the forced disappearance of at least 10,000 people. Alfonsín quickly instituted a series of measures aimed at investigating and prosecuting human rights violators and providing redress for victims. He created the National Commission on Disappeared Persons (CONADEP), headed by novelist Ernesto Sabato, and charged it with investigating the fate of those who had disappeared. Although it was unable to subpoena witnesses or compel testimony, the Commission produced a detailed and widely read report, *Nunca Más*.

Another central plank of the Alfonsín government's platform was the trial of persons considered responsible for the campaign of disappearances and assassinations. Trying the military required annulling, as void *ab initio*, a self-serving amnesty law that had been issued by executive decree shortly before the military left power. Once the judiciary annulled the amnesty law,[7] cases of human rights violations by the military were to be tried initially before the Supreme Council of the Armed Forces, with appeal to the civilian courts. The Law to Amend the Code of Military Justice, enacted on February 9, 1984, gave the military court 180 days to complete each trial, made appeal to civilian courts mandatory, and exculpated those who had acted under orders, unless they had exceeded those orders or had committed "atrocious and aberrant acts."[8] This initial due obedience clause did not prevent prosecutions, because whether defendants had committed the prohibited acts could be established only by trial on the merits. The idea was to allow the military to cleanse itself. This approach proved to be a mistake, however, as the military courts dithered after indicting some of the members of the first two juntas but refused later to pursue the cases further. Eventually the cases of human rights violations were removed to civilian courts, but valuable time, and a reservoir of political support, had been lost.

In deciding whom to prosecute, the government focused on the commanders of the three branches of the armed services, who had made up the members of the governing juntas. In December 1984, the federal court of appeals of Buenos Aires took over the conduct of the trials against the commanders. After a highly publicized five-month trial, the court sentenced General Jorge Videla and Admiral Emilio Massera to life imprisonment and three other junta members to terms of sixteen, eight, and four years and acquitted four others. The Supreme Court upheld the decision in December 1986. Several other high-ranking military officers were also tried.

As time went on, however, the bulk of the military became increasingly opposed to the trials, and protests from the military sectors were accompanied by bomb blasts throughout the country. Under pressure, the government had pushed through Congress a law — known as the *punto final*, or "full stop" — which limited new complaints brought for crimes committed during the dirty war to a sixty-day period; existing complaints would be considered moot unless the courts took action during that time. The result was a flurry of complaint filings by human rights groups and victims' families. The law was insufficient to quell military unrest, however, and in April 1987 a group of young Army officers, led by Lieutenant-Colonel Aldo Rico, took over a military compound after an officer accused of torture sought refuge there rather than face the questions of a civilian court. Although the government, backed by widespread popular support, put down the rebellion, months later it passed a "due obedience" law that had the effect of an amnesty for many potential defendants. This second law was aimed at appeasing the intermediate ranks who claimed that they were unjustly bearing the weight of the "dirty war." They claimed that they were being put to trial for their direct involvement in human rights violations, whereas their superior officers who had issued the orders — but had neither designed nor carried them out — remained untouched or were even promoted. This new initiative ensured that officers beneath the rank of colonel — and some above that rank who did not hold positions as chiefs of security areas or forces — would not be criminally prosecuted. It created an irrebuttable presumption that lower officers were following orders and thus were not liable. The Supreme Court promptly upheld the constitutionality of the law. Those officers excluded from the operation of the "due obedience" law, together with the convicted commanders, were pardoned by incoming President Saul Menem in decrees dated October 6, 1989 and December 29, 1990. Given the vagaries of the political context in which the commanders were tried and sentenced, the question as to the value of the trials is still a matter of speculation today.

There are several reasons for claiming that retributive sanctions will contribute to establishing democracy by reasserting the authority of institutions, largely the judiciary, thus awakening individuals' sense of their rights. Trying state criminals affirms the principle that nobody is beyond the reach of the law and that citizens have rights the exercise of which is essential to a working democracy. By this token transitional administrations have a moral obligation to try persons responsible for human rights violations[9]. As one who has argued this way, I have claimed that punishment plays an important role in reversing the citizens' adaptation to a dictatorial system in which fear drove them from pursuing their ideals and political activities, into apathy, isolation, and self-disdain. A rights-based community is unlikely to emerge from populations in which persecution and fear compelled individuals to give up their personal values and ideals. To limit the category of victims of repression to those who disappeared, the tortured, and the jailed ignores the social repercussions of state crime. Protracted repression not only caused pain and anguish to those who were related to or associated with the murdered and the disappeared but it also debased the large majority of the population.[10] Brutality brings about a culture of fear and insecurity that pervades the community at large. The notion that almost everybody qualifies for state abuses penetrated most aspects of social life.[11]

Fear demands adjustment. Afraid that by the most whimsical criteria they will become victims of repression, individuals break social ties and throw away any possibly "incriminating evidence," such as books, that could link them to the left.[12] In dictatorial regimes, the state systematically represses the pursuit of individual ideals and values it considers undesirable. As members of the community abandon walks of life that make existence meaningful to them, they surrender self-respect and self-esteem.[13] This feature of dictatorships represents one of the most burdensome legacies transitional governments must overcome and often leads to an inescapable paradox. The crueler the infringements, the more retributive justice is needed; yet the more retributive justice is needed, the less the courts will retain whatever authority they might have had. Prospects for impartial justice depend on a community's sense of moral responsibility, and this sense is determined by individuals' perception of their own worth and by authoritative institutions that ensure and promote that perception. Minimally, state repression blurs such perception.[14]

As an argument against prosecuting military officers, a sizable number of Argentine politicians claimed from 1983 on that allotting resources to avert future violations was the state's priority.[15] But the choice of not trying human rights violators and securing respect for individual rights in the future is nonexistent. The failure to exact punishment on state criminals will, in and of itself, frustrate attempts to lessen society's authoritarian tendencies. Citizens who bore — or feared to bear — state persecution are not likely to spontaneously develop self-respect once the dictatorship is over.[16] Incapable of self-respect, they will also deem other people's choices unworthy.

The oppressor kills our ideals, our self-respect, the perception of our rights. Compromising our goals makes us feel shame; deserting our principles and loyalties instills guilt in us. Our sense of worthlessness, of shame, and of guilt demands a "political remedy."[17] Only public admission by political institutions that we were wronged will legitimize us in our own eyes. Punishment of the violators of our rights is the clearest and strongest statement an authoritative institution may issue to that effect.[18] Citizens need to learn that they have rights—not only to be able to act on these rights but to respect other people's liberties as well. A rights-based community is unlikely to emerge spontaneously from populations in which individuals adapted to dictatorial violence by giving up their personal values and ideals. Two reasons to punish those responsible for these practices seem self-evident. First, trials of human rights abusers will expectedly generate awareness of recent history, and this recognition is a prerequisite for effecting change. Second, brutal repression not only causes anguish for those directly touched by the assassinations but it also deeply affects the large majority of the population. Public admission that a large sector of society was wronged will help legitimize government institutions in the eyes of the citizens; and punishment of human rights violators is the most authoritative and strongest statement to that effect.

But the policy of trying "state criminals" has visible weaknesses. First, experience has revealed the difficulties posed by selecting those persons to be brought to trial. An inevitable air of artificiality surrounds establishing the boundaries of responsibility. By pinning the blame on a limited sector of society, human rights trials reinvent history. The meaning of the resulting "truth" inevitably becomes controversial if not plainly factious. Dissatisfaction with the Argentine trials was conveyed not only by those who defended the convicted officers but also by human rights activists such as the Madres de Plaza de Mayo.[19] While the former claimed the culprits were scapegoats, the latter protested that too few of the accused were actually convicted and that their sentences were too light. For both parties, the trials were clearly political: Instead of bringing about justice, the judiciary was adjusting to the political convenience of the executive. Thus, the underlying authoritativeness of the institution that should tell us about our rights becomes itself open to discussion.

The most perplexing feature of this fragmentation of public opinion as a result of the lack of authoritativeness of the courts is that few people, including lawyers, ground their positions on the December 1985 decision[20] of the federal appellate court of Buenos Aires concerning the responsibility of the military juntas that ruled the country between 1976 and 1982. The verdict of the Supreme Court,[21] delivered one year later, is equally irrelevant to the citizenry's view of its recent political history. This verdict shows that despite the theoretical claim that a judicial determination will establish an authoritative truth, in Argentina judicial decisions lack authoritativeness both in establishing the facts brought to trial and in evaluating these facts. Thus, controversies about what should have been done about past human rights violations continue unabated, with no hope that any arbiter will bring them to an end.

The Argentine judiciary lacks authority for many reasons. One reason is a general distrust of the impartiality of the courts in trying politically related cases that arise during dictatorial periods. I believe there are three reasons specifically connected to the human rights trials: (1) the absence of a clear idea of how the human rights trials may have contributed to the democratization of the Argentine polity;

(2) the inevitable shortcomings of truncated and selective prosecutions; and (3) the lack of an adequate system of prosecutorial discretion.

A Victim-Centered Theory of Punishment

I have argued elsewhere that neither a deterrence-based nor a full-blooded retributivist rationale for punishment adequately applies in cases of state crimes.[22] I do not claim that the examined utilitarian and retributivist approaches do not contribute to the justification for punishing state criminals. Utilitarians are correct to expect criminal convictions to have dissuasive effects. But at their best these effects are, as I have explained, limited to a few officers at the top. Retributivists also provide a cogent argument for protecting individual rights: Persons who are not guilty of wrongful acts ought not be punished.[23] This negative aspect of retributivism is modest; it refers solely to restraints on the utilization of punishment. It does not offer a (positive) justification for criminal convictions. I have argued that punishment should contribute to the making of a rights-based democracy. I have also suggested that institutional regard for the victims of crime is crucial to the furtherance of that goal. In that respect, utilitarianism and full-blooded retributivism, as "perpetrator-centered" theories, are intrinsically inappropriate. I propose a "victim-centered" theory of punishment as an independent ground for justifying the conviction of state criminals.

Redress for victims is nonessential to a utilitarian justification. By giving key significance to the deterrence of potential offenders, utilitarians will have no qualms about overlooking the plight of persons who have suffered degradation as a consequence of having their basic rights infringed upon or threatened. The notion of justice for the victims would be excluded from the utilitarian calculus when discretion is exercised. Full-blooded retributivists invite a similar criticism. By disregarding all consequences of punishment, proponents of this version of retributivism focus only on wrongdoers' facing the consequences of their deeds.

But there is another variant of retributivism — a goal-oriented variant. According to this version, punishment ought to be directed at redressing the valued sentiments of those who were wronged. I am not referring to vindictive sentiments but rather to the victims' loss of a sense of purpose and of their own worth. As I have explained, the persons who endured unwarranted actual — or potential — chastisement from the oppressor experience feelings of shame and a lack of self-respect for renouncing the personal ideals that made their lives meaningful. Goal-oriented retributivists will attach to punishment the function of restoring this lost trust.

There is a salient pragmatic difference between full-blooded and goal-oriented retributivists. Whereas the former are compelled to impose punishment given the presence of a set of conditions that render an act criminal, such generality does not apply to goal-oriented retributivists. In seeking redress for the victims, the latter may consistently choose to forgo punishment or else content themselves with merely condemning the offender — or solely the offender's deed. If goal-oriented retributivists believe that imposing pain upon the perpetrator will do nothing substantial to improve the victim's sense of self-respect and confidence, punishment will lack warrant. So if the victims of certain forms of state crimes have already regained self-respect and are confident that they will be protected against future violations because the heads of the criminal organization have been convicted, goal-oriented retributivists may refrain from punishing other members of the group. There is room for considerable discretion. This discretion would legitimately allow a transitional government, for example, to limit prosecutions to certain heinous offenses, to the most notorious perpetrators, or to those individuals most closely associated with the design and implementation of a policy of terror. Thus, moral justification exists for the "full stop" law proposed by President Alfonsín.

Nonetheless, I believe that the 1985 trials did not adequately employ the approach to punishment espoused here. On the one hand, some officers, such as the members of the last junta, were known to have had no direct responsibility over the scattered abuses perpetrated shortly before the government was handed over to elected authorities. On the other hand, generals—whom overwhelming evidence singled out as the protagonists of the worst acts of repression—were also tried for forgery and usurpation of property.[24] These offenses have no connection with gross human rights abuses and are not comparable in either nature or moral gravity, thus blurring the lessons of the trials. At the same time, the mid- and upper-level officers who were most deeply involved in planning and executing the crimes at a regional and local level were exempted. Although admittedly prosecuting all 2,000 or so officers and their civilian aides and instigators involved in one way or another was impossible, if the Alfonsín government had, for example, initially prosecuted a larger group of some sixty to one hundred officers, the lesson would have been clearer. As it was, the initial choice of a few officers, and the subsequent restrictions and later forgoing of their punishment, had the opposite effect on many victims. The trials also blurred the citizenry's perception of recent history.

Blaming as Social Practice

Both official and popular versions of recent Argentine history suggest that state-sponsored human rights violations were the result of the military regime's strategy following its 1976 takeover. However, situating the massive abuses between March 1976 and December 1983, when the military was formally in power, is a misguiding version of that history. State violence actually began in the early 1970s. Felt to be a necessary response to the activities of insurgent groups that had emerged in the late 1960s, a large portion of the middle class supported a wave of assassinations and abductions perpetrated by paramilitary gangs directly associated with the elected Peronist government in office. Perón's minister of social welfare, José Lopez Rega, ran the most prominent of these groups, the Triple A,[25] aided by factions in the police, the Army, and right-wing civilians. Between 1974 and the end of 1975 hardly a day passed without reports of disappearances and assassinations.

Immediately after the military takeover of March 1976, assassinations by the

Army and the security forces increased, and a wave of abductions — many performed in broad daylight — rocked the country. Labeled as subversives, the targets of state-sponsored terrorism were varied: workers, students, writers, lawyers, and even priests and nuns.

The military was not alone in staging the "antisubversive" campaign. A rightwing sector of the citizenry actively contributed to brutal repression as paramilitary squads and vigilante groups.[26] Conspicuous members of the Catholic Church praised the assassination of students and workers by underscoring the spiritual value of the crusade and the "patriotic merit of eliminating the 'unrecuperable elements' of society."[27] Beyond these organized groups, the middle class actively or passively supported state brutality. A vast sector of the population justified the official strategy by either denying what was happening or pinning the blame for torture and assassinations on the victims themselves. Whenever someone disappeared one was often confronted with the phrase, "There is something she must have done" or, "She must have been up to something," placing the blame on the victim and not on the perpetrator. This social environment is vividly described in the Prologue to *Nunca Más*, the official report of the Commission on the Disappearance of People, headed by writer Ernesto Sábato:

> The idea of insecurity became increasingly entrenched in society: the dark fear that anybody, no matter how innocent, could fall victim to that infinite witch hunt. Some were absorbed by overwhelming fear, while others were controlled by the conscious or unconscious proclivity to justify horror: "There is something she must have done" was the whisper, as wanting to favor inscrutable gods, looking at the children or parents of the disappeared as if they were pest ridden. These sentiments were vacillating, because it was known that so many had been swallowed up by that abyss without bottom without being guilty of anything; because the struggle against the "subversive," with the drift that characterizes the hunting of witches and the possessed, had turned into a demential generalized repression. Because the epithet "subversive" had such a vast and unpredictable reach.[28]

The initiation of-state sponsored terrorism by right-wing activists — most of them civilians — before the 1976 military takeover, active participation of civilians in the campaign of terror during the military dictatorship, and mass support of the citizenry of the dictatorship's campaign of terror demonstrate that responsibility was shared by many sectors of society. The persistent appeal of violence indicates that the 1983 collective demand that the "military assassins" (*milicos asesinos*) be punished was based on a (conscious or unconscious) biased representation of past events. The moral and legal responsibility for Argentina's tragic past appears to be oversimplified by narrowly ascribing political terror to the military and by limiting it to the abuses perpetrated by military officers during the 1976–83 dictatorship. This rationalized reinterpretation explains why one of the judges responsible for convicting military officers for human rights abuses confessed to me in private: "I often feel we have treated the military like scapegoats. It is now clear to me we have done nothing about the civilians who marched with the military and later turned their backs upon them."[29]

By establishing fault we are able to "understand" an array of social processes.

In many cases "fault" is not the result of our causal findings but rather an identifiable, "external," "aberrant" element that makes social events intelligible.[30] In this latter sense, in the seventies a large sector of Argentine society "understood" massive disappearances and torture by placing blame on the victims and their conjectured behavior: "She must have been up to something." In the eighties this "understanding" changed radically as blame for these abuses shifted to the military as a group clearly disconnected from the rest of society: *"milicos asesinos."* Yet narrowly connected to our political interests, the social practice of blaming is a selective process by which we attempt to control the behavior of the people we blame. Intimately related to the balance of power, blaming is essentially the practice one sector of society uses to change some other sector's future conduct.[31] Earlier in Argentina it was left-wing students, progressive trade union leaders, and workers. Later it was the military.

In part, narrowing the focus of blame was the result of partisan political interests rather than the more "sincere" outcome of an open debate that would reflect the far more complex and wider allocation of responsibility. The issue of blame was tied to a host of political restrictions in 1983, the most important being avoiding direct confrontation with the largest opposition group — the Peronist Party, which ruled between 1973 and 1976. The fledgling democracy had too much to lose by clashing with the Peronists, who were temporarily allied in order to press for general elections. Thus, blaming deepened political conflict and further fragmented the social perception of reality.

In part, too, the very mechanism of trials divides the world into *guilty* and *innocent,* with those not declared guilty judged to be innocent of the terror campaign regardless of their direct or indirect involvement in the campaign or in the creation of the political environment that led to it. On the one hand, this process led necessarily to the view that only a limited number of citizens were responsible for the extreme violence the country had experienced; on the other hand, the process led to a perceived scapegoating as members of a sector were accused by, among others, those who also should have shared the brunt of a widely supported strategy. It thus perpetuated the "us versus them" war mentality that makes one's political adversaries the proper subjects of repressive measures.

The Role of the Judiciary

Like the criminal justice systems of most Latin American countries, Argentina's adopted the so-called principle of legality. According to this principle, neither the prosecutors nor the courts are entitled to dismiss cases that are legally defined as criminal. Cogent with the full-blooded retributivist tradition, actions defined as crimes create the duty to prosecute and convict. This feature of the country's law poses a serious obstacle to the credibility of judges when they are trying state-sponsored human rights violations. In such situations, the perpetrators who must stand trial — usually a large number of people — and the corporatist powers behind them, impose overwhelming pressure upon the judiciary. In Argentina, while the military and their supporters pressed for acquittals, vast sectors of the population demanded convictions. Under such circumstances, putting the judiciary in the spotlight turned the judiciary itself into the centerpiece of one of Argentina's most critical political struggles. The military pompously called this struggle the judicial battle.

Judges during the transitional period in the establishment of a democracy play the key role of instilling among the citizenry a sense of self-respect — and the respect of other people — by making rights an essential part of the political arrangement. This idea, I think, is a sufficient reason to refrain from passing amnesty laws. Placing the judges at the center of the transitional process by having them bear the weight of such significant political conflict, however, threatens to jeopardize the impartiality of the judiciary, given the intensity of the debate that takes place outside the courtroom. During my tenure in office, a day did not pass when I did not receive numerous telephone calls or visits from people who had strong views on these issues. Indeed, these individuals often expressed concern — if not alarm — about the upheaval the human rights trials were causing within the armed forces, the negative impact that trying certain officers would have on their comrades, or the "senselessness" of confronting the most powerful sector of society.

Army officers and numerous politicians were apprehensive. Presidential military aides did not miss a single occasion to convey their alarm. High officials and an array of sympathizers with the military regime, and even personal friends among the civilians, shared concern about what the trials could lead to. Directly or indirectly, thousands of officers were implicated in human rights abuses. The reasons for urging restraint in the scope of the trials or for giving up the trials altogether ranged from practical grounds to ideological allegiances.

For the judges, the pressure placed on the judiciary by the trials of human rights violators rapidly became unbearable. As a consequence of the permanent pressure exerted by different sectors of society with direct interest in the outcome of the trials, the members of the Buenos Aires federal court gradually abandoned their life-tenured positions. By the end of 1987, that court had been replaced entirely by newly appointed judges. For many observers, the resignations of these judges severely undermined the credibility of the human rights trials. The military and their sympathizers viewed their move as an admission that the trials were politically biased[32] and that once their mission of convicting a few generals was accomplished, some members of the tribunal would seek to aggrandize themselves by obtaining important government positions in the Alfonsín regime, whereas others successfully went into private practice. Although I do not believe there are serious grounds for defending such a thesis, the fact that one of the judges was appointed secretary of the interior and another attorney general by President Alfonsín himself makes it difficult to argue convincingly for the impartiality of the court.[33]

Human rights organizations also believed that the court's decision had been tainted by an allegiance to the administration in power. They claimed that the sentences imposed upon some commanders were unjustifiably light and that the acquittal of other officers was a sign that the court had set out to help President Alfonsín in his undeclared effort to favor the armed forces by creating a facade of an impartial trial. History has confirmed, however, that it was impossible for the judges to have borne the burden of trying the sizable number of accused officers.

It is arguable that the pressure could have been ameliorated had the judges been conferred the power to select the cases to be tried. Such an approach, however, would not have been a solution because the pressure to impose sentences one way or another would have simply shifted to the point of deciding who would be tried; and suspicions would have been equally drawn from both quarters. The military would have still accused the court of turning those indicted into scapegoats. Human rights activists would have raised the objection that the exercise of discretion was but a masquerade of justice. The authoritativeness of the justice system depends to a great degree, then, on prosecutorial discretion.

Nor can an adequate selection of cases be made by individual prosecutors: The issue is too critical to be left to the temptations of quick political solutions adopted on the basis of expediency by the administration in power. Although practical reasons such as political necessity and limited resources make it crucial that the government have a say, it seems indispensable to merge short-term political views with farsighted policy making. Both Professor Julio Maier[34] and Judge Andres D'Alessio[35] suggested to me that a criminal policy department should be created in Argentina. The attorney general (or the solicitor general), as a member of the judiciary, and the ombudsman, or special prosecutor,[36] would integrate this office together with that of the minister of justice. Whereas the latter would embody the government's immediate priorities, the former would represent society's long-term interests. Maier suggested that a board headed by the three officials could serve the purpose of exercising discretion.

The possibility of prosecutorial discretion, exercised in light of the victim-centered justifications I referred to earlier, would go some way toward imbuing judicial decisions with the authority they require if they are to serve a democratizing effect. Disregard for the victims as a reason to punish state criminals has been an important factor in the failure to transform an authoritarian society into a rights-based community. But the dismal path the case for individual rights has taken in Argentina in the 1990s is also a consequence of not taking the judiciary seriously.[37] Blatantly neutralizing convictions for human rights violations, Menem's pardons of officers undercut the nascent authority of the judiciary. Until such authority is restored, a rights-based society will never flourish in Argentina.

13

Chile: Truth and Justice under the Democratic Government

Jorge Mera

Chile returned to democratic government in March 1990 when President Patricio Aylwin was elected after seventeen years of military rule. The process of transition was designed by the military, which allowed elections in exchange for agreement by the political parties to respect the constitutional structure put in place by the military. Despite the election of a civilian president, the ex-head of government, General Augusto Pinochet, remained head of the Army, and the military structure remained intact. These were the circumstances in which the new president was faced with the problem of human rights violations—summary executions, forced disappearances, widespread torture, and clandestine detention—committed during the military regime. The coherence of the Aylwin government's policy in dealing with this problem is the subject of this chapter.

Despite a lack of explicitly articulated goals, the government's actions correspond to a definite political rationale, which can be summed up in the presidential formula of "truth, and justice to the extent possible." We will return to the question of feasibility—that is, what really was possible—later; for now, let us note that the political rationale revolves around two approaches that are not only incompatible but, in the end, contradictory. On the one hand, there is the government's overriding concern not to provoke a confrontation with the armed forces over the latter's institutional responsibility for human rights violations. One of the main political-institutional goals of the transition was the normalization of civilian-military relations, which had been seriously strained under the previous regime. The Aylwin government apparently assumed that a more aggressive attitude with respect to past human rights violations would provoke clashes or friction with the armed forces that might jeopardize the success of the transition itself.

On the other hand, there is (within limits) the government's sincere desire to seek out the truth, apply justice, and provide reparations to the victims of the violations. The government attempted to adopt policies in this area that would be favorably received by public opinion, both so it would be perceived as keeping the promises it made during the presidential campaign and to be consistent with the historically severe criticism of human rights violations that those now in power had leveled against the military.

The government has had to strike a balance between these two policy imperatives and has ended up choosing the first over the second. The government's failure to carry out its own campaign platform and the design and functioning of its main initiative, the Commission on Truth and Reconciliation, (the Commission), must be understood within the context of this overriding goal. This is not to minimize the positive and important contributions of the government's main initiatives — the Commission and the Corporation for Reparation and Reconciliation. These have been favorably received by most Chileans and have allowed significant progress to be made in resolving the human rights problems still outstanding. However, that progress should not obscure the limits of the government's chosen policy nor impede an open discussion of the whole issue. I believe the government has been unduly cautious and could have done much more — or at least made the effort to — without jeopardizing the transition to democracy.

Seeking Out the Truth: The Commission on Truth and Reconciliation

The most important initiative of the incoming government was the creation of the Commission on Truth and Reconciliation.[1] The Commission's mandate was, inter alia, to "contribute to the overall clarification of the truth about the worst violations carried out in recent years," establishing "the most complete picture possible of these grave acts, their background and circumstances," and "bringing together evidence to identify individual victims and establish their fate or whereabouts." The mandate to identify individual victims was restricted to cases of death or disappearance because these were the most serious violations and the ones consistently denied by the military. Expanding the mandate to encompass torture was felt to have been too unwieldy an enterprise to be completed within the allotted time. The Commission was also to propose measures for reparation and prevention.

The Commission, chaired by a well-known jurist, was composed of eight people, including several conservative scholars and jurists as well as people with a record of advocacy on human rights. The even number of Commission members was intended to send a signal that the matter was to be decided without partisan majorities and minorities. The Commission worked for nine months with a staff of sixty, interviewing thousands of witnesses throughout the country and at embassies abroad. Commission members made extensive use of the documents and files of domestic and international human rights groups.

The Commission presented its final, unanimous report in February 1991. President Aylwin accepted the report and a month later (on national television) announced its main findings; he also offered a formal apology on behalf of the government for the acts of its agents. The report's main contribution was individualized information on a large number of victims. The report declared 2,025 cases to involve fatal victims of human rights violations committed by state agents; 90 to involve fatal victims of violent opposition groups; and 164 to be cases involving political violence that could not be attributed to any side. In another 614 cases the Commission could not come to any conclusions due to lack of evidence. In contrast, the Commission could not establish the fate or whereabouts of most victims, although it assumed those who had disappeared had been killed.[2]

The report also included a number of recommendations regarding reparations to the victims of past violations, including both moral and material compensation. These recommendations were taken up by the legislature, and on February 8, 1992 a law was passed creating the National Corporation for Reparation and Reconciliation.[3] The law provides for a monthly pension of ¢140.000 (U.S. $350) for the families of those named in the Commission's report and those subsequently recognized as victims by the Corporation for Reparation and Reconciliation, up to a deadline of July 15, 1993. According to the head of the Corporation, yearly outlays for annuities should come to $22 million (U.S.).[4] The law also provides for medical benefits, including psychological counseling for the families. The health benefits offered extend beyond the families of those killed and those who disappeared to cover families in which a member was detained and tortured as well as returning exiles. Finally, the law provides a subsidy for high school and college education and waives tuition at public institutions of higher education for the children of the victims. The associations of family members of victims have accepted these benefits, considering them a positive step, although an insufficient one.

Finally, the report established some of the significant circumstances that surrounded the violations and made them possible. Nonetheless, the objective of global clarification through a comprehensive picture of the violations, their antecedents and circumstances, was not fully met and has actually been undermined by the chosen treatment of the armed forces and their institutional responsibility for state terrorism. A detailed critique of these aspects of the report follows.

The Concept of Human Rights and Their Violation

Both the decree creating the Commission and the work of the Commission itself suffer from a mistaken view of the very concept of human rights violations. This is not simply an academic concern, but has important implications for social education and the creation of a collective culture of human rights, as well as for public perception of the specific nature and seriousness of the violations at issue.

According to the terms of paragraph 2, article 1, of the decree creating the Commission, for purposes of its work

> serious violations are here to be understood as situations of those persons who disappeared after arrest, who were executed, or who were tortured to death, in which the moral responsibility of the state is compromised as a result of actions by its agents or persons in its service, as well as kidnappings and attempts on the life of persons committed by private citizens for political purposes.[5]

The decree thus diverges from the universally accepted political-legal concept of a human rights violation, which refers exclusively to acts committed by the state or its agents. The formula used was intended to include within the Commission's mandate those kidnappings and killings carried out by armed groups opposed to the Pinochet dictatorship against members of the armed forces and security forces and to cover the most serious acts of political violence no matter what their origin.

To equate genuine human rights violations with criminal acts committed by dissident armed groups represents a concession to the armed forces that not only blurs the importance of the former but distorts their specific nature. The net effect is to pervert the very concept of human rights. To prevent future violations — the goal recognized by the Commission — Chile needs to develop a national education in, and culture of, human rights. To do so, the concepts must be clear.

The Commission's report recognizes the problem, maintaining that the question of whether human rights violations can be commmitted by private persons or only by the state "has been the object of a good deal of controversy."

> One reason that it is so controversial is that the term "human rights violation" has taken on a symbolic power far beyond its technical meaning both in our country and in the concert of nations. Hence, while some take one side or other of the issue without any ulterior motive, others do so for political reasons.[6]

The Commission recognizes that what it calls the "traditional position" restricts the possibility of human rights violations to those committed by the state or its agents. The truth is that the concept of human rights violations has always been limited to the actions of the state. Human rights arise historically as demands to limit state power and are now a limit on state sovereignty. Legally, they are obligations assumed by the state both internationally and domestically; the need for international protection of human rights stems from the lack of protection of such rights from the state. With regard to crimes committed by private individuals, the victims have access to the criminal justice system to restore their rights. If that system does not act, a violation of human rights arises from the state's failure to develop an effective criminal justice system or the state's tolerance or condonation of the crimes of private actors, thus guaranteeing their impunity.

While acknowledging the strength of this position, the Commission insists that it is now starting to change. The opposite position, it asserts, is also supported by valid theoretical arguments (which the report omits). "Furthermore," the report continues,

> in practice it has been observed that when the expression "human rights violations" is limited to government actions, public opinion very often tends to interpret it as an effort to condone or justify abuses or atrocities that may be committed by certain opposition political groups. There is no doubt that public opinion overwhelmingly condemns resorting to abuses or atrocities whether in order to retain or seek power or to resolve political conflicts. The idea that there are certain values of humane behavior that not only the state but all political actors must respect has become enshrined in the public conscience. Those norms of humane behavior derive partly from the norms of human rights and partly from the norms

of international humanitarian law or the laws of war. In peacetime, they govern all political actors, governmental or non-governmental; and in the case of armed conflict, whatever its nature, they are obligatory for all combatant forces. Public opinion has a deep intuition of these norms of humane behavior, which it has taken to be synonymous with the expression "human rights." Thus in practice people have been moving beyond the more restricted historic or technical meaning of this term.

The Commission believes that these reasons explain why its founding decree regards as human rights violations not only certain acts committed by agents of the government, but also other politically motivated acts of private citizens.[7]

The difficulties the Commission confronted were clear in its last paragraph on the issue:

> The Commission is certainly bound to follow the terminology set down in the decree. However, it wants to make clear that in carrying out its assigned task, it also accepts the need to acknowledge this broader interpretation of the term "human rights" that has gradually become prevalent in public opinion. This does not mean that such broader interpretation is to be regarded as universally valid, nor does it entail a disregard for the power of the arguments that originally led to a more restricted use of the term. Indeed, the Commission believes that it should always be emphasized that acts of terrorism or other illegitimate actions committed for political reasons cannot be used to seek to justify human rights violations committed by the state and that the state's use of its monopoly over public force to violate the rights of persons is a matter of the gravest concern.[8]

In my view, the real reasons for the language of the decree are to be found in political considerations. They are tied to the central objective of avoiding frictions with the armed forces, which could, in the government's view, jeopardize the success of the transition.

The problem is that by privileging these political considerations, the impression is left that rather than state terrorism, what happened in Chile was merely a skirmish between rival criminal gangs. This is not to undervalue the need for the truth, not just with regard to human rights violations but also with regard to the most serious crimes committed against members of the armed forces and security forces. However, this latter goal (more easily achieved given that the majority of those involved were arrested and punished by military courts) could have been achieved some other way—for example, through the creation of a separate commission for this purpose. It is the mixture of the two situations that produces confusion and detracts from the educational objectives of the Commission.[9]

It is true that there have been some doctrinal proposals and efforts by some governments to broaden the concept of human rights to encompass certain private entities or organizations that possess enough power to affect people's rights on a massive and grave level, in situations in which the state is actually incapable of effectively safeguarding rights. In these situations—for example, concerning multinational corporations or certain terrorist organizations—international protection and control of the violations are justified because these private organizations seriously jeopardize the state's ability to carry out its essential functions of ensuring and protecting human rights. The government of Peru, for example, has turned to the Inter-American system of human rights to ask that the acts of the Shining Path guerrilla group be considered human rights violations, which would allow for the intercession of the system.

The Chilean situation under the military government was entirely different. The groups that attacked the military and the police never had any real military strength — certainly not enough to create a situation in which the rules of international humanitarian law applied. Their members were, for the most part, tried and sentenced (except for those whose right to life was violated, as the Commission points out). The state was never in danger, nor did the actions of these groups create a generalized sense of insecurity in the population because their acts were generally narrowly aimed at the armed forces and security forces. In short, there is no justification for departing from the universally held definition of human rights violations. If the problem is that a majority of the population does not understand this definition, the answer should have been to educate the people, not perpetuate the error.

Defining the Responsibility of the Armed Forces

One of the most delicate and controversial aspects of the report is its treatment of the degree and type of responsibility of the armed forces as an institution, and of individual members of the institution, in the human rights violations that took place. The Commission's treatment of the role of the armed forces as essentially similar to that of other institutions of political life — say, that of the political parties — for not knowing how to avoid the breakdown of the democratic regime is profoundly and dangerously mistaken.

> Indeed it is correct to say that the responsibilities of a criminal character and other legal responsibilities that may derive from human rights violations are personal in nature and do not affect the institution to which the perpetrator belongs. It is also true that the fundamental role played by the armed forces and security forces in the history of the country should be fully appreciated, as should be their character as permanent and essential national institutions. Finally, it is praiseworthy to strive to avoid any use of the issue of human rights to attempt to sully these institutions, or to detract from their contribution to the country and the role they are called to play in the future.
>
> Nevertheless, these points cannot be invoked to deny the historic or moral responsibility that may befall one institution or another as a result of the practices it ordered, or to which it consented, or with regard to which it failed to do all that was required to impede or prevent their recurrence. Just as we have spoken of the moral responsibility of the state, which would be inconceivable if the actions of its officials could never affect it, we can also speak properly of the moral or historical responsibility of political parties, of other institutions or sectors of national life, and of society as a whole. The armed forces and the security forces are no exception. It is human beings who forge and make institutions great, and it is also human beings who can affect them negatively. . . .[10]

Although this downplaying of the specific nature of the role of the armed forces is no doubt aimed at making the Commission's findings and recommendations more palatable to the military, it represents a serious impediment to establishing the truth, which is, after all, the main objective of the report. The responsibility of the armed forces cannot be compared to that of other institutions of national life: It constituted the decisive factor that explains the massive and systematic character of the violations and the impunity enjoyed (then and now) by their authors. Military structures and procedures made possible the extended and prolonged practice of state terrorism. During the initial period of military government, repression was carried out directly by the armed forces throughout the country. Repression was later institutionalized and professionalized through the Directorate of National Intelligence (DINA) and its successor agency, the National Intelligence Central (CNI). Both were military institutions composed of members from all branches of the defense establishment.

By avoiding and downplaying the institutional responsibility of the armed forces, the report fails to live up to its mandate to "contribute to the overall clarification of the truth," establishing the "most complete picture possible" of the events, their causes, and their circumstances. The report cannot help but present a partial and limited vision of the truth. Although in some places one can glimpse a more than moral/historical view of the armed forces' responsibility, it remains without elaboration. It is not just a question of responsibility (which might also be attributed to the political parties or other institutions) but of direct, institutional participation, which explains both the possibility of massive violations, their carefully planned nature, and the institutional cover-up of criminal acts that form their most direct and immediate conditions. These institutional aspects in no way detract from the existence of individual criminal responsibility for those members of the armed forces who committed such criminal acts, either as material or intellectual authors, instigators, accomplices, or as part of the cover-up.

Naming Names?

The report fails to make public the names of the persons who appear to have been responsible for the violations. This decision, reportedly unanimous, was made on the grounds that to reveal the names would have been tantamount in practice (and would have been seen by public opinion) to bringing criminal charges, an act beyond the Commission's competence. The precedent of the Sábato Commission in Argentina was invoked, even though that commission's report indicates that it communicated the names of the alleged perpetrators to the government confidentially (and even though the names were quickly leaked to the Argentine press).

The Commission has a point. Like it or not, by making public the names it would have been seen to be attributing criminal responsibility to individuals without the ability, due to the Commission's terms of reference, for those named to defend themselves. To do so would have constituted a violation of due process. The problem is rather that the Commission chose not to comply with its mandate to place *all* information regarding possible crimes, including the names of the authors, before the competent courts. Instead, it selected among the available information, sending to the courts only that information which was "new, useful and relevant to judicial investigations." This selection was up to the courts, not the Commission, to make. Moreover, a court hearing a case is in a position to judge the relevance of a piece of information that might seem unimportant to an outside observer. The Commission exceeded its jurisdiction by making a preliminary selection of the information to be passed on to the courts. The net result is that much of that information, including names of alleged perpetrators, was not made available to the courts assigned to proceed with criminal investigations.

The failure of the Commission to make public all the information it had available is only one of a number of ways in which the current government has made it more difficult to identify the persons responsible for past violations. Domestically, the Human Rights Commission of the Chamber of Deputies and the Senate can investigate acts occurring only after the current regime came to power. Internationally, the government accepted the jurisdiction of both the Inter-American Court of Human Rights and the U.N. Human Rights Committee, but with the reservation that its acceptance is valid only for events initiated after March 1990. Thus, while averring that it would do everything within its power to facilitate identification of the perpetrators, the government in practice has done much less.

Problems of Methodology

The Commission was empowered to receive information directly from possible victims, their representatives, and successors or family members as well as to collect and evaluate information from national and international organizations. According to the Group of Family Members of the Disappeared, the Commission used both sources effectively. However, according to the Group of Family Members, the Commission underutilized its ability to carry out its own investigations. It had broad investigative powers:

> Within the scope of their competency, government authorities and agencies are to offer the Commission all the collaboration it may request, furnish the documents it may need, and provide access to such places as it may determine necessary to visit.[11]

Despite this apparently broad language, the Commission was able to do little independent investigation into the names of perpetrators or the institutional participation of the armed forces. In large part this was due to a lack of collaboration by the armed forces. The Commission chose to negotiate quietly with the armed forces to improve its cooperation rather than to apply public pressure. According to the Group of Family Members, this approach was a mistake, and it explains why so little information was obtained on the fate of the victims or the names of those who were responsible for their deaths.

The Need for Justice

In cases of human rights violations it is not enough to know the truth of what happened. Justice must also be done, and the guilty punished. Criminal sanctions for grave human rights violations are required by both domestic and international law and are an unavoidable responsibility of the state. Disclosure of the truth is part of ensuring that justice will be done, but it does not replace justice. Although the two are interrelated, they are separate categories.

This point was understood by the incoming government from the start. The military regime's policy of impunity stands as an obstacle to justice. The policy ranged from denying that violations existed, through an institutional cover-up, to the enactment in April 1978 of legislative decree 2,191, which granted amnesty for crimes including all murders, mayhem, batteries, unlawful detention, kidnappings, disappearances, and torture, committed by agents of the state during the period of martial law imposed after the coup, which lasted from September 1973 until March 1978.[12]

The Aylwin government's platform referred to the need to rescind or annul the military's self-amnesty and thus recognized the imperative of criminal prosecutions. The presidential decree that created the Commission stresses that justice is an additional and separate requirement, affirming that "only upon a foundation of truth will it be possible to meet the basic demands of justice and create the necessary conditions for achieving true national reconciliation." Moreover, article 1 of the decree points out that truth finding should be understood "without affecting any legal proceedings to which those events may give rise," and article 2 adds that "If while it is carrying out its functions the Commission receives evidence about actions that appear to be criminal, it will immediately submit it to the appropriate court."

The Commission's report, in its section on preventative measures, refers to the need for justice as follows:

> From the standpoint of prevention alone, this Commission believes that for the sake of national reconciliation and preventing the recurrence of such events it is absolutely necessary that the government fully exercise its power to mete out punishment. Full protection for human rights is conceivable only within a state that is truly subject to the rule of law. The rule of law means that all citizens are subject to the law and to the courts, and hence that the sanctions contemplated in criminal law, which should be applied to all alike, should thereby be applied to those who transgress the laws safeguarding human rights.[13]

In presenting the Commission's report, President Aylwin referred to the need for justice, which he described as "the greatest of social virtues, the irreplaceable basis for peace." He noted that the disclosure and acceptance of the truth is an important part of rendering justice to the victims, as are the moral vindication of the dignity of the victims and reparations to their families proposed in the report. But, he continued, these are not enough. Justice also requires revealing the whereabouts of the persons who have disappeared and assigning personal responsibility for the crimes. Although he noted that the Commission was unable to find the remains of most victims, he asserted that the question of assigning responsibility is, in a law-based state, a matter for the courts under existing law and according to the dictates of due process. He noted that the Commission could not go into that area because it had no power to do so under its founding decree, which followed clear institutional rules. In both cases, the Commission had forwarded the relevant data to the competent court. The president concluded by saying he hoped that the courts would do their duty and investigate. The amnesty law now in force, he averred, could not impede those investigations.

Thus, the president's policy was to allow the ordinary courts to go forward in investigating complaints of deaths and disappearances, even though the courts would quickly run up against the obstacle of the self-amnesty if they proceeded beyond the investigatory stage.

Some people, including members of the governing coalition, have tried to minimize the importance of the amnesty as a meaningful obstacle to justice. They have argued that the amnesty (1) does not cover acts that occurred after March 10, 1978; (2) does not include cases of persons who disappeared after being arrested; (3) does not prevent the investigation of what happened but only bars punishment for the acts committed; and (4) does not cover certain acts because in theory the judges could interpret the law to exclude the most serious violations (which would not be subject to amnesty).

Scope of the Amnesty

The amnesty by its terms applies only to human rights violations that took place during the initial period of military rule when the country was under a state of siege. According to some people, the amnesty is therefore justified because during the years of military rule an atmosphere close to that of civil war existed, so that the violations might legitimately be described euphemistically as the more or less inevitable "excesses" of armed conflict. There are two problems with this argument: First, the period in question covers the most serious and significant violations, including all the cases of persons who disappeared and most of the summary executions. Second, and more important, the large majority of cases concerned unarmed and defenseless victims who were not members of armed groups. These victims were killed or forcibly disappeared by members of the armed forces, who only a few days after the coup assumed total control over the country. Thus, these were not the transgressions of opposing sides committed in the heat of battle. Under these circumstances, the military's argument that the violations took place within a framework of the aftermath of civil war, or during combat against armed subversives, is patently untrue, as the Commission's report makes clear. There is therefore no basis for an amnesty, which is based on the need, recognized by most of the populace, to restore social harmony and peace. Here, in contrast, most of the population opposed the amnesty, which was really a self-pardon granted by the military regime to those that carried out its repressive policies.

It is true that, technically speaking, the amnesty cannot apply to cases of forced disappearances. Forced disappearance is a continuing offense that remains in force so long as the fate and whereabouts of the victim are unknown. Thus, if the fate of the person was still unknown as of 1978, the offense would continue beyond that date. Nonetheless, the amnesty remains an obstacle to justice. Should judicial investigation successfully uncover the fate of the persons who disappeared — unfortunately, their deaths, almost certainly before March 10, 1978 — the offense would then become that of homicide, subject to the amnesty if committed by military personnel.

Amnesty and Investigations: The Aftermath

The amnesty does not prevent investigation of the facts. That interpretation has broad support in Chilean jurisprudence (both civil and military). It explains why there are as of 1993 more than 200 cases before the courts and another 800 cases that are temporarily closed, which could be reopened if new evidence comes to light. Still, investigation without the possibility of penal sanction does not satisfy the demands of justice.

President Aylwin, as mentioned, initially supported the continuation of investigations into the crimes covered by the amnesty. As time passed, the army became increasingly dissatisfied with this state of affairs; in fact, it led on May 28, 1993 to a military show of force outside the presidential palace to demand an end to the investigations. The president, in a speech explaining his proposed solution to the conflict, said that the military disliked "hateful situations prejudging the possible responsibility of military personnel as a result of the publicity generated by the judicial investigations, especially the subpoenas of active-duty officers to testify." According to President Aylwin, the Army complained that

> the frequent citing of active-duty officers to testify before the courts regarding events covered by the amnesty, and the wide coverage of this testimony in the media, in addition to taking time away from their jobs and tarnishing their image before their subordinates, forms part of a campaign of harrassment or denigration of the Army.

The Army therefore demanded that the cases be speeded up and that the hearings avoid the creation of demeaning situations for the military or other persons involved. In response, several politicians and members of Congress proposed variants on a "full stop" law, bringing an end to the investigations altogether. President Aylwin spent some time in discussion and negotiation, in which he reportedly asked the military to accept publicly its responsibility for having wrongfully killed those who had disappeared. He also asked the military to come forward with whatever information it had on the location of the victims' remains, which it refused to do.[14] On August 4, 1993, the president proposed a law mandating the appointment of special, additional judges who would take up the remaining cases, as well as allowing for secret testimony by persons with information about these crimes and their circumstances.

The president's bill failed in Congress, due basically to the opposition of the left wing of the governing coalition. Those opposed argued that, among other things, allowing the declarations before the court and the information contained in them to remain secret undermined the objective of truth seeking. At the same time, given the historical refusal of the armed forces to collaborate with the courts over the years, the proposed law was unlikely to act as a potent incentive to produce new information concerning what had happened. Moreover, the proposed law allowed the designation of military judges as ad hoc investigatory judges in these cases. The military courts have never shown any interest in seriously investigating human rights abuses, and the military members of those courts are active-duty officers with no independence from their institutions. Finally, opponents noted that the proposed new judges would not have sufficient powers to carry out fruitful investigations — for example, to investigate military installations — and that without such powers it would be impossible to advance the truth-finding process.

Interpreting the Amnesty in Accordance with National and International Law

The correct legal interpretation of the amnesty law is that it need not stand in the way of criminally punishing the guilty. The amnesty cannot cover the most serious human rights violations because the human rights treaties to which Chile is a party are part of its constitutional law, and they preclude such amnesty.[15] Unfortunately, in practice this theoretical argument has not been applied either by the courts or by the legal community in general. The general interpretation, mistaken in my view, that the amnesty applies across the board is no doubt due to the lack of information and sensitivity to the existing international norms.

As discussed earlier, rather than a true amnesty, the law in question constituted yet another violation of the rights of Chileans by the dictatorship, which took advantage of its illegitimate seizure of legislative power to pervert the country's legal institutions. As a question of international human rights law, the amnesty is illegitimate to the extent that it covers serious human rights violations which must be prosecuted and cannot, therefore, be subject to amnesty. Within the Inter-American system, for example, the Inter-American Court of Human Rights, in the *Velasquez Rodriguez* case, held that states must prevent, investigate, and prosecute violations of the rights contained in the American Convention. The Inter-American Commission on Human Rights has found specifically that laws such as those passed in Uruguay and Argentina, which impede or create obstacles to the prosecution of serious human rights violations, contravene the provisions of the American Convention on Human Rights and the American Declaration on the Rights and Duties of Man.[16]

The same conclusion applies with even greater force to the amnesty law passed by the military government in Chile. The democratic government has a duty to deny any legal effect to this law, so that Chile can comply with its obligations under the American Convention. It is not enough, as some people have argued, that the current government refrain from passing its own amnesty. The report of the Commission on Truth and Reconciliation provides more than enough evidence that the violations at issue were true human rights violations, not lamentable "excesses" of military combats, and that they were serious enough to come within the ambit of the Convention's requirement of prosecution. It is up to the legislature to take the appropriate action directing the courts to ensure justice is done.

The option of leaving it to the courts, through judicial interpretation, to deny effect to the amnesty law in cases of the most serious human rights violations is not feasible. Although technically possible, this option ignores the reality of the courts, especially the Supreme Court, which has repeatedly interpreted the amnesty decree to impede absolutely any prosecution.[17] Legislative action is therefore needed to allow the lower courts to apply the law correctly.[18]

There are several legal options. One, annulling the amnesty decree, as presidential candidate Aylwin proposed, was followed in Argentina. However, unlike the Argentine legal tradition, the Chilean does not formally allow for annulment of laws. Another option, derogation, also proposed in the Aylwin government's platform, would not achieve the desired result because it would not have retroactive effect. What is needed, rather, is an interpretative law that excludes from the scope of the amnesty the most serious violations of human rights — specifically, forced disappearances and other violations (summary executions, torture) that resulted in deaths of individuals. Socialist members of Congress have introduced such a proposal, which has not yet been debated. Such a law would not violate the principle of nonretroactivity of penal laws, since under both national and international law the amnesty was never able legally to cover these serious violations of human rights. Moreover, article 15.2 of the International Covenant on Civil and Political Rights makes clear that the principle of nonretroactivity does not "prejudice the trial and punishment of any person for any act or omission which, at the time when it was committed, was criminal according to the general principles of law recognized by the community of nations." The acts at issue come within that principle.

The Problem of Feasibility: Truth, and Justice to the Extent Possible

The government of President Aylwin coined the formula "truth, and justice to the extent possible" to summarize its position regarding the human rights violations committed during the military regime. The government insisted that had it given equal priority to both truth and justice, it would have achieved neither because the military, fearing prosecutions, would have opposed even efforts to establish the truth and compensate the victims. Concretely, with respect to justice, this position has meant accepting the 1978 amnesty as a fixed legal obstacle that the courts must apply. The government insists nothing can be done because it has neither the parliamentary strength to legislate changes to the amnesty nor the ability to force the courts to overturn it.[19]

The government's formula could be considered correct, depending on whether the possibility of truth and justice to which it refers is understood as an ex post and not ex ante judgment. It is true that no one is obligated to do the impossible: Only that amount of truth and justice which are possible can be obtained. But the "possible" then refers to the result — that is, what it is possible to *obtain*. This means, therefore, that it is necessary to carry out a serious effort to obtain the desired result — the maximum truth and justice possible. If, despite the efforts made, little or nothing is obtained, then these will constitute the extent of truth and justice that is possible. Nothing more was possible. This is a judgment made a posteriori: judging the results in light of the efforts expended to achieve them. However, this is not the interpretation the Aylwin government gave its formula. For the government it constitutes an ex ante prejudgment, in which the government beforehand sets its own limits on what it believes possible, without any effort to obtain the results it desires.

When discussing the problem of feasibility we should distinguish between the *possible,* as an after-the-fact judgment, and the *demandable.* The latter refers to the attempt to obtain the desirable result, the value of the attempt itself, independent of the result. The possible is not defined beforehand; circumstances can broaden or restrict its limits. For example, the presentation at the proper moment (that is, when the Commission made public its report) of a proposed law aimed at limiting the effects of the amnesty, put forward with the necessary ethical, legal, and political force by all those groups and entities that support the government, could well have provoked an informed, high-level national debate; such a debate could have changed the balance of forces in unexpected ways.

An interpretative law along these lines, reasonable and prudent, could well have generated a favorable political climate and garnered the support of the Church, some sectors of the democratic right, and even of the armed forces, who might have wished public repudiation of the atrocities committed not to fall indiscriminately on its members and on the military as an institution. Such a law would have excluded from the amnesty's scope only those serious violations that matter most (deaths and disappearances), would have provided for some recognition of the role of due obedience in cases in which subordinates had no possibility of moral choice, and would have contained full due process guarantees for the persons implicated.

This, I believe, is what could have been demanded and what should have been attempted. And if the effort had failed, then we could agree that what was done was what was possible. However, the government and the political forces that support it have not sought what is possible. Rather, they defined in a before-the-fact and abstract manner the limits of the possible in a politically convenient way, a way that accorded with their overriding objective. That objective, unfortunately, has been to favor the normalization of civilian-military relations, as they understood them, over demands for truth and justice.

14

Haiti: Searching for Alternatives

Irwin P. Stotzky

The challenges posed by Haiti's rocky transition from the Duvalier era to one of democracy have been as difficult as any in the world. As this book goes to press, international efforts to restore the democratically elected government have successfully reinstated President Aristide to office. It remains unclear, however, whether the international efforts will again founder on the intransigence of the most powerful forces in Haiti—the economic elite and the military and paramilitary forces. Even assuming that these corporative forces can be brought under democratic control, the difficulties of creating a viable economy, an institutional structure, and respect for the rule of law, which must undergird both, remain formidable. The question of whether to prosecute those who have committed serious human rights violations played a key role in the events leading up to the September 1991 coup. That question continued to be significant in negotiations for President Jean-Bertrand Aristide's return and is now a key question in the consolidation of the democratic government. Indeed, dealing with the past will be crucial to opening up new possibilities for establishing the rule of law in both the institutions and the minds of the Haitian people.

The Origins of Dictatorship

The history of Haiti is a tragic tale of political corruption and military violence. With the singular exception of one regime that governed between 1818 and 1843, Haiti has been marked by ceaseless coups, assassinations, and massive violations of human rights.[1] The only period of relative stability[2] was between 1915 and 1934 when the U.S. Marines occupied the country in order to ensure U.S. commercial privileges.[3] When the troops were finally removed, conventional hostilities with the Dominican Republic resumed.[4]

Any notion of stability from that point meant dictatorship. First, it was the regime of François (Papa Doc) Duvalier, who ruled with an iron fist between 1957 and his death in 1971 with the aid of a maniacal private security force known as the Tonton Macoutes.[5] Papa Doc consolidated his power quickly and ruthlessly, eviscerating individual liberties and political opposition with equal dispatch.[6] Indeed, over 40,000 Haitians reportedly lost their lives as the victims of official brutality.[7] Duvalier stole over $500 million in foreign aid and taxes and deposited the money into personal accounts in Haiti and abroad.[8] Officials at all levels of government, taking their cue from Duvalier, took part in similar acts of corruption.[9]

Papa Doc remained in power for over fourteen years, and in order to ensure a legacy of Duvalier control over the country, organized a referendum on January 31, 1971, in which voters approved his nineteen-year-old son, Jean-Claude (Baby Doc), as his successor.[10] When his father died, Jean-Claude became "President for Life." His rule was as repressive as his father's. In 1986, however, when the levels of economic disparities and political corruption reached ungovernable proportions, Baby Doc fled Haiti for exile in France.[11]

Following the Duvaliers came a series of political regimes[12] that owed their survival to a large military caste which operated with the indefatigable support of a small upper class.[13] None of these regimes, however, had the support of the Haitian people. Each ruled through the power of the gun.[14]

Nonetheless, the fall of the Duvaliers raised expectations that some of the military and security forces, including the Duvalier-associated Tonton Macoutes, would be brought to justice. In the weeks after Duvalier was ousted, mobs killed a number of known Macoutes. After crowds looted the home of former secret police chief Luc Desir and prevented him from leaving the country, the Namphy government promised to arrest and bring to justice the persons suspected of committing serious crimes during the twenty-eight years of Duvalier rule. Spurred by large demonstrations demanding justice, the government did prosecute several low-ranking Army officers, and three Macoutes were tried and convicted of killing political prisoners. However, the regime also allowed a number of high-ranking officers, including the head of the Macoutes and the former Army intelligence chief, to leave the country; others known to have committed crimes were freed after Army courts found insufficient evidence to convict them. According to human rights activists, intimidation of witnesses and jurors made bringing such cases to trial extremely difficult.[15] Whatever small advances were made initially soon became buried under a new wave of Army shootings, repeated coups, and instability.

The popular will was finally expressed in 1990. The Haitian people elected Jean-Bertrand Aristide to the office of president in December 1990 in the first fully democratic election to take place in Haiti in nearly 200 years.[16] Popular support for Aristide was astonishing: He received two thirds of the vote, giving him an unprecedented mandate for reform.[17]

Equally impressive was the election process. It represented the culmination of an extraordinary international effort to launch Haiti on the path to democracy. Both the Organization of American States (OAS) and the United Nations actively participated in helping Haitian officials assure the security and dignity of the election process.[18] Voter turnout was remarkably high; 75 percent of the eligible voters — approximately 2.7 million out of the 3.2 million registered voters — turned out to vote despite extremely difficult logistical problems.[19] The dirt roads and mountain paths of rural Haiti, where three quarters of the population lives, made the distribution of election materials particularly hazardous. Moreover, the high illiteracy rate of Haitians compounded the challenge of registering and voting.[20] Nevertheless, despite these problems, virtually all observers who monitored the voting claimed that the elections were fair and that voters experienced no intimidation.[21] In addition, the military helped assure that violence would not occur.[22]

This peaceful, positive election, however, soon gave way to violence. Even before Aristide took his oath of office, the military challenged his legitimacy in an unsuccessful coup, and coup attempts continued throughout his tenure.[23] The September 1991 coup was not only successful but it has also resulted in a widely publicized reign of terror in Haiti.[24]

During its short tenure, the Aristide government took important steps to improve the rule of law in Haiti.[25] In one of his first official acts,[26] President Aristide announced the retirement of senior military officials who had either been involved in past human rights violations or had failed to punish persons responsible for such abuses.[27] He also appointed several new public prosecutors and removed corrupt officials linked to the military.[28] Simultaneously, Aristide announced the creation of a human rights commission charged with investigating some of the most notorious human rights abuses that had been committed in the past.[29] The new president also closed down Fort Dimanche, known as a torture center, and dedicated a museum to its victims on the site. In addition, under the Aristide government, a number of people believed to have been involved in a 1987 massacre were arrested, as were others alleged to have directed killings and torture under past regimes. Unfortunately, Aristide was overthrown before these individuals could come to trial.[30]

The most significant step Aristide took to improve respect for the rule of law was the dissolution of the institution of rural section chiefs who were accountable solely to the military authorities.[31] These section chiefs had unfettered control over the lives of the peasants in rural areas. This unchecked power led to systematic disregard of human rights with complete impunity.[32] The Aristide government replaced the section chiefs' system with a system of rural police under the jurisdiction of the ministry of justice. It appointed a completely new corps of rural agents made up of individuals untainted by the abuses of the old system.[33]

But these reforms did not last long. The overthrow of the Aristide government has resulted in the deaths and torture of thousands of innocent people that continues to the present day.[34] Moreover, after the overthrow of Aristide, the military rapidly took steps to consolidate power. It named a civilian government, including an interim president, to complicate the return of President Aristide.[35] It reversed the systemic changes made by the Aristide government. First, the military fired or hunted down many of the prosecution and judicial officials who had been appointed by Aristide.[36] Next, it released prisoners, including Tonton Macoutes, who had been convicted of human rights violations during Aristide's presidency.[37] The military also restored the old section chief structure, thus returning to power individuals who were known to have committed massive human rights abuses.[38] These section chiefs, in turn, enlisted their old private armies, formerly known as the Tonton Macoutes but now referred to as attachés, and reasserted their control over the countryside.[39]

International Efforts to Restore Aristide to the Presidency

Over the next two years the international community made serious efforts to help restore Aristide to power and to support the nascent democratic movement in Haiti.[40] The diplomatic reaction of the OAS and the United Nations was vigorous and forceful. The member states of the OAS froze the assets of Haiti and imposed a trade embargo on the country.[41] There followed a round of negotiations, under U.N. and OAS auspices, that stretched out over the next year and a half. By April 1993, the outlines of a settlement were visible. The sticking point turned out to be amnesty for the past human rights violations of the military.

As part of the price for Aristide's reinstatement, the military demanded a complete amnesty. In February 1993, Aristide agreed to a general amnesty for political crimes but refused to extend the amnesty to "common criminals." He argued that the Haitian Constitution forbade such an amnesty, adding that he believed the killings and torture by Army leaders would subject the latter to prosecution as common criminals. Intense negotiations took place in March and April. The U.S. and U.N. negotiators made no secret of their belief that a full amnesty was necessary and that Aristide was being unrealistic as well as intransigent. Aristide supporters, for their part, accused the United Nations and the U.S. administration of exerting enormous pressure on Aristide to accept an illegal amnesty, thus making the cost of a settlement prohibitively high in order to blame the exiled president if the talks collapsed.[42] Finally, Aristide apparently gave in to the increasing pressure to settle, agreeing to guarantee freedom from criminal prosecutions and not to oppose future parliamentary efforts to preclude civil suits against the military. In exchange, the settlement was to include creation of a "Truth Commission" to investigate the most serious abuses.[43] The military rejected this deal, however, and, as a result, the international community imposed stricter sanctions, including an oil embargo.[44]

The culmination of these negotiations was the July 1993 Governors Island Agreement.[45] Under this agreement, President Aristide agreed to appoint a prime minister who would be subject to confirmation by parliament,[46] after which the embargo would be suspended. The agreement further provided that the U.N. and OAS sanctions would be suspended at the initiative of the respective secretaries-general of the two organizations immediately after the new prime minister "is confirmed and assumes office."[47] President Aristide would return to Haiti on October 30, 1993.[48] Shortly before his return, Cédras would retire from the high command in favor of an Aristide appointee, who would then name new members to the high command "in accordance with the constitution."[49] Other coup participants would be allowed to remain in the military, but they would be posted outside Haiti.[50] The agreement also gave Aristide the right to appoint a new chief of police to head a reorganized police force for Port-au-Prince, which would no longer be part of the military.[51] An international police force would be stationed in

Haiti, and other steps would be taken to "modernize" the Army.[52] Moreover, in connection with the agreement, an international aid program amounting to $1 billion over five years would be instituted. Finally, there would be international cooperation in matters of technical and financial development aid and assistance for administrative and judicial reform.[53]

The Governors Island Agreement provided for full amnesty granted by the president to the coup leaders and supporters within the framework of article 147 of the national constitution and "implementation of other instruments which may be adopted by the Parliament."[54] Article 147 allows a presidential amnesty only for political matters "as stipulated by law." Thus, if parliament defines the military's human rights violations as "political," they would be covered by the amnesty. Violence and intimidation and the total abrogation of the Governors Island Agreement by the military kept Parliament from meeting to define the issue, although Aristide's government at one point agreed to the amnesty.

The Governors Island Agreement was a total failure. Neither Cédras nor François resigned. Instead, Cédras broke every part of the brokered deal[55] and employed every kind of delay while subordinates known as attachés continued to terrorize the population.[56] Their terror knew no bounds. They assassinated the largest financial backer of Aristide, Antoine Izmery, pulling him from a church in broad daylight and shooting him in the streets. They also assassinated the minister of justice, Guy Malary. The Haitians who could, fled the capital, hoping the countryside would be safer. Like the attachés, the men at the top appeared determined not to lose the power they amassed since the coup. Indeed, they made huge amounts of money from control of the ports and taxation, and some shared in the drug trade that moved through Haiti at a rapid clip.[57]

When Cédras reneged on the agreement, the United Nations imposed a new embargo on oil and arms shipments,[58] and U.S. and allied warships encircled the nation. The new sanctions included freezing all assets in the United States owned by Haitians residing in their homeland. The freezing of these assets represented the Clinton administration's attempt to show the powerful Haitian elite that they would not be allowed to escape the consequences of their support for an illegitimate and illegal government.[59] The U.N. sanctions also called for a total trade embargo. The immediate and most significant result of the embargo was the discontinuation of all commercial air travel to and from Haiti.[60] The freeze and the embargo, however, did not result in the removal of the military coup leaders. The effectiveness of the sanctions was weakened by the almost free flow of contraband goods, especially gasoline, across the Dominican Republic border. Only under significant U.S. pressure did Joaquin Balaguer, President of the Dominican Republic, agree to take steps to enforce the international embargo.[61]

Although sanctions hurt, they may not have been enough without a credible threat of force. Though impoverished Haitians suffered severe deprivation under an on-again, off-again embargo, the military bosses prospered from rising prices and trade in smuggled goods. While the latest embargo eventually pushed Cédras toward another negotiation, it was not likely to destroy the power of the military. So how was the United States and the international community to fulfill its pledge not just to restore President Aristide to office but also to ensure the growth of a lasting democratic nation?

The United States, of course, was particularly concerned with this question. As of now, there is only one way Haiti makes its problems matter in the United States (or elsewhere internationally, for that matter) — by having thousands of desperate asylum-seeking refugees attempt the hazardous 600-mile journey by sea to Miami. Indeed, Haitian boat people are a large concern to President Clinton, who until very recently continued the Bush policy of returning the boat people to Haiti without hearings on their asylum claims, in flagrant violation of international law.

The Clinton administration, under intense political pressure from many members of Congress, especially the Congressional Black Caucus, and human rights groups, changed its policy of forcibly returning Haitians stopped at sea.[62] Instead, the administration agreed to hold interviews on board vessels docked at third countries and to take those Haitians found to have a well-founded fear of persecution to the United States for further processing of their asylum claims.

Because of this change in policy and increased acts of violence against the Haitian people by the Haitian military, thousands of Haitians fled Haiti in boats. In response to this newest flood of refugees, President Clinton changed his policy once again. Instead of allowing those refugees with a well-founded fear of persecution to come to the United States for processing, his latest policy required sending those Haitians to third countries.[63] As exemplified by the Clinton administration's vacillating Haitian refugee policy, as well as the United States and international communities' shifting policy toward Haiti during the past century, establishing a functioning democracy in Haiti may, over the long term, not maintain the support of the international community.

At the same time, the United Nations gave the Clinton administration its backing for the use of force in Haiti. On July 31, 1994, the Security Council, by a 12-to-zero vote, authorized a U.S. invasion and occupation of Haiti if the international sanctions and embargo failed to remove the illegitimate military regime.[64] After this chapter was completed, and as this book was going to press, U.S. troops entered Haiti pursuant to a last-minute deal between the U.S. government and Haiti's military leaders. While the full outlines are not yet known, the deal called for Cédras and François to leave their posts (although not necessarily the country) by October 15, 1994 or the date the Haitian Parliament passed a sweeping amnesty law, whichever came first. U.S. troops were to ensure that the deal went through as well as help retrain the Army and the police; the current military structure was to remain intact.[65] The embargo was to be lifted immediately. President Aristide and his advisers, however, questioned the ability of the accord to protect Aristide supporters while the military still retained full power. In addition, according to press reports, Aristide expressed opposition to the amnesty provisions of the deal, which provide not only amnesty for political crimes but also for murder, rape, and other crimes committed by military and security forces from 1991 on.[66] Aristide pointed out that the "notion that crimes against humanity, murders and tortures can be amnestied by Parliament" would "contradict the Haitian Constitution."[67]

While an invasion may solve the immediate problem by removing the military leaders, it does not solve the more difficult task of creating the conditions for a viable democracy to flourish in Haiti. Indeed, the last time the Marines invaded Haiti, in 1915, they stayed for almost two decades and achieved very little in the way of building a democratic nation. Haiti has never had a secure democratic government, and it is not clear that there are enough functioning elements of civil society left to provide a proper foundation for such a government within the period of time the U.S. public and the international community will support an international presence. The successors of Cédras and François are still present, and the country is still split between a tiny elite and a vast poor majority. What, if any, alternatives exist? The answer begins with a focus on the complex issues involved in any transition to democracy, especially one that may take place in Haiti.

Institutions, Imagination, and the Rule of Law

Several thorny and intertwined problems in Haiti's movement toward democracy must be resolved if the transition is to succeed without causing great harm to masses of people. Institutional structures must be developed and secured. Economic and political stability must be assured. Corporatist social and political structures must be transformed so that the powerless receive their fair share of the basic necessities of life. The rule of law must become paramount in the formal institutions and practices of government and in the affairs of daily life. Yet virtually no nation that has undergone a transition from dictatorship to democracy has been entirely successful in resolving these problems.

In working toward these goals, the poverty of structural imagination acts as an inhibiting factor in an age in which the focus of social innovation and ideological controversy around the world has begun to shift away from the old quarrels about statism and privatism and toward an emerging experimentalist rivalry among alternative institutionalized versions of economic and political pluralism. For example, the dominant political regimes of the less-developed economies, and even their critics, often start with the desire merely to imitate and import the institutional arrangements of the rich industrial democracies. These countries take this approach in the hope that from similar institutional devices similar economic and political consequences will result. In practice, however, imitation has not led to the desired results. The failure of these efforts at emulation may, nevertheless, be useful in the development of new institutional structures. Put another way, such efforts may end up driving less-developed political economies into an involuntary institutional experimentalism, which may shed light on the suppressed opportunities for transformation. So it is possible that if Haiti begins on this path, positive results will follow.

Predictions about the success of any political process, and particularly the process of change in Haiti, however, are problematic at best. Therefore, I do not intend to make such predictions. I shall, however, discuss briefly some of the most prominent features of democratic consolidation and apply these features to the circumstances in Haiti. These aspects of the transition process are useful in formulating predictions on which depend the claim that the transition to democracy in Haiti can succeed.

The first significant feature of the consolidation that may occur in Haiti is that the democratization process must take place during one of the worst economic and social crises in the history of the country. In general, this crisis manifests itself in enormously high rates of human rights abuses, including murders, disappearances, and torture, very high unemployment rates, unacceptably high increases in infant mortality, epidemics, and a variety of other social catastrophes.[68] Furthermore, there is great controversy in the international community about whether this crisis may lead to changes in the economic and social structures of Haiti that are necessary to revitalize the economy. The great unknown factor is whether the previous dominant economic groups will remain all powerful or instead have been reduced to mere puppets of the military. During most of Haiti's history the military did the bidding of the elite classes by protecting their economic monopolies and brutally suppressing the vast majority of the poor. In turn, the rich paid off the dictators. But after the 1991 coup the military took over the country's ports and landing strips and as a consequence prospered in the illicit drug trade. Even more significant, the military increasingly prospered through its control of state monopolies, such as the telephone company. For example, Colonel François took over from the rich the old monopolies in flour, sugar, rice, and cement.[69] The military's voraciousness caused some of the traditional economic elite to support the Governors Island Agreement. But the question remains: What will this economic elite do now that Aristide is returned to power?

It is possible that if international aid is forthcoming, Haiti will be able to streamline its economic structure to create more efficient schemes of production and, thus, improve all sectors of society. But, of course, such a possibility requires massive changes in the Haitian economic, political, and social structure. These changes would need to encompass, at a minimum, an overhaul of the tax system to redistribute wealth, strategies to overcome the internal division of Haiti into two or more weakly connected economies, the imposition of real competition on the private sector, and massive investment in people and infrastructure, all backed by the strength of the international community.

A second and integrally connected feature of the consolidation is the required transformation of the corporatist political and social structure that characterizes Haiti. This corporatism[70] has been described as bifrontal. On the one hand, it serves the state by allowing it to control different sectors of civil society; on the other hand, it involves the establishment of cleavages of privilege and domination by different social groups within the structure of the state. The groups that form the constellation of corporative power in Haiti include the armed forces; the Catholic Church;[71] trade groups; a variety of civic organizations, including peasant associations; grass-roots development projects; independent radio stations and the like; and the economic elite. Unlike many nations that have attempted to make the transition from dictatorship to democracy, Haiti's civil society is extremely advanced. Moreover, political parties are among the least advanced parts of this civil society. The strength of civil society is to be found in its diversity and breadth outside electoral politics.

The armed forces and their civilian front (attachés) consolidated their rule by ruthlessly suppressing Haiti's once diverse and vibrant civil society. The military systematically repressed virtually all forms of independent associations in an attempt to deny the Haitian people any organized base for opposition to the dictatorship and to push Haiti back into an atomized and fearful society reminiscent of the Duvalier era. The strategy appeared to be that even if Aristide was returned to power, he would have great difficulty transforming his popularity into the organized support he would need to exert civilian control over the Army and to create a democratic institutional structure that could aid in that endeavor.

The Rule of Law and Judicial Independence

Strongly interconnected with the economic, social, political, and institutional aspects is a third feature of the process of democratic consolidation: the deficiency in the fulfillment of the requirements of the rule of law.[72] This deficiency pervades Haiti, acting as an inhibiting incubus to any possible positive democratic development.

Haiti does not, however, lack a comprehensive legal structure that would support a democracy. The blueprint is set forth in the 1987 Constitution, which the Haitian people overwhelmingly approved in a March 29, 1987 election.[73] The Constitution contains specific guarantees of personal liberty and political and civil rights.[74] It provides citizens with the basic freedoms associated with a democratic state: the right to life (article 19), freedom of expression (article 28), freedom of association and assembly (article 31), freedom of the press (article 28-1), and freedom of religion and conscience (article 30). The Constitution also provides citizens protection from prosecution, arrest, or detention unless pursuant to law (article 24-1). For example, no one may be detained without a warrant unless caught in the act of committing a crime, and no arrest may be made between 6 P.M. and 6 A.M. (articles 24-2 and 24-3d). No one may be kept under arrest for more than forty-eight hours without being brought before a judge, who must rule on the legality of the arrest and detention (article 26). Article 276-2 expands all of these protections, providing that all international treaties ratified by Haiti are incorporated directly into Haitian law and supersede any laws in conflict with them. This provision is significant because Haiti has ratified several international human rights conventions.[75]

Despite these provisions, the Haitian judicial system is in disarray. The nation needs not only to develop institutions but to train large numbers of people to run the institutions. Even more ominous for the success of any possible transition to democracy is the fact that Haiti's institutional structure — particularly its judicial structure — is less developed than that of virtually any nation which has attempted this precarious transition. The majority of judicial officials fail to apply the law because they are intimidated, corrupt, or incompetent. The problem is even more deeply rooted. Deeds of corruption by the highest government officials (the military) occurred daily during the coup years, yet judicial procedures did not prove helpful in investigating these acts.[76]

Perhaps even more destructive to the creation of a democracy than these sources of corruption, however, was the domination by the military dictatorship of all other state power and branches of government.[77] The military monopolized the civilian justice system to such an extent that it failed to investigate or identify the persons responsible for massive human rights violations. There was no judicial independence. Judges were appointed and removed at the will of the military. Persons arrested or detained by the military had no access to judicial protection. Judges themselves have been detained and beaten for ruling against members of the military. Moreover, attorneys have been harassed, threatened, and even murdered. The armed forces routinely ignored judicial orders, including orders to arrest soldiers or officers accused of human rights violations.[78]

The violation of legal norms, however, is not restricted to the military coup leaders or their supporting cast. Unfortunately, such behavior is a distinguishing mark of Haitian political and social life that has been evident throughout the nation's history. Failure to follow the rule of law is apparent both in social practice and in the actions of government bodies. The tendency to unlawfulness infects not only public officials but the general society, and it correlates with a general trend toward anomie. It manifests itself in such matters as corruption in private economic activities, nonobservance of efficient economic norms, and noncompliance with the most basic rules of society. This general tendency toward illegality in public and social life normally manifests itself in one of two ways: People in Haiti may adopt a "finalist attitude," where they agree with the goals of a rule but do not follow the commands of the rule. Conversely, they may adopt a "formalistic attitude," where they blindly comply with the commands of the rule but ignore the goals. Both attitudes are incompatible with and thus contribute to the continuing difficulty of securing adherence to the rule of law.

The problem is even more complicated. The tendency toward unlawfulness in Haitian public and social life is often the product and the cause of collective action problems, like those that game theory labels "prisoner's dilemma," "assurance game," "chicken game," and so forth. Frequently, the combination of expectations, interests, possibilities of actions, and their respective payoffs are such that the rational course of action for each participant in the process of political or social interaction advises the person not to comply with a certain norm. This is so despite the fact that general compliance with the norm would have been for the benefit of everybody, or almost everybody. Anomie of this kind may be called dumb anomie[79] because it refers to situations in which compliance with a certain norm would have led the social actors to a more efficient result — in Pareto's terms — than what they obtain in the actual situation of not observing norms.

Moreover, dumb anomie is connected with the stunting of Haiti's economic and social development. First, there is a direct conceptual connection between that kind of anomie and failures in economic productivity. Indeed, dumb anomie is identified by the inefficient results of processes of interaction, including economic ones, that do not observe certain norms. Second, it is clear that anomie affects the process of capital accumulation. For example, when the behavior of people intervening in the process of production — even that of judges and government officials — is not sufficiently predictable, productive investments decline or claim disproportionate profits.

Therefore, it is critical for the life of the Haitian nation to consolidate the rule of law. This is important not only to secure respect for fundamental rights and for the observance of the democratic process but also to achieve satisfactory degrees of economic and social development. Moreover, it is obvious that the consolidation of the rule of law, with the consequent overcoming of dumb anomie, requires strengthening the independence, reliability, and efficiency of the judicial process.

The macropolitics of institutional change in Haiti remains inadequate to the aims of democratization and practical experimentalism unless it is complemented by a micropolitics that confronts the logic of habitual social interactions. Haitian culture appears to be strongly resistant to the internalization of universal standards of achievement and competition that are necessary to an equitably functioning democracy. Rather, Haitians appear to have internalized a belief in the overpowering importance of status and connections, thus crippling the transition to a constitutional democracy. In Haitian society there is a predominance of patron–client relations, with their pervasive mingling, in the same associations and encounters, of exchange, power, and sentimental allegiance. There is frequently an oscillation between rule formalism and personal favoritism, and each creates the opportunity and the need for the other. Finally, there is a stark contrast between the treatment of *insiders* (anyone with whom, by virtue of the role you occupy, you have a pre-existing relationship) and *outsiders* (everyone else) and the consequent shortage of impersonal respect and reliability.

A "transformative" politics capable of challenging and changing both the established arrangements of the economy and the polity and the intimate habits of sociability must combine a strategic approach to the satisfaction of recognized material interests with the visionary invocation of a reordered society. In Haiti, a nation trapped in these impoverished visions, nothing is more important than to encourage the belief in the Haitian people that structural change is possible.

Coming to Terms with the Past

One way to begin enlarging the collective sense of the possible and to achieve some of the other suggested goals — making the rule of law an essential part of public and private life, changing the habits of social interaction, and creating viable democratic institutions — is to address the question of how to deal with the massive human rights violations committed by the military dictatorship. These cases involve what Kant referred to as "radical evil" — offenses against humanity that are so widespread, persistent, and organized that normal moral assessments seem inadequate.

Hannah Arendt claimed that we know very little about these offenses and that they exhibit a structural element in the realm of human affairs, which is that "men are unable to forgive what they cannot punish and that they are unable to punish what has turned out to be unforgivable."[80] She concluded that these offenses, for which we can neither punish people nor forgive them, "transcend the realm of human affairs and the potentialities of human power, both of which they radically destroy wherever they make their appearance."[81]

This image of powerlessness in the face of these deeds may seem at first sight as merely a literary image that reflects our awe of the inadequacy of human justice and social evolution and its punishments for such deeds. But when actual cases of massive human rights abuses are analyzed, it becomes clear that there are strong barriers to going forward even with measures that are applied to common criminals.

One problem, on a level of moral assessment, is the possibility that the persons who commit these acts have concepts, such as "the natural good," which are incomprehensible to us and lead to actions that are incommensurable under our conceptual schemes. This poses the problem of whether a state can legitimately carry out moral discourse outside its boundaries and thus subject agents who do not share the assumptions of that discourse to courses of action based on its findings. This problem, of course, destroys any possibility of grounding public moral responsibility in consensus because even moral disagreement is foreclosed by conceptual divergence.

Other moral problems exist even if the problem of conceptual relativism is overcome. For example, the type of collective behavior that is necessary for the commission of these acts would not have been successful without strong conviction by the perpetrators of the deeds. Sincere conviction poses problems for moral evaluations even if the society does not agree with the substantive content of the conviction. Moreover, the mistaken character of the conviction has to be demonstrated. This, of course, raises questions about the foundations of human rights and about their scope and balance when several of them conflict.[82]

Another moral problem concerns the diffusion of responsibility. These deeds cannot be committed without the assent of numerous and very different people in the society. There are those who planned the acts and those who executed them. There are those who in some way supported the actions by giving information to the perpetrators or by lending material support. Indeed, this assent even includes the eventual victims. There are also a large number of people who cooperated by acts of omission: Are we to punish all of the numerous judges who failed to enforce the rule of law; journalists who failed to report on the atrocities; diplomats who concealed or attempted to justify the position of their governments; and everyday citizens who decided to turn a blind eye to what was happening, refrained from telling other people about the atrocities, or even justified the deeds? To reach this point leads to the view that if almost everyone had some complicity in these acts, then everyone is guilty and thus nobody is guilty.

This set of moral concerns translates into political and legal considerations that the Aristide government must face in any attempt to take action against the military.[83] The conditions under which Aristide has resumed office will, of course, determine in part the limits of the possible. Whether or not the shape of the amnesty agreed upon at Governors Island remains intact under new conditions is a key unknown factor as of this writing — as is the extent to which other measures of purge, investigation, or reparations will be possible. Clearly, there will be no prosecutions for the coup itself or for affronts against democracy. But what about the crimes that under international law cannot be subject to a blanket amnesty? The direct incorporation of international human rights treaties into Haitian law gives rise to an obligation on the government's part to take action against the individuals who have assassinated, caused to disappear, tortured, and arbitrarily jailed thousands of Haitians. Complying with that obligation will require staunch international and domestic support. But even assuming the best possible scenario, significant impediments remain to prosecutions or even to investigations of the abuses that were committed.

A key problem is defining the chain of responsibility for both criminal and civil purposes. Although the military has a clear-cut command structure, the relationship among the military, the police, and the "attachés" and other private goon squads is less clear for purposes of attributing both state and command responsibility. The lines of communication between the coup leaders and the attachés and rural section heads are ambiguous — the attachés and section chiefs are adjuncts who both receive orders and act independently. Nonetheless, a plausible argument can be made that these individuals have over time become agents of the state, so that all their actions may be attributed to the state.[84] A similar problem arises with respect to members of the economic elite who bankrolled and otherwise supported the coup and who may have been involved in death squad–type activities. Should these individuals be held criminally or civilly liable for the results of their actions?

In October 1993, with the Governors Island accord still in place and Aristide's return to Haiti imminent, the democratic government convened a group of international experts to help it, as a priority, elucidate a policy on human rights trials, among other issues. With the assassination of Minister of Justice Malary and the disintegration of the accord, the seminar never took place. Presently, with a new limited amnesty law in place, President Aristide continues to stress the need for national reconciliation as well as for justice. He has established a National Commission for Truth and Justice, whose mandate will be to

> establish worldwide the truth with regards to all serious violations of human rights committed between September 29, 1991 and October 5, 1994, both in the interior as well as abroad against all Haitians, provided that these violations are related with the Haitian state or Haitian politics.[85]

Still, both the promise and the paradoxes of coming to terms with the past remain unexplored.[85]

The transformation of Haitian society is fraught with many dangers. How the Haitians deal with these massive human rights crimes of the past will not pose the least of these dangers. The answers to these issues will indeed help determine whether and to what extent Haiti will become a viable democracy.

15

El Salvador:
A Negotiated End to Impunity?

Margaret Popkin

The Salvadoran transition differs from others in Latin America because it is the product of a negotiated agreement between an undefeated military and an unde-feated insurgency. During the 1980s El Salvador was ravaged by a genuine civil war. Unlike countries in the Southern Cone in which a debilitated or defeated guerrilla movement served as the pretext for the state terrorism employed by mili-tary dictatorships, the Salvadoran military faced the most effective guerrilla movement on the continent. Because the Farabundo Martí National Liberation Front (FMLN) had not been defeated and enjoyed substantial support inside El Salvador as well as international recognition, it was able to negotiate a far-reach-ing peace accord as the price for ending hostilities. Nonetheless, the "transition" government was the same government that had fought the war.

Another distinguishing feature of the Salvadoran transition has been the unprecedented involvement of international actors, notably the United Nations, in the resolution of the conflict and the implementation of the peace accords. The Salvadoran peace process was the first in which the United Nations success-fully mediated the resolution of an internal armed conflict as well as its first expe-rience in peace building after an accord had been reached.[1] International human rights experts working with the United Nations have played crucial roles in this process.[2]

Through the negotiations that ended the Salvadoran conflict, several mecha-nisms were established aimed at overcoming impunity and guaranteeing human rights. These included a commission to purge the military of human rights viola-tors (the Ad Hoc Commission), a commission to examine major human rights cases that occurred during the war (the Truth Commission), a new Human Rights ombudsman, a U.N. office to monitor and promote human rights (the United Nations Observer Mission in El Salvador, ONUSAL), the replacement of military security forces with a new civilian police force, and constitutional reforms to increase the independence of the judiciary. Although it is still too soon to judge their ultimate effectiveness, this chapter reviews key mechanisms established in El Salvador and their implementation, difficulties, and prospects.

The Context: Rampant Impunity

El Salvador's effort to overcome impunity must be viewed in the context of the country's recent history. Put simply, the Salvadoran state, controlled by the military allied with a tiny economic elite, never assumed its responsibility to guarantee human rights. Eventually, its all-out effort to control an armed insurgency exacerbated the existing lack of protection.

The Salvadoran military and its civilian allies waged a no-holds-barred attack on the rebels and anyone thought to be associated with them. During the first years of the war the military massacred thousands of *campesinos* (peasants) as part of a deliberate strategy mandated by the high command and intended to eliminate or terrorize the peasant population in guerrilla zones and eliminate sources of supply and information for the guerrillas. The authorities failed to investigate these massacres, which were repeatedly reported, and dismissed such reports as libelous propaganda on the part of their adversary. The military and the police forces were also responsible for killings and forced disappearances of individuals they considered political opponents.

Rebel forces violated international humanitarian law through some of their policies and tactics. For example, the guerrillas condemned and executed civilians considered opponents without providing judicial due process guarantees.[3] And death squads linked to security forces and powerful civilians targeted persons who were considered political opponents. Their best-known victim was San Salvador's Archbishop, Monsignor Oscar Arnulfo Romero, who was gunned down on March 24, 1980 as he said mass in a hospital chapel.[4] According to the Truth Commission:

> The death squads, in which members of State structures were actively involved or to which they turned a blind eye, gained such control that they ceased to be an isolated or marginal phenomenon and became an instrument of terror used systematically for the physical elimination of political opponents. Many of the civilian and military authorities in power during the 1980s participated, encouraged and tolerated the activities of these groups.[5]

Salvadoran authorities maintained that death squad actions were outside government and military control. Yet in December 1983, Vice President George Bush visited El Salvador with a list of death squad-linked officers who had to be removed from their posts to assure continued U.S. military assistance. Shortly thereafter, U.S. military assistance reached an all-time high, while the number of death squad killings plummeted and Army massacres in the countryside became less common. Still, extrajudicial executions continued, prisoners were routinely tortured, and no real effort was made to investigate past abuses.

Early efforts to investigate past crimes, prodded by the United States, were halfhearted and ineffectual. A U.S.-funded Commission to Investigate Criminal

Acts came into being in 1985 as part of a larger judicial reform effort funded by U.S. dollars.[6] This new investigative body was intended to tackle sensitive human rights cases, especially those with military involvement. Although the Commission was nominally under civilian leadership, military officers controlled all investigations and shielded the military.[7] The Truth Commission called for the dissolution of the Commission to Investigate Criminal Acts because its omissions had covered up serious human rights violations.[8]

The U.S. Congress made specific action on certain cases a condition for U.S. military aid.[9] During the 1980s only two cases — both involving the death of U.S. citizens, U.S. conditions on aid and significant assistance from U.S. investigators — resulted in trials and convictions of the triggermen.[10] Similar efforts were not made in cases involving only Salvadoran victims, nor were any officers punished for ordering or covering up political murders.

The Role of the Judiciary

One cause of the war was the lack of recourse for victims of human rights violations. Salvadorans — even before the war — did not look to the justice system for solutions. The challenge in El Salvador in this area, as in many others, was not to restore democratic institutions temporarily suspended but to build them for the first time.

El Salvador's judiciary has not been independent. Judicial appointments were based on political criteria and family ties.[11] Political and military influence, corruption, and fear made the justice system ineffective. Military officers responsible for serious human rights violations were protected from prosecution. Political crimes and unnatural deaths were rarely investigated. In cases in which some kind of investigation had to be carried out, judges were intimidated or persuaded to assist in guaranteeing impunity through rulings that ignored the facts and the law. Torture was commonplace, yet the persons responsible for torture were never called to account.[12]

In the predawn hours of November 16, 1989, during the largest FMLN offensive, uniformed soldiers from an elite United States-trained unit entered the campus of the Central American University and murdered six Jesuit priests — including the university rector, vice rector, and head of the human rights institute — a woman who worked for the priests, and her teenage daughter. The military sought to cover up the crime, maintaining that the FMLN was responsible.[13]

The Jesuit murders tested the Salvadoran judicial system and the Salvadoran military. A police and judicial investigation proceeded, but strictly within the limits set by the military. The Truth Commission revealed that the chief police investigator not only failed to pursue leads pointing to higher orders but actually counseled the principal defendant on how to destroy evidence.[14] The judge proceeded against the nine defendants identified by the military but failed to develop significant additional evidence in the face of military lies and stonewalling. The president of the Supreme Court orchestrated the trial. Despite the triggermen's detailed confessions of how the crime was committed, the jury convicted only the colonel alleged to have given the order (for all eight counts of murder) and a lieutenant who served with him, who was inexplicably convicted solely for the murder of the teenage girl.

Although the conviction of the two officers was heralded as a break in the tradition of military impunity, the failure to identify the persons who gave the orders and to convict the confessed triggermen was widely questioned.[15] Observers noted that the outcome seemed to have little to do with the justice system, which had served as a vehicle for a political decision. Rather than establishing a new standard for Salvadoran justice, this test case graphically illustrated key problems in the judicial system. Although for the first time military officers were convicted for political murder, foreign pressures — especially from the U.S. Congress — again seemed to have required the result.

The Negotiated Solution

The November 1989 FMLN offensive showed that neither side was in a position to win the war militarily. The U.S. government was confronted with its failure to inculcate respect for human rights in the Salvadoran armed forces: Almost ten years after the death squad killing of Archbishop Romero, six Jesuit priests had been gunned down by uniformed soldiers on the orders of high-level officers who had benefited from years of U.S. training. The hard lessons of the offensive and the Jesuit murders, as well as the end of the cold war, paved the way for serious negotiations.

It was in this context that the negotiators sought to overcome impunity and establish institutions capable of guaranteeing human rights. They included human rights and judicial reform as agenda items during the negotiations process.[16] Ultimately, the peace accords included a variety of measures designed to address impunity and prevent the recurrence of past violations.

The Human Rights Accord

The San José Agreement on Human Rights was the first substantive agreement between the parties.[17] Its preamble recognized the state's obligation to respect and guarantee human rights as established in Salvadoran law and in the "many international conventions" to which El Salvador is a party. It further stated that the FMLN "has the capacity and the will and assumes the commitment to respect the inherent attributes of the human person." The preamble clarified that "human rights" included the declarations and principles on human rights and humanitarian law adopted by the United Nations and the OAS.[18]

The San José Agreement called for immediately taking all necessary steps and measures to avoid any act or practice that constitutes an attempt upon the life, integrity, security, or freedom of the individual.

> Similarly, all necessary steps and measures shall be taken to eliminate any practice involving enforced disappearances and abductions. Priority shall be given to

the investigation of any cases of this kind which may arise and to the identification and punishment of the persons found guilty.[19]

The San José Agreement further provided for the establishment of a U.N. verification mission with broad powers to oversee the human rights situation. This mission was to make a special effort "to clarify any situation which appears to reveal the systematic practice of human rights violations and, in such cases, recommend appropriate measures for the elimination of the practice to the Party concerned."[20] The U.N. mission, known as ONUSAL, was authorized to take any steps it deemed appropriate to promote and defend human rights. The parties pledged "not to hinder the fulfillment of the Mission's mandate."[21]

Although its positive and dissuasive impact is widely recognized, ONUSAL encountered difficulties in carrying out some aspects of its mission.[22] A major concern was the lack of an established mechanism to ensure that the recommendations of its Human Rights Division were actually considered and implemented. In its Eighth Human Rights Report, ONUSAL reviewed earlier recommendations and steps to comply taken by the Government. Although in some cases government bodies had prepared draft legislation to overcome specific problems, the bulk of the recommendations had not been fully carried out. In late 1994, most of the legislation proposed had yet to be enacted into law, leading ONUSAL to conclude that this "unaccountable delay is currently one of the main hurdles to improving the administration of justice and machinery for protecting human rights in El Salvador."[22]

ONUSAL has provided human rights training to the new civilian police, the new ombudsman's office, and judges, among others. It has become the authoritative voice on human rights violations and practices, having been given nationwide coverage and unprecedented access to Salvadoran authorities and their records. ONUSAL has also worked with Salvadoran officials to find ways to end patterns of abuse. Nonetheless, it is still unclear whether ONUSAL's presence will leave a lasting impact on the practices of Salvadoran institutions.

Confronting the Past

Thus, from an early stage of the negotiations the parties explicitly recognized the state's obligation to respect and guarantee human rights and the urgent need to take steps to fulfill these obligations. The peace accords addressed this problem on two fronts. One issue, on which agreement was reached without great difficulty, was the need to take steps to improve respect and guarantees for human rights in the present and future. The question that proved more difficult was how to address past violations.

The peace accords established two specific mechanisms for dealing with the past. The Ad Hoc Commission was designed to cleanse the military, and the Truth Commission was given the broader task of examining the most serious "acts of violence" committed by all sides during the war. The Ad Hoc Commission could only recommend the transfer or discharge of military officers, whereas the Truth

Commission had a broad mandate to investigate and make any recommendations it deemed appropriate regarding cases investigated and measures necessary to prevent the repetition of such cases. The government reaction to the reports issued by these two commissions suggests that, despite having signed the agreements that established their mandates and powers and agreeing to their members, the government negotiating team did not anticipate the potential consequences of these agreements or that either commission would go as far as it did.

The Ad Hoc Commission

One of the most difficult aspects of the peace talks had been negotiating civilian control over and a cleansing *(depuración)* of existing forces. The Ad Hoc Commission that was established to cleanse the military was to be made up of three Salvadorans "of recognized independence of judgment and unimpeachable democratic credentials." Two military officers were included in the Commission but were not to participate in the investigations or decision making. The Secretary-General of the United Nations consulted with the parties to find three civilians both parties would accept as members of the Commission, based on lists presented by the parties. President Alfredo Cristiani named the military representatives. Two Commission members had ties to the Christian Democratic Party, and the third member was an international lawyer who had served as the United Nation's special rapporteur for Iran. The government insisted that the Ad Hoc Commission members be Salvadorans because the military would not accept such a procedure if it were carried out by foreigners.[24]

The accords gave the Commission three months to evaluate active-duty officers and make binding recommendations for discharge or transfer of officers whose records revealed they had committed or had tolerated human rights violations. The conclusions of the Commission were to be reached after "hearing the parties concerned." The Commission cited officers for interviews to hear their explanation of charges against them. The agreement did not require that officers be afforded full due process protections or the use of any particular standard of evidence. The Commission was free to "avail itself of information from any source which it considers reliable."[25]

On September 23, 1992 the Ad Hoc Commission presented its report to President Cristiani and the U.N. secretary-general.[26] At the Salvadoran president's request, the Ad Hoc recommendations remained confidential. The Commission recommended the discharge or transfer of 102 active-duty officers.[27] No explanation was provided for the recommendations.

The military leaders and their allies rejected the recommendations as biased and unfair. They protested that the officers affected had been denied due process rights, and they threatened constitutional challenges.[28] Ad Hoc Commission members received threats and were accused of leftist ties. President Cristiani balked at carrying out the Ad Hoc recommendations, delaying action concerning certain officers and arguing that the names of some officers should not have been included on the list. The president objected that the process had not been fair—

that officers had not been granted legal due process, that some of the officers named had been instrumental in implementing the peace process, and that carrying out the recommendations could have a destabilizing effect on the process. The willingness of some FMLN leaders to discuss modifications to the Ad Hoc recommendations made it easier for President Cristiani to delay compliance.[29]

The full implementation of the Ad Hoc recommendations became a particularly sensitive aspect of the peace process, because President Cristiani refused to carry out an agreement on implementation he had made with U.N. envoy Alvaro de Soto less than two months before.[30] Although not within the calendar established, most of the Ad Hoc recommendations were carried out. In fifteen cases, however, the U.N. secretary-general found that the government's proposed action did not conform with the Ad Hoc recommendations.[31] These fifteen officers included the defense minister, General René Emilio Ponce, who reportedly ordered the Jesuit killings but was also considered to have played a crucial role in the peace process. It was only after the Truth Commission report was published, with its finding that Ponce had ordered the Jesuit killings, and the U.S. Congress had conditioned $11 million in aid on full implementation of the Ad Hoc recommendations that the government finally agreed to remove the disputed officers from their duties by June 30, 1993.[32]

Despite its inherent limitations and the difficulties in implementing the Ad Hoc recommendations, the Ad Hoc process constituted an unprecedented civilian evaluation of military officers. Given the brief time allowed and the limited information available to the Ad Hoc Commission, the process was inevitably incomplete. Many of the aspects criticized by the military were directly attributable to the agreement itself, which gave the Ad Hoc Commission members broad latitude in determining how to carry out their task and precluded a thorough review of all 2,000 plus active-duty officers. The Commission's recommendations had symbolic importance precisely because they reached the highest echelons of the armed forces. Instead of doing what earlier investigations on specific cases had done — affixing blame on lower-ranking officers and soldiers while leaving high-ranking officers untouched — the Ad Hoc Commission focused on Army commanders.

The Ad Hoc Commission's work contributed to cleansing the military. Yet hundreds of officers who committed serious human rights violations remain in command positions. Of particular concern are those who worked in intelligence units, which were heavily involved in death squad activities and torture. Although no long-term mechanism for cleaning out the military was established, reforms stemming from the negotiations were designed to reform the military and remove internal security functions from the armed forces.[33] Nonetheless, it remains unclear whether the military will truly limit its role and introduce adequate safeguards against human rights abuses, including discharge and prosecution in civilian courts of military personnel who violate rights.

The Truth Commission

Because the Ad Hoc Commission did not have to explain the basis for its recommendations and because its report remained confidential, it in no sense constituted a truth-telling process. During the negotiations, the parties presented different proposals for addressing the past, including lists of well-known cases that should be investigated to serve as examples. Unable to agree on the list of cases, they ultimately accepted a U.N. proposal to establish a Truth Commission to determine the official truth about the most "important acts of violence" that occurred during the war. The parties recognized the need to make the complete truth known and to strengthen "the resolve and means to establish the truth." This mechanism was designed to yield quick results "without prejudice to the obligations incumbent on the Salvadoran courts to solve such cases and impose the appropriate penalties on the culprits."[34] The final article of the agreement stated that "the provisions of this agreement shall not prevent the normal investigation of any situation or case, whether or not the Commission has investigated it, nor the application of the relevant legal provisions to acts contrary to law."

In the Chapultepec Peace Agreements, the parties specifically recognized

> the need to clarify and put an end to any indication of impunity on the part of officers of the armed forces, particularly in cases where respect for human rights is jeopardized. To that end, the Parties refer this issue to the Commission on the Truth for consideration and resolution. All of this shall be without prejudice to the principle, which the Parties also recognize, that *acts of this nature, regardless of the sector to which their perpetrators belong, must be the object of exemplary action by the law courts so that the punishment prescribed by law is meted out to those found responsible.*[35] (emphasis added)

Thus the parties explicitly recognized the need for prosecution as well as establishing and disseminating the truth about past rights violations. The apparent intent of the negotiators was not to use the Truth Commission as a substitute for judicial proceedings.[36]

Nor was the Commission to be limited by the Ad Hoc Commission's recommendations. The accords authorized the Truth Commission to have an observer to the Ad Hoc Commission and established that the Ad Hoc Commission's recommendations were without prejudice to any recommendations the Truth Commission might make.

The Truth Commission's Mandate

The Commission was given broad powers to carry out its mandate. The government and the FMLN agreed to provide full cooperation, as well as to carry out the Commission's recommendations.[37] The Mexico Agreements assigned the Truth Commission the tasks of:

- Investigating serious acts of violence that occurred since 1980 and whose impact on society urgently demands that the public should know the truth. The Commission was to take into consideration in choosing cases the "exceptional importance that may be attached to the acts to be investigated, their characteristics and impact, and the social unrest to which they gave rise" as well as the need to build confidence in the positive changes being

promoted by the peace process and to assist in the transition to national reconciliation.
- Making recommendations regarding legal, political, or administrative measures based on the results of the Commission's investigations. These recommendations could include measures designed to prevent the repetition of the
kinds of acts that occurred in the past and initiatives to promote national
reconciliation.

By giving the Commission the task of examining the most "serious acts of
violence" the parties avoided entering into a legal discussion about which acts
constitute human rights violations. The Commission's mandate was intended to
permit examination of serious acts of violence committed by government forces,
members of paramilitary groups, and insurgent forces.

The FMLN did violate international humanitarian law in various actions,
some as a result of particular policies and strategies. However, the vast majority
of violations were committed by government forces or paramilitary groups connected to the military and tolerated by the government, and were directed against
noncombatants considered to be aligned with the left. The FMLN understood that
the government would allow no accounting for the past if its own violations were
not also scrutinized. Yet the government clearly anticipated that the two parties to
the conflict would be found equally responsible — an expectation that was neither
realistic nor realized. Aside from the numerical imbalance — only 5 percent of the
cases presented to the Truth Commission were attributed to the FMLN, whereas
government forces or paramilitary groups were reported responsible for almost 85
percent — the Salvadoran state had abdicated its responsibility to prevent, investigate, and sanction these acts, much less compensate the victims. The Commission
noted the fundamental distinction in its recommendations:

> [W]ith the armed conflict at an end, it is natural that the bulk of the recommenda-
> tions, being institutional in nature, should be addressed to the official sector. The
> most crucial recommendation which would have had to be made to the FMLN
> would have been to abandon the use of arms as a means of political struggle and,
> in any case, to renounce acts and practices such as those described in this report.
> This objective has been achieved through the peace agreements and their imple-
> mentation.[38]

An International Commission

The negotiators agreed that the Truth Commission would be headed by three individuals appointed by the U.N. secretary-general. Given the extreme polarization
of Salvadoran society, many persons involved in the negotiations, particularly the
FMLN, felt that it would be virtually impossible to find three Salvadorans who
would be able to carry out this sensitive mission. Ultimately, the parties agreed to
entrust the task to foreigners. After consultation with both parties, the U.N. secretary-general named former Colombian president Belisario Betancur, former
Venezuelan foreign minister Reinaldo Figueredo, and U.S. law professor Thomas
Buergenthal to the Truth Commission. For the first time, an inquiry commission

of this kind was U.N. sponsored. To protect the Commission's independence, both in reality and in appearance, all funds and staff came from outside El Salvador. No Central Americans were included in the Commission's professional staff. Donations of $2.5 million from other countries (including $1 million from the United States) were channeled through the United Nations.[39]

The decision to have an international commission under U.N. auspices instead of a commission of national notables had several ramifications. On the negative side, foreigners, especially staff, unfamiliar with El Salvador may not have been sufficiently attuned to perceive the relative importance of certain cases and issues as well as the consequences of some of their decisions and recommendations. Unlike the intent of similar commissions in the Southern Cone, this process did not serve to bring together diverse national actors to write a common history. Moreover, the international nature of the Commission became a target of attack from quarters dissatisfied with its findings and recommendations who charged that Salvadoran sovereignty had been violated and judicial functions usurped.

Outside the country, however, and in many quarters in El Salvador, U.N. sponsorship enhanced the Commission's credibility. Precisely because they were outsiders, the three commissioners and their staff could ask hard questions and push to get information on cases in a way that would have been difficult for Salvadorans or those closer to the conflict. Their efforts were strengthened by their U.N. status, which led many people to come forward who had never presented their testimony to national human rights groups. The sponsorship of the United Nations and international involvement increased the likelihood that international actors would press for compliance with the Commission's recommendations.

Methodology

The Truth Commission undertook to establish the truth about the violence that occurred in El Salvador during twelve years of war. With a six-month mandate to carry out its enormous task, the Commission could investigate only a sampling of the tens of thousands of cases that occurred during the war. The Commission received testimonies from more than 2,000 people about violations involving more than 7,000 victims. The Commission devoted much of its energy to investigating a smaller group of cases chosen either because of their serious repercussions or as illustrations of practices.

The commissioners and their staff interviewed hundreds of witnesses or individuals who might have had information about specific cases or practices, including victims, military men of all ranks, FMLN members, lawyers and court personnel, and government officials and employees. They also collected information from a variety of sources, which included human rights groups inside and outside El Salvador, Salvadoran institutions, and foreign governments and agencies.

Unlike prior commissions of inquiry, the Truth Commission focused on assigning individual responsibility for violations through findings of fact. The Commission stressed that responsibility should fall not on the institution but on those who committed violent acts, who being in a position to take preventive or investigative action failed to do so, who took steps to cover up criminal deeds, or who themselves gave the order that led to the respective action.[40] The Commission reasoned that the peace accords made very clear that the Truth Commission was created because the full truth must be made known, which necessarily implied naming the persons responsible

> where there is reliable testimony available, especially when the persons identified occupy senior positions and perform official functions directly related to violations or the cover-up of violations. Not to name names would reinforce the very impunity to which the parties instructed the Commission to put an end.[41]

The Salvadoran government opposed the decision to publish the names and engaged in a diplomatic offensive to convince the United Nations to omit them, or at least to delay publication of the report until after the March 1994 elections.[42] Despite these efforts, the Commission published the results of its investigation of some thirty cases. In roughly half those cases, the Commission found sufficient evidence to name individuals found to have committed, ordered, or covered up the acts investigated. Some forty military officers were named. Six leaders of the People's Revolutionary Army (ERP), one of the five component organizations of the FMLN, were named as responsible for implementing a policy of killing mayors in areas under FMLN control. Others named included civil defensemen, judges, an Army lawyer, and several other civilians. Although it emphasized that civilians, along with members of the military, plotted and carried out death squad killings, the report named few of the civilians involved. Nor did it examine the role of the United States.

The Commission was not and was never intended to be a tribunal with full due process guarantees. In explaining its work, the Commission emphasized that it was not a judicial or quasijudicial body, which could determine legal rights or obligations. Due process protections such as disclosing the identity of witnesses or permitting the accused to confront them were denied because witnesses in El Salvador still risk reprisals and fear for their safety. The peace agreement authorized the Commission to carry out its activities on a confidential basis and to use any sources of information it deemed useful and reliable.[43]

In arriving at its findings and naming the persons responsible, the Commission considered no single source or witness sufficiently reliable to establish the truth about any question of fact necessary to allow the Commission to reach a conclusion.[44] In other words, perpetrators were named only when multiple sources or witnesses had confirmed their role. Still, the criteria for naming some names and omitting others has raised questions, especially since the sources relied on were not identified.

The Truth Commission's work was inevitably incomplete. Time and the availability of information precluded a thorough review of the thousands of human rights cases that occurred in El Salvador during the war. The Commission denounced the "destruction or concealment of documents, or the failure to divulge the locations where numerous persons were imprisoned or bodies were buried." It noted that it "will be up to those who administer the new system of justice to pursue these investigations and take whatever final decisions they consider appropriate at this moment in history."[45]

The Commission's Recommendations

The Commission recommended a series of measures under four headings:

1. Those arising directly from the results of the Commission's investigations: dismissal of persons found responsible for violations from the armed forces and civil service; the drafting of a law to disqualify those named from holding public office for at least ten years and bar them permanently from positions in national defense and public security; judicial reform, including the voluntary resignation of the current Supreme Court to permit election of new justices, as set forth in the negotiated constitutional reforms, and a thorough evaluation of all sitting judges.

2. Eradication of structural causes linked directly to the acts investigated: reforms in the armed forces and those in charge of public security, and an investigation of illegal groups (death squads) as a necessary preventive step.

3. Institutional reforms to prevent the repetition of these acts: judicial reform, including constitutional reforms to end the concentration of power in the Supreme Court and transfer authority to name lower court judges to the National Council on the Judiciary; and measures to enhance human rights protection, including strengthening the new ombudsmen's office; making the remedies of *amparo* and habeas corpus truly effective, implementing the recommendations made by ONUSAL's Human Rights Division, changing the system for administrative detentions, ratifying international human rights instruments, and accepting the compulsory jurisdiction of the Inter-American Court on Human Rights.

4. Measures for national reconciliation: material compensation for victims, from a fund to be created by using 1 percent of foreign assistance, and moral compensation.

Recommendations ranged from highly specific to very general and called for action by the judiciary, the legislature, COPAZ,[46] the executive branch, and, in a few instances, the FMLN. The substantial number of recommendations regarding the judicial system reflected the Commission's view of its central role in perpetuating impunity.

Prosecutions

The Salvadoran experience raises the question of how countries with a weak and compromised judiciary can prosecute past violations. The Truth Commission stopped short of recommending prosecutions because of the unreliability of the existing judiciary. The legal system in general and the judiciary in particular were indicted as major contributing factors to rampant impunity. The report singled out Supreme Court president Mauricio Gutiérrez Castro for criticism, particularly his improper interference in the El Mozote massacre case. The Commission suggested that without a drastic overhaul of the judiciary, prosecutions might be counterproductive and would be unlikely to achieve fair results.

The Commission made clear its view that the persons responsible for human rights violations should be tried and punished. In one case, the Las Hojas massacre, it endorsed the recommendations of the Inter-American Commission on Human Rights, which called on the government to prosecute and punish the persons responsible for the 1983 killings, despite a 1987 amnesty law.[47] Still, the report failed to call for prosecutions in the other cases it examined. Nor did it specifically exclude the possibility of an amnesty.

The Truth Commission was undeniably accurate in its assessment that prosecutions were unlikely and untenable under current conditions. Nonetheless, human rights groups questioned the Truth Commission's decision not to recommend prosecutions, noting that it missed an opportunity to call for the application of principles of international law.[48] To a large degree, the Commission accepted that its task had become a substitute for judicial action, despite the contrary language of the peace accords. It left open the possibility of prosecutions in the future, once the judicial system was prepared to handle them. Its position seemed calculated to focus attention on judicial malfeasance and the urgent need for fundamental judicial reform. By failing to call for prosecutions or advising against an immediate amnesty, however, it may have facilitated early passage of a comprehensive amnesty decree.

Reaction to the Report

The Truth Commission's findings and recommendations won little favor in government and military circles. Members of the government's negotiating team made it clear that the Commission had not done what they had anticipated. The government's head negotiator and minister of the presidency, Dr. Oscar Santamaria, termed the report "not serious, not complete . . . not balanced. It is an insult to Salvadoran society and very explosive."[49] He noted that "We did not want these gentlemen . . . to come and propose situations that would destabilize institutions and the system."[50] The military's representative on the negotiating team found the report "biased, incomplete, unfair, totally unacceptable."[51] Defense minister Ponce, in an unusual nationally televised appearance of the High Command, flanked by other military commanders, said the report "exceeded the authority" granted in the peace agreements and "invaded the constitutional field, the authority of government institutions, and the fair administration of justice." Ponce denounced the report as "unjust, incomplete, illegal, unethical, partisan, and insolent."[52]

The Commission's focus on the failings — and complicity — of the judicial system was unexpected and hit a raw nerve. The Supreme Court rejected the Commission's conclusions and recommendations as "harmful to the dignity of the administration of justice in El Salvador in general, and in particular, against the president of the Supreme Court of Justice, Mauricio Gutiérrez Castro."[53] The military and government representatives argued that the Commission had not devoted the same attention to FMLN cases and practices as it had to those in which the armed forces were implicated.[54] The suggestion that the Supreme Court justices voluntarily step down to facilitate the process of reform established in the peace accords met with a particularly virulent reaction. Supreme Court president Gutiér-rez Castro responded that "only God" could remove him from his post before the end of his term.[55] The Supreme Court president went so far as to term the decision to create the Truth Commission a "stupidity."[56]

Although government officials, members of the ruling party, and military officers rejected and attacked the report, a public opinion poll conducted in June 1993 indicated wide acceptance of the Commission's findings. The poll, carried out by the Public Opinion Institute of the Central American University (UCA), found that 45 percent of the Salvadorans questioned were satisfied with the Truth Commission's report and 27 percent were dissatisfied. Three fourths of those polled favored the removal from office of officials found to have violated human rights.[57] However, the failure of the report to name the civilians who financed the death squads was widely criticized.[58]

Internationally, the report was well received, with its findings and recommendations widely accepted. Although the report itself said little about the U.S. role in tolerating or covering up abuses, it sparked renewed concern in Washington about U.S. policy and actions during the war years. Some congressional outrage seemed disingenuous given the considerable information available to U.S. policy makers when the events examined by the Truth Commission occurred.[59] Since then, the United States, upon congressional urging, has declassified documents detailing U.S. knowledge of high-ranking government participation in death squads.[60] A July 1993 report commissioned by the State Department, nonetheless, was mild in its critique of past U.S. actions.[61]

Amnesty

Three days after the Truth Commission report was published, President Cristiani called for a general amnesty, noting that the report did "not respond to the wishes of the majority of Salvadorans who seek to forgive and forget everything having to do with that very sorrowful past."[62] Only five days after the publication of the report and over the objection of opposition forces, the governing ARENA party pushed through the Assembly an immediate and sweeping amnesty law.[63] Within days, the amnesty was applied to free, among others, the two officers convicted for the Jesuit murders.[64]

Decree 486 granted unconditional amnesty for political crimes, common crimes connected to political crimes, and common crimes in which more than twenty persons took part. In addition to the crimes usually considered to be political, the law includes a series of crimes against the justice system, such as judicial resolutions that knowingly disregard the law or the facts and inadequate representation of clients. This unusual extension of the concept of political crimes reflects the Truth Commission's emphasis on the judiciary's complicity in the massive rights violations that occurred during the war. The amnesty law provided for the extinction of civil as well as criminal responsibility. The law also superseded an amnesty law passed at the time of the peace accords.[65]

The issue of amnesty was not specifically addressed in the peace accords.[66] Because of the immediate need to legalize the situation of FMLN leaders who were returning to the country and would be involved in implementing the peace accords, on January 23, 1992 the political parties rushed through a National Reconciliation Law. At the time, the governing ARENA party expressed its view that a total amnesty was needed: National reconciliation required forgetting and forgiving. Any attempt to prosecute past rights violations, the party said, would destabilize the peace process. Opposition parties urged exempting certain kinds of crimes from the amnesty law. The compromise agreement that was ultimately reached amounted to a delayed general amnesty. It excluded from its benefits:

1. Persons convicted by juries, to prevent the release of the two officers convicted four months earlier for the killing of the six Jesuit priests, their housekeeper, and the housekeeper's daughter.
2. Persons named in the Truth Commission report as being responsible for serious human rights violations, to allow the Truth Commission to carry out its work before the application of amnesty in all cases. The amnesty law was passed on January 23, 1992, whereas the Truth Commission report was not made public until March 15, 1993.

The same article that provided for these exceptions established that the legislature could overrule the exceptions six months after the Truth Commission issued its report.[67] Human rights groups objected to the law, which permitted amnesty for crimes that cannot be granted amnesty under international law. Even the exceptions to the 1992 amnesty were explicitly overruled by the 1993 law, which eliminated the six-month waiting period for legislative action.

The U.N. secretary-general expressed concern about the immediate sweeping amnesty and said that it would have been preferable to have achieved a broad degree of national consensus before approving an amnesty law.[68] A public opinion poll conducted by the Jesuit Central American University in June 1993 found strong public sentiment against the amnesty law (55.5 percent), with 77 percent of persons polled favoring punishment of the individuals who violated rights.[69] Amnesty International called for immediate repeal of the law.[70] The Inter-American Commission on Human Rights in February 1994 found the Salvadoran amnesty to be a violation of El Salvador's commitments under the American Convention on Human Rights "regardless of any necessity that the peace negotiations might pose." It found the amnesty unlawful

> because it makes possible a "reciprocal amnesty" without first acknowledging responsibility (despite the recommendations of the Truth Commission); because it applies to crimes against humanity, and because it eliminates any possibility of obtaining adequate pecuniary compensation, primarily for victims.[71]

Salvadoran human rights groups petitioned the Supreme Court to declare the law unconstitutional on a number of grounds.[72] Among the provisions challenged was the extension of the concept of political crime to include crimes against judicial actions and "those committed because or as a result of the armed conflict, without taking into consideration the condition, membership status, affiliation, or political ideology."[73] These extensions have no basis in the constitutional authorization for granting amnesty.[74] The Salvadoran human rights groups argued that the amnesty decree deprived victims and their relatives of their rights to seek legal redress for human rights violations, of the state's protection, and of their right to know the truth. The Salvadoran Constitution includes guarantees of judicial protection, due process, and the right to seek compensation. It also imposes special responsibilities on public officials, civilian and military, to report "official crimes" committed by their subordinates or to face sanctions for cover-ups.[75] Along the same lines, the Salvadoran Constitution does not permit amnesty for civilian or military officials who committed constitutional crimes during President Cristiani's term.[76] Moreover, the amnesty plainly violated El Salvador's obligations under international conventions to which it is a party. These obligations, according to article 144 of the Constitution, supersede Salvadoran laws.

The constitutional chamber of the Salvadoran Supreme Court avoided these constitutional challenges by ruling that the amnesty was a political question outside its realm.[77] The Court thus abdicated its constitutional role of reviewing the legality of the terms and scope of any amnesty.

Barring repeal by a future legislature or a finding of unconstitutionality by the new Supreme Court, the amnesty has effectively blunted the Truth Commission's role, turning its findings into a substitute for judicial action. This leaves El Salvador with some measure of truth and reinforcement of the notion that justice is not yet possible.

Implementation of the Truth Commission's Recommendations

In evaluating the implementation of the Truth Commission's recommendations, it is important to keep in mind that the ARENA government's domestic political mandate was for continuity, with the least number of changes possible to end the war and disarm the FMLN. Thus, implementing the Ad Hoc and Truth Commission's recommendations—especially when these were perceived as going beyond what was agreed to in the negotiations—was not high on President Cristiani's agenda nor that of his successor, Armando Calderon Sol. Indeed the government's reluctance to implement key Truth Commission recommendations contributed to the appearance that it had flatly rejected the report.

Initially, the Salvadoran government disputed the applicability of the Commission's recommendations. The U.N. secretary-general reminded the parties that the recommendations were binding on them. The only exception cited by the United Nations was the recommendation that would legally disqualify the persons named in the report from holding public office because that recommendation apparently contradicted the Salvadoran Constitution. Nonetheless, the United Nations suggested that implementation could be achieved through a political decision—that is, voluntary recusals by those implicated or by their parties.[78]

After an exchange of opinions between the Salvadoran government and U.N. officials, President Cristiani raised the strongest reservations about those recommendations that (1) involved dismissal from public service and disqualification from holding public office; (2) required constitutional reforms; and (3) the judicial branch would have to implement.[79] The government has also been unwilling to accept the compulsory jurisdiction of the Inter-American Human Rights Court.

The Truth Commission's findings were important in assuring President Cristiani's belated compliance with the Ad Hoc Commission's recommendations. Yet the government was unwilling to discharge eight military officers named by the Truth Commission who remained on active duty after implementation of the Ad Hoc recommendations. Government officials argued that those named were denied due process and that requiring their discharge exceeded the authority of the Truth Commission (and was an issue put to rest by implementation of the the Ad Hoc Commission recommendations).

Nor have the civilians cited for their role in blocking investigations been dismissed from public service. The civilian Army lawyer found to have been instrumental in the Jesuit case cover-up subsequently represented the government in COPAZ. The Supreme Court conducted its own investigation and exonerated a judge and a forensics official who were found by the Truth Commission to have covered up or failed to investigate properly an extrajudicial execution.[80] The Salvadoran government nominated then-Supreme Court president Gutiérrez Castro to the OAS Inter-American Juridical Committee, a prestigious post.[81]

Despite the government's initial rejection of many key recommendations, some of these had a profound influence on subsequent developments. Although not binding on the government and rejected by the members of the Court, the recommendation urging the Supreme Court to resign ensured that Supreme Court President Gutiérrez Castro and his fellow justices would not be elected to the new Court chosen in June 1994 under the new constitutional formula. The Truth Commission's condemnation of the judicial system and the new mechanisms for electing justices established in the Peace Accords led to an unprecedented effort to appoint respected lawyers from across the political spectrum, the majority of whom had no known party affiliation. The new Court, in turn, recognized that it faced the challenge of cleaning out the judiciary and confronting impunity.

Several of the Commission's recommendations to reform the judicial system implied constitutional reforms to end the dangerous concentration of powers in the Supreme Court. The Commission called for ending the concentration of functions in the Supreme Court and its president; transferring the power to appoint and remove judges to the National Council on the Judiciary; establishing an independent body to authorize and regulate the legal profession; ending the Supreme Court's exclusive jurisdiction over habeas corpus and *amparo*. The government initially showed little enthusiasm for further constitutional reforms (beyond those agreed to in the peace negotiations). President Cristiani pointed out that the executive branch lacked authority to initiate constitutional reforms, while key legislators maintained that constitutional reforms negotiated between the government and the FMLN in April 1991 and the then-imminent March 1994 elections precluded further reforms.

Because constitutional reforms must be passed and ratified by two successive legislatures, the U.N. Secretary General stressed the urgency of initiating action as a new legislature would take office on May 1, 1994. Under pressure from the United Nations, the Cristiani government maintained its public opposition to constitutional reforms while it authorized an effort to draft a packet of proposed reforms that included the issues raised by the Truth Commission. The proposed reforms were not presented to the legislature until after the second round of elections on April 20, 1994, leaving a very short time for discussion. COPAZ also reached an agreement on key constitutional reforms, yet forces opposed to limiting the powers of the Supreme Court succeeded in blocking approval of those reforms that would have transferred power for naming judges to the National Council on the Judiciary. The reforms ultimately approved by the outgoing legislature did little to lessen the concentration of power in the Supreme Court, although they did establish a separate body to oversee the legal profession and broaden jurisdiction over habeas corpus petitions. Due process protections were also strengthened. As of December 1994 these reforms had not been ratified by the new Assembly. The election in June 1994 of a far more independent Court, committed to reforming the judiciary, raised hopes that the grim situation highlighted by the Truth Commission might nonetheless begin to change.

The need to investigate illegal groups operating in the country became increasingly evident in late 1993 because of an increase in apparently politically motivated attacks and death squad actions, particularly against FMLN leaders and former combatants.[82] These attacks and the lack of effective investigations threatened the stability of the peace process. Initially reluctant to form a new body to investigate these crimes, the Cristiani government finally agreed, under heavy pressure from the United Nations, to the formation of a Joint Working Group in late 1993 after two ranking FMLN leaders had been murdered. Composed of the Human Rights Ombudsman, two independent representatives of the government, and the director of ONUSAL's Human Rights Division, the Joint Working Group was charged with investigating politically motivated illegal armed groups after the signing of the peace accords. The Joint Group's report, published in July 1994,[83] stressed the need for enhanced investigative efforts by Salvadoran institutions — notably the new civilian police, the state prosecutor's office and the judiciary — to combat politically motivated and organized crime. Its report did not name names, instead providing to the president and a few other government officials an additional appendix with confidential information obtained in the course of the Working Group's investigations. While it has become well recognized that impunity continues in El Salvador and that those responsible for organized crime can be found in the military, the police, the government, and the ARENA party, there is still a total unwillingness to look at the past or any connections between current criminal activity and former death squad structures.

No steps have been taken to implement the Truth Commission's recommendation to establish a compensation fund for victims. Given the magnitude of the losses suffered during the war and the potential difficulties of establishing criteria for compensation, it is unclear how much compensation can realistically be expected. Nor has the government undertaken any effort to rehabilitate the victims or create the kind of memorial that could provide some moral compensation.

Much will depend on the extent to which civil society takes up the issues addressed in the Truth Commission report, and insists on further implementation of the recommendations and on related measures to combat impunity that go beyond the Commission's recommendations. The international community has an important role to play in this regard given its involvement in the resolution of the

Salvadoran conflict. Indeed, United Nations pressure has been behind most recommendations implemented, even those ostensibly required by the peace accords. Yet if the degree of compliance with the report's recommendations depends on international pressure, Salvadorans will once again see that action on human rights issues comes only in response to international pressure. Thus, a crucial challenge confronting El Salvador as the United Nations prepares to depart is for Salvadoran institutions and actors within and outside the government to assume the watchdog function currently played by the United Nations and to insist on full compliance with the peace accords and the establishment of the rule of law.

The FMLN — and indeed the UN — placed top priority on structural changes agreed to in the peace negotiations. Among the most important of these was the replacement of military security forces by a new civilian police force. This ambitious undertaking has encountered a series of obstacles,[84] yet if it were ultimately implemented as foreseen in the peace accords, it stands to establish an independent, professional police force capable of investigating crimes and protecting the public. In late 1993, failure to adhere to established guidelines designed to prevent the militarization of the new civilian force, including the incorporation of former military and security force personnel without adequate screening or training threatened to pervert the effort. Under new leadership appointed by President Calderon Sol in June 1994, an effort to rectify some of the principal problems pointed out by the U.N. was initiated. These changes reflect an increased societal awareness of the need for a reliable independent police force not linked to former military security forces, whose members have themselves been implicated in criminal activities. Nonetheless, in late 1994 ONUSAL reported increasing complaints about the new police force and an uneven track record of dealing with abuses.[85]

The new office of the Ombudsman for Human Rights has been slow to establish a strong presence in the country and faces the daunting task of assuming many of ONUSAL's Human Rights Division's tasks as the U.N. withdraws from El Salvador. Both the Truth Commission and ONUSAL have made important recommendations on ways to fully implement the steps designed to protect human rights and promote judicial reform included in the peace accords, as well as additional measures needed to create an effective and independent judiciary and a professional and independent criminal investigative capacity.

The peace accords thus foresaw that impunity is overcome by holding past violators accountable *and* by taking steps to ensure that their actions cannot be repeated. Past violators have not been, nor apparently will they be, held accountable. No political force in El Salvador currently advocates prosecuting those responsible for past violations, although how important the issue is to civil society is hard to detect. Institution building and strengthening will be effective, however, only in a climate conducive to the rule of law, one in which those who violate human rights are prosecuted and sanctioned and victims can seek legal redress.

The United Nations, through ONUSAL, the Truth Commission, and independent expert Pedro Nikken as of September 1994 continued to emphasize that the Salvadoran institutions still do not fulfill their obligation to guarantee human rights — an obligation overtly recognized in the peace accords. Salvadoran public opinion resoundingly confirms how much remains to be done: Only 5 percent of the Salvadorans polled in a the June 1993 UCA survey believed that impunity no longer exists in El Salvador; and 46 percent said impunity continues as before.[86]

ONUSAL reports continue to emphasize that crimes are rarely properly investigated and still more rarely result in punishment for those found responsible. It remains to be seen whether sufficient political will exists to effect necessary changes such as: rectifying serious problems in the National Civilian Police and providing necessary training and oversight; profoundly reforming the judiciary starting with a thorough evaluation of all sitting judges; approving and implementing law reforms; creating an effective, law-abiding, independent criminal investigative capacity; making the Ombudsman's office an effective oversight/protective institution.

As other countries undergo negotiated transitions to end internal conflicts, they are bound to confront many of the difficulties faced by El Salvador in coming to terms with the past. The specificity of the Salvadoran situation should not be overlooked in applying the lessons learned elsewhere. The obstacles to overcoming impunity encountered in El Salvador — despite a detailed negotiated agreement that included measures to address this key problem — highlight the tremendous complexity of this urgent task.

IV

CASE STUDIES: AFRICA AND ASIA

16

Overview

Naomi Roht-Arriaza

Africa

The late 1980s and early 1990s have seen a spate of African countries move from one-party or military rule to governments resulting from multiparty, contested elections. In some cases efforts to democratize have been thwarted by recalcitrant military establishments; in others ethnic or tribal tensions or economic problems have pushed newly elected governments toward repeating some of the human rights abuses of the past. The new governments have faced the issues of investigating and prosecuting the perpetrators of past human rights violations and of compensating their victims in situations of continuing political instability. The responses of the new regimes have varied; in many countries the new government has granted an amnesty covering all acts of the former ruler and/or his supporters. In Benin, for example, ex-President Mathieu Kerekou, whose government was accused of torture and the killing of prisoners, was nonetheless granted personal immunity.[1] In the Congo, the National Conference held in February 1991 declared a general amnesty for political crimes or human rights violations. On the other hand, other countries have taken steps to investigate, although only a few have prosecuted. Some of the more important experiences are summarized below. The cases of Zimbabwe and South Africa are considered in separate chapters. That of Rwanda is too recent to be dealt with adequately here, although international efforts to prosecute genocide arc touched on in the concluding chapter.

Uganda

Up to 800,000 people disappeared in Uganda between 1962 and 1986 as a result of civil wars and dictatorships, including the notorious rules of Idi Amin and Milton Obote. In 1986, the National Resistance Movement, headed by President Yoweri Museveni, came to power. One of the new government's first acts was to establish a Commission of Inquiry into Violations of Human Rights. The five commissioners, supported by a fifty-person staff, include two lawyers, a doctor, a historian, and a farmer/writer; two are members of Parliament.[2] The Commission's mandate is to

> inquire into all aspects of violations of human rights, breaches of the Rule of Law and excessive abuses of power, committed against persons in Uganda by the regimes in government, their servants agents or agencies whatsoever called, during the period from 9th day of October 1962 and to the 25th day of January 1986, and possible ways of preventing the recurrence of the aforesaid matters.[3]

The Commission, established by decree, was to pay special attention to cases of mass murder and arbitrary execution, arbitrary arrests and detention, denial of a public trial, torture, expulsion, official discrimination, and the "extent to which the State security agencies may have interfered with the funcitoning of the law-enforcement agents," as well as "the protection by act or omission of any person that perpetrated any of the aforesaid things from due process of law." Power to call witnesses and ask for production of evidence was granted. The decree also provided due process protections for anyone who "in the opinion of the Commissioners is adversely affected by the evidence given before the Commission"; such persons were to be given an opportunity to be heard and to cross-examine the person giving the adverse evidence, unless the commissioners found that departure from such procedures was essential. Given the existence of these safeguards, the Commission has "named names" of a number of people, including members of the current Parliament and well-known public figures. According to press reports, ex-dictator Amin has agreed to testify before the Commission in the near future on his role in killings and disappearances.

Although the decree called for the Commission to report with "all due diligence and speed," no fixed time limit was set. The Commission's work has now entered its eighth year without a final report. In part this is due to the thoroughness with which the Commission has approached its broad mandate: The decree establishing it was widely circulated in local languages; public, televised hearings were held on representative cases in each of thirty-three districts; and voluminous testimony has been compiled and tabulated. In part the delays are also due to a lack of resources and may also reflect some fear on the part of the government that a final report will exacerbate regional or ethnic tensions or will implicate figures close to the current government.

In addition to the Commission, several ad hoc commissions have been set up to investigate cases of Army abuses in areas of continuing civil conflict, but almost all of their reports remain secret. Few prosecutions for human rights violations have taken place, with the exception of three top officials of the Amin government. In June 1993 a former Army commander and provincial administrator under Amin was convicted for a 1972 arrest and murder.[4] On the other hand, several persons implicated in torture or massacres not only have not been indicted but continue in 1994 to hold high positions in Parliament or government, again in part because of fears that prosecutions will fuel ethnic- or region-based opposition to the current government.

Chad

The government of President Idriss Deby has named several investigatory commissions since coming to power in December 1990. One commission focused on the crimes of former president Hissein Habre, finding that during the Habre regime more than 40,000 people died in prison or were executed.[5] Another was empaneled in November 1991 after international pressure was brought to bear to look into repression by the military forces of the current government against the Hadjeray ethnic group. Although it was to report within two months, a year later little testimony had been received, none of it from the military. A third commission, which included the Minister of Interior and an adviser to the president, was charged with investigating massacres in the Logone Oriental region, an area in which antigovernment insurgents operate. The investigatory mission blamed civilian and military authorities for the massacres, specifically naming the commanders of the local military region, a number of soldiers, the subprefect, and the public prosecutor of the area. The delegation called for dismissal of all the military commanders involved, prosecutions, and replacement of the military by the *gendarmerie* in the area. However, to date the government has apparently not acted on these recommendations.[6]

In Chad, as in Uganda, one of the main problems in obtaining a complete and authoritative inquiry stems from conditions of continuing ethnic unrest, which limit the commissions' freedom of action, lead to continuing violations, and make any conclusions less authoritative.

Mali

On February 13, 1993, ex-president Moussa Traore, who had ruled Mali for twenty-three years with military backing, was found guilty of mass murder and sentenced to death.[7] Convicted along with Traore were three high-ranking military officers: his defense and interior ministers and the ex-Army chief under his government. Twenty-eight other officials accused of complicity were acquitted. A seven-judge panel, after a ten-week trial marred by threats against the defendants and their lawyers, found the four responsible for ordering security forces to fire on opposition demonstrators in March 1991, killing 106 people. Traore was overthrown soon afterward, and his successor was replaced by an elected president. In addition to the case brought by the state, some 430 private individuals filed civil suits against Traore and his co-defendants, which were joined to the state's case.

The military officer who overthrew Traore, Lieutenant Colonel Amadou Toumani Toure, warned Malians not to try to avenge their martyrs, but added that "we will never stop paying tribute to their memory" and that "whoever caused their loss" should be fairly tried and punished.[8]

Traore argued that he did not order the shootings but found out about them only after the fact and that only those who actually opened fire should be tried.

The death sentences were upheld by the Supreme Court in May 1993. In addition, several other high-ranking officials of the former regime are to be tried for economic crimes.[9]

Ethiopia

As in Nicaragua, the current government came to power after a complete military victory in a bloody civil war. The previous regime of President Mengistu Haile Mariam had been responsible for the deaths of hundreds of thousands of people through deliberate starvation and mass killings known as the "Red Terror." The transitional government demobilized the former Army, disbanded the security forces, and detained thousands of members of the Army, police, security forces, and the former ruling party and civil service. Although most of these people were released following scrutiny of their record, some 1,000 remain detained, and arrests continue as new evidence is discovered.

The government created a Special Prosecutor's Office (SPO) to investigate and charge detainees from the former regime. Its mandate is to investigate and prosecute "any person having committed or responsible for the commission of an offence by abusing his position in the party, the government or mass organizations under the Dergue-WPE regime."[10] The detainees are to by tried by the ordinary courts.

The detainees fall into several categories: some are military officers who allegedly ordered the summary execution of political opponents; others are soldiers and officers who allegedly bombed (or ordered the bombing) of civilian areas and burned crops in violation of the Geneva Conventions. About 70% of the detainees are mid-level officials of the *kebele* (local peasant or neighborhood groups created by the Mengistu government). These are thought to have participated in the "Red Terror," in which thousands of people were killed or disappeared, as well as in war crimes or the misuse of food aid and the forced relocation, through starvation, of parts of the population.[11]

Delays in setting up, funding and organizing the SPO have resulted in serious due process problems. By the time the SPO was established, some ex-officials had been jailed for 18 months without charges. The Central High Court heard over 1,300 habeas corpus petitions and ordered nearly 200 of the detainess released on bail or unconditionally. The SPO released another 900 or so on its own. However, a newly created legal loophole allows the SPO to detain the ex-officials indefinitely without charge or trial. While originally promising that charges would be filed by June 1994 with trials to start shortly thereafter, by December charges had been filed only against 73 defendants.[12]

This first batch of defendants is composed of high-level Mengistu officials. They have been charged both under Article 281 of the Ethiopian 1957 Penal Code, which includes crimes against humanity and genocide, as well as directly under the United Nations Genocide Convention. The Special Prosecutor's Office also filed charges of aggravated homicide and homicide in the first degree under Ethiopian law and indicated it will add new charges for war crimes and related offenses. Article 281 of the Penal Code contains an expanded definition of genocide: Unlike the international convention, it covers intent to destroy political groups as well as racial and religious ones. It also covers "the compulsory movement or dispersion of peoples or children, or their placing under living conditions calculated to result in their death or disappearance."[13]

The SPO has gathered tens of thousands of documents and conducted over 5,000 witness interviews. Unlike other countries where many of the orders given were unwritten or indirect, the Mengistu regime kept careful records that have been collected, organized and fed into a computer database. In addition, domestic and international forensic teams have uncovered mass graves, and that evidence too will be available at trial.[14]

The sheer number of potential defendants and volume of evidence may overwhelm Ethiopia's justice system. When and if trials do occur, many of the attorneys will be inexperienced, some fresh out of law school, as will be many judges. They will be called on to apply difficult concepts of international as well as domestic law. In addition, Ethiopia has no tradition of plea bargaining, which might reduce the load on both the SPO and the judiciary.[15]

In addition to criminal prosecutions, the transitional government denied the right to vote and to stand for election to members of the former ruling party and has dismissed judges who were party members. The government justified the dismissals on grounds both that the judges might undermine reform efforts and that the public would have no confidence in the judiciary if it were not purged. About half the country's Supreme Court and appellate judges were dismissed, making the normal function of the judiciary more difficult.[16]

If all the detainees are eventually charged and tried, Ethiopia will become the site of the largest human rights/war crimes trials since World War II. A combination of the complete defeat and disbanding of the pro-Mengistu Army and political structure, the existence of well-preserved evidence of chains of command and of criminal orders, some international funding and technical help, and the political will of both the new government and of local non-governmental organizations make successful investigations and prosecutions more likely. These advantages could, however, be overwhelmed by continuing delays and problems regarding the due process rights of detainees. That would be a shame for both the long-suffering Ethiopian people and for the international community.

Asia

The Asian case studies in this volume represent different types of incomplete transitions from a repressive, authoritarian government to a more open and representative one. In the Philippines, the indebtedness of Corazon Aquino's government to sectors of the Army for turning against Ferdinand Marcos and, later, for holding off coup attempts, hobbled any attempts by those both within her government and in the human rights community to come to terms with the violations of the Marcos era. Ironically, it may be the case against Marcos in U.S. courts that — despite its limitations — provides the best measure of both redress and truth telling for the Filipino people. The complexities of settling accounts in the context of internationally brokered peace negotiations are well illustrated by the Cambodian experience with the leaders of the former government of Democratic Kampuchea.

Similar variants have taken place elsewhere in Asia. The Nepalese experience is another example of an incomplete process of coming to terms with the past. That of Bangladesh after its independence war provides insight into the problems of dealing with genocide in the aftermath of war or civil conflict. In other notorious situations, little has been done to come to terms with past violations.

In the Japanese case, for example, after World War II some twenty-five former leaders, including ten from the military, were convicted by the International Military Tribunal for the Far East of waging aggressive war, and another some 5,500 Japanese were tried by Allied Military Commissions for war crimes.[17] Nonetheless, Japan has been slow to recognize and make reparations for its acts during the war. The war crimes trials, conducted with glaring lapses of due process and without any acknowledgment of Allied responsibility for civilian deaths, created scarce moral opprobrium for those convicted.[18] Especially notorious has been the failure to acknowledge and redress the forced abduction and enslavement of hundreds of Korean "comfort women." Only after intense international pressure did the Japanese government, in 1993, even recognize that the women had been enlisted against their will. While the Japanese government has offered one billion dollars in cultural and student exchanges as atonement, it has to date refused to pay direct compensation to the women.[19]

Bangladesh

In 1971, a civil war in East Pakistan led to the declaration of independence of the territory now known as Bangladesh. During the conflict, which ended with Indian Army intervention, some one million people were reportedly killed.[20] Soon after, the new Bangladeshi government passed a law entitled "an Act to provide for the detention, prosecution and punishment of persons for genocide, crimes against humanity, war crimes and other crimes under international law." Special tribunals were established to try Bangladeshi citizens who had collaborated with the Pakistani armed forces, and India and Bangladesh agreed to bring criminal charges under the act against some 195 Pakistanis held by India as prisoners of war. Pakistan objected to the trial of its nationals, arguing that under the Genocide Convention it had jurisdiction to try any violators in its own courts; it also stated that "the extreme emotionally charged situation" in Bangladesh made a "competent tribunal" impossible to find there. The parties eventually brought the question of India's detention of Pakistani war criminals to the International Court of Justice, but the case was never decided because a political agreement was eventually reached. As a result of the settlement, Pakistan recognized Bangladesh, and in exchange India returned the detainees, including those accused of genocide. The question of accountability had been sacrificed to what the Indian government saw as larger political objectives. Nonetheless, the Bangladeshi experience is one of the few post-World War II attempts to prosecute either genocide or crimes against humanity.

Nepal

Prior to April 1990, Nepal was ruled by individual edict, not by rule of law. The 1962 Constitution of Nepal vested all powers in the king, with the crown the sole source of power for all branches of the government. The king ruled through peremptory command, which could override any law, even the Constitution. The independence of the judiciary was effectively limited by such royal supremacy.

Nepal's legislature also failed to assert any independence from the royal edicts. Although the Parliament was elected, it merely served as a rubber stamp for carrying out the royal decisions. Members were elected on the understanding that they would carry out policy directives elaborated in the name of the king.

The lack of independence of the various branches of government and the prevalence of a heavy-handed monarchy combined effectively to deprive the Nepali people of their individual and collective rights. A variety of laws were enacted that restricted civil liberties, including the Public Security Act of 1989, Offenses Against the State (Punishment) Act of 1989, and the destructive Crimes (Special Control and Punishment) Act of 1985. This act provided for six-month detention with no charges, for secret trials, and for the death penalty.

This situation allowed the government to infringe continually upon the human rights of the Nepali people. After Nepal had suffered the excesses of non-democratic, monarchy-dominated rule for thirty years, a movement began for the restoration of democracy. The movement continued for eight weeks, culminating on April 6, 1990, when people took to the streets in defiance of the king and his government. Tens of thousands of people came out to demand multiparty democracy and human rights. The police opened fire on the crowds as they sought to reach the royal palace, Darbar Marga. Hundreds were killed in the fight for democracy.

After the populist protest, the transition to democracy continued on the political level. Two weeks later, a final settlement was reached between King Birewandra and the leaders of the Nepali Congress and the United Left Front. On April 19, 1990 the king accepted the resignation of Lokendra Bahadur Chand's transition government; appointed Nepali Congress's acting president, Krishna Prasad Bhattarai, prime minister in his place; and allocated portfolios to a coalition cabinet according to Bhattarai's recommendation. The king also directed the new government to "have the responsibility of conducting general elections in future."

The new government sought to ride the wave of popular euphoria by quickly forming a new constitution. These parties were in a hurry to hold elections as soon as possible in order to establish their popular legitimacy before the glow of the recent popular triumph had faded. The new constitution emerged from a six-month process of complex, difficult, and delicate negotiations among all parties, with the chairman of the Constitutional Recommendations Commission, Chief Justice Bishwa Nath Upadhyaya, providing advice and consultations. The end result was a hastily improvised constitutional document.

The new Constitution now explicitly states in its preamble that sovereignty resides in the people. It guarantees their fundamental rights to freedom of expression, assembly, and association and — most important — their right to the rule of law. Article 116(1) provides that the fundamental rights, multiparty democracy, constitutional monarchy, and an effective independent judiciary are to be henceforth regarded as inalienable. In addition, Nepal became a party to the International Covenants and the Convention Against Torture. The Special Control and Punishment Act was repealed, and persons who had been sentenced under its provisions were released.

In the first flush of democratic triumph in Nepal, the interim government was determined to take legal action against the persons responsible for serious violations of human rights during past regimes. With this end in view, the government established two commissions. One was the "Disappearances Commission" to investigate "disappearances under the previous governments during the last thirty years." The second commission (also known as the Mallik Commission), headed by regional court judge Janardan Lall Mallik, was charged with the duty of investigating the "loss of life and property" during the movement for the restoration of democracy from February to April 1990.

The Disappearances Commission was initially established in July 1990 under the chairmanship of additional Supreme Court judge Hiraneshwar Man Pradhan. It consisted of Professor Surya Bahadur Shakya, a former vice Chancellor of Tirbhuvan University, and an adviser to the Human Rights Organization of Nepal; Sachche Kumar Pahadi, a doctor, who was then president of the Nepal Medical Association; Basudev Prasad Dhungana, a senior advocate of the Nepal Supreme Court and president of the Nepal Bar Association at that time; and Prakash Kafle, general secretary of the Forum for Protection of Human Rights.

Five days after Pradhan's appointment as chairman, he ceased to be an additional Supreme Court judge and for that reason did not deem it fit to continue as the head of the commission without further instructions from the government. It took the government three and a half months to name another member of the Commission — Professor Shakya — chairman in his place. The unnecessary delay in naming the chairman was interpreted by some people as a sign that the government's enthusiasm for bringing to justice those responsible for past serious violation of human rights was declining. Despite these encumbrances, the Commission completed its task in six months and presented its report to the government in April 1991.

The Commission called for information on all disappearances during the previous thirty years and carried out detailed investigations into all such cases that were brought to its notice. Unfortunately, it received little information detailed enough to provide some hope of resolving the cases. Although some military and police officers voluntarily appeared before the Commission, most did not. The Commission had no ability to subpoena reluctant witnesses. It therefore chose to focus, despite its broad mandate, on a single notorious case. In addition to the political significance of the case, the Commission benefited from investigatory groundwork laid by Amnesty International starting as far back as 1987.

The Commission focused on the cases of eight people who disappeared in police custody after the explosion of bombs in the country on June 20 and 21, 1985 in which six people were killed. In the spring of 1985, a peaceful noncooperation movement, or *satyagraha,* had been launched by the banned Nepali Congress. This movement was still on when the bombings took place. There was no doubt that many persons in authority panicked when the bombs went off, the first such incident to take place in Katmandu. Hundreds of people were rounded up by the police for rough treatment and lengthy detention, and a palpable state of terror prevailed among Nepalis of all classes.

The Disappearances Commission narrowed its investigation to eight persons who were arrested during the postbomb roundups and were never seen alive again. In the course of its investigations, the Commission interviewed people who witnessed those who disappeared being arrested or saw them during detention; at least one witness mentioned that he saw evidence that one of those who had been detained was being tortured. In a newspaper report, a police officer confessed to killing four of the persons who had been detained on the orders of his superiors. But the report has not been published officially, nor has the government made any public statement about how the report will be acted on. However, home minister Sher Bahadur Deupa of the 1991 elected Nepali Congress government told Parliament that the findings of the Disappearances Commission do not warrant further action of any kind with regard to persons who disappeared.

The Mallik Commission's full report has not yet been published, although a copy has been made available for consultation in the parliamentary library. According to press reports, the Commission has reached the conclusion that from February to April 1990 "about 45 persons were killed and 2,300 were injured." This figure is not the same as that of sixty-three dead given by the home ministry in November 1990. Upon submission of the report, the interim prime minister promised that appropriate action would be taken against persons found guilty and that the victims or their families would be compensated. So far, only token compensation has been paid, and no further action has been taken. At one point the interim government seized the passports of high-ranking officials of the past *panchayati* government, but was forced to back down when the Supreme Court, composed of judges appointed under the old government, declared the seizures illegal.

Reportedly, the attorney general is of the opinion that no action can be taken on the findings of the Commission because the Commission failed to specify the laws under which actions could be taken, because it had been unable to identify the individual policemen who fired on demonstrators, and because too much time had passed. In July 1993, Justice Mallik issued a statement denying that there were any legal obstacles to prosecuting persons implicated in the report and urging the government to take action. Justice Mallik's comments take on special weight because he now heads the Commission for Prevention of Abuse of Power by Government Authorities, which is in charge of preventing and investigating current human rights violations. If the attorney general's reported opinion is true, that report is all the more reason for having further legal safeguards and improved investigation procedures, including full protection for witnesses and investigators. Although it is essential to identify the persons who carried out the fatal shootings, it is equally necessary to determine whether higher authorities were also responsible for the shootings and to identify those authorities.

Nepal has no law granting immunity to security forces from prosecution for causing disappearances and for extrajudicial executions. Rather, the interim and now elected government's inability to end impunity mainly arises from the prevalence even now of old laws and practices that are clearly inconsistent with the letter and spirit of the constitution. This inability also stems from the government's reliance on the same old administrative and security personnel for policy implementation without being able to bring about any change in their outlook. Both the Nepali Congress–United Left Front interim coalition government and the elected Nepali Congress government have not, to date, been able to bring a single human rights violator to justice for the simple reason that they have continued with the security and the administrative machinery staffed by the same persons who were in positions of authority when serious human rights abuses took place. Prime Minister Bhattarai, the head of the interim government, cited his concern for the rule of law and a lack of popular mandate as grounds for being helpless to bring human rights violators to justice immediately. But as time went on political and economic difficulties made it more difficult to keep focused on the problem.

As a result, serious human rights violations continue, albeit on a smaller scale. There have been reports of torture of suspects held in police custody.[21] In addition, a number of people have been killed by the police mostly during crowd control operations.[22]

Both the Nepali Congress party and the opposition coalition made firm commitments in their respective electoral platforms to do everything possible to punish the culprits of the previous regimes. However, according to newspaper reports published about the time the 1990 Constitution was promulgated, the interim government felt compelled to give assurances to the security personnel that they would be exempt from future legal action concerning their past deeds before the loyalty and cooperation of this group could be secured for the conduct of the general elections. Whatever may be the case, it goes without saying that international standards require governments to take action against human rights violators to prevent extrajudicial executions or other unlawful killings and attach considerable weight to effective investigations into such acts. The question is not merely one of bringing the guilty to justice in a particular case but of sending a clear message to all concerned that human rights violations will no longer be tolerated and that the violators will be held fully accountable. If the Nepali government does not act on these issues on some pretext or other, not only its honesty, integrity, and credibility but also its democratic credentials will become largely suspect, and the people of Nepal may begin to despair of democracy.

17

The Human Rights Debacle in the Philippines

Belinda A. Aquino

This chapter examines the attempts to redress countless human rights violations in the Philippines, which reached their peak during the martial law regime of Ferdinand Marcos between late 1972 and early 1986. It focuses on the administration of Corazon Aquino (1986–92), which replaced the Marcos regime in the dramatic 1986 "people power revolution." The Aquino government put into place a new constitution guaranteeing "full respect for human rights" and restraining the military from carrying out arbitrary actions. It also established a Commission on Human Rights to investigate the numerous cases of human rights crimes and offenses that came to light following the overthrow of the Marcos dictatorship.

A close look at the performance of the Aquino administration with regard to the human rights issue reveals a very poor record. Its vigorous commitment after the 1986 revolution to bring to justice human rights violators turned out to be more symbolic than real. It took a landmark decision in a Honolulu district court in September 1992 to bring a measure of justice to some 10,000 victims of torture and other atrocities under the Marcos regime.

Initial Steps of the Aquino Presidency

At the onset of Aquino's presidency in February 1986, Filipinos held high hopes that the notorious human rights violators in the fourteen-year Marcos dictatorship would be brought to justice and meted out due punishment. This belief was strengthened by a personal dimension, the fact that President Aquino had suffered herself during the Marcos years. Her husband Benigno, more popularly known as "Ninoy," was incarcerated for nearly eight years, at times held incommunicado. She visited him every day when permitted and watched his intense physical and psychological suffering. And on August 21, 1983, he was murdered at high noon at the Manila International Airport in the most brazen assassination in recent

231

memory. "Cory" became an overnight symbol of the escalating popular resistance against Marcos. She was drafted to run against Marcos in the 1986 "snap election," which Marcos called fully expecting to win easily. Following a stunning series of events before millions of people in February 1986, Aquino was proclaimed president of the Philippines.

Aquino immediately released 500 political prisoners, including top Communist leaders held in the Marcos detention camps. She also formed the Presidential Committee on Human Rights (PCHR) and picked José Diokno, a respected politician and well-known human rights lawyer, to head the new body. She appointed to the Committee Sister Mariani Dimaranan, one of the best-known human rights advocates in the country and the founder of the Task Force Detainees of the Philippines (TFDP), which regularly monitored human rights violations nationwide during the Marcos dictatorship. Several human rights lawyers and activists, who had been active in the opposition to the dictatorship and in pursuing human rights cases under very trying circumstances, were also appointed to key positions in the new government.

The newly created PCHR was inundated with cases far beyond its capacity to handle them. Sister Mariani herself brought 700 cases before the Committee on behalf of TFDP. Diokno, himself a political detainee in the Marcos regime, devised a long-term strategy for prosecuting human rights cases, believing the Aquino government needed to stabilize first and consolidate its power base. In the short term, a few "test cases" would be pursued, partly for symbolic value.

The PCHR was put under the jurisdiction of the office of the president as an "advisory and consultative body." As such, it had no prosecutorial powers. Its broad mandate was to

> investigate complaints it may receive, cases known to it or to its members, and such cases as the Presidency may, from time to time, assign to it, of unexplained disappearances, extra-judicial killings ("salvaging"), massacres, torture, hamletting, food blockades and other violations of human rights, past or present, committed by officers or agents of the national government or persons acting in their place or stead or under their orders express or implied.[1]

The Committee was further mandated to report its findings to the president and make them public, "suggesting such action or actions by the new government to compensate the victims and punish culprits as it may deem appropriate," and similarly to "propose procedures and safeguards to ensure that, under the new government, human rights are not violated by officers or agents of the government, or by persons acting in their name and stead or under their orders, express or implied."[2] In addition to these functions, the PCHR was given powers to issue subpoenas to Committee hearings, grant immunity from prosecution to any person whose testimony was necessary for an investigation, and call upon any ministry or agency of the government for assistance.

At this point, the Aquino government was in possession of numerous reports, many of them prepared by both national and international organizations, on human rights abuses committed by military personnel during the Marcos era.[3] The data and legal evidence against known torturers in the previous regime were there, but the critical ingredient to bring the violators to justice was the political will to prosecute.

As time passed the momentum for proceeding against human rights violators seemed to slow down. René Saguisag, President Aquino's first spokesperson, conceded that prosecuting military officials accused of human rights offenses might prove destabilizing. Sensing that nothing substantial would happen in these human rights cases, Sister Mariani and other committee members resigned en masse after working fourteen months with the new government. Senator Diokno also resigned in disgust, and because by that time he was seriously ill. The PCHR eventually became the Commission on Human Rights (CHR) in May 1987, but by then the initial impetus had been lost.

Complicating the mass resignation of the entire PCHR membership, the Committee was overtaken by the ratification of the new constitution in February 1987. One of its provisions was the creation of an "independent" Commission on Human Rights. This would be a constitutional body with greater powers and a more or less permanent tenure, rather than just an appendage to the president's office in Malacañang. In fact, in a test case involving the new Commission's first chairperson, the Supreme Court ruled that the chair's appointment was not subject to confirmation by the Senate Commission on Appointments. The new body therefore appeared to have more autonomy or clout than its predecessor, which was just an ad hoc committee. The Commission would also act as a watchdog overseeing the government's human rights agenda. But its functions were really not substantially different from the old Committee. Like its predecessor, the new Commission was given the power "to investigate on its own or on the complaint by any party, all forms of human rights violations involving civil and political rights."[4] To chair the new CHR President Aquino appointed a human rights lawyer, Marcos opponent, and former member of the Presidential Commission on Good Government (PCGG), Mary Concepcion Bautista.

Bautista looked promising at first, noting that from the time of its establishment

> the Commission has suffered from setbacks due to the lack of funds and personnel, and was buffeted and pressured on all sides by the forces of the left and the right, even by other sectors, who all had their own set of ideas as to whose rights should be protected and who should be prosecuted.[5]

However, she then proceeded to her own interpretation of the Commission's role, which was "to protect equally the human rights of soldiers, policemen, government officials, ordinary citizens as well as those opposing the government." Bautista added that this line of thinking regarding protecting the human rights of even soldiers and policemen was not welcomed by "activists, human rights organizations and even legislators."[6]

Indeed, during her entire tenure as chairperson of the Commission, Bautista remained controversial because of her insistence on equating the serious human rights violations committed by the military with abuses committed by the rebel New People's Army (NPA). This is not to excuse the abuses of nongovernmental criminal groups or political movements, but by definition the concept of human rights violations must focus on those committed by or with the support or condonation of the state. Nor was there even remote parity between the abuses committed by military and paramilitary forces and those committed by the rebels — in these circumstances, equating the two meant obfuscating the role of the military. In any case, Bautista's strange perspective led to criticism that she was more of "a public relations agent of the Government and the military rather than one concerned about human rights and what is happening to the people."[7]

In both the PCHR and CHR a serious drawback was the lack of real power to prosecute human rights violators. The powers vested in the new Commission by the president and the Constitution were essentially investigative. According to a Filipino legal scholar, the Commission delineated on July 26, 1988 the violations that were covered by its investigative powers. These were (1) civil and political rights guaranteed in the Constitution and (2) violations of basic human rights as defined in the Universal Declaration of Human Rights and international covenants on human rights to which the Philippines was a party.[8] The specific abuses of government military personnel were lost somewhere in these broad categories.

What would it have meant had the Commission been given not only investigative but prosecutorial powers to deal with violations of human rights? First, the Commission's placement within the government bureaucracy was problematic. It could not be investigator, watchdog, ombudsman, and prosecutor at the same time without creating potential conflicts of interest. A solution advanced was to create an office of special prosecutor for human rights to prosecute cases referred to it by the CHR, nongovernmental organizations (NGOs), and other private parties.[9] To complement this new office, special courts were proposed to try violations not only of Philippine laws but also of international human rights instruments that the Philippines had pledged to uphold.

A special prosecutor would have meant removing from the jurisdiction of the military courts the power to try offenders in uniform for crimes against civilians. This objective was partially fulfilled by the repeal of presidential decree No. 1850, a Marcos directive that gave military tribunals the sole right to prosecute erring personnel of the armed forces. As far as can be determined, however, the new law, Republic Act 7055, signed on June 20, 1991 by President Aquino, has yet to be implemented. And the proposed office of special prosecutor was never created.

Second, the demand for a special prosecutor and special courts reflected the public's perception that the regular machinery for prosecution in the Philippine legal system was ineffectual, vulnerable to corruption or manipulation, or simply unable to deliver justice. The courts under the Marcos regime had lost their autonomy and integrity. Marcos had required standing resignations of judges. The system was notorious for interminable delays and inordinate postponements of hearings, intimidation or influence peddling by powerful elements in the society, bribery, and whitewashing of cases. To assign the cases resulting from human rights investigations to these bodies was to consign them essentially to oblivion.

The Aquino Assassination Trial

The most celebrated case exemplifying many of the classic problems of the justice system in the Philippines was the Aquino assassination trial, which ended in a brazen travesty of justice during the Marcos regime. Leading Marcos opponent Benigno Aquino, Jr., was shot to death at the Manila International Airport on August 21, 1983 under suspicious circumstances that eventually pointed to elements of the military as the perpetrators of the crime. The Marcos regime made up the incredulous tale that a lone gunman, Rolando Galman, who had links with the Communist leadership in the country, was Aquino's assassin.

The following October, nearly two months later, the Marcos government created an independent ad hoc fact-finding board with plenary powers to determine the facts and circumstances surrounding the killing and to allow for a free, unlimited, and exhaustive investigation into all aspects of the tragedy.[10] The board was composed of a chairperson and four members. Marcos appointed a retired justice of the court of appeals, Corazon Agrava, to chair the body and Ernesto Herrera, Dante Santos, Amado Dizon, and Luciano Salazar, representing a cross section of the professional groups, as members. The body subsequently became known as the Agrava Board. Considering that Marcos himself was, in the minds of the people and the Aquino family, the "primary suspect" behind the killing, the integrity of the board immediately became an issue.

Nevertheless, the board conducted hearings for almost a year. A total of 193 civilian and military witnesses gave testimonies. The witnesses coming from the military invariably supported the government's version that they saw "a man in a light blue shirt with a gun in hand" on the day of the assassination.[11] The first civilian witness to dispute the military version was Ramon Balang, a ground engineer of Philippine Air Lines, who testified that Aquino was shot from behind as he descended the narrow airline stairs upon his arrival.

Balang and other actual and potential witnesses were intimidated, harassed, or caused to disappear. A day before he made up his mind to testify, Balang's mother said a Captain Dantes and two other Central Intelligence Service officials came to the Balang home looking for her son. Fortunately, Balang hid until it was time to give his testimony to the board. Other witnesses or would-be witnesses were not as fortunate. Galman's mother and sister were picked up by the military and moved to various places despite their protests. Lina Lazaro, Galman's common law wife, was abducted and eventually disappeared. Lazaro's daughter Roberta told the board her mother had said, "General Ver was sending for her but that she, Roberta, was not to tell anybody as their lives were in danger."[12] (General Fabian Ver was the armed forces chief of staff and the top military adviser to Marcos.) Anna and Catherine Oliva, sisters working as nightclub hostesses who were friends of Galman's, likewise disappeared.

In the end, the board, over the objections of its chairperson, indicted twenty-six individuals for the "premeditated killing" of Senator Aquino and Rolando Galman on August 21, 1983. The list was headed by General Ver, Major General Prospero Olivas, and Brigadier General Luther Custodio. The other accused included two colonels, three captains, one second lieutenant, twelve sergeants, and four corporals or privates. Only one civilian was indicted.

Marcos received the report in September 1984 and submitted its conclusions to the Sandiganbayan (a special court for cases of corruption involving government personnel) for litigation purposes. The Sandiganbayan was a creation of

Marcos and its presiding judge a Marcos appointee. To expect that the court would act against Marcos's wishes was simply not realistic.

True to expectations, the Sandiganbayan acquitted Ver and the other persons accused in December 1985; Ver, who had been temporarily suspended, was promptly restored to office. It was a mockery of justice. The world was dismayed, especially the U.S. government, which had been exerting pressure on Marcos to dismiss Ver and undertake major reforms in his deteriorating government. Filipinos, knowing how the justice system works, had no such illusions.

When the new government came into power, it was expected that the Aquino assassination case would be revived. But for some reason the victim's widow, Cory Aquino, seemed indifferent to the matter. Either she had put it behind her as a matter of forgiveness or she did not want to be perceived as vindictive. Again her diffidence got the better of her; if she had shown decisiveness, or even aggressiveness, on the question — after all, it involved the ultimate sacrifice on the part of her husband — the people would have supported her to the utmost.

Despite her reluctance or indifference, the Supreme Court ordered a retrial of the case on April 29, 1987. This time the main defendant, General Ver, was no longer in the Philippines, having joined Marcos in exile in Hawaii. Special prosecutor Raúl Gonzalez stressed the "impartiality of the Court," now that the democratic process and "rule of law" had returned to the country. He allotted nine months for the trial the second time around, adding three civilians to the original list of indictees. There were thirty-six accused in the second trial.

It was an optimistic timetable. The trial dragged on, typical of the inordinate delay that characterizes criminal court cases in the Philippines. It would take another three years, in 1990, before a verdict could be handed down by a division of the Sandiganbayan. The court found sixteen military men — headed by Brigadier General Custodio, Captain Romeo Bautista, and Lieutenant Jesus Castro — guilty and sentenced them to *reclusion perpetua,* or life imprisonment, the maximum punishment because the new Constitution promulgated in 1987 abolished the death penalty. The twenty other accused, including the four civilians, were "not proved guilty beyond reasonable doubt" and were acquitted. Thus ended the so-called trial of the century in the country, the most successful human rights trial to date. It had been seven years since Aquino was assassinated.

Aquino's Relationship with the Military

But the problems of investigating and prosecuting human rights violations under Aquino went deeper than just the sluggish nature of the judicial system or the inadequate powers of the commissions on human rights. The military is a powerful institution in any country; in the Philippines it played a particularly crucial role in helping to oust Marcos.

Reflecting on the history of the 1986 "people power revolution," many Filipinos believe that it could not have happened without the turnabout of Juan Ponce Enrile and Fidel V. Ramos, defense minister and armed forces of the Philippines vice chief of staff, respectively, at the time. Their defection from Marcos accelerated the massing of "people power" that subsequently toppled the dictator. Thus, even before Aquino could assume the presidency, she was constrained by the need to make compromises with the military, which had suddenly been catapulted to center stage after the Marcos overthrow. The military assumed a new vitality, if not respectability, and was basking in its new glory. After a while, Enrile was revising the history of the 1986 upheaval, claiming that the military handed power over to Aquino and should logically become a "partner" in the ensuing ruling coalition in the country. The old notion that the military was subordinate to civilian supremacy was a thing of the past.

The military thus became part of Aquino's power base, and she immediately reappointed Enrile defense minister and promoted Ramos to armed forces chief of staff. In such a situation, Aquino and her advisers considered it imprudent to bring up the topic of punishing the military human rights violators under Marcos, knowing that Enrile and Ramos were part of the whole apparatus of martial law that perpetrated the abuses. Ramos, for instance, was the chief of the Philippine Constabulary/Integrated National Police, which was reported to have the most abusive military and paramilitary personnel. With the exception of General Ver and other Marcos cronies, the military apparatus remained intact. Some officers known to have violated human rights, like Colonel Rolando Abadilla, were elected or appointed to public office. The military was not about to chastise its own members who were charged with infractions against human rights.[13]

In particular, Enrile immediately recoiled when Aquino released all the political prisoners, including the top Communist leaders. It was a politically difficult situation for Aquino: How would a military purge square with her earlier decision to pardon and release the Communists and other prisoners of a left-wing persuasion? It was obvious that Aquino opted for caution to avoid a head-on collision with her erstwhile colleagues in the post-Marcos era. In doing so, she lost the opportunity to mobilize the still-feverish "people power" to press for greater changes, particularly reforming the abusive military.

Aquino's caution proved to do her no good. Despite her kid-glove treatment of the military, before long Enrile and his senior aides were hatching a coup plan, code named "God Save the Queen," which was designed to reduce Aquino to a mere figurehead. Within a few months of her presidency, Aquino was under siege, and pressure from the military continued to build up against her fledgling administration. In the end it would be the same circle — Enrile and others — who would scheme repeatedly to oust her from power. Aquino managed to survive politically, but in the process she became dependent on, or even a captive to, another sector of the military consisting of the loyal soldiers under Ramos. Owing her survival to the military, she was hesitant to pursue harsh measures against officers in the ranks, even those who were reputed to have been "criminals in uniform" during the Marcos years. She may not have been the most astute politician, but she probably understood that, once she depended on the military, insisting on punishing military offenders would mean the end of her presidency.

With the sacking of Enrile in November 1986 and the continuing specter of potential coups, Aquino became even more dependent on the loyal military for survival. She became beholden to the military, which renamed itself the New

Armed Forces of the Philippines (NAFP) under Ramos. The latter spent much of his time and energies keeping coup plotters in tow, sparing Aquino from numerous military-inspired destabilization attempts. In time, by inclination or circumstance, or both, Aquino drifted to the right. *"Nakalimutan na ang human rights"* ("She has forgotten human rights") was a common observation.

By the end of 1987, her first year as president, the complexion of Aquino's administration had changed dramatically in favor of the right. All the progressive, liberal human rights activists whom Aquino had appointed to key positions in her administration had either resigned or been pressured out of office by military or right-leaning elements. Augusto Sanchez, Reli German, Alex Padilla, and Joker Arroyo were all victims of the witch hunt from the right.

Prospects for bringing human rights offenders to justice became dimmer. The political situation between 1986 and 1989 was exacerbated by the rise of vigilantism and an escalation of the government's policy of "total war" against the Communist insurgents. The "dirty war" against the NPA continued, and once again the number of human rights abuses began to rise.[14]

Behavior of the Military and the Police in Human Rights Cases

The power of the military and former President Aquino's lack of decisive leadership, not to mention her debts to the military for her political survival, essentially explain why her government's record in prosecuting human rights cases is extremely poor. This had been the consistent finding of Amnesty International and the Lawyers Committee on Human Rights.[15] The body of evidence unearthed by human rights groups relating to military obstruction in efforts to prosecute violations against ordinary citizens is considerable. "The military leadership has fostered an environment where disincentives for prosecuting fellow officers and subordinates are great and incentives few." The national police, which has become part of the Department of the Interior and Local Government since the Aquino administration, has also been unwilling to take serious action against offenders in its ranks. "Consequently, at virtually every stage of criminal proceedings, military and police act to shield their colleagues from accountability for even the most serious violations."[16]

Military tribunals, the most common venue for prosecutions in human rights cases, are worse than useless, consistently exonerating defendants. A blatant case in point was the massacre of seventeen civilians in a *barangay* (village) in Lupao, Nueva Ecija province, which several witnesses and survivors attributed to soldiers from the 14th Infantry Battalion looking for NPA insurgents. Twenty-one military defendants were accused of the killings. In a trial before a military tribunal that lasted seventeen months, survivors and witnesses provided detailed testimony "making clear that the villagers had been deliberately killed — and not, as the defendants claimed, killed in the cross fire of a military encounter." On July 14, 1989, General Court Martial No. 1 issued its verdict, finding the twenty-one defendants not guilty on all charges. To aggravate matters, President Aquino accepted the verdict of the military court, saying it was not a whitewash because there was no substantial evidence to convict due to the "noncooperation of certain witnesses."

Military and police interference in cases before civilian courts has likewise been pervasive. Warrants and subpoenas issued by the courts cannot or will not be served by law-enforcement officers. Police claim they cannot locate the suspect — even when he is visibly present in the community.[17] Consequently, human rights cases are dismissed or filed away for lack of witnesses or sufficient evidence. Plaintiffs are further deterred by threats of reprisals, by bearing the costs of producing witnesses, and by having to pay for engaging a "private prosecutor" who acts instead of the public prosecutor in preparing and presenting cases. And to make matters more painful still, a "blaming the victim" attitude prevails. No wonder few crimes ever reach investigation, let alone trial.

Between 1987 and 1990, the Commission on Human Rights received 7,944 complaints of human rights violations, ranging from disappearance to "salvaging," or summary execution. The Commission established enough evidence for valid administrative or judicial cases in 1,509 of these. Of this number, 603 involved murder, homicide, and extrajudicial execution of victims; 119, arrests or detention; and 19, disappearances. As of December 1990 complaints had been filed in 994 cases; in 37 cases there were dismissals, seven acquittals, six convictions, one demotion, three suspensions, and one dismissal from military service. Thus, over a three-year period only eleven cases of the more than 1,500 had resulted in sanctions — a dismal record by any account.[18]

Aquino's successor, Fidel Ramos, has not made a strong commitment to redress human rights issues. Given his military background, it is unlikely that he will take a hard line against men in uniform accused of various violations. As defense secretary under President Aquino in 1989, he asserted that "93 percent of all cases against the military [filed before the CHR] are baseless."[19] Now as president, he has not put forward a bold human rights agenda. But committed human rights advocates are determined to seek justice, even if it means going to foreign territory.

Venue Shifts to Hawaii

Recognizing the futility of ever obtaining any justice, let alone some form of restitution, for the injuries inflicted on them by the Marcos regime, the human rights victims and their counsel decided to pursue a different tactic. A 1789 U.S. statute allows non-U.S. citizens to sue in federal courts for torts committed in violation of the law of nations.[20] Once Marcos and his family sought exile in Hawaii, they became open to suit under this law. Several individual torture victims and family members of people killed by the military under Marcos's orders filed civil suits alleging that Marcos was personally responsible for summary executions, torture, disappearances, and prolonged arbitrary detention and asked for compensation. The suit brought on behalf of the family of Archimedes Trajano, a student who was murdered by elements of the military in 1977, was typical. He was reportedly picked up by soldiers on orders of Imee Marcos Manotoc, the daughter of the

Marcos couple, who headed a national youth organization. Archimedes apparently had asked Imee embarrassing questions in a public forum. His body was retrieved by his mother in a public morgue a few days later. It bore marks of severe torture, and his skull was cracked.

Other individual suits were filed on behalf of José Maria Sison, a Communist Party of the Philippines (CPP) leader who had been tortured; former legislative aide Fluellen Ortigas; former political prisoner Jaime Piopongco; and others. These suits on behalf of about thirty named individuals were soon joined by a class action suit, the first ever filed in an Alien Tort Claims Act (ATCA) case, on behalf of some 10,000 victims of torture, disappearance, or summary execution from Marcos's declaration of martial law in 1972 until his departure from the Philippines. The suits, filed in three separate venues, were eventually consolidated for trial in Hawaii. Preliminary dismissals on act of state grounds[21] were reversed by the Ninth Circuit Court of Appeals, and the trial judge eventually denied subsequent motions to dismiss on sovereign immunity and other grounds.[22]

More than thirty plaintiffs traveled to Hawaii from the Philippines and various parts of the United States to testify at the jury trial, which started on September 9, 1992, at the U.S. District Court in Honolulu, with Judge Manuel Real presiding. It had been six years since the first cases were filed. Although several other cases brought under the ATCA had obtained default judgments, this case marked the first trial on the merits with an active defense. The trial testimony was widely covered by the Filipino press. Attorneys for the plaintiffs introduced depositions and testimony of victims, who said they were told they had been picked up on orders of the "highest authority." They produced arrest orders personally signed by Marcos or then minister of defense Juan Ponce Enrile, including several naming representatives of the class. Witnesses testified that Marcos personally had been in charge of state security and must have known about or even ordered the widespread torture and summary executions.

On September 25, 1992, a jury found the Marcos estate liable for damages for torture and other abuses during the martial law period. (Marcos died in exile in September 1989.) The verdict was widely reported in the Philippines and caused great rejoicing among human rights groups. However, the victims still faced several obstacles regarding receiving actual compensation.

First, because the suit is in part a class action, the actual number of victims was unknown. The figure of 10,000 victims was based on calculations of the Task Force Detainees of the Philippines, which monitored yearly the number of arrests, tortures, and murders during the Marcos martial law period. To identify the potential claimants, plaintiffs' attorneys published a claim form in newspapers in the United States, Europe, and the Philippines. The forms, translated into the major Philippine languages for publication in regional newspapers, explained the nature of the suit and requested potential claimants to complete a form giving details of torture, summary execution, or disappearance of themselves or a family member. Philippine human rights groups also helped to disseminate the information.

Once the class size had been ascertained and claims authenticated, trial on actual and exemplary damages commenced. On February 23, 1994, a jury awarded plaintiffs $1.2 billion in punitive damages. Trial on the compensatory damages owed was set for December 1994, and a special master was appointed to take the testimony of selected class members in the Philippines before the December trial. In addition, the Ninth Circuit Court of Appeals on June 16, 1994, affirmed the district court's issuance of a preliminary injunction enjoining the Marcos' estate from transferring or dissipating any of the estate's assets. The court also dismissed the defendant's objections to the suit.

It may take years, however, for the case to finally exhaust any appeals. For many plaintiffs who are old or infirm, the damages award may come too late; others may have problems proving actual damages for acts that occurred many years ago.

The second area of contention involves the competing claims to the "ill-gotten wealth" of the Marcos family and its cronies. The Philippine government, through the Philippine Commission on Good Government (PCGG) (in charge of trying to recover the Marcos "ill-gotten wealth"), has asserted that it has a prior claim on the assets of the Marcos estate, particularly the $386 million reportedly deposited in secret accounts in Swiss banks. Conceivably some of these funds could be used to compensate the winning plaintiffs. But the Philippine government has given contradictory statements on whether it is willing to "share" the money if any is recovered. Although PCGG chairman Magtanggol Gunigundo stated that he would have no objections to using part of the funds recovered from the Marcoses to indemnify the victims, the form such indemnification would take is unclear. Of course, the Philippine government has still to prove that the assets were "ill-gotten" to have claim to them, whereas the Honolulu torture trial plaintiffs need only identify any assets belonging to Marcos. It is obvious at this point that negotiations are needed between the plaintiffs and their lawyers and representatives of the Philippine government.

Conclusion

Despite the restoration of democratic rule in the Philippines in 1986, efforts to redress human rights abuses by successor governments to the Marcos regime have been extremely disappointing, although not surprising. There were only six convictions among thousands of cases brought before the courts by the Human Rights Commission during the Aquino administration. The current Ramos government does not seem inclined to prosecute — and indeed has articulated a "total amnesty" policy for both military rebels and left-wing insurgents. Thus, under the guise of a "peace process," crimes committed by agents of the state will be swept under the rug.

A number of factors have made breaking the cycle of impunity more difficult. The structural and political constraints of the existing judicial system, the assignment of crimes committed by the military to military tribunals interested in protecting their own, the intimidation or killing of lawyers disposed to bring human rights cases to trial, and the high degree of institutional loyalty within the armed forces have all made both investigation and prosecution more difficult. President Aquino's debt to the military at the beginning for helping to overthrow Marcos, and later to one sector of the military for staving off destabilization attempts by another sector, hemmed in her administration and did not allow it to act. Even if Aquino had had a free hand, her own temperament and the perceived need for national unity might have led her to stress forgiveness rather than justice.

Thus the struggle to redress human rights in the Philippines has been set back by these factors. Consequently, the forum for airing and litigating cases of human rights victims has moved to international circles. The landmark decision in Honolulu in September 1992 is the first human rights victory for scores of Filipino torture victims after all these years. It is ironic that their search for justice had to be carried out in a foreign country. The U.S. setting for the trial meant it was limited in terms of providing truth telling for the Filipino people: Few witnesses could afford to come and testify, and a U.S. jury's verdict, although an important victory, is far from an official government acknowledgment of wrongdoing. In addition, the trial necessarily focused on Marcos as an individual, leaving in the background the institutional structures of repression that a fuller process of truth telling would have exposed. Nonetheless, the impact of the foreign trial on the Filipino people has been substantial, especially because of the large Filipino expatriate population (with its own press and media) in Hawaii and the United States, and because the language and procedure of the trial were less foreign to the Philippines than to many other countries in which similar acts took place.

But this is really just a beginning. Unfortunately, the real measure of justice — imprisonment or punishment of the perpetrators of countless human rights atrocities and compensation for their victims — may never come.

18

Human Rights in Cambodia

Michael Vickery and Naomi Roht-Arriaza

Factual Background

From 1975 to 1979 Democratic Kampuchea (DK) was a regime that many people have called worse than Hitler's and that has become a paradigm for oppression, arbitrary imprisonment, torture, and murder by a state of its own citizens. Earlier, between 1970 and 1975, under the U.S.-backed Khmer Republic, all guarantees of civil rights, fair trial, and freedom from arbitrary police harassment were de facto suspended; the justification, if there was any, was that a state of war prevailed in the country. Even during Cambodia's best peace time years under Prince Sihanouk before 1970, the right to a quick, fair trial without risk of torture during preliminary police investigation was not guaranteed in practice; and political suspects could be judicially murdered in widely publicized executions.[1]

The Cambodian experience must also be situated in relation to its late colonialist background. Cambodia became a French protectorate in 1863, a de facto colony in 1884, and an independent nation again in 1953–54. In Cambodia before the French experience the first principle of modern Western law — equality of all before the law — was not even known in principle, and torture was explicitly provided for in local law.

In most of Asia and Africa the Western type of legal system was imposed by force during the period of colonial expansion. "Human rights" were imposed at gunpoint on societies in which equality before the law would have been revolutionary if it had been truly applied, but where it appeared as the most hypocritical device of political manipulation used to maintain the position of a new, and foreign, ruling class.

In Indochina the people learned *liberté, égalité, fraternité* and learned at the same time that those fine words were not for them. As a true protectorate, Cambodia preserved the structure of its traditional state, including the privileges of the ruling class. French practice simply added another rung at the top of the ladder of social and legal privilege, and colonial police practices preserved the worst of both systems.

This is the heritage that has weighed on modern Cambodia, under whatever regime. When Cambodia became independent in 1953–54, the French police and judicial systems, both in practice and in personnel, were inherited and continued operation in a society that preserved ascriptive class differences and corresponding degrees of privilege, including freedom from the law.

Throughout the 1950s and 1960s Cambodians were convinced that police were routinely brutal, judges almost universally corrupt, and the legal system a dangerous spider web for the ordinary citizen. Privileges for the elites were accepted as normal, and there was little protest, not only because protest itself would have been viewed as antiregime activity but because Cambodians in general did not fully realize that standards in the rest of the world might be different.[2]

Beginning in 1968 Cambodia was rapidly engulfed by war, which by late 1970 was almost total; and as is usual in a war zone, whatever guarantees of legality and human rights prevailed in peacetime were suspended. Both sides were guilty of violations, and local contempt for legal standards was encouraged by the cynical U.S. support of an incompetent regime at the same time as U.S. bombing was physically destroying the heart of the countryside.

The war was won by a party with a fierce commitment to revolutionary equality, with leaders who knew the principles of Western justice. These leaders had, however, also directly experienced the way such principles could be manipulated in support of privilege, both by a colonial power and a postcolonial local regime. With reason they may have thought that the high ideals were a sham and that their new Democratic Kampuchea must devise its own principles. Inevitably, their regime was brutal and in the end lost whatever support it had initially enjoyed.

Protests were voiced in the West, but since the DK existed in hermetic isolation, international influence could not be brought to bear except by invasion, which was advocated even by some sincere political figures.[3] Finally there came an invasion. In 1979 the war that DK had started with its neighbor Vietnam resulted in the overthrow of DK and its replacement by the Peoples Republic of Kampuchea (PRK), since 1989 called State of Cambodia (SOC), which is still in place. Almost overnight there was a full swing of the pendulum with respect to civil and human rights—freedom of movement, of family life, and of choice of work were immediately acknowledged; and the normal infrastructures of society (administration, education, health, markets, currency) gradually began to be reconstructed and recreated, with great difficulty given the near total destruction of material—including documentation and archives—and trained personnel. By the end of 1980 there could be no reasonable doubt that in terms of personal freedom, legality, and human rights the post-1979 PRK was an enormous improvement over its predecessor, in some respects over all three of its predecessors since the late 1960s.

This conclusion was accepted by most observers. Yet instead of praise, diplomatic recognition, and generous aid to encourage and hasten the improvement, the dismantling of the DK was greeted with dismay by most of those Western countries, led by the United States, who had been shedding crocodile tears over DK atrocities. There was a campaign of denigration because the improvement had been brought about by Vietnam.

With the full support of China and Thailand and the acquiescence of the Association of Southeast Asian Nations (ASEAN) and most Western countries, a huge international campaign was developed to block the peaceful development of the PRK — if possible to destroy it, no matter who might replace it. This effort included the physical rehabilitation, military supply, and encouragement of the remnants of DK, which until 1990 was allowed to retain Cambodia's U.N. seat. Finally, when the military overthrow of the PRK/SOC became clearly recognized as impossible, the Western countries, led by the United States and joined by China, mounted a campaign to bring the DK leaders back into the government through a peace process that legitimized their existence and consolidated their control over part of Cambodian territory.

Efforts by Phnom Penh to Identify and Prosecute DK violators

When the PRK came to power in 1979 there were severe objective impediments to the realization of the rule of law. These included the penury of surviving legally trained personnel, the destruction of archives and legal documentation, the total absence of formal courts and legality under the DK, preceded by the neglect of all of these during the 1975–79 war. Legal and judicial systems had to be recreated from zero, in a situation in which no one had experienced normal legal procedures for at least nine years — often longer, or never — and in which persons with prewar police experience may never have heard of the rights of accused.

This situation inevitably gave rise to instances of rough military justice for malefactors, real or suspected, and it provided welcome ammunition for organizations ill disposed to the PRK. As PRK officials willingly admitted, legality in the first years was below the desired standard, and police practices were not beyond reproach. Beginning in 1980 with laws on criminal offenses, new law codes were gradually developed, culminating in 1986 with a detailed law on arrest, search, temporary detention, and treatment of arrested persons. This law is not inferior to similar laws promulgated by the capitalist regimes of ASEAN.[4] Perhaps for the first time in the country's history, police training involved formal instruction against the use of torture.[5]

The new PRK did not begin a campaign to investigate and prosecute violators and compensate victims of human rights violations under the DK, nor was there a great popular demand for such action. This again reflects the peculiar circumstances of Cambodia. The DK victory in 1975 was a victory of one half of Cambodia's people over the other half, and much of the violence, especially in 1975–76 was spontaneous, unrecorded, and anonymous. By 1979 most of the population who had supported the victors had also become victims until, with respect to recognition of victims, the problem was too huge. All of the six million survivors considered that they had been victims, and compensation, beyond restoration of normal basic living conditions, family life, education, and so on, was beyond the capabilities of the state.[6]

Very few perpetrators of violations during the DK could be identified. The anonymous DK soldier who in irritation shot a few evacuees on the road out of Phnom Penh in 1975, or a peasant who denounced — or himself killed — a former rich neighbor, could hardly be traced. Most official killings were clandestine, carried out by anonymous executioners; in most cases their very names were unknown. The few who were identified and apprehended by the populace in 1979 met swift, rough justice; and the concern of the new state was to prevent a mass of revenge killings, which would have been as arbitrary as DK executions and which would have hindered the sorely needed restoration of social peace.

Probably most of the surviving perpetrators were among the DK administration and troops who fled the Vietnamese and by autumn 1979 reached the Thai border, where they have since benefited from U.S., Chinese, and Thai largesse. They were thus outside the range of PRK authority.

By 1980 there were probably very few people within the PRK who could have been credibly identified as direct participants in murder or torture under the DK, although there was some official effort to discover the few who might have remained. One provision in the first rather lenient criminal legislation obviously aimed at former DK criminals was that the death penalty could be inflicted on those who "are guilty of many crimes against the population in the past." On a trip to Takeo in 1984 I met a man who told me he worked for the special police and was assigned to search for former "Pol Potists."[7]

There was no lack of truth telling and symbolic redress. A major theme in state propaganda was the injustice and brutality of the DK past; among themselves and with foreigners Cambodians were eager to tell of their experiences; and the Tuol Sleng prison, one of the few places where records of arrest, torture, and executions had been preserved, was made the object of much publicity. Even in those records, however, hardly more than a half dozen names of jailers and torturers were discovered; all but two, the prison director and deputy director, nonentities who if they have survived would be unidentifiable.

The trial of DK leaders Pol Pot and Ieng Sary, which was held in Phnom Penh in August 1979, may be seen as symbolic redress because there was no chance that the defendants could be apprehended from the Thai border and extradited to Phnom Penh. The trial provided an opportunity to bring a certain number of Western legal personnel to Phnom Penh, to give a number of witnesses the chance to tell their stories to a wide public, and to publicize DK crimes, not only within Cambodia but to the whole world. The sentence was death in absentia, and perhaps, in the opinion of Phnom Penh, it still stands. The sentence was never recognized internationally, both because of due process objections to the trial procedures and because of the diplomatic isolation of the PRK regime.

International Efforts to Redress Violations

The flight of top DK leaders to Thailand made further internal attempts to bring these individuals to justice futile, and the protection granted by Thailand to DK survivors with the support of China and the United States, together with non-recognition of the PRK, made extradition impossible.

There were attempts by Western nongovernmental groups to use international legal institutions to achieve some measure of justice. In 1980 Dr. Gregory H.

Stanton's Cambodian Genocide Project "proposed that a case be brought to the World Court," where "the government that would have been served with the charges was the Khmer Rouge's Democratic Kampuchea itself, which still represented Cambodia in the U.N."[8] David Hawk's Cambodia Documentation Commission tried to obtain materials documenting the extent of DK human rights violations. Hawk also tried to convince governments either to set up an international tribunal or to bring a case before the International Court of Justice, contending that Cambodia had violated the Genocide Convention by failing to punish the persons responsible for committing genocide.[9] Human rights lawyers have argued that article 9 of the Genocide Convention allows disputes relating to the responsibilities of a state for genocide to be submitted to the World Court; that Cambodia had long been a party to the 1948 Genocide Convention and had accepted the compulsory jurisdiction of the court; and that representatives of the DK government continued to represent Cambodia internationally through 1992. The lawyers tried to present evidence of genocide by alleging the DK's intent to destroy religious and ethnic groups, including Chams, Buddhist monks, Chinese, and Vietnamese, as well as people from the eastern zone of Cambodia, who were massacred in 1978 allegedly because they had "Vietnamese minds."[10] A World Court decision would not be a criminal conviction and would apply to the state rather than to individuals. Nonetheless, the proponents argued that it would be important to establish authoritatively who ordered the killings, provide some measure of vindication for victims, and reduce international support for the DK.

Nonetheless, no state was willing to bring such a case before the International Court of Justice—even those states like Australia, Canada, Norway, and the United Kingdom, which in 1978 presented evidence of genocide to the U.N. Commission on Human Rights. Australia proposed the establishment of an international tribunal to try the Khmer Rouge at a June 1986 ASEAN foreign ministers' meeting but dropped the idea when the United States and China objected.

Rivalry among the nongovernmental organizations, as well as their internal regulations, may have hindered a common effort. According to Stanton, David Hawk and Michael Posner of the Lawyers' Committee for Human Rights used their influence to block sponsorship by the American Bar Association (ABA) of a commission of inquiry to Cambodia; at the same time the International Commission of Jurists refused to participate in an investigation in Cambodia unless it would include present conditions under the Phnom Penh government.[11]

Both Amnesty International and the Lawyers' Committee for Human Rights wrote reports that were highly critical of the PRK and that gave little or no recognition to the improvements over the prior regime or even improvements from the 1979 invasion until the mid-1980s.[12] Although some of the criticisms voiced in the reports may have been deserved, the unfortunate result was to shift the attention of the human rights community from the atrocities of the DK to the admittedly much better, although still flawed, record of the PRK and to create a climate in which it was more difficult to bring international pressure or support to bear on bringing DK leaders to justice.

Why was it so difficult to garner international support for action against the DK, either before or after 1979? Before 1979, unilateral U.S. intervention was unthinkable so soon after the Vietnam War, nor would a U.S.-led international intervention have been supported by any significant group of nations. Even by 1978, when atrocities in Cambodia had been better authenticated and when respectable figures such as George McGovern were calling for intervention, the appalling record of the United States in Southeast Asia still made U.S. military intervention impossible. And non-United States–led U.N. intervention would have been blocked by Chinese and Soviet vetoes and been opposed by most of the Third World states out of sympathy for Cambodian sovereignty over internal affairs. Furthermore, it is important to recall that in 1975–77 at least there was a great deal of uncertainty about what was happening in Cambodia; and the charges of genocide – or abuses approaching genocide – were not coming from sources with sufficient credibility.[13]

After 1979 and on the part of the U.S. government probably as early as 1977, anti-Vietnamese sentiment and the utility of the DK to destabilize Vietnam, together with a reluctance to antagonize the DK's Chinese backers, argued against intervention. Such a climate led to continued U.S. recognition of the DK leadership internationally and reluctance to refer to its past acts. The CIA did its part by issuing a report that whitewashed the worst period of DK massacres and that tried to make the first year of the PRK appear even worse.[14] The press too played its part. Probably in no controversial foreign policy issue has the press been so united in support for the state policy – that is, the isolation and condemnation of Vietnam and the PRK – with implied lenience for the DK.

The later alliance of the Khmer Rouge with two smaller anti-Communist groups, led by Prince Sihanouk and Son Sann, established in 1982 as the Coalition Government of Democratic Kampuchea, provided a cover for the United States, ASEAN, and most Western countries to isolate the PRK and support the DK. In fact, the Coalition was established only under U.S. and Chinese pressure, with that purpose in mind.

Redress under the Current Peace Agreement

The nature of the peace agreement signed in October 1991[15] will make investigation, apprehension of violators, and compensation for victims of the DK even less likely in the future. The agreement, to the extent it deals with human rights, focuses almost entirely on future safeguards, with only a vague mention of the past. This sparsity is a result of the 1988–91 process of negotiating a peace settlement, brokered by the United Nations. These negotiations attempted at almost any cost to bring the Khmer Rouge into a process of disarmament and electoral participation, on the assumption that it could be controlled better from within than from without. After the May 1993 elections not only was the Khmer Rouge not under anyone's control but its own but it was poised to play a major role in the new government.

The issue of genocide played a major role in the negotiations from the start, and from the start the negotiation process was held hostage by Chinese and U.S. rejection of any formula that would exclude the Khmer Rouge from the government. At the first Jakarta Informal Meeting in July 1988, the final communiqué noted a Southeast Asian consensus on preventing a return to the "genocidal policies and practices of the Pol Pot regime."[16] During the unsuccessful 1989 Paris Conference on Cambodia, the Hun Sen government stressed the issue of genocide, the nonreturn of those who had been responsible, and the setting up of a tribunal to try the perpetrators as key points in the negotiations. The Khmer Rouge, backed by the United States and China, was able to scuttle language to that effect. Eventually, in June 1991, Indonesia and France, the co-chairs of the Paris Conference, accepted Phnom Penh's proposal that the final agreement include provisions that the new constitution would be "consistent with the provisions of . . . the U.N. Convention on the Prevention and Punishment of Crimes of Genocide."[17] However, the permanent Five Security Council members rejected this formulation, so it too was dropped.

In October 1991 the nineteen states that had participated in the Paris Conference, the state of Cambodia, and the three opposition parties, including the Khmer Rouge, signed an Agreement on a Comprehensive Political Settlement of the Cambodia Conflict. The agreement set up an interim Supreme National Council, to be made up of representatives of all the factions, which would act as a repository of Cambodian sovereignty internationally until elections could be held. Also established under the agreement was the U.N. Transitional Authority on Cambodia (UNTAC), whose mandate was to administer the country during an interim period, monitor and enforce cease-fire and demobilization of the various armed forces, and prepare for free and fair elections.

The electoral provisions raised the thorny question of whether former DK high officials would be allowed to run for office. There were no explicit provisions preventing them from doing so. The only possible limit was that party platforms and candidates must be consistent with the principles and objectives of the agreement and that candidates must adhere to an UNTAC-prepared code of conduct — vague stipulations easy to evade.[18] Although in practice the point proved moot once the Khmer Rouge withdrew altogether from the electoral process, there is no reason why even the individuals personally identified with past genocide or crimes against humanity cannot hold future office.

The human rights provisions of the agreement focused on future prevention as the best way to avoid the horrors of the past. UNTAC was charged with implementing a human rights education program, overseeing human rights compliance, and investigating and acting upon current human rights complaints.[19] What little is left of the determination to confront the past was embodied in article 15 of the agreement: Cambodia was to guarantee respect for human rights; take effective measures "to ensure that the policies and practices of the past shall never be allowed to return"; and adhere to "relevant international human rights instruments."[20] Other signatories also agreed to promote respect for human rights in Cambodia.

Some analysts have argued that the "adhere to" language of article 15 is broad enough to include instruments to which Cambodia has long been a party, as well as those to which it acceded as a result of the accords. Thus, under this view, "the accords commit Cambodia to fulfilling its duties under the Genocide Convention by prosecuting those accused of genocide."[21] A less sanguine view, however, sees the watered-down language, with no specific mention of either a historical period, the identity of the perpetrators, or the international obligations assumed under both the Genocide Convention or the general principles of international law, as leaving the new government free to argue that "adhere to" involves only becoming a party to the major human rights treaties and future compliance with those instruments. (Cambodia signed the International Covenants, the Convention Against Torture, and the Convention Against Racial Discrimination, among others, in 1992.) The long alliance of the party that won the May 1993 elections with the Khmer Rouge make this result even more likely unless international pressure is brought to bear.

The evolution of international statements on the issue has been somewhat encouraging. For years the General Assembly had been passing resolutions on Cambodia, demanding the withdrawal of foreign forces; in 1988 and 1989 it added an oblique reference to past violations. The resolution, no doubt to avoid Chinese opposition, made no reference to the Khmer Rouge, alluding only to the "universally condemned policies and practices of the recent past."[22] The U.N. Sub-Commission on Prevention of Discrimination and Protection of Minorities in 1990 dropped from its agenda a draft resolution that would have called on states to detect, arrest, extradite, or bring to trial persons responsible for crimes against humanity committed in Cambodia and to prevent the return to government positions of persons who were responsible for genocidal actions during the 1975–78 period.[23] According to one account, the resolution was dropped to avoid rendering a disservice to the negotiations on a U.N. peace plan. By 1991, however, the Sub-Commission passed a milder resolution, noting "the duty of the international community to prevent the recurrence of genocide in Cambodia." The U.S. and Australian governments have both expressed support for bringing to trial the persons responsible for the mass murders of the 1970s, *if* the new government chooses to do so.[24]

For the peace plan what have been the results of international ambivalence (or worse) toward efforts to bring the DK leaders to justice? First, it strengthened the sense of impunity on the part of the Khmer Rouge. The Khmer Rouge denied the UNTAC access to territory under its control and refused to disarm or to take part in elections. Thus, attempts to investigate current violations completely excluded those carried out by the Khmer Rouge, even in the face of repeated attacks against civilians (most of them Cambodian citizens of Vietnamese origin) as well as against UNTAC personnel. Because UNTAC had no access to parts of the country in which many of the worst violations took place, its focus on the violations of the Hun Sen regime did not reflect the overall reality of the situation that prevails in Cambodia.

Second, as the head of the UNTAC's Civil Administration Component noted in January 1993, "this absence of firmness with the Khmer Rouge was a sort of signal for the other parties who saw there the proof of UNTAC's weakness towards the group that from the start eschewed all cooperation." UNTAC head Yasushi Akashi agreed that as a result of the Khmer Rouge's failure to abide by the agreement, the other factions, especially the SOC, had been "less than consistent" in their adherence.[25] The SOC's cooperation with UNTAC human rights monitors in cases of military shootings and alleged disappearances of civilians has been deficient, and few government officials have been arrested — much less tried — despite alleged widespread abuses.[26]

Finally, there is the effect on the legitimacy and consistency of international law. Although early attempts to punish the massive crimes committed by the government of Cambodia in the 1970s may have foundered on cold war antagonisms, the impunity of high officials of the DK regime has continued past the end of the cold war and has been exacerbated by the role of the five permanent Security Council members. Whereas the human rights organs of the United Nations have developed clearer and more elaborate guidelines on the required treatment of past human rights violations, the peacemaking branches of the United Nations have subordinated those guidelines to an ill-advised effort to bring even mass murderers into the political process, in the hopes they can be placated, reformed, or at least isolated.

Developments since the May 1993 election have been unexpected. Under Prince Sihanouk's guidance the FUNCINPEC party, which won 58 out of the 120 seats in the Constituent Assembly, and the Cambodian People's Party of the Phnom Penh government, which won 51 seats, have become equal partners in a coalition government, with proportional participation of Son Sann's BLDP party, which won 10 seats. Prince Ranariddh of FUNCINPEC and Hun Sen are co-prime ministers, and their parties share an equal number of ministerial posts.

The first announcements by the new leaders with respect to the Khmer Rouge were discouraging for the persons who sought to bring the DK leaders to justice. It appeared instead that eventually the DK leaders would be integrated into the new government and into the new joint military that had already been formed from the armies of Phnom Penh, Sihanouk, and Son Sann by the end of June 1993.

Since mid-1993, however, the new joint army has launched victorious attacks against Khmer Rouge bases. The implication may be that Prince Ranariddh, instead of pursuing his old policy of reconciliation with the Khmer Rouge, has been persuaded of the wisdom of Hun Sen's announced preelection policy of inflicting military defeat on them. If this is the case, the exclusion of old DK leaders from the new government may be assured, although there is no guarantee that a Cambodian government will undertake to punish these individuals. Moreover, the entire situation within Cambodia is still too fluid and unstable to permit any predictions that are more than crude guesses.

19

Zimbabwe: Drawing a Line Through the Past

Richard Carver

We were trying to kill each other; that's what the war was about. What I am concerned with now is that my public statements should be believed when I say that I have drawn a line through the past.

—Prime Minister Robert Mugabe, on retaining the head of Rhodesian intelligence in charge of Zimbabwe's Central Intelligence Organization, quoted in Ken Flower, *Serving Secretly*

Nothing the police are doing now is new. The police have learned all their bad habits from the Rhodesian police. The beatings, the electric shock. . . .

—Former Rhodesian police officer, quoted in Lawyers' Committee for Human Rights, *Zimbabwe: Wages of War*

The issue of the accountability of security force personnel for human rights violations is seldom debated in Africa. In Latin America and, more recently, in Eastern Europe, the issue of whether to bring to justice officials who violated human rights under past regimes has been a subject of national debate. But in most African countries the choice has been scarcely considered and has tended to be decided by default. South Africa is clearly an exception. Already embarked on a process of constitutional transformation after decades of gross human rights violations, the new government and the leading political parties must consider what attitude to take toward the members of the security forces and others responsible for these abuses. Will their crimes be investigated? Will they be brought to justice? Will there be a blanket amnesty for human rights violators? Will they be allowed to continue to hold positions of responsibility in the security forces?

Neighboring Zimbabwe confronted a similar range of options at independence some fourteen years ago, in circumstances that were similar to those in South Africa today. A white minority government finally conceded democratic rule to the black majority after decades of political repression. The culmination was a brutal counterinsurgency war in the 1970s. The Army, the police, and the security agencies had been responsible for widespread detention without trial and torture of persons who opposed the government, for extensive judicial and extrajudicial executions, and for forced disappearances. All of these abuses had been thoroughly documented by both international and domestic human rights bodies. At independence in 1980, however, essentially political considerations dictated that not only would human rights violators not be brought to justice for past abuses but that they would be retained within the security apparatus, with no investigation or calling to account for the deeds of the past. The serious consequences of this decision are explored in this chapter.

Focusing on past human rights abuses is a timely subject because it is an ongoing issue in Zimbabwe. The subject is also timely because of recent debates over whether South Africa will follow the same path of a blanket amnesty for human rights violators, based upon similar political considerations. It is reasonable to assume that the consequence — the continued recurrence of similar types of human rights violations — would also be the same.

1980—The Hidden Amnesty

After years of armed struggle and international diplomacy, Zimbabwe's independence settlement came suddenly. Between September and December 1979 all the major parties in the country assembled in London for a conference at Lancaster House, chaired by the United Kingdom, the colonial power. These parties were the white minority Rhodesian government and the leaders of a number of black parties co-opted into an "internal settlement" a year earlier and the two major nationalist parties, the Zimbabwe African National Union (ZANU), led by Robert Mugabe, and the Zimbabwe African People's Union (ZAPU), led by Joshua Nkomo. At this stage ZANU and ZAPU were linked in an alliance known as the Patriotic Front (PF).[1]

The Lancaster House settlement included an amnesty for all acts carried out in the course of the war. Earlier, the nationalist movement had been vocal in calling for Rhodesian leaders to be brought to trial, yet these demands were not reflected in the agreement. The amnesty and the entrenched guarantees of land and pension rights were seen as political imperatives if the independence agreement was to be acceptable to the economically important white community.

After independence the Zimbabwean government adhered to the provisions of the Lancaster House settlement in a number of other matters it found obnoxious — such as the maintenance of a racially segregated voters' roll. Arguably, it would have been unrealistic to expect the government to break the agreement over the amnesty issue because it depended on continued good will from the white minority as well as from the international community. However, the new government went far beyond its Lancaster House obligations by not investigating past human rights violations at all and by keeping human rights violators in crucial positions in the security apparatus. Little disquiet was expressed over these developments, and the international community heaped praise on the new prime minister, Robert Mugabe, for his "statesmanlike" compromises with the white community. The general view was that the new government, dominated by ZANU—which was regarded as the more radical of the two main nationalist organizations—could have sought "vengeance" against the white settler population but instead opted for "reconciliation."

Ken Flower, the head of the Rhodesian Central Intelligence Organization (CIO), was the most prominent security official retained by the new government. He later described how Prime Minister Mugabe told him that he was being kept on despite allegations by the commissioner of police that he had orchestrated attempts to kill Mugabe:

> He had no wish to talk of the allegations against me, dismissing the Commissioner as just another police informer, and he laughed when I showed readiness to confirm some of our attempts to kill him.
>
> "Yes, but they all failed, otherwise we would not be here together," he remarked. "And do not expect me to applaud your failures."
>
> He paused for a moment and then continued: "As far as I have realised the position, we were trying to kill each other; that's what the war was about. What I am concerned with now is that my public statements should be believed when I say that I have drawn a line through the past."[2]

Thus the amnesty to human rights violators was rationalized by describing all abuses committed before independence as being in the context of war. Yet this is simply untrue. Rhodesia, like South Africa, was a system of institutionalized racial domination that depended upon systematic and legalized human rights violations for its maintenance. Mugabe himself and thousands of other nationalists were detained—and in many cases tortured—not for armed activities but for attempting to express their political views. During the war the Rhodesian security forces carried out large numbers of extrajudicial executions of prisoners, civilians, or others who were placed *hors de combat*, in clear contravention not only of international human rights standards but also of the laws of war. To take one of the clearest examples: In August 1976 the Rhodesian security forces launched raids on the Zimbabwean refugee camp at Nyadzonia in Mozambique, leaving nearly 1,000 people dead. A member of the elite Selous Scouts, who took part in the massacre, later described the preraid briefing:

> We were told that Nyadzonia was a camp containing several thousand unarmed refugees who could be recruited to join the guerrillas. It would be easier if we went in and wiped them out while they were unarmed and before they were trained rather than waiting for the possibility of them being trained and sent back armed into Rhodesia.[3]

This was not a normal military operation. It was a human rights violation—and a war crime—that was echoed in hundreds of smaller incidents throughout the country and in neighboring states. For Mugabe to pardon Flower for attempts to kill him might be seen as a personal act of forgiveness. But the other victims of Rhodesian human rights violations—or their surviving families—were not consulted when the decision was made that their tormentors should go unpunished.

The rationale for retaining human rights violators in the security forces was explained by Emmerson Mnangagwa, now minister of justice but then minister of state responsible for security, in an interview by journalist Joseph Lelyveld in 1983:

> The first thing he did, he said, when he took over his department was to revisit a room in a police station where he had been tortured by white officers who hung him upside down by leg irons from butchers' hooks that ran along a track on the ceiling. This enabled the interrogators, the minister said, to bat his suspended body back and forth on the track from one end of the room to the other, as if he were the puck in an adaptation of hockey. The game continued until he lost consciousness. The day after the independence ceremonies, the butchers' hooks were still on the ceiling, and astonishingly, his former interrogators were now on his staff, as was another official who acknowledged having once sent him a letter bomb. They told him they had just been doing their jobs; he then promised they could start in independent Zimbabwe with a "clean slate." Some had later proved to be South African agents, but others still appeared to be loyal officers, the minister said. In the beginning he had no choice but to trust them, he explained. Zimbabwe could not be expected to dismantle its only security agency.[4]

This rationale is important and should be placed alongside the reluctance to frighten the white community. But it also reveals that the new government conceived of the nature of the state — at least the coercive aspects of the state — in much the same way as did its Rhodesian predecessors. This attitude was to have pernicious consequences later on.

A third element that perpetuated a general atmosphere of impunity was the continuation for ten years after independence of the state of emergency that had been in place since 1965, which provided the legal framework for ongoing human rights violations. Most important, the emergency state provided powers of detention without trial under the Emergency Powers (Maintenance of Law and Order) Regulations, which remained in force with only minor amendments. Similarly, the Law and Order (Maintenance) Act, the statute most widely used to prosecute nationalist guerrillas and their alleged supporters, was retained and frequently used. These broad and often arbitrary legal powers provided a sense that the security forces operated beyond the reach of the normal provisions of the law. It also meant that normal law-enforcement officials, such as police officers, failed to gain the basic skills to properly investigate criminal cases and prosecute them in court. Instead, ill treatment and torture of both criminal and political prisoners was widespread.

Indemnity and Compensation in Rhodesian and Zimbabwean Law

The right to sue for compensation for government abuses has a turbulent history. In 1975 several torture victims brought actions for damages in the High Court. The response of the Rhodesian government was to introduce the Indemnity and Compensation Act. This legislation indemnified members of the security forces and other government servants for any actions that had been carried out in good faith in defense of national security since December 1972. The act also gave the minister for law and order authority to terminate actions for damages before the High Court.

The Zimbabwean government retained the act after independence. A senior government minister, Edgar Tekere, successfully invoked the act when he faced charges of murdering a white farmer in August 1980, with the result that the government was obliged to give way to political pressure and repeal the law. However, the government promptly reintroduced almost identical provisions as regulations under its emergency powers—which meant that it avoided any parliamentary scrutiny. In 1984 a Harare lawyer, Denis Granger, sued the minister of state for Security for damages for wrongful arrest by the CIO. The minister of home affairs used his powers under these emergency powers (security forces indemnity) regulations to issue a certificate disallowing the proceedings. The constitutionality of the certificate was then tested in the Supreme Court, which ruled unanimously that the regulations were in breach of the constitutional provision allowing a person who is wrongfully arrested to sue for compensation. As a result, the government was obliged to repeal the regulations.

Yet, despite this constitutional guarantee of the right to sue for compensation, in practice government policy has been to disregard court rulings in such cases; the judiciary has not risked a direct confrontation with the executive over this point. Prime Minister Mugabe told Parliament in 1986:

> If Government—and I want to say this as a matter of principle— were to be awarding damages and paying huge sums of money that are involved in these cases, some of which are of a petty nature, Government would in my view be using the taxpayers' money wrongfully. . . .
>
> [W]here people take advantage of our liberal situation to go to court and win on technicalities, they should not expect that Government is going to use the people's resources to enrich them.[5]

Granger himself never received the damages payment awarded by the court, although he deducted the amount from his income tax bill and the matter was left there. Member of Parliament Wally Stuttaford, who was awarded damages for torture in 1982, received nothing either. Aged in his sixties, Stuttaford had been kicked, punched, made to do strenuous exercise, and had his hair pulled. Pencils were inserted between his fingers, and his hands were squeezed. It is unclear if this is what the prime minister had in mind when he talked of cases of a "petty nature," which were won "on technicalities."

Zimbabwe's past practice has clearly been in breach of the provisions of the International Covenant on Civil and Political Rights guaranteeing a right to a remedy, including enforcement of the remedies provided. Zimbabwe became a party to the Covenant in 1991, and more recent cases suggest that the authorities have become readier to abide by damages awards made by the courts.

In May 1989 Parliament passed another indemnity law, this time shielding national park game wardens and other security force personnel from criminal prosecution for acts carried out in good faith in the course of antipoaching activities. This indemnity does not apply to civil proceedings for compensation and is therefore not affected by the Supreme Court ruling in the Granger case. According to official figures, between July 1984 and September 1991 antipoaching patrols killed 145 suspected poachers. The Protection of Wildlife (Indemnity) Act was introduced after senior national park officials faced criminal charges in connection with the deaths of poachers. There were widespread allegations that the charges had been fabricated by police personnel who were themselves involved in elephant poaching, and eventually the charges were dropped. It is understood that national park officials insisted on the enactment of indemnity provisions. It appears that the Protection of Wildlife (Indemnity) Act has encouraged the use of lethal force against poachers, including possible extrajudicial executions. It is alleged in some quarters that the security forces follow a shoot-to-kill policy.

In summary, Zimbabwe embarked upon its existence as an independent state by sending a clear message to its security forces that they would enjoy the same impunity their Rhodesian predecessors enjoyed. Officials responsible for human rights violations had been granted amnesties without any investigation or accounting for past abuses. Many of these individuals were retained in similar positions of authority. Members of the security forces were indemnified from any future prosecution for human rights violations, and much of the legal apparatus that had provided the framework for abuses in the 1970s remained intact. The consequences were clear and predictable:

- Respect for the rule of law was weakened, and the security forces continued to operate within a culture that saw human rights violations as part of an acceptable method of working.
- Specific methods of human rights abuses were passed on from the Rhodesian to the Zimbabwean forces — and these methods were often practiced by the very same individuals.

The legacy of Rhodesian human rights violations was not confined within Zimbabwe's borders. Many Rhodesian personnel left the country at independence and placed themselves beyond the reach of Zimbabwean law. Even so, a proper truth telling, or the issuance of arrest warrants, might still have inhibited their further abuses. Many ex-Rhodesians ended up in the service of the South African state, with some actively engaged in subverting Zimbabwe's security. Others found employment with the nominally independent black "homelands" within South Africa, such as Transkei. Among the most prominent, Ron Reid-Daley, head of the Selous Scouts — who were responsible for gross abuses, including the Nyadzonia massacre — became commander of the Transkei Defence Force. Many other Rhodesians also found senior positions in the Transkei security apparatus. During Reid-Daley's period in Transkei there were frequent reports of armed attacks on neighboring Lesotho by the South African-backed Lesotho Liberation Army and the Transkei Defence Force itself.

Most seriously, Rhodesia bequeathed to South Africa an entire institution dedicated to the abuse of human rights — RENAMO, the Resistencia Nacional Mocambicana, or Mozambique National Resistance. The Rhodesian CIO created RENAMO in the mid-1970s as a means of countering ZANLA, the military wing of ZANU, which operated from rear bases inside Mozambique. The organization grew into a full-fledged opposition to the Mozambique government and engaged in widespread killing, mutilation, and enslavement of Mozambique's rural population. RENAMO was initially recruited from among the Shona-speaking Ndau, who straddle the Zimbabwe-Mozambique border. (Its present leader, Afonso Dhlakama, is Ndau, as are many of the movement's senior officials.) At Zimbabwean independence in 1980 control of RENAMO was transferred lock, stock, and barrel to the South African military, according to its creator, Ken Flower, who became Prime Minister Mugabe's trusted security adviser. Flower later wrote: "I began to wonder whether we had created a monster that was now beyond control."[6]

Nothing in the political and military situation in southern Africa remains confined within national borders. Thus the Zimbabwean army engaged for some years in a counterinsurgency war against RENAMO in Mozambique, in the course of which it committed human rights violations against Mozambican civilians. RENAMO, launched to counter the Zimbabwean nationalist movement and then transformed into a Mozambican insurgent force, until a recent cease-fire carried out attacks — and commited gross abuses — against civilian targets inside independent Zimbabwe. And Portuguese speakers, possibly South African-trained RENAMO members, have been identified as members of the death squads operating in South Africa's townships. The Special Forces of the South African Defence Force were also known to contain former personnel from Koevoet (Crowbar), the paramilitary police unit responsible for extensive human rights abuse before independence in Namibia. As in Zimbabwe, Namibian human rights violators benefited from an amnesty at independence.

The Effects of Impunity: Repression in Matabeleland

From the earliest months of Zimbabwe's independence there was tension and potential insecurity. Three armies were to be integrated to form a single Zimbabwe National Army: ZANLA, the military wing of ZANU; ZIPRA, the military wing of ZAPU; and the Rhodesian Army. Although the former Rhodesian Army continued to be housed in barracks and draw full Army pay, the nationalist guerrillas awaiting integration were housed in makeshift camps in poor conditions. Resentment against these problems aroused latent rivalries between ZANLA and ZIPRA, which broke out into open conflict in Bulawayo's Entumbane township in November 1980 and again in February 1981. During the second round of fighting Prime Minister Mugabe deployed the Rhodesian Air Force and the Rhodesian African Rifles against the ZIPRA forces in Bulawayo, killing more than 100. There were a number of reports of killings of civilians and prisoners. In Mzilikazi township, more than two kilometers from the fighting, three children were killed when a helicopter gunship attacked a civilian township. In Bulawayo's industrial area former Rhodesian police reservists reportedly executed five ZAPU officials. A judicial commission of inquiry investigated the events, but its report was never made public. Many former ZIPRA guerrillas were disillusioned by the government's use of the Rhodesian state against them, deserted from Entumbane and other assembly points, and returned to the bush to continue their armed struggle. Over the next six years the Army's counterinsurgency campaign against these former guerrillas, now termed "dissidents," was to provide the occasion for gross violations of human rights.

The government's anti-"dissident" campaign, launched in early 1982, reprised many of the tactics, including serious human rights abuses, that had been used by the Rhodesian forces in their campaign against nationalist forces. The government first deployed a task force in Matabeleland North under the command of Lieutenant Colonel Lionel Dyke, a former officer in the Selous Scouts. The force was composed of former Rhodesian African Rifles and Rhodesian Light Infantry. There were frequent reports of detention and torture of villagers. The task force was later replaced by the Fifth Brigade, an elite unit. In press accounts the Fifth Brigade's poor human rights record was usually attributed to its training by North Korean instructors. In the rainy season of early 1983, and again at the same time the following year, the Fifth Brigade carried out systematic killings of civilians in Matabeleland. There is a clear linguistic divide between the Ndebele speakers of southwestern Zimbabwe — Matabeleland — and the Shona speakers of the north and east. This division had come to be almost coterminous with the political divide between ZANU, which controlled the government, and ZAPU, which drew its support from Matabeleland. Unlike other Army units, which were ethnically and politically integrated, the Fifth Brigade drew exclusively from Shona-speaking former ZANLA guerrillas. What is remarkable is the extent to which the Zimbabwe national Army had distanced itself from ZANLA's guerrilla past. The roots of ZANLA's success had been in the extent to which it was able to organize the rural population politically. The Fifth Brigade, on the contrary, made no effort to promote any political identification with the peasants of Matabeleland, resorting instead to crude tribalist stereotypes to justify its abuse of the civilian population. Its members came to resemble the Rhodesian Army more than they resembled their former guerrilla selves. The deployment of army units with no roots in the local community was clearly a conscious tactic for reasons that went beyond mere tribalism. In the late 1980s when the Mozambican rebel group RENAMO began to operate in the Shona-speaking areas along Zimbabwe's eastern borders, the Army units that were deployed were dominated by Ndebele speakers. These included the Grey's Scouts, an elite counterinsurgency unit inherited from the Rhodesian Army.

In some respects the tactics used by the Fifth Brigade in Matabeleland differed markedly from those of the Rhodesian Army in the 1970s. The Fifth Brigade did not, for example, employ the "fireforce" method of swift, concentrated helicopter-borne attacks against rebels. Indeed, its aim often seemed to be to avoid the "dissidents" altogether, concentrating its attack on suspected civilian supporters of the "dissidents." However, two counterinsurgency tactics, both entailing gross human rights violations, were directly inherited from the Rhodesians. The first was named, with grim irony, Operation Turkey. The ostensible aim of this tactic used by the Rhodesian security forces was to eliminate any surplus food held by the rural population so that they had none to share with the guerrillas. In practice the purpose was to demoralize the civilians in the rural areas by a policy of starvation. This tactic was combined with a policy of herding three-quarters of a million people into some 220 "protected villages." The aim of this strategy — which had been practiced by Britain and the United States in Southeast Asia—was to isolate the civilian population from the guerrillas by forced removals and strict dusk-to-dawn curfews. The result often was that people were unable to reach their fields to cultivate them. The combined effect of Operation Turkey and the protected-village policy was that at independence Zimbabwe, the breadbasket of the region, faced an acute food crisis.

In 1984 Operation Turkey was revived in Matabeleland South, then in the grip of a three-year drought. As before, food supplies were destroyed, shops were closed, and food was confiscated from travelers. A strict curfew was imposed, and violators were shot. There were reports that food relief was supplied only to those who produced a ZANU(PF) party card. The Rhodesian government had used a similar tactic to compel support for the black parties involved in its "internal settlement" in the late 1970s. (The protected-village policy was also revived at a later stage in eastern Zimbabwe. From late 1988 onward people were concentrated near main roads to protect them from attacks by RENAMO. In this instance no major human rights violations on the part of the Army were reported.)

The second Rhodesian tactic that was widely emulated by the Zimbabwean Army was the use of "pseudogangs"—groups of soldiers posing as guerrillas, either to expose civilian supporters of the rebels or to commit abuses that could be blamed on the insurgents. This tactic could have the effect both of turning the civilian population against the rebels and of creating propaganda that would favor the security forces. Amnesty International documented two clear examples of this tactic in 1985. Both involved figures known to be sympathetic to ZAPU who were killed while military or police forces located nearby did nothing to intervene. The Zimbabwe government resisted calls for independent inquiries into these two incidents, and the culprits have never been identified. It is impossible to know how many other killings officially attributed to "dissidents" may in fact have been the work of pseudogangs. Similarly, it seems likely that some of the hundreds of people who served sentences under the Law and Order (Maintenance) Act for "failure to report" the presence of rebels were the victims of entrapment by security force pseudogangs.

Sometimes the very individuals who had carried out torture and other abuses under the Rhodesian government continued to do so under new political masters. Of course, not all—nor even most—human rights violations in Zimbabwe have been committed by former Rhodesian personnel. However, the continued presence of Rhodesian human rights violators has provided a fund of expertise. The tortures used by the Rhodesian police became commonly used by the Zimbabwean security forces against political detainees. But more important, these former Rhodesians legitimated a culture of human rights abuse and a sense of impunity.

The 1988 Amnesty

This sense of impunity was reinforced by the government's own ineffectual response to allegations of human rights violations. The commission of inquiry into the Entumbane disturbances has already been mentioned, along with the government's failure to publish its report. Similarly, in 1983 the government set up a commission to investigate allegations of Army killings of civilians in Matabeleland, and again there was no public report. The failure to publish any report only underscored the government's inability or disinclination to confront the issue publicly.

This official culture of forgetfulness reached its apogee in June 1988 when seventy-five members of the security forces serving sentences or awaiting trial for human rights violations were granted amnesties. One of those released was Robert Masikini, a CIO officer who only a week earlier had been found guilty of murdering a political detainee. Masikini's release, with press reports of his crime still fresh and without any expressions of remorse on his part, caused a good deal of public outrage. Also released were four Fifth Brigade soldiers, under sentence of death for murder, who were among the very few ever to have been brought to justice. Probably the reason they were charged in the first place was that one of their four victims was an off-duty Army officer, Lieutenant Edias Ndlovu. The inquest had found that "the deceased were tied with pieces of fibre, were got down on the ground and repeatedly stabbed with bayonets, much as a hunter slaughtering a wounded animal with a spear."

The government claimed to have a clear political justification for the 1988 amnesty. It was a direct parallel with an amnesty earlier the same year granting immunity from prosecution to "dissidents," which followed the signing of a unity agreement between ZANU(PF) and ZAPU. The amnesty for "dissidents" was successful in bringing peace to Matabeleland, but it created serious public misgivings because some of the rebels granted amnesty were believed to have been responsible for atrocious abuses, such as the hacking to death of sixteen people, including babies and children, at a Protestant mission in Esigodini in November 1987. However, by its amnesty for security force members the government appeared to attach no particular significance to the fact that, unlike the "dissidents," their crimes had been carried out when they were charged with the responsibility of protecting the human rights of Zimbabwe's citizens. Essentially the government's rationale was the same as in 1980, when all past abuses were placed in a closed file labeled acts of war.

The Debate Over Impunity

Remarkably few voices were raised within Zimbabwe to criticize the amnesties of either 1980 or 1988. However, particularly after the 1988 amnesty, there has been criticism of the government's failure to explain and learn from past human rights violations. There has also been a tenacious legal struggle by the families of one group of people who "disappeared."

The 1980 amnesty scarcely figured in political debate at the time. Even persons who were critical of the new government's alleged failure to fulfill other aspects of its preindependence program, such as land reform, seemed content to accept the view that a line should be drawn through the past. Once the step had been taken to grant amnesty to people like Rhodesian Prime Minister Ian Smith — prominent figures in the demonology of Zimbabwean nationalism — it seemed natural that similar magnanimity should extend to persons who had committed offenses in defense of the Zimbabwean state. Thus, historian Lawrence Vambe, interviewed after the 1988 amnesty, stated:

> We could have tried and hanged Mr Smith. We could have tried all those who participated in Smith's war who had blood on their hands. If there was a compulsion to settle old scores, this country would have seen much more suffering than we have seen, especially with the whites.[7]

The 1988 amnesty did arouse some disquiet, especially the releases already mentioned of CIO official Masikini and the murderers of Lieutenant Ndlovu. In legal terms the issue was rather different from that in 1980. At independence a decision was made not to investigate or undertake any accounting for past human rights violations. By contrast, some of the persons released under the 1988 amnesty had already been tried and convicted, so the government could not reasonably be accused of concealing its actions. In that sense, perhaps, the later amnesty may have been less objectionable. Although few people actually opposed the amnesty for security force personnel, human rights activists pointed out the inconsistency of the government's position because prisoners serving sentences for far less serious offenses under the Law and Order (Maintenance) Act did not benefit from the amnesty.

Once again there was almost no support in political circles for the notion that there should be a thorough accounting for abuses that took place between independence and 1988. Many government supporters argued that if "dissidents" could be let off scot free, then it was only fair that persons who committed abuses "in good faith" in defense of national security should also go unpunished. Kembo Mohadi, a ZAPU member of Parliament who had successfully sued the government for damages for torture, dropped the case after the unity agreement between his party and ZANU(PF): "I personally don't really accept retrospective condemnation. A new chapter was opened on 22 December [when the unity agreement was signed]." Another ZAPU member of Parliament, Sidney Malunga, was detained three times and beaten on the soles of the feet. He expressed similar sentiments: "I believe political leaders must be magnanimous. We don't want to open up old wounds." Underlying these reactions may be an acceptance by the political elite, in Zimbabwe as in other parts of Africa, that imprisonment, and even torture, are a normal part of the "swings and roundabouts" of the political process. Demanding accountability not only violates the rules of the political game but also may be dangerous, because you yourself may be held to account for similar actions while in government.

The reaction of ordinary people was different. Joseph Khumalo from Silobela was interviewed shortly after the unity agreement and amnesty:

> The memory is very powerful. Even people who I played with disappeared. A friend in our area, Matanda Fuzane, they shot him directly. Ah, that was terrible. It was done publicly, that shooting, at night. His father witnessed it. It was the Fifth Brigade. They shot him in front of his family. [The unity agreement] has done nothing to help the souls of the people. The people were suffering, now it has come to a rest. But you can't just say, "Gentlemen, it's over." There is nothing that proves to me that we are over this matter.[8]

An Ndebele lawyer spoke of how his brother still suffered "psychological withdrawal" five years after having been given electric shock torture by the CIO. He commented:

> For those who were untouched, they might as well have been reading about Lebanon. Those people have nothing to forget, nothing to forgive. But in Matabeleland, every family was touched. Every family suffered.[9]

One group of families has tried with only partial success to use the legal system to call the government to account for human rights violations. They are the relatives of nine men who were detained and "disappeared" from the Silobela area of Midlands province on the night of January 30, 1985. Dozens — possibly hundreds — of people disappeared in Matabeleland and Midlands in the space of a few weeks in January and February 1985. Most of them were abducted at night by armed men driving vehicles without license plates. The victims were overwhelmingly Ndebele speaking — although Midlands has a mixed population of Shona and Ndebele speakers — and many were local ZAPU officials. The government alleged that the persons who disappeared had slipped across the border to Botswana to join the "dissidents." Quite aside from the inherent improbabilities in this account — many of those who disappeared were elderly, and there are no reported instances of "dissidents" driving vehicles — it remains a fact that when the amnesty for "dissidents" was declared in 1988, not a single person reappeared of those who had vanished in January or February 1985.

In 1986 a lawyer for the Catholic Commission for Justice and Peace in Zimbabwe filed a suit in the High Court on behalf of nine women from Silobela. In their supporting affidavits the women described how their husbands had been threatened by ZANU(PF) officials before they disappeared; how their abductors did not speak proper Ndebele and appeared to be government officials rather than people who lived in the bush; how they beat the men and drove them away in vehicles that looked like the Nissan trucks used by the security forces; and how the police failed to carry out proper investigations into the disappearances. The High Court ordered a police investigation into the case, which finally reported its findings in early 1989. However, the findings did not go beyond the women's affidavits. There was no proper investigation into a number of aspects of the case. The police failed to interview all relevant witnesses, such as the man who swore an affidavit saying that he had seen his nephew, a special constable, driving toward the scene of the abductions on the night of January 30. Nor did they interview the ZANU(PF) officials who had issued threats against local people. The police also failed to check the movements of police and other security force vehicles on the night of January 30. In 1985 a BBC television crew was shown a mass grave in nearby Nkayi, which was alleged to contain the bodies of some of those who had disappeared earlier that year. There were said to be four other graves in the vicinity. Yet the police apparently made no attempt even to look at the graves, let alone commission a forensic examination of their contents.

Finally, in early 1992 the nine men from Silobela were declared dead. While this resolved certain financial problems connected with the administration of their estates, the conclusion of the case was unsatisfactory because it failed to account for the circumstances surrounding the men's disappearance, to assign responsibility, or to pay damages to the families. An independent commission of inquiry employing its own impartial investigating team might have come nearer to the truth of what happened in Silobela. Instead, the security forces have received another reassurance of their impunity.

Some Conclusions: The Need to Come to Terms with the Past

It is important that discussion of the impunity issue not oversimplify or exaggerate its effects. The amnesty for Rhodesian human rights violators did not "cause" the continuation of abuses in independent Zimbabwe. However, it did provide the environment — and the means — for new human rights violations.

At one level the new government consciously used the repressive apparatus of the Rhodesian state: emergency laws, intelligence personnel, specialized military units, and counterinsurgency tactics. But more broadly it allowed a culture of abuse and impunity to permeate the security structures. Many observers were surprised by the ease with which former Rhodesian personnel worked side by side with Zimbabwean nationalist guerrillas. Yet their shared military ethos — including the notion that they were beyond the reach of the law — proved stronger than their previous differences. The lessons for South Africa need hardly be elaborated.

The paradox is that impunity for human rights violators has flourished in a country that since 1980 has been a functioning multiparty democracy. Zimbabwe has a vigorous independent judiciary and a Declaration of Rights that is enforceable by the courts. It does not lack the institutional means to enforce respect for human rights. However, the government has chosen to place the security forces above the law. The problem is essentially political rather than institutional. Interestingly, since 1987 the strengthening of institutions of civil society has created greater pressure on the government to act against human rights violators. The emergence of an independent press has been particularly important in this regard. For example, independent newspapers have highlighted the disappearance of a woman, Rashiwe Guzha, who was last seen in CIO custody in 1990. The elevation of the case into a cause célèbre forced the government to bring charges against a senior CIO official. There have been calls from the press, academics, and human rights groups for an independent commission of inquiry into the whole functioning of the CIO.

It should be stressed that the aim of calling human rights violators to account is not retribution. Probably few within the human rights movement are advocates of purely retributive punishment. Instead, accountability is about three things, none of which has really been accomplished in the Zimbabwean cases cited:

- *Telling the truth:* Human rights abuses, by their very nature, are often obscured by a fog of lies and deceit. The victims of such abuses have a right to have their fate properly recounted, and an accurate historical record is essential to fulfill the other two elements.
- *Prevention:* Only by understanding the reality of human rights abuses — and their causes — can such violations be stopped in the future. Removing

human rights violators from positions of responsibility and bringing them to justice is part of this process.

- *Redress:* There can be no real compensation for the loss of a loved one, but exemplary financial damages may help families deal with some of the consequences of extrajudicial executions and disappearances, as well as deter the authorities from perpetuating abuses.

It is not too late for the Zimbabwean government to initiate a thorough process of investigation and truth telling about past human rights violations. The government should understand that this is part of the process of healing wounds both at the individual level — among the families of the dead and of those who disappeared — and nationally. It might be added that the government would emerge with a small amount of credit from such an investigation: Since 1987 it has made significant steps to overcome past human rights violations. The danger is that without a proper accounting such improvements will not be institutionalized. The situation on Zimbabwe's eastern border, where domestic political opposition has occurred in the context of RENAMO guerrilla attacks and unsympathetic Army operations, contains the seeds of another Matabeleland. The behavior of the Zimbabwean Army across the border in Mozambique has not been fully documented, but there is no doubt that it continues to commit abuses.

Zimbabwe can be viewed only in a regional context. The readiness of the Patriotic Front to agree in 1979 to the amnesty for Rhodesian personnel was undoubtedly based upon the experience of Mozambique, where skilled white colonialists had fled by the thousands at independence in 1975, causing economic disaster. Similarly, the ANC and other nationalist forces in South Africa will almost certainly draw positive lessons from the experience of Zimbabwe. Like Zimbabwe, a democratic South Africa will inherit security forces with a history of legal immunity and practical impunity for acts that violate human rights. As in Zimbabwe, there will no doubt be much talk about the need to heal old wounds and effect national reconciliation. At the level of political leadership it is not difficult to envisage such a reconciliation. Nor is it hard to imagine an integration of the security branches of the state and the nationalist movement, as happened in Zimbabwe. What is impossible to visualize is any healing of the wounds inflicted on the population by decades of human rights violations until the truth is told in full.

The persons who are engaged in designing South Africa's future might also ponder the rationale that the Zimbabwean government offered for retaining human rights violators from the Rhodesian state — namely, that they were the "only security agency" that the country had. Yet former Rhodesian CIO officials were responsible for the murder in 1981 of Joe Gqabi, the African National Congress representative in Harare. The following year these individuals oversaw the destruction of the most modern planes of the Zimbabwean Air Force in a commando raid on the Thornhill air base. A group of innocent (white) Air Force officers were arrested and tortured as a result of the attack. In January 1988, Kevin Woods, a former senior official in CIO anti-"dissident" operations in Matabeleland was responsible for a bomb attack that killed a man in Bulawayo. Woods's accomplices were a former Rhodesian soldier and a former police officer. The previous year Woods and his colleagues had carried out a car bomb attack in Harare that nearly killed antiapartheid activist Jeremy Brickhill. Most serious, it has emerged that Matt Calloway, a former Rhodesian who headed the CIO in Hwange after independence, was responsible for organizing the caching of arms by former ZIPRA combatants. The discovery of the caches led to the arrest of senior ZAPU officials and the expulsion of ZAPU ministers from the government in 1982, sparking armed "dissident" activity and leading thence to the appalling response by the Army in Matabeleland. Calloway later defected to South Africa where he organized arms and training for the "dissidents."

One cannot help but think that if this was Zimbabwe's "only security agency," the country might have managed better without one.

20

South Africa: Negotiating Change?

Lynn Berat

When the ruling National Party (NP) came to power in South Africa in 1948 with its slogan "apartheid,"[1] the country, which had long had discriminatory laws, rapidly adopted an elaborate system of legislation aimed at enforcing its racist social engineering programs. Over time, as antiapartheid protests within the country grew, the government enacted an ever-more draconian array of security laws that gave its security forces — the police and the military — sweeping powers to arrest and detain without trial persons opposed to its reign.[2] In the early 1960s, following one particularly marked period of unrest, the government banned the leading antiapartheid organizations such as the African National Congress (ANC) and imprisoned their leaders, most notably Nelson Mandela. Consequently, many antiapartheid groups went underground while thousands of their members fled the country.

The political situation then remained relatively calm until the 1976 Soweto uprisings, occasioned by the police shooting of African schoolchildren who were peacefully protesting the use of Afrikaans in the schools. Months of unrest followed throughout the country, during which time the government augmented its arsenal of security legislation and eventually achieved relative quiet. It was, however, the proverbial calm before the storm.

By 1983, protest began anew with the formation of a broad-based umbrella organization of antiapartheid groups known as the United Democratic Front (UDF). With the emergence of the UDF, antigovernment protests reached unprecedented heights. So great was the perceived threat to the government that then-President P. W. Botha elevated the security forces to a new level of authority within the government. From the mid-1980s, the country was ruled under a nationwide state of emergency accompanied by especially stringent security legislation. Troops were omnipresent in the black townships, and thousands of people, including children as young as eight years, were detained without trial.[3] Allegations of torture were widespread. At the same time, the rise of vigilantism in the townships and a series of assassinations of prominent antiapartheid activists led to suspicion that the government or its agents were conducting an extralegal campaign of terror. As the decade came to a close, Botha, who had suffered a stroke, was replaced by F. W. de Klerk. De Klerk, in a series of moves that startled both South Africans and foreign observers, set South Africa on the road toward a negotiated settlement of the political crisis.

Almost from the start, the question of the treatment of those both within the government and within the opposition who had committed human rights abuses became a contentious issue.[4] The identification and punishment of persons responsible for extralegal killings and massacres, the fate of political prisoners, and the role of an amnesty all continue to be major points of discussion and discord. As South Africa moved toward—and beyond—its first election based on universal suffrage, it faced hard questions of how, and to what extent, to deal with the past.

Negotiations and the Move Toward a New Order

On February 2, 1990, President de Klerk announced the lifting of the ban on the ANC, the Pan-Africanist Congress (PAC), the South African Communist Party (SACP), and other groups;[5] the removal of restrictions on thirty-three other organizations, including the powerful Congress of South African Trade Unions; the release of most political prisoners; the repeal of restrictions on 374 freed detainees; the limiting of detention without trial to six months, with provision for legal representation and medical treatment; and a moratorium on hangings. De Klerk also indicated that he would free ANC leader Nelson Mandela, perhaps the world's most famous political prisoner, after twenty-seven years in jail.[6] Thus began the process of political transformation of South Africa.

Mandela's release a few days later was accompanied by jubilation on the part of many of his compatriots as millions of people the world over watched the events on television. Mandela proceeded to tour numerous foreign countries, where he was greeted by adoring crowds. At home, the ANC opened offices throughout the country, and other political groups began to organize their newly legalized operations. In addition, the ANC held meetings with the government on "talks about talks." These discussions yielded the Groote Schuur Minute of May 4, 1990 and the Pretoria Minute of August 6, 1990; the documents established procedures for the release of political prisoners and for the granting of an official indemnity to political exiles. It was envisaged that all political prisoners would be released by April 1991. In fact, the established procedure proved unwieldy, so that by August 1992, the ANC insisted that 400 political prisoners remained incarcerated, a charge the government denied.

Meanwhile, in June, de Klerk announced the lifting of the four-year-old state of emergency.[7] Shortly thereafter, the ANC abandoned the armed struggle,[8] although it did not disband its military wing Unkhonto we Sizwe (Spear of the Nation), a condition the government continued to insist upon.[9]

Many people came to believe de Klerk's promise in his February speech that "[H]enceforth, everybody's political points of view will be tested against their realism, their workability and their fairness. . . . The time for negotiation has arrived."[10] Graffiti in some African townships even proclaimed, "Viva Comrade de Klerk!"[11] Yet euphoria quickly evaporated as people recognized that despite the unprecedented occurrences, the main pieces of apartheid legislation — the Land Acts of 1913 and 1936, the Group Areas Act, and the Population Registration Act — remained intact.[12] By year's end, South Africa teetered perilously on the brink of collapsing in internecine convulsions as Africans, allegedly with security force or other government complicity, brutalized and murdered one another in areas throughout the country in conflicts fueled by urban-rural, class, and ethnic tensions.[13]

The February 1991 opening of Parliament brought further changes. De Klerk announced his intention to remove the pillars of apartheid.[14] However, because blacks lacked the vote, the rescission of the legislation did not alter the balance of power in South Africa. The NP remained firmly in control of the country, commanding the allegiance of the largest and most sophisticated military machine in Africa.

In September, some people saw grounds for cautious optimism when representatives of the government, the ANC, and Inkatha became the major signatories to the National Peace Accord. Thereafter, the NP, in an effort to lead any negotiations in a way that would produce a settlement favorable to its interests, agreed to sit down at the bargaining table with the ANC and members of all political parties that wished to participate. The forum, which became known as the Convention for a Democratic South Africa (CODESA), included representatives from eighteen political parties. Analysis reveals that the perception Pretoria sought to create that CODESA was a vigorous multiparty free-for-all was but an illusion. With the exception of the ANC, Inkatha, and the NP itself, all parties to the left[15] and right[16] with the potential to disrupt the democratization process or undermine a new democratic order chose to absent themselves. With one exception,[17] the other fourteen parties, including the Colored and Indian parties and those from the African homelands,[18] were essentially NP puppets, which owed their existence to Pretoria's largesse and had negligible support from the populace.

On December 20, 1991, sixteen of the eighteen parties[19] signed the Declaration of Intent.[20] The Declaration provided that CODESA would "set in motion the process of drawing up and establishing a constitution"[21] guaranteeing that South Africa would be "a united, democratic, nonracial and nonsexist state,"[22] with a constitution as the supreme law and "an independent, nonracial and impartial judiciary"[23] to interpret that constitution. In addition, the parties subscribed to the ideas that South Africa would be a multiparty democracy with universal adult suffrage, a common voters' roll, and a basic electoral system based on proportional representation.[24] The parties also agreed upon "a separation of powers between the legislature, executive and judiciary with appropriate checks and balances."[25] "[T]he diversity of languages, cultures and religions of the people of South Africa" also was to be recognized.[26] All were to enjoy "human rights, freedoms and civil liberties . . . protected by an entrenched and justiciable Bill of Rights and a legal system that guarantees equality of all before the law."[27]

De Klerk at first indicated that an interim government might be quickly established, but almost immediately retreated from that position.[28] On March 17, 1992, in an effort to show that he had broad support for his initiatives, de Klerk staged a referendum among white voters. They were asked to respond yes or no to the question, "Do you support the continuation of the reform process which the State President began on February 2, 1990 and which is aimed at a new constitution through negotiation?" With an 87.6 percent voter turnout, 68.7 percent voted in favor of de Klerk's policies.[29] The white voters did so perhaps out of fear that a "no" vote would plunge the country into civil war and in spite of a vigorous campaign by the official parliamentary opposition Conservative Party. De Klerk's ostensible victory cleared the way for negotiations to proceed apace. However, further talks deadlocked over the power of the executive until an interim government could be formed, the fate of the remaining political prisoners, and the percentage of votes required for decisions by the proposed interim assembly with regard to regional borders, government powers, and various regional issues.

Violence and the Goldstone Commission

The NP, ANC, and Inkatha (now formally known as the Inkatha Freedom Party, or IFP) continued to express their desire for talks about change. However, they did so against a backdrop of increasing violence in the black community. Indeed, from July 1990 through June 1992, some 6,229 South Africans died in violent incidents, approximately the same number killed during the unrest of the 1980s.[30] The ANC alleged that the deteriorating conditions were not merely the result of black animosities but rather were being orchestrated by a "third force" operating either under government auspices or with government approval.

After considerable public outcry, de Klerk appointed a commission of inquiry, known officially as the Commission of Inquiry into Public Violence and Intimidation. The Commission quickly became known as the Goldstone Commission, after the judge who presided over the Appellate Division, South Africa's highest court.[31] The Commission's mandate included investigating certain particularly notorious massacres and other acts of violence and attempting to discover the extent of involvement by security forces or forces under the control of the ANC, Inkatha, PAC, or other groups.[32] Despite its official mandate, the Commission initially had few resources and no investigative capacity of its own, but relied instead on reports by the police or independent human rights groups. The Commission had no mandate in the nominally independent black homelands; nor did the government have to act on the evidence of misconduct it produced.[33] It carried out over forty investigations and won a reputation for evenhandedness.

The Goldstone Commission was called upon regularly to investigate incidents of violence that threatened to derail the negotiation process. In May 1992, the Commission issued a report on the causes of violence, placing primary blame on the ANC and Inkatha and finding no evidence of government complicity.[34] A month later, on June 17, forty-five ANC supporters were killed in Boipatong township south of Johannesburg by Inkatha Freedom Party members who lived in a hostel for migrant workers.[35] The ANC pulled out of negotiations, accusing government security forces of abetting the perpetrators.[36] De Klerk denied such suggestions and asked that the Goldstone Commission add the Boipatong massacre to its investigative agenda.[37]

Over a year later, the Commission found no conclusive evidence that the South African Defence Force had trained Inkatha supporters to perpetrate violence.[38]

After considerable jockeying and in the midst of escalating violence, the government and the ANC agreed to meet in a two-day "bush summit" at the end of October.[39] By then, commentators were arguing that the ANC favored bilateral over multiparty negotiations[40] and that the government was interested in a power-sharing arrangement with the ANC.[41] The planned summit stalled for months on the issues of power sharing and a decentralized federal government.[42]

The United Nations Becomes Involved

The impasse over further negotiations led the ANC to propose international involvement in halting the violence and accelerating the transition to majority rule. Speaking at a U.N. Security Council emergency meeting over the Boipatong massacre, Mandela called for a permanent U.N. presence in the country in the form of a special envoy who would investigate the causes of the violence and "provide the council with information for further measures to end the violence, including continuous monitoring of the situation."[43] In response, the United Nations sent former U.S. Secretary of State Cyrus Vance as a special envoy on a ten-day mission aimed at getting the government and the ANC to resume their talks.

One outcome of the U.N. visit was the stationing of international observers to monitor the violence. Secretary-General Boutros Boutros-Ghali, favoring a return to the bargaining table, proposed in a report to the Security Council that thirty U.N. observers be stationed in South Africa to bolster the National Peace Accord;[44] by September, fifty observers had arrived. By that time the international community was becoming increasingly involved in efforts to stop the violence in South Africa and ensure a smooth transition to democracy. In addition to the U.N. monitors, teams from the World Council of Churches, the European Community, the Commonwealth, and the Organization of African Unity were either beginning operations or planning to begin them in the near future.[45] In addition to a National Peace Secretariat composed of representatives of the political parties,[46] the Goldstone Commission helped coordinate the observers and used them to buttress the commission's fact-finding abilities.

In addition, the secretary-general's report of August 7 commended the Goldstone Commission's work and called on it to investigate the behavior of not only the government-controlled security forces but also various private security agencies, the military wings of the ANC and PAC, and the Buthelezi-controlled police force of the KwaZulu homeland.[47] The report also called upon the government to give the Commission greater powers of investigation into the causes of violence and asked for international assistance for its operation. Finally, the secretary-general recommended an amnesty for all political offenders.[48]

The Question of Amnesty

The Commission responded positively to the U.N. suggestions and asked for a general amnesty so that its work could be made "more efficient."[49] In other remarks, Justice Goldstone suggested that some form of amnesty would be needed to encourage people with inside knowledge of violent events to come forward.[50] Shortly thereafter, the government and the ANC were reported to be discussing a general amnesty plan put forward by the United Nations aimed at restarting the move toward an interim government.[51] Under the plan members of the security forces who had been involved in actions against the ANC as well as antiapartheid activists were to receive blanket immunity; the 420 captives the ANC insisted were political prisoners were also to be freed.[52]

From the beginning, the NP government had tried to tie the question of an amnesty for its own forces to the freeing of the remaining prisoners. One early stumbling block was the government's steadfast refusal to release prisoners sentenced for offenses such as murder, terrorism, and arson on behalf of political organizations. In November 1991, the government issued Guidelines for Defining Political Offenses, which extended the definition of a political prisoner to include those who had advanced apartheid policies.[53] Now, ostensibly viewing the idea as a way to build on its own earlier Guidelines and to protect its agents, the NP government immediately seized upon the U.N. suggestion and proposed that the ANC accept such a policy in exchange for the release of the political prisoners.

The ANC rejected the suggestion of a blanket amnesty. On August 13, an ANC press release emphasized that the discussion of amnesty should be reserved for "an interim government of National Unity" and that such an amnesty could be granted only if the people agreed.[54] In addition, the document pointed out that an amnesty would not further the Goldstone Commission's investigations because the courts already had the authority to grant individuals immunity from prosecution. Furthermore, both the ANC and Bishop Desmond Tutu indicated that any amnesty would have to be accompanied by full disclosure of the past activities of the security forces, including their complicity in factional violence in the townships.[55] An ANC spokesperson added that the ANC might be more willing to consider an amnesty for older crimes, but certainly not for those committed while the negotiations were under way.[56] Finally, the ANC refused to let the problem of the political prisoners be tied to the amnesty question and suspended all discussion of both subjects.

Shortly thereafter, de Klerk, who clung to his long-held position that he knew of no one in the government engaged in nefarious activities, on October 16 introduced into Parliament an amnesty bill just as testimony began before the Goldstone Commission's inquiry into alleged police involvement and complicity.[57] The bill, which gave the president sweeping powers of indemnity, was debated in committee on October 18.[58] It immediately became a contentious issue; debate required postponing the conclusion of a special session of Parliament when it appeared the bill was going down to defeat.[59]

On October 19, de Klerk publicly expressed his support for the measure at the Transvaal Law Society's centenary celebration. De Klerk said the bill's purpose was to "level the playing field" between the government and its opponents.[60] He insisted that as

> head of the government I do not know of any single individual by name employed by the state in the police, in the defence force, or in any other capacity, who committed any crime. I don't have a list, I don't have any plans to take any

initiative to submit any names to the board which is to be established in terms of the legislation. No doubt, there might be such individuals. I don't know who they are. If we knew who they were we would have charged them . . . with the crimes they committed. I would like to stress that this legislation is not aimed at clearing the decks for intransigent government which participated behind the scenes in all sorts of criminal activities.[61]

Still, despite this public plea, the bill failed to receive the necessary majorities in the segregated tricameral Parliament.[62] The bill passed handily in the NP-dominated white House of Assembly over the objections of the Democratic Party, which insisted that there be public disclosure of the behavior of those indemnified. It also passed readily in the Colored House of Representatives, despite criticism from the minority Labour Party. However, Solidarity, the majority party in the Indian House of Delegates was steadfast in its refusal to ratify the bill. The discussion over amnesty was further complicated when the Goldstone Commission revealed that top military officers had been involved in a campaign to discredit the ANC.[63]

Consequently, de Klerk overcame his rebuff by resorting to the president's council, the parliamentary body that resolved legislative disputes among the three houses. The council was dominated by the National Party, which had thirty-five votes in the sixty-member body, a 58 percent majority.[64] The council had last been called upon by P. W. Botha, de Klerk's predecessor, in 1986 when he used it to enact security legislation opposed by the Labour Party.[65] In 1989, the council itself suggested that it be restructured.[66] By using this route, on November 9, de Klerk enacted the Further Indemnity Act.[67]

The act provided the state president with the authority to grant amnesty to those who "advised, directed, commanded, ordered or performed any act with a political object."[68] Although the act applied to acts committed before October 8, 1990, a discretionary clause gave the state president the power to enlarge the period as he deemed appropriate, and there was some indication that the government intended to amend the law to extend to late 1992.[69] Persons seeking amnesty applied individually to a National Council on Indemnity, which heard their case in secret. Not only Council members but also those present at the proceedings were to take an oath of secrecy.[70] Any contravention of the secrecy provision was a crime punishable by a fine or a one-year prison term.[71] Although the names of those granted indemnity would be published, their offenses and the identities of their victims would not be disclosed. Those granted indemnity would no longer be subject to either criminal prosecution or civil suits. Because it required individual presentation to the council on indemnity, government spokespersons argued the bill did not constitute a blanket amnesty but merely a "procedural mechanism."[72]

The ANC, of course, vociferously opposed the legislation, which it considered an effort by the government to pardon police, military, and security force members implicated in the commission of heinous acts.[73] It was adamant that criminals could not pardon themselves and indicated that it would not abide by the legislation if it came to power. Nonetheless, on November 18, the ANC formally adopted a discussion document, entitled Strategic Perspectives, which supported a possible power-sharing arrangement with the NP.[74] The document recognized the desirability of a general amnesty for security force and civil service members because such individuals have the power to obstruct the transition.

Before leaving office, de Klerk commuted the sentences of almost 100 convicted prisoners and granted amnesty to several former security officials, thus attempting to remove any chance that information on their activities would become public.[75] These indemnities and sentence reductions were frozen and referred to President Mandela for judgment.[76]

The ANC's Own Abuses

The ANC also worked to bolster opposition to the amnesty bill by the carefully timed release of a report conducted by an ANC commission of inquiry into atrocities committed in ANC refugee camps in Zambia, Angola, Tanzania, and Uganda.[77] The commission, which was composed of three lawyers—one independent and two ANC members—had been appointed in March 1992 after former refugees repeatedly alleged that torture and other forms of mistreatment were widespread. The commission completed its report in August.

The findings, which Mandela announced at a news conference, recognized that the acts committed included torture, which contravened both the ANC's code of conduct and former ANC President Oliver Tambo's 1980 pledge to honor the Geneva Conventions. The commission warned that the ANC would suffer from continued accusations, malaise, and recriminations unless the organization expanded the investigation.[78] Thus, it recommended that the ANC "cleanse" itself of persons who had committed atrocities and urged that the guilty be barred from positions of authority.[79] Recognizing that its own membership was weighted in favor of the ANC, the commission urged that a more independent commission of inquiry be formed to explore allegations of disappearance and murder of which it had become aware and bring those responsible to justice. Furthermore, the commission urged that victims receive compensation for their treatment as well as psychological, medical, and educational assistance. Acknowledging these recommendations, at his press conference Mandela stated that "as a leadership we accept ultimate responsibility for not adequately monitoring and therefore eradicating such abuses."[80] He pledged that the ANC would immediately examine the recommendations and act appropriately. The obvious intent was to contrast the ANC's handling of humanitarian law violations and abuses within its own ranks with the government's attempted blanket amnesty.

As 1993 began, the amnesty issue, and that of the ANC's conduct, continued to draw attention. The right-wing International Freedom Foundation had appointed a commission led by a British barrister named R. S. Douglas to investigate the behavior of the ANC in its camps for political exiles. In mid-January, the Douglas Commission issued a report condemning ANC behavior as a gross violation of human rights. The ANC's response was not to deny the charges—which it could not do in light of its own earlier revelations about atrocities—but to minimize the severity of what had occurred. The controversy deepened when the conservative Europe-based

International Society for Human Rights endorsed the Douglas Commission Report and argued that "[i]f the ANC were a government, then the U.N. would have already appointed a special human rights rapporteur to investigate."[81] Also in this vein, the *Sunday Times,* not known for its radical views, in an editorial castigated the behavior of both the government and the ANC and called for an accounting to the international community.[82] The paper opined,

> [T]his attempt to exonerate the "security establishment" of the ANC, and to cover up its crimes, bears striking resemblance to the government's attempts to exonerate its own security establishment and to cover up its own crimes . . . the guilty—all the guilty—must be brought to justice—if necessary, by the international community.[83]

The ANC followed up in January 1993 by appointing a commission to examine allegations of human rights abuses in its detention centers in exile.[84] The commission was led by a black South African businessman who was assisted by a Zimbabwean judge and an American lawyer.[85] The commission's August 1993 report found that at least two senior ANC officials had violated the rights of detainees. These were Joe Modise, commander of the ANC's military wing and a central figure in negotiations over the structure of the new national defense force, and Jacob Zuma, former ANC intelligence chief and executive committee member who was thought by observers of South African politics to be a likely candidate for a major role in a reconstructed police force. The commission also found that several security officials, including three members of the ANC's security department, were involved in violations, including torture, execution, arbitrary detention, and various types of inhuman treatment. Although the ANC's code of conduct provided a maximum penalty of suspension or expulsion from the organization, the commission went much further in its recommendations. It suggested that the ANC apologize and give compensation to victims of abuse. To this end, it recommended the ANC create a claims settlement agency to give awards to persons who suffered abuse as well as to the families of those who perished. The commission also recommended that the organization keep relatives of those missing in the camps informed of continuing investigations. Finally, those former detainees who wished to rejoin the ANC should be permitted to do so. Commenting on the report, Mandela, reflecting the views of many ANC members who were never in exile and who have favored disclosure of wrongdoing, said that the ANC was taking the commission's recommendations "very seriously. . . . We have taken the first important step of taking the public into our confidence as to what the commission has recommended."[86] The report was heralded by the diplomatic and academic communities as an important act of self-criticism not typical of South African political organizations.[87] In contrast, the NP was quick to try to capitalize on the findings for political advantage.[88] It claimed that the report revealed the ANC could not run the country by itself. The NP also challenged the ANC to have persons accused of abuses submit to the legal process. However, the NP's call for ANC action made no suggestion that a similar course of behavior be followed by the NP with regard to its agents.

The Outcome of the Negotiations

On November 26, 1993, de Klerk announced that he wanted a fully representative government of national unity in place no later than the first half of 1994.[89] In response, the ANC criticized de Klerk for anticipating the outcome of the pending bilateral talks and for refusing to accede to its prior demand for elections before the end of 1993.[90] Days later, Buthelezi announced that he had plans for a new constitution in Natal province, an area including the KwaZulu homeland, which would result in an autonomous state. The danger of secession orchestrated by Buthelezi was bad enough; shortly thereafter the Azanian People's Liberation Army (APLA), the military wing of the Pan-Africanist Congress (PAC), in a series of attacks on a golf club and a steakhouse, declared war on all white South Africans.[91] The government then broke off all talks with the PAC.

In the midst of this instability, the chance of insurrection by elements within the military and a campaign of right-wing terror was exacerbated by a December 19 announcement by de Klerk. In contrast to his prior defense of the security forces, de Klerk dismissed or suspended twenty-three military officers, including six generals who were suspected of activities, including assassination, aimed at thwarting racial reconciliation.[92] While de Klerk's actions could be construed as a major concession to the ANC, which had urged a purge of the military as a condition for the resumption of multiparty discussions, there was the danger that his actions would push increasing numbers of whites into the arms of the Conservative Party and extraparliamentary groups to its right.

In mid-August, as negotiations continued, widespread suspicion about government efforts to cover-up past misdeeds was bolstered by revelations that the state security council had instructed government departments to destroy classified documents.[93]

Although the question of dealing with human rights violators remained unresolved, in October, as the prospect loomed large of concluding the multiparty negotiations with a new constitutional arrangement, de Klerk and Mandela shared the Nobel Peace Prize for their work toward effecting a peaceful transition in their country. Shortly thereafter, on November 18, de Klerk, Mandela, and the leaders of eighteen of the nineteen other parties remaining in the negotiations endorsed a new constitution that combines provisions for majority rule with those safeguarding minority rights.[94] Inkatha and a number of right-wing Afrikaner groups refused to endorse the agreement, seeking greater autonomy. The 142-page constitution is to remain in effect until the Parliament—a 400-seat assembly and a 90-seat senate, which chooses the president—elected April 27, 1994, drafts a permanent one, a process estimated to take two years. The constitution provides for minority seats in a twenty-seven member cabinet for five years; safeguards the positions and pensions of white civil servants and military personnel; divides the country into nine provinces—the four currently existing provinces and the homelands that were abolished—with considerable power over their police, educational system, hospitals, and other public services. The constitution also contains a long list of fundamental rights, including a prohibition of torture and three pages of limitations on the president's power to declare a state of emergency. An eleven-member constitutional court, whose members are appointed by the president from a list drawn up by an independent commission, is to construe these rights. The interim constitution's final paragraphs deal with the issue of reconciliation and amnesty:

> The pursuit of national unity, the well-being of all South African citizens and peace require reconciliation between the people of South Africa and the reconstruction of society. The adoption of this Constitution lays the secure foundation for the people of South Africa to transcend the divisions and strife of the past, which generated gross violations of human rights, the transgression of humanitarian principles in violent conflicts and a legacy of hatred, fear, guilt and revenge. These can now be addressed on the basis that there is a need for understanding but not for vengeance, a need for reparation but not for retaliation. In order to advance such reconciliation and reconstruction amnesty shall be granted in respect of acts, omissions and offenses associated with political objectives and committed in the course of the conflicts of the past. To this end Parliament . . . shall adopt a law determining a firm cut-off date, which shall be a date after 8 October 1990 and before 6 December 1993, and providing for the mechanisms, criteria and procedures, including tribunals, if any, through which such amnesty should be dealt with at any time after the law has been passed.[95]

The April 1994 parliamentary elections, the inauguration of Nelson Mandela as President of South Africa, and his appointment of de Klerk and Buthelezi as members of an ANC-dominated cabinet of national unity ushered in a new epoch in South African politics. The elections themselves were described by one government official as "unmitigated chaos"[96] and were boycotted by most of the white right-wing groups.[97] A spate of bombings in the two days preceeding the elections resulted in the arrest of thirty-five white rightists.[98]

The new government was welcomed internationally. On June 23, 1994, South Africa reclaimed its seat at the United Nations General Assembly. The Security Council terminated the mandate of the United Nations Observer Mission in South Africa five days later.[99]

The Mandela Government's Proposed Measures
to Deal with Past Violators

The question of how to treat human rights violators from the days of NP rule on the side of the government and abuses on the side of its foes has come to occupy considerable space in the political landscape. President de Klerk's hurried passage of the Further Indemnity Act over the objections of his own Parliament did not display a willingness on his part to subject persons suspected of nefarious activities to standards of international law. The act had three especially glaring shortcomings. First, the aura of secrecy that surrounded the entire process created the impression that the government would use the process to name only a few token perpetrators while concealing the extent of government-sanctioned or officially orchestrated abuses of human rights of the type revealed in forums such as the Goldstone Commission hearings. Second, the provision forbidding criminal penalties evinced the government's unwillingness to bring the guilty to justice. Third, the language barring civil suits indicated a lack of empathy for victims and their families, who may have been irreparably harmed — physically, psychologically, financially, or otherwise — by their experience. Thus, the passage of the legislation, rather than becoming a symbol of the government's desire for reconciliation, may have heightened suspicions in the black community that the former government took the behavior of its agents lightly and has little interest in witnessing the creation of a legal system marked by equality for all under the law.

In contradistinction to the NP government's position, the ANC's posture on the issue of prosecutions is seemingly accepting of international legal standards, its reaction to the Douglas Commission Report notwithstanding. In late 1992, the organization maintained that

> [i]t is not a question of victors punishing the vanquished, or of anyone losing or saving face, but of joint responsibility undertaken by all South Africans to affirm norms and standards of accountability that become part and parcel of the new democratic society and bind all future governments. People in positions of power, now and in the future, must know that they will be held accountable for abuses of the law and violations of human rights no only by history but by the agencies of law."[100]

The ANC's commitment to this view seems to have been affirmed by its behavior with regard to the most recent report on abuses.

Thus, one of the new government's acts was to announce the formation of a Commission of Truth and Reconciliation. The mandate and proposed working methods of the Commission reflect the South Africans' study of the experience of other countries as well as the advantage of a negotiated transition period in which to think through appropriate guidelines.

As of September 1994, the new government announced that the Truth Commission will establish, in line with international law and the constitution, "as complete a picture as possible of gross human rights violations relating to the conflicts of the past" in and outside South Africa. It will cover events from March 1, 1960, through December 6, 1993; thus, those involved in bombings or other terrorist acts in the pre-electoral period are excluded.[101] It is to prepare a report on such violations and to recommend legal and administrative measures to ensure respect for, and observance of, human rights. The commission is to be made up of eight to ten members appointed by the president. It will have one year to complete its job, with the option of a six month extension.[102]

One of the commission's most interesting and innovative features is its treatment of the issues of amnesty and prosecution. Those members of political organizations, liberation movements, law enforcement agencies, and security forces who were involved in political crimes may apply to the commission for amnesty and indemnity. However, the commission will only recommend amnesty or indemnity on the basis of full disclosure of the applicant's involvement in the crime, and where the action claimed had a political motive that was capable of being realized. Moreover, the commission's recommendations will not be binding on President Mandela, who will make the final decision as to when amnesty shall apply to a specific individual. As of September 1994, it was unclear the extent to which the commission's proceedings would be public: whereas human rights groups were pushing for open hearings, the National Party and some ANC members preferred secrecy.[103] It is also unclear whether those persons implicated by the testimony of others will be notified and invited to present their own evidence before the commission, and if doing so will automatically constitute an application for amnesty.

The scheme provides a strong incentive for individuals to come forward and seek amnesty. If implicated parties do not come forward by the cut-off date for applications for amnesty, their names may be forwarded to the attorney general to consider prosecution.[104] Thus, rather than a blanket amnesty, the commission's mandate seems to incorporate a massive plea-bargaining arrangement. To receive amnesty, perpetrators may not only have to accept their own responsibility for political crimes but provide any information they may have on the fate of victims or on those higher-ups involved in giving illegal orders. Any prosecutions will take place using existing laws and courts. Nonetheless, where the commission has reasonable grounds to believe there is a risk evidence will be destroyed or tampered with, it may enter premises to search for and seize evidence. These search and seizure provisions are likely to be among the first legal challenges brought under the new Bill of Rights.[105]

The commission's work also evinces a primary concern with victims. Among the commission's objectives is to gather information to make it possible to identify victims and determine their fate or whereabouts, as well as to provide victims with a platform on which they can "express their plight and tell their story."[106] It is to recommend reparations, which may take the form of financial payments or education grants.[107] Indeed, Mandela stressed in a speech marking his first 100 days in office that the "challenge is to ensure that amnesty helps to heal the wounds of the past by also addressing the plight of the victims."[108]

Of course, one of the major challenges confronting the commission will be to design reparations measures that are feasible in light of the enormous economic and social needs of the majority of South Africans and the government's budgetary restraints. An emphasis on government services or grants rather than monetary compensation is likely. Moreover, the commission will face the delicate problem of deciding whether to pass on for possible prosecution the names of high-ranking members of the army or government—who are now partners in national unity—if they do not come forward voluntarily. The same is true of those members of the ANC responsible for political crimes, and for members of Inkatha. A declared intent to prosecute Inkatha members for the pre-electoral violence if they do not seek amnesty, for example, could unravel an already fragile peace.

The creation of the Truth Commission is, of course, only one part of the larger process of dismantling the apartheid state and creating a new one in its place. The former guerrilla forces of the ANC are being integrated into the South African National Defence Force, and old officers are being retired. More broadly, apartheid infected every aspect of South African life, from urban design to land tenure to the educational and health systems. The extent to which South Africa can afford to — or can afford not to — make reparation for these broader injustices is one of the central issues facing the Mandela government.[109]

Nonetheless, the outline of the Truth Commission, including the government's rejection of a blanket amnesty and declared intent to abide by international law on the subject, provides hope that South Africa can provide a successful model of dealing with the past. It remains to be seen whether the operation of the commission bears out that hope.

21

Conclusion: Combating Impunity

Naomi Roht-Arriaza

It is time now to sum up the experiences of the case studies, drawing out the commonalities and lessons to be learned. These lessons are theoretical and practical, legal, ethical, and political. They point to dilemmas for future attempts to come to grips with the past, and to some future directions for the contribution of international law and outside actors in assisting the transitional process.

The Lessons Learned

Transitional governments must initially choose whether to confront the past at all or to attempt to draw a thick line between the past and the present. There are admittedly cogent reasons for doing the latter. This is especially so when new governments with a limited amount of political capital and bureaucratic control confront a past in which the line between victim and victimizer is unclear, or in which both sides to a full-fledged civil war can point to a rough equivalence of violations by armed forces on either side and the sheer number of victims makes action daunting. Bruce Ackerman has argued, for example, that in the Eastern European case an emphasis on corrective justice will undermine and divert energies from the more fundamental need for constitution building.[1] Although the question of squandering limited political moments is indeed crucial, it is more one of how, rather than whether, to proceed. Certainly the results of efforts to avoid corrective justice entirely and to draw a line through the past in the interest of social peace seem less than ideal. Where such line drawing has been attempted, the issue often proved divisive despite the rationale of preventing divisiveness. In some cases, as in Poland, the debate over where line drawing was appropriate was used as a weapon against political opponents. In others, such as Uruguay, a substantial part of the population disagreed with the government's decision to avoid confronting the past and so expended a great deal of energy fighting that position. Moreover, the lesson of Zimbabwe, among others, indicates that leaving the military and security forces intact and unrepentant in the long term results in a resurgence of abuses against the civilian population — whether this takes the form of new repressions of political opponents or of the brutal squelching of street crime. Nor does a policy of forgetting have any necessary relationship to forging social consensus and constitution building: In Latin America, for instance, where amnesties are common, constitutions have been easily enacted and as easily ignored, with little effect on actual social peace. There are, no doubt, counter-examples (post-Franco Spain comes to mind) but not too many. In addition to the moral and legal arguments raised against a policy of wholesale forgetting, on a practical level as well such a policy seems ill advised.

Those governments — a majority — that chose to take some action to come to terms with the past used a combination of one or more of five different kinds of measures: investigations, prosecutions, purges, commemoration, and compensation. The choice depends on a number of variables, including how widespread and how severe the earlier repression was, how much social support the prior regime enjoyed, how strong the prior regime's adherents remain, how quickly the new government moves to confront these issues, and how strong the institutions of civil society are just after the transition. Each type of measure brings its own series of conundrums and difficulties. All nonetheless confront a paradox of timing and scope.

A basic paradox of all measures against impunity is that such measures must be put into effect relatively quickly, before the new government loses the widespread legitimacy it enjoys, before the political unity engendered by opposition to the old regime evaporates and apathy sets in, before the old guard can reorganize, and before the new government is overwhelmed by intractable economic and social problems. At most, the window is usually about a year. Yet effective measures against impunity require either the overhauling of existing institutions or the creation of new ones, and such restructuring takes time. So too does the easing of emotions needed to turn implacable enemies into political adversaries within a democratic framework.

Transitional governments facing this paradox tend to turn, if they are acting in good faith, to institutions that are easy to create from scratch. Investigatory commissions, ad hoc groups, parliamentary commissions, and the like are within the power of the legislative and/or executive branches to create, and they require little special infrastructure to begin functioning. Reforming or creating an independent, capable judiciary and a court system to go with it tends to be more difficult, more expensive, and more time consuming. Whereas courts can be created anew and untainted judges appointed quickly, their independent functioning, and the revised substantive and procedural codes under which they are to operate, are not so swiftly produced. Nor can such rules and machinery be introduced willy-nilly: Scrupulous attention to due process and the avoidance of both ad hoc courts and ex post facto application of the criminal laws limit the options of a new or post-war government. Perhaps this is one reason prosecutions, administrative sanctions, and civil suits have been much less common than investigations and civil service purges.

Investigations

Investigations of past human rights violations are by far the most common method of coming to terms with the past.[2] In incomplete transitions such as those of Nepal or the Philippines investigations tend to focus on one or two signal events, usually those that are well known internationally. Such limited investigations, if the results are made public, may well prove helpful in bringing to light patterns or methods of repression and in providing succor to the immediate victims. If, however, they are carried out without a wider context, the effect may be to "exceptionalize" the events at issue and thus to obscure the wider truth.

There are two principal means of pursuing investigations: through ad hoc commissions appointed by the executive branch or through normal parliamentary channels. Given a breakdown in democratic institutions, in law enforcement, and in the judiciary, ad hoc commissions are by far the more common channel. Such commissions, to be successful, must command widespread support and respect and must be able by that token to establish an authoritative version of the truth. The inclusion of well-known figures considered independent of both the past and the current regime or of persons representating a spectrum of political opinion is the most common means of ensuring respect. Although the latter option raises the danger of degeneration into endless political wrangling, a unanimous result is by the same token more likely to be authoritative.

The experience of the Truth Commission in El Salvador (Chapter 15) raises the question of whether investigations carried out by nonnationals under the auspices of the United Nations or other international organizations might provide a more authoritative and more easily accepted accounting of recent history. Undoubtedly, an international commission enjoys several advantages: distance from domestic political squabbles, a claim to objectivity and disinterestedness, a greater degree of protection from reprisals, and the clout to bring its recommendations to the attention of international public opinion and to use international pressure to have its recommendations implemented. Yet this very distance may prove problematic, giving rise to both a perception and, possibly, the reality that commission members are unattuned to the nuances of the domestic political moment and that their conclusions and recommendations may on this score be discounted.

Moreover, part of the internal process of coming to terms with the past depends on the persons in charge of the state itself recognizing the official responsibility of the state for the acts of the prior regime, listening to the victims, and validating the victims' stories. Although to some degree representatives of the international community may fulfill these functions of validation and recognition, if the state is not required to make the commission's conclusions and recommendations its own, an essential part of the healing process may be lost. Nor—as the Salvadoran experience seems to show—does an external authority necessarily resolve debates over the authoritativeness of the conclusions that are reached. A better solution may be to invest a national commission with an international or regional mandate, and if necessary provide outside protection for its members and staff, resorting to an international commission only if sufficiently prestigious and independent nationals cannot be recruited.

Another set of dilemmas related to the method of investigations arises from the scope and nature of the commission's findings. The findings must be broad enough in scope to encompass the most prevalent harms and to avoid the perils of exceptionalism. At the same time, constraints of time, money, and access to evidence will mean that some limits must be imposed. Commissions seem to be most effective when they must present their findings within a fixed time limit; although an open-ended mandate, like that of the Uganda commission, allows for greater thoroughness, it runs the risk of eventual political and legal irrelevancy. Given time constraints, however, an initial question concerns the scope of the harms themselves: Should inquiry be limited to a few particularly heinous types of crimes, or should it be comprehensive, showing the interrelationships or patterns on which a system of repression was built? Thus, for instance, while torture was widespread in Chile under Pinochet, the national Commission investigated only those cases in which torture had led to death in detention. A second, related question concerns the degree to which a commission chooses to focus in depth on a limited number of exemplary cases while listing minimal data for others—as, for example the Salvadoran Truth Commission did—or rather tries to provide information on a wider range of events. The former has the advantage of allowing more pointed and well-researched conclusions as to the origins and meaning of the events chosen, but such inquiries should be careful to stress the representative, not exhaustive, character of the events chosen. Of course, to some degree the choice can be made only in context because it depends on the underlying patterns and scope of repression.

One obstacle to effective investigation is the limited powers of most ad hoc commissions to compel testimony and document production. This is one reason groups of family members of the disappeared, for example, in Argentina, pushed for a parliamentary commission, which would have had such powers: The executive-appointed Sábato Commission that was set up (see Chapter 12) lacked them. The inability to call hostile witnesses, preserve or obtain documents, and/or visit military or police installations has made it particularly difficult for investigatory commissions to go beyond descriptions of general patterns. For example, little information has been gleaned regarding the remains of the disappeared. The lack of broader powers is usually justified on grounds that compulsory process is reserved for the courts—although there seems little reason why that should be the case so long as minimal due process is followed. More cogent is the argument that powerful actors under investigation will not comply with orders to testify or produce documents, leading to an unnecessary standoff. But this objection is not limited to investigatory commissions; it is as relevant to orders to testify in court. The problem forms part of the more general problem of obtaining information from reluctant institutional actors. One answer is to employ variants on plea bargaining aimed at inducing cracks in monolithic institutions, as discussed below. A variant, proposed in Chile but rejected, is to allow testimony to be taken secretly, without identifying the persons involved. If the substance of the testimony is kept secret, the procedure raises questions about its validity as a truth-seeking device. However, concealing the identity of—or even protecting—the persons agreeing to provide useful information may seem a worthwhile bargain. Another variant comes from recent proposals in South Africa: Persons who come forward with evidence regarding their crimes become eligible for relief from criminal prosecution. This provision may be enough of an incentive to some members of the military or security forces to voluntarily make the information available.

Without the ability to subpoena, most commissions have relied on a combination of direct witness testimony, contemporaneous records of human rights groups, and access to government records — which may be incomplete or even falsified — cross-checking one source against another. Such careful corroboration and cross-checking may well lead to undercounting of the actual victims of the violations at issue. The process is necessary, however, to avoid accusations of sensationalism and, more important, of violations of due process. Investigation is a civil, not criminal, procedure, so the formal international guarantees of judicial due process applicable in criminal cases do not directly apply. Nonetheless, being labeled a violator of human rights can harm the lives or careers of the individuals or even the groups named and therefore raises due process concerns. Different countries have dealt with the due process question differently: The Chilean (and Argentine) commissions declined to name individuals, arguing that only a judicial proceeding could responsibly do so. The Salvadoran Truth Commission did name names, justifying that choice by noting that public exposure is probably the only punishment that will be meted out to most of the persons implicated, that the commission made findings of fact but did not adjudicate guilt, and that the careful corroborative methods used minimized the chances of error. Naming the names should present no serious ethical difficulty: Either those named will be indicted by a court in due time, at which point they will have full opportunity to come forward and defend themselves, or political constraints will make prosecution impossible, in which case the persons facing public opprobrium are free to come forward with the information that would exonerate them before public opinion; if they do not, such opprobrium is a small price to pay for participation in heinous acts.[3] Perhaps providing the persons to be named with an opportunity beforehand to present exonerating evidence (in private, if they wish) — as was done by the Ad Hoc Commission in El Salvador and suggested in the Czech parliamentary lustration cases — would minimize both error and the perception of unfairness. A full-fledged hearing, with opportunity for cross-examination of hostile witnesses and representation of counsel, is probably not necessary and is certainly not required under existing law.[4]

Another major difficulty concerns the treatment of organized government opponents, especially armed guerrilla organizations. The tendency has been, in the interests of enlisting a broad base of political support for the findings of an investigatory commission, to include both government-initiated or government-sponsored human rights violations and the violent acts of opponents within the same investigation. This, as Jorge Mera (see Chapter 13) points out, dilutes the focus of the investigation. The danger is that the two types of violence will be seen as functionally equivalent and thus equally worthy of moral blame and legal sanction. In fact, not only are the two types of violence generally numerically disproportionate, with the immense number of victims a result of government acts, but their legal status is fundamentally dissimilar because the government has the legal responsibility to protect the citizenry and uphold the law. In addition, under international law, with a few exceptions it is governments, not private individuals, that take on the commitment not to violate human rights.[5]

The Chilean Commission attempted to justify its mixture of human rights violations and political crimes by arguing that the traditional legal categories had broken down, yet it provided little justification beyond the existence of erroneous public perceptions on the issue. The Salvadoran Truth Commission, acknowledging that its negotiated mandate required it to consider crimes committed by both sides, tried to assign the weight of responsibility to the government; indeed, the Commission was criticized for letting the opposition FMLN off too lightly.[6] Given these difficulties, it might be preferable, if inquiry into the crimes of nongovernmental groups is important, to separate the two investigations. This has been done to some degree in South Africa, where the ANC created its own independent commission of inquiry. The danger is that confusion on this point in investigation can feed into arguments that, since an amnesty is required to reintegrate former opponents into civil life, it is only "fair" that such an amnesty also apply to government officials accused of human rights violations. Such arguments served as a cover for amnesties in Central America, for example, which benefited primarily the armed forces.

A final caveat regarding investigations and investigatory commissions comes from their very popularity: the tendency to conceive of them as a substitute for judicial action. While "truth even if not justice" may at least arguably be a necessary compromise in certain cases, it should be conceived as a necessary evil, not an equally desirable choice. Judicial action by a credible court — criminal, civil, or both — comports a solemnity and authority in individual cases that a "truth commission," even one that names names, cannot equal.

Prosecutions and Purges

Judicial action is, nonetheless, extraordinarily complex and fraught with difficulties. To begin with, the same conditions that made widespread human rights violations possible also stunted and compromised the judicial system. A transitional government may take years to build — or rebuild — a judiciary and courts with both the ability and the independence to render respected decisions in human rights cases, especially where there may be so many as to overwhelm the system. In countries with little tradition of judicial independence, whatever result the courts reach in highly charged cases of past human rights violations may only feed perceptions that political motivations are at work. Furthermore, the machinery of justice is not cheap. The paradox of both the need and impossibility of quick action asserts itself most strongly where the judiciary is concerned.

Compounding the problem is the need for both judicial action and judicial independence, values that in transitional situations tend to conflict. Old-guard judges may drag their feet or worse in preparing and trying cases of past human rights violators. At the least they may employ differing and idiosyncratic evidentiary standards. The new government may not have the constitutional or legislative authority to replace judges, or may lose so much in overall legitimacy by doing so that such a course becomes unadvisable. Court-packing and the creation of new courts (albeit based on existing law) remain as options but carry their own dangers for regimes that must also seek increased judicial independence to break with executive arbitrariness. And, as in cases of investigatory commissions, it may be hard to find figures of sufficient stature and independence. In the case of the judiciary, years of deficient legal education, the existence of a separate judicial career track, and the low status of the legal profession may make it hard even to fill new positions with minimally qualified personnel. "Loans" of foreign investigators and support personnel to overburdened court systems might be an appropriate way to enable the judiciary to fulfill its function.

This series of conundrums leads inexorably to attempts to limit the scope of prosecutions to the most notorious offenders, the highest-placed, or the easiest to prosecute (who tend to be the direct perpetrators rather than high-placed planners). Appropriately limiting prosecutions requires both an ability to exercise discretion and to plea bargain, trading leniency for information and breaking down the institutional bonds that make prosecutions of military or party officials particularly difficult. Limiting prosecutions also requires a great deal of clarity in the reasons for the choice of particular targets for prosecution. That clarity has not always been present: Prosecutions have mixed crimes of venality with human rights violations in Argentina, Germany, and elsewhere; similar confusions between crimes against the institutional order and human rights-related crimes have been common. Along related lines, criminal charges should be precise enough to withstand charges of vagueness and conform to internationally recognized definitions: In Romania, for example, the process was undermined by loose and unjustifiable use of charges of genocide.

Beyond this type of confusion lies the question of what level of actor to focus on. Many countries have opted for prosecuting persons at the top of the hierarchy, following the precedent set at the International Tribunal at Nuremburg and reasoning that the persons in charge planned and organized the acts of their subalterns. The problem with this approach is that by removing the top layer of a hierarchy in which almost everyone was involved in at least aiding and abetting crime, the next layer down — of younger officials often more directly involved in heinous acts — is rewarded by accession to the top posts. Another problem, that of lack of proof that those at the top actually gave orders to commit crimes, seems more manageable with the help of concepts like command responsibility.[7] And despite the drawbacks, the alternative is worse: If those who pulled the trigger or ran the torture chambers are prosecuted while those who gave ambiguous or unwritten orders to "take care of" putative political or social opponents are let free, both the credibility of the process and hopes of nonrepetition suffer. In addition, those lower in the hierarchy will no doubt raise a defense of superior orders. Although, as we have seen, the defense is actually quite a narrow one legally, its political resonance may be much greater.

Although the availability of admissible evidence and limiting prosecutions to only the most serious crimes will provide some natural limits, there will always be charges of arbitrariness in defining the limits of prosecutions. It is important for the prosecutors to be able to justify their choice of defendants on some principled basis: victim-centered justice, as proposed by Malamud-Goti, or some other.

Another consideration is the ability of the government to maintain its policy over time: Some writers have argued that whatever the constraints, it is important for the government's legitimacy and credibility to initiate a policy it can carry through on — not one that will be forced back by overwhelming pressure from the persons affected. Thus, for example, in the Chilean case it would be better to start out accepting the limits of a prior amnesty law rather than, as in Argentina, attempting prosecutions and being unable to carry through due to military pressure;[8] alternatively, better to focus on a few well-prepared cases than to cast too widely and end up bungling the opportunity.[9] Of course, political balances of forces change, sometimes overnight, and the limits to action can be known only with hindsight: The question of how much can be done before the government itself is endangered, rather than merely challenged or inconvenienced, will change over time. And international as well as domestic support for doing more may accelerate that change.

In addition to the superior orders defense, prosecutions for past violations have confronted two major issues of criminal law: the maxim *nullum pena sin lege*, or the ex post facto law issue, and the question of statutes of limitation. The first has proved much more problematic in Eastern Europe, where the conduct at issue may have been lawful under prior domestic law, than in other parts of the world where domestic penal codes clearly prohibit behavior that could persist only because state agents were at work. Nonetheless, even in Eastern Europe, the earlier Nuremburg precedents and human rights treaties allowing prosecution for violations of general principles of law have given courts the tools they need to sidestep the ex post facto problem — even if, as the German case exemplifies, the results are unsettling. Even so, the prohibition on ex post facto laws would, for example, limit efforts to criminalize membership per se in institutions or party organizations. Notions of the imprescriptability of crimes against humanity and of equitable tolling have helped ameliorate problems raised by short statutes of limitations.

Civil Sanctions

The considerable difficulties involved in criminal prosecutions, as well as the more diffuse nature of the violations, for example, in Eastern Europe, have led many transitional governments to focus instead on administrative or civil sanctions, exemplified by the loss of position or rank. Such sanctions target members of the institutions considered responsible for past violations, usually the military, police, or Communist Party members. While civil sanctions are generally applied on the basis of individual acts, in a few Eastern European cases individuals have been subject to lustration, or banning, based merely on membership in a proscribed organization. Categorical sanctions raise the issue, already alluded to, of the degree to which due process applies during proceedings to strip someone of his or her job, rank, or ability to vote and hold public office. The language of international law focuses to a large extent on criminal due process,[10] but certain procedural guarantees extend to any "suit at law."[11] Human rights bodies have found that determinations prohibiting an individual from exercising her profession or relating to pension rights come under the minimal guarantees of a hearing before an independent and impartial tribunal.[12] It could also be argued that the existence of at least minimal due process protections of a hearing for civil forefeitures in the world's major legal systems gives these protections the status of general principles of law to be universally respected.

Again, a paradox ensues: Ideally, due process in civil deprivation cases entails a right to a predeprivation hearing, to present exonerating evidence, and to appeal. However, individualized hearings are time-consuming, messy, and require both procedures and machinery that may take considerable time and resources to set up, thus subjecting them to all the drawbacks of judicial adjudication with few of the advantages. Moreover, individualized adjudications may be more damaging to the persons discharged, who will face the stigma of a case-by-case adjudication rather than the relatively nonjudgmental discharge or banning of all individuals holding certain positions.

Special concerns arise when the civil sanctions take the form of prohibitions on voting or standing for public office. Rights to take part in public affairs, to vote, and to be elected are guaranteed in human rights treaties. While article 25 of the International Covenant allows reasonable restrictions on such rights, the American Convention specifies that such rights, including the right of everyone "to have access, under general conditions of equality, to the public service of his country" may be restricted, for present purposes, only after sentencing by a competent court in criminal proceedings.[13] Thus, even temporary bans on civic participation unrelated to a criminal conviction may be problematic.

From a policy viewpoint, of course, the purpose of such limitations is to keep those responsible for disastrous state policies in the past from influencing future ones, or from regrouping and again seizing a measure of power before democratic institutions can be consolidated. Thus, the bans are usually limited to five or ten years, and generally apply only to high political or military operatives. From the viewpoint of both justice for past acts and allowing for a fresh start, such measures seem reasonable and prudent. Yet one goal of democratic transition has been to broaden the spectrum of political participation, not simply replace the names and political coloration of those excluded. Civic virtue is a value that should be nourished above all in persons who have disdained it in the past; it may be preferable, therefore, to let those whose ideas led to disaster, or worse, enter those ideas into public debate within a democratic framework rather than being left to scheme outside it. Perhaps public naming as a perpetrator of human rights violations (although it might raise the due process issues mentioned above) might dampen public enthusiasm for members of the old order as candidates for office, without denying them other rights of civic participation. On the other hand, the Argentine experience is a depressing reminder that identification as a human rights violator is not necessarily a sufficient stigma, and formal banning measures may be warranted.

A third issue revolves around loss of employment or pension rights as civil sanctions. Job loss has extended in some cases far beyond what would seem necessary to remove remnants of the old guard from decision making and to have taken on distinctly punitive aspects — for example, the government lunchroom workers subject to lustration in Czechoslovakia. If such government employment bars extend even indirectly (through informal blacklisting or the like) to private employment, the transitional government may find itself in violation of international guarantees of the right to work.[14] At the same time, those persons with skills or connections needed to restart the economy have largely remained untouched no matter what their past. While such concessions to economic needs may be inevitable, they should not be passed off as virtue: Again, the clarity of goals of measures dealing with the past is crucial to their success. Where persons without real decision-making power are purged while the managers or financiers remain, the legitimacy of the entire transition suffers.

Perhaps the focus on the future operation of government rather than on disabling those unworthy to serve explains in part the notable underuse of economic sanctions. Occasionally, as in Germany, pension benefits have been forfeited, but in general neither administrative sanctions nor civil suits by victims have been widely used as mechanisms of settling accounts. In the case of civil suits, the potential for overwhelming the judicial apparatus, the cost to potential victims who must come forward and pay for attorneys, and the difficulties in obtaining access to the assets of most potential civil defendants are all disincentives to suit. So too are a culturally ingrained reluctance to litigate, a sense that mere monetary sanctions are insufficient as instruments of justice, and procedural constraints on the use of private, civil litigation.

The underuse of targeted economic sanctions by the new government itself, however, seems less justified.[15] In addition to sanctions such as loss of pensions or rank aimed at individuals, sanctions explicitly aimed at institutions — reductions in the military budget, for instance, with the proceeds to be used to pay compensation to victims of human rights violations perpetrated by the military — would seem to have symbolic as well as practical value. Although most transitions include reductions in those institutions associated with past violations — for instance, reductions in the size of the armed forces or security forces or disbanding of the Communist Party and seizure of its assets — such measures are not explicitly tied to reparations for past acts.

Compensation

A majority of cases have provided some form of compensation for victims of past violations and their families. Again, there are line-drawing problems: Should only death or disappearance receive compensation, or should it extend to torture, imprisonment, or even further to loss of a job or access to university education for one's children? Given limited resources, most countries have focused on deprivations of life or personal liberty. A second question relates to the kinds of compensation: In poor countries facing daunting economic problems, monetary compensation may be out of the question. Cambodia and Russia are cases in point; suffering was so widespread and money is so scarce that meaningful monetary compensation has proved elusive. In several places money has been supplemented by services such as access to special stores or housing or by dispensations like Argentina's exemption from military service for family members of persons who disappeared. In some places individuals who lost their jobs for political reasons have been reinstated, although this practice produces tensions in societies with significant unemployment. Creative use of these types of mechanisms can allow even poor countries to meet their obligations. In addition, the Salvadoran Truth Commission's recommendation that one percent of foreign aid to El Salvador be designated for victims' compensation might make it easier for incoming governments to maintain payments to victims of past abuses in the face of other overwhelming economic demands. Such a policy would seem especially just where the government providing the aid had some part in prolonging or fostering the past abuses. In addition to compensation in money or preferential access to services, counseling and rehabilitation are required to help victims and their families come to terms with their personal tragedies.

Another issue revolves around the mechanisms used to provide compensation. The general practice has been a government commission that takes in and processes the claims of persons who come forward as victims or family members. In Chile, for instance, the individuals who testified to the National Commission for Truth and Reconciliation that a family member had disappeared became eligible for pension payments. The utility of such payments has been debated: Members of the Argentine Mothers of the Plaza de Mayo, for instance, for a long time rejected all payments as "blood money" that could not substitute for the return of their children who disappeared. In addition, while compensation mechanisms require survivors or family members to tell their stories to a (it is to be hoped sympathetic) state official, such procedures must be quick and streamlined and must not rob survivors or their dependants of dignity, force them through a bureaucratic maze, or make them relive traumatic experiences. The liberal use of presumptions (i.e., that someone imprisoned between certain dates was tortured) and the separation of the truth-telling and compensation functions may be helpful.[16] Useful too may be the organization of nongovernmental entities made up of survivors and family members, such as Memorial in Russia, to oversee the compensation process because these groups may be perceived as more understanding and less bureaucratic than a state agency. Furthermore, such organizations of family members and victims may be in a better position to speak for those — children, for instance, or persons killed whose family members are unknown or unwilling to step forward — who cannot speak for themselves and whose right to compensation would otherwise be ignored. Such funds, if they cannot go to make whole those directly affected, should be used for commemorative or educational purposes.

Commemoration

The series of country experiences points up the importance of commemoration as an integral part of the confrontation and healing of the past. Commemorative measures have included exhumation and public reburial of persons secretly buried, days of remembrance, the naming of streets and schools after victims, public apologies, the creation of museums, works of art, drama, television series, movies, and books dedicated to educating about the past, and the rehabilitation of victims' names and reputations. Psychological research confirms the importance of these types of measures in promoting both individual and societal healing.

Especially where the number of victims and the lack of resources make individual compensation problematic, resources used for commemorative efforts may be among a new government's most well-spent funds.

Impunity and the Building of Democracy

Of course, the measures outlined above, with their myriad problems and choices, do not by any means describe those required overall to move from repressive regimes to those based on democracy and rule of law. It would require another whole volume (probably several) to do so, but a few initial thoughts should be mentioned here. Many of these suggestions have been made by the various investigatory commissions and other reform-minded bodies. Although these notes focus on civil and political institutions, a good part of the preconditions for rule of law are rooted in economic and social systems that provide for the basic needs of all, and opportunities for a wide spectrum of citizens, and that therefore give a majority of the society's citizens a stake in its future.

One set of changes has to do with building an independent and creative judicial capacity with both the will and the wherewithal to challenge arbitrary, discriminatory, or illegal action by other branches of government and semiautonomous institutions. Beginning to do so means strictly limiting the jurisdiction of military courts to try civilians, for instance, and insisting that common crimes by the military against civilians be tried in civilian courts. Strict limits on the government's ability to impose a state of emergency, the restructuring of judicial education to lessen the isolation of judges and allow those educated as attorneys rather than judges to enter judicial service, separation from the judiciary and professionalization of the investigative function, and reforms in overall criminal procedure will also be helpful.[17]

Civilian control over previously autonomous institutions like the military, changes in military recruitment procedures and education to stress a smaller, better educated, more professional force, and clear separation of military and police functions are also part of what is required. Moreover, in many countries the military itself, or at least a large military, may be superfluous in the post-cold war era and should be abolished. Also, the police are as susceptible as the military were to becoming autonomous bastions of abuse of power, especially where, as in many transitional societies, the secuelae of social and economic breakdown includes burgeoning street crime. Avoiding a backlash of popular yearning for authoritarianism, prompted by a sense of personal insecurity, is one of the biggest challenges of transitional and newly democratic societies. Although there may be no magic bullets to solve the problem of street crime, early planning, external control, and clear checks on police action may help avoid a recreation of past repressions with different actors. The use of ombudsmen or similar offices is a way of channeling and empowering citizens to take action against official arbitrariness, although experience in several countries shows that ombudsmen are effective only where both the holder of the office and her superiors have the resources and the political will to take on powerful adversaries.

Finally, there is the role of collective memory in coming to terms with the past and preventing its return. Although disagreements may persist as to *why* certain events happened, the fact that they did happen must be beyond reproach and must be part of school curricula and training courses for lawyers, judges, politicians, the military, and the police. Commemoration includes rescuing historical memory, both in formal, educational settings and in popular culture. Plays, movies, fine arts, literature, and music are an integral part of the process of coming to grips with the past and may have a more profound influence on a people and their historical memory than any legal process.

Beyond these specifics, the larger question remains one of forging a civil society in which disputes are settled through peaceful political means and citizens tolerate difference, a society that provides a modicum of political freedom as well as economic security and social integration. Past cultural and political history may weigh heavily on transitions away from repressive regimes: A history of legalism, respect for elected governments, and tolerance of differing political discourse may prove more important in predicting the future course of a transition than all the specific measures discussed in this book. Thus, for example, a transition to democracy in Chile or Uruguay, with long civilist and legalist traditions of government, might have been more successful than one in Argentina or El Salvador, with long traditions of military coups and instability, independently of the antiimpunity measures taken or forgone. I do not mean to be mechanical or overly deterministic here, merely to acknowledge the weight of a past history and political culture in helping or hindering movement toward democracy and the limits to legal measures, domestic or international, in shaping national consciousness.

One way of breaking with longstanding authoritarian traditions is to provide counterweights to an overly dominant central executive branch: a vigorous press and nongovernmental sector, responsive local-level institutions, strong unions, peasant and neighborhood groups, universities, and religious institutions. These have historically been the loci of opposition to dictatorship, but in new conditions of formal democracy they may find their mission unclear or their support dwindling. This has happened, for instance, with human rights and other nongovernmental groups in the Southern Cone of Latin America. At the same time, a new line of scholarship and activism recognizes the importance of building civil society as a bulwark against new repressions. A conscious effort to encourage grassroots organizations aimed at debating and influencing national policies rather than taking power themselves is one bulwark against a return to the bad old days. And here again, the international community has a supportive role to play.

Increasing Compliance with the Law

Chapters 3, 4, and 5 focused on the international law imperatives regarding investigation, prosecution, and redress. Comparing these imperatives with the case studies yields a mixed outcome. While most countries undertook some measures to investigate, prosecute, and provide redress, few complied fully with the stated imperatives. The grant of amnesty provoked the greatest divergence of declared law and actual practice. In several countries, governments considered amnesties as necessary for "national reconciliation." Still, in most of those cases amnesty was combined with some form of investigation.

What is even more striking when comparing those imperatives with actual practice is the extent to which, even where transitional governments have complied fully or partially with them, they have done so with little or no reference to these norms of international law. In part this is a function of the fact that many countries became parties to the relevant treaties only with the advent of the transitional government. But beyond the specific treaty language, longstanding law on crimes against humanity and general principles of law would seem to be applicable to all countries, and yet national policy making has rarely made reference to these principles. Moreover, international peacemaking, mediation, and reconciliation efforts have often similarly ignored the relevant principles, even when the peacemakers are from the international organizations that developed the guiding principles on the subject.

That said, I believe the reality is more nuanced. Over the last ten years or so, the insistence by human rights lawyers and institutions on the legal limits to government choices in this area has had an impact, albeit an indirect one. That impact has come through norm creation and diffusion, the creation of an authoritative vision of what is right.

This process of norm creation and diffusion takes place simultaneously at the national and international levels. It operates through the interaction of actors on both planes and the passing of information and legal-policy arguments from one to the other and back again. A first step has been the recognition that the problem at issue belongs to the realm of international human rights and can and should be discussed using existing concepts and categories. Thus, before the 1980s, it was widely believed that decisions about prosecution, investigations, amnesties, and the like were entirely within the sphere of each country's domestic jurisdiction. That has now changed; both governments and nongovernmental organizations now compile information, issue protests, rate government performance, and condition aid and trade on the treatment of past human rights violations as well as on the prevention of current abuses.[18]

More important, within a number of countries internal political forces and human rights advocates have used international law-based arguments to buttress their position in favor of prosecutions or against the granting or maintenance of an amnesty for government officials involved in crimes against civilians.[19] Chilean legislators, for example, in proposing laws "interpreting" the military's 1978 self-amnesty, turned to article 3 of the Geneva Conventions to provide a definition of what crimes would be excluded from the amnesty's scope.[20] A few government human rights officials in the 1990s, for example, in Honduras[21] and Ethiopia,[22] have cited their country's international obligations as a rationale for investigations or prosecutions. President Jean-Bertrand Aristide in Haiti has repeatedly stressed that a blanket amnesty for crimes like murder, rape, and torture would violate Haiti's obligations under international law as well as the Haitian constitution. South African President Nelson Mandela has stressed that the investigation/plea bargaining "amnesty" scheme proposed by the ANC-led government is consistent with South Africa's international law obligations.

International law serves in these cases as one strand of argument to bolster a political-legal position. In contrast, in early transitions such as those of Argentina and Uruguay, although there were fierce national debates over the proper policy, these made little or no reference to international law strictures. In the interim several international bodies, including the U.N. General Assembly, the Inter-American Commission on Human Rights, and the Inter-American Court, have spoken specifically on issues of amnesty, redress, and state responsibility to clarify violations. A plausible explanation is that these international decisions and declarations, often influenced by human rights lawyers and nongovernmental organizations with members in countries facing problems of impunity, are in turn carried back to the national level and become part of the operative political discourse domestically. The linkage is clearest in the Honduran case, where Commissioner Leo Valladares's report was obviously heavily influenced by his work on the Inter-American Commission.

Thus, international law becomes effective through the creation of a transnational community of scholars and activists able to transmit legal and normative arguments from one country to another, directly or by way of international institutions. Such an international "epistemic community"[23] of lawyers, scholars, and human rights activists was instrumental in disseminating arguments based on international law, which were then picked up and used in subsequent national debates. In the same way government officials learned from the limits and pitfalls of earlier attempts to deal with the past,[24] so too political actors who favored measures to deal with the past learned from each other.

Moreover, a number of courts have used international law to conclude that prosecutions are permissible in the face of contrary domestic law. The Hungarian Constitutional Court found that international law on the imprescriptibility of war crimes and crimes against humanity allowed the Hungarian Parliament to override the statute of limitations on murder to reach back to the violent suppression of the 1956 uprising. The court used the 1949 Geneva Conventions and the 1968 Convention on the Non-Applicability of Statutes of Limitation to War Crimes and Crimes Against Humanity to find that the Hungarian government had specifically agreed not to impose a statute of limitations on war crimes and crimes against humanity. As noted above,[25] the court's decision follows a prior, contrary decision that security of expectations in a law-based society required forgoing changes in the statute of limitations. It was the international law argument that overcame the court's initial reluctance. The German Appeals Court similarly used international law to interpret the law of the former East Germany, concluding that prosecution of former border guards for the unjustified killing of several wall jumpers did not violate a prohibition on ex post facto laws.[26] In these cases international law has served as a welcome way out of a thorny domestic legal as well as moral problem.

Significantly, where international law is invoked in a criminal setting, it is often used for its norm-establishing and reaffirming value rather than as a basis for the precise statutory definitions required for valid criminal conviction. In Bolivia the Supreme Court found former dictator Luis Garcia Meza, his interior minister, and forty-six other persons guilty of genocide, among other crimes, for the assassination of eight opposition political leaders. Although the court's opinion refers to the Convention on the Prevention and Punishment of the Crime of Genocide, it is based on a domestic law definition of the crime, which is broader than the international definition and includes "bloody massacres" as a basis for conviction. Similarly, in Romania several persons close to the Ceausescu government were originally convicted on charges of genocide resulting from large-scale political killings. International law serves to validate, to legitimize, and to universalize a course of action, not directly to provide the rule of decision.

Despite the increasing use of international law, much remains to be done in making the law effective within national political-legal systems. The effort must be to better integrate existing and emerging international law on investigation, prosecution, and redress with emerging guidelines regarding amnesties and peace-making, on the one hand, and with an emerging consensus regarding the defense of the right to democracy, on the other. Such integration will help provide better solutions to the real difficulties transitional governments face in complying with their obligations.

Investigation, Prosecution, Redress, and the Right to Democracy

One of the most cogent objections raised to full-fledged prosecution as well as investigation of past human rights violations is that it ignores the political realities of those transitions where the perpetrators and their supporters are still a force to be reckoned with. In many cases these groups conserve the armed forces of the state as well as significant political support. Any attempt to prosecute systematically their crimes leads to threats to overthrow the new civilian regime and return to the dark old days. Thus, although a government may recognize that both truth and justice regarding the past are desirable, even necessary, attributes of a full democracy, it may be unable to fully or partially provide either. Although there is consensus that mere inconvenience or cowardice (or connivance) of the new government does not excuse complying with its international obligations, the dilemma remains a real one if the threat is credible. Thus, some scholars and activists argue that the transitional government must act responsibly, doing whatever can be done within the constraints of the existing political balance and no more.[27]

But if the investigation and prosecution of past crimes has become a matter of international concern, so too have these constraints on the ability of governments to investigate and prosecute them. There must be a clear understanding that attempts to disable or overthrow a democratically installed transitional regime in order to avoid legitimate prosecutions or investigations will not be tolerated by the international community. Only when it is clear to would-be coup plotters that a successful coup will result in international isolation, sanctions, and economic chaos, as well as a loss of political legitimacy, will the plotters think twice and newly emerging governments find their hand strengthened enough to resist such threats. Such an understanding is beginning, albeit unevenly, to emerge in the law regarding the right to democratic governance.

International law scholars[28] have noted two trends: the number of governments turning to the international community for legitimation and, conversely, the emergence of a community expectation that legitimate governments are those that obtain the honest and periodic consent of the governed. A sanctions regime enforcing this emerging norm of democratic governance is still in its infancy; and it has yet to overcome a legacy of justified mistrust of (neo)colonial interventions and of big-power politics disguised as commitment to the rule of law.

The clearest declarations of an international responsibility to protect democratically elected governments come from the Conference on Security and Cooperation in Europe (CSCE). In its 1990 Copenhagen meeting, for example, the CSCE Conference on the Human Dimension declared:

> (6) The participating states declare that the will of the people, freely and fairly expressed through periodic and genuine elections, is the basis of the authority and legitimacy of all government. . . . They recognize their responsibility to defend and protect . . . the democratic order freely established through the will of the people against the activities of persons, groups or organizations that engage in or refuse to renounce terrorism or violence aimed at the overthrow of that order or of that of another participating state.
>
> (7) [T]o ensure that the will of the people serves as the basis of the authority of government, the participating States will . . . (7.9) "ensure that candidates who obtain the necessary number of votes required by law are duly installed in office and are permitted to remain in office until their term expires."[29]

Thus, the participating states recognize an obligation to "defend and protect" the democratically elected government of another state. The document places no limits on either the type of action to be taken or the need for collective agreement on such measures. Both unilateral action and the use of force to restore a democratically elected government appear to be contemplated.[30]

In 1991 the member states of the OAS adopted the Santiago Commitment to Democracy and the Renewal of the Inter-American System, along with resolution 1080.[31] These agreements established a procedure whereby the OAS Permanent Council would meet "in the event of any occurrences giving rise to the sudden or irregular interruption of the democratic political institutional process or of the legitimate exercise of power by the democratically elected government in any of the Organization's member states." The Council may convene a meeting of the ministers of foreign affairs to take action, which will be legally binding on OAS member states. Thus, the Santiago Commitment allows for OAS action in cases of military or other threats to a democratically elected government.

The aftermath of the overthrow of Haiti's democratically elected president Jean-Bertrand Aristide in September 1991 provided the opportunity to see both the promise and the limits of this principle in action. Aristide was overthrown by a military coup;[32] a few weeks later the OAS recommended that its member states take "action to bring about the diplomatic isolation of those who hold power illegally in Haiti" and "suspend their economic, financial and commercial ties" until the elected government was restored.[33] On October 11, the U.N. General Assembly unanimously voted to demand the return of Aristide to office, full application of the country's constitution, and respect for human rights.[34] A series of negotiations and increased sanctions followed over the next three years. As of December 1994, United States troops have landed in Haiti, Aristide has returned to office together with pro-Aristide legislators, and the military chiefs are in exile. It is still unclear whether the results of the deal struck between the Haitian Army chiefs and U.S. negotiators will allow Aristide not only to return but to carry out his program, or will rather perpetuate the rule of the military and their civilian backers under a civilian facade. Nonetheless, it is undeniable that the overthrow of a democratically elected government, even without significant international security ramifications, can now be adjudged a matter of international concern.[35]

Events in Russia, Nigeria, Peru, and Guatemala reinforce this view, albeit somewhat equivocally. In both Peru and Guatemala elected presidents staged "auto-coups," dissolving Congress and the courts and imposing curbs on the press and on civil liberties. In the Peruvian case the OAS immediately protested President Alberto Fujimori's decision and called for sanctions unless there was a quick return to representative democracy. The sanctions were subsequently dropped after Fujimori presented a timetable for new elections. In Guatemala President Jorge Serrano was forced to resign only days after his own auto-coup in June 1992, in large part because of the threat of international sanctions against his regime. Nonetheless, neither country has yet established a full democracy, although some of the trappings are there.

In Nigeria General Ibrahim Babangida and other military leaders voided the June 1993 elections, turning over the government instead to a handpicked successor and later to a military general. Both the United States and Britain, the two countries with the most external influence on Nigeria, protested the annulment of elections by terminating aid, withdrawing military personnel and training funds, and threatening stronger sanctions. Despite these measures, as of this writing the military is still in power and the elected president has been imprisoned. In several cases it is possible to argue that international pressure has been insufficient or halfhearted and that more could have been done. The selective nature of international action, without any apparent principled criteria, rules, or constraints, threatens to undermine the future legitimacy of such actions. Why is Haiti a different case from Nigeria, or Myanmar-Burma? As of now, the answer comes down to pragmatic politics and resources of the large powers; eventually, a better answer is required.

Moreover, the use of economic sanctions or military force to restore democracy must raise a number of cautions given a historical tendency to abuse, especially by large countries acting to protect their interests in the name of manifest destiny or the fight against communism. A number of commentators and countries have concluded from this history of abuse that interference in the internal form of government, or at the least the use of force to interfere, may never be justified because it has no principled limits. Like the earlier, and related, controversy over the legality of humanitarian intervention, the debate seems to be swinging away from such categorical refusals. Rather, the search now is for a set of neutral criteria that would avert the risks of international intervention while accruing the benefits.

An initial answer is to limit permissible sanctions and interventions to the restoration of existing elected democracies rather than the overthrow of "unacceptable" ones. As Halberstam points out, where the state has already held elections and the elected government is prevented from taking office or deposed by threat or violence, the form of government has already been chosen by the population and is not being externally imposed.[36] Imposing a requirement of collective action, although admittedly it holds action hostage to cumbersome processes of big-power consensus, is another possible safeguard. Defining democracy to mean more than elections, to imply full respect for human rights and channels for popular participation in policy making, will limit interventions in aid of a democracy in form only. Whereas the borders that distinguish legitimate use of the right of rebellion from illegitimate usurpation of democracy may be fuzzy, in most real-life cases they will be clear enough.

In summary, an international obligation to defend and protect elected democracies is emerging in international law parallel to the obligation to investigate, prosecute, and provide redress. Transitional governments contemplating measures for confronting the past in situations where military or security-force destabilization or attempts to overthrow the new government are possible will need a coordinated strategy that contemplates marshalling international pressure early on in defense of the civilian regime. As such pressure becomes more of a credible threat, the arguments for restraint in the name of responsibility or realpolitik lose some of their force.

Amnesties and Peacemaking

Another major area of debate has centered on the use of amnesties as an incentive to settle a civil conflict or permit the exit of a dictator. As discussed in Chapter 5, emerging declaratory law holds that blanket amnesties for certain particularly grave human rights violations are illegal under international law. Of course, consistency in application is crucial if an emerging rule is to crystallize as law. And if the primary purpose of such a rule is deterrence, consistency is essential to the efficacy of the deterrent threat.

Nonetheless, this view has been lacking not only in some domestic settlements but, more disturbingly, in the mediation or peacemaking efforts of the United Nations and of states acting under United Nations auspices. One such instance is the involvement of the United Nations in peace negotiations over Cambodia, described in Chapter 18. While the ASEAN powers were prepared not only to exclude the Khmer Rouge from a settlement but to accuse them of genocide, under U.N. sponsorship mentions of past grave human rights violations were watered down to the point of nonrecognition, and all attempts to include provisions for prosecution, or even for keeping former Khmer Rouge leaders out of government, were ruled out. Similarly, in attempting to mediate negotiations over a transition to a democratic government in South Africa, representatives of the U.N. secretary-general apparently were willing to contemplate an unconditional amnesty that would cover acts not open for amnesty under international law.

The involvement of OAS, U.N., and U.S. mediators in negotiating the return of President Aristide to Haiti, described in Chapter 14, is another case in point. While Aristide himself, and some human rights groups, have consistently objected to the idea of a blanket amnesty for the military as part of the terms of the 1993 Governor's Island Agreement as well as the September 1994 "Carter deal," U.N. and U.S. officials urged Aristide to accept those terms as the price of return.[37] The proposed amnesty would have covered not only crimes against the democratic order but abuses, including killings, disappearances, and torture, for which amnesty is clearly proscribed under international human rights law. While as of this writing it appears that the Haitian legislature has narrowed the scope of an amnesty, neither U.S. nor U.N. officials have apparently been sympathetic to — or even aware of — any necessary limits to an amnesty grant.

A fourth example is the Truth Commission's report on El Salvador, discussed in Chapter 15, which made no mention of amnesty. It is true that the Salvadoran legislature had already passed a version of an amnesty bill. It is also true that the Commission's report rightly pointed out the futility of recommending criminal prosecutions in the face of a dysfunctional judicial system. However, the complete absence of any mention of the terms of an amnesty or its relation to compliance with the Commission's recommendations in its report probably emboldened military-aligned parties to push through an immediate, sweeping amnesty bill that precludes civil suit as well as criminal prosecution. Although the secretary-general eventually criticized the granting of amnesty, an earlier statement of concern might have been more effective.

In part these examples demonstrate the gulf between the human rights machinery of the United Nations and the newly empowered peacemaking functions centered in the secretary-general's office and the Security Council. In larger part, however, these inconsistencies reflect a deeper ambivalence product of the deep moral and ethical dilemma posed: When is it permissible to "bargain with the devil"? On one level this is the quintessential question of all politics, that of ends justifying means. Others have posed the question as an issue of an "ethics of responsibility," which takes into account the likely consequences of proposed actions.[38] Posed this way, many people would probably say that it is worth letting criminals go free to end wars or dictatorships, and the law be damned. On the other hand, excusing states from complying with their international obligations because of pressure from recalcitrant military and security forces in effect rewards the use of threats and pressure, encouraging further acts of insubordination and highhandedness, which may, in the long run, facilitate a return to war or dictatorship. The dilemma seems insoluble. But perhaps there is another way of framing the question, one that avoids all-or-nothing dichotomies as well as the constant undermining of admittedly necessary principles by appeals to pragmatism and exceptionalism.

One possible initial distinction has already been mentioned: that between amnesty and pardon. Although amnesty implies no investigation or acknowledgment of responsibility, pardon comes after both and merely constitutes a suspension of punishment. Moreover, amnesty implies a categorical decision, whereas pardon requires individualized consideration. Many of the functions of criminal prosecution — judicial inquiry into the truth, acknowledgment of responsibilities, public delegitimation — may be carried out without anyone actually going to jail. Indeed, it is noteworthy how uniformly the victims of past abuses indicate they are uninterested in seeing their former tormentors imprisoned, so long as their pardon is based on an acceptance of responsibility rather than its denial. While a promise of pardon may not satisfy some reluctant perpetrators, it may be enough for others. As of this writing, the Mandela government in South Africa seems to have chosen a variant of this approach, described in Chapter 20: Within the framework of a truth commission, individuals will be able to come forward and confess their crimes. Those who do so will receive a recommendation of pardon; President Nelson Mandela will individually determine whether to accept each recommendation.[39] Although billed as an "amnesty," this is far from blanket preinvestigation amnesia. It is, in effect, a scheme for pardons.

A similar rationale applies to the possibility of plea bargaining, either within or outside a strictly judicial context. Of course, the lack of an amnesty is not the same as a decision to prosecute all those involved in mass killings, disappearances, or torture. It may well be that some of those whose crimes are not subject to amnesty are nonetheless not prosecuted due to lack of enough evidence or for other reasons. One such reason may be the striking of a plea bargain, a technique well-known to the United States criminal justice system but little used in Latin America and elsewhere. Trading a promise of leniency for the information necessary to convict the persons most responsible for the commission of massive crimes or to reconstruct the structures and methods of repression may facilitate the changes needed to avoid future repressions and provide a tangible benefit to truth seeking. The difference between a plea bargain and an amnesty resides in the individualized, tailored nature of one versus the blanket nature of the other. Of course, if all of the persons implicated in past violations strike a bargain, the practical effect may be much the same, but the principle remains very different, and at least what is obtained in return is directly related to the goal of confronting the past. Plea bargains for individuals toward the bottom of a hierarchy, in exchange for information about either the whereabouts of victims or the involvement of high officials, seem less objectionable than bargains with those at the top of a hierarchy. Similarly, questions arise over the propriety of maintaining in secret the evidence obtained: Although the individual sources of pieces of evidence may remain anonymous, the overall outlines of the information obtained probably should be available to the public as a requirement of any bargain.

A third possibility is to give up the ability to prosecute, but allow individual victims to bring civil suits during a certain period against those responsible for grave violations of their rights. This approach provides the benefits of a judicial process and may give important symbolic as well as monetary redress to victims without the threat of incarceration. However, significant disadvantages include possible overload of a fragile judicial system, the lack of available assets for most potential defendants, objections from persons who are to be eased from power, and the potential to undercut the principle that such crimes offend both society and individual victims. In addition, in many states access to the evidence necessary to prove liability is available only through the coercive power of the prosecutor — private discovery is much more limited. Indeed, this was part of the basis for the complaints brought against Uruguay and Argentina for enacting de facto amnesties. A civil suit solution would be feasible only if appropriate provisions for access to testimony and documents were part of the package.

A final option is suggested by the rules of procedure of the International Tribunal on the former Yugoslavia. Faced with the reality that the most important potential defendants are unlikely to be surrendered by the states harboring them, and unable to resort to trials in absentia, the Tribunal's staff sought a way to at least make public the evidence of crimes committed and subject the defendants to public opprobrium. Rule 61 allows the prosecutor, after demonstrating that she has taken all reasonable steps to execute an arrest warrant but has been unable to do so, to submit the indictment to a trial chamber. If the judges are satisfied that the evidence provides reasonable grounds for believing that the accused has committed all or any of the crimes charged in the indictment, it shall so determine. The prosecutor may then read out the relevant parts of the indictment in open court. An international arrest warrant is to be issued for the defendant, making him, in effect, unable to leave his country.[40] On the domestic level, the equivalent action would be the release of the names of those implicated in certain grave human rights violations. It would then be up to other states to prohibit the entrance of those names, freeze their assets, or otherwise restrict their movements internationally.

The International Aspect

What of the role of the international community, and international institutions? A starting place must be the need for consistency in norm articulation and application, at'least on the international level. The development of international legal norms cannot be subject to the vicissitudes of political negotiation without the norms themselves becoming open to question. Although it may be true that some countries will be unable to comply fully with the articulated norms, this is true in the case of many human rights, without the international community accepting such noncompliance in the name of another social good. The obligation of states to refrain from torture, for instance, exists whether or not the use of torture would facilitate the identification and elimination of terrorist groups, an admitted social good. There will be lapses, but they should not be dignified internationally as acceptable policy.

Rather, international institutions must support those transitional governments attempting to comply with their obligations. As discussed, a first type of support comes from an international willingness to support democratically elected governments in the face of pressure from disgruntled perpetrators of past violations. A second involves refraining from proposing or ratifying peace agreements, negotiations, or compromises that are based on blanket amnesties, no matter what the short-term gains. Such amnesties may, in practice, be granted anyway, but they should not receive the imprimatur of international acceptance.

A third type of support comes from continued insistence on the application of the established norms regarding past abuses in diplomatic and international settings. In addition to their record on current protection of human rights, states should be publicly judged on how well they have dealt with problems of impunity, in human rights forums and when governments are deciding on aid and trade concessions. As noted earlier, steps in this direction have already been taken. Such insistence will strengthen the hands of the persons within each country who are trying to assert the primacy of law and the subordination of military or security forces to civilian rule. It will make efforts to bring them to acccount seem less like political revanchism and more like an ineluctable duty whose dereliction itself brings consequences.[41]

International and regional organizations may also play a useful role in the sharing of experiences and of the difficulties and options available to governments that are newly confronting these issues. The U.N. Advisory Services program, for example, could profitably develop expertise in measures not only to reform judicial and administrative systems for the future but in the design of measures aimed at finding out the truth and dispensing justice and redress in past cases.

Another useful change might come in the international law of political asylum. Asylum law prevents a grant of asylum to certain persons suspected of crimes against humanity or "acts contrary to the purposes and principles of the United Nations."[42] Although this is generally a useful rule, it has had perverse consequences in cases of military or death squad members who have had second thoughts about their actions and have been willing to testify as to the methods, masterminds, and financiers of their activities if they are assured of safe haven elsewhere. Even individuals who have given very useful information have been unable to avoid their deportation back to the country in which those they denounced remain in powerful positions. As an incentive for such low-level officials to come forward, a discretionary grant of asylum abroad for persons whose information proves useful in investigating or prosecuting human rights violations in their home country would be a beneficial modification.

Yet another possibility of international support, mentioned in the case studies, is the use of transnational civil litigation to overcome some of the barriers to domestic civil suits. The United States has gone the farthest in allowing this type of suit, which has been brought against torturers and persons accused of summary execution and disappearance in Paraguay, the former Yugoslavia, Argentina, Guatemala, Haiti, the Philippines, Ethiopia, and Chile.[43] Such suits may serve as truth telling and redress in a way that affects the political climate in the parties' home country, especially if the evidence presented is transmitted to the home country, if the defendants are well chosen, and if the strangeness of the legal system does not overwhelm, in the public mind, the value of a trial in a foreign venue. To date, the Marcos trial remains the most ambitious effort along these lines, going beyond individual damages to compensation for a broad class of victims, most of them still in the Philippines. But the confluence of an accessible defendant with known assets and a reasonably similar, and therefore understandable, legal system and culture seem unlikely to be repeated elsewhere.

Finally, international support may come from the establishment of an international criminal tribunal with the power to try gross violators of human rights. Much has been written about the need for, and possible structure and functions of, such a court, and this is not the place to repeat that discussion.[44] The situation in the former Yugoslavia has given a new impetus to decades-long attempts to create such a court. The International Law Commission has presented a draft statute for comment, and debate on the draft will be taken up in the coming years.

The precedential effect of the Yugoslav tribunal on future acceptance of a permanent international criminal court is unclear. To gain Security Council approval, especially from Brazil and China, Resolution 827 authorizing the Tribunal is cautiously worded, referring to the "particular circumstances of the former Yugoslavia" and the fact that the Tribunal is an "ad hoc measure." The secretary-general's report makes clear that the Security Council's decision does not relate to the establishment of either international criminal jurisdiction or an international court.[45] The Tribunal faces many problems, including evidentiary and financial difficulties, an inability to gain jurisdiction over the most appropriate defendants, and the temptation of states to trade off its existence or effectiveness for diplomatic concessions. On the other hand, it may provide the infrastructure, practical experience, and some of the law that could subsequently be applied by an international criminal court. Moreover, the U.N. Security Council has now established a second international tribunal on the 1994 genocide in Rwanda as an outgrowth of the Yugoslav tribunal. This raises the possibility that, rather than a permanent court, a series of ad-hoc tribunals for specific situations will develop precedents and methodology for at least the near future.[46]

Nonetheless, even establishment of an international criminal court will not obviate the need for rules requiring states to investigate, prosecute, and provide redress within domestic legal systems. Most obviously, a permanent court will focus only on criminal convictions, not on other forms of investigation or redress. It will, with minor exceptions, apply only to a narrow range of crimes and depend on state consent to try its nationals. Current proposals may well result in a tribunal focused more on drug dealers and hijackers than on persons committing torture and mass murder. Furthermore, the risks facing transitional governments regarding domestic investigation and prosecution of perpetrators of past offenses will extend to decisions to turn them over for prosecution to an international court. Moreover, once an international tribunal has done its job, many tasks will remain: those of working through to a shared national history, of establishing new institutions and new ways of thinking, and of getting practice in the unaccustomed exercise of a functional system of law, at least.

Ultimately, responsibility to investigate, prosecute, and provide redress will remain largely with each state for the foreseeable future. In an ideal world these obligations would be of minor importance as democratic governments refrained from violating human rights and the issue was reduced to ensuring adequate responses to isolated instances of rogue officials. They remain crucial, nonetheless, in our less than ideal circumstances. International actors can help move us closer to the ideal by providing support for governments attempting to overcome impunity, by refusing to recognize or support de facto regimes that overthrow elected governments, and by consistent and steadfast enunciation and application of the applicable legal norms. We owe the victims of mass executions, disappearances, and other crimes no less.

Notes

Chapter 1

1. Thus, for instance, the Chilean government and human rights groups were both heavily influenced by the Argentine and Uruguayan examples.

2. *See* J. Van Dyke and G. W. Berkley, "Redressing Human Rights Abuses," 20 *Denver Journal of International Law* 243 (1992).

3. Eastern Europe presents a slight variant, but the violations at issue to a greater or lesser degree still involved rights to physical integrity.

4. For example, the extent of economic, social, and cultural rights, or of "third-generation" rights such as development, have been subjects of longstanding controversy. Some writers are reluctant to establish hierarchies of rights, but in practice such hierarchies exist.

5. *See* the section on derogability in Chapter 5, pp. 58–59.

6. Peremptory norms are a small subset of widely shared norms that arise from a state's status as such, rather than its consent, and that cannot be overcome by a treaty provision to the contrary. *See, e.g., Restatement (Third) of the Foreign Relations Law of the United States,* section 702, comment n and reporter's note 11.

7. This is true at least for torturers and those who commit genocide or crimes against humanity. *See* K. Randall, "Universal Jurisdiction Under International Law," 66 *Texas Law Review* 785 (1988).

8. *See* "Summary of the Discussions," *Seminar on the Right to Restitution, Compensation and Rehabilitation for Victims of Gross Violations of Human Rights and Fundamental Freedoms,* T. van Boven, C. Flinterman, F. Grünfeld, and I Westendorp, eds. (Maastricht: Netherlands Institute of Human Rights, 1992), pp. 3–15. *See also* U.N. Sub-Commission on Prevention of Discrimination and Protection of Minorities, Working Paper prepared by Mr. Guisse and Mr. Joinet, On the Question of Impunity for Perpetrators of Human Rights Violations, U.N. Doc. E/CN.4/Sub.2/1994/11, June 22, 1994 (preliminary report on economic, social, and cultural rights).

9. G.A. Res. 217 (III), arts. 3, 5, 9, U.N. Doc. A/810, p. 71 (1948).

10. Dec. 19, 1966, 999 U.N.T.S. 171, arts. 6, 7, 9.

11. Nov. 22, 1969, 36 O.A.S.T.S. 1, arts. 4, 5, 7, OEA/ser. L./V/II.23, doc. 21 rev. 6 (1979) (entered into force July 18, 1978).

12. Done at Rome, Nov. 4, 1950. Entered into force Sept. 3, 1953. Europ. T.S. No. 5., arts. 1, 3, 5.

13. Convention Against Torture and Other Cruel, Inhuman or Degrading Treatment or Punishment, adopted 10 Dec. 1984, opened for signature Feb. 4, 1985, G.A. Res. A/Res/39/46 (1984).

14. *See, e.g.,* Inter-American Convention on the Forced Disappearance of Persons, resolution adopted by the OAS General Assembly, seventh plenary sess., OEA/ser. P, AG/doc. 3 114/94 rev. 1, June 9, 1994.

15. *See* Chapter 4 for a discussion of U.N. pronouncements.

16. *Filartiga v. Pena-Irala,* 630 F.2d 876 (2nd Cir. 1982).

17. *Forti v. Suarez Mason,* 694 F. Supp. 707, 710 (N.D. Cal., as amended 1988).

18. *See Barcelona Traction, Light and Power Co. (Belg. v. Spain)* case, 1970 I.J.C. 3, regarding some obligations being *erga omnes*—that is, owing to all. To the extent these

obligations are not merely customary but rather *jus cogens,* they arise from a nation's status as part of the international community and are independent of its consent. *See Restatement (Third) of the Foreign Relations Law of the United States, supra* note 6; T. Franck, *The Power of Legitimacy among Nations* (New York: Oxford University Press, 1990).

19. Inter-American Convention on the Forced Disappearance of Persons, *supra* note 14; *see also Forti v. Suarez-Mason,* 694 F. Supp. 707, 710 (N.D. Cal., 1988) (finding that "causing disappearance" is a universally proscribed tort in violation of the law of nations).

20. *See* the discussion in Chapter 2, especially notes 11, 39, 41, and accompanying text.

21. M. Osiel, "The Making of Human Rights Policy in Argentina: The Impact of Ideas and Interests on a Legal Conflict," 18 *Journal of Latin American Studies* 135, 145 (1986).

22. *See* L. Weschler, *A Miracle, A Universe* (New York: Pantheon Books, 1990), for a discussion of the Brazilian Church's investigation into torture in Brazil in the 1960s.

23. *Id.,* p. 4.

24. Malamud-Goti, "Trying Violators of Human Rights: The Dilemma of Transitional Democratic Governments," in *State Crimes: Punishment or Pardon* (Aspen Institute: Queenstown, Maryland, 1989), pp. 71, 81–84.

25. Frank Newman, for example, argues that these nonpenal measures may be more effective in both punishment and deterrent terms.

Chapter 2

1. C. L. Ten, *Crime, Guilt and Punishment* (Oxford, U.K.: Clarendon Press, 1987), p. 3.

2. This philosophy may include using the punishment of innocent people as a means to convey the desired message. *Id.,* p. 14.

3. In fact, in many cases people who were not directly affected by the human rights abuses of totalitarian regimes claim that they "miss" those regimes. For example, the Fallangists in Spain fondly remember that there was very little crime or social disturbance during the reign of Francisco Franco. A similar phenomenon of longing for a "strong hand" against crime now exists in Argentina as well. *See* Chapter 12.

4. Detractors of utilitarian punishment theories claim that the theory allows the punishment of innocent people. If a person's punishment is minimal and the benefit to society of that punishment is great, utilitarians would say that the person should be punished. Ten, *supra* note 1, p. 14.

5. *Id.,* p. 4.

6. Andrew von Hirsch, *Past or Future Crimes* (New Brunswick, NJ: Rutgers University Press, 1987), p. 8.

7. Johannes Andenaes, "General Prevention–Illusion or Reality," in *Theories of Punishment,* Stanley E. Grupp, ed. (Bloomington: Indiana University Press, 1971), p. 138.

8. Johannes Andenaes, *Punishment and Deterrence* (Ann Arbor: University of Michigan Press, 1974), p. 8.

9. For example, the Argentine government under Isabelita Perón supported the kidnapping and murder of "guerrillas" by paramilitary organizations as a form of social control. Later, some people supported the military's actions, including some human rights abuses, because they believed that the military "deterred" crime.

10. Jaime Malamud-Goti, "Transitional Governments in the Breach: Why Punish State Criminals?" 12 *Human Rights Quarterly* 1, 9 (1990). I am indebted to Jaime Malamud-

Goti, whose writings and discussions with me provided many of the ideas in this chapter. For a further exposition of his views, *see* Chapter 12.

11. *See* Jaime Malamud-Goti, "Punishment and a Rights-Based Democracy," *Criminal Justice Ethics* (Summer/Fall 1991), p. 7.

12. Ronald J. Rychlak, "Society's Moral Right to Punish: A Further Exploration of the Denunciation Theory of Punishment," 65 *Tulane Law Review* 299, 311 (Dec. 1990).

13. Of course, this assumes that the rehabilitator knows what would be a meaningful life for the offender.

14. Von Hirsch, *supra* note 6, p. 5.

15. *Id.,* p. 441, fn. 59.

16. *See* Malamud-Goti, *supra* note 10, pp. 10–11.

17. *Id.,* p. 8.

18. Wrongs can be moral, social, and/or legal, and this is not an exclusive list. Some retribution theorists focus on the moral conduct of the offender; others focus on the legal wrong committed.

19. Rychlak, *supra* note 12, p. 327.

20. *See* Jeffrie Murphy and Jean Hampton, *Forgiveness and Mercy* (New York: Cambridge University Press, 1988), pp. 18–25.

21. Sadurski, "Theory of Punishment, Social Justice and Liberal Neutrality," 5 *Oxford Journal of Legal Studies,* 47, 55 (1985).

22. Malamud-Goti, *supra* note 10, p. 8.

23. Ralph D. Ellis and Carol S. Ellis, *Theories of Criminal Justice* (Wolfeboro, NH: Longwood Academic, 1989), p. 2.

24. *See, e.g.,* Wesley Cragg, *The Practice of Punishment: Towards a Theory of Restorative Justice* (London: Routledge, 1992), pp. 67–72.

25. Rychlak, *supra* note 12, pp. 331–35.

26. Gary B. Melton, "The Law Is a Good Thing (Psychology Is, Too): Human Rights in Psychological Jurisprudence," 16 *Law & Human Behavior* 381, 384 (1992).

27. Malamud-Goti, *supra* note 11, p. 9.

28. In a study of litigants in purely civil cases, a researcher found that the parties were most satisfied with the justice system when the proceedings matched the litigants' expectations. The litigants also felt that judicial proceedings were fairer if the proceedings were dignified. The researchers speculated that the dignified ceremony of court lent importance to the litigants' problems, thus acting as a symbolic form of satisfaction. E. Allan Lind, Robert J. MacCoun, Patricia A. Ebener, William L. F. Felstiner, Deborah R. Hensler, Judith Resnik, and Tom R. Tyler, "In the Eye of the Beholder: Tort Litigants' Evaluation of Their Experiences in the Civil Justice System," 24(4) *Law and Society Review* 953, 971–73, 981 (1990).

29. Quoted in Cherif Bassiouni, *Crimes Against Humanity in International Criminal Law* (Dordrecht, Netherlands: M. Nijhoff, 1992), p. 544.

30. Stephen Schafer, "Victim Compensation and Responsibility," 43 *Southern California Law Review* 55, 55–57 (1970).

31. *See* S. Schafer, *Compensation and Restitution to Victims of Crime,* 2nd ed. (Montclair, NJ: Patterson Smith, 1970), pp. 3–12.

32. For the early utilitarians, including Jeremy Bentham and John Austin, the distinction was meaningless. Justice Holmes concluded that "the general principles of criminal and civil liability are the same." O. W. Holmes, *The Common Law* 44 (1881). Other scholars, especially Jerome Hall, disagreed. *See* Hall, "Interrelation of Criminal Law and Torts: I & II," 43 *Columbia Law Review* 753, 967 (1943).

33. Richard S. Frase, "Comparative Criminal Justice as a Guide to American Law

Reform: How Do the French Do It, How Can We Find Out, and Why Should We Care?," 78 *California Law Review* 542 (1990).

34. *See* Alan Harland, "Monetary Remedies for the Victims of Crime: Assessing the Role of the Criminal Courts," 30 *UCLA Law Review* 52 (1982).

35. Schafer, *supra* note 30, pp. 58–59.

36. Lynne Henderson, "The Wrongs of Victims Rights," 37 *Stanford Law Review* 937, 956 (1985).

37. *Id.,* p. 958.

38. *Id.,* p. 959.

39. *See* Y. Danieli, "Preliminary Reflections for a Psychological Perspective," in *Seminar on the Right to Restitution, Compensation and Rehabilitation for Victims of Gross Violations of Human Rights and Fundamental Freedoms,* T. van Boven, C. Flinterman, F. Grünfeld, and I. Westendorp, eds. (Maastrict: Netherlands Institute of Human Rights, 1992), pp. 196, 197.

40. *See* Henderson, *supra* note 36, n. 128.

41. Ana Julia Cienfuegos and Cristina Monelli, "The Testimony of Political Repression as a Therapeutic Instrument," 1983 *Journal of the American Orthopsychiatric Association* 43, 44, 49–50. There is a significant psychological literature on the effects of repression and on the failure of successor regimes to deal adequately with the past. *See, e.g.,* S. Salimovich, E. Lira, and E. Weinstein, "Victims of Fear: The Social Psychology of Repression," in *Fear at the Edge: State Terror and Resistance in Latin America,* Juan E. Corradi, P. W. Fagen, and M. A. Garreton, eds. (Berkeley: University of California Press, 1992), pp. 72–89; Instituto Latinoamericano de Asistencia Social (ILAS), *Todo es Segun el Dolor con que se Mira,* E. Lira, ed. (Chile: Ed. Sur, 1989).

42. For a detailed discussion of international standards for a compensation program, *see* Ellen Lutz, "After the Elections: Compensating Victims of Human Rights Abuses," in *New Directions in Human Rights*, E. Lutz, H. Hannum, and K. Burke, eds. (Philadelphia: University of Pennsylvania Press, 1989), p. 195.

43. Tom R. Tyler, *Why People Obey the Law* (New Haven, CT: Yale University Press, 1990), ch. 9, p. 116.

44. Lind et al., *supra* note 28, pp. 957–59.

45. *See* Tyler, *supra* note 43, p. 150.

46. Lind et al., *supra* note 28. Another study compared an "inquisitorial" method of procedure, in which most fact development and presentation of evidence is in the hands of an impartial decision maker, to an "adversarial" model, in which these tasks are left to the parties and their attorneys. Through a series of simulations and controlled experiments, researchers found that an adversary procedure produced the greatest satisfaction with a judgment, based in large part on the separation of presentations of the contending parties, the alignment of attorneys with their client rather than as neutral fact finders, and a free choice of attorneys rather than an appointed investigator. They also found that key properties contributing to the superiority of an adversarial system were the degree of control over the process by the disputants, the ability to discover and present their own evidence, and the acknowledged contentiousness — albeit kept within limits — of the disputants themselves. J. Thibaut and L. Walter, *Procedural Justice: A Psychological Analysis* (New York: John Wiley, 1975).

47. K. Leung and E. A. Lind, "Procedural Justice and Culture: Effects of Culture, Gender and Investigator Status on Procedural Preferences," 50 *Journal of Personality and Social Psychology,* 1134–40 (1986).

48. E. Allan Lind and Tom R. Tyler, *The Social Psychology of Procedural Justice* (New York: Plenum Press, 1988), pp. 83–88.

49. The Thibaut and Walter study used cross-cultural data from French subjects for parts of its analysis, but not for others. *See* Thibaut and Walter, *supra* note 46, pp. 97–101.

50. Henry Rousso, *The Vichy Syndrome: History and Memory in France since 1944* (Cambridge, MA: Harvard University Press, 1991), p. 215.

51. Daniel T. Kobil, "The Quality of Mercy Strained: Wresting the Pardoning Power from the King," 69 *Texas Law Review* 569, 575 (1991).

52. Courts and commentators have disagreed on this point: *cf.* R. Golfarb and L. Singer, *After Conviction* (New York: Simon & Schuster, 1973), pp. 350–51, with *Knote v. U.S.,* 95 U.S. 149, 152–53 (1877). Although usages may differ, the underlying concepts are similar: I will use "pardon" and "amnesty" with these meanings throughout.

53. J. Bentham, *Introduction to the Principles of Morals and Legislation* (1789) (Darien, CT: Hafner Publishing, 1948), cited in Kathleen Dean Moore, *Pardons: Justice, Mercy and the Public Interest* (New York: Oxford University Press, 1989).

54. The phrase is from Immanuel Kant's *The Metaphysical Elements of Justice* (New York: Bobbs-Merrill, 1965), p. 100.

55. Moore, *supra* note 53, p. 33.

56. *Id.*

57. *See* Ignacio Martin-Baro, S.J., "Reparations: Attention Must Be Paid," 186 *Commonweal* (Mar. 23, 1990).

58. Murphy and Hampton, *supra* note 20, pp. 179–80.

Chapter 3

1. The Statute of the International Court of Justice, in the most widely recognized formulation, lists the sources of international law in article 38. *See* 59 stat. 1055, T.S. No. 993 (June 26, 1945).

2. States acquire jurisdiction to prosecute criminal acts that have a significant connection to that state—because the crime occurred within the state's territory (territorial jurisdiction) or had important effects within that territory (effects jurisdiction) or because it was committed by (nationality jurisdiction) or against (passive personality jurisdiction) a national of that state. In addition, some crimes are considered so heinous they are subject to universal jurisdiction; any state finding the offender in its territory may prosecute. *See* K. Randall, "Universal Jurisdiction under International Law," 66 *Texas Law Review* 785 (1988).

3. H. Grotius, *De Jure Belli et Pacis* (The Rights of War and Peace), bk. II, ch. XXI, sec. IV(1), p. 347 (W. Whewell trans. and ed., 1853).

4. Geneva Convention for the Amelioration of the Condition of the Wounded and Sick in Armed Forces in the Field, Aug. 12, 1949, arts. 49, 50, 6 U.S.T. 3114, 3146, T.I.A.S. No. 3362, 75 U.N.T.S. 31 62; Geneva Convention for the Amelioration of the Condition of Wounded, Sick and Shipwrecked Members of Armed Forces at Sea, Aug. 12, 1949, arts. 50, 51, 6 U.S.T. 3217, 3250, T.I.A.S. No. 3363, 75 U.N.T.S. 85, 116; Geneva Convention Relative to the Treatment of Prisoners of War, Aug. 12, 1949, arts. 129, 130, 6 U.S.T. 3316, 3418, T.I.A.S. No. 3364, 75 U.N.T.S. 135, 236; Geneva Convention Relative to the Protection of Civilian Persons in Time of War, Aug. 12, 1949, arts. 146, 147, 6 U.S.T. 3516, 3616, T.I.A.S. No. 3365, 75 U.N.T.S. 287, 386.

5. Protocol Additional to the Geneva Convention of 12 August 1949 relating to the protection of victims of International Armed Conflicts. Protocol I, sec. III, ch. I, art. 75(7) (1977).

6. *Id.,* arts. 86, 91.

7. The distinction between international and noninternational conflicts in this regard is becoming increasingly blurred. *See* Chapter 4.

8. U.N. GAOR Supp. (No. 30), p. 75, U.N. Doc. A/9030 (1973), reprinted in 13 I.L.M. 50 (1974). Apartheid is defined as a series of inhuman acts, including murder, arbitrary arrest and illegal imprisonment, forced labor, and denial of full participation in the life of the country "committed for the purpose of establishing and maintaining domination by one racial group of persons over any other racial group of persons and systematically oppressing them." *Id.,* art. II.

9. *See, e.g.,* 1926 Slavery Convention, 60 U.N.T.S. 253, 46 Stat. 2183 (1927), amended by Protocol, Dec. 7, 1953, 212 U.N.T.S. 17 (1953). Cherif Bassiouni provides an exhaustive list of conventions prohibiting slavery and the slave trade; *see* Cherif Bassiouni, *Crimes Against Humanity in International Criminal Law* (Dordrecht, Netherlands: M. Nijhoff, 1992), pp. 767–83.

10. Convention for the Suppression of Unlawful Seizure of Aircraft, Dec. 16, 1970, art. 7, 22 U.S.T. 1641, 1646, T.I.A.S. No. 7192, 860 U.N.T.S. 105, 109.

11. Convention for the Suppression of Unlawful Acts Against the Safety of Civil Aviation, Sept. 23, 1971, art. 7, 24 U.S.T. 565, 571, T.I.A.S. No. 7570, 1971 U.N. Jurid. Y.B. 143, 145, U.N. Doc. ST/LEG/SER.C/9.

12. International Convention Against the Taking of Hostages, Dec. 17, 1979, art. 8, U.N.G.A. Res. 34/146, 34 U.N. GAOR Supp. (No. 46), pp. 245, 246, U.N. Doc. A/C6/34/46 (1979).

13. European Convention on the Suppression of Terrorism, Jan. 27, 1977, art. 7, Europ.T.S. No. 90, p. 3.

14. Convention on the Prevention and Punishment of the Crime of Genocide, adopted Dec. 9, 1948, G.A. Res. 260 A (II), 78 U.N.T.S. 227, entered into force Jan. 12, 1951.

15. Genocide is defined in article II as "any of the following acts committed with intent to destroy, in whole or in part, a national, ethnical, racial, or religious group as such:

   a. Killing members of the group;
   b. Causing serious bodily or mental harm to members of the group;
   c. Deliberately inflicting on the group conditions of life calculated to bring about its physical destruction in whole or in part;
   d. Imposing measures intended to prevent births within the group;
   e. Forcibly transferring children of the group to another group."

Thus, genocide requires a specific intent absent from the definition of crimes against humanity; it also excludes political opposition groups from the list of protected groups.

16. Proposals for an international criminal court are again before the United Nations. *See* the discussion in Chapter 21.

17. Convention Against Torture or Other Cruel, Inhuman or Degrading Treatment or Punishment, GA Res. 39/46, 39 U.N. GAOR Supp. (No. 51) at 197, U.N. Doc. A/39/51 (1984).

18. Torture is defined as: "any act by which severe pain or suffering, whether physical or mental, is intentionally inflicted on a person for such purposes as obtaining from him or a third person information or a confession, punishing him for an act he or a third person has committed or is suspected of having committed, or intimidating or coercing him or a third person, or for any reason based on discrimination of any kind."

19. *Id.,* p. 197.

20. Inter-American Convention on the Forced Disappearance of Persons, resolution adopted by the OAS General Assembly, seventh plenary sess., OEA/ser.P,AG/doc. 3 114/94 rev. 1, June 9, 1994. The convention is not yet in force.

21. Similarly, the Inter-American Convention to Prevent and Punish Torture provides

in article 8 that if there is an accusation or well-grounded reason to believe that an act of torture has been committed within their jurisdiction, the States Parties shall guarantee that their respective authorities will proceed ex officio and immediately to conduct an investigation into the case and to initiate, whenever appropriate, the corresponding criminal process. 67 O.A.S.T.S., Dec. 9, 1985, art. 8, reprinted in 25 I.L.M. 519 (1986). The Convention entered into force in 1987.

22. A group of criminal law experts developing implementation principles for a U.N. declaration on victims (*see* Ch. 4) defines redress as including "such matters as financial reparation and the public acknowledgement (through the criminal justice process) of the wrong done to the victim." G.A. Res. 40/34, 40 U.N. GAOR Supp. (No.53) at 213, U.N. Doc. A/40/53 (1985) (adopted by consensus), Commentary to sec. 4, reprinted in *International Protection of Victims,* C. Bassiouni, ed. (Toulouse, France: ERES, International Criminal Law Association, 1988), p. 48.

23. J. Herman Bergers and Hans Danelius, *The United Nations Convention Against Torture* (Dordrecht, Netherlands: M. Nijhoff; Boston: Norwell, 1988), pp. 146–47.

24. As of the end of 1990, twenty-six of the fifty-five states parties had accepted the competence of the Committee to hear individual cases. The Committee is made up of independent experts. In addition, the Committee receives reports from parties on their implementation of the Convention.

25. For a full explanation of these laws, *see* Chapter 12. For another view on the legality of these provisions, *see* the discussion of the Inter-American Human Rights Commission cases in Chapter 5.

26. Report of the Committee Against Torture to the General Assembly at its forty-fifth session, A/45/44, Annex VI, decision of Nov. 23, 1989. The Inter-American Commission on Human Rights has come to a different conclusion. *See* Chapter 5.

27. Opened for signature Mar. 7, 1966, entered into force Jan. 4, 1969. 660 U.N.T.S. 195, reprinted in 5 I.L.M. 352 (1966).

28. These conventions are the International Covenant on Civil and Political Rights, the American Convention on Human Rights, and the European Convention for the Protection of Human Rights and Fundamental Freedoms, signed Nov. 4, 1950, 213 U.N.T.S. 222, Europe T.S. No. 5 (hereafter European Convention). In addition, the Banjul (African) Charter on Human and Peoples' Rights, adopted June 27, 1981, O.A.U. Doc. CAB/LEG/67/3/Rev.5, reprinted in 21 I.L.M. 58 (1982) and the International Covenant on Economic, Social and Cultural Rights, Dec. 19, 166, U.N.G.A. Res. 2200 (XXI), 21 U.N. GAOR, Supp. (No. 16) 49, U.N. Doc. A/6316 (1967), reprinted in 6 I.L.M. 360 (1967) also define broad categories of rights but are not considered here because they do not address investigation, prosecution, or compensation of victims of the narrow set of violations I am considering here.

29. The International Court of Justice has drawn a distinction between "the obligations of a State towards the international community as a whole" and those arising among individual states. Because all states have an interest in the former, they are "obligations *erga omnes.*" *Barcelona Traction Light and Power Company* case, 1970 I.C.J. 4, p. 33.

30. T. Buergenthal, "State Obligations and Permissible Derogations," in *The International Bill of Rights*, L. Henkin ed. (New York: Columbia University Press, 1981), pp. 25, 72, 77.

31. Optional Protocol to the International Covenant on Civil and Political Rights, Dec. 19, 1966, G.A. Res. 2200 (XXI), 21 U.N. GAOR Supp. (No. 16) at 59, arts. 1, 2, U.N. Doc. A/6316 (1967), reprinted in 6 I.L.M. 383 (1967). The Human Rights Committee is composed of eighteen experts, elected for four-year terms by states parties to the covenant, who serve in their personal capacities. It is not a judicial body but rather considers individ-

ual complaints submitted to it under article 5(4) of the Protocol and forwards its views on the complaint to the state party concerned and to the individual. Its final report is made public. Centre for Human Rights, United Nations Office at Geneva, *Fact Sheet No. 1: Human Rights Machinery* (1987), pp. 12–14. As of July 1990, the Committee had formulated its views on 110 complaints. Report of the Human Rights Committee to the General Assembly at its forty-fifth session, A/45/40, vol. I, para. 589.

32. General Comments under art. 40, para. 4, of the Covenant, *Report of the Human Rights Committee,* 37 U.N. GAOR Supp. (No. 40) Annex V, General Comment 7 (16), at 94, para. 1 (1982). The Committee has dealt with individual complaints alleging torture in much the same terms. In cases in which it has found violations of articles 7 (prohibiting torture) and 10 (prescribing humane treatment in detention), it has called on the state party to "provide effective remedies to the victim," including providing compensation for physical and mental injury and suffering caused by the inhuman treatment, conducting an inquiry into the circumstances of torture, punishing those found guilty of torture, and taking steps to ensure that similar violations do not occur in the future. *Tshitenge Muteba v. Zaire*, case No. 124/1982, 39 U.N. GAOR Supp. (No. 40), Annex XIII, U.N. Doc. A/39/40 (1984).

33. General Comment No. 20(44), art. 7, General Comments Adopted by the Human Rights Committee under article 40, para. 4, of the International Covenant on Civil and Political Rights, U.N. Doc. No. CCPR/C/21/Rev.1/Add.3, April 7, 1992.

34. *Irene Bleier Lewenhoff and Rosa Valino de Bleier v. Uruguay,* case No. 30/1978, U.N. Doc. CCPR/C/OP/1 (1985).

35. *Id.,* p. 112, para. 13.3. Article 4(2) of the Optional Protocol states: "Within six months, the receiving State shall submit to the Committee written explanations or statements clarifying the matter and the remedy, if any, that may have been taken by that State." Optional Protocol, *supra* note 31.

36. Similar language may be found in the case of *Baboeram v. Suriname*, case No. 146/1983 and 148–54/1983, 40 U.N. GAOR Supp. (No. 40), Annex X, U.N. Doc. A/40/40 (1985) (government must take effective steps to investigate killings, bring to justice any persons found to be responsible, pay compensation to surviving families, and ensure that right to life was duly protected); *Dermit Barbato v. Uruguay*, case No. 84/1981, 38 U.N. GAOR Supp. (No. 40), Annex IX, U.N. Doc. A/38/40 (1983) (government must establish the facts of the death [in detention], bring to justice any persons found to be responsible for his death, and pay appropriate compensation to his family).

37. It found that the mother of a woman who disappeared "had the right to know what had happened to her daughter" and that, due to the "anguish and stress caused . . . by the disappearance of her daughter and by the continuing uncertainty concerning her fate and whereabouts, . . . [the mother] too is a victim of the violations of the Covenant suffered by her daughter." *Quinteros v. Uruguay*, case No. 107/1981, 38 U.N. GAOR Supp. (No. 40), Annex XXII, U.N. Doc. A/38/40 (1983).

38. The Inter-American Court of Human Rights was created as part of the enforcement machinery of the American Convention. The court may issue both advisory opinions as well as binding, adjudicatory judgments in cases involving countries that have made a separate declaration accepting the court's adjudicatory jurisdiction, either unconditionally or on a case-by-case basis.

The Convention also empowers the Inter-American Commission on Human Rights to receive and review complaints regarding governmental human rights violations. Only the Commission or state parties to the Convention can refer a case to the court. *Id.,* art. 61.1. Individual petitioners must bring their cases to the Commission, which then decides whether they are admissible and whether to refer them to the court. States not parties to the

Convention are still tied into the Inter-America Commission through the Commission's oversight of the O.A.S. Charter and the American Declaration of the Rights and Duties of Man. For a full description, *see* T. Buergenthal, R. Norris, and D. Shelton, *Protecting Human Rights in the Americas*, 2nd ed. (Kehl, Germany; Arlington, VA: N. P. Engle, 1986). *Velasquez* was heard with two companion cases: *Fairen Garbi and Solis Corrales* case, Inter-Am. Ct. H.R., No. 7951 (1989) and *Godinez Cruz* case, Inter-Am. Ct. H.R., No. 8097 (1989). *Fairen Garbi and Solis Corrales* involved a Costa Rican couple who disappeared while driving through Honduras en route to Mexico. The case was eventually dismissed for lack of evidence. *Godinez Cruz* concerned a Honduran schoolteacher who disappeared in July 1982 after a witness saw him arrested by men in military uniforms. In all three cases, after requesting information from the Honduran government, the Commission declared the petitions admissible and, pursuant to article 42 of its regulations, presumed the truth of the facts as stated in the petitions brought to the Commission by relatives of the individuals who disappeared. *Velasquez Rodriguez* case, Inter-Am. Ct. H.R. (ser. C), No. 4 (1988) (judgment), para. 4.

39. Judgment, *supra* note 38, para. 4.

40. *Id.,* para. 166.

41. *Id.,* para. 174.

42. *Id.,* paras. 166–67.

43. *Id.,* para. 177. Thus, for instance, an investigation conducted by the military was inadequate because military officials were accused of the crime.

44. *Id.,* paras. 170, 172–73. Thus, the court's judgment covers situations in which the state fails to prevent, investigate, or prosecute death squad activity. In paragraph 184 the court asserts: "If the State apparatus acts in such a way that the violation goes unpunished and the victim's full enjoyment of [protected] rights is not restored as soon as possible, the State has failed to comply with its duty. . . . The same is true when the State allows private persons or groups to act freely and with impunity to the detriment of the rights recognized by the Convention."

45. *Id.,* para. 184.

46. In establishing the government's responsibility for the Velasquez disappearance, the court relied on evidence presented by the Commission to establish that the Honduran government carried out or tolerated a pattern of disappearances between 1981 and 1984. Acknowledging that the disappearance of particular individuals may be difficult to prove, the court allowed the Commission to establish, first, that a policy or practice of disappearances occurred; and, second, through circumstantial evidence and inference, that Velasquez's disappearance was part of this pattern. Judgment, para. 124.

47. International tribunals are familiar with the idea of a pattern or practice or "administrative practice." The European Court of Human Rights described an administrative practice as "an accumulation of identical or analogous breaches which are sufficiently numerous and inter-connected to amount not merely to isolated incidents or exceptions but to a pattern or system." The court stated that such a pattern serves as constructive notice to higher government officials. *Ireland v. United Kingdom*, 25 Eur. Ct. H.R., para. 159 (ser. A) (1978). *See also* "The Greek Case," *1969 Y.B. Eur. Conv. on Hum. Rts.,* 511 (Eur. Comm'n on Hum. Rts.) (resolution); "Second Greek Case," *1970 Y.B. Eur. Conv. on Hum. Rts.,* 132–34 (Eur. Comm'n on Hum. Rts.) (decision on admissibility); Restatement (Third) of the Foreign Relations Law of the United States, sec. 702 (consistent pattern of gross violations a separate violation under customary law); Foreign Assistance Act sec. 502B, 22 U.S.C. sec. 2304 (1988) (U.S. law prohibiting military and security sales and aid to countries whose governments engage in a "consistent pattern of gross violations of internationally recognized human rights").

48. *Gangaram Panday* case (*Comm'n v. Suriname*), Inter-Am. Ct. H.R., sentence of Jan. 21, 1994.

49. *Id.*, para. 62.

50. Judgment, para. 194. Article 63.1 of the American Convention empowers the court to guarantee the victim the enjoyment of the affected right or liberty, repair the consequences of the breach, and assure payment of fair compensation to the injured party. Thus, the court has the power to order broad injunctive measures.

51. Letter from Claudio Grossman and Juan E. Mendez, attorneys for the family of Saul Godinez, to the president of the Inter-American Court of Human Rights, Mar. 10, 1989, p. 5 (discussing appropriate remedies for the client's family and for civil society); Brief of Twelve Jurists as *Amici Curiae, Sobre la Reparacion de las Consecuencias de las Violaciones a los Derechos Humanos y la Justa Indemnizacion que Prescribe el Articulo 63.1 de la Convencion Americana de Derechos Humanos* (Mar. 10, 1989), pp. 17–18.

52. *See* D. Orentlicher, "Settling Accounts," 100 *Yale Law Journal* 2537 (1991), note 173.

53. Compensation judgment of July 21, 1989, Inter-Am. Ct. on H. R. (ser. C), No. 7 (1989).

54. Compensation judgment, para. 26.

55. *Id.*, para. 51.

56. *Id.*, paras. 32–39.

57. *Id.* In August 1990 the court further ruled that Honduras should compensate for the losses caused by devaluation of the Honduran lempira during its delay in making payments, as well as pay prejudgment interest. Although the government paid the original damages, as of 1992 it had still not paid these extra amounts. U.S. Department of State, *Country Reports* (1992), pp. 651–52; letter from Judge Hector Fix-Zamudio of the court to the Honduran ambassador, dated Nov. 12, 1990.

58. The European Commission on Human Rights considers both interstate and individual complaints alleging violations of the Convention. European Convention, arts. 24, 25. The Commission may refer cases to the court for a binding determination of whether there has been a breach; arts. 48–52.

59. *Ireland v. U.K., supra* note 47, para. 239 (judgment). However, the court found that it could not direct the United Kingdom to institute criminal or disciplinary proceedings against those members of the security forces who were responsible for the breaches of the Convention or against those who condoned or tolerated them. *Id.*, Judgment I (10), 2 E.H.R.R., p. 107. Like the Inter-American Court, the European Commission has found that "although one single act contrary to the Convention is sufficient to establish a violation, it is evidence that the violation can be regarded as being more serious if it is not simply one outstanding event but forms part of a number of similar events which might even form a pattern." Op. Com., Jan. 25, 1976, *Ireland v. U.K.,* Y.B. Eur. Conv. on Hum. Rts. XIX, para. 762.

60. *Mrs. W. v. United Kingdom,* application on admissibility, 32 Collection of Decisions 190, 200 (Feb. 28, 1983). The headnote to the decision goes even further, asserting that "the obligation to protect the right to life is not limited for the High Contracting Parties to the duty to prosecute those who put life in danger but implies positive preventive measures appropriate to the general situation." *Id.*, p. 190.

61. *Id.* (emphasis added).

62. Universal Declaration, G.A. Res. 217, U.N. Doc. A/810 (1948), art. 8. The Universal Declaration is not a treaty but a resolution adopted unanimously by the U.N. General Assembly in 1948. It is considered either an authoritative interpretation of the U.N. Charter or a statement of customary law; in either case, at least its basic provisions are now consid-

ered binding on U.N. member states. T. Buergenthal, *International Human Rights* (St. Paul, MN: West, 1988), pp. 29–33; *Restatement (Third) of the Foreign Relations Law of the United States*, sec. 701, reporter's notes 4, 6.

63. Schachter, "The Obligation to Implement the Covenant in Domestic Law," in *The International Bill of Rights, supra* note 30, p. 326; 10 U.N. GAOR Annex (Agenda Item 28) ch. V, para. 15, U.N. Doc. A/2929 (1955).

64. Commission on Human Rights, 6th Sess., U.N. Doc. E/CN.4/SR.195 (1950), para. 24. The proposal was justified on the following basis: "This addition places upon the State the responsibility of taking the initiative in the investigation and prosecution of abusive acts. The victim is too often under the influence of fear, so the Government itself should act with energy to bring the criminals swiftly to justice. The last words, 'especially when they are public officials', are designed particularly to curb abuse of power by such government agents." Commission on Human Rights, 6th Sess., U.N. Doc. E/CN.4/365 (PI), (1950), para. 15. *See also* M. Bossuyt, *Guide to the 'Travaux Préparatoires' of the International Covenant on Civil and Political Rights* (Dordrecht, Netherlands; Hingham, MA: M. Nijhoff, 1987), p. 65.

65. Commission on Human Rights, 6th Sess., U.N. Doc. E/CN.4/SR.195 (1950), para. 25 (statement of Mr. Mendez).

66. Schachter, *supra* note 63, p. 325.

67. *Id.* In many countries, civil suits and criminal prosecutions are intertwined, with the victim playing an active role in the criminal case. In these countries, criminal prosecution is even more clearly part of the victim's remedy. *See, e.g.*, article 7 of the Geneva (Swiss) Code of Criminal Procedure, cited in *Klein v. Superior Court*, 198 Cal. App. 3d 894, 244 Cal. Rptr. 226, 228 (1988) (civil action for damages caused by crime may be brought at the same time and before the same court as criminal action). Several Latin American countries have similar provisions. *See* the discussion of Uruguay and Argentina in Chapters 11 and 12.

68. Commission on Human Rights, 5th Sess., U.N. Doc. E/CN.4/SR 102 (1949); 6th Sess., U.N. E/CN.4/SR147, 148 (1950); 8th Sess., U.N. Doc. E/CN.4/SR313–14 (1952).

69. Article 25(1) provides that "[e]veryone has a right to simple and prompt recourse ... to a competent court or tribunal for protection against acts that violate his fundamental rights recognized by the constitution or laws of the state concerned or by this Convention, even though such violation may have been committed by persons acting in the course of their official duties." Note that the rights covered are both those enumerated in the Convention (as in the International Covenant) and in national law (as in the Universal Declaration).

70. Judgment, para. 80. The record in *Velasquez* showed that of three habeas corpus petitions filed on his behalf, one was denied and the other two had been pending since 1981 and 1982, respectively. *Id.* at para. 74. In addition, Velasquez's family had brought two criminal complaints against military officers, one of which had been pending since 1982, and the other had been dismissed for lack of evidence.

71. American Convention, art. 63.

72. *See, e.g.*, Case 7821, Inter-Am. C.H.R. 86, OAE/ser. L/V/II.57, doc. 6, rev. 1 (1982), p. 87 (disappearance); Case 6586, Inter-Am. C.H.R. 91, OEA/ser. L/V/II/61, doc. 22, rev. 1 (1983), p. 93 (torture, arbitrary arrest).

The Inter-American Commission has recently addressed the right to a remedy, along with other provisions of the Convention, in several cases involving government amnesties for security forces. These cases are discussed in detail in Chapter 5.

73. This provision has been criticized as ambiguous by commentators. *See, e.g.*, J. E. S. Fawcett, *Application of the European Convention on Human Rights* (Oxford, UK: Clarendon

Press, 1987), p. 289 ("Article 13 is an unsatisfactory Article, difficult . . . to construe"); F. Castberg, *The European Convention on Human Rights* (Leiden, Netherlands: Sijthoff; Dobbs Ferry, NY: Oceana, 1974), p. 157 (terms of the provision are puzzling). Part of the ambiguity stems from confusion over whether the article requires a remedy only when the Committee of Ministers, the Human Rights Court, or a domestic court (in countries in which the Convention is directly applicable as domestic law) has already found a violation of the Convention, as favored by Fawcett and Castberg (Fawcett, pp. 291–92; Castberg, p. 158), or whether part of the remedy is precisely a determination of whether or not there has been a violation. If the former view is adopted, the scope of the right is very limited.

74. Case of *Klass and others* (F.R.G.), 28 Eur. Ct. H.R. (ser. A) (1978) (German nationals brought suit against their government for allegedly violating the Convention by enacting a certain surveillance law).

75. Ser. A, No. 91, judgment of Mar. 26, 1985.

76. *Id.,* paras. 27, 36.

77. Report of the U.S. Delegation to the Inter-American Conference on a Protocol of Human Rights, San Jose, Costa Rica, Nov. 9–22, 1969; reprinted in OAS, *Human Rights: The Inter-American System* 53–54, No. 15, August 1982, release 2 (OAS, Washington, DC).

78. *Donnelly and others v. The United Kingdom,* 1976 *Y.B. Eur. Conv. on Hum. Rts.,* pp. 234–36.

79. *See supra* note 47 for a discussion of administrative practices. The court and the commission found that domestic remedies need not be exhausted in cases in which an administrative practice is alleged, because by definition there is no effective domestic remedy. *See, e.g.,* "The Greek Case," *1969 Y.B. Eur. Conv. on Hum. Rts.* 194, paras. 24, 25.

80. Commission on Human Rights, 5th Sess. (1949), U.N. Doc. A/.2929, chap. VI, sec. 73; cited in Bossuyt, *supra* note 64, pp. 279–80.

81. M. Nowak, *The U.N. Covenant on Civil and Political Rights, C.C.P.R.,* Commentary (Kehl, Germany; Arlington, VA: N. P. Engle, 1993), p. 239.

82. American Declaration, O.A.S. Res. XXX, adopted by the Ninth International Conference of American States (March 30–May 2, 1948), Bogota, O.A.S. Off. Rec. OEA/ser. L/V/I.4 Rev. (1965).

83. Article 6(1) reads: "In the determination of his civil rights and obligations or of any criminal charge against him, everyone is entitled to a fair and public hearing within a reasonable time by an independent and impartial tribunal established by law."

84. Judgment of May 29, 1986, ser. A; reprinted in Mark Janis and R. Kay, *European Human Rights Law* (Hartford: University of Connecticut Law School Foundation Press, 1990), p. 330.

85. *Feldbrugge* case, para. 21; reprinted in Janis and Kay, *supra* note 84, p. 343.

86. *See* Castberg, *supra* note 73, p. 117; Fawcett, *supra* note 73, p. 143; P. van Dijk, "The Interpretation of 'civil rights and obligations' by the European Court of Human Rights — One More Step to Take," in *Protecting Human Rights — The European Dimension,* F. Koln, ed. (Cologne: C. Heymann, 1988), p. 31.

87. Frank C. Newman, "Natural Justice, Due Process and the New International Covenants on Human Rights 'Prospectus,'" 274 *Public Law* (London: Stevens and Sons, Ltd., Winter 1967). The Human Rights Committee has interpreted the "suit at law" language broadly, indicating that analysis must be based on the nature of the right in question, not on the status of one of the parties or "particular form in which individual legal systems may provide that the right in question is to be adjudicated upon . . ." (emphasis mine). *Y.L. v. Canada,* case No. 112/1981, 38 U.N. GAOR Supp. (No. 40), Annex IX, U.N. Doc. A/38/40 (1983).

88. Application No. 4618/70, 21 Mar. 1972, 40 Collection of Decisions of the European Commission of Human Rights 11; cited in Castberg, *supra* note 73, pp. 116–17.

89. Commission on Human Rights, 5th Sess. (1949), E/CN.4/SR.96, p. 4; 6th Sess. (1950), E/CN.4/SR.102, p. 6.

90. Commission on Human Rights, 6th Sess. (1950), E/CN.4/SR.148, paras. 31, 38; 8th Sess. (1952), E/CN.4/SR.314, p.13.

91. *See, e.g.,* Third Committee, 14th Sess. (1959), A/C.3/ser. 964, para. 24; Commission on Human Rights, 5th Sess. (1949), E/CN.4/SR.106, p.15; E/CN.4/SR.107, p.3.

Chapter 4

1. Different bodies have interpreted the non-retroactivity requirement differently. *See* the discussion in Chapter 5 of the differing views of the Committee Against Torture and the Inter-American Commission on Human Rights.

2. *Restatement (Third) of the Foreign Relations Law of the United States,* at sec. 102(2). In proving that a rule has become law through custom, courts and other tribunals look at several types of evidence. They accord substantial weight to judgments and opinions of international judicial and arbitral tribunals, the writings of scholars, and resolutions of universal international organizations, if adopted by consensus or virtual unanimity or if explicitly declaratory of customary law. *Id.,* sec. 103, and comment c. Confirmation of the right in many national laws may also be persuasive in the case of human rights norms. T. Meron, *Human Rights and Humanitarian Norms as Customary Law* (Oxford, UK: Clarendon Press, 1989), p. 94.

3. *See, e.g.,* J. S. Watson, "Legal Theory, Efficacy and Validity in the Development of Human Rights Norms in International Law," 3(3) *University of Illinois Law Forum* (1979).

4. *See, e.g.,* Meron, *supra* note 2; *Military and Paramilitary Activities in and against Nicaragua (Nicar. v. U.S.),* 1986 I.C.J. 14 (1986).

5. A good example is the debate over the law-creating capacity of U.N. General Assembly resolutions. For a discussion, *see Arbitral Award on the Merits in Dispute between Texaco Overseas Petroleum Co. and the Government of the Libyan Arab Republic,* reprinted in 17 I.L.M. 1, 27 (1978).

6. *See* Marti Koskenniemi, *From Apology to Utopia* (Helsinki: Finnish Lawyers' Publishing Co., 1989), pp. 362–88.

7. For an authoritative treatment of the role of treaties in generating custom, *see* A. D'Amato, *The Concept of Custom in International Law* (Ithaca, NY: Cornell University Press, 1971), pp. 103–66. *But see* A. M. Weisburd, "Customary International Law: The Problem of Treaties," 21 *Vanderbilt Journal of Transnational Law* 1 (1988) (concluding that treaties are simply one form of state practice and that one cannot answer questions as to the content of customary international law by looking at the language of treaties).

8. North Sea Continental Shelf (*W. Ger. v. Den.; W. Ger. v. Neth.*), 1969 I.C.J. 3, 41–42 (Feb. 20, 1969).

9. Nottebohm (second phase) (*Liechtenstein v. Guat.*), 1955 I.C.J. 4, 21–23 (Apr. 6, 1955).

10. U.S. courts have also used treaties to demonstrate the existence of a customary norm. For example, in the landmark *Paquete Habana* case, 175 U.S. 677, 686–700 (1900) the Supreme Court used numerous treaties that did not formally bind either party to the dispute in deciding that international law prohibited the capture of non-belligerent fishing vessels. More recently, in *Filartiga v. Pena-Irala,* 630 F. 2d. 876, 883–84, 887 (2d Cir. 1980) the Second Circuit reviewed several sources of customary international law but placed substantial emphasis on numerous multilateral instruments prohibiting torture to

support its holding that torture constitutes a tort "committed in violation of the law of nations."

11. R. R. Baxter, "Multilateral Treaties as Evidence of Customary International Law," 1965–66, *British Yearbook of International Law* 275, 286.

12. Reservations to the Convention on Genocide (Advisory Opinion), 1951 I.C.J. 15 (1951).

13. Meron, *supra* note 2, pp. 92–93.

14. Vattel, in *Le Droit des Gens,* bk. II, ch. 6, sec. 76–77 (1758), recognized a duty to extradite those accused of serious crimes.

15. For a list, *see* Cherif Bassiouni, *Crimes Against Humanity in International Criminal Law* (Dordrecht, Netherlands: M. Nijhoff, 1992), p. 788 *et seq.*

16. *Restatement, supra* note 2, sec. 702. Despite this agreement, in practice more than one third of world governments used or tolerated torture or ill treatment of prisoners in the 1980s. *See* Amnesty International, *Torture in the Eighties* (London: Amnesty International, 1984), p. 2.

17. *Nicaragua* case, *supra* note 4, pp. 98–108. *See also Western Sahara* case, 1975 I.C.J. 12, 30–37 (Advisory Opinion of Oct. 16, 1975) (using U.N. General Assembly resolutions as evidence of customary law). *See also* Meron, *supra* note 2, pp. 42, 113. Baxter also approved of this method, writing that "[t]he firm statement by the State of what it considers to be the rule is far better evidence of its position than what can be pieced together from the actions of that country at different times and in a variety of contexts." Baxter, *supra* note 11, p. 300.

18. Americas Watch, *Challenging Impunity* (New York: Americas Watch, 1988), p. 12. One year later, Uruguay's permanent delegation to the United Nations made a similar pledge to the Human Rights Committee that oversees compliance with the Covenant on Civil and Political Rights. *Id.*

19. Human Rights Committee, 22nd Sess., 529th mtg., *Consideration of Reports Submitted by States Parties Under Article 40 of the Covenant (Chile)*, pp. 4–5, U.N. Doc. CCPR/C/SR.529 (1984) (remarks of Mr. Calderon). Members of the Committee also implied that Chile had an obligation to investigate and prosecute human rights violators. For example, referring to disappearances, Mr. Ermacora asked "what had the authorities done to establish the facts. The same question applied to the mass graves and secret burial places which had been found." *Id.,* p. 2. Mr. Graefrath "wished to have details of the number of persons prosecuted for performing secret executions, of public bodies other than the courts which had been responsible for making investigations and of any compensation to which the families of the victims had been entitled." *Id.,* p. 3. Mr. Errera asked about the number and result of complaints filed alleging torture, the police or military rank of the culprits, whether the prosecutions or sentences had been affected by a claim of superior orders or by an amnesty, and whether disciplinary measures had been taken against certain members of the police or army. *Id.,* p. 6. Finally, Mr. Prado Vallejo stated that it was Chile's duty to put an end to the impunity with which acts of torture were committed. *Id.,* p. 7.

20. Human Rights Committee, 29th Sess., 719th mtg., *Consideration of Reports (El Salvador),* p. 4, U.N. Doc. CCPR/C/SR.719 (July 7, 1987) (remarks of Mr. Trejo Padilla). *See also* Human Rights Committee, 24th Sess., 596th mtg., *Consideration of Reports (United Kingdom),* p. 3, U.N. Doc. CCPR/C/SR.596 (1985); Human Rights Committee, *Initial Reports of States Parties Due in 1978 (Zaire),* p. 17, U.N. Doc. CCPR/C/4/Add.10 (1987); Human Rights Committee, 31st Sess., 783rd mtg., *Consideration of Reports (Rwanda),* p. 7, U.N. Doc. CCPR/C/SR.783 (1987).

21. *See* Chapter 15 on El Salvador and Chapter 13 on Chile.

22. "U.S. Warns Salvador on Rights Cases," *New York Times,* Jan. 7, 1989, sec. 1, p. 3, col. 4; *see also* "Quayle Pressed Salvador for Inquiry on Massacres," *New York Times,* Feb. 15, 1989, p. A6, col. 4.

23. "Guatemalan Says U.S. Is Unfair on Rights," *New York Times,* Mar. 7, 1990, p. 3, col. 1.

24. "Chile Agrees to Pay Compensation in Case of Diplomat Slain in U.S.," *New York Times,* May 13, 1990, p. 1, col. 4.

25. Chile-United States Commission Convened under the 1914 Treaty for the Settlement of Disputes: *Decision with Regard to the Dispute Concerning Responsibility for the Deaths of Letelier and Moffit,* done at Washington, Jan. 11, 1992, reprinted in 31 I.L.M. 1 (1992).

26. "Chile Arrests Ex-Secret Police Chief," *Miami Herald,* Sept. 24, 1991, p. A10. *See also* "Jail Sentence May Not Spell End for Chile's Letelier Case," *Los Angeles Times,* Nov. 19, 1993, p. A4.

27. "Poles Urge Charges in Katyn Massacre," *New York Times,* Apr. 14, 1990, p. 5, col. 3. The admission of Soviet guilt was termed important for future Polish-Soviet relations.

28. G.A. Res. 36/157, para 4(e) (1981). *See also* numerous resolutions on El Salvador and Guatemala, *e.g.,* G.A. Res. 37/185 (1982), urging prosecution and punishment of those found responsible for torture and assassination.

29. *See Report of the Working Group on Enforced or Involuntary Disappearances,* 47 U.N. ESCOR Comm'n on Hum. Rts., p. 86, para. 406, U.N. Doc. E/CN.4/1991/20 (impunity is perhaps the single most important factor in disappearances); *Report prepared by the Special Rapporteur on the situation of human rights in Chile in accordance with paragraph 11 of the Commission on Human Rights resolution 1983/38 of 8 March 1983,* U.N. Doc. A/38/385, para. 341 (1983) (impunity of security forces is the cause, and an undoubted encouragement in the commission, of multiple violations of rights).

30. ECOSOC Res. 1989/65 of May 24, 1989, Annex, ECOSOC Off Rec., 1989, Supp. No. 1, p. 5 (1990), endorsed by G.A. Res. 44/162 of Dec. 15, 1989, GAOR 44th Sess., Supp. No. 49, p. 235 (1990).

31. G.A. Res. 40/34, 40 U.N. GAOR Supp. (No.53) at 213, U.N. Doc. A/40/53 (1985) (adopted by consensus), reprinted in *International Protection of Victims,* C. Bassiouni, ed. (Toulouse, France: ERES, International Criminal Law Association, 1988), p. 201.

32. *Id.,* p. 214; *Implementation Principles* at 66. The Declaration continues: "[i]n cases where the Government under whose authority the victimizing act or omission occurred is no longer in existence, the State or Government successor in title should provide restitution to the victims."

33. "Implementation Principles for § R4(d)," reprinted in Bassiouni, ed., *International Protection of Victims, supra* note 31, principles R4(d) 4, 5, 6, 8.

34. *Id.,* secs. 18, 19, "Implementation Principles," *supra* note 33, pp. 77–79. The Declaration distinguishes between crimes and abuse of power, the latter defined as acts or omissions "that do not yet constitute violations of national criminal laws but of internationally recognized norms relating to human rights." Those norms that are criminalized under national laws are considered "crimes." *Id.,* pp. 20–21.

35. G.A. Res. 47/133 (18 Dec. 1992), U.N. Doc. A/RES/47/133, Feb. 12, 1993.

36. Declaration on the Protection of All Persons from Being Subjected to Torture and Other Cruel, Inhuman or Degrading Treatment or Punishment, adopted by the General Assembly on Dec. 9, 1975 (res. 3452 [xxx]).

37. U.N. Commission on Human Rights, 47th Sess., Report of the Working Group on Enforced or Involuntary Disappearances, U.N.Doc. E/CN.4/1992/18, Dec. 30, 1991.

38. U.N. Commission on Human Rights, 49th Sess., Report of the Working Group on Enforced or Involuntary Disappearances, ch. 1F, U.N. Doc E/CN.4/1993/25, Jan. 7, 1993.

39. U.N. Sub-Commmission on Prevention of Discrimination and Protection of Minorities, Working Paper prepared by Mr. Guisse and Mr. Joinet, On the Question of Impunity for Perpetrators of Human Rights Violations, U.N. Docs. E/CN.4/Sub.2/1992/18, Aug. 12, 1992; E/CN.4/Sub.2/1993/6, July 19, 1993 (first preliminary report); E/CN.4/Sub.2/1994/11, June 22, 1994 (preliminary report regarding economic, social, and cultural rights).

40. Sub-Commission on Prevention of Discrimination and Protection of Minorities, Study concerning the right to restitution, compensation and rehabilitation for victims of gross violations of human rights and fundamental freedoms, Mr. Theo van Boven, Special Rapporteur, U.N.Doc. E/CN.4/Sub.2/1992/8, July 29, 1992 (interim report); E/CN.4/Sub.2/1993/8, July 2, 1993 (final report).

41. Proposed Basic Principles and Guidelines, in E/CN.4/Sub.2/1993/8 (final report), *supra* note 40.

42. World Conference on Human Rights, Declaration and Programme of Action, Vienna, June 1993, U.N. Doc. A/Conf./57/23, second part.

43. Julio Barberis, "Los Principios Generales de Derecho Como Fuente del Derecho Internacional," 14 *Revista IIDH* 11, 39–40 (1992).

44. Cited in Cherif Bassiouni, "A Functional Approach to General Principles of International Law," 11 *Michigan Journal of International Law* 768, 782 (1990).

45. General principles are "obvious maxims of jurisprudence of a general and fundamental character. . . . a comparison, generalization and synthesis of rules of law in its various branches — private and public, constitutional, administrative, and procedural — common to various systems of national law." E. Lauterpacht, ed., 1 *International Law, Being the Collected Papers of Hersch Lauterpacht* 69, 74 (Cambridge, UK: Cambridge University Press, 1970). The main difference among scholars refers to whether these principles are an international common law growing out of the composite concepts, rules, and norms of state legal systems or whether they are in themselves part of international law. *See* Bassiouni, "Functional Approach," *supra* note 44, p. 772.

46. For example, the rule requiring exhaustion of local remedies before seeking intercession by an international tribunal could be considered a general principle, since it is generally applied by international courts and arbitrators and not therefore a question of state practice.

47. Bassiouni, "Functional Approach," *supra* note 44, pp. 768–69.

48. *See* the discussion in Chapter 21.

49. In a variant on these arguments, at the 1993 World Conference on Human Rights, several Asian states raised the idea of the relativity of human rights. However, the final statement of the conference reaffirms the universality of such rights despite differences in culture and political systems. Vienna Declaration and Programme of Action, *supra* note 42, para. I(5).

50. J. L. Brierly, *The Law of Nations*, 6th ed. (New York: Oxford University Press, 1963), p. 63. *See also* Judge McNair's separate opinion in *International Status of South-West Africa*, Advisory Opinion, 1950 I.C.J. 148 (international tribunals should view private law rules and institutions as an indication of policy and principles rather than directly importing them).

51. Certain rights, especially so-called third-generation rights, may concern the state's relationship to groups or collectivities. These relationships also must be ruled by a set of procedures as well as principles.

52. Linda J. Maki, "General Principles of Human Rights Law Recognized by All

Nations: Freedom from Arbitrary Arrest and Detention," 10 *California Western International Law Journal* 272, 280 (1980).

53. Wolfgang Friedmann found these two types of general principles to be relatively straightforward. *See* Friedmann, "The Uses of 'General Principles' in the Development of International Law," 57 *American Journal of International Law* 279, 287–90 (1963).

54. P. van Dijk, *Judicial Review of Governmental Action and the Requirement of an Interest to Sue* (Leiden, Netherlands: Sijthoff & Noordhoff, 1980), p. 481.

55. *See, e.g.,* Argentine Penal Code arts. 144(3), 144(4), and 144(5), which provide additional penalties for torture if carried out or condoned by officials acting under color of authority; in the United States, sec. 18 U.S.C. 242 provides for federal criminal penalties additional to those of state law for deprivations of civil rights carried out under color of law.

56. *Chorzow Factory (Ger. v. Pol.)*, 1928 P.C.I.J. (ser. A), No. 17, p. 47.

57. L. Hurwitz, *The State as Defendant* (Westport, CT: Greenwood Press, 1981), pp. 22–23, 194.

58. For the general role and extent of use of ombudsmen, *see* H. Fix Zamudio, "Global Survey of Government Institutions," 13 *Denver Journal of International Law and Policy* 1, 39–40 (1983); Kent Weeks, *Ombudsmen Around the World: A Comparative Chart* (Berkeley: Institute of Government Studies, University of California, 1978); C. Bell, "Local Government Ombudsmen — Progress through Persuasion," *New Law Journal* 635 (June 11, 1981); J. Hatchard, African Ombudsmen Revisited," 40 *International and Comparative Law Quarterly* 937 (1991).

59. U.S. Department of State, 1990 Country Human Rights Reports.

60. Interestingly, the justifications of U.S. constitutional law scholars for allowing suits by victims parallel those made here in the international context. *See, e.g.,* Christina Whitman, "Constitutional Torts," 79 *Michigan Law Review* 5, 21–25 (1980) (symbolic message of providing a federal remedy is important to demonstrate official commitment to vindicated rights).

61. For example, Guatemala and Costa Rica have an Office of the Human Rights Procurator.

62. For a discussion of the limits of immunity in U.S. law, *see Harlow v. Fitzgerald,* 457 U.S. 800 (1982).

63. *See* A. Feller, *The Mexican Claims Commissions 1923–1934* (New York: Macmillan, 1935), secs. 143–45, pp. 149–54; *see also* M. Whiteman, *Damages in International Law,* Vol. 1 (Washington, DC: U.S. Government Printing Office, 1937), pp. 40–60.

64. The international law rules governing state responsibility during this time reflected the balance of power favoring strong nations like England and the United States over weak ones like Mexico or Venezuela; thus the rules favored aliens since they were usually from the dominant states. Reacting to this imbalance, Latin American nations developed the "national treatment" standard, arguing that international law required only that aliens and nationals be treated alike.

65. *Neer* case (*U.S. v. Mex.*), 1927 U.S. and Mexico General Claims Commission 71, 4 R. Int'l Arb. Awards 60 (1926).

66. The Commission stated that the treatment of an alien, in order to constitute an international delinquency, should amount to an outrage, to bad faith, to willful neglect of duty, or to an insufficiency of governmental action so far short of international standards that every reasonable and impartial man would readily recognize its insufficiency. Whether the insufficiency proceeds from deficient execution of an intelligent law or from the fact that the laws of the country do not empower the authorities to measure up to international standards is immaterial.

67. *Janes* case (*U.S. v. Mexico*), 1927 U.S. and Mexico General Claims Commission 108, 11419, 4 R. Int'l Arb. Awards 82 (1926).

68. *Id.,* p. 115, 4 R. Int'l Arb., p. 87.

69. *Id.,* p. 114, 4 R. Int'l Arb., pp. 86–87.

70. *Id.,* p. 118, 4 R. Int'l Arb., p. 89.

71. *Id.,* p. 119, 4 R. Int'l Arb., p. 89.

72. State responsibility for injury to aliens is based at least in part on the idea that an injury to a national injures the state to which the individual belongs. Because the state's traditional sovereignty over its nationals did not apply, international law could question a state's internal processes.

73. "Report to the President from Justice Robert H. Jackson, Chief of Counsel for the United States in the Prosecution of Axis War Criminals, June 7, 1945," reprinted in 39 *American Journal of International Law* 178, 184 (Supp. 1945). Of course, others attributed less laudable motives to the trials, labeling them "victors' justice."

74. The Charter of the International Military Tribunal (IMT), annexed to the London Agreement for the Prosecution and Punishment of Major War Criminals of the European Axis, Aug. 8, 1945, art. 6(c), 59 Stat. 1544, 1547, E.A.S. No. 472, 82 U.N.T.S. 279, 288. It is worth noting that while disappearances are not mentioned in the definition, the phrase "other inhumane acts" would cover them. The original Charter version of article 6(c) used a semicolon rather than a comma after the word "War." The change to a comma was made in the Berlin Protocol of Oct. 6, 1945. By making clear that *all* the listed crimes came within the IMT's jurisdiction only when the crimes were connected to war crimes or crimes against peace, the drafters hoped to avoid criticism that they were creating an entirely new category of crimes.

75. Consistent with the latter justification, the IMT could prosecute crimes against humanity only when committed "in execution of or in connection with" war crimes or crimes against peace. In contrast, the law drafted to allow prosecution of Germans within Germany by Allied-administered courts rather than by an international tribunal contains no such limitation. Allied Control Council Law No. 10 of Dec. 20, 1945 does not require a connection to the war. The law was promulgated to provide a legal basis for prosecution by German courts of suspected war criminals and other offenders. Some commentators have argued that the nexus requirement of the IMT was simply a limit on its jurisdiction, due to its extraordinary international status, rather than part of the definition of the offense. *See, e.g.,* R. Clark, "Codification of the Principles of the Nuremberg Trial on the Development of International Law," in *The Nuremberg Trial and International Law,* G. Ginsburg and V. Kudriavtsev, eds. (Dordrecht, Netherlands: M. Nijhoff; Boston: Norwell, 1990), pp. 195–97.

In addition, the case law of both the IMT and the tribunals set up within Germany under Allied supervision limits the actionable offenses to those involving large numbers of people (civilian *populations*), although individual atrocities could be prosecuted if they were part of a pattern of similar crimes. *See also United States v. Altstoetter* (Case No. 3), III Trials of War Criminals Before the Nuremberg Military Tribunals Under Control Council Law No. 10, p. 982 (isolated cases of atrocity excluded from the definition of crimes against humanity). Furthermore, crimes against property were excluded from the definition of crimes against humanity. *See United States v. Flick* (Case No. 5), VI Trials of War Criminals, p. 1215.

For a more extensive discussion of Nuremberg and crimes against humanity in the context of a duty to prosecute, *see* D. Orentlicher, "Settling Accounts," 100 *Yale Law Journal* 2537, 2588–96 (1991). For another view on the "nexus" requirement, *see* C. Bassiouni, *Crimes Against Humanity in International Criminal Law* (Dordrecht, Netherlands: M. Nijhoff, 1992), pp. 185–86.

76. *See* Jackson Report, *supra* note 73, pp. 184, 186.

77. *See* article 15(2) of the International Covenant on Civil and Political Rights and article 7(2) of the European Convention for the Protection of Human Rights and Fundamental Freedoms.

78. The definition of what constitutes "state action or policy," of course, must be broad enough to take into account situations in which the state condones, encourages, or fails to take appropriate action to prevent or punish the acts of others, whether of its officials or private parties. *See Velasquez Rodriguez* case, Inter-Am. Ct. H.R. (ser. C), No. 4 (1988) (judgment), para. 176.

79. *See United States v. Ohlendorf* (Case No. 9), IV Trials of War Criminals, *supra* note 75, p. 498 ("crimes against humanity . . . can only come within the purview of this basic code of humanity because the state involved, owing to indifference, impotency or complicity, has been unable or has refused to halt the crimes and punish the criminals").

80. International Law Commission Report on Principles of the Nuremberg Tribunal, July 29, 1950, 5 U.N. GAOR Supp. (No. 12) 11, U.N. Doc. A/1316 (1950).

81. G.A. res. 2712, 15 Dec. 1970, U.N.G.A. Res. 2538 (XXIV), reprinted in Bassiouni, *Crimes Against Humanity, supra* note 15, p. 698.

82. Principles of International Cooperation in the Detection, Arrest, Extradition, and Punishment of Persons Guilty of War Crimes and Crimes Against Humanity, G.A. Res. 3074, 28 U.N. GAOR Supp. (No. 30), p. 79, U.N. Doc. A/9030 (1973).

83. *Id.,* principle 1. Principle 2 provides that every state has the right to try its own nationals for crimes against humanity, whereas principle 5 makes clear that trial and punishment shall, as a general rule, be held in the countries in which the crimes were committed.

84. 177(II), Nov. 21, 1947, cited in *1991 Y.B. Int'l Law Comm.* 198 (1991).

85. *Draft Articles on the Draft Code of Crimes Against the Peace and Security of Mankind,* Report of the International Law Commission on the work of its Forty-Third Session, U.N. GAOR, 46th Sess., Supp. No. 10, U.N. Doc. A/46/405, Sept. 11, 1991.

86. *Id.,* arts. 6, 13.

87. Such crimes include aggression; genocide; apartheid; systematic or mass violations of human rights, including murder, torture, slavery, or deportation of populations but not, as yet, disappearances; exceptionally serious war crimes; use of mercenaries; terrorism; large-scale drug dealing; and causing willful and severe damage to the environment. Draft Code, arts. 15–26.

88. Draft Code, arts. 7, 11, 12, 14. *See* the discussion in Chapter 5.

89. For example, "intervention" is defined in article 17 as "fomenting [armed] subversive or terrorist activities or by organizing, assisting or financing such activities, or supplying arms for the purpose of such activities, thereby [seriously] undermining the free exercise by that State of its sovereign rights." However, "nothing in this article shall in any way prejudice the right of peoples to self-determination as enshrined in the Charter of the United Nations." How an individual is to tell what conduct is prohibited under this language seems an entirely subjective and inherently ideological task, raising serious concerns both about vagueness and about whether the existence of such a crime can be universally agreed on.

90. Security Council Res. 780 (Oct. 6, 1992); Secretary-General's report of Oct. 14, 1992, S/24657, reprinted in 32 I.L.M. 1159 (1993).

91. Security Council Res. 808 (Feb. 22, 1993).

92. Security Council Res. 827 (May 25, 1993).

93. International Tribunal for the Prosecution of Persons Responsible for Serious Violations of International Humanitarian Law Committed in the Territory of Former

Yugoslavia since 1991, Rules of Procedure and Evidence, U.N. Doc. IT/32, March 14, 1994.

94. Rules, *supra* note 93, rules 88, 105.

95. *Id.,* rule 106.

96. Larisa Gabriel, "Victims of Gross Violations of Human Rights and Fundamental Freedoms Arising from the Illegal Invasion and Occupation of Kuwait by Iraq," in *Seminar on the Right to Restitution, Compensation and Rehabilitation for Victims of Gross Violations of Human Rights and Fundamental Freedoms,* T. van Boven, C. Flinterman, F. Grünfeld, and I. Westendorp, eds. (Maastrict: Netherlands Institute of Human Rights, 1992), pp. 29–39.

97. Rules, *supra* note 93, rule 61.

98. The statute of the Tribunal is annexed to S.C. Res. 827, *supra* note 92. *See* art. 29.

99. For a fuller discussion of the international law of the statute, *see* T. Meron, "War Crimes in Yugoslavia and the Development of International Law," 88 *American Journal of International Law* 78 (1994).

100. Diane Orentlicher, "Yugoslavia War Crimes Tribunal," 1 *ASIL Focus* (1993); Meron, *supra* note 99, p. 85.

101. "Rwanda Agrees to a U.N. War-Crimes Tribunal," *New York Times,* Aug. 9, 1994, A6, col. 3.

102. For more detailed discussion, *see* J. Crawford, "The ILC's Draft Statute for an International Criminal Tribunal," 88 *American Journal of International Law* 140 (1994); C. Tomuschat, "A System of International Criminal Prosecution Is Taking Shape," 50 *The Review, International Commission of Jurists* 56 (1993).

103. Report of the International Law Commission on the work of its forty-fifth session, U.N. GAOR, 48th Sess., Supp. No. 10, Annex, U.N. Doc. A/48/10 (1993), p. 274.

Chapter 5

1. *See* Robert K. Goldman, "Amnesty Laws and International Law: A Specific Case," in International Commission of Jurists, *Justice Not Impunity* 209 (Geneva: ICJ, 1993).

2. Art. 3, para. 2, Treaty of Leusenne (frontiers between Turkey and Iraq), 1925 P.C.I.J. (ser. B), No. 12, p. 32 (Nov. 21, 1925).

3. Allied Control Council Law No. 10, Punishment of Persons Guilty of War Crimes, Crimes Against Peace and Against Humanity, 20 Dec. 1945, Official Gazette of the Control Council for Germany, No. 3, Berlin, 31 Jan. 1946.

4. *See* L. Joinet and E.-H. Guisse, "Study on the Question of the Impunity of Perpetrators of Human Rights Violations," U.N. Sub-Commission on Prevention of Discrimination and Protection of Minorities, U.N. Doc. E/CN.4/Sub.2/1993/6, July 19, 1993.

5. 1977 Protocol Additional to the Geneva Conventions of 12 August 1949, and Relating to the Protection of Victims of Non-International Armed Conflicts (Protocol II), entered into force, Dec. 7, 1978. U.N. Doc. A/32/144, Annex II (1977), reprinted in 16 I.L.M. 1442 (1977).

6. Plenary Meeting, 3 June 1977 (CDDH/SR.50/Annex; VII, 99, explanations of vote, representatives of Zaire, Cameroon), reprinted in H.S. Levie, *The Law of Non-International Armed Conflict* (Dordrecht, Netherlands: M. Nijhoff, 1987, pp. 301-2).

7. Levie, *supra* note 6, p. 262.

8. *Id.,* p. 270.

9. *Id.,* p. 295. The Spanish delegation went further, arguing that

The adoption of measures of clemency in general and of an amnesty in particular is necessarily subject, as regards application, to considerations of expediency which can be neither appreciated nor forseen by the drafters [];
for the same reasons, such measures fall within the exclusive competence of States, which, bearing always in mind the common good of the community they govern, can alone decide whether or not an amnesty is conducive to the restoration of public peace.

Id., p. 301.

10. The clearest statement came from the Zairian delegate, who thought it important to "encourage the widest degree of reconciliation in order to bring back into the fold those strayed members of the flock who unwittingly contribute to the destruction of their nation in order to please outsiders." *Id.*, p. 302.

11. The trend is not altogether new: In the *West* case (*United States v. Mexico*), 1927 U.S./Mexico General Claims Comm'n 404, 4 R. Int'l Arb. Awards 270 (1927), decided by an early U.S.–Mexico arbitral commission, the commissioners awarded $10,000 to the survivors of an American oil well driller killed by rebel forces who were subsequently granted amnesty. The commission held that if an amnesty renders an assailant immune from prosecution, it has the same effect as a failure to punish a crime, rendering the state indirectly responsible. It refused to look into whether the amnesty was properly applied under Mexican law or to recognize that reasons of national policy might dictate granting an amnesty.

12. "Study on Amnesty Laws and their Role in the Safeguard and Promotion of Human Rights," Preliminary Report by Louis Joinet, Special Rapporteur, U.N. Commission on Human Rights, U.N. Doc. E/CN.4/Sub.2/1985/16 (1985).

13. *Id.*, p. 17, notes 19, 20.

14. Americas Watch, *Truth and Partial Justice in Argentina* (New York: Americas Watch, 1987), p. 19.

15. *See* the discussion in Chapter 4, note 35, and accompanying text; *see especially* art. 18.

16. *See* the discussion in Chapter 4, note 30, and accompanying text.

17. *See* the discussion in Chapter 4, notes 31–33, and accompanying text.

18. The 1992 draft by the Inter-American Commission on Human Rights provided that "perpetrators of forced disappearances shall not benefit from any act of law adopted by the Executive or Legislature which could result in impunity with respect to such disappearances." Inter-American Commission on Human Rights, text approved at first reading by the Working Group, Mar. 30, 1992, art. 7, OEA/ser.L/V/II.74 (1992). By the time the OAS General Assembly approved the convention, formal references to impunity were gone. However, a blanket amnesty would still violate the state parties' obligation to punish the authors of forced disappearances as well as attempt, abetting, and complicity in forced disappearances (art. 1). *See* Inter-American Convention on the Forced Disappearance of Persons, resolution adopted by the OAS General Assembly, seventh plenary sess., OEA/ser. P,AG/doc. 3 114/94 rev.1, June 9, 1994.

19. General comment No. 20(44) (art. 7), General Comments Adopted by the Human Rights Committee under article 40, para. 4, of the International Covenant on Civil and Political Rights, U.N. Doc. No. CCPR/C/21/Rev.1/Add.3, April 7, 1992. *See* the discussion in Chapter 3.

20. *See* the discussion in Chapter 11.

21. Comments of the Human Rights Committee, Uruguay, Consideration of Reports Submitted by States Parties Under Article 40 of the Covenant, U.N. Doc. CCPR/C/79/Add.19, May 5, 1993.

22. *See* the discussion of that case in Chapter 3.

23. Inter-American Commission on Human Rights, Report No. 26/92 (El Salvador),

82nd Sess., OEA/ser. L/V/II.82 (Sept. 24, 1992) [hereafter El Salvador report]; 29/92 (Uruguay), 82nd Sess., OEA/ser. L/V/II.82, Doc. 25 (Oct. 2, 1992) [hereafter Uruguay report]; Report No. 24/92 (Argentina), 82nd Sess., OEA/ser. L./V/II.82, Doc. 24 (Oct. 2, 1992) [hereafter Argentina report].

24. Uruguay report, *supra* note 23, para. 53.

25. Article 29 reads in full:

No provision of this Convention shall be interpreted as:

    a. permitting any State Party, group, or person to suppress the enjoyment or exercise of the rights and freedoms recognized in this Convention or to restrict them to a greater extent than is provided for herein;

    b. restricting the enjoyment or exercise of any right or freedom recognized by virture of the laws of any State Party or by virture of another Convention to which one of the said States is a party;

    c. precluding other rights or guarantees that are inherent in the human personality or derived from representative democracy as a form of government; or

    d. excluding or limiting the effect that the American Declaration of the Rights and Duties of Man and other international acts of the same nature may have.

26. *Id.*, paras. 22, 26.

27. *See* Chapter 12.

28. The Committee on Torture came to the opposite conclusion on similar facts. *See* Report of the Committee Against Torture to the General Assembly at its forty-fifth session, A/45/44, Annex VI, decision of Nov. 23, 1989.

29. J. Kokott, "No Impunity for Human Rights Violations in the Americas," 14 *Human Rights Law Journal* 153, 157 (1993).

30. International Covenant on Civil and Political Rights, Dec. 19, 1966, 999 U.N.T.S. 171, art. 4(1); European Convention for the Protection of Human Rights and Fundamental Freedoms, done at Rome, Nov. 4, 1950. Entered into force Sept. 3, 1953. Europ. T.S. No. 5., art. 15; American Convention on Human Rights, Nov. 22, 1969, 36 O.A.S.T.S. 1, art. 27(1). Article 4 of the International Covenant is typical:

(1) [i]n time of public emergency which threatens the life of the nation and the existence of which is officially proclaimed, the States Parties to the present Covenant may take measures derogating from their obligations . . . to the extent strictly required by the exigencies of the situation, provided that such measures are not inconsistent with their other obligations under international law.

31. Eur. Ct. of Hum. Rts., "The Greek Case," *1969 Y.B. Eur. Conv. on Hum. Rts.,* 511 (Eur. Comm'n on Hum. Rts.) (resolution), para. 153. It is up to each state initially to decide whether an emergency exists, the measures necessary to cope with it, and if any such measures derogate from obligations under human rights instruments, whether those measures are strictly required. However, the state must inform other treaty parties of the reasons for the emergency and the range of rights affected, so that other states may decide whether to challenge the legality of the derogations. International Covenant, art. 4(3); European Convention, art. 15(3); American Convention, art. 27(3).

32. C. Schreuer, "Derogation of Human Rights in Situations of Public Emergency: The Experience of the European Convention on Human Rights," 9 *Yale Journal of World Public Order* 113, 129 (1982); T. Buergenthal, "State Obligations and Permissible Deroga

tions," in *The International Bill of Rights,* L. Henkin, ed. (New York: Columbia University Press, 1981), p. 82.

33. European Convention, art. 15(2); American Convention, art. 27(2); International Covenant, art. 4. Although none of these conventions explicitly prohibits disappearance, it might be considered nonderogable under the general protection of the right to life.

34. American Convention, art. 27(2).

35. Inter-American Court of Human Rights, "Habeas Corpus in Emergency Situations," Advisory Opinion No. OC- 8/87, Jan. 30, 1987, reprinted in 9 *Human Rights Law Journal* 94, 101 (1988).

36. International Law Commission, Draft Articles on State Responsibility (1980) 2 *Yearbook of the International Law Commission* 26, 33, U.N. Doc. A/CN.4/ SER.A/1980/Add.1.

37. United Nations Convention on the Non-Applicability of Statutory Limitations to War Crimes and Crimes Against Humanity, Nov. 26, 1968, 754 U.N.T.S. 73.

38. The Convention was drafted primarily to avoid the running of the statute of limitations on Nazi war criminals; however, the inclusion of apartheid as a crime against humanity among the listed offenses reduced support for its adoption and led to the drafting of a European treaty on the same subject which does not mention apartheid. European Convention on the Non-Applicability of Statutory Limitation to Crimes Against Humanity and War Crimes, opened for signature Jan. 25, 1974, reprinted in 13 I.L.M. 540 (1974). *See generally* R. Miller, "The Convention on the Non-Applicability of Statutory Limitations to War Crimes and Crimes Against Humanity," 65 *American Journal of International Law* 476 (1971).

39. European Convention on the Non-Applicability of Statutory Limitation to Crimes Against Humanity and War Crimes, Strasbourg, Jan. 25, 1974, E.T.S. No. 82, reprinted in 13 I.L.M. 540 (1974).

40. Draft Articles on the Draft Code of Crimes Against the Peace and Security of Mankind, art. 7, Report of the International Law Commission on the Work of its Forty-Third Session, GAOR 46th Sess., Supp. No. 10, U.N. Doc. A/46/405 (Sept. 11, 1991).

41. *Barbie* case, Judgment of Jan. 26, 1984, Cass. Crim., Fr., 78 I.L.R. 132, 135 (1988).

42. *See* discussion in Chapter 7 and Chapter 10.

43. *Forti v. Suarez-Mason,* 672 F. Supp. 1531, 1550 (N.D. Cal. 1988).

44. Inter-American Convention, *supra* note 18, art. 7. When the constitutional provisions in domestic law require a limitations period, it shall be that of the most serious crime. *Id.*

45. While Nuremberg developed and publicized the international law on superior orders, instances of a court rejecting a plea of superior orders in cases of egregious crimes go back to 1474, when Peter von Haganbach, governor of Breisach under Charles of Burgundy, was convicted of murder, rape, perjury, and other *malefacta,* despite his plea that he had received the orders from the Duke of Burgundy and had no right to question them. L.C. Green, *Superior Orders in National and International Law* (Leiden, Netherlands: A. W. Sijthoff, 1976), pp. 263–64. Professor Green also refers to the World War I case of the *Llandovery Castle,* in which a German U-boat commander and his subordinates were convicted for firing on the helpless survivors of a sunken hospital ship. The tribunal held that the subordinate officers, being Naval officers by profession, must have known that the order to fire was illegal under international law; therefore, the fact that they acted under orders was no defense, although it could mitigate their punishment. *Id.,* pp. 266–73.

46. The Charter of the International Military Tribunal (IMT), annexed to the London

Agreement for the Prosecution and Punishment of Major War Criminals of the European Axis, Aug. 8, 1945, arts. 7, 8, 59 Stat. 1544, 1547, E.A.S. No. 472, 82 U.N.T.S. 279, 288.

47. "International Tribunal (Nuremberg), Judgment and Sentence," Oct. 1, 1946, reprinted in 41 *American Journal of International Law* 172 (1947).

48. *United States v. Ohlendorf* (Case No. 9), IV Trials of War Criminals Before the Nuremberg Military Tribunals Under Control Council Law No. 10, pp. 665–68.

49. Draft Code, *supra* note 40, arts. 11, 12.

50. *See* Y. Dinstein, *The Defense of "Obedience to Superior Orders" in International Law* (Leiden, Netherlands: A. W. Sijthoff, 1965), pp. 220–25.

51. 17 Pesakim Mehoziim 90, 44 Pesakim Elyonim 362 (1958/59), cited in Green, *Superior Orders, supra* note 45, pp. 99–103 (1976).

52. For a discussion of the relationship among superior orders, moral choice, and duress, *see* Cherif Bassiouni, *Crimes Against Humanity in International Criminal Law* (Dordrecht, Netherlands: M. Nijhoff, 1992), pp. 436–46.

53. *See, e.g.,* J. Hall, *General Principles of Criminal Law* (Indianapolis: Bobbs-Merrill, 1974).

54. D. Orentlicher, "Settling Accounts," 100 *Yale Law Journal* 2537 (1991).

55. Vojin Dimitrijevic, "Dimensions of State Responsibility for Gross Violations of Human Rights and Fundamental Freedoms Following the Introduction of Democratic Rule," in *Seminar on the Right to Restitution, Compensation and Rehabilitation for Victims of Gross Violations of Human Rights and Fundamental Freedoms,* T. van Boven, C. Flinterman, F. Grünfeld, and I. Westendorp, eds. (Maastrict: Netherlands Institute of Human Rights, 1992), pp. 214, 217.

56. S. Chernichenko, Definition of Gross and Large-Scale Violations of Human Rights as an International Crime, U.N. Sub-Commission on Prevention of Discrimination and Protection of Minorities, 45th Sess., U.N. Doc. E/CN.4/Sub.2/1993/10, June 8, 1993.

57. *See* Preliminary Report on Opposition to the Impunity of Perpetrators of Human Rights Violations (Economic, Social and Cultural Rights), prepared by Mr. Guisse and Mr. Joinet, U.N. Sub-Commission on Prevention of Discrimination and Protection of Minorities, 46th Sess., item 10(a), U.N. Doc. E/CN.4/Sub.2/1994/11, June 22, 1994.

58. Restatement (3rd) of the Foreign Relations Law of the United States, §702.

59. The Restatement distinguishes between aliens and nationals with respect to the need for a state policy of condonation; *cf.* T. Meron, *Human Rights and Humanitarian Norms as Customary Law* (Oxford, UK: Clarendon Press, 1989).

60. *See* A. Cassese, "Genocide and the International Community: The Case of Sabra and Shatila," in *New Directions in Human Rights*, E. Lutz, H. Hannum, and K. Burke, eds. (Philadelphia: University of Pennsylvania Press, 1989).

61. *See, e.g., In re Janes* (*U.S. v. Mexico*), 4 Rep. Int'l Arb. Awards 82, 89–90 (1926), discussed in Chapter 4.

62. *See* the earlier discussion of the differing viewpoints of the Committee Against Torture and the Inter-American Human Rights Commission on this point, *supra* note 28 and accompanying text.

63. *Velasquez Rodriguez* case, Inter-Am. Ct. H.R. (ser. C), No. 4 (1988) (judgment), para. 177.

Chapter 6

1. Commission on the Responsibility of the Authors of War and on Enforcement of Penalties — Report Presented to the Preliminary Peace Conference, Versailles, Mar. 29, 1919, reprinted in 14 *American Journal of International Law* 95 (Supp. 1920).

2. L. Parks, "Command Responsibility for War Crimes," 62 *Military Law Review* 1, 12–13 (1963).

3. The Treaty of Peace Between the Allied Powers and Turkey (Treaty of Sèvres), Aug. 10, 1920, 15 *American Journal of International Law* 179 (Supp. 1921) (not ratified).

4. *See* E. Schwelb, "Crimes Against Humanity," 23 *British Yearbook of International Law* 178, 182 (1946).

5. The Charter of the International Military Tribunal (IMT), annexed to the London Agreement for the Prosecution and Punishment of Major War Criminals of the European Axis, Aug. 8, 1945, 59 Stat. 1544, 1547, E.A.S. No. 472, 82 U.N.T.S. 279, 288. For detailed accounts of the genesis and evolution of the law and practice of the tribunal, *see* C. Bassiouni, *Crimes Against Humanity in International Criminal Law* (Dordrecht, Netherlands: M. Nijhoff, 1992); *see also generally* Schwelb, *supra* note 4; T. Taylor, Final Report to the Secretary of the Army on the Nuremberg War Crimes under Allied Control Council Law No. 10 (1949); B. Smith, *Reaching Judgment at Nuremberg* (New York: Basic Books, 1977); R. Woetzel, *The Nuremberg Trials in International Law* (London: Stevens; New York: Praeger, 1962); *The Nuremberg Trials and International Law,* G. Ginsburg and V. N. Kudriavtsev, eds. (Dordrecht, Netherlands: M. Nijhoff; Boston: Norwell, 1990); and law review articles too numerous to cite.

6. *See* R. Bierzanek, "War Crimes: History and Definition," in C. Bassiouni, *International Criminal Law: Enforcement* (Dobbs Ferry, NY: Transnational Publishers, 1989), p. 3.

7. High-ranking Nazi official Adolph Eichmann, who was found in Bolivia, was taken to Israel and was tried and hanged in 1962. *See Attorney General of Israel v. Eichmann* (Israel Dist. Ct. of Jerusalem, 1961), 36 I.L.R. 5 (1962), (S. Ct. of Israel 1962), 36 I.L.R. 277 (1962). John Demjanjuk, accused of being "Ivan the Terrible," a particularly sadistic camp guard at Treblinka, had his U.S. citizenship revoked and was extradited to Israel for trial. *Demjanjuk v. Petrovsky,* 776 F.2d 571 (6th Cir. 1985), *cert. den.* 475 U.S. 1016 (1986). In 1993, the Israeli Supreme Court found that sufficient doubts had been raised about Demjanjuk's identity as "Ivan" to overturn his conviction. Decision of Israel Supreme Court on the Appeal of John (Ivan) Demjanjuk (July 1993) (Translation on file with Embassy of Israel, Washington, D.C.). *See also New York Times,* July 29, 1993, p. A1.

8. *Barbie* case, Judgment of Jan. 26, 1984, Cass. Crim., Fr., 78 I.L.R. 132, 135 (1988). *See* the discussion later in this chapter.

9. *R. v. Finta,* 50 C.C.C. (3d) 247; 61 D.L.R. 85 (4th 1989). Gendarmerie Captain Finta was acquitted.

10. For a description and analysis, *see* John Herz, "Denanzification and Related Policies," in J. Herz, ed., *From Dictatorship to Democracy* (Westport, CT: Greenwood Press, 1982).

11. 162 U.N.T.S. 265 (1952). Three billion DM were payable for settlement of those victims of racial persecution in Europe who immigrated to Palestine or Israel; another 450 million DM were earmarked to a consortium of Jewish organizations for Jews living outside Israel; and 50 million was provided for nonreligious Jews who had been persecuted. Karl Josef Partsch, "The Federal Republic of Germany," in *Seminar on the Right to Restitution, Compensation and Rehabilitation for Victims of Gross Violations of Human Rights and Fundamental Freedoms,* T. van Boven, C. Flinterman, F. Grünfeld, and I. Westendorp, eds. (Maastrict: Netherlands Institute of Human Rights, 1992), pp. 130–45.

12. *See* B. Ferencz, *Less Than Slaves* (Cambridge, MA: Harvard University Press, 1979).

13. Roy C. Macredis, "France: From Vichy to the Fourth Republic," in Herz, ed., *From Dictatorship to Democracy, supra* note 10. I have also relied on the following books for this account: Henry Rousso, *The Vichy Syndrome: History and Memory in France since*

1944 (Cambridge, MA: Harvard University Press, 1991); Robert Paxton, *Vichy France: Old Guard and New Order, 1940–44* (New York: Knopf, 1972). For a detailed account of post-World War II anti-collaborationist measures in Belgium, *see* Luc Huyse and Steven Dhondt, *La Répression des Collaborations 1942–1952: Un Passé Toujours Présent* (Brussels: CRISP, 1991).

14. Rousso, *supra* note 13, p. 20.

15. Cited in Macredis, *supra* note 13, p. 170.

16. Rousso, *supra* note 13, p. 22.

17. "Frenchman Convicted of Crimes Against Jews in '44." *New York Times,* Apr. 20, 1994, p. A3.

18. Rousso, *supra* note 13, pp. 214–15.

19. This account is taken from Harry Psomiades, "Greece: From the Colonels' Rule to Democracy," in J. Herz, ed., *From Dictatorship to Democracy, supra* note 10, p. 251 *et seq.*; Constantine Danopoulous, "Beating a Hasty Retreat: The Greek Military Withdraws from Power," in Danopoulos, ed., *The Decline of Military Regimes: The Civilian Influence* (Boulder, CO: Westview Press, 1988), p. 225 *et seq.*; and Amnesty International, *Torture in Greece: The First Torturers Trial 1975* (London: Amnesty International, 1977).

20. *See* Carolyn P. Boyd and James M. Boyden, "The Armed Forces and the Transition to Democracy in Spain," in *Politics and Change in Spain,* T. D. Lancaster and G. Prevost, eds. (New York: Praeger, 1985).

Chapter 7

*Acknowledgment—*I am grateful to the Einstein Institution for financial support during the writing of this essay.

1. I exclude from consideration East European countries outside Central Europe—that is, Yugoslavia, Albania, Romania, and Bulgaria—because by 1989 their political development had greatly diverged from that of Central European regimes.

2. Prague Radio, Oct. 13, 1991, in *Foreign Broadcast Information Service, Daily Report on Eastern Europe* [hereafter *FBIS-EE*], Oct. 15, 1991, p. 13.

3. For the term "replica regimes," *see* Ken Jowitt, "Moscow 'Centre'," *East European Politics and Societies* 1(3) (Fall 1987).

4. The Soviets first used former concentration camps to intern suspected Nazis; East Germans then used them to hold purge victims. Henry Kamm, "East Germans Unlock a Murky Past: Nazi Prisons Turned Soviet Prisons," *New York Times,* Mar. 28, 1990.

5. Statistics on the number of political prisoners remain unreliable despite greater access to official records; nevertheless, approximately 200,000 appeals for rehabilitation have been filed in both Hungary and Czechoslovakia. Celestine Bohlen, "Victims of Hungary's Past Press for an Accounting, but with Little Success," *New York Times,* Aug. 4, 1991; *Radio Free Europe Report on Eastern Europe* [hereafter *Report on EE*], no. 27, July 5, 1991, p. 50.

6. J. F. Brown, *Eastern Europe and Communist Rule* (Durham, NC: Duke University Press, 1988), p. 42.

7. Albert P. Van Goudoever, *The Limits of Destalinization in the Soviet Union: Political Rehabilitations in the Soviet Union since Stalin,* Frans Hijkoop, trans. (London: Croom Helm, 1986), p. 31.

8. On everyday repression under late Communist systems, *see* Krzysztof Nowak, "Covert Repressiveness and the Stability of a Political System: Poland at the End of the Seventies," *Social Research* 55 (Spring/Summer 1988).

9. Jan Urban, "The Politics and Power of Humiliation," in *After the Velvet Revolution:*

Vaclav Havel and the New Leaders of Czechoslovakia Speak Out, Tim D. Whipple, ed. (New York: Freedom House, 1991), p. 276.

10. One effective sanction adopted by Communist regimes in the 1970s was allowing dissidents to emigrate voluntarily or, alternatively, expelling them.

11. Vaclav Havel, "The Power of the Powerless," in *The Power of the Powerless,* Havel et al., eds. (New York: Palach Press, 1985), pp. 23–96.

12. J. F. Brown, *Surge to Freedom: The End of Communist Rule in Eastern Europe* (Durham, NC: Duke University Press, 1991), p. 113.

13. *Id.,* pp. 119–23.

14. *Id.,* p. 145.

15. Prague Radio, Feb. 25, 1990, in *FBIS-EE,* Feb. 26, 1990, p. 15.

16. *Id.,* p. 16.

17. As noted earlier, Havel argued that everyone shared some degree of responsibility in the maintenance of Communist rule.

18. Tim D. Whipple, "After the Velvet Revolution: The First Six Months," in *After the Velvet Revolution,* Whipple, ed., *supra* note 9, pp. 40, 49–51.

19. Prague Radio, Feb. 5, 1990, in *FBIS-EE,* Feb. 6, 1990, p. 21.

20. Ultimately, the Federal Assembly addressed this problem by amending its law on the StB to make quick firing possible for persons who were either redundant or lacking in the moral and professional qualifications necessary to serve. Prague CTK, May 9, 1990, in *FBIS-EE,* May 16, 1990, p. 13.

21. For charges against Lorenc, *see* Prague CSTK, Oct. 8, 1991, in *FBIS-EE,* Oct. 9, 1991, p. 12; for Civic Forum's response to this smear campaign, *see* Prague CTK, Apr. 4, 1990, in *FBIS-EE,* Apr. 6, 1990, pp. 11–12.

22. *Report on EE,* no. 35, Aug. 24, 1990.

23. Jiri Pehe, "Reforming the Judiciary," *Report on EE,* no. 34, Aug. 23, 1991, pp. 9–13.

24. Bratislava Radio, Feb. 7, 1990, in *FBIS-EE,* Feb. 9, 1990, p. 37.

25. Jiri Pehe, "The Controversy over Communist Managers," *Report on EE,* no. 36, Sept. 7, 1990, pp. 6–10.

26. "Conservative Reflections on Czechoslovak Politics," an interview with Pavel Bratinka, in *After the Velvet Revolution,* Whipple, ed., *supra* note 9, pp. 213–14.

27. Paris, Agence France Presse, May 12, 1990, in *FBIS-EE,* May 14, 1990, p. 16.

28. Prague CSTK, Dec. 11, 1991, in *FBIS-EE,* Dec. 13, 1991, p. 9.

29. *Lidove Noviny,* May 2, 1990, in *FBIS-EE,* May 9, 1990, pp. 21–22.

30. *Hospodarske Noviny,* Jan. 8, 1992, in *FBIS-EE,* Jan. 13, 1992, p. 14.

31. Prague Radio, Jan. 12, 1990, in *FBIS-EE,* Jan. 16, 1990, p. 38; Prague CTK, Jan. 4, 1990, in *FBIS-EE,* Jan. 25, 1990, p. 24.

32. *Mlada Fronta,* Feb. 19, 1990, in *FBIS-EE,* Feb. 22, 1990, p. 19.

33. Jiri Pehe, "The First Weeks of 1991: Problems Solved, Difficulties Ahead," *Report on EE,* no. 10, Mar. 8, 1991, pp. 5–7.

34. Bratislava Radio, Feb. 19, 1991, in *FBIS-EE,* Feb. 21, 1991, p. 26.

35. Jan Oberman, "Two Landmark Bills on Privatization Approved," *Report on EE,* no. 11, Mar. 15, 1991, pp. 12–15.

36. Jan Oberman, "Laying to Rest the Ghosts of the Past," *Report on EE,* no. 24, June 14, 1991, pp. 4–11. Among those "outed" was the well-known Czech dissident Jan Kavan. His complicated case illustrates the intricacies and deficiencies of the lustration process. For an excellent account of Kavan's odyssey, *see* Lawrence Weschler, "The Velvet Purge: The Trials of Jan Kavan," *The New Yorker,* Oct. 19, 1992, pp. 66–96.

37. A poll taken in July 1991 by the Prague Institute for Public Opinion Research

found 58 percent in favor of publication of the names of all former secret police collaborators. *Report on EE,* no. 37, Sept. 13, 1991, p. 44.

38. The minister of the interior, the director of the Federal Information and Security Service, and the director of the Federal Police Corps may also make individual exceptions for their employees where it serves state security.

39. *Rude Pravo,* Oct. 5, 1991, in *FBIS-EE,* Oct. 11, 1991, pp. 14–15.

40. Prague CSTK, Oct. 4, 1991, in *FBIS-EE,* Oct. 7, 1991, p. 8.

41. Prague Radio, Oct. 13, 1991, in *FBIS-EE,* Oct. 15, 1991, p. 13.

42. Petr Toman in presenting the report of the Commission on the Events of November 17 regarding the screening of the Federal Assembly. Prague Radio, Mar. 22, 1991, in *FBIS-EE,* Mar. 25, 1991, p. 12.

43. Prague CSTK, Oct. 11, 1991, in *FBIS-EE,* Oct. 16, 1991, p. 11.

44. International Labour Organization, Decision on the Lustration Law, GB.252/16/19, 252nd Sess., reprinted in International Labour Office, "Report of the Director General, Governing Body," Mar. 2–6, 1992 (Geneva). The ILO Committee carefully examined each occupation covered by the lustration law and found that the law discriminated on the basis of political opinion, thus violating ILO Convention No. 111 forbidding discrimination in employment. The committee found that the screening requirements in most cases did not come within either the exceptions for national security or for the inherent requirements of a particular job, especially since they concerned past affiliations, not current ones. *Id.*

45. Weschler, "The Velvet Purge," *supra* note 36.

46. *Lidove Noviny,* May 25, 1991, cited in Oberman, "Ghosts," *supra* note 36, p. 11.

47. "Informer Charge on Prague Dissident Upheld," *New York Times,* Oct. 18, 1992, p. 5.

48. Testimony from informers' reports were cross filed in dossiers on their objects — and all these files were continuously paginated, thus making additions and alterations difficult. Petruska Sustrova, "The Lustration Controversy," *Uncaptive Minds* 5 (Summer 1992), pp. 132–33.

49. Prague Radio, May 3, 1990, in *FBIS-EE,* May 4, 1990, pp. 19–20.

50. "Taking the Communists to Court Can Be Nettlesome, Czechs Find," *New York Times,* Jan. 24, 1992, p. 4.

51. *Report on EE,* no. 11, Mar. 16, 1990.

52. John Tagliabue, "East German's Past Is Subject of an Inquiry," *New York Times,* Feb. 5, 1992, p. 4.

53. Bohlen, "Victims of Hungary's Past," *supra* note 5, p. 3.

54. Law on the Right to Prosecute Serious Criminal Offenses Committed Between Dec. 21, 1944 and May 2, 1990 That Had Not Been Prosecuted for Political Reasons, Nov. 4, 1991. *See* Krisztina Morvai, "Retroactive Justice Based on International Law: A Recent Decision by the Hungarian Constitutional Court," *East European Constitutional Review* (Fall 1993/Winter 1994), pp. 32–34.

55. Judgment of Mar. 5, 1991, 1992/11, Alkotmanybirosag Hatarozatai 77, pt. V(1) (unofficial translation). For more extensive discussion of this initial decision, *see* Ruti Teitel, "Paradoxes in the Revolution of the Rule of Law," 19 *Yale Journal of International Law* 239 (1994); Forum, "Dilemmas of Justice," *East European Constitutional Review* (Summer 1992), p. 17.

56. *See* Laszlo Solyom, "The Hungarian Constitutional Court and Social Change," 19 *Yale Journal of International Law* 223 (1994).

57. Act 53/1993 (X.13), Judgment of Oct. 13, 1993, Alkotmanybirosag Hatarozatai [Constitutional Court], 1993/147 MK. 8793 (unofficial translation).

58. Art. 7, cited in Morvai, "Retroactive Justice," *supra* note 54, p. 34.

59. Judgment, *supra* note 57, p. 8800. As discussed in Chapter 5, other courts have

found that the non-applicability of statutes of limitations to crimes against humanity is a rule of customary law.

60. Common Article 3 prohibits murder of all kinds, cruel treatment, torture, outrages upon personal dignity, and the passing of sentences and carrying out of executions without proper judicial guarantees against persons taking no active part in the hostilities. Unlike crimes against humanity, there is no requirement of numerosity or that the acts be part of a plan. *See* the discussion in Chapter 3.

61. *Id.*

62. Jane Perlez, "Hungarian Arrests Set off Debate: Should '56 Oppressors be Punished?," *New York Times,* Apr. 3, 1994, p. 10, col. 1.

63. *Wochenpresse* [Vienna], Jan. 12, 1990, in *FBIS-EE,* Jan. 31, 1990, p. 51.

64. Warsaw Radio, Oct. 4, 1991, in *FBIS-EE,* Oct. 10, 1991, pp. 20–25.

65. Louisa Vinton, "Poland's Government Crisis: An End in Sight?" *RFE/RL Research Report* 1(30) (July 24, 1992).

66. Prague Radio, Jan. 1, 1992, in *FBIS-EE,* Jan. 2, 1992, pp. 11–12.

67. Vinton, "Poland's Government Crisis," *supra* note 65.

68. Weschler, "The Velvet Purge," *supra* note 36, p. 85.

Chapter 8

Acknowledgments — I am indebted to Jörg Arnold, Helmut Gropengießer, and Georg Hermes for constructive criticism and to Emily Silverman for assiduous scrutiny and thoughtful suggestions concerning questions of language, style, and content. An earlier version of this chapter appeared in Vol. 1 of the *European Journal of Crime, Criminal Law and Criminal Justice* (1993), pp. 104–25.

German abbreviations: BGH = Bundesgerichtshof; *BGBl.* = *Bundesgesetzblatt; BGHSt* = *Entscheidungen des Bundesgerichtshofs in Strafsachen;* BVerfG = Bundesverfassungsgericht; *BVerGE* = *Entscheidungen des Bundesverfassungsgerichts; DtZ* = *Deutsch-deutsche Rechts-Zeitschrift;* EGStGB = Einführungsgesetz zum Strafgesetzbuch; *EuGRZ* = *Europäische Grundrechte Zeitschrift; GA* = *Goltdammers' Archiv;* GDR = German Democratic Republic; *JuS* = *Juristische Schulung; JZ* = *Juristenzeitung; KritJ* = *Kritische Justiz;* LG = Landgericht; *NJ* = *Neue Justiz; NJW* = *Neue Juristische Wodienschrift; NStZ* = *Neue Zeitschrift für Strafrecht; SJZ* = *Süddeutsche Juristenzeitung;* StGB = Strafgesetzbuch; StPO = Strafprozeßordnung; StrEG = Gesetz über die Entschädigung für Strafverfolgungs in ßuahmen; *StV* = *Strafverteidiger;* UZwG = Gesetz über den unmittelbaren Zwang bei Ausübung öffentlicher Gewalt durch Vollzugsbeamte des Bundes; *VVdStRL* = *Veröffentlichungen der Vereinigung deutscher Staatsrechtslehrer;* WStG = Wehrstrafgesetzbuch; ZaöRV = Zeitschrift für ausländishes öffentiches Redit und Völkrrecht; ZRP = Zeitschrift für Rechts-Politik.

1. Further complexities are added because the issue of collective *Vergangenheitsbewältigung* arises for the second time in recent German history. For many people it may be tempting to equate the legacy of the Socialist Unity Party (SED) with that of the Nazis. Whether the comparison bears any legitimacy at all is clearly beyond the scope of this chapter; historians and political scientists have just begun their work. *See* E. Jesse, "Entnazifizierung und Entstasifizierung als politisches Problem. Die doppelte Vergangenheitsbewältigung," in J. Isensee, ed., *Vergangenheitsbewältigung durch Recht?* (Berlin: Duncker and Humblot, 1992), pp. 9–36.

2. For an instructive overview, *see* A. Eser, "Deutsche Einheit: Übergangsprobleme im Strafrecht," *GA* 1991, p. 263 *et seq.*

3. *See* G. Schmidt, "Aus der Arbeit der unabhängigen Ausschüsse zur Überprüfung von Strafurteilen der ehemaligen DDR in Strafsachen," in *Festschrift für Rudolf Schmidt* (Tübingen: Mohr, 1992), pp. 344–56. For example, in the so-called Waldheim trials that took place in the GDR in 1950, over 3,000 Soviet camp prisoners who were classified as Nazi criminals were tried in nonpublic, summary fashion, without defense attorneys, and sentenced to harsh terms of imprisonment and even death. *See* "Das waren Blutrichter," *Der Spiegel,* Sept. 7, 1992; F. Werkentin, "Scheinjustiz in der früheren DDR," *KritJ* 1991, pp. 333–50; *see also* the declaration of nullity and declaratory quashing of judgment by the Bezirksgericht Dresden of Oct. 28, 1991, *NJ* 1992, p. 69.

4. According to § 16a StrEG (prosecution compensation law) in combination with § 369 *et seq.* GDR Criminal Procedure Code; *see* Eser, *supra* note 2, pp. 264–65.

5. *See* W. Pfister, "Das Rehabilitationsgesetz," *NStZ* 1991, pp. 165–71 (pt. 1).

6. In 1993, two more judgments were rendered by the BGH (one in review of the first *Mauerschützen* case tried before the LG Berlin); BGH, Judgment of Mar. 25, 1993 (5 StR 418/92), *NJW* 1993, 1932; BGH Judgment of June 8, 1993 (5 StR 88/93), *Dtz* 1993, 255. In both judgments the court confirmed the principles expressed in its first decision.

7. Federal High Court, with appellate jurisdiction in civil and criminal cases. Criminal cases originating in a Landgericht may be appealed directly to the BGH if specific grounds for appeal are established.

8. BGH, Judgment of Nov. 3, 1992 (5 StR 370/92), *NJW* 1993, pp. 141–49.

9. BGH Judgment of July 26, 1994 (5 StR 98/94) (citations are to unpublished opinion).

10. App. I, ch. III A, sec. III 1z, Treaty between the Federal Republic of Germany and the GDR on the creation of German unity (Unification Treaty) of Aug. 31, 1990 (BGBl. II 889), with Amendment Clause of Sept. 9, 1990 (BGBl. II 1239) and Unity Treaty (ratification) law Sept. 23, 1990 (BGBl. II 885); a special working group was established to investigate government criminality. For a comprehensive overview of the historic developments leading up to the treaty, *see* Eser, *supra* note 2.

11. LG Berlin, Judgment of Jan. 20, 1992, *JZ* 1992, p. 691.

12. With regard to three defendants, this judgment was later reversed by the BGH. K. was acquitted because, according to the federal judges, it was not proved that he had acted with the requisite intent to kill. Concerning H., the BGH remanded the case for resentencing. The court regarded the initial sentence of three years and six months of imprisonment as too rigid and opined that a sentence within the range of eligibility for probation (i.e., up to two years) would reflect the defendant's guilt more adequately. The BGH also lifted the acquittal and remanded for retrial the case of another defendant (I.), who in his role as sentinel leader had yelled the command "Shoot!" at defendant H. BGH, Judgment of Mar. 25, 1993 (5 StR 418/92), *NJW* 1993, pp. 1932–38.

13. LG Berlin, Judgment of Feb. 5, 1992, *NStZ* 1992, p. 492.

14. § 17 German Criminal Code.

15. Before the Grundlagenvertrag (Basis Treaty) of 1973 between the two Germanys, the courts treated the GDR the way it treated its own *Länder* (states), generally applying East German law as the *lex loci* according to West German (customary) rules of interlocal jurisdiction. *See* Eser, *supra* note 2, p. 256 *et seq.*; H.-H. Jescheck, *Lehrbuch des Strafrechts, Allgemeiner Teil,* 4th ed. (Berlin: Duncker and Humblot, 1988), p. 169.

16. As provided in the Unification Treaty, West German criminal law superseded East German criminal law with only a few exceptions, the most significant concerning abortion and homosexuality.

17. § 2 German Criminal Code (StGB), art. 315, Introductory Law to the German Criminal Code (EGStGB); LG Berlin (*Mauerschützen* I), *supra* note 13; LG Berlin

(*Mauerschützen* II), *supra* note 11; BGH, *supra* note 8, p. 142; *but see* the differing view of G. Küpper and H. Wilms, "Die Verfolgung von Straftaten des SED-Regimes," ZRP 1992, pp. 91–96. The provisions of the Unification Treaty do not expressly condition the application of GDR law by an *ordre public* clause. *See* J. Polakiewicz, "Verfassungs- und völkerrechtliche Aspekte der strafrechtlichen Ahndung des Schußwaffeneinsatzes an der innerdeutschen Grenze," *EuGRZ* 1992, p. 180.

18. Punishable under § 112 GDR Criminal Code as murder, in minor cases as manslaughter.

19. German criminal law theory generally defines "intent" (*Vorsatz*) as a state of mind in which the perpetrator fulfills all the elements of the crime "knowingly and willfully" (*Vorsatz,* or *dolus directus* of the second degree). It recognizes one stronger form of intent, *Absicht,* or *dolus directus* of the first degree, in which the perpetrator acts out of direct interest in the fulfillment of certain crime elements; and one weaker form, *bedingter Vorsatz,* or *dolus eventualis,* the definition of which is a longstanding controversy among German scholars. *See* Jescheck, *supra* note 15, p. 266 *et seq.* Generally, it can be said that the perpetrator acts with contingent intent when he or she is aware that the conduct may fulfill the elements of crime but still chooses to act, more or less putting up with or accepting the result. In U.S. criminal law doctrine, the term "reckless" appears to encompass such forms of conduct; *cf. Black's Law Dictionary,* 6th ed. (St. Paul, MN: West, 1990), "Reckless," p. 1270.

20. § 27, cl. 2 Border Law.

21. § 213, cl. 3, Nr. 2 Criminal Code, GDR.

22. § 27, cls. 1 and 5 Border Law.

23. *See* LG Berlin (*Mauerschützen* I) *supra* note 11, p. 692; LG Berlin (*Mauerschützen* II), *supra* note 13, p. 492 ("Border violations are intolerable under all circumstances. Border violators must be stopped or destroyed."); BGH, *supra* note 8, pp. 143–44.

24. Art. 103, cl. 2, Grundgesetz für die Bundesrepublik Deutschland, May 23, 1949, BGBl. 1 (Constitution).

25. Art. 7, cl. 2, European Convention for the Protection of Human Rights and Fundamental Freedoms, Nov. 4, 1950, 213 U.N.T.S. 222.

26. J. Polakiewicz, *supra* note 17, p. 187 *et seq.*; G. Jakobs, "Vergangenheitsbewältigung durch Strafrecht?" in Isensee, *supra* note 1, pp. 39, 52 *et seq.*; J. Arnold and M. Kühl, "Forum: Probleme der Strafbarkeit des Schußwaffengebrauchs von 'Mauerschützen,'" *JuS* 1992, p. 994 *et seq.*

27. Polakiewicz, *supra* note 17, p. 190. Some authors contend, however, that the ex post facto prohibition applies not only to the law as written but also to the law as practiced, a view that would, in effect, amount to something like a general *Vertrauensprinzip* (reliance principle). *See* Jakobs, *supra* note 26, p. 44. Neither the LG Berlin nor the BGH has shared such a far-reaching interpretation of the prohibition.

28. LG Berlin, *supra* note 13, p. 493.

29. BGH, *supra* note 9, p. 144.

30. *See* D. Oehler, *Internationales Strafrecht,* 2nd ed. (Köln-Heymanns, 1983), p. 640; U. Vultejus, "Verbrechen gegen die Menschlichkeit," *StV* 1992, pp. 602–7; for an instructive summary of the relevant international law, *see* Polakiewicz, *supra* note 17, p. 181 *et seq.*

31. As suggested by Polakiewicz, *supra* note 17, p. 186, this may be different for government officials responsible for implementation of a shooting policy. *But see* discussion *infra.*

32. *BGHSt* 2, 234, p. 237 (1952). This and following translations are by the author.

33. *BGHSt* 2, 234, p. 237 (1952).

34. *BGHSt* 2, 234, p. 239 (1952); *see* G. Radbruch, *SJZ* 1946, p. 105.

35. *BGHSt* 15, 214, p. 216 (1961) (with reference to art. 2, European Convention on Human Rights).

36. LG Berlin, *supra* note 11, p. 693.

37. Federal Constitutional Court, with jurisdiction to review on constitutional grounds in cases and controversies as specifically provided in the Grundgesetz (Basic Law), art. 93.

38. BVerfG 3, 225, p. 232 (1953).

39. The court emphasized that a violation of the Federal Republic's *ordre public* in itself would not be sufficient to disregard the bases for justification in domestic law. BGH *supra* note 8, p. 144, contrary to Küpper and Wilms, *supra* note 17, pp. 91, 93. The notion of *ordre public* is found in the German customary rules of interlocal criminal jurisdiction; the principle that the *lex loci* is applied is suspended when it contradicts "inalienable principles" of the *lex fori*. For instance, under the application of interlocal rules of jurisdiction between two crimes committed in the GDR, a defendant convicted of murder based on GDR law could not, even though provided by GDR law, be sentenced to death in a West German court because the Grundgesetz expressly abolished the death penalty; *see* Jescheck, *supra* note 15, pp. 169–70.

40. BGH, *supra* note 8, pp. 146–47.

41. *Id.*, p. 147.

42. International Covenant on Civil and Political Rights, Dec. 19, 1966, 999 U.N.T.S. 171.

43. *BGH, supra* note 8, p. 144.

44. At the same time, the court pointed to the inherent limitations of the prohibition with respect to conduct that was punishable at the time of commission under principles of law commonly recognized by the community of nations. BGH, *supra* note 8, p. 147; art. 15, cl. 2, International Covenant on Civil and Political Rights of 1966; *see also* art. 7, cl. 2, European Convention on Human Rights of 1950.

45. *BGH, supra* note 8, p. 148.

46. The argument has been advanced, for instance, by Arnold and Kühl, *supra* note 26, p. 995.

47. BGH, *supra* note 8, p. 145.

48. According to I. Seidl-Hohenveldern, *Völkerrecht,* 6th ed. (Köln: Heymanns, 1987), "Comments," pp. 561–62, only a few states, like the Federal Republic of Germany, Austria (with exceptions), Switzerland, and the United States seem to recognize such an "automatic" transformation if the treaty has been ratified and officially published.

49. BGH, *supra* note 8, p. 145.

50. *See* Polakiewicz, *supra* note 17, p. 186 *et seq.*

51. *See id.*, p. 183. In at least one West German case, a court found lawful the use of firearms where deadly force was a possible outcome. In 1988, the BGH in the "motorcycle case," *BGHSt* 35, 379, acquitted a customs officer charged with the offense of inflicting dangerous bodily injury under § 223a of the German Criminal Code. A motorcyclist had evaded the border check, and the customs officer, after firing two warning shots, had directly aimed and shot at the fleeing motorcyclist's passenger. The court held that this conduct was in accordance with West German border-security laws authorizing the use of firearms against persons evading a stopping order or the checking of their person, vehicle, or carry-on items. The use of firearms must be reasonable, firearms must be used only "to render impossible attack or flight," and there must be a warning. §§ 12, 13 UZwG. However, whether and when this may be achieved at the price of a deadly outcome is left open. The use of firearms is generally banned if the endangerment of "identifiable third parties" is highly probable, except if it is unavoidable "when proceeding against a crowd." § 12, cl.

2 UZwG. The law contains an unqualified shooting ban only with regard to persons who appear to be of tender age. § 11 UZwG. Thus, even under West German law, whether the use of deadly force is acceptable has no clear textual answer and is left up to the legal "interpreter"—just as it was in the GDR border law, where the court acknowledged that "how the life of the fleeing person had to be weighed against the inviolability of the border could not be read in the law." BGH, *supra* note 8, p. 143. Of course, East German interpretation in practice differed from West German interpretation: whereas the GDR practice was characterized "by the precedence of flight prevention over the protection of life" (*id.,* p. 144), shoot to kill orders for persons evading border control have never been officially supported or condoned in West Germany. The BGH in its 1988 decision made clear in dicta that such conduct would not be lawful. *See BGHSt* 35, 379, p. 386 *et seq.* In its recent *Mauerschützen* judgment, the BGH distinguished the border soldiers' subjective element of contingent intent (recklessness) as compared to the "motorcycle case," where the defendant was found not to have taken into account a deadly outcome. BGH, *supra* note 8, p. 148. More convincingly, perhaps, the court criticized the vagueness of the "arbitrariness" standard qualifying the protection of life under art. 6, cl. 1 of the International Covenant and pointed to the tendency, discernible in other states as well, to emphasize strongly the principle of reasonableness and limit the possibly deadly use of firearms by state authorities to the defense of seriously endangered third parties. BGH, *supra* note 8, p. 146; *see also* Polakiewicz, *supra* note 17, pp 184–85.

52. Universal Declaration of Human Rights, G.A. Res. 217 (III), U.N. Doc. A/810 (1948).

53. For the following, *see* Polakiewicz, *supra* note 17, pp. 186–87.

54. BGH, *supra* note 8, p. 145.

55. BVerfG 6, 32, pp. 33, 44 (1957). According to the *Elfes* decision, the protection of "the security and substantial concerns of the state" was sufficient for the restriction of general personal liberty, protected in art. 2, cl. 1 Basic Law (GG), which is also deemed to protect the right to leave. The citizen in this case had repeatedly and publicly, even abroad, voiced "his very critical opinion on the Federal Government's policy." He was denied the renewal of his passport, which he needed to travel to an international peace congress in Vienna where he intended to read a *Gesamtdeutsche Erklärung* (all-German declaration). *See also* G. Grünwald, "Die strafrechtliche Verantwortlichkeit in der DDR begangener Handlungen," *StV* 1991, p. 37.

Of course, the personal and national bonds between East German and West German citizens could also be viewed as constituting the particular peril of the GDR's "bleeding to death" in the post-World War II political circumstances, a peril that the building of the Wall in 1961 sought to avoid.

56. The BGH had taken this view in 1962 in the case of the Soviet secret agent Stachinskij, who had carried out a mission to kill; *BGHSt* 18, 87.

57. On the dark chapter of the failures of the German justice system in the postwar era, *see* I. Müller, *Furchtbare Juristen* (München: Knaur, 1989), p. 240 *et seq.*

58. § 25 StGB (1975) defines as principals those who commit the crime themselves, through another, or in concert with others. Thus, an actor who fulfills all the elements of crime cannot be a mere accomplice.

59. BGH, *supra* note 8, p. 148.

60. *See* Arnold and Kühl, *supra* note 26, p. 996; BGH, *supra* note 8, pp. 148–49. *But see* BGH, Judgment of June 8, 1993 (5 StRl 93), *DtZ* 1993, 256, where the court sees no difference between the two legal orders in this respect: no defense of superior orders where the criminal nature of the conduct is obvious beyond all doubt.

61. § 5, cl. 1 WStG (Military Criminal Code); BGH, *supra* note 8, p. 149.

62. BGH, *supra* note 8, p. 149.

63. § 17, cl. 1 German Criminal Code.

64. LG Berlin, *supra* note 13, p. 495. *But see* BGH (5 StR 88/93), *Dtz* 1993, 256, holding that the illegality of bodily injury by the use of firearms was not obvious to the indoctrinated young soldier.

65. BGH, *supra* note 8, p. 149.

66. BGH, *supra* note 8, p. 149.

67. *See also* Arnold and Kühl, *supra* note 26, pp. 996–97.

68. Strong criticism was voiced by R. Augstein, "Die Justiz-Farce," *Der Spiegel,* Oct. 26, 1992, who argued that "the Soviet satraps in East Berlin" are really responsible ("Honecker was about as independent of the Kremlin as Herod the Great in Jerusalem was of Emperor Augustus in Rome").

69. *BVerfG* (third chamber of the second Senate), Order of Feb. 21, 1992, *DtZ* 1992, 216; BGH, *supra* note 8, p. 142.

70. According to § 206a of the German Criminal Procedure Code, the trial ends automatically and without judgment on the merits upon the death of the defendant; for criticism of "trials against the dying," *see* K. Lüderssen, *Der Staat geht unter — Das Unrecht bleibt? Regierungskriminalität in der ehemaligen DDR* (Frankfurt a. M.: author, 1992), p. 97 *et seq.*

71. Berlin VerfGH, constitutional court of the Land Berlin, established in 1992, with jurisdiction over questions of state constitutional law. According to § 49 VerfGHG of Nov. 8, 1990 (Law on the Constitutional Court, GVBl. 1990, 2245), the court hears constitutional complaints of persons claiming that state action constitutes a violation of rights guaranteed by the Berlin Constitution.

72. For the German courts, the Honecker case was not finished on the day of his departure for Chile. Only a day later, the Berlin court of appeals had to rule on a complaint against the termination of Honecker's detention, which was rejected (KG Berlin, Judgment of Jan. 13, 1993, 4 WS 7 u. 8/83, *NJW* 1993, pp. 673–75). Complaints against the termination of the proceedings were brought before the Federal Constitutional Court but summarily rejected; there exists no constitutionally protected right to have another person subjected to criminal prosecution by the state (BVerfG, Judgment of Jan. 21, 1993, 2 BvQ 1/93, *NJW* 1993, 915–16, and Judgment of Mar. 31, 1993, 2 BvR 236/93, *NJW* 1993, p. 1577). Honecker died in Chile more than a year later.

73. Initially, manslaughter charges were also brought against former minister president Willi Stoph and former state security chief Erich Mielke. Stoph was found unable to stand trial, and the charges against Mielke were severed because he was at the time being tried before another chamber of the Landgericht Berlin for the killing of two policemen in 1931. In September 1994, after Mielke, who was eighty-six years old, had been convicted on those charges and sentenced to six years imprisonment, he was made to stand trial for the killing of six people trying to flee across the inter-German border.

74. § 22, cl. 1 GDR Criminal Code. Other recognized forms of indirect perpetration, defined under the term "participation," are instigation, complicity, and aiding and abetting. § 22, cl. 2.

75. The statutory punishment for manslaughter is a minimum of five years imprisonment; in particularly severe cases it can be life imprisonment, and in minor cases it can be six months to five years (§§ 212, 213 StGB). Instigators are punishable like principals; for aiders, however, the minimum is lowered to two years (§§ 26, 27, 49 StGB). Seventy-three-year-old Heinz Keßler was sentenced to seven years and six months, sixty-six-year-old Fritz Streletz was sentenced to five years and six months, and seventy-three-year-old Heinz Albrecht was sentenced to four years and six months; *see Deutschland Archiv* (1993), p. 1121.

76. BGH, *supra* note 9.

77. The court applied the law of the Federal Republic, based on the rule that where two laws potentially apply in a criminal case, the defendant should be given the benefit of the milder law ("milder-law rule"). The court did so on the basis of comparing the statutory ranges for intentional homicide. It did not, however, apply the milder-law rule with regard to the provisions and doctrine regarding complicity in homicide. This ruling appears questionable, but further analysis is beyond the scope of this chapter.

78. § 25 StGB.

79. BGH, *supra* note 9, p. 29.

80. *Id.,* p. 31. The court further noted that while Honecker's power had been "very great," the defendants' role with respect to him was not an "entirely subordinate" one since they themselves held high party and government offices.

81. The court itself mentions organized crime and white-collar crime; BGH, *supra* note 9, pp. 30–31.

82. In June 1994, a company commander was convicted for his role in administering the routine "guard mount." As a result of the guard mount, a border soldier shot at a fugitive a few hours later. *Süddeutsche Zeitung,* Sept. 1, 1993; June 5–6, 1994; June 11–12, 1994. Whether under the new BGH precedent intermediate ranks will be held as principals appears doubtful, given that the court still holds on to a subjective element of "crime interest."

83. § 213 German Criminal Code.

84. LG Berlin, *supra* note 11, unpublished part IX. of opinion, p. 184; similarly LG Berlin, *supra* note 13, unpublished part V. of opinion, p. 63.

85. § 212 German Criminal Code.

86. According to §§ 22, 23, 49 German Criminal Code; LG Berlin (*Mauerschützen* I) (unpublished advance copy), p. 186.

87. *See* LG Berlin, *supra* note 11. This sentence was later reversed; *see supra* note 6.

88. Technically, the sanctioning system of the Federal Republic of Germany does not know a "sentence of probation," but rather the suspension of a specified sentence of imprisonment for a probationary period, which the court sets between two and five years. The court may also order conditions of probation. § 56 *et seq.* German Criminal Code.

89. BGH, *supra* note 9, p. 149.

90. *Id.*

91. As a side note, I want to point out that in the sentencing phase as well, the judge ought to apply the more lenient law of the two systems; this becomes relevant, for instance, with regard to probation periods that are between two and five years under West German law and between one and three years under GDR law (§ 56a German Criminal Code, § 33 GDR Criminal Code). It also applies to the possibility of abstention from punishment (§ 25 GDR Criminal Code).

92. *See* W. Stree, in *Strafgesetzbuch, Kommentar,* A. Schönke and H. Schröder, eds., 24th ed. (München: 1991), § 56, comment 3. Whether and what other purposes of criminal policy are served by probationary sentencing appear to be controversial; *see* K. Lackner, *Strafgesetzbuch mit Erläuterungen,* 19th ed. (München: Beck, 1991), § 56, comment 3.

93. This implies the issue of whether the granting of probation is grounded in the reasonable expectation that the offender will not engage in any criminal conduct in the future or whether it is only relevant that the offender can be expected not to commit crimes of the kinds and severity he is presently convicted of — an issue that appears to be controversial. For the first view, *see* F. Streng, *Strafrechtliche Sanktionen* (Stuttgart: Kohlhammer, 1991), p. 66; for the second view, *see* Stree, *supra* note 92, § 56, comment 15.

94. The court may choose abstention from punishment if "the consequences of the

crime for the offender have been so severe that punishment would clearly be mistaken," provided, however, that the offender not have forfeited a term of imprisonment in excess of one year. § 60 German Criminal Code.

95. For a more general discussion of theories of punishment and redress in the context of past human rights violations, *see* Chapter 2.

96. In Germany, the traditionally prevailing view is that no single theory succeeds in explaining sufficiently the purpose of punishment and that instead a combined approach is most appropriate, uniting, in essence, "rehabilitation," "deterrence," and "retribution." The sentencing provision in § 46 German Criminal Code lays down the basic criteria in sentencing without ultimately resolving the dispute. It does, however, establish as the basic tenet that "the guilt of the offender is the basis for the determination of punishment."

97. The theory of "positive" general prevention or "integrative prevention" (as opposed to "negative" general prevention, or deterrence) has gained a lot of academic attention and support in recent years. Günter Jakobs and Claus Roxin have been two of its main advocates.

98. N. Roht-Arriaza, "State Responsibility to Investigate and Prosecute Grave Human Rights Violations in International Law," 78 *California Law Review* 451, 509 (1990).

99. *See* P. A. Köhler, "Völker-, verfassungs- und sozialrechtliche Probleme bei der Überführung von DDR-Zusatz- und Sonderversorgungssystemen in die gesetzliche Rentenversicherung," *NJ* 1993, p. 5.

100. Unification Treaty *supra* note 10, App. II, ch. VIII H, sec. III 9.b.; Köhler, *supra* note 99, p. 5. Regardless of such violations, recent social security legislation provides for the reduction of pension benefits for persons in higher government or party positions; yet another regulation provides that pension rights will be suspended if the beneficiary is being charged with a crime against bodily integrity or personal liberty in his or her capacity as a state official or political or societal functionary and evades prosecution by leaving the country; arts. 3 and 4 Renten-Überleitungsgesetz (RÜG), July 21, 1191 (*BGBl.* I, 1606).

101. As to political rights, § 45 German Criminal Code provides for the deprivation of eligibility to serve in public office, of eligibility to acquire rights in public elections, and of the right to vote. These sanctions are statutorily labeled "collateral consequences," not "punishment," and thus cannot stand alone. The loss of eligibility to serve in public office and to acquire rights in public elections for five years (but not forfeiture of the right to vote) are automatic, collateral consequences (only) for offenders convicted of a felony and sentenced to imprisonment of at least one year, and the loss is coupled with the loss of rights acquired while in office. Otherwise these sanctions are in the discretion of the court if specifically provided by the law. The fact that according to prosecution statistics for 1988 courts have employed this sanction in only one case evinces our justice system's reluctance. This sanction applied in the Mauerschützen cases (except for defendant W., who had been sentenced under juvenile law) because manslaughter is a felony even if it is reduced to a minor degree.

102. *See, e.g.,* H. Schöch, "Empfehlen sich Änderungen und Ergänzungen bei den strafrechtlichen Sanktionen ohne Freiheitsentzug?" *Gutachten C zum* 59. Deutschen Juristentag, Hannover, 1992.

103. § 43a StGB.

104. Whether the ex post facto prohibition as embodied in art. 103, cl. 2 is subject to any "inherent boundaries" analysis absent textual qualification in the Constitution itself is a pivotal issue of constitutional doctrine, but clearly beyond the scope of this chapter.

105. N. Roht-Arriaza (*supra* note 98), p. 489 *et seq.*; *see also* J. Kokott, "Völkerrechtliche Beurteilung des argentinischen Gesetzes Nr. 23.521 über die Gehorsamspflicht (due obedience), in ZaöRV (1987) p. 509 *et seq.*

106. At least for its conceptual starting point, the approach taken here can draw sup-

port from R. Alexy's and M. Kriele's comments in *VVdStRL* 51 (1992), pp. 131–33, defending application of the Radbruch formula on the idea that extreme and therefore evident un-law does not merit protection of the ex post facto prohibition. Furthermore, both Alexy and Kriele distinguish between "general" justification grounds and "special" justification grounds, the latter being characteristic of totalitarian regimes. Both the criteria of "evidence" as well as the distinction between elements of crime and general justification grounds on the one hand and "special" grounds of justification or excuse on the other have been rejected by M. Herdegen (*loc. cit.*), pp. 139–40. For an "open" break with the ex post facto prohibition by way of constitutional amendment, *see* K. Günther (Comment), *StV* (1993), pp. 23–24.

107. This latter view was taken by the BGH not only in the *Mauershützen* cases but also in prosecutions of judges for judicial abuse of power (perversion of justice). BGH, Judgment of Dec. 13, 1993 (5 StR 76/93), *NStZ* 1994, p. 240.

108. *See* Lüderssen, *supra* note 70, p. 15; *see also* J. Limbach as quoted in Fran Limbach, "Gefen Amnestie für politische DDR-Verbrechen," in *Frankfurter Allgemeine Zeitung,* Oct. 20, 1991; Jesse, *supra* note 1, p. 24.

109. Some people contend that they are questionable under the rule of law, at least if their purpose ultimately amounts to an allocation of individual criminal responsibility. *See* Lüderssen, *supra* note 70, p. 129 *et seq.*; *see also* the sharp criticism by H. Prantl, "Tribunal! Tribunal?" *Süddeutsche Zeitung,* Dec. 6, 1991; favoring the idea of "public forum," *see* R. Schröder, "Gesinnungsjustiz ist Unrecht," *Die Zeit,* Dec. 6, 1991; *see also* Cherif Bassiouni and C. L. Blakesley, "The Need for an International Criminal Court in the New Transnational World Order," 25 *Vanderbilt Journal of Transnational Law* 151, 173 (1992).

110. *See* Cherif Bassiouni, International Criminal Law, Vol. III, *Enforcement* (Dordrecht, Netherlands: M. Nijhoff, 1987), p. 181 *et seq.*; and Cherif Bassiouni, "Chronology of Efforts to Establish an International Criminal Court," Draft Statute International Criminal Tribunal, 9 *Nouvelles Etudes Pénales* 1992, p. 29 *et seq.*

111. *Cf.* Draft Statute International Criminal Tribunal, 9 *Nouvelles Etudes Pénales* 1992, art. XXI, pp. 86–87, providing for these "penalties": "(i) Deprivation of liberty or any lesser measures of control where the person found guilty is a natural person; and (ii) Fine to be levied against a natural person, organization, or State; and (iii) Confiscation of the proceeds of proscribed (or criminal) conduct." The Draft Statute further provides for "sanctions," which are: "(i) Injunctions against natural persons or legal entity restricting them from engaging in certain conduct or activities; and (ii) Order restitution and provide for damages."

Chapter 9

1. Nikita Khrushchev and Leonid Brezhnev imprisoned political and religious dissidents in labor camps and psychiatric wards. Even under Mikhail Gorbachev, the authorities harassed and sometimes detained citizens who engaged in political activism.

2. In August 1991 an alliance of conservative Party, military, and KGB leaders detained President Gorbachev and seized control of the Soviet government. The putsch collapsed in a matter of days because of resistance by democratic forces led by Boris Yeltsin and the coup plotters' own indecisiveness.

3. Roy Medvedev and Giulietto Chiesa, *Time of Change: An Insider's View of Russia's Transformation,* Michael Moore, trans. (New York: Pantheon, 1989), pp. 101–4.

4. *Id.,* pp. 104–5.

5. These distinctions are adapted in somewhat altered form from Albert Van Goudo-

ever, *The Limits of Destalinization in the Soviet Union: Political Rehabilitations in the Soviet Union since Stalin,* Frans Hijkoop, trans. (London: Croom, Helm, 1986), p. 7.

6. "Iz 'otcheta o rabote komiteta partiinogo kontrolia pri TsK KPSS za period s XX po XXII s"ezd KPSS (1956–1961 gg.),'" *Reabilitatsiia: Politicheskie protsessy 30–50-kh godov* (Moscow: Politizdat, 1991).

7. "O dopolnitel'nykh merakh po zaversheniiu raboty, sviazannoi s reabilitatsiei lits, neobosnovanno repressirovannykh v 30–40-e gody i nachala 50-kh godov" (July 11, 1988) and "O dopolnitel'nykh merakh po vosstanovleniiu spravdelivosti v otnoshenii zhertv repressii, imevshikh mesto v period 30–40-kh i nachala 50-kh godov" (Jan. 5, 1989), *Reabilitatsiia, supra* note 6, p. 16–18.

8. Interview with Olga Matlash, Moscow City Procuracy, May 21, 1991.

9. In May 1991, the council of ministers, however, had still not worked out a procedure for restoring the rights of dekulakized peasants. This meant the procuracy and courts were powerless to resolve questions about the return of confiscated land.

10. Several republics, including the Baltic states and Ukraine, had already adopted comprehensive legislation on rehabilitation and reparations. For a comparison of republican laws, *see* L. V. Voitsova and V. V. Voitsova, "Vosstanovlenie i okhrana prav zhertv massovykh repressii: sostoianie i perspektivy zakonodatel'nogo regulirovaniia," *Gosudarstvo i pravo,* no. 6 (1992).

11. "Zakon Rossiiskoi Sovetskoi Federativnoi Sotsialisticheskoi Respubliki o reabilitatsii zhertv politicheskii repressii," *Vedomosti S"ezda narodnykh deputatov RSFSR i Verkhovnogo Soveta RSFSR,* no. 44 (1991).

12. The law excludes from rehabilitation real traitors (spies, defectors, and terrorists), those who committed violence against civilians or prisoners of war, Nazi collaborators, and common criminals.

13. Resettlement of repressed ethnic groups in their historic homelands is one of the most difficult tasks facing the parliament because it infringes on the rights of the current residents of the contested areas.

14. For the story of one woman's struggle to take advantage of the new conditions governing archives, *see* Lucan Way, "Exhuming the Buried Past," *The Nation,* Mar. 1, 1993, pp. 267–77.

15. "O kul'te lichnosti i ego posledstviia: doklad Pervogo sekretaria TsK KPSS tov. Khrushcheva N.S. XX s"ezdy Kommunisticheskoi partii Sovetskogo Soiuza" (Feb. 25, 1956), *Reabilitatsiia, supra* note 6, pp. 56–58.

16. Bertram D. Wolfe, "Operation Rewrite: The Agony of Soviet Historians," *Foreign Affairs,* Oct. 1952, p. 39.

17. Cited by Merle Fainsod, "Soviet Russian Historians, or: the Lesson of Burzhdalov," *Encounter,* Mar. 1962, p. 86.

18. Liberal writers also faced many obstacles, including opposition from conservatives. For instance, Aleksandr Solzhenitsyn's *Day in the Life of Ivan Denisovich* passed censorship in 1961 only after gaining Khrushchev's personal approval. On literary politics in the Khrushchev era, *see* Priscilla Johnson, *Khrushchev and the Arts: The Politics of Soviet Culture, 1964–64* (Cambridge, MA: MIT Press, 1965); Dina Spechler, *Permitted Dissent in the USSR: Novy Mir and the Soviet Regime* (New York: Praeger, 1982).

19. R. W. Davies, *Soviet History in the Gorbachev Revolution* (Bloomington: Indiana University Press, 1989), pp. 180–81.

20. Cited in *id.,* p. 129.

21. "Chebrikov Decries Abuses of Openness," *Izvestiia,* Sept. 11, 1987, in *Current Digest of the Soviet Press,* Oct. 7, 1987, p. 8.

22. A prime example of consolidation of liberal critiques of Stalinism may be found in

Aleksandr Yakovlev's response to the infamous conservative manifesto by Nina Andreeva. *Pravda,* Apr. 5, 1988; *Sovetskaia Rossiia,* Mar. 13, 1988.

23. William B. Husband, "Rewriting Soviet History Texts: The First Phase," in *Facing Up to the Past: Soviet Historiography under Perestroika,* Takayuki Ito, ed. (Sapporo, Japan: Hokkaido University Slavic Center, 1989).

24. *Id.,* p. 84.

25. "Obsuzhdenie shkol'nogo uchebnika po istorii SSSR," *Voprosy istorii,* no. 1 (1990), pp. 188–91.

26. *XXII S"ezd Kommunisticheskoi partii Sovetskogo soiuza 17–31 Oktiabria 1961 goda stenograficheskii otchet,* Vols. 2–3 (Moscow: Politizdat, 1962).

27. Amy W. Knight, *The KGB: Police and Politics in the Soviet Union* (Boston, MA: Unwin Hyman, 1988), p. 51.

28. N. Petrov, "Spravka-dopolnenie (sudy nad rabotnikami NKVD-MGB)," *Zven"ia* (Moscow: Progress, 1991), pp. 430–36.

29. Anatolii Golovkov, "Vechny isk," *Ogonek,* no. 18 (1988), p. 31.

30. *Supra* note 6.

31. Adam Hochschild, "The Secret of a Siberian River Bank," *The New York Times Magazine,* Mar. 28, 1993, pp. 29–31, 38, 40, 78; Yegor Ligachev, *Inside Gorbachev's Kremlin,* Catherine A. Fitzpatrick, Michele A. Berdy, and Dobrochna Dyrcz-Freeman, trans. (New York: Pantheon, 1993), pp. 254–56.

32. Yevgeniya Albats, "Not to Be Pardoned," *Moscow News,* no. 19, May 16–23, 1988, and "Will There Be an End to the Lubyanka?" no. 10, Mar. 18–25, 1990.

33. Lyudmila Saraskina, "I Shall Defend Comrade Stalin's Honour and Dignity as Long as I Live," *Moscow News,* no. 40, Oct. 9–16, 1988; Bill Keller, "Stalin Has Lots of Friends in Court," *New York Times,* Jan. 30, 1989, p. A4.

34. *See* the discussion in Chapter 7.

35. S. Sulakshin, "KPSS: Vnezakonnost', prestupnost', otvetstvennost'" (Tomsk, 1990); "Obshchestvennyi sud nad KPSS," *Volia Rossii,* no. 1, Dec. 1990, pp. 1–2; "Obshchestvennyi sud nad KPSS," *Gospodin narod,* no. 1, 1990, p. 11.

36. T. Reprintseva, *Ogonek,* no. 42, Oct. 14–21, 1989, p. 25.

37. Ironically, one of the difficulties facing the judges was that they had to decide whether the Communist Party was unconstitutional based on a constitution written by that same party.

38. Kronid Liubarskii, "Sud nad grazhdaninom Lui Kapetom," *Novoe vremia,* no. 29, 1992.

Chapter 10

Acknowledgments — The author is grateful to Bill McPherson, Gabriel Andreescu, Diane Orentlicher, Gail Kligman, and Mona Nicoara, who shared insights and provided valuable advice on earlier drafts of this essay. The author also gratefully acknowledges the research assistance of Cynthia Stewart.

1. The "truth" in Romania is something of a national obsession, perhaps because the concept has been so abused for the past half century. For astounding anecdotes regarding the big lie as practiced under Ceausescu, *see* Ion Mihai Pacepa, *Red Horizons* (Washington, DC: Regnery Gateway, 1987), the memoirs of Ceausescu's foreign intelligence chief who defected to the United States in 1978. Pacepa's book is as reliable as can be expected, written as it was by a man whose main occupation under Ceausescu was providing disin-

formation. Nevertheless, it is an interesting product of the atmosphere of disinformation and lies even if its "clarification" of specific episodes is not to be believed. *See also* Matei Calinescu and Vladimir Tismaneanu, "Epilogue," in Vlad Georgescu, *The Romanians: A History* (New York: I. B. Taurus & Company, 1991), for a description of Ceausescu's manufactured cult of personality and the intensive use of nationalistic hagiography, ultimately resulting in Ceausescu himself losing touch with reality, according to the authors. For an historical argument that deception was characteristic of Romanian politics long before the advent of the Communist regime, *see, generally,* Martyn Rady, *Romania in Turmoil* (New York: I. B. Taurus & Company, 1992), chs. 1 and 2.

2. *See, e.g.,* Calinescu and Tismaneanu, *supra* note 1, p. 268. They write: "What happened was actually the abduction of the revolution by a group of seasoned aparatchiks, well versed in palace intrigues and behind-the-scenes maneuvers. It was also likely that their actions had the blessing of the Soviet leadership, who had every reason to favor Ceausescu's replacement with an 'enlightened autocrat' in the Gorbachev mold instead of the uncompromising and unpredictable anticommunist forces already manifest in Poland, Hungary, and Czechoslovakia."

3. *See* Nestor Ratesh, *Romania: The Entangled Revolution* (New York: Praeger, 1991), p. 28, quoting excerpts from a transcript of a Political Executive Committee meeting (Dec. 17, 1989) printed in *Romania Libera,* Jan. 10, 1990. Members of the Political Executive Committee claimed at their trial that the transcript printed in *Romania Libera* had been falsified, but they admitted that the meeting had taken place and that they had, at least implicitly, approved Ceausescu's decision to use live ammunition.

4. Admissions and other testimony at the "Timisoara trial" later confirmed that at least forty dead bodies were shipped secretly to Bucharest for incineration to erase all traces of the bloodshed. "Prosecution Testimony Heard in Genocide Trial — ROMPRES — March 15, 1990," *FBIS Daily Report (FBIS-EEU),* Mar. 16, 1990, p. 54; and "Timisoara Trial Ends; Witnesses' Hearing Starts — ROMPRES — March 14, 1990," *FBIS Daily Report (FBIS-EEU),* Mar. 16, 1990, p. 54. Lists of the dead and wounded at the Timis County Hospital were also destroyed; *id.* The Cenusa crematorium in Bucharest today bears a plaque honoring forty-five victims who were disposed of this way.

5. Violent repression of street protests also broke out in Cluj, Sibiu, Brasov, Targu Mures, and Arad.

6. *See* Ratesh, *supra* note 3, pp. 70–73, for a detailed and dramatic account of the Ceausescus' aborted escape.

7. Some of the videotape footage from the days after Ceausescu's fall, as well as from the protests later that spring, are compiled in a video documentary produced by the Group for Social Dialogue in Bucharest.

8. Radio Bucharest, Dec. 23, 1990, cited in Ratesh, *supra* note 3, p. 73.

9. It wasn't until 4 A.M. that Romanian television showed a hastily edited version of the trial to an anxiously waiting public, many of whom had stayed up through the night awaiting the broadcast. When the segment was finally shown, a television announcer implied that the editing had been done in order to protect those present from retribution. The long wait and the heavily edited result perhaps planted the first seeds of doubt about the self-proclaimed leadership.

10. For an account of the trial, *see* Rady, *supra* note 1, ch. 11.

11. The National Salvation Front disclosed two weeks after the trial that, contrary to the impression created at the time, the figure of 63,000 victims was intended to cover the entire twenty-five years of Ceausescu's rule and that only 10,000 of the victims had died during the uprising. Official figures released in June 1990 contradicted both earlier statements by putting the figure at 144 killed during the uprising, with 727 wounded. The offi-

cial, nationwide figures for the period after the Ceausescus fled is 889 dead and 1,417 wounded. *See* Ratesh, *supra* note 3, p. 78.

12. From a transcript reprinted in "Revolution in Romania: Ceausescus Defiant to the End," *Financial Times,* Dec. 28, 1989.

13. *See* the transcript reprinted in *id.*

> Counsel for the defense: "As a lawyer, I consider that all the conditions under the law for putting the defendants on trial have been fulfilled. They can be sentenced if there is evidence, whether or not they sign anything. Had they pleaded mental incompetence, they would have had some chance of saving themselves. But they are in perfect control of their mental capacities. In view of the evidence, I find them guilty. Nevertheless, I ask the court that the verdict be not revenge. This court is as legitimate as the indictment against Nicolae Ceausescu and his wife."

14. The Ceausescus were asked at the trial if they wanted to appeal the verdict. They refused to treat the offer of appeal any more seriously than the trial itself.

15. Dan Ionescu, "Old Practices Persist in Romanian Justice," *Report on Eastern Europe,* Mar. 9, 1990, p. 44.

16. A videotape of the trial in its entirety was not shown on Romanian television until eight months after the event took place.

17. *See, e.g., Financial Times,* Dec. 27, 1993; Amnesty International, *1990 Report,* p. 199.

18. "Extraordinary Military Tribunals to Try Terrorists—Bucharest Domestic Service—January 7, 1990," *FBIS Daily Report (FBIS-EEU),* Jan. 8, 1990, p. 81.

19. *Id.*

20. Originally twenty-four defendants were charged, but three died before the trial opened, and four defendants were added later.

21. In addition, a number of high-ranking Securitate and interior ministry officials were convicted of illegal deprivation of liberty and abuse of power; one of them, former Securitate chief General Vlad, was sentenced in July 1991 to nine years in prison for complicity in genocide. There is widespread speculation that the persons in power have ensured that Vlad stay in prison because if he were free his knowledge and contacts could jeopardize their own positions. Trials also took place of local officials involved in the December violence in several cities, and four of the Ceausescus' bodyguards were acquitted on charges relating to the ruling couple's escape.

22. Sean Hillen and Tim Judah, "Ceausescu, the Freed Playboy Prince Dons Dissident Halo," *The Times,* Nov. 25, 1992.

23. Decree-Law Regarding the Amnesty of Some Crimes and Pardon of Some Sentences, no. 3/1990, published in *Monitorul Oficial,* Jan. 5, 1990, art. 1.

24. Decree-Law on the Pardon of Some Sentences, no. 23/1990, published in *Monitorul Oficial,* Jan. 14, 1990, art. 2. A full text of the decree, as read on Bucharest Radio, is translated in "Decree-Law on Pardons—Bucharest Radio—January 15, 1990," *FBIS Daily Report (FBIS-EEU),* Jan. 16, 1990, p. 92.

25. *Id.*

26. Article 268 of the Romanian Penal Code provides: "The deed of initiating criminal prosecution against, of making the arrest of, of suing or convicting a person, while knowing that he/she is not guilty, is punished with prison from 2 to 7 years."

27. "Former Securitate Generals, Colonels Sentenced—ROMPRES—March 18, 1991," *FBIS Daily Report (FBIS-EEU),* Mar. 19, 1991, p. 43. Two months later, two Securitate officers, Gheorghe Goran (sentenced to three years) and Gheorghe Vasile (sentenced to two and a half years), who had been convicted on the same charge, were also pardoned.

The charges against four other officers tried for the same offense, however, was changed to "illegal arrest and abusive investigation" under article 266 of the criminal code. Yet two of them, who were accused only of illegal arrest, received suspended sentences. The two others, who were convicted of abusive investigation, were sentenced to three year prison terms. "Sentences Passed on Former Securitate Generals — ROMPRES — May 10, 1991," *FBIS Daily Report (FBIS-EEU)*, May 13, 1991, pp. 40–41.

28. For instance, Ioan Furcoiu and Maria Cebuc, members of the Brasov County secretariat of the Romanian Communist Party, were acquitted of some charges and then released because other charges against them were covered by the amnesty. "Two Defendants Released in Brasov Trial — ROMPRES — September 26, 1990," *FBIS Daily Report (FBIS-EEU)*, Sept. 27, 1990, p. 48.

29. *See* the discussion in Chapter 4.

30. *See* Convention on the Prevention and Punishment of the Crime of Genocide, adopted Dec 9, 1948, G.A. Res. 260 A (II), 78 U.N.T.S. 227, entered into force Jan. 12, 1951 and the Romanian Penal Code, art. 357.

31. "Former Dissident Cornea on Communists, Elections — *Liberation* — January 10, 1990," *FBIS Daily Report (FBIS-EEU)*, Jan. 26, 1990, p. 84.

32. "Newspaper's Director on Post-Revolution Trials — ROMPRES — March 16, 1990," *FBIS Daily Report (FBIS-EEU)*, Mar. 22, 1990, p. 70.

33. "Justice Minister Issues Statement — ROMPRES — December 24, 1990," *FBIS Daily Report (FBIS-EEU)*, Dec. 27, 1990, p. 29. The justice minister at the time was Victor Babiuc. Roman's resignation was forced by a fourth incursion of the miners in September 1991. After local elections in the fall of 1992, Babiuc joined with Roman and other former ministers in an internal split of the National Salvation Front. The Roman wing, which retained the party's name, thereafter cultivated the image of a reform-minded party of pragmatic technocrats. Iliescu's wing became the Democratic National Salvation Front and has been more closely associated with nostalgic Communist ideologies. In 1993, both parties changed names: the former became the Democratic Party (FSN) and the latter the Party of Social Democracy in Romania.

34. "Prosecutor on Efforts to Find Guilty Criminals — ROMPRES — January 4, 1991," *FBIS Daily Report (FBIS-EEU)*, Jan. 5, 1991, p. 51.

35. A human rights group, the League for the Defense of Human Rights, submitted to the prosecutor a document signed by Draghici assigning a released prisoner to work at the canal. The document makes reference to a law for "determining the place of work for counterrevolutionary convicts who have both served their sentences and fulfilled other categories of elements hostile to the popular-democratic regime of the People's Republic of Romania." The human rights group believes the file represents merely one of thousands of identical cases. Nevertheless, the file was returned by the prosecutor, rejected without justification.

36. The most commonly cited figure is 750,000 victims sent to prisons and labor camps, attributed to the Association of Former Political Prisoners. The documentation to back up this claim is, however, incomplete.

37. "Intelligence Service Reports to Parliament on Threat to National Security," ROMPRES, June 30, 1993, in *BBC Summary of World Broadcasts,* July 3, 1993. The investigations were apparently part of an internal censure within the Communist Party of the excesses of the Gheorghiu-Dej regime. Interview with Paul Niculescu Mizil, Oct. 3, 1993.

38. The incident, in which the Securitate opened fire on a bus filled with hostages, leaving six dead and twelve wounded, gained renewed notoriety when it was captured in the popular 1992 Romanian film *Balanta* (The Oak). Ceausescu was reportedly infuriated that the three hostage takers had been captured alive.

39. The Romanian Intelligence Service does, however, sometimes provide information from the files to prosecutors, as in the Draghici case; *supra* notes 35–37 and accompanying text.

40. *See* Rady, *supra* note 1, ch. 6.

41. *See, generally,* Gail Kligman, "The Policies of Reproduction in Ceausescu's Romania: A Case Study in Political Culture," *East European Politics and Societies* 6(3):364, Fall 1992. Between 1965 and 1989, 9,452 women died because of complications arising from illegal abortions. *Id.,* p. 398.

42. *See* Rady, *supra* note 1, ch. 6.

43. Constantin Ticu Dumitrescu, "The Trial of Communism — The Revolution's Last Chance," *Rezistenta* (Journal of the Association of Former Political Prisoners), no. 4, p. 3.

44. Interview with Gabriel Andreescu, Aug. 5, 1993.

45. "Former Political Prisoners to Demand Reparation — AFP — January 4, 1990," *FBIS Daily Report (FBIS-EEU),* Jan. 4, 1990, p. 84.

46. Interview with Constantin Ticu Dumitrescu, August 30, 1994.

47. "Intelligence Service Reports to Parliament on Threat to National Security," ROMPRES, June 30, 1993, in *BBC Summary of World Broadcasts,* July 3, 1993.

48. At the beginning of 1993, a scandal broke out when it was discovered that many people had obtained the certificates for their economic advantage without legitimate justification.

49. Other associations inspired by the popular uprising in December 1989 include the Group for Social Dialogue, founded immediately afterward by a group of intellectual dissidents, including Gabriel Andreescu, Andrei Plesu, and Radu Filipescu; and the December 21 Association. An overlapping group of well-known cultural and political leaders formed the Civil Alliance at the end of 1990. Some members of the Civic Alliance subsequently splintered off into a political party known as the Civic Alliance Party, fielding candidates in the 1992 local and national elections.

50. The exact text of point 8 reads as follows: "For the first three consecutive legislatures, it is prohibited to include former Communists and former Securitate officers on any list for central and local elections. Likewise, during the same period, it is prohibited to nominate former Romanian Communist Party activists for the position of Romania's president." "Appeal to Ban Former Securitate from Elections — *Dreptatea* — April 12, 1990," *FBIS Daily Report (FBIS-EEU),* Apr. 20, 1990, p. 59.

51. Calinescu and Tismaneanu, *supra* note 1, p. 291. The estimate that four million individuals registered in support of the Timisoara Proclamation has been challenged, especially in light of the fact that far fewer than four million voted with the opposition in the May elections.

52. At first, the National Salvation Front assured the Romanian public that it was not a political party and would not run candidates when elections were scheduled. The National Salvation Front leaders went back on their word on January 23, 1990.

53. Other demands of the demonstrators included postponing elections and eliminating the subordination of Romanian television to the current leadership of the country.

54. "Warns Against 'Witch Hunt' — ROMPRES — March 15, 1990," *FBIS Daily Report (FBIS-EEU),* Mar. 16, 1990, p. 55. Similar issues arise in the disqualification of judges. As a practical matter, however, it would be especially difficult to disqualify judges on the basis of membership in the Communist Party because membership was a prerequisite for a judicial career. Indeed, the judiciary has been chronically understaffed since Ceausescu fell, a situation that became even worse when hundreds of new positions were created by a judicial reorganization law that went into effect in July 1993. Many positions remained vacant months after the law took effect. Nevertheless, then minister of justice Victor

Babiuc claimed that over 90 percent of the presidents and over 80 percent of the vice presidents of the regional Judet tribunals, as well as 170 other judges, had been replaced as of November 1990. However, there has never been an established disqualification procedure. Michael Shafir, "Toward the Rule of Law," *RFE/RL Research Report,* July 3, 1992, p. 34.

55. Student leader Marian Munteanu, transcribed from a video documentary produced by the Group for Social Dialogue, Bucharest.

56. Iliescu won with an overwhelming majority of 85 percent, but there were many flaws in the conduct of the elections, including violent intimidation during the campaign. *See, e.g.,* International Human Rights Law Group, *Report on the Romanian Campaign for President and Parliament,* May 9, 1990; and National Democratic Institute for International Affairs and National Republican Institute for International Affairs, *The May 1990 Elections in Romania,* (Washington, DC, 1991).

57. On June 13, members of the IMGB (Intreprinderea de masini grele-Bucuresti— "Heavy Equipment Enterprise of Bucharest") were out on the streets trying to restore order before the miners, who came on June 14, arrived.

58. The Bucharest-based League for the Defense of Human Rights (LADO) filed a 121-page complaint with the general prosecutor's office on June 28, 1990, but three years later the authorities had not issued any indictments based on the information provided. League for the Defense of Human Rights, *Informative Bulletin,* May 4, 1993.

59. At least four people died in street violence when miners stormed Bucharest to demand the resignation of Prime Minister Petre Roman. Amnesty International, *Report 1992,* p. 221. In addition, ethnic violence in Targu Mures in March 1990 gave rise to inconsistent prosecutions resulting in impunity for many.

60. Interview with Dan Stanescu, Vice President of the League for the Defense of Human Rights, June 2, 1993.

61. *Id.*

62. Interview with Alexandru Paleologu, Oct. 1, 1993.

63. The draft law would also require background checks for public officials to ensure that they had not been informers or secret police officers.

64. Virgil Ierunca, *Fenomenul Pitesti* (The Pitesti Phenomenon) (Bucharest: Humanitas, 1991). As noted, the Pitesti Phenomenon involved a brutal psychological and physical torture process that converted torture victims into torturers.

65. Cornel Dragoi, *Povestea Elisabetei Rizea din Nucsoara* (The Story of Elisabeta Rizea from Nucsoara) (Bucharest: Humanitas, 1991).

66. For instance, *Memoria: revista gandirii arestate* (Memory: Journal of Arrested Thoughts), published by the Union of Romanian Writers, put out its eighth edition in 1993. *Din documentele rezistentei* (From the Documents of the Resistance), the Archives of the Association of Former Political Prisoners, also published its eighth edition in 1993.

67. As of the summer of 1994, the initiative was still awaiting funds from the Council of Europe.

68. Interview with Alexandru Paleologu, Oct. 1, 1993.

69. In 1993, for instance, the International Human Rights Law Group and *Equipo Argentino de Forense Antropologica* (Argentine Forensic Anthropology Team) assisted in the excavation of what purported to be a mass grave site discovered in 1991 in Caciulati, a small town near Bucharest, on the site of an estate that had been used by the Securitate for several years in the late 1940s and early 1950s. The prosecutor's office and other officials had been insisting that the site was merely an ancient cemetery whose proximity to the former Securitate office was a coincidence. The Association of Former Political Prisoners, however, claimed that the bodies buried there were victims of Securitate torture and executions of people who had been internally displaced and housed in Caciulati under hard con-

ditions. An independent analysis of the available evidence showed that neither side's experts had any substantial basis for their "scientific" conclusions. Ironically, the announcement was greeted by widespread skepticism, with many newspapers presenting one-sided versions of the available evidence.

The lesson of Caciulati was that the "truth" in Romania does not always correspond with the underlying facts, rendering more difficult the process of reshaping collective memory and acknowledging past human rights abuses.

70. In October 1993 Romania was admitted to the Council of Europe, and the U.S. Congress voted to restore most-favored-nation trade status to Romania.

Chapter 11

1. Unless otherwise cited, the information in this chapter is drawn from newspaper accounts of the events.

2. *See, e.g.*, Americas Watch, *Challenging Impunity: the Ley de Caducidad and the Referendum Campaign in Uruguay* (Washington, DC: Americas Watch, 1989); Lawrence Weschler, *A Miracle, A Universe* (New York: Pantheon, 1990).

3. The report was published in English as SERPAJ, *Uruguay: Nunca Mas: Human Rights Violations 1972–1985,* Elisabeth Hamsten, trans. (Philadelphia: Temple University Press, 1992).

4. The text of the law reads:

Article 1. It is recognized that, as a consequence of the logic of the events stemming from the agreement between the political parties and the Armed Forces signed in August 1984 and in order to complete the transition to full constitutional order, the State relinquishes the exercise of penal actions with respect to crimes committed until March 1, 1985 by military and police officials either for political reasons or in fulfillment of their functions and in obeying orders from superiors during the de facto period.

Article 2. The above article does not cover:
a) judicial proceedings in which indictments have been issued at the time this law goes into effect;
b) crimes that may have been committed for personal economic gain or to benefit a third party.

Article 3. For the purposes contemplated in the above articles, the court in pending cases will request the Executive branch to submit, within a period of thirty days of receiving such request, an opinion as to whether or not it considers the case to fall within the scope of Article 1 of this law. If the Executive branch considers the law to be applicable, the court will dismiss the case. If, on the other hand, the Executive branch does not consider the case to fall under this law, the court will order judicial proceedings to continue. From the time this law is promulgated until the date the court receives a response from the Executive branch, all pretrial proceedings in cases described in the first paragraph of this article will be suspended.

Article 4. Notwithstanding the above, the court will remit to the Executive branch all testimony offered until the date this law is approved, regarding persons allegedly detained in military or police operations who later disappeared, including minors allegedly kidnapped in similar circumstances.

The Executive Branch will immediately order the investigation of such incidents.

Within a 120-day period from the date of receipt of the judicial communication of the denunciation, the Executive branch will inform the plaintiffs of the results of these investigations and place at their disposal all information gathered. (Unofficial translation by Americas Watch)

5. All those convicted have appealed. U.S. Department of State, 1993 Human Rights Report, Paraguay Human Rights Practices 1993, Jan. 31, 1994.

6. Don Podesta, "Ruling Party Wins in Paraguay," *Washington Post,* May 11, 1993, p. A14.

7. For a description of the full scope of the convictions, *see* International Commission of Jurists, "Bolivia: A Historic Ruling Against Impunity," 51 *The Review* 1 (1993).

8. Corte Suprema de Bolivia, *Sentencia Pronunciada en los Juicios de Responsabilidad Seguidos por el Ministerio Público y Coadjuvantes contra Luis Garcia Meza y sus Colaboradores,* Apr. 21, 1993, Sucre, Bolivia. Interestingly, none of the charges against these defendants involved forced disappearances. In addition, the U.N. Declaration on Forced Disappearances, discussed in Chapter 4, typifies the act as "in the nature of" a crime against humanity, leaving open the question of whether it fits within the Nuremberg definition.

9. *See, generally,* M. Lippman, "The Drafting of the 1948 Convention on the Prevention and Punishment of the Crime of Genocide," 3 *Boston University International Law Journal* 1 (1984). The court also noted that the United Nations had declared punishable conspiracy to commit genocide, incitement, and attempt and complicity in genocide and had decreed the maximum sentence for responsible rulers. *Sentencia, supra* note 6, p. 16.

10. The Nuremberg definition refers to crimes against civilian "populations." *See* discussion in Chapter 4.

11. *See, e.g.,* NotiSur, "Bolivia: Former Dictator Sentenced to 30-Year Prison Term," Apr. 30, 1993; Malcolm Coad, "Ex-Dictator Guilty But Free in Bolivia," *The Guardian,* Apr. 23, 1993.

12. Reuters, "Bolivia Puts Price on Former Leader's Head," May 5, 1993.

13. Doyle McManus, "Nicaragua Courts, Jailings Criticized by Rights Group," *Los Angeles Times,* Apr. 5, 1985, p. 9.

14. The Commissioner's office was established by Decree-Law 26-92 of June 8, 1992, and its independence was further guaranteed by Executive Decree 6/51-92 of Sept. 8, 1992. The office is responsible for overseeing acts and measures necessary to ensure respect for human rights, investigate violations, and oversee Honduras's compliance with international human rights norms. *See* Comisionado Nacional de Protección de los Derechos Humanos, *Los Hechos Hablan por Si Mismos: Informe Preliminar sobre los Desaparecidos en Honduras 1980–93* (Tegucigalpa, Honduras: ed. Guaymuras, 1994) (hereinafter CNPDH Report or Valladares Report). The report has been translated into English by the Center for Justice and International Law (CEJIL) and Human Rights Watch/Americas (New York: Human Rights Watch, 1994).

15. The *Velasquez* case in the Inter-American Court, discussed in Chapter 3, concerned a Honduran student who was a victim of a forced disappearance.

16. For a complete account of the Mack case, *see* Lawyers Committee for Human Rights, *An Interim Report on the Investigation of the Murder of Myrna Mack* (March 1992); *Decision in the Myrna Mack Case: A Question of Command Responsibility Unresolved* (June 1993); Fundación Myrna Mack, *Informe Sobre el Caso Myrna Mack: su Estado Actual* (May 1994).

17. As in many Latin American countries, crime victims and their families may intervene in prosecutions. Most of the impetus for continuing action in this case has come from the tenacity of Helen Mack rather than from the public prosecutor.

18. To cite two, six enlisted men and a captain were convicted for killing U.S. citizen

Michael Devine, but the captain subsequently escaped from the military base where he was being held and is in hiding. In August 1992, a military court acquitted a naval captain, two lieutenants, and three soldiers of killing eleven people near the town of Escuintla. "Guatemalan Soldiers Acquitted in Massacre," *San Francisco Chronicle,* Aug. 13, 1992, p. A4, col. 1. Members of civil patrols organized by the Army have also regularly been accused of killings and disappearances, but few have been convicted. *See Report by the independent expert, Mr. Christian Tomuschat, on the situation of human rights in Guatemala, prepared in accordance with paragraph 11 of Commission resolution 1991/51,* U.N. Doc. E/CN.4/1992/5 (1992).

19. Acuerdo Global sobre Derechos Humanos entre El Gobierno de la Republica de Guatemala y la Unidad Revolucionary Nacional Guatemalteca, Mar. 29, 1994, Mexico, D.F., U.N. Doc. A/48/928-S/1994/448, Apr. 8, 1994, reprinted in 1 *Verdad y Vida* xxv (Jan.–Mar. 1994).

20. *Supra* note 19, p. xxvi (author's unofficial translation).

21. Compare the Chilean and Salvadoran Truth Commissions, discussed in Chapters 13 and 15.

22. "Presiones no Cambiarán Propósitos de Comisión de la Verdad, dice De Leon," *Prensa Libre,* June 26, 1994, p. 3. The defense minister has stated that any amnesty aimed at allowing the URNG insurgents to return to legal life should extend to the military. "Enriquez: Militares Dispuestos a Acorgerse a Amnistia Política," *Siglo Veintiuno,* July 6, 1994, p. 2.

23. "Diputados Impulsan Amnistia por Delitos Politicos y Evasión Fiscal," *Siglo Veintiuno,* July 5, 1994, p. 2.

24. Both the Solicitor General, Acisclo Valladares Molina, and the head of the government Human Rights Ombudsman's Office, Jorge Garcia, oppose the proposal. "CACIF Rechaza Tajantemente," *Siglo Veintiuno,* July 6, 1994, p. 2; "Qué Piensa de una Eventual Amnistia?" *El Gráfico,* July 6, 1994, p. 12.

25. Guatemala's constitution privileges international law over contrary domestic law, including constitutional provisions.

Chapter 12

Acknowledgments — This paper is a part of a larger research effort the author is carrying out under the sponsorship of the U.S. Institute of Peace and the John D. and Catherine T. MacArthur Foundation. Naomi Roht-Arriaza has put together the pieces I once gave her, managing to even make sense of them. I wish to thank her for the content and shape of this chapter.

1. *See Página 12* (newspaper, Buenos Aires) Aug. 16, 1991, p. 7. Despite his reputation for having ordered ruthless political repression as a military delegate in the province of Tucuman, General Domingo Bussi received 43 percent of the vote in that province. David Ruiz Palacios, deputy minister of the interior during the military dictatorship, was favored by the polls to win the elections in the Chaco province. When Ruiz Palacios was barred from running because he lacked the requisite years of residence in the state, he named his own substitute, who managed to win the elections by a landslide.

2. In the province of Buenos Aires alone, 500,000 citizens voted for Aldo Rico. *See Página 12,* Sept. 10, 1991, p. 4; Raul Kollman, "El Identikit de los Votantes," *Página 12,* Sept. 15, 1991, p. 2.

3. *See* Horacio Verbitsky, *Civiles y militares* (Buenos Aires: Editorial Contra punto,

1987), p. 360 (provides an account of Aldo Rico's revolts); and Iain Guest, *Behind the Disappearances: Argentina's Dirty War Against Human Rights and the United Nations* (Philadelphia: University of Pennsylvania Press, 1990), p. 555, n. 22.

4. Kollman, *supra* note 2, p. 3.

5. *See* Kollman, *supra* note 2, p. 6; *Buenos Aires Herald* (newspaper, Buenos Aires), Aug. 26, 1991, p. 7.

6. I am referring to law 23.492 of December 1986, known as the "Full Stop Law," and law 23.521 of June 1987, usually called the "Due Obedience Law," discussed below.

7. Before the Supreme Court invalidated the "self amnesty," Congress passed law 23.040. Although the legislature does not have the power for such invalidation, the legislative act sought to make a strong statement against the amnesty.

8. *See* Carlos Fontan Balestra, *Tratado de Derecho Penal*, 2d ed. (Argentina, 1980). The Argentine military justice code endorses the principle that only the officer who issues the order is criminally accountable for offenses perpetrated by his subordinates. This principle, however, is tempered by the rule that inferior officers are accountable for the "excesses" they may commit. Furthermore, to diminish the number of prosecutions, Congress passed law 23.049, which prescribed that military personnel who had lacked "decision capacity" would benefit from the presumption that they had acted on the basis of an excusing mistake, except for "atrocious and aberrant" offenses. As it was, the systematic perpetration of torture and assassination rendered over a thousand officers liable for prosecution.

9. This topic was discussed at length at a seminar hosted by the Aspen Institute for Humanistic Studies: "State Crimes: Punishment or Pardon," Wye Woods, MD, Nov. 4–6, 1988. As a participant of this seminar I greatly profited from the ideas expounded there.

10. The military governor of the province of Buenos Aires, General Iberico Saint-Jean, reflected the South American dictators' conception of society's potential enemies when he said: "We will first kill all the subversives; later, we will kill those who collaborate with them; then we will kill those who remain indifferent; and, finally, we will kill the timid." *See* Carlos H. Acuna and Catalina Smulovitz, "Ni Olvido ni Perdón: Derechos Humanos y Tensiones Cívico-Militares en la Transición Argentina," paper submitted at the XVI International Congress of the Latin American Studies Association, 1991.

Consistent with this view, one of the chief officers in the repression campaign in the province of Buenos Aires, Colonel Roberto Roualdes, stated to human rights campaigner Emilio Mignone that it was worthwhile killing a hundred suspects if just five of these suspects proved to be actual subversives. *See* Mignone, *infra* note 27, p. 67.

11. The fact that the military's enemy was designated as the "subversives" instead of "terrorists," "guerrillas," or "insurgents" was the cause for greater confusion. The fact that "subversion" is more linked to ideological antagonism than the direct or indirect exercise of violence implied in "terrorism" developed an environment in which the military divided allies and enemies. In the "if you are not with us you are against us" approach, there is no room for neutrality: Those who do not spontaneously march with us, who are not our friends, are our actual or potential foes. Jon Elster, "Active and Passive Negation: An Essay in Ibanskian Sociology," in *The Invented Reality: How Do We Know What We Believe We Know? Contributions to Constructivism*, Paul Watzlawick, ed. (New York: Norton, 1984), p. 175.

12. Juan E. Corradi describes the general adaptive behavior of the population under military rule: People abandoned, first, their political activities and, second, their political beliefs; they reduced associational activities and denied any evidence that inhumane practices were being carried out. Members of groups that were potential targets of state terror developed ignorance about what was going on. Selfish strategies of survival, like competi-

tion and speculation, were adopted. *See* Corradi, "The Culture of Fear in Civil Society," in *From Military Rule to Liberal Democracy in Argentina,* Monica Peralta Ramos and Carlos H. Waisman eds. (Boulder, CO: Westview Press, 1987), p. 113.

13. In this paper I treat "self-esteem" and "self-respect" indiscriminately. I endorse, however, Waltzer's version, according to which self-esteem consists of the opinion we have of ourselves, whereas self-respect is the "proper regard for the dignity of one's own person or one's own position." Democratic citizenship is thus narrowly related to the self-respect all individuals enjoy as "full and equal members" of the community. *See* Michael Waltzer, *Spheres of Justice* (Oxford, U.K.: M. Robertson, 1983), p. 227.

14. Constructivist authors have insisted on the pervasiveness of our adaptive behaviors. Once a strategy has been developed to protect us from a hostile environment, this adaptive strategy becomes a character trait and a "theory" to understand the world in general. Thus, we will tend to cling to this theory to view reality in the same light even once the external danger has disappeared. *See* Gregory Bateson, "Social Planning and the Concept of Deutero-Learning," in *Steps in the Ecology of Mind* (New York: Ballantine Books, 1972), p. 159; *see also* Juergen Ruesch and Gregory Bateson, *Communication: The Social Matrix of Psychiatry* (New York: Norton, 1951), p. 212.

15. There were many members of the cabinet and other high officials who opposed the trials on pragmatic grounds. The president strongly defended the view that human rights violators should be tried.

16. Amartya K. Sen points out that subjugated people will abandon their belief in their own and other persons' rights in order to accommodate themselves to the attainment of "small mercies." Sen, *On Ethics and Economics* (Oxford, U.K., and New York: Blackwell, 1990), p. 45.

17. *See* L. Wechsler, *A Miracle; A Universe: Settling Accounts with Torturers* (New York: Pantheon, 1990), p. 241.

18. A former political prisoner told me that the pardoning of the generals made him feel the same way that a raped woman in a *machista* society sees herself. If the rapist is not convicted, she is likely to feel guilty as a blameworthy participant in the wrongdoing. She needs an institutional response to the wrongdoing to support her dignity.

19. The Madres de Plaza de Mayo is a group of mothers of youths who were made to disappear during the military dictatorship. Staunchly denouncing the human rights abuses perpetrated during the 1976–83 period, the Madres paraded wearing white scarfs around the square across the street from the Government House in Buenos Aires. This group was an important organization in the late seventies. Though currently split, it is still active today.

20. Judgment in Case No. 23, Federal Criminal and Correctional Court of Appeals for the Federal District of Buenos Aires, Dec. 5, 1985, reprinted in 26 *I.L.M.* 317 (1987). The charges against the junta members included illegal deprivation of liberty, torture, homicide, robbery, being an accessory after the fact, reduction to involuntary servitude, and false statements. The defendants raised defenses of necessity and self-defense based on the existence of terrorist groups. The court rejected both arguments, finding that the danger to the government was not imminent enough to constitute a "state of necessity" and that in any case the means employed to combat the terrorist threat were unnecessary and illegal. The defendants also argued that the state of internal war existing in Argentina justified their acts. To rebut this argument the court turned to both domestic and international law. It looked at the Geneva Conventions of 1949 and at the works of international law publicists to conclude that the laws of war prohibited, rather than justified, the acts charged. The court then turned to issues of command responsibility, finding the commanders responsible for the acts of their subordinates.

21. Supreme Court of Argentina, Dec. 30, 1986, *Revista de Jurisprudencia Argentina*, no. 5513, Apr. 29, 1987.

22. *See* Jaime Malamud-Goti, "Punishment and a Rights-Based Democracy," *Criminal Justice Ethics*, Summer–Fall 1991, pp. 3–13.

23. *See* John Mackie, "Morality and Retributive Emotions," 1 *Criminal Justice Ethics* 3, nn. 1–4 (1982).

24. *See* "Sentencia de la Cámara Nacional de Apelaciones en lo Criminal y Correc-cional Federal de la Capital Federal" of December 9, 1985, in *Proceso a los Ex-Integrantes de las Juntas Militares,* with the collaboration of Guillermo Palombo (Buenos Aires, n.d.), p. 46.

25. Argentine Anti-Communist Alliance.

26. *See Nunca Más: Informe de la Comisión Nacional sobre la Desaparición de Personas* (Report of the National Commission on the Disappearance of People) (Buenos Aires: Editorial Universitaria, 1986), p. 2.

27. *See* Emilio F. Mignone, *Witness to the Truth: The Complicity of Church and Dictatorship in Argentina,* 1976–1983, Phillip Berryman, trans. (New York: Orbis Books, 1986). José Maria Ghio, researcher on the Church in Latin America, conveyed to me his conclusion that without the support of the Church, the Argentine military would not have dared to wage the campaign of terror between 1976 and 1980. If their confessors had turned their backs on them, the officers of the armed forces would have been left in total isolation.

28. Ernesto Sábato, Prologue to *Nunca Más,* translation by the author. *Supra* note 26, pp. 7–11.

29. Conversation with one of the members of the Buenos Aires Federal Criminal Appellate Court, Sept. 18, 1991.

30. Joel Feinberg, *On Doing and Deserving: Essays in the Theory of Responsibility* (Princeton, NJ: Princeton University Press, 1970), ch. 8.

31. *See* Marion Smiley, *Moral Responsibility and the Boundaries of Community: Power and Accountability from a Pragmatic Point of View* (Chicago: University of Chicago Press, 1992), p. 179.

32. Interview with Cavalry Army Colonel Federico Toranzo, Buenos Aires, Sept. 29, 1991. Colonel Toranzo reflected the opinion of 90 percent of his comrades.

33. I strongly believe in these two judges' commitment to their bench as much as in President Alfonsín's impartiality in their appointments, which they doubtlessly honored. The pressure at their posts, however, did not make their judicial careers attractive.

34. Julio B. Maier, *The Criminal Justice System Today: Between the Inquisition and the Composition,* unpublished manuscript.

35. Andres D'Alessio, "The Role of the Prosecutor in the Transition to Democracy in Latin America," in *The Transition to Democracy in Latin America: The Role of the Judiciary,* Irwin P. Stotzky, ed. (Boulder, CO: Westview Press, 1993), p. 187.

36. Before Menem's cashiering of the head of the administrative affairs' prosecutor in 1990, this official enjoyed life tenure for obvious reasons. The attorney general was by law a member of the Supreme Court and therefore also a tenured official. Menem, however, issued a decree removing Andres D'Alessio and appointing a political sidekick in his place, thus ending the life tenure of the attorney general.

37. In July 1992 Menem confronted a strike to improve the impoverished state of public education by stating that "subversion" had permeated the ranks of the protestors and that parents now supporting the dissent campaign should be wary that they might become the future Madres de Plaza de Mayo, striving to establish their children's whereabouts. (*See,* for instance, *Buenos Aires Herald,* July 10, 11, 12, 1992).

Chapter 13

Acknowledgments — This chapter was edited and translated from the Spanish by Helen Geffen Roht and Naomi Roht-Arriaza. Quotes from the Report of the Chilean National Commission are from the English translation of the Report, *infra* note 2.

1. The Commission was created by ministry of the interior decree 355, Apr. 25, 1990, published in the *Diario Oficial* (May 9, 1990). The Commission was established by presidential decree after opposition parties in the legislature indicated they would oppose a legislative commission.

2. Ministerio Grl. de Gobierno, *Report of the National Commission for Truth and Reconciliation* (Santiago, Chile, 1991) [hereinafter Report]. The English translation of the report was published in October 1993 by the Center for Civil and Human Rights, Notre Dame Law School. Several accounts of the Commission's work have appeared in English. In addition to the Introduction to the English version of the report, *see* Jose Zalaquett, "Balancing Ethical Imperatives and Political Constraints: The Dilemma of New Democracies Confronting Past Human Rights Violations," 43 *Hastings Law Journal* 1425 (1992); Jorge Correa S., "Dealing with Past Human Rights Violations: The Chilean Case after Dictatorship," 67 *Notre Dame Law Review* 1455 (1992); D. Weissbrodt and P.W. Fraser, "Report of the Chilean National Commission on Truth and Reconciliation," 14 *Human Rights Quarterly* 607 (1992).

3. Law 19.123 (Feb. 8, 1992).

4. Alejandro Gonzalez, "The Treatment of Victims and of Their Families: Rehabilitation, Reparation and Medical Treatment," in *Justice Not Impunity* (Geneva: International Commission of Jurists, 1993), pp. 323, 332.

5. Report, *supra* note 2, p. 6.

6. *Id.,* p. 30.

7. *Id.,* p. 31.

8. *Id.*

9. It is interesting to note that the February 1992 law creating the Corporation for Reparations and Reconciliation does distinguish between the families of the victims of human rights violations and the families of victims of political violence, although each receives the same benefits.

10. Report, *supra* note 2, pp. 34–35.

11. *Id.,* p. 9.

12. The law made an exception in the cases of Manuel Contreras and Pedro Espinoza. Contreras, a retired general and ex-head of the secret police (DINA), and Brigadier Espinoza, ex-operations chief of DINA and an active-duty army officer, were convicted in November 1993 for the 1976 murder of former foreign minister Orlando Letelier in the United States. Contreras was sentenced to seven years in prison and Espinoza to six; both have appealed. In large part due to continuing U.S. pressure to bring the culprits to justice, the amnesty decree excluded this crime, and in 1991 Judge Banados began his investigation. Although the sentences normally meted out for this type of crime are double those given to Contreras and Espinoza, the judge decided to reduce the sentence. *See, e.g.,* Julia Meehan, "Former Secret Police Chief to Appeal Jail Sentence," *Reuters,* Nov. 13, 1993. Other cases have fared less well. For example, in the case of Carmen Soria, a U.N. official and Spanish citizen tortured and killed in 1976, the government argued that the impact on Chile's foreign policy meant the amnesty should not be applied. After several appeals, an investigating judge was appointed, but that judge soon ruled that the amnesty applied and closed the case. *See* William R. Long, "Prosecution Barred in U.N. Official's Death," *Los Angeles Times,* Jan. 1, 1994, p. A6.

13. Report, *supra* note 2, p. 885.

14. *See, e.g., La Nacion,* Aug. 1, 1993, p. 8.

15. Chile has been a party to the International Covenant on Civil and Political Rights since 1972. While admittedly it was not a party to the American Convention on Human Rights at the time the violations in question took place, it was bound by similar obligations under the American Declaration of the Rights and Duties of Man. In any case, the continuing denial of judicial remedies created by the amnesty is a separate violation of the Convention, one that continues until today. *See* the discussion in Chapter 5.

16. The Argentine law is discussed in Chapter 12 and the Uruguayan law removing the state's power to prosecute in Chapter 11. For an extended treatment of both the *Velasquez* case and the Inter-American Commission's findings on the Uruguayan and Argentine laws, *see* Chapters 3 and 5.

17. The Supreme Court upheld the amnesty in 1990, in a case called *Insunza Bascunan*. It rejected equal protection arguments based on the fact that by excluding people who had been tried or condemned, in effect the main beneficiaries were the security forces. It then rejected arguments based on the Chilean Constitution's right to life provisions. The Court considered arguments that the amnesty violated Chile's international obligations under the Genocide Convention and the 1949 Geneva Conventions. It held that the Genocide Convention was inapplicable because Chilean criminal law did not include a specific crime of genocide, and that the Geneva Conventions were inapplicable because the acts subject to amnesty did not take place during an international or noninternational armed conflict. Finally, the Court *sua sponte* considered whether the International Covenant on Civil and Political Rights—which was ratified and became part of Chilean law in 1989— applied. It decided that the Covenant was inapplicable, because the acts subject to amnesty occurred before Chile became a party to the Covenant. It also held that the victims' right to compensation was not affected because civil remedies were still open to them, and it was up to the victim to decide how to obtain the necessary information without a criminal investigation. Corte Suprema de Chile, Aug. 24, 1990, *Insunza Bascunan, Ivan Sergio (recurso de inaplicabilidad), Revista de Derecho y Jurisprudencia y Gaceta de los Tribunales,* t. LXXXVII, No. 2, May–Aug. 1990, pp. 64–86.

18. The lower courts have continued to hear cases involving military and police abuses during the Pinochet years. One court eventually sentenced three former police officers to life imprisonment, and another three to shorter terms, for the notorious slaying of three human rights workers in 1985. *See* "Chile Court Raises Cut-Throat Sentences to Life," *Reuters,* Sept. 30, 1994. In July 1994, a lower court ordered the arrest of another ex-head of the DINA on charges of kidnapping and illicit association stemming from the forced disappearance of four political activists in 1975. The court held the amnesty did not apply to kidnapping because the offense continued until the victims' bodies were found. *See* Gustavo Gonzalez, "Chile: Another Trial Pits Civilian Courts Against Military," *Inter-Press Service,* July 12, 1994; "Chilean Ex-Colonel Arrested in Human Rights Case," *Reuters North American Wire,* July 10, 1994. Two active-duty army officers were also charged in the case. An intermediate appeals court in September 1994 denied a request by secret police agent Osvaldo Romo to dismiss charges against him under the amnesty law. The court found that the amnesty cannot apply to the killing of prisoners in violation of the Geneva Conventions. *See* "Court Punches Hole in 1978 Amnesty: 'State of War' Argument Backfires on its Authors," *Latin American Newsletters, Ltd.* 465, Oct. 13, 1994. How these cases will fare when they arrive at the Supreme Court is, however, another story. Prior cases leave little room for optimism.

19. Although the governing coalition won a majority in the Chamber of Deputies and 22 of 38 Senate seats, it remained a minority in the Senate given the existence of nine appointed senators. These appointed terms will eventually expire, and at that point legislative action may become more feasible—if the political will exists.

Chapter 14

1. Although Haiti enjoyed relative political stability under Jean-Pierre Boyer (1818–43), his methods were certainly not always just. *See* David Nicholls, *From Dessalines to Duvalier: Race, Colour and National Independence in Haiti,* (Cambridge, U.K.: Cambridge University Press, 1979), pp. 67–82. *See also* Michel-Rolph Trouillot, *Haiti–State Against Nation: The Origins and Legacy of Duvalierism* (New York: Monthly Review Press, 1990), pp. 47–50.

2. Although the occupation of Haiti by the United States stabilized the currency and briefly reduced administrative corruption, the overall effect of the occupation severely damaged Haiti in a variety of ways. *See* Trouillot, *supra* note 1, pp. 102–8.

3. *See, e.g.,* Charles R. Foster and Albert Valdman, eds., *Haiti–Today and Tomorrow: An Interdisciplinary Study* (Lanham, MD: University Press of America, 1984), pp. 255–56; Trouillot, *supra* note 1, pp. 100–4; Amy Wilentz, *The Rainy Season: Haiti Since Duvalier* (New York: Simon and Schuster, 1989), p. 77; Jonathan Power, "Haiti Still Has a Chance to Survive," *Calgary Herald,* Nov. 1, 1993, p. A4. For a more detailed account of the U.S. occupation of Haiti, *see* Hans Schmidt, *The United States Occupation of Haiti 1915–1934* (New Brunswick, N.J.: Rutgers University Press, 1971).

4. Interview with Cathy Maternowska (November 8, 1993), an anthropologist who lived in Haiti from 1985 to 1993. Maternowska worked extensively with the poor of Haiti and was instrumental in the preliminary attempts by the Aristide government to reform the nation.

5. *See* George DeWan, "Reigns of Terror," *Newsday,* Oct. 26, 1993, p. 24; "Haiti Coup Leader Sentenced to Life," *New York Times,* July 31, 1991, p. A5. *See generally,* Bernard Diederich and Al Burt, *Papa Doc: Haiti and Its Dictator* (Port-au-Prince, Haiti: Bodley Head, 1986); James Ferguson, *Papa Doc, Baby Doc: Haiti and the Duvaliers* (Oxford, UK: B. Blackwell, 1987), pp. 30–59.

6. DeWan, *supra* note 5, p. 24.

7. *See id.,* p. 25 (estimating the number as up to 60,000, with millions more exiled). *See also* Ferguson, *supra* note 5, p. 57.

8. Trouillot, *supra* note 1, pp. 213–14, 226.

9. *Id.,* pp. 175–77.

10. On January 22, 1971 the official gazette, *Le Moniteur,* carried the amendments that were to be voted on in the national referendum. One amendment included lowering the age for the presidency from forty to eighteen. The ballot stated that Jean-Claude had been chosen to succeed his father and listed two questions plus the answer:

Does this choice answer your aspirations? Do you ratify it?

Answer: yes. (*Le Moniteur,* Jan. 22, 1971).

The official count was 2,391,916 in favor and, of course, not a single vote opposed. *See, e.g.,* Diederich and Burt, *supra* note 5, p. 397.

11. Ferguson, *supra* note 5, pp. 60–89. The popular will had been expressed in other ways before 1990. In 1984, for example, there were food riots in Gonaives, where the masses attacked the warehouses of nine charitable organizations. This was the first mass demonstration against the regime. The 1987 Constitution was another expression of the popular will. Interview with Cathy Maternowska, *supra* note 4.

12. At least five different governments ruled the country until the election of Aristide. *See, e.g.,* Special Economic and Disaster Relief Assistance to Haiti: Note by the Secretary-General, p. 10, U.N. Doc. A/45/870/ADD.1 (1991) (report on mission).

13. Interview with Cathy Maternowska, *supra* note 4.

14. Steven Forester, "Haitian Asylum Advocacy: Questions to Ask Applicants and

Notes on Interviewing and Representation," 10 *New York Law School Journal of Human Rights* 351, 357 (1993).

15. *See* Americas Watch, The National Coalition for Haitian Refugees, and Caribbean Rights, "Haiti: The Aristide Government's Human Rights Record," Nov. 1, 1991 (pamphlet).

16. *See, e.g.,* Howard W. French, "Haitians Overwhelmingly Elect Populist Priest to the Presidency," *New York Times,* Dec. 18, 1990, p. A1; Lee Hockstader, "Haiti's Army Chiefs Defend Overthrow; OAS Delegation Holds 2nd Day of Talks," *Washington Post,* Oct. 6, 1991, p. A29.

17. *See, e.g.,* Forester, *supra* note 14, p. 359; Don A. Schanche, "Populist Priest Wins in Haiti, Is Backed by U.S.," *Los Angeles Times,* Dec. 18, 1990, p. A1; Human Rights Watch, *Human Rights Watch World Report 1992: Events of 1991,* (New York: Human Rights Watch, 1992), pp. 259–69.

Aristide actually received even greater popular support. Approximately 400,000 votes in his favor had to be nullified because the ballots were so complex that many of the illiterate people could not understand how to cast their votes. These people were, of course, Aristide supporters. Interview with Cathy Maternowska, *supra* note 4.

18. *See, e.g.,* Council of Freely-Elected Heads of Government, *The 1990 General Elections in Haiti* (Washington, DC: National Democratic Institute for International Affairs, 1991), pp. 87, 92. Similarly, both the United Nations and the OAS took leading roles in post-coup efforts to restore democracy in Haiti. So far their attempts have been tentatively successful. *See* Peter Hakim, "Saving Haiti from Itself: How a New OAS Effort Can Build Democracy," *Washington Post,* May 3, 1992, p. C1. *See also* Barbara Crossette, "Accord to Resume Constitutional Rule in Haiti Is Reported," *New York Times,* Nov. 16, 1991, p. 5.

19. For a useful account of the 1990 elections in Haiti, *see* Council of Freely-Elected Heads of Government, *supra* note 18; U.N., *supra* note 12.

20. 70 percent of Haiti's population is illiterate and desperately poor. *See, e.g.,* Howard W. French, "Haiti Premier's Installation Reflects Division of Rich and Poor," *New York Times,* June 21, 1992, p. 8. *Cf.* "Haitian Vote, So Bloody Before, Is Peaceful," *St. Louis Post-Dispatch,* Dec. 17, 1990, p. 1A (citing the illiteracy rate as high as 80 percent).

21. Pamela Constable, "For the U.S. No Choice but Optimism after Haiti Vote," *Boston Globe,* Dec. 23, 1990, p. 4. *See generally,* "Haitian Vote, So Bloody Before, Is Peaceful," *supra* note 20, p. 1A.

22. Kenneth Roth, "Haiti: The Shadows of Terror," *The New York Review of Books,* Mar. 26, 1992, pp. 62–63 (pointing out that Raoul Cédras, whom Aristide selected to head the Army, was credited with supervising the relatively peaceful December 1990 elections). This behavior directly contradicts claims by apologists for the military that the Army is nothing more than a coalition of competing gangs and that the military hierarchy is unable to control the actions of its subordinates.

23. *See, e.g.,* Howard W. French, "Troops Storming Palace, Capture Plotters and Free President," *New York Times,* Jan. 8, 1991, p. A1; "High Abstention in Second-Round Polls; At Stake Is Who Will Be Aristide's Prime Minister," *Latin America Weekly Report,* Jan. 31, 1991, p. 10.

24. This reign of terror has resulted in the deaths and torture of thousands of innocent people. *See, infra* note 34. The coup itself resulted in the death of at least thirty people. *See, e.g.,* "Haitian President Is Ousted; At Least Thirty Reported Killed as Army Troops Mutiny," *Chicago Tribune,* Oct. 1, 1991, p. 4.

25. Interview with Ira J. Kurzban (Nov. 8, 1993) attorney and adviser to President Aristide.

26. This was his inaugural address. *Haiti Progress,* a New York Haitian-language daily newspaper published the full text of his address on February 1, 1971. A copy of the address cannot be obtained because the newspaper did not keep a copy of it.

27. Interview with Ira J. Kurzban, *supra* note 25.

28. *Id.;* Roth, *supra* note 22, p. 62.

29. Interview with Ira J. Kurzban, *supra* note 25; interview with Cathy Maternowska, *supra* note 4.

30. Americas Watch, *supra* note 15.

31. Aristide replaced section chiefs with unarmed "communal police agents." These agents were under the supervision of the local judiciary. This action was in line with the requirement of the 1987 Constitution of putting police under civilian control and thereby separating police from control of the Army. Americas Watch, *Silencing a People: The Destruction of Civil Society in Haiti* (New York: Human Rights Watch, 1993), p. 104.

32. Interview with Ira J. Kurzban, *supra* note 25; interview with Cathy Maternowska, *supra* note 4.

33. Roth, *supra* note 22, pp. 62–63.

34. *La Plate-Forme des Organismes Haïtiens de Défense des Droits Humains* (The platform of Haitian Organizations for the Defense of Human Rights) documented 1,021 cases of extrajudicial executions from October 1991 to August 1992 and estimates the number of cases could be as high as 3,000. Memorandum to the OAS Commission to Haiti, Aug. 17, 1992, p. 3. Perhaps several thousand more Haitians have been murdered since that time, and thousands have been illegally arrested, detained, and tortured. Indeed, recent estimates suggest that over 4,000 people have been executed since the 1991 coup. A knowledgeable observer in Haiti estimates that between 200,000 and 400,000 people have also been forced into hiding. Interview with Cathy Maternowska, *supra* note 4. Indeed, even after the restoration of the democratic government, attachés continue to kill people, albeit at a reduced rate. One report cited 50 political murders in the month following Aristide's return. *See* Rachel L. Swarnes, "Haitian Kids, Alone at Base, Face Return in Three Months," *Miami Herald,* Jan. 6, 1995, p. 1A.

35. *See, e.g.,* "Haitian Troops Threaten Assembly," *St. Louis Post Dispatch,* Oct. 8, 1991, p. 1A.

36. Interview with Ira J. Kurzban, *supra* note 25; interview with Cathy Maternowska, *supra* note 4. The systematic seizure and torture of other democratically elected officials ensued as well. *See, e.g.,* Evans Paul, "A Mayor in Hiding Speaks Out," *Miami Herald,* Nov. 3, 1991, p. 1C.

37. "Macoutes Stand to Reap Benefit as Haiti Gives Political Pardons," *Florida Sun-Sentinel,* Dec. 26, 1991, p. 10A; interview with Ira J. Kurzban, *supra* note 25; interview with Cathy Maternowska, *supra* note 4.

38. *Id.*

39. *Id.*

40. For a detailed description of the attempt of the OAS to enforce the "Santiago Commitment to Democracy and the Renewal of the Inter-American System" in Haiti, *see* Stephen J. Schnably, "The Santiago Commitment as a Call to Democracy and Human Rights in the United States" (unpublished manuscript on file with Irwin P. Stotzky).

41. The Aristide government had long been urging a total trade embargo, including a boycott of travel into and out of Haiti. But the United States persistently refused to impose a total embargo. John Donnelly, "Haitian Army Leaders Snub Negotiations: More Sanctions Are Likely," *Miami Herald,* Nov. 6, 1993, p. 26A. Several months before the return of the elected government, the boycott became more serious. An Aristide adviser even suggested peppering Haiti with radio transmissions of speeches by President Aristide in the

hope of creating enough hostility in the citizenry to force the military leaders to step down. The United States finally provided President Aristide with the technology to send weekly addresses to the Haitian people. Haitian exiles in Montreal had an idea that went even farther: They called for a volunteer force of exiles to invade Haiti. In addition, they urged President Aristide to seek help from Canada and the United States to arm, train, and finance their group. "Haiti Envoy Flies to U.S. for Meetings," *Miami Herald,* Nov. 7, 1993, p. 26A.

The effects of the series of international embargoes since Aristide's ousting seemed to cause more hardship for the Haitian people than for the intended victims, the military leaders, and their supporters. *See, e.g.,* Kenneth Freed, "Next Step Haiti: A Society Burning with Sorrow," *Los Angeles Times,* Oct. 26, 1993, p. 1 (estimating that more than 10,000 people starved to death since the first international embargo went into effect in October 1991). *See also* Howard W. French, "Study Says Haiti Sanctions Kill Up to 1,000 Children a Month," *New York Times,* Nov. 9, 1993, p. A1 (estimating that as a result of the latest embargo an additional 1,000 Haitian children were dying each month).

42. *See* Howard W. French, "Haiti Talks Stall Over Amnesty for Coup Leaders," *New York Times,* Apr. 7, 1993, p. A11; Pamela Constable, "U.S. Readies for Return of Aristide," *Boston Globe,* Apr. 8, 1993, p. 1.

43. Howard W. French, "Two Rights Groups Protest Offer of an Amnesty in Haiti," *New York Times,* Apr. 16, 1993, p. A11. Americas Watch and the National Coalition for Haitian Refugees criticized U.N. and U.S. support for a blanket amnesty as contrary to international law. *Id.*

44. Howard W. French, "Haiti Army Leaders Reject Offer of Amnesty by Exiled President," *New York Times,* Apr. 17, 1993, p. A1.

45. *See* Agreement between President Jean-Bertrand Aristide and General Raoul Cédras, July 3, 1993, reprinted in *The Situation of Democracy and Human Rights in Haiti: Report of the Secretary General,* A/47/975, S/26063, July 12, 1993, pp. 2–3. *See also* Howard W. French, "Haitian Military Is Said to Accept Plan to End Crisis," *New York Times,* July 3, 1993, p. A1.

46. Governors Island Agreement, July 4, 1993, paragraphs 2, 3. It was also understood that Aristide would name a consensus prime minister. In addition, the confirmation of the prime minister would not take place until the matter of the election of nine new members to the Parliament in sham elections conducted by the military in January 1993 had been resolved.

47. *Id.,* paragraph 4.

48. *Id.,* paragraph 9.

49. *Id.,* paragraph 8.

50. Elaine Sciolino, "Haiti's Man of Destiny Awaiting His Hour," *New York Times,* Aug. 3, 1993, p. A1.

51. Governors Island Agreement, paragraph 7.

52. *Id.,* paragraph 5C.

53. *Id.,* paragraph 5B.

54. *Id.,* paragraph 6.

55. Aristide, on the other hand, lived up to every requirement of the agreement.

56. Yet international efforts to resolve the impasse continued. Garry Pierre-Pierre, "Haitian Talks End on a Hopeful Note," *New York Times,* Nov. 4, 1993, p. A6; John Donnelly, "New Round of Talks Tentatively Set," *Miami Herald,* Nov. 4, 1993, p. 19A. The most recent effort to revive the negotiations failed because Cédras refused to attend the planned meeting. *See, e.g.,* Donnelly, *supra* note 41, p. 1A; Garry Pierre-Pierre, "Effort to Save Haitian Accord Fails as Military Shuns Talks," *New York Times,* Nov. 6, 1993, p. A1.

57. *See, e.g.,* Joseph B. Treaster, "Drug Flow through Haiti Sharply Cut by Embargo," *New York Times,* Nov. 4, 1993, p. A6. Indeed, the military built a modern paved highway into the Dominican Republic to help avoid the embargo and to aid in its drug trade. *See, e.g.,* French, *supra* note 41, p. A6.

58. Cédras's actions had the effect of persuading the United States and the international community to make the embargo even more severe. Indeed, discussion of doing so had been going on since the coup. *See, e.g.,* Donnelly, *supra* note 41, p. 26A; *cf.* French, *supra* note 41, pp. A1, A6 (discussing the possibility of persuading other nations to follow the U.S. lead in freezing the overseas assets of leaders and supporters of the military government); Pierre-Pierre, *supra* note 56, pp. A1, A4 (doubting the effectiveness of freezing assets abroad, since the funds are believed to have been moved under other names).

59. *See* Christopher Marquis, "Clinton Freezes U.S. Assets of Haitians in Homeland," *Miami Herald,* June 23, 1994, p. 16A.

60. Most commercial air travel ended on June 24, 1994 at midnight as a result of the U.N. embargo. Air France, the last commercial airline servicing Haiti, ended all flights July 30, 1994 because of the Haitian government's decision to expel human rights observers. *See* Susan Benesch and Tim Johnson, "Today's Last French Flight Out Leaves Haiti Increasingly Isolated," *Miami Herald,* July 30, 1994, p. 22A; Andres Viglucci and Yves Colon, "The Door to Haiti Slams Shut," *Miami Herald,* June 25, 1994, p. 1A.

61. *See* Susan Benesch and Christopher Marquis, "Fuel Still Flows to Haiti from Dominican Republic," *Miami Herald,* June 22, 1994, p. 26A; John Kifner, "Balaguer Says He'll Enforce Curbs on Haiti," *New York Times,* June 30, 1994, p. 4.

62. The political pressure exerted against the Clinton administration by human rights groups was especially intense. The actions of one of the most prominent human rights activists, Randall Robinson, the executive director of TransAfrica, seems to have been very effective in causing Clinton to change his refugee policy. In the midst of intense media coverage, Robinson fasted for several weeks until the Clinton administration, apparently embarrassed by Robinson's actions, stopped repatriating Haitian refugees without an interview. *See* Bob Herbert, "Fasting for Haiti," *New York Times,* June 4, 1994, p. A15.

63. Originally, Panama, Suriname, Dominica, St. Lucia, and the Turks and Caicos Islands agreed to allow the Clinton administration to process Haitian refugees on their soil. However, three days after making this offer, Panamanian President Guillermo Endara rescinded it. Nevertheless, the Clinton administration's latest change in policy seems to have slowed the flow of Haitian refugees and significantly decreased the need for third-country processing.

64. *See* Richard P. Lyons, "U.N. Authorizes Invasion of Haiti to Be Led by U.S.," *New York Times,* Aug. 1, 1994, p. A1. Before the U.S. troops entered Haiti, President Artistide had been equivocal regarding an invasion. The exiled president publicly refused in August 1994 to support a military intervention to restore him to power, claiming that such an action would be unconstitutional. At the same time, however, he called for "swift and determined action" against the military government. *See* Christopher Marquis, "Aristide Rejects Invasion as U.S. Leans Toward One," *Miami Herald,* July 13, 1994, p. 8A; "Aristide Urges Action to Restore Democracy," *Miami Herald,* July 30, 1994, p. 26A.

65. Subsequent reports indicate that the size of the military is to be reduced from 7,000 to 1,500 men, and that several high-ranking officers have been reassigned. A number of groups and individuals within Haiti have called for complete abolition of the army. *See, e.g.,* Kathy Grey, "Haiti Grassroots Leaders Press for Army Banishment," *Reuters,* Dec. 29, 1994.

66. Subsequent reports on the amnesty law passed by the Haitian Parliament after President Aristide's return note that the amnesty covers political crimes only, leaving open

the possibility of prosecutions for common crimes or international crimes. The amnesty law also leaves considerable discretion to President Aristide to decide whether to proceed with prosecutions. In addition, it calls for the creation of a "truth commission" to hear complaints, gather evidence, and convey it to the criminal justice system if warranted. *See, e.g.,* Rogers Worthington, "Haiti Mobs Settling Old Scores: Vigilantes Kill, Burn Out Allies of Military," *Chicago Tribune,* Oct. 18, 1994, p. 8.

67. Steven Greenhouse, "Aristide Is Angered by Amnesty Pledge to Haitian Military," *New York Times,* Sept. 20, 1994, p. A6, col. 6.

68. Crises of this magnitude would surely and unavoidably lead to the destruction of any nascent democratic system. Yet before the intervention of the U.S. military, the brutal dictatorship in Haiti appeared to grow stronger with each passing day. This clearly shows the force of the repression in Haiti and its intractable staying power.

69. *See, e.g.,* Howard W. French, "Power Means Brutality; Practice Makes Perfect," *New York Times,* Oct. 17, 1993, p. E1.

70. The concept of corporatism refers to two distinct situations. In the traditional sense, corporatism refers to the control exercised by the state over organizations and interest groups. The more technical meaning, usually used in the political arena, refers to the contrary phenomena: where these same organizations and interest groups acquire considerable influence and exert persistent pressure against state decision makers. *See generally,* J. Malloy, ed., *Authoritarianism and Corporatism in Latin America* (Pittsburgh, PA: University of Pittsburgh Press, 1977).

71. The Catholic Church has played both a positive and a negative role in the life of Haiti. The organized Church has been siding with the military. Indeed, the Vatican is the only nation that recognized the political legitimacy of the military coup. *See, e.g.,* Alan Cowell, "Aristide Has Long Posed Problem for Vatican," *New York Times,* Oct. 28, 1993, p. A4. *But see* "Friendship and Solidarity Visit by Aristide," *European Report,* Oct. 30, 1991, p. 5. On the other hand, local churches have nurtured popular groups in the rural areas.

72. For a comprehensive look at the role of the judiciary and the rule of law in the transition to democracy, *see* Irwin P. Stotzky, ed., *Transition to Democracy in Latin America: The Role of the Judiciary* (Boulder, CO: Westview Press, 1993).

73. Constitution of the Republic of Haiti.

74. Haiti's court system is based on the Napoleonic Code that was in effect in France almost 200 years ago.

75. For example, Haiti ratified the American Convention on Human Rights on September 14, 1977 by a declaration signed by Jean-Claude Duvalier.

76. A U.N. special expert concluded in 1988 that

> The ordinary system of justice, organized along traditional lines . . . did not play its role. The cases of torture, ill treatment, and arbitrary detentions led to practically no checks on its part, no arrests, no proper investigations. . . . The independence of the judicial authorities is not safeguarded and their powers are very restricted . . . [T]hey have been unable to clear up any of the numerous crimes committed during the past few years. F. Texier, "Advisory Services in the Field of Human Rights," E/CN.4/1989/40, [Feb. 6, 1989] paragraphs 89, 48.

77. For example, article 263 of the Haitian Constitution requires the separation of the police from the military, but the police during the coup era remained under control of the Army. In the rural areas, section chiefs, charged with performing police duties, were little more than gang leaders who reported to military officials rather than to civilian authorities. These chiefs possessed absolute power in the region and were immune from civilian con-

trol. They imposed arbitrary taxes, maintained private armies, and arrested and murdered people. Some chiefs even maintained their own private prisons. Haitian prisons were also controlled by the military. Prison conditions clearly continue to constitute severe and systematic violations of Haitian law and international standards: There is overcrowding, the food is poor, and prisoners lack access to water, medical care, and legal counsel.

78. Lawyers Committee for Human Rights, *Paper Laws, Steel Bayonets: Breakdown of the Rule of Law in Haiti* (New York: Lawyers Committee for Human Rights, 1990), p. 1.

79. Carlos S. Nino used this term in describing this phenomenon in Argentina. *See, generally,* Nino, *Un País al Margen de la Ley* (Argentina, Emece Editores, 1992).

80. Hannah Arendt, *The Human Condition,* pbk. ed. (Chicago: University of Chicago Press, 1958), p. 241.

81. *Id.*

82. For example, the defenses raised by the perpetrators, such as self-defense, necessity, and so forth, raise these questions.

83. There are, of course, other moral, political, and legal concerns that, while central to human rights trials in general, are less pressing in Haiti.

84. In any case, even if these acts cannot be directly attributed to the state, the state is still responsible for not adequately investigating and prosecuting them.

85. Decree of Dec. 17, 1994 (on file with author).

Chapter 15

1. *See* U.N. Secretary-General Boutros Boutros-Ghali, *Agenda for Peace,* U.N. Doc. A/47/277, June 17, 1992.

2. Venezuelan jurist Dr. Pedro Nikken was the United Nations' adviser on human rights during the peace negotiations and subsequently the United Nations' Independent Expert on the Situation of Human Rights in El Salvador. His mandate, established in Resolution 1992/62 of March 3, 1992, included examining the effects of the peace agreements on the effective enjoyment of human rights and investigating the manner in which both parties apply the recommendations made by the U.N. Observer Mission in El Salvador and the Commissions established during the negotiating process. Nikken was a member of the Inter-American Human Rights Court when the *Velasquez Rodriguez* case was heard and decided. Truth Commission member Thomas Buergenthal was the president of the Inter-American Human Rights Court during that period. The 1988 decision of the Inter-American Human Rights Court was critical in defining the state's obligation to guarantee human rights.

3. *See* Commission on the Truth, *From Madness to Hope* (San Salvador, Mar. 15, 1993, reprinted Report of the Sec. Grl. S/25500, "Truth Commission Report," pp. 148–168; Americas Watch, *Violations of Fair Trial Guarantees by the FMLN's Ad Hoc Courts, May 1990* (New York: Americas Watch, 1990).

4. The Truth Commission Report confirmed that the governing ARENA party's founder masterminded the killing of the archbishop. *See* Truth Commission Report, *supra* note 3, pp. 127–131.

5. *Id.* p. 132.

6. An earlier commission had been set up to investigate five well-known cases. The cases included (1) the murder of Archbishop Romero; (2) the January 1981 murder of two U.S. agrarian reform advisers and the head of the Salvadoran agrarian reform institute in the Sheraton Hotel; (3) the disappearance and murder of U.S. journalist John Sullivan in December 1980; (4) the killing of various people by civil defensemen in the Armenia area in 1981, known as the Armenia "well" case; (5) and the Las Hojas massacre in which at

least sixteen peasants were killed in a combined Civil Defense and Army operation. Only in the "Sheraton" case was anyone convicted, and after years of U.S. pressure and assistance, only the triggermen faced trial. Efforts to prosecute officers involved in the case and civilians reportedly involved in the planning were thwarted at every turn. The uncle of one of the officers sat on the Supreme Court. In late 1991 thirteen civil defensemen were finally tried and acquitted in the Armenia "well" case. Prosecutors cited the jurors' proximity to the defendants and the military presence outside the courtroom as intimidating factors. In late 1987 the Supreme Court quashed efforts to proceed against at least one of the officers reportedly involved in the Romero killing when it voided an extradition effort and rejected new testimony on the case. Efforts by the attorney general's office to proceed in the Las Hojas case in 1987 were abruptly halted by the application of a broad amnesty law, *see infra* note 65, whereas no progress was ever made in the Sullivan case. The commission was soon disbanded.

7. *See* Lawyers Committee for Human Rights, *Underwriting Injustice: AID and El Salvador's Judicial Reform Program* (New York: Lawyers Committee, 1989), for a thorough critique of the Commission to Investigate Criminal Acts.

8. Truth Commission Report, *supra* note 3, p. 184. The United Nations' Independent Expert and ONUSAL have also called for the dissolution of the Commission. Instead, however, it was incorporated wholesale into the new civilian police force.

9. An amendment introduced by Sen. Arlen Specter (R. Pa.) and Rep. Clarence D. Long (D. Md.) blocked $21 million (one-third) of one of President Reagan's supplemental requests for military aid for El Salvador until the Salvadoran government obtained convictions in the churchwomen's case. Act of Nov. 14, 1983, Pub. L. No. 98–151, 97 Stat. 970 (1983). In the Jesuit case Congress passed a provision calling for the suspension of all military aid to El Salvador if the President were to determine that the Salvadoran government had failed to conduct a thorough and professional investigation of the Jesuit murders.

10. One of these cases, resolved before the presidential commission was formed, involved the murder of four U.S. churchwomen in December 1980. The other was the January 1981 killing of two U.S. agrarian reform advisers and the Salvadoran head of the Agrarian Reform Institute. Pressure by the United States, including the conditioning of $21 million on a conviction in the churchwomen's case, led to the May 1984 conviction of five former national guardsmen. Those who might have given the order to kill the four women and the officers who covered up the crime were never investigated. *See* Truth Commission Report, pp. 62–66. In the Sheraton case, the persistence of AIFLD, the AFL-CIO–linked American Institute for Free Labor Development, which assigned a full-time investigator to the agrarian reform murders, ultimately resulted in the conviction of the triggermen, two former members of the national guard. Those who planned the killings, gave the orders and covered up the crime, including several officers known to be involved in death squad activities, were never tried. *See* Truth Commission Report, *supra* note 3, pp. 144–147.

11. *See* U.S. Department of State, *Country Reports on Human Rights Practices for 1991* (1992), p. 598.

12. *See, generally,* Lawyers Committee for Human Rights, *El Salvador: Human Rights Dismissed, a Report on Sixteen Unresolved Cases, 1986* (New York: Lawyers Committee and Human Rights Watch, 1986); Lawyers Committee for Human Rights, *Underwriting Injustice: AID and El Salvador's Judicial Reform Program* (New York: Lawyers Committee, 1989); A. DeWind and D. Kass, *Justice in El Salvador: A Report of a Mission of Inquiry of the Association of the Bar of the City of New York,* 38 Rec. A. B. City N.Y. 112,129 (1983).

13. *See, generally,* Martha Doggett, *Death Foretold: The Jesuit Murders in El Salvador* (Washington, DC: Lawyers Committee for Human Rights and Georgetown Univer-

sity Press, 1993). The Truth Commission's report subsequently confirmed that members of the High Command and other ranking officers planned and ordered the murders as well as orchestrating the coverup. Truth Commission Report, *supra* note 3, pp. 45–54.

14. Truth Commission Report, p. 51.

15. *See El Proceso por el Asesinato de los Sacerdotes Jesuitas en El Salvador,* Informe del Observador Eduardo Luis Duhalde, Asociación Americana de Juristas, p. 78; Amnesty International, *El Salvador Army Officers Sentenced to 30 Years for Killing Jesuit Priests,"* AMR 37/WU 01/92 a 5 (Feb. 7, 1992); *Informe sobre el proceso judicial por los asesinatos de Seis Jesuitas y dos Colaboradoras en El Salvador,* unpublished report prepared by José María Tamarit for Ministry of Foreign Affairs of Spain, pp. 19–20 (1991). Report to the Lawyers Committee for Human Rights on the Jesuit Murder Trial by Robert Kogod Goldman, Appendix C to *Chronicle of Death Foretold, supra* note 13, pp. 344–346; International Commission of Jurists, *A Breach of Impunity, the Trial for the Murder of Jesuits in El Salvador, Report of the Observer for Latin America of the International Commission of Jurists* (New York: Fordham University Press, 1992), pp. 71–73.

16. The agenda for the negotiations was established in the Caracas Agreement of May 21, 1990. Agreements were to be reached in the following areas: armed forces, human rights, judicial system, electoral system, constitutional reform, economic and social issues, and verification by the United Nations. *See* United Nations, *El Salvador Agreements: The Path to Peace* (New York: United Nations, 1992), p. 4.

17. Signed July 26, 1990, in San José, Costa Rica; *Path to Peace, id.,* pp. 7–12.

18. When the war started, El Salvador had already ratified a number of international instruments, including the International Covenant on Civil and Political Rights, the American Convention on Human Rights, and Protocol II to the Geneva Conventions of 1949.

19. *Id.,* art. 1, p. 8.

20. *Id.,* art. 11, p. 9.

21. *Id.,* art. 15, p. 11.

22. *See, generally,* Americas Watch, *El Salvador — Peace and Human Rights: Successes and Shortcomings of the United Nations Observer Mission in El Salvador (ONUSAL),* Sept. 2, 1992; Lawyers Committee for Human Rights, *El Salvador's Negotiated Revolution: Prospects for Legal Reform* (New York: Lawyers Committee, June 1993), pp. 40–50.

23. Twelfth Report of the Director of the Human Rights Division of the United Nations Observer Mission in El Salvador (ONUSAL) covering the period from 1 July to 30 Sept. 1994. U.N. Doc. A/49/585, S/1994/1220, Oct. 31, 1994, p. 7.

24. Americas Watch, *El Salvador: Accountability and Human Rights* (New York: Americas Watch, 1993) p. 8.

25. *Path to Peace, supra* note 16, Chapultepec Agreements, Chapter I.Armed Forces.3 Purification.G, E.

26. The Commission was granted an additional month to complete its work.

27. The exact number of officers involved became known only when the United Nations published a January 7, 1993 letter from U.N. Secretary-General Boutros Boutros-Ghali to the Security Council. U.N. doc. S/25078, Jan. 9, 1993.

28. *See, generally,* Lawyers Committee for Human Rights, *El Salvador's Negotiated Revolution: Prospects for Legal Reform, supra* note 22, pp. 53–56.

29. *See, generally, id.,* pp. 53–62.

30. A letter of November 11, 1992 from the U.N. secretary-general to the Security Council indicated that the president had agreed to carry out the Ad Hoc recommendations within a specific time frame. Although not spelled out in the secretary-general's letter, the Ad Hoc Commission's decisions were to be incorporated into the year-end "general order"

of military promotions and retirements. *See* Lawyers Committee for Human Rights, *El Salvador's Negotiated Revolution, supra* note 22, p. 55.

31. Letter from U.N. Secretary-General Boutros Boutros-Ghali to the Security Council, Jan. 7, 1993, note 32.

32. Lawyers Committee for Human Rights, *El Salvador's Negotiated Revolution, supra* note 22, p. 61. Ponce publicly offered his resignation to the president three days prior to publication of the Truth Commission Report, blasting the United States for suspending military aid pending compliance with the Ad Hoc Commission Report. His resignation was not immediately accepted, however, and he remained in office until July 1, 1993.

33. Constitutional reforms limited the role of the armed forces and called for the establishment of a national civil police independent of the armed forces and under the authority of a different ministry. The final Chapultepec Agreements included an extensive chapter on the armed forces, which addressed Doctrinal Principles of the Armed Forces, separating national defense from public security and emphasizing that the armed forces' mission of defending the sovereignty of the state and the integrity of its territory is inseparable from democratic values and strict respect for all parts of the Constitution. *Path to Peace, supra* note 16, p. 47. The peace accords also called for major reform in the army's educational system, including the incorporation of civilians in the military academy's academic council. State intelligence responsibilities were to be transferred to the Executive. The accords called for dismantling paramilitary bodies such as civil defense patrols. The president was authorized to name a civilian defense minister. Any appointee was to be "fully committed to observing the peace agreements." *Path to Peace, supra* note 16, p. 55. Preventive and Promotional Measures called for supervision of armed forces operations by the legislative assembly; effective functioning of the Armed Forces General Inspectorate; creation of an armed forces court of honor to try acts contrary to military honor (without prejudice to the requirement that soldiers who violate the law must be brought before the regular courts).

34. *See* Mexico Agreements of April 27, 1991; *Path to Peace, supra* note 16, p. 29.

35. Chapultepec Agreements, Chapter I, Armed Forces, §5 End to Impunity; *Path to Peace, supra* note 16, p. 53.

36. In contrast, the question of amnesty for the perpetrators of human rights violations was not directly addressed in the peace accords. The two amnesties granted in the wake of the accords are discussed below.

37. *Path to Peace, supra* note 16, p. 31. (Truth Commission Agreement, Undertaking by the Parties)

38. Truth Commission Report, *supra* note 3, p. 175.

39. Douglass W. Cassel, Jr., "International Truth Commissions and Justice," *The Aspen Institute Quarterly,* Summer 1993, p. 5. Professor Cassel was one of three special advisers to the Truth Commission. For another fascinating "insider's" view of the Commission's work, *see* Thomas Buergenthal, "The United Nations Truth Commission for El Salvador," 27 *Vanderbilt Journal of Transnational Law* 497 (1994).

40. Truth Commission Report, *supra* note 3, p. 4.

41. Truth Commission Report, p. 25.

42. Americas Watch, *El Salvador: Accountability and Human Rights, supra* note 23, pp. 12–13.

43. Truth Commission Agreement, Powers; *Path to Peace, supra* note 16, p. 30.

44. *Id.,* p. 24.

45. *Id.,* p. 13.

46. COPAZ, the Commission to Consolidate Peace, was established in the peace accords to oversee and participate in the implementation of the peace agreements. It was

composed of two representatives from the government and the FMLN and one representative from each of the political parties.

47. Informe No. 26/92, Case N. 10.287, Sept. 24, 1992, cited in Truth Commission Report, *supra* note 3, pp. 80–81. For a full discussion, *see* Chapter 5.

48. *See, e.g.,* Americas Watch, *El Salvador: Accountability and Human Rights, supra* note 23, pp. 27–29.

49. Channel 12, television interview, Mar. 19, 1993, as cited in El Rescate, *Report from El Salvador,* 4:11.

50. Tracy Wilkinson, "A Matter of Justices," *Los Angeles Times,* Mar. 23, 1993.

51. Interview, JSU radio, Mar. 20, 1993, as quoted in El Rescate, *Report from El Salvador, supra* note 49.

52. Posición de la Fuerza Armada de El Salvador ante el Informe de la Comisión de la Verdad, Mar. 23, 1993, published in *Diario de Hoy* (San Salvador), Mar. 24, 1993.

53. Resolution of the Supreme Court of Justice, Mar. 22, 1993, signed by all fourteen members of the Court.

54. Americas Watch, *El Salvador: Accountability and Human Rights, supra* note 23.

55. Tracy Wilkinson, "Salvadoran Leader Blasts UN Report," *Los Angeles Times,* Mar. 19, 1993.

56. Interview on Channel 2 television, San Salvador, Apr. 14, 1993.

57. Universidad Centroamericana José Simeón Cañas, Instituto Universitario de Opinion Publica, *Boletín de Prensa,* "La Opinión de los Salvadoreños sobre la Comisión de la Verdad," Año VIII, No. 2.

58. Critics ranged from military officers who said it was unfair to blame them without also naming the persons who gave them orders; members of the judiciary who felt that the report's harsh criticisms of the administration of justice were disproportionate when those who financed the death squads had not been named; members of the political opposition, including the FMLN, who worried that death squad involvement by those in the governing party had not been sufficiently exposed.

59. *See* Lawyers Committee for Human Rights, *El Salvador's Negotiated Revolution: Prospects for Legal Reform, supra* note 22, p. 72.

60. In late 1993, the State Department, the Defense Department, and the Central Intelligence Agency released more than 12,000 documents that reportedly provided "powerful evidence that the Reagan and Bush Administrations" continued to work with right-wing leaders in El Salvador despite having collected detailed information about assassinations they conducted. *See* Clifford Krauss, "U.S., Aware of Killings, Worked with Salvador's Rightists, Papers Suggest," *New York Times,* Nov. 9, 1993. *See also* Buergenthal, *supra* note 39, pp. 507–10, for a description of the Commission's difficulties obtaining U.S. information.

61. The panel, composed of two retired career ambassadors and two academic advisers, to "examine the implications of the U.N.-sponsored El Salvador Truth Commission report for the conduct of U.S. foreign policy and the operations of the Department of State," praised the State Department for its efforts to advance human rights in El Salvador, while limiting its criticisms to specific actions. U.S. Department of State, "Report of the Secretary of State's Panel on El Salvador," Washington, D.C., July 1993. For a critique of this report, *see* Americas Watch, *El Salvador: Accountability and Human Rights, supra* note 23, pp. 33–36. "Estados Unidos Conocía La Violencia en El Salvador," commentary in 534–35 *Estudios Centroamericanos* 420 (April/May 1993).

62. *Diario Latino* (San Salvador), Mar. 18, 1993.

63. Legislative Decree 486, Mar. 20, 1993, published in *Diario Oficial* 318(56), Mar. 22, 1993.

64. The U.S. government maintained that, because of the protected diplomatic status of the victims, amnesty should not be granted to those persons convicted for the 1985 "Zona Rosa" murders of four U.S. Marines and nine civilians, and to those persons awaiting trial for the killing of two U.S. military advisers after rebel fire brought down their helicopter in January 1991. Amnesty was denied in the Zona Rosa case, as it had been after the 1987 amnesty, but was granted to the two FMLN members imprisoned in the more recent case because the victims were found not to have had diplomatic status in El Salvador when the incident occurred. Amnesty was again denied to the convicted killers of four U.S. church-women because the court held that their conviction had been for a common rather than a political crime.

65. Legislative Decree 147, Jan. 23, 1992, *Diario Oficial* 314(14), Jan. 23, 1992. An earlier, broad amnesty law had been passed in 1987 as part of El Salvador's effort to com-ply with the regional Esquipulas II peace effort spearheaded by Costa Rican President Oscar Arias. Conceived as a mechanism to create a political opening by pardoning govern-ment opponents, the Salvadoran version was drafted so broadly that it allowed judges to apply it to state agents as well as to political prisoners allied with the FMLN.

66. The San José Agreement on Human Rights provided that during the course of the negotiations, appropriate legal procedures and timetables would be determined for the release of individuals imprisoned for political reasons (art. 3). The Chapultepec Agree-ments included a chapter on political participation by the FMLN, which called for the "adoption of legislative or other measures needed to guarantee former FMLN combatants the full exercise of their civil and political rights, with a view to their reintegration, within a framework of full legality, into the civil, political, and institutional life of the country." These measures were to be adopted in the two-week period between the signing of the Chapultepec Agreements (Jan. 16, 1992) and the initiation of the formal cease-fire (Feb. 1, 1992). The agreements further provided for the release of all political prisoners within thirty days of the initiation of the cease-fire period and full guarantees and security for the return of exiles, war-wounded, and other persons outside the country for reasons related to the armed conflict within forty days of the cease-fire.

67. Legislative Decree 147, art. 6.

68. United Nations, Report of the Secretary General on the United Nations Observer Mission in El Salvador, U.N. Doc. S/25812/Add.1, May 24, 1993.

69. Instituto Universitario de Opinión Pública, Universidad Centroamericana José Simeón Cañas, *Boletín de Prensa,* Año VII, No. 2, July 14, 1993.

70. Amnesty International, *El Salvador: Peace without Justice* (New York: Amnesty International, June 1993) p. 9.

71. Inter-American Commission on Human Rights, Report on the Situation of Human Rights in El Salvador, OEA/ser.L/V/II.85 Doc. 28 rev., Feb. 11, 1994, p. 77.

72. The nongovernmental Human Rights Commission of El Salvador filed a petition with the Supreme Court on April 21, 1993, while Socorro Jurídico Cristiano "Archbishop Oscar A. Romero," and the Human Rights Institute of the Central American University filed another petition on May 11, 1993.

73. Decree 485, art. 2.

74. Article 130, 26º of the Constitution authorizes the legislature to decree amnesty for political crimes, common crimes connected to political crimes, or common crimes commit-ted by twenty persons or more.

75. Salvadoran Constitution, art. 241.

76. Article 244 of the Constitution prohibits granting amnesty to public or military officials who violated the Constitution during the same presidential period the crime was committed.

77. Resolution of the Salvadoran Supreme Court, May 20, 1993. While ignoring the petitioners' international law arguments, the Court cited Additional Protocol II to the Geneva Conventions (art. 6, no. 5) to support the granting of the broadest possible amnesty to persons who took part in the armed conflict or who have been deprived of liberty, interned, or detained for reasons related to the armed conflict.

78. United Nations, "Report of the Secretary-General on the United Nations Observer Mission in El Salvador," S/25812/Add.3, May 25, 1993, p. 3.

79. Letter from President Cristiani to U.N. Secretary-General Boutros-Ghali, dated July 13, 1993, as cited in Further Report of the Secretary-General of the United Nations: Observer Mission in El Salvador, U.N. Doc. S/26581, Oct. 14, 1993.

80. U.S. Embassy Report, San Salvador, July 1993: Status on Compliance with the Truth Commission Recommendations.

81. Further Report of the Secretary-General, *supra* note 78, p. 6.

82. Doyle McManus, "Worried Over Political Slayings, U.S. Sends Top Diplomat to El Salvador," *Los Angeles Times,* Nov. 11, 1993.

83. Report of the Joint Group for the Investigation of Politically Motivated Illegal Armed Groups in El Salvador, July 28, 1994, Annex to U.N. Doc. S/1994/989, Oct. 22, 1994.

84. *See, e.g.,* Tracy Wilkinson, "Salvador Civilian Police Facing Uphill Struggle," *Los Angeles Times,* Nov. 15, 1993.

85. ONUSAL, Twelfth Report of the Director, *supra* note 23.

86. Instituto Universitario de Opinion Publica, Universidad Centroamericana José Simeón Cañas, *Boletín de Prensa* Año VII, No. 2, July 14, 1993. 22.7 percent of the persons polled said impunity had decreased, while 18.4 percent thought it was worse.

Chapter 16

Acknowledgments — The section on Nepal was written by Rishikesh Shaha, founder and member of the Human Rights Organization of Nepal (HURON). Mr. Shaha has been Nepal's representative at the United Nations, its ambassador to the United States, and the head of the Nepal section of Amnesty International. He is the author of many books on Nepalese society and politics. I am deeply indebted to him for his participation in this project.

1. Emmanuel Decaux, "International Law and National Experiences," in International Commission of Jurists et al., *Justice Not Impunity* (Geneva: International Commission of Jurists, 1992), pp. 27, 49.

2. For a full description of the Commission and its work, *see* Joan Kakwenzire, "Identification and Investigation Methods," in International Commission of Jurists, *Justice Not Impunity, supra* note 1, p. 123.

3. Commission of Inquiry Act, Legal Notice No. 5 of 1986, May 16, 1986.

4. Agence France Presse, "Former Idi Amin Minister Sentenced to Death in Uganda," June 11, 1993.

5. Mahamat Hassan Abakar, "Investigating Commissions on Human Rights Violations: The Case of Chad," in *Justice Not Impunity, supra* note 1, p. 141.

6. *See* BBC, "Central Africa: Chad: Inquiry Commission Names People It Says Were Responsible for Massacres," May 5, 1993.

7. *See, e.g.,* "Mali's Ex-Ruler Condemned," *Washington Post,* Feb. 13, 1993.

8. "Mali's Democracy, Begun in Bloodshed, Completes Orderly Transition," *Africa News,* June 22, 1992.

9. "Mali: Death Sentence on Former President and Other Officials Upheld," British

Broadcasting Corporation, BBC Summary.of World Broadcasts, May 21, 1993; "Officials of Traore Regime Released on Bail," BBC Summary of World Broadcasts, Jan. 21, 1994.

10. *See Foreign Broadcast Information Service* (FBIS-AFR) for Feb. 5, 1992.

11. Human Rights Watch/Africa, *Ethiopia: Reckoning Under the Law* (New York: HRW/Africa, Dec. 1994), p. 11.

12. *Id.,* pp. 13–14. Human rights groups have expressed concern that whatever benefits are to be gained by the SPO's work are being seriously undermined by the delays in charging.

13. *Id.,* p. 19.

14. *See The Economist,* London, July 30, 1994.

15. Human Rights Watch/Africa, *supra* note 11, p. 27.

16. *See* Africa Watch, *Ethiopia, Waiting for Justice: Shortcomings in Establishing the Rule of Law* (New York: Human Rights Watch/Africa, May 8, 1992).

17. *See, generally,* A. C. Brackman, *The Other Nuremberg: The Untold Story of the Tokyo War Crimes Trials* (New York: Morrow, 1987).

18. *See* Arthur E. Tiedemann, "Japan Sheds Dictatorship," in *From Dictatorship to Democracy,* John H. Herz, ed. (Westport, CT: Greenwood Press, 1982), p. 198.

19. James Sterngold, "Seoul Women Protest Offer by Japanese on War Sex," *New York Times,* Sept. 1, 1994, p. 11, col. 6.

20. *See* "Case Concerning Trial of Pakistani Prisoners of War (*Pak. v. India*)," 1973 International Court of Justice *Pleadings,* pp. 3–7. *See, generally,* J. Paust and A. Blaustein, "War Crimes Jurisdiction and Due Process: The Bangladesh Experience," 11 *Vanderbilt Journal of Transitional Law* 1 (1978); Bassiouni, *Crimes Against Humanity in International Criminal Law,* (Dordrecht, Netherlands: M. Nijhoff, 1992), pp. 228–30.

21. In the district of Baglung more than 500 people were arrested following the murder of a police inspector in January 1992. Although most were quickly released, ten were kept incommunicado for between thirty and fifty-five days. When they finally appeared in court, all ten alleged that they had been tortured in the presence of senior police officers and in two cases, before the prosecutor, to make them sign false confessions. Human rights groups called for an investigation, but to no avail.

22. For example, a nineteen-year-old student was killed by police in July 1991 during a public protest. Although opposition legislators found a possible case of extrajudicial execution, no investigation followed. In April 1992 seven more people were killed by police.

Chapter 17

1. Executive Order No. 8, Malacañang, Manila, Mar. 18, 1986.

2. *Id.*

3. *See, e.g.,* Virginia Leary et al., *The Philippines: Human Rights after Martial Law* (Geneva: International Commission of Jurists, 1984), p. 116–23.

4. Executive Order No. 163, President Corazon Aquino, Malacañang, Manila, May 5, 1987.

5. Quoted in Fe An Taro, *Human Rights: The Philippine Perspective* (Manila: 1991), pp. 37–38.

6. *Id.*

7. John J. Carroll, "Deaths That Should Outrage Us," *Manila Chronicle,* Oct. 5, 1986, p. 4.

8. *See* Alberto T. Muyot, "The Human Rights Situation under the Aquino Government," 1986–91, Part I, *Philippines Human Rights Monitor* 5(3) (Manila, Mar. 1992), p. 29.

9. *Id.,* p. 43.

10. Presidential Decree No. 1886, Ferdinand E. Marcos, Malacañang, Manila, Oct. 14, 1983.

11. For a complete account of the board's proceedings, *see Reports of the Fact-Finding Board on the Assassination of Senator Benigno S. Aquino Jr.* (Manila, 1984).

12. *Id.,* p. 61.

13. Many of Enrile's security aides had belonged to the Reform the Armed Forces Movement (RAM), the clandestine group in the military that started in the early 1980s to plot the overthrow of Marcos. Coming from the ranks of the best and the brightest in the military, these RAM officers, mostly lieutenant colonels, while becoming disenchanted with Marcos, were part of the "torture apparatus" in the martial law regime. RAM personalities like Rodolfo Aguinaldo and Billy Bibit were dreaded in the military. Other officers in their league were reported to be notorious human rights violators. After the 1986 revolution they came back with a vengeance. They were led by Colonel Gregorio "Gringo" Honasan, chief security aide to Enrile.

14. Between March 1986 and September 1991, 167 people had been "salvaged" (the Filipino term for summary execution), and 2,756 had been tortured among persons arrested for political offenses. *See* Muyot, *supra* note 8, p. 9. During the same period, there were 171 massacres in which 746 persons were killed and 297 wounded. These were mostly in Mindanao, but the Visayas and Luzon regions also had their share of various forms of human rights excesses by military and paramilitary elements. In Cagayan Valley there were 236 political arrests, 34 "salvage" victims, and another 27 killings for no apparent reason during 1986 alone. *See* Northern Luzon Human Rights Organization, *1986 Human Rights Report* (Manila: TFDP, 1987), p. 5. This unabated pattern of killings was basically a function of the fact that instead of being dismantled, the notorious bastions of abuse, such as the paramilitary Civilian Home Defense Forces (CHDF), were retained and renamed Citizen Armed Force Geographical Units (CAFGU). These units and the vigilante groups that mushroomed in 1987–88 exacerbated the human rights problem inherited by the Aquino government.

15. *See* Lawyers Committee for Human Rights: *Impunity: Prosecutions of Human Rights Violations in the Philippines* (1991); *Militia Abuses in the Philippines (1990)*; *Vigilantes in the Philippines: A Threat to Democratic Rule* (1988); and *Lawyers Under Fire: Attacks on Human Rights Attorneys in the Philippines* (1988).

16. Lawyers Committee, *Impunity, supra* note 15.

17. *Id.*

18. These figures were compiled by Alberto Muyot of the College of Law, University of the Philippines, from records at the Commission on Human Rights. The total of 7,944 complaints includes 1,658 cases stemming from events prior to 1986. Muyot, *supra* note 8, p. 12.

19. *Philippine Journal* (July 1989), quoted in Lawyers Committee, *Impunity, supra* note 15, p. 58. (The accurate name, however, is *People's Journal.*)

20. Alien Tort Claims Act, 28 U.S.C. 1350.

21. The act of state doctrine is a prudential one, which states that U.S. courts will not judge the acts of foreign sovereigns within their own territory. The district court originally dismissed the Marcos cases on these grounds, but in a short opinion, the Ninth Circuit Court of Appeals held that the acts at issue — orders to torture, disappear, and murder — were not official acts subject to the act of state doctrine. *See Trajano v. Marcos,* 878 F.2d 1439 (9th Cir. 1989).

22. Marcos argued he was immune as either the de jure or former president of the Philippines, as well as because of a lack of personal and subject-matter jurisdiction.

Although these grounds were rejected by the trial judge, in a 1992 decision on the *Trajano* case, the Ninth Circuit Court of Appeals considered contentions by Marcos's daughter Imee that (1) the Foreign Sovereign Immunities Act of 1976 provided immunity to the Marcos defendants, and (2) the court lacked subject-matter jurisdiction under the Alien Tort Claims Act (ATCA). The court rejected both arguments, holding that while Marcos's acts in ordering Trajano arrested, tortured, and killed were under color of law and thus sufficient to give rise to substantive liability under the ATCA, they were not the acts of a "sovereign" under the FSIA. In *Re Estate of Ferdinand E. Marcos Litigation,* 978 F.2d 493, 498 (9th Cir. 1992).

Chapter 18

1. *See Far Eastern Economic Review,* May 21, 1987, pp. 6–7.

2. This is based on my own observations in Cambodia during 1960–64 and 1970–72.

3. Uncritical propaganda attacks on DK as a Communist regime, without consideration for the destruction wrought on Cambodia by the United States as a contributing factor in its radical policies, were John Barron and Anthony Paul, *Murder of a Gentle Land* (New York: Reader's Digest Press, 1977); Francois Ponchaud, *Cambodia Year Zero* (New York: Penguin Books, 1977); David Aikman, "Cambodia: An Experiment in Genocide," *Time,* July 31, 1978. Among sincere figures who thought the situation justified international military intervention was Senator George McGovern (*see* Noam Chomsky and Edward S. Herman, *After the Cataclysm: Postwar Indochina and the Reconstruction of Imperialist Ideology* [Boston: South End Press, 1979], p. 138).

4. For an English translation, *see* Michael Vickery, "Criminal Law in the People's Republic of Kampuchea," *Journal of Contemporary Asia* 17(4) (1987), pp. 508–18. For references to the earlier PRK laws, *see* Michael Vickery, "A Critique of the Lawyers Committee for International Human Rights, Kampuchea Mission of November 1984," *Journal of Contemporary Asia* 18(1) (1988), pp. 108–16.

5. Amnesty International, *Kampuchea Political Imprisonment and Torture,* (London: Amnesty International Publications, 1987), p. 36.

6. All quantitative statements about Cambodia's population assume a high margin of uncertainty. Thus "half" in the text paragraph is to be understood in the loosest possible sense. For estimates of total survivors, *see* Michael Vickery, "Democratic Kampuchea—CIA to the Rescue," *Bulletin of Concerned Asian Scholars* 14(4) (Oct.–Dec. 1982), pp. 45–54; Michael Vickery, *Cambodia 1975–1982* (Boston: South End Press, 1984), pp. 184–88; Michael Vickery, "Comments on Cham Population Figures," *Bulletin of Concerned Asian Scholars* 22(1) (Jan.–Mar. 1990), pp. 31–33.

7. *See* Vickery, "A Critique of the Lawyers Committee," *supra* note 4, p. 111. The law in question was Decree-Law No. 02 k.c., "concerning sentences for treason against the revolution and sentences for other crimes."

8. Gregory H. Stanton, "The Cambodian Genocide and International Law," typescript [n.p.], in *Genocide and Democracy in Cambodia: The Khmer Rouge, the U.N., and the International Community,* Ben Kiernan, ed. (New Haven, CT: Yale Center for International and Area Studies, 1993).

9. *Id.,* Hurst Hannum, "International Law and Cambodian Genocide: The Sounds of Silence," 11 *Human Rights Quarterly* 82 (1989).

10. *Id.*

11. These details are reported by Stanton, *supra* note 8. He does not explain the reasons for blocking ABA efforts, but the Lawyers' Committee is on record through its *Kampuchea: After the Worst* (New York: Lawyers' Committee, August 1985), and even more so

in the preliminary report that preceded it, as being more interested in condemning the People's Republic in Phnom Penh than the DK.

12. *See* Lawyers' Committee, *Kampuchea: After the Worst, supra* note 11; Amnesty International, "File on Torture in Cambodia" (London: Amnesty International, 1986); Amnesty International, "Kampuchea Political Imprisonment and Torture," *supra* note 5. For a critique of the Lawyers' Committee report, *see* Vickery, "A Critique of the Lawyers' Committee, *supra* note 4.

13. *See supra* note 3.

14. *See* Vickery, "Democratic Kampuchea," *supra* note 6.

15. For the text of the Agreements, *see* Letter dated Oct.30, 1991, from the Permanent Representatives of France and Indonesia to the United Nations addressed to the Secretary-General, U.N. Doc. A/46/608-S/23177, Annex (1991), *reprinted in* 31 I.L.M. 180 (1992). The Agreements were signed by Australia, Brunei, Cambodia, Canada, China, France, India, Indonesia, Japan, Laos, Malaysia, the Philippines, Singapore, the USSR, the United Kingdom, the United States, Vietnam, and Yugoslavia.

16. *Far Eastern Economic Review,* August 11, 1988, p. 29, cited in Ben Kiernan, "The Cambodian Crisis, 1990–92: The UN Plan, the Khmer Rouge, and the State of Cambodia" [hereinafter Cambodian Crisis], 24 *Bulletin of Concerned Asian Scholars* 3 (Apr.–June 1992).

17. Kiernan, *Cambodian Crisis, supra* note 16, p. 19.

18. Settlement Agreement, *supra* note 15, ann. 3, paras. 5, 7.

19. Agreement, art. 16 and ann. 1, sec. E.

20. Settlement Agreement, *supra* note 15.

21. Steven R. Ratner, "The Cambodia Settlement Agreements," 87 *American Journal of International Law,* 1, 26 (1993). Ratner argues that the difference between "adhering to" and "complying with" "appears more cosmetic than legally substantive in light of the dictates of *pacta sunt servanda. Id.,* p. 26, note 158.

22. GA Res. 43/19, UN GAOR, 43d Sess., Supp. No. 49, p. 24, UN Doc. A/43/49 (1988).

22. Ben Kiernan, "Deferring Peace in Cambodia: Regional Rapprochement, Superpower Obstruction," in *Beyond the Cold War: Conflict and Cooperation in the Third World,* (Berkeley: University of California, Berkeley, International and Area Studies, 1991), p. 59.

24. Press statements of U.S. Secretary of State James Baker and Australian Foreign Minister Gareth Evans, quoted in Kiernan, *Cambodian Crisis, supra* note 16, p. 20.

25. Commentary, "Hopes for Cambodia Peace Dim as Vote Nears," *Asian Wall Street Journal Weekly,* Apr. 19, 1993.

26. *See, e.g.,* "Cambodia Sees No End to Brutality by Officials," *New York Times,* July 11, 1993, p. A1 col. 1.

Chapter 19

An earlier version of this paper was presented at an Amnesty International conference on political killings and disappearances at Noordwijkerhout, the Netherlands, September 4–6, 1992, and published in the *Journal of African Law* in 1993.

1. At independence the PF broke up and the two organizations contested the elections separately. ZANU(PF) — as it became known — won a majority of seats and formed the government, with a minority of ZAPU ministers. Most ZAPU ministers were dismissed in

1982 with the worsening of political tensions. In December 1987 the two parties agreed to unite and now form the government under the name of ZANU(PF).

2. Ken Flower, *Serving Secretly: An Intelligence Chief on Record* (London: J. Murray, 1987), pp. 1–3. Aside from the general point of principle, Mugabe's remarks as reported are inaccurate. The assassination attempts took place after the war, in the course of the 1980 general election campaign.

3. Quoted in David Martin and Phyllis Johnson, *The Struggle for Zimbabwe* (Harare/London: Zimbabwe Publishing, 1981), p. 241.

4. Joseph Lelyveld, *Move Your Shadow: South Africa, Black and White* (New York: Time Books, 1985), p. 213.

5. Speech of July 16, 1986, cited in G. Feltoe, *A Guide to Zimbabwean Cases Relating to Security, Emergency Powers and Unlawful Arrest and Detention* (Harare: Legal Resources Foundation, 1988), p. 8.

6. Flower, *Serving Secretly, supra* note 2, pp. 261–62. Flower also reprints a secret CIO memorandum from 1974 detailing negotiations with the Portuguese and South African intelligence agencies about the formation of RENAMO (pp. 300–302).

7. Quoted in Bill Berkeley, "One Party Fits All," *The New Republic*, March 6, 1989.

8. Interview carried out by Bill Berkeley, Zimbabwe, 1988.

9. *Id.*

Chapter 20

1. "Apartheid" means "separateness" in Afrikaans. The rise of the National Party is described in Leonard Thompson, *A History of South Africa* (New Haven, CT: Yale University Press, 1990).

2. The history of this legislation is described in detail in Lynn Berat, "Doctors, Detainees, and Torture: Medical Ethics v. the Law in South Africa," 25 *Stanford Journal of International Law* 499 (1989).

3. It is estimated that some 54,000 people were detained under the state of emergency between 1985 and 1990. By contrast, an estimated 25,000 persons were detained between 1963 and 1984.

4. Many scholars and practitioners of international human rights law have long taken the position that human rights violations require state action, whether or not officially sanctioned. In contradistinction, they posit that the behavior of nonstate actors may violate international humanitarian law, which applies to combatants regardless of whether they represent a state, or may constitute a crime under international law; however, it is not a violation of human rights. This article takes a contrary view, maintaining that the universality of human rights norms demands that such rights attach to all individuals. Whether the rights were violated by state or nonstate actors is irrelevant because the damage to the victim is the same. With regard to South Africa, this position also accords with the way the issue of bringing violators to task has been treated by the ANC, which has conducted inquiries into human rights violations committed in its camps in exile and not into breaches of humanitarian law or international criminal law.

5. The history of these groups is described in Tom Lodge, *Black Politics in South Africa since 1945* (London; New York: Longman, 1983).

6. On Mandela, *see* Fatima Meer, *Higher Than Hope* (London: Hamish Hamilton, 1990).

7. *New York Times*, June 15, 1990. The state of emergency remained in place in Natal for several months longer, due to fighting between those loyal to Chief Mangosuthu Buthelezi's rural, Zulu Inkatha movement and a successor to the UDF.

8. *Id.*, Mar. 19, 1992.

9. *Id.*, Mar. 27, 1992.

10. *Id.*

11. Such slogans were also shouted when de Klerk visited African townships. Bill Keller, "De Klerk's Gorbachev Problem," *The New York Times Magazine,* Feb. 1, 1993, p. 38.

12. This legislation, which is often referred to as the pillars of apartheid, is described in Leonard Thompson and Andrew Prior, *South African Politics* (New Haven, CT: Yale University Press, 1982); *see also* Thompson, *supra* note 1.

13. *New York Times,* Oct. 30, 1990.

14. *Id.*, Feb. 2, 1991.

15. These included the Pan Africanist Congress, the Communist Party, and the Azanian People's Organization. The willingness of the ANC's leadership to negotiate with the de Klerk government alienated many young Africans, who joined the PAC, the ANC's main rival. Unlike the ANC, the PAC has historically been more nationalist in orientation, rejecting the ANC's willingness to find accommodation with whites. The argument can be made that the Communist Party did, in fact, have representation because many of its members are also prominent in the ANC. On the Communist Party, *see, generally,* Lodge, *supra* note 5. Further to the left of the CP and PAC was the strongly nationalist AZAPO, which indicated that it would negotiate with whites only in the context of a constituent assembly.

16. Notably the Conservative Party, which many people believe enjoyed widespread support from members of the security forces, the civil services, and a host of ultra-right-wing neo-Nazi groups.

17. The Democratic Party, a white group slightly to the left of the NP but without broad backing.

18. Homelands were the names given to reserves for Africans when, under the apartheid system, the government argued in international forums that in these desiccated areas Africans could exercise their legitimate rights to self-determination. Under the scheme, four such homelands—the Transkei, Bophuthatswana, Venda, and the Ciskei—received sham independence recognized by no state but South Africa.

19. The exceptions were the party representing the "independent" homeland of Bophuthatswana and the Inkatha Freedom Party. The party from the "independent" homeland of the Ciskei initially refused to sign but then reversed its position.

20. Convention for a Democratic South Africa, Declaration of Intent, December 20, 1991, reprinted in South African Consulate General, New York, *This Week in South Africa,* Dec. 18–23, 1991, p. 1.

21. *Id.*, sec. 5.

22. *Id.*, sec. 5.a.

23. *Id.*, sec. 5.b.

24. *Id.*, sec. 5.c.

25. *Id.*, sec. 5.d.

26. *Id.*, sec. 5.e.

27. *Id.*, sec. 5.f.

28. *Citizen* (Johannesburg, South Africa), Dec. 21, 1991.

29. The vote was 1,925,065 in favor and 875,676 against. Embassy of South Africa, South Africa Update, no. 2, 1992, p. 1.

30. *Id.*

31. Justice Goldstone was later appointed chief prosecutor of the International Tribunal on crimes committed in the former Yugoslavia. *See* Chapter 21.

32. Earlier, in 1990, a government-appointed commission under Justice Louis Harms,

known as the Harms Commission, had considered state-sponsored violence by means of hit squads and state operatives of the Civil Cooperation Bureau and other organizations. It emerged that hit men were used to assassinate government "enemies." The commission's report recommended that those responsible be brought to justice, but de Klerk never acted. "National Party Suffers Humiliating Defeat Over Attempts to Cover Up State Terrorism with Amnesty Bill," *Southern Africa Report,* Oct. 23, 1992, p. 3 [hereinafter cited as Amnesty Bill].

33. Agence France Presse, Aug. 29, 1992.

34. David Ottaway, "Judge Blasts ANC, Rival on Violence," *The Washington Post,* May 29, 1992.

35. David Ottaway, "De Klerk's Call for Talks with ANC Is Turned Down," *The Washington Post,* June 24, 1992, p. A38.

36. John Battersby, "Growing Violence, Stalled Talks Dim Prospects for South Africa," *Christian Science Monitor,* June 22, 1992.

37. *Id.*

38. BBC Summary of World Broadcasts, June 26, 1993.

39. Billy Paddock, "ANC, Government to Meet in 'Bush Summit,'" *Business Day,* Oct. 2, 1992, p. 1.

40. "No Rush to Multi-Party Negotiations," *New Nation,* Oct. 2–8, 1992.

41. Phillip van Niekerk, "Still Searching for a Heart of Stone," *Weekly Mail,* October 16–22, 1992.

42. John Battersby, "Disclosures of Covert Military Activities Weaken de Klerk in S. African Impasse," *Christian Science Monitor,* Nov. 18, 1992, p. 1.

43. John Goshko, "Permanent U.N. Presence in South Africa Sought," *The Washington Post,* July 16, 1992, p. A1.

44. John Battersby, "S. African Leader Is Set to Allow Security Probe," *Christian Science Monitor,* Aug. 10, 1992.

45. Arthur Gavshon, "SA Accepts EC Offer to Retrain Policemen," *Weekly Mail,* Sept. 25–Oct. 1, 1992.

46. Agence France Presse, Aug. 13, 1992.

47. U.N. Doc. S/24389, Aug. 7, 1992, Report of the Secretary-General on the Question of South Africa.

48. Agence France Presse, Aug. 13, 1992.

49. Goldstone Commission Report (1992).

50. *Chicago Tribune,* Aug. 14, 1992.

51. *Id.*

52. *Id.*

53. National Party, Guidelines for Defining Political Offenses, Nov. 1990.

54. African National Congress, Press Release, Aug. 13, 1992.

55. *The Washington Post,* Aug. 14, 1992; Xinhua General News Service, Aug. 11, 1992.

56. Liz Sly, "ANC Unwilling to Back a General Amnesty," *Chicago Tribune,* Aug. 14, 1992.

57. Amnesty bill, *supra* note 32, p. 2.

58. *Id.*

59. *Id.*

60. *Id.*

61. *Id.*

62. *Id.*

63. *Id.*

64. *Id.,* pp. 2–3.

65. *Id.,* p. 2.

66. *Id.,* p. 3.

67. *Id.*

68. *Id.*

69. Agence France Press, Oct. 21, 1992.

70. *Id.*

71. *Id.*

72. *Id.*

73. Amnesty bill, *supra* note 32, p. 2. The complicated relations among the police, military, and security forces in South Africa is described in Lynn Berat, "Conscientious Objection in South Africa: Governmental Paranoia and the Law of Conscription," 22 *Vanderbilt Journal of International Law* 127 (1989).

74. *Cape Times,* Nov. 19, 1992.

75. "Mandela Will Grant Amnesty to Some: Waivers for Political Crimes Will Depend on Full Confessions," *The Chicago Tribune,* June 8, 1994.

76. John Battersby, "South Africa Creates Commission to Judge Apartheid-Era Crimes." *The Christian Science Monitor,* June 9, 1994.

77. ANC Wins and Loses with Horror Camps Report," *Southern Africa Report,* Oct. 23, 1992, p. 3.

78. *Id.,* p. 4.

79. *Id.,* p. 3.

80. *Id.*

81. *Citizen,* Jan. 19, 1993.

82. *Sunday Times,* Jan. 18, 1993.

83. *Id.*

84. John Battersby, "ANC Goes Public on Abuses in Exile Camps," *Christian Science Monitor,* Aug. 25, 1993.

85. John Battersby, "Escalating Violence in South Africa Prompts Calls for U.N. Intervention," *Christian Science Monitor,* Aug. 6, 1993.

86. *Id.*

87. *Id.*

88. *Id.*

89. *Weekly Mail,* Nov. 27, 1992; *Cape Times,* Nov. 27, 1992.

90. *Star,* Nov. 30, 1992.

91. *Star,* Dec. 2, 6, 7, 1992; *Citizen,* Dec. 7, 1992.

92. Alan Cowell, "De Klerk Concedes Military Had Role in Township Strife," *New York Times,* Dec. 20, 1992, p.1.

93. Gaye Davis, "Civil Servants Told to Destroy Secret Files," *Weekly Mail and Guardian,* Aug. 13–19, 1993, p. 3.

94. Bill Keller, "South African Parties Endorse Constitution Granting Rights to All," *New York Times,* Nov. 18, 1993, p. 1.

95. South African Constitution, quoted in Justice Richard Goldstone, "Exposing Human Rights Abuses — A Help or Hindrance to Reconciliation?," The Matthew O. Tobriner Memorial Lecture, Hastings School of Law, January 18, 1995 (to be published in Hastings Law Journal, 1996).

96. Richard Ellis, "Free, fair — and flawed," *Sunday Times,* London, May 1, 1994.

97. Accadoga Chiledi, "South Africa — Politics: Battle Rages over Government Amnesty," *Inter Press Service,* June 10, 1994.

98. Rich Mkhondo, "South Africa Keeps Ban on Elections," *Reuters Limited,* May 27, 1994.

99. "Monday Highlights," United Nations Package, *Federal News Service,* June 28, 1994.

100. ANC Policy Document, quoted in Lawyers' Committee for Civil Rights under Law, Southern Africa Project, *Amnesty for the South African Government* (n.d.), p. 7.

101. "Mandela Will Grant Amnesty," *supra* note 75; Oxfam, *South Africa Watch,* No. 43, September 9, 1994 (published by oxcape@wn.apc.org on-line service). The language regarding human rights violations outside South Africa presumably refers to the killings of ANC members and other opponents of apartheid in neighboring countries as well as to the ANC's actions in refugee camps. For example, *see* David Beresford, "Pretoria Death Squad 'Killed Swapo Leader,'" *The Guardian,* June 24, 1994.

102. *South Africa Watch, supra* note 101.

103. *South Africa Watch,* No. 37, July 6, 1994.

104. Battersby, "South Africa Creates Commission," *supra* note 76.

105. *South Africa Watch, supra* note 101.

106. *Id.*

107. *Id.; see also* "Mandela Will Grant Amnesty," *supra* note 75.

108. African National Congress press release, August 18, 1994.

109. For discussion of this larger context, *see* Kader Asmal, "Victims, Survivors and Citizens — Human Rights, Reparations and Reconciliation in the South African Context," 1 *East African Journal of Peace and Human Rights* 1 (1993).

Chapter 21

1. Bruce Ackerman, *The Future of Liberal Revolution* (New Haven, CT: Yale University Press, 1992), esp. ch. 5.

2. In addition to the studies mentioned in the relevant country chapters, *see* Pricilla B. Hayner, "Fifteen Truth Commissions — 1974 to 1994: A Comparative Study," 16 *Human Rights Quarterly* 597 (Nov. 1994); Naomi Roht-Arriaza and Margaret Popkin, "Truth As Justice? Investigatory Commissions in Latin America," *Law and Social Inquiry* (forthcoming Feb. 1995).

3. This is the idea behind public indictments in the Yugoslav war crimes tribunal, for example. *See* the discussion in Chapter 5.

4. The International Commission of Jurists has elaborated certain basic principles of fairness to be followed in administrative adjudications. These include adequate notice to the interested parties of the nature and purpose of the proceedings; adequate opportunity for them to prepare the case, including access to relevant data; their right to be heard, and adequate opportunity for them to present arguments and evidence, and to meet opposing arguments and evidence; their right to be represented by counsel or other qualified persons; adequate notice to them of the decision and of the reasons therefor; and their right of recourse to a higher administrative authority or to a court. International Commission of Jurists, *The Rule of Law and Human Rights* (1966), p. 21; cited in F. C. Newman, "Natural Justice, Due Process and the New International Covenants on Human Rights: Prospectus", *Public Law* (London Stevens, 1967), p. 312. While truth-finding commissions have adhered to most of these principles, they have generally not allowed representation by counsel or included rights to appeal. Of course, it is unclear whether the work of such commissions, even those naming individual perpetrators, constitutes "administrative adjudication." Such guidelines may be more clearly applicable in the cases of civil sanction addressed later in this chapter.

5. Exceptions include humanitarian law, which applies to all combatants and international criminal law. This position is by no means unanimous: Contrast Chapter 13 with Chapter 20, note 4. Of course, as a non-state group acquires control over territory, population, and other indicia of statehood, the arguments against holding it responsible for human rights violations lose their force.

6. *See* C. Arnson, *El Salvador, accountability and human rights* (New York: Americas Watch, 1993).

7. *Cf.* Ackerman, *supra* note 1, pp. 75–77.

8. *See, e.g.,* the writings of Chilean attorney José Zalaquett, a member of that country's Commission on Truth and Reconciliation. "José Zalaquett propone caminos de solucion para los juicios a militares," *La Segunda* (Santiago de Chile), June 30, 1993, p. 17.

9. This was the view, for instance, of Senator José Dionko in the Philippines immediately after the Aquino government took power.

10. *See* International Covenant on Civil and Political Rights, articles 14, 15. The only requirements in noncriminal cases are that all persons are "entitled to a fair and public hearing by a competent, independent and impartial tribunal established by law." However, the public nature of trials is qualified and may be restricted for any number of reasons. A judgment rendered in a suit at law must be made public, but nothing is said about administrative hearings. *See* Newman, *supra* note 4. The U.S. Supreme Court has established that certain minimal due process requirements apply in civil cases in which a person is to be deprived of benefits.

11. *See* the discussion of the contours of this phrase in Chapter 3.

12. M. Novak, *The International Covenant on Civil and Political Rights* (Dordrecht, Netherlands: Martinus Nijhoff, 1993), pp. 242–43, citing decisions of both the Human Rights Committee under article 14 of the International Covenant and of the European Commission and Court of Human Rights under article 6 of the European Convention on Human Rights and Fundamental Freedoms.

13. American Convention on Human Rights, San Jose, Nov. 22, 1969, reprinted in 9 I.L.M. 673 (1970), art. 23. The Convention also allows regulation of these rights to participation in government "on the basis of age, nationality, residence, language, education, [or] civil and mental capacity."

14. For instance, article 6 of the International Covenant on Economic, Social and Cultural Rights pledges states parties to take appropriate steps to safeguard "the right of everyone to the opportunity to gain his living by work which he freely chooses or accepts." Of course, article 4 of the same Covenant allows the state to limit this right for the purpose of "promoting the general welfare in a democratic society."

15. Although such sanctions might raise issues of vesting or of a loss of settled expectations, it is generally within the state's prerogative to modify contracts unilaterally.

16. *See generally* Ellen Lutz, "After the Elections," in E. Lutz, H. Hannum, and K. Burke, eds., *New Directions in Human Rights* (Philadelphia: University of Pennsylvania Press, 1989).

17. *See, e.g.,* the reforms proposed in A. Garro, "Nine Years of Transition to Democracy in Argentina," 31 *Columbia Journal of Transnational Law* 1 (1993).

18. For example, recent U.S. State Department Country Reports and Amnesty International and Human Rights Watch Reports all refer to how countries are taking action against past human rights violations. *See also* the evidence presented in Chapter 4.

19. Diane Orentlicher has written that "international pressure to institute prosecutions can help shift the balance of power between civilian and military sectors in situations where that balance is relatively fluid and where civilian institutions already possess significant, if limited, power vis-a-vis the military."

D. Orentlicher, "The Role of the Prosecutor in the Transition to Democracy in Latin America," in Irwin Stotzky, ed., *The Transition to Democracy in Latin America: the Role of the Judiciary* (Boulder, CO: Westview Press, 1993). Actors within countries facing these issues seem to share this insight.

20. Legislators turned to the Geneva Conventions rather than to human rights treaties because the military itself had justified imposition of a state of siege by characterizing the Chilean situation as one of "internal war." Therefore, legislators argued, common article 3 of the Conventions, setting out minimal standards of humanitarian conduct in noninternational conflicts, applied. Summary executions, torture, and the taking of hostages, inter alia, are prohibited under common article 3. Robert J. Quinn, "Will the Rule of Law End? Challenging Grants of Amnesty for the Human Rights Violations of a Prior Regime: Chile's New Model," 62 *Fordham Law Review* 905, 957 (1994).

21. *See* discussion in Chapter 11. *See also* Leo Valladares, *Los Hechos Hablan por Si Mismos* (Tegucigalpa, Honduras: Editorial Guaymuras, 1994).

22. *See* Chapter 16.

23. For a discussion of the role of "epistemic communities" of scholars — for example, scientists — in the creation of international legal regimes, *see* the writing of recent "regime theorists" such as Peter Haas and Oran Young. *See, e.g.,* Peter M. Haas, "Banning Chloroflourocarbons: Epistemic Community Efforts to Protect Stratospheric Ozone," 46 *International Organization* 187 (1992). Whereas human rights activists obviously differ from scientists in the strength and specificity of shared knowledge and assumptions, the two communities share many common traits.

24. *See* José Zalaquett, "Balancing Ethical Imperatives and Political Constraints," 43 *Hastings Law Journal* 1425 (1992), regarding the Chilean government's reflections on the earlier Uruguayan and Argentine experiences in formulating its policy; *but see* David Pion-Berlin, "To Prosecute or to Pardon? Human Rights Decisions in the Latin American Southern Cone," 15 *Human Rights Quarterly* 105, 123–24 (1993) (little "contagion effect" in policy formulation).

25. *See* the discussion in Chapter 7.

26. In addition to the cases cited in Chapter 8, a July 1994 decision of the German Appeals Court (BGH) used the U.N. Charter, the Universal Declaration of Human Rights, as well as the International Covenant on Civil and Political Rights to evaluate East Germany's border practices in 1972. Although the GDR had not ratified the Covenant at that time, the court argued that the Universal Declaration already embraced the rights to life and to leave one's country contained in it. The Declaration expressed the will of the international community, and served to make concrete the obligations all U.N. member-states took on by signing the U.N. Charter. BGH, Judgment of July 26, 1994, 5 StR 167/94, NJW 1994, 2708, 2710.

27. José Zalaquett has been one of the most articulate exponents of this view. *See, e.g.,* Zalaquett, *supra* note 24.

28. *See, e.g.,* Thomas Franck, "The Emerging Right to Democratic Governance," 86 *American Journal of International Law* 46 (1992).

29. Document of the Copenhagen Meeting of the Conference on the Human Dimension of the Conference on Security and Cooperation in Europe (CSCE), June 29, 1990, reprinted in 29 I.L.M. 1305 (1990). The CSCE includes the nations of Eastern and Western Europe, Canada, and the United States; its documents, although not treaties, represent the views of a fair number of the world's governments. The Conference on the Human Dimension was set up to deal with human rights-related concerns in the CSCE. *See* Thomas Buergenthal, "The CSCE Rights System," 25 *George Washington Journal of International Law and Economics* 333 (1991).

30. *See* Malvina Halberstam, "The Copenhagen Document: Intervention in Support of Democracy," 34 *Harvard International Law Journal* 163 (1993), for an argument that the use of force in these circumstances neither violates the U.N. Charter's prohibitions on the use of force nor requires collective action by the Security Council or otherwise.

31. AG/Res. 1080 (XXI-0/91), *Representative Democracy,* General Assembly, Organization of American States (1991).

32. *See* the discussion in Chapter 14.

33. Support to the Democratic Government of Haiti, OEA/Ser.F/V.1/MRE/RES.1/91, corr.1, paras. 5,6 (1991).

34. U.N. Doc. A/46/L.8/Rev.1 (1991).

35. For an account of the limits of the Haitian example, *see* Tom Farer, "Collectively Defending Democracy in a World of Sovereign States: The Western Hemisphere's Prospect," 15 *Human Rights Quarterly* 716 (1993).

36. Halberstam, *supra* note 30, p. 170.

37. *See* "Haiti Talks Stall Over Amnesty for Coup Leaders," *New York Times,* Apr. 7, 1993; "Rights Groups Oppose Proposed Amnesty in Haiti," *New York Times,* Apr. 16, 1993.

38. *See* Zalaquett, *supra* note 24.

39. *See* "South African Commission to Investigate Past Political Violence," *New York Times,* June 8, 1994, p. A5.

40. Rule 61, Rules of Procedure and Evidence, International Tribunal for the Prosecution of Persons Responsible for Serious Violations of International Humanitarian Law Committed in the Territory of the Former Yugoslavia since 1991, IT/32, Mar. 14, 1994.

41. *See* Diane Orentlicher, "The Role of the Prosecutor in the Transition to Democracy in Latin America," in Irwin Stotsky, ed., *The Transition to Democracy in Latin America: The Role of the Judiciary* (Boulder, CO: Westview Press, 1993).

42. This language comes from Article 1F. of the Convention Relating to the Status of Refugees, Geneva, July 28, 1951, 189 U.N.T.S. 137. United States law goes further, prohibiting a grant of asylum to anyone who "ordered, incited, assisted or otherwise participated in the persecution of any person on account of race, religion, nationality, membership in a particular social group, or political opinion." 8 C.F.R. sec. 208.8 (f)(1)(iii); 8 U.S.C. sec. 101(a)(42) (1994).

43. Most of these suits were brought under the Alien Tort Claims Act, 28 U.S.C. 1350, a 1789 law that allows suit against an alien for a tort against the law of nations. Those that name the state rather than the individual official as defendant face, in addition to other obstacles, the hurdle of sovereign immunity. For detailed descriptions of these cases, *see* Joan Fitzpatrick and Paul Hoffman, "Human Rights Litigation Update," in ACLU, *International Civil Liberties Report,* (Los Angeles: ACLU, July 1994).

44. *See, e.g.,* Cherif Bassiouni, *A Draft International Criminal Code and Draft Statute for an International Criminal Tribunal* (Dordrecht, Netherlands; Boston: M. Nijhoff, 1987); Benjamin B. Ferencz, "An International Criminal Code and Court: Where They Stand and Where They're Going," 30 *Columbia Journal of Transnational Law* 375 (1992).

45. *See* S.C. Res. 827 (May 25, 1993); Report of the Secretary-General Pursuant to Paragraph 2 of Security Council Resolution 808 (1993), U.N. Doc. S/25704, May 3, 1993, both discussed in Chapter 4.

46. *See* Raymond Bonner, "U.N. Panel Backs Rwanda 'Genocide' Tribunal," *New York Times,* Sept. 29, 1994, p. A4, col. 1.

Index